COMPENDIOUS SYRIAC GRAMMAR

COMPENDIOUS
SYRIAC GRAMMAR

BY

THEODOR NÖLDEKE

WITH A TABLE OF CHARACTERS
BY
JULIUS EUTING

TRANSLATED
FROM THE SECOND AND IMPROVED GERMAN EDITION
BY
JAMES A. CRICHTON

AND WITH AN
APPENDIX
THE HANDWRITTEN ADDITIONS IN
THEODOR NÖLDEKE'S PERSONAL COPY
EDITED BY
ANTON SCHALL
TRANSLATED BY
PETER T. DANIELS

EISENBRAUNS
Winona Lake, Indiana
2001

Library of Congress Cataloging-in-Publication Data

Nöldeke, Theodor, 1836–1930.
    [Kurzgefasste syrische Grammatik. English]
    Compendious Syriac grammar / by Theodor Nöldeke ; with a table of
        characters by Julius Euting ; translated from the second and improved
        German edition by James A. Crichton. And with an appendix, The
        handwritten additions in Theodor Nöldeke's personal copy / edited by
        Anton Schall ; translated by Peter T. Daniels.
            p.   cm.
    First work originally published: London : Williams & Norgate, 1904. 2nd
    work originally published as an appendix in: Kurzgefasste syrische
    Grammatik. Darmstadt : Wissenschaftliche Buchgesellschaft, 1966.
    Includes bibliographical references and index.
    ISBN 1-57506-050-7 (cloth : alk. paper)
        1. Syriac language—Grammar. I. Nöldeke, Theodor, 1836–1930.
    Handschriftlichen Ergänzungen in dem Handexemplar Theodor Nöldekes und
    Register der Belegstellen. English.   II. Title: Handwritten additions in
    Theodor Nöldeke's personal copy.   III. Title.

PJ5423.N6813 2000
492′.35—dc21
                                                              00-064686
                                                                   CIP

The paper used in this publication meets the minimum requirements of the American
National Standard for Information Sciences—Permanence of Paper for Printed Library
Materials, ANSI Z39.48-1984.♾™

TRANSLATOR'S PREFATORY NOTE.

It appears desirable that the leading modern grammars of the four best-known Semitic languages, in their classical forms, should be readily accessible to English-speaking students. And in this connection, probably few competent judges will dispute the claims of the following treatises to be regarded as authoritative and leading, viz:— Wright's Arabic Grammar (as revised by Robertson Smith and De Goeje); Kautzsch's Gesenius' Hebrew Grammar; Nöldeke's Syriac Grammar; and Dillmann's Ethiopic Grammar. Of these the first two already exist in English, Wright's work having been in that form from the outset, at least under his own name, and Kautzsch's Gesenius' having been presented in a similar form a few years ago, in Collins and Cowley's excellent translation. The grammars of Nöldeke and Dillmann, however, have not hitherto appeared in English, although their pre-eminent position in their respective departments of Semitic philology is perhaps even less open to challenge, than that of the other two. It is to supply this want in the educational apparatus available for English students, so far at least as Nöldeke's Grammar is concerned, that the present translation has been attempted.

Of course it may be said, that students of Syriac will in all liklihood be sufficiently well acquainted with German, to be able to consult the original for themselves. I trust that such is the case; but those students and scholars amongst us, who are most familiar with German, will probably be the first to welcome a translation of such a work, if only it has been executed with reasonable fidelity and care. There are obvious advantages in an English version for an English eye, however accomplished a linguist its owner may be. At all events it is in that belief, and with no other desire than to do something for this branch of study, that I have ventured upon the present edition.

No attempt has been made to alter in any way either the substance or the arrangement of the Grammar. Citations, it is true, have been again verified, and slight errors here and there have been tacitly corrected. To facilitate reference, not only has the very full Table of Contents been set in its usual place, but its items have also been applied throughout the book, in the form of rubrics to the several sections. With a similar design an Index of Passages, wanting in the original, has been drawn up and placed at the end of the volume.

Among other friends who have been helpful towards the preparation of this version, I have specially to thank Professor Robertson of Glasgow University, for much kindly encouragement and wise counsel. Above all I must express my deep indebtedness to the distinguished author himself, Professor Nöldeke, for the unfailing courtesy and unwearied patience with which he lent his invaluable guidance and assistance, as the proof-sheets passed through his hands. Thanks are also due to Herr W. Drugulin and his staff, for again encountering, with a very considerable measure of success, the typographical difficulties, which a work of this nature must present.

JAMES A. CRICHTON.

PREFACE TO THE FIRST EDITION.[1]

This book does not claim to be in any respect a *complete* Syriac Grammar. It is true that with the material at my disposal I might have added very considerably to not a few sections; but any treatment of grammatical phenomena which aimed at completeness in every detail required quite other manuscript studies, than were at all open to me. Practical considerations too imposed a severe limitation. I trust however, that even within restricted limits, I have succeeded in producing something which may be of use.

I have taken my material from the best sources within reach, entirely disregarding Amira and the other Maronites. Besides the Jacobite and Nestorian grammarians and lexicographers now in print, I have made use of Severus of St. Matthaeus (usually, but incorrectly, styled "of Tekrit") as he appears in the Göttingen manuscript. The Directorate of the Göttingen Library, with their accustomed liberality, farther sent me, at my request, from their manuscript treasures, the large grammar of Barhebraeus together with his Scholia; and, with no less readiness, the Library-Directorate of Gotha sent me the Vocabulary of Elias of Nisibis. These manuscripts yielded produce of many kinds. It would have been an invaluable assistance to me, if I had had before me the *Masoretic* tradition of the Syrians, with some degree of completeness. Of this, however, I had at command at first—in addition to the epitomes which are found in printed works—only a few extracts, which

---

[1] Somewhat shortened at the close.—The first edition (1880) was dedicated to J. P. N. Land (Died 30. Ap. 1897).

I had myself noted down in earlier years, from the well-known Nestorian
Masora of the year 899 (Wright's Catalogue 101 *sqq.*) and from the
London "Qarqafic" manuscripts (Rosen-Forshall 62 *sqq.*; Wright 108 *sqq.*).
The deficiency was made up, at least to some extent, by the amiability
of Wright, Zotenberg and Guidi, who—in answer to a host of questions
about the mode of writing this or that word in the Masoretic manuscripts
in London, Paris and Rome—furnished me with information which in
many cases had been gained only after prolonged search. A careful collation
of the entire Masoretic material, allowing for the chance mistakes of
individual scribes, especially if it were accompanied by an attentive
observation of good, vocalised manuscripts of the Bible, would let us
know pretty accurately and fully how the Jacobites on the one hand,
and the Nestorians on the other, were wont to pronounce Syriac in the
Church use. Any point in which these two traditions are found to be in
agreement must have been in use prior to the separation of the two
Churches, that is, at the latest, in the 5th century. Although in the
recitative of the Church Service there was doubtless a good deal of
artificiality, yet we have in it a reflex at least of the living speech. The
Grammar of Jacob of Edessa (*circa* 700) is unfortunately lost, all but
a few fragments. What the later systematisers give, has, generally
speaking, no more authority than can be traced to the Church tradition.
Even the observant Barhebraeus, towering as he truly does by a head
and shoulders over the rest of his countrymen, has not always surveyed
this tradition completely, while sometimes he explains it incorrectly.
Now and then too, following mere analogy, he presents forms which
can with difficulty be authenticated in the genuine speech. Accordingly
if here and there I do not notice Barhebraeus' data, I trust it will not
be attributed to a want of acquaintance with them on my part. Still
less could editions like Bernstein's "Johannes", or Joseph David's
"Psalter" (Mosul 1877)—which unfortunately gives an "improved" text
of the Peshitā—constitute an absolute authority for me, although I am
greatly indebted to them. I need hardly mention that in the matter of
vocalisation I have made large use of the well-known complete editions
of the Old Testament and the New Testament, and of both the Nestorian

and the Jacobite-Maronite tradition. In this process, however, I have endeavoured to observe a due spirit of caution. Even the examination of the metrical conditions found in the old "poets" (*sit venia verbo!*) has not been without results for determining grammatical forms.

Still, even when all authoritative sources have been disclosed, a good deal will continue to be obscure in the Phonology and Morphology of Syriac, as it is only for the Bible and a few ecclesiastical writings that an accurate tradition of the pronunciation exists. So much the less will the expert be disposed to find fault with me, for having left here and there, upon occasion, a mark of interrogation.

As regards the *Orthography* of the consonantal writing, we are very favourably situated at the present time, when a long series of texts reproduces for us with accuracy the style of writing followed in manuscripts, from the 5th century onwards.

The *Syntax* I have based wholly upon original authors belonging to the age in which Syriac was an absolutely living speech. I have relied specially upon prose works, and among the poets I have given preference to those who write a simple style. Only a very few of my supporting-passages come down as far as the 7th century: the others range from the 2nd to the 6th. To bring in Barhebraeus or Ebedjesu for the illustration of the Syntax, is much the same as if one sought to employ Laurentius Valla, or Muretus, as an authority for *original* Latin. All the examples I have myself collected, with the exception of about a dozen. Naturally I have made much less use of strongly Graecising writings, than of those which adhere to a genuine Aramaic style. From the ancient versions of the Bible I have, without farther remark, adduced such passages only as are free from Hebraisms and Graecisms. Looking to the great influence of the Peshitā on the style of all subsequent writings, I might perhaps have gone somewhat farther in quoting from it. All the citations from the O. T. I have verified in Ceriani's edition, so far as it has proceeded. Other translations from the Greek I have used only very exceptionally,—in fact almost never except to illustrate certain Graecisms which were in favour. No doubt even the best original writings in Syriac give evidence of the strong influence of Greek Syntax; but, on

the other hand, everything is not immediately to be regarded as a Grae-
cism, which looks like one. The Greek idiom exercised its influence with
all the greater force and effect, precisely at those points where Syriac
itself exhibited analogous phenomena.

Although, in the composition of this book, I have continually kept
an eye upon kindred dialects and languages, I have nevertheless refrained
almost wholly from remarks which touch upon Comparative Grammar.
Not a few observations of that character, however, will be found in my
"Grammar of the New-Syriac Language" (Leipzig 1868) and my
"Mandaean Grammar" (Halle 1876). Here and there, besides, I have
tacitly rectified a few things which I had said in those works. The great
resemblance of Syriac to Hebrew—and that especially in Syntax—
will, I hope, be brought into clearer light than heretofore, by the mere
description of the language given in this book. A similar remark may
be made with regard to special points of contact in the case of Syriac
and Arabic.

I have been obliged to avoid almost entirely any reference to my
authorities in the Phonology and the Morphology. I have also refrained
from quoting the works of modern scholars. A brief manual cannot
well separate between widely-known facts and special stores either of
others or of one's own. But yet I do not mean to miss this opportunity
of referring to the fact, that I am peculiarly indebted to Prof. G. Hoffmann's essay, contained in ZDMG XXXII, 738 *sqq.*, even as I am
farther under deep obligation to this dear friend of mine, for many an
epistolary communication and encouragement, with reference to the
present work. Prof. Hoffmann also enabled me to make some use, at
least for the Syntax, of his edition of the Julianus-Romance (Leyden
1880) before it was given to the public. Unfortunately it was then too
late to permit my utilising that story still more thoroughly. I have
farther expressly to declare my adherence to the conception of the roots
עו׳ and עע׳, which Prof. August Müller has set forth in ZDMG
☞ p. 341 XXIII, 698 *sqq.*, and which Prof. Stade coincidently follows in his Heb.
Gramm., although I am not blind to the difficulties which cling even to
that theory.

As I wished to avoid extreme prolixity, I was obliged to seek for some adjustment between the two systems of vowel-marking. Whoever weighs the practical difficulties, and particularly the typographical difficulties, will, I trust, find the plan which I have adopted here, to be fairly suitable, although I cannot myself regard it as entirely satisfactory. In the latter part of the Syntax I have made an attempt to employ the One-point System, occasionally introducing the Two-point System, and applying proper Vowel-signs only where they seemed to be required in order to ensure clearness. That attempt was bound to show a certain amount of arbitrariness and vacillation. The reader may always reflect, that in many cases different ways of marking have prevailed according to place and time, and that very seldom indeed does an old manuscript, which employs the points with any degree of fulness, continue to be perfectly consistent in this matter. As regards the carrying-out of this marking, I must apologise for the circumstance that the points are not of the same size throughout: distance from the place of printing made it difficult to correct this slight inequality.

The division into *paragraphs* aims in nowise at logical consistency: still less is this to be looked for in the process of subdivision which has been applied to not a few of the paragraphs. In every case my sole concern was to break up the subject-matter into comparatively small sections, so as to facilitate the survey and the reference from one passage to another.

I take for granted in those who mean to use this Grammar-some acquaintance at least with Hebrew. Whoever desires to learn Syriac from it, without the help of a teacher, will do well to impress upon his memory at first merely the fundamental characteristics of the Orthography, the Pronouns, something of the Flexion of the Nouns, the Paradigm of the Strong Verb, and the most important deviations of the Weak Verbs, — as also to acquire some acquaintance with the attachment of the Pronominal Suffixes. Then let him read easy, vocalised texts, next, extracts from the Bible, as they are to be found, for example, in Rödiger's "Chrestomathia"—a compilation to be highly commended even on other grounds. The learner may at first pass many difficulties by, but in time he should with increasing care try to find out in the Grammar the explanation of anything which may arrest his attention. If, at a later stage, he goes systematically over the whole of the Grammar, including the Syntax, there will no longer be so much that is strange in appearance to him. And even to a teacher—dealing with beginners in Syriac, or any other Semitic language, who already understand something of Hebrew — an analogous procedure may be recommended. Familiarity with the Nestorian punctuation will be gained most readily from Urmia- [and New York-] editions of the Bible, although these do not give the system in completeness — doubtless for typographical reasons—and, besides, are not free from mistakes.

The Table of Characters, from Euting's master-hand, will suffice to exhibit the development of the Aramaic Character, at least in several of its leading types, from its earliest form up to the oldest Estrangelo, and the farther development of this last, up to the more modern script.

In conclusion I beg once more to tender an emphatic expression of my warmest thanks to the Library-Authorities, as well as to the personal friends, who have been helpful to me in the composition of this book.

Strassburg i. E. 30th Septr., 1880.

TH. NÖLDEKE.

PREFACE TO THE SECOND EDITION.(¹)

Although I did not reckon upon the necessity arising during my lifetime for a new edition of the Syriac Grammar, I still have continued to note down in my own copy—following my general practice—many additions and improvements. A good deal of this material, accordingly, I was able to devote to the new edition. Amongst other things, I have compared the citations already given from the Life of Simeon Stylites, with a transcript of the London Codex lent me by Prof. Kleyn of Utrecht, now deceased. It would appear however, that the Vatican text is upon the whole nearer the original, than the one in the British Museum.   ☞ p. 341

I have endeavoured to introduce a considerable number of improvements in points of detail, but I have abstained from radical alterations except in a very few cases. In the Syntax I have added to the number of the examples. The Syriac Bible has been more largely drawn upon than in the former edition, particularly as regards the Gospels, and especially the Synoptic Gospels. These last exhibit almost invariably an exceedingly flowing, idiomatic style of Syriac, which upon the whole reads better than the Semitic Greek of the original. This feature comes into still stronger relief in the more ancient form of the text—as contained in C. (*Curetonianus*) and S. (*Sinaiticus*)—than in our usual text   ☞ p. 341 P. (*Peshitā*). The Syriac Old Testament frequently approximates the original Hebrew text too closely; and, precisely because of the intimate relationship of the languages, we sometimes find ourselves at a loss as to whether the verbal reproduction is still in conformity with the true

---

(¹) [This edition in the original is dedicated to Prof. Guidi].

Syriac idiom, or is really a Hebraism. It should farther be noticed, that the genuine Syriac Canon is of much less compass than that of the Western Churches, and lacks, for instance, the Book of Esther and the Chronicles. The punctuation, therefore, of these last books in the Urmia edition, is of more slender authority than that of the others, which reproduces an ancient and established tradition, although it is not free from mistakes.

Many Syriac words, of which the form is not in keeping with the rules of Aramaic, have been proved now to be loan-words from the Assyrian. I have frequently drawn attention to such strangers. In this matter I follow Jensen's data in Brockelmann's Syriac Lexicon, and partly, direct communications from Jensen himself, as well as Delitzsch's Assyrian Dictionary. In the case of some words however, which are now indeed looked upon as being borrowed from the Assyrian, it is perhaps a matter of doubt whether the supposed borrower may not be the lender, or whether the words concerned may not be part of a common stock.

I have increased the number of references from one paragraph to another, but the order of these paragraphs remains the same. As the figures indicating that order have not been altered, quotations made in accordance with the paragraphs of the old edition are suitable also for the new. The few additional paragraphs which have been introduced, bear severally the number of the one which immediately precedes, a *b* being attached thereto.

The new edition has received much benefit from the discussion of the first by Prof. G. Hoffmann in the "Lit. Centralblatt" of 4th March, 1882,—as well as from other printed and written notices from his hand.

The late Prof. Bensley, as well as Dr. J. O. Knudson and Dr. H. Schulthess farther earned my gratitude by pointing out various inaccuracies, particularly errors of the press. And after all, in preparing the second edition, I came upon a few more blunders, some of them rather serious. If, as I venture to hope, the new form of the book should turn out to be tolerably free from annoying mistakes of the press, this is due very especially—seconded by the dexterity of the compositor—to the careful first correction of proofs, undertaken by Dr. Chamizer, the director of the printing house of W. Drugulin.

The abbreviations which I have adopted are for the most part clear enough in themselves. Besides those which have already been mentioned as indicating the three Texts of the Gospels, viz. P. C. and S. the following perhaps should be noticed: —

Addai = The Doctrine of Addai, The Apostle (ed. by G. Phillips)

Aphr. = The Homilies of Aphraates (ed. by W. Wright).

Anc. Doc. = Ancient Syriac Documents (collected and edited by W. Cureton, with a preface by W. Wright).

Apost. Apocr. = Apocryphal Acts of the Apostles. Vol. I (ed. by W. Wright).

Barh. = Barhebraeus.

Ephr. = S. Ephraem Syri Opera (Roman edition).

Ephr. Nis. = S. Ephraemi Syri Carmina Nisibena (ed. by G. Bickell).

Isaac = Isaaci Antiocheni Opera (ed. by G. Bickell).

Jac. Ed. = Jacob of Edessa.

Jac. Sar. = Jacob of Sarūg.

John Eph. = The Third Part of the Ecclesiastical History of John, Bishop of Ephesus (ed. by W. Cureton).

Joseph = Histoire complète de Joseph, par St. Ephraem[?] ed. by Paul Bedjan, 2. ed. Paris 1891).

Jos. Styl. = The Chronicle of Joshua, The Stylite (ed. by W. Wright). [wrongly attributed to Joshua.]

Jul. = Julianos der Abtrünnige (ed. by J. G. E. Hoffmann).

Land = Anecdota Syriaca (ed. by J. P. N. Land).

Mart. = Acta Martyrum Orientalium et Occidentalium (ed by Steph. Ev. Assemanus).

Moes. = Monumenta Syriaca ex Rom. codd. Collecta (ed. by G. Moesinger).

Ov. = S. Ephraemi Syri, Rabulae Episcopi Edesseni, Balaei Aliorumque Opera Selecta (ed. by J. Jos. Overbeck).

B

Sim. = Life of St. Simeon Stylites,—in the 2nd Volume of the Acta Martyrum (ed. by Steph. Ev. Assemanus).

Spic. = Spicilegium Syriacum (ed. by W. Cureton).

☞ p. 341 Of Syriac abbreviations note 'ܡܘ = ܡܘ̈ܬܐ "and the rest" = &c.

Strassburg i. E. August 1898.

TH. NÖLDEKE.

NOTE ON THE ENGLISH EDITION.

I am glad to have the opportunity of expressing here my satis-faction with Dr. Crichton's translation of my book, and my hearty re-cognition of the great care and ability with which he has performed his task. Special thanks are also due on my part to the translator, for recti-fying certain errors which had crept into the original work in the case of several of the citations. I venture to hope that the book, in its new form, will prove useful to a still wider circle of readers.

Strassburg i. E. March 1904.

TH. NÖLDEKE.

CONTENTS.

INTRODUCTION.

PART FIRST. ORTHOGRAPHY AND PHONOLOGY.

I. ORTHOGRAPHY.

Letters.

Vowel Expression.

(a) By Vowel Letters.

(b) By Other Signs.

Other Reading-Signs.

B*

II. PHONOLOGY.

1. CONSONANTS.

General Statement.

Rukkākhā and Quššāyā.

Liquids.

Gutturals.

The Vowel-Letters ꞅ and ꞈ.

2. VOWELS.

Long and Short Vowels in open and closed Syllables.

PART SECOND. MORPHOLOGY.

I. NOUNS.

1. PRONOUNS.

Personal Pronouns.

XX CONTENTS.

2. NOUNS IN THE STRICTER SENSE.
(Substantives and Adjectives.)

A. GENDER, NUMBER, STATE.

II. VERBS.

PART THIRD. SYNTAX.

I. THE SEPARATE PARTS OF SPEECH.

1. NOUNS.

B. ABSOLUTE STATE: EMPHATIC STATE.

C. GENITIVE AND CONSTRUCT STATE.

D. CO-ORDINATION.

E. ﻟﺐ.

2. VERBS.

A. PERSON AND GENDER.

B. TENSES AND MOODS.

Perfect.

Imperfect.

Participles.

Participles used as Nouns.

C. GOVERNMENT OF THE VERB.

Infinitive with Object.

Infinitive Absolute.

D. ܗܘܐ.

E. ܐܝܬ.

II. THE SENTENCE.

1. THE SIMPLE SENTENCE.

A. THE SIMPLE SENTENCE IN GENERAL.

B. RELATIVE CLAUSES.

Attributive Relative Clauses.

Conjunctional Relative Clauses.

C. INDIRECT INTERROGATIVE CLAUSES.

D. CONDITIONAL CLAUSES.

APPENDIX.

INTRODUCTION.

From the time the Greeks came to have a more intimate acquaintance with Asia, they designated by the name of "Syrians" the people who called themselves "Aramaeans". *Aramaic* or *Syriac,* in the wider sense of the word, is a leading branch of the Semitic speech-stem,— particularly of the Northern Semitic. This language, extending far beyond its original limits, prevailed for more than a thousand years over a very wide region of Western Asia, and farther did duty as a literary language for less cultivated neighbouring populations. It separated into several dialects, of which some have been preserved for us in literary documents, and others only in inscriptions.—It is one of these Aramaic dialects which we purpose to describe in the present work. This particular dialect had its home in Edessa and the neighbouring district of Western Mesopotamia, and stretched perhaps as far as into Northern Syria. Accordingly it is called by the authors who make use of it, the "*Edessan*" or "*Mesopotamian* tongue", but usually it lays claim to the name of *Syriac* pure and simple, as being the chief Syriac dialect. Occasionally indeed it has also been designated *Aramaic,* although, in Christian times, the name "Aramaic" or "Aramaean" was rather avoided, seeing that it signified much the same thing as "heathen".

Syriac, in the narrower meaning,—that is to say, the dialect of Edessa—, appears to have come somewhat nearer to the Aramaic dialects of the Tigris regions, than to those of Central Syria and Palestine. As far, however, as our imperfect knowledge goes, the dialect stands out quite distinctly from all related ones.

c

In Edessa this dialect was employed as a literary language, certainly long before the introduction of Christianity. But it attained special importance, from the time the Bible was translated into it (probably in the 2nd century) and Edessa became more and more the capital of purely Aramaic Christianity (in a different fashion from the semi-Greek Antioch). With Christianity the language of Edessa pushed its way even into the kingdom of Persia. By the 4th century, as being then Syriac pure and simple, it serves (and that exclusively) the Aramaean Christians on the Tigris as their literary language. During that period, so far as we know, it was only in Palestine that a local Aramaic dialect was — to a certain extent — made use of by Christians, for literary purposes. The Syriac writings of the heathen of Ḥarrān, the neighbouring city to Edessa,— of which writings, unfortunately, nothing has been preserved for us—, must have exhibited but a trifling difference at the most from those of the Christians.

The language and its orthography already present such a settled appearance in the excellent manuscripts of the 5th century, that we can hardly doubt that scholastic regulation was the main factor in improving the popular tongue into the literary one. The Greek model has been effective here. The influence of Greek is shown directly, not merely in the intrusion of many Greek words, but also in the imitation of the Greek use of words, Greek idiom and Greek construction, penetrating to the most delicate tissues of the language. Numerous translations and imitations (such as the treatise on Fate, composed after Greek patterns by a pupil of Bardesanes, about the beginning of the 3rd century) furthered this process. But we must carefully distinguish between Greek elements which had made good their entry into the language, and such Graecisms as must have been forced upon it by pedantic translators and imitators. Many Hebraisms also found their way into Syriac through the old translations of the Bible, in which Jewish influence operated strongly.

The golden age of Syriac reaches to the 7th century. The Syrians of that day belonged partly to the Roman empire, and partly to the Persian. The cleavage was made more pronounced by the ecclesiastical divisions, occasioned specially by the unhappy Christological controversies.

The Persian Syrians decided mostly for the teaching of the *Nestorians*,
—the Roman Syrians for that of the *Monophysites* or *Jacobites*. And
when the Academy of Edessa, the intellectual capital, was closed (489)
to the former as declared heretics, they founded educational institutions
of their own,—of which in particular the one at Nisibis attained to
high repute. This separation had as a consequence an abiding severance
of tradition, even with respect to the language and the mode of writing
it. Assuredly the variety of the common dialects in olden time cannot
have been without influence upon the pronunciation of Syriac, in the
mouths even of cultivated persons in different localities,—just as in
Germany the Upper-Saxon language of polite intercourse assumes a very
perceptible colouring, conditioned by the local dialect it meets with, in the
case of the inhabitant for instance of Holstein or the Palatinate or Upper
Bavaria,—or as in Italy the Tuscan tongue is similarly modified, in the case
of the native of Lombardy, Genoa or Naples. Many of these differences,
however, rest doubtless upon rules of art laid down by the Schools. So
far as we find here a genuine variety in the forms of the language, it is
sometimes the Eastern, sometimes the Western tradition, which preserves
the original with the greater fidelity. Naturally the more consistent of
the two is the Western, which as a whole restores to us the pronunciation
of the Edessans, in the remodelled form in which it appeared about the
year 600 or 700,—that is, at a time subsequent to the golden age of
the language.

The conquest of the Aramaean regions by the Arabs brought the
commanding position of Syriac to a sudden close. True, it lived on for
sometime longer in Edessa, and Aramaic dialects long maintained themselves in remote districts, as they partly do up to the present day; but
Syriac speedily lost its standing as a language of cultivated intercourse
extending over a wide region. The very care which was now devoted to
the literary determination of the old speech is a token that men clearly
perceived it was passing away. It can hardly be doubted that about the
year 800 Syriac was already a dead language, although it was frequently
spoken by learned men long after that time. The power of tradition,
which keeps it up as an ecclesiastical language, and the zealous study

of ancient writings,—had the effect of leading even the later Syriac authors, among whom were several considerable men, to wield their ancestral speech with great skill. Besides, the influence of the actually living tongues—the Aramaic popular dialects and the Arabic—did not attain its prevalence with such a disturbing effect as might have been expected. But on the whole, for more than a thousand years, Syriac—as an ecclesiastical and literary language—has only been prolonging a continually waning existence.

PART FIRST.

ORTHOGRAPHY AND PHONOLOGY.

I. ORTHOGRAPHY.

LETTERS.

§ 1. A. The character most in use in Syriac printing is that of Form of the
letters. the West-Syrians (Jacobites and Maronites), of which the proper name is *Serṭā* (*Serṭō*). It has been developed out of the older one, which is called *Estrangelo*, properly στρογγύλη. This character also is pretty often employed in printing, particularly in more recent times. The same thing may be said of the Nestorian character, which comes nearer the Estrangelo than the Serṭā does. We accordingly give, in the following Table not only the Serṭā letters of the alphabet but also the old or Estrangelo letters, as well as the Nestorian letters.

B. All Syriac styles of writing are *Cursive*; the most of the letters must be connected right and left within the word,—and thus several small modifications of shape arise. In the case of the Serṭā, we give all these forms; for the Estrangelo and the Nestorian character it may iffice to give the special final forms, in addition to the main forms. [1]

The form, which is given here in European character, of the names of the letters, aims at representing the older pronunciation: brackets enclose the diverging pronunciation of the later West-Syrians. Secondary forms, varying both in sound and character, are also met with.

---

[1] Cf. besides, the Plate of Alphabetical Characters by Euting, appended to this work.

Usual Syriac Character				Estrangelo.	Nestorian.	Names.	Sound-Value and Transcription.	Hebrew Equivalents.	Numerical Value.
1. Unconnected— (Detached finals).	2. Connected on right— (United finals).	3. Connected on left.	4. Connected right and left.						
						Ālaf (Ōlaf)	Spiritus lenis (')	א	1
						Bēth	b; v (β)	ב	2
						Gāmal (Gōmal)	g (hard); gh (γ)	ג	3
						Dālath or Dāladh (Dōlath or Dōladh)	d; dh (ò)	ד	4
						Hē	h	ה	5
						Wau	w	ו	6
						Zain, Zēn, or Zai	soft s (z)	ז	7
						Ḥēth	hard h (ḥ)	ח	8
						Ṭēth	emphatic t (ṭ)	ט	9
						Yōdh (Yūdh)	y	י	10
						Kāf (Kōf)	k; kh	כ	20
						Lāmadh (Lōmadh)	l	ל	30
						Mīm	m	מ	40
						Nūn, Nōn	n	נ	50
						Semkath	s	ס	60
						Ē	peculiar guttural (')	ע	70
						Pē	p; f, ph	פ	80
						Ṣādhē (Ṣōdhē)	emphatic s (ṣ)	צ	90
						Qōf	guttural k (q)	ק	100
						Rēsh (Rīsh)	r	ר	200
						Shīn	sh (š)	שׁ	300
						Tau	t; th (ϑ)	ת	400

At the end of a word we can only have a form from the 2nd column or the 1st, and from the one or the other according as the preceding letter has a form connecting to the left (Col. 3) or not. Forms from Col. 4 can only appear in the interior of a word; while initial forms must be taken from Col. 1 or 3.

Rem. The most judicious course for the beginner will be to impress upon his memory only Cols. 1 and 3.

C. ﹅ with ﹇ is generally written 𝗅𝗅 (𝗅𝗅), but initial ﹇ with ﹅ thus, ﹅﹅. For ﹇﹅ one sometimes puts ﹅, and thus draws in this case two words together. In Nestorian script ﹅ is given for final ﹅ (﹅).

For ﹅, ﹅ as single letters or as ciphers, one generally writes ﹅, ﹅.

In manuscripts ﹅ and ﹅ are often mistaken for each other from their resemblance; so is it with ﹅ and ﹅, and also with ﹅ on the one hand and ﹅, ﹅, ﹅, and ﹅ on the other. Farther it is frequently difficult to distinguish ﹅ from a simple ﹅, and occasionally even ﹅ from a simple ﹅. Even in many printed copies ﹅ and ﹅ are far too like one another:[1] farther, ﹅ and ﹅, and ﹅ and ﹅ are not sufficiently discriminated.

☞ p. 341

§ 2. The *pronunciation* of the letters can of course be determined only approximately. Notice the following: ﹅ ﹅ ﹅ ﹅ ﹅ ﹅ have a twofold pronunciation, one hard, answering to our *b g d k p t*, one soft, aspirated or rather sibilated. Soft ﹅ is nearly the German *w*, or the English and French *v*; soft ﹅ = γ (*gh*) is nearly the Dutch *g* (like the Arabic غ); soft ﹅ = ð (*dh*) is the English *th* in *there, other*; soft ﹅ = *kh*, or the German *ch* in *ach* (not that in *ich*); soft ﹅ the German, English, and French *f*; soft ﹅ = ϑ (*th*) is the English *th* in *think, both*. [2] On the changes of the hard and soft pronunciations v. §§ 15, 23 *sqq.*

Pronun- ciation.

﹅ is always the vowel-sounding English *w*, never the German *w*, and accordingly it quiesces easily and completely into a *u*. ﹅ has also more of a vowel character than the German *j*, being nearly the English *y*.

---

[1] *Translator's Note*: The same may be said for ﹅ and ﹅.

[2] *Translator's Note*: In the transcription followed in this Edition, soft ﹅ will be represented by *v*, soft ﹅ by *kh*, soft ﹅ by *f* or *ph*, and soft ﹅ by *th*; while soft ﹅ and ﹅ will be rendered by γ and ð respectively.

‍ = ‍ẕ is a soft *s* as in *chosen*, German *s* in *Rose*, French in *choisir* or French *z* in *zéro*.

ܚ = *ḥ* is quite a foreign sound to us, an *h* rattled in the throat (Arabic ‍). The East-Syrians pronounce it as a very hard Swiss *ch* (Arabic ‍).

‍ = *ṭ* is an emphatic and completely unaspirated modification of ܠ *t*, in which the tip of the tongue is pressed firmly against the palate; ‍ is a similar modification of ‍ *k*, produced in the back part of the mouth. ‍ and ‍ are employed by the Syrians as equivalents for the Greek sounds *τ* and *κ*, which at all events were quite unaspirated.

‍ = *ṣ* is an emphatic articulation of the sound of ܣ *s*, by no means to be rendered as a German *z* (= *ts*).

‍ = ʿ is a guttural breathing, again quite foreign to us, which is formed by a peculiar compression of the upper part of the windpipe. It is nearly related to ܚ, and even to the Spiritus lenis (ʾ). Those who render it by the latter sound will make the least considerable mistakes.

‍ = *š* is the German *sch*, the English *sh*, or the French *ch*.

‍ seems to have been a lingual-dental, not a guttural.

The remaining consonants have nearly the same sound as the corresponding German or English ones.

DISPOSITION OF WORDS.

Disposition of words.

§ 3. Particles, which consist of only a single letter, *i. e.* of a consonant with a short vowel, are attached as prefixes to the following word, thus ܒܡܠܟܐ *bêmalkā*, "in rege", not ܒ ܡܠܟܐ, ܘܩܛܠ *waqṭal*, "and killed", not ܘ ܩܛܠ, &c.

Certain short words, and to some extent even longer ones, which together belong to the same idea, are also frequently written as one, though not invariably. Thus ܐܦܠܐ or ܐܦ ܠܐ *āf lā* "neither", "not even"; ܒܪܢܫ or ܒܪ ܢܫ *bar nāš*, "son of man", *i.e.* "man"; ܟܠܝܘܡ or ܟܠ ܝܘܡ *kul yōm* "every day"; ܟܠܡܕܡ or ܟܠ ܡܕܡ *kul meddem* "quicquid"; ܪܘܚܩܘܕܫܐ, more commonly ܪܘܚ ܩܘܕܫܐ *rūḥ quḏšā* "spirit of holiness", "the Holy Ghost"; even ܡܪܢܝܫܘܥܡܫܝܚܐ instead of ܡܪܢ ܝܫܘܥ ܡܫܝܚܐ *māran Ješūʿ mešīḥā* "our Lord Jesus Christ", appears. On the fusion together of two words, of which the one ends in ܠ, while the other begins with ܐ (ܠܐ), see above § 1 C.

VOWEL EXPRESSION (A) BY VOWEL LETTERS.

Vowel expression: (a) By vowel letters. Actual use.

§ 4. A. The letters ܐ ܝ ܘ are frequently made use of by the Syrians to express vowel sounds.

ܐ denotes every final *ā* and *ē*, and in certain cases *ē* within the word; that *ā* was pronounced *ō* by the later West-Syrians, and that *ē* in part *ī*. Thus ܡܐ *mā* (*mō*); ܡܠܟܐ *malkā* (*malkō*), ܡܡܣܐ *mamsē*; ܢܐ *nē* (*nī*); ܦܐܪܢ *pēran* (*pīran*).

ܝ denotes every *ī* in the middle and end of a word, also certain cases of *ē* in the middle: ܒܝܫ *bīš*; ܒܝ *bī*; ܕܝܢ *dēn*; ܥܝܢ *ʿēn* (*ʿīn*). For *ē* there appears also ܐܝ: ܟܐܝܢ or ܟܝܢ *kēn* (§ 46). In an open syllable *ē* is frequently not expressed at all, *e. g.* ܡܣܟܢܐ *meskēnā* (*meskīnā*); in ancient MSS. it is sometimes unindicated even in a closed syllable, *e. g.* ܐܚܪܢ *ḥêrēn*.

ܘ in the middle and end of a word denotes any long or short *u* or *o*: ܩܘܡ *qūm*; ܦܘܪܩܢܐ *purqānā*; ܢܓܠܘܢ *neγlōn* (*neγlūn*); ܬܫܒܘܚܬܐ *tešboḥtā* (*tešbuḥtō*); ܡܠܟܘ *malkū*; ܐܘ *ō*. Only the very common words ܟܘܠ *kol*, *kul* "all", "every", and ܡܛܘܠ *meṭṭol*, *meṭṭul* "because of" are often in old times, and always in later times, written without ܘ, thus ܟܠ, ܡܛܠ. The Cod. Sin. frequently leaves out the ܘ even in other words, *e. g.* ܠܩܒܠ for ܠܘܩܒܠ *luqval*. ☞ p. 341

ܘ and ܝ farther express the diphthongs *au* and *ai*: ܠܘ *lau*; ܒܝܬܐ *baitā*; the diphthongs *īu* and *ēu* are written ܝܘ: ܓܠܝܘ *gallīu*; ܢܓܠܝܘܗܝ *neγlēu*.

B. A final and originally short *a* in Greek words is expressed by ܐ: in pronunciation it was doubtless always lengthened. Greek *α* in the middle of a word is also often written ܐ, *e. g.* ܕܘܓܡܐܛܐ or ܕܘܓܡܛܐ δόγματα &c. Even the Syriac *a* is sometimes thus expressed, *e. g.* ܛܐܠܐ *ṭallā* for the usual ܛܠܐ. In the very same way ܝ appears pretty often for *ĭ* in the middle of a word, *e. g.* ܐܦܝܣܩܘܦܐ (or ܐܦܣܩܘܦܐ) *episkopā*, ἐπίσκοπος; ܟܪܝܣܝܣ (ܟܪܣܝܣ) χρῆσις. In quite isolated examples this happens even in Syriac words, as ܓܝܫܪܐ (ܓܫܪܐ) *gišrā*; ܫܝܓܪܐ (ܫܓܪܐ) *šiγrē*.

Greek ε and αι are in some writings expressed by ܘܝ, e. g. ܠܟܣܘܣܘܣ
λέξις. The desire to render Greek vowels with accuracy gave rise to
various strange forms of transcription among learned Syrians.

Greek ο on the other hand is frequently left entirely unexpressed,
e. g. ܚܣܝܠܝܣܩ Βασίλειος, alongside of ܚܣܝܠܝܣܩ; ܐܦܝܣܩܘܦܐ, ܐܦܣܩܘܦܐ
alongside of ܐܦܣܩܘܦܐ, ܐܦܣܩܘܦܐ ἐπίσκοπος. Thus the placing of the
vowel letters in Greek words is far more fluctuating than in native ones.

Apparent use of ܐ.

§ 5. A distinction is to be made between the employment of ܐ as
a vowel sign and those cases in which it has its place from etymological
considerations,—especially from having been formerly an audible *spiritus lenis*: e. g. ܡܠܐܟܐ *malakhā* "angel", from מַלְאֲכָא; ܒܐܪܐ *bērā* (*bīrō*) "a
well" from בְּאֵרָא (Hebrew בְּאֵר); ܥܐܠܝܢ *ʿāllīn* "enter" (pl. part.), because of the sing. ܥܐܠ *ʿāʾēl* "enters" (sing. part.) &c.

**Vowel ex-
pression:
(b) By other
signs.
Simple
points.**

VOWEL EXPRESSION (B) BY OTHER SIGNS.

§ 6. This insufficient representation of vowel sounds was gradually
made up for by new signs. At first, in some words which might be pronounced in various ways, *a point over* the letter concerned was employed
to signify the fuller, stronger pronunciation, and *a point under* it to
denote the finer, weaker vocalisation, or even the absence of vowel sound.
Thus there was written (and is written) ܥܒܕܐ *ʿevāḏā* "a work", set over
against ܥܒܕܐ *ʿavdā* "a servant"; ܡܢ *mān* "what?" and *man* "who?", ܡܢ
men "from"; ܩܛܠ *qāṭel* "he kills" (part.) and *qaṭṭel* "he murdered"
(Paël), ܩܛܠ *qēṭal* "he killed" (Peal); ܫܢܬܐ *ša(n)tā* "a year", ܫܢܬܐ *šenthā*
"sleep"; ܡܠܟܐ *malkā* "king", ܡܠܟܐ *melkā* "counsel"; ܛܒܐ *ṭāvā* "good";
ܛܒܐ *ṭebbā* "fame"; ܗܘ *hau* "that" (masc.), ܗܘ *hū* "he"; ܗܝ *hāi* "that"
(fem.), ܗܝ *hī* "she"; ܗܢܘܢ *hānōn* "those", ܗܢܘܢ *hennōn* "they" &c.
Frequently it is held to be sufficient to indicate by the upper point the
vowels *ā, a*,—e. g. in ܣܝܡܐ *sēyāmā* "setting", ܐܝܕܐ *aidā* "what?" (fem.),
ܕܚܝܠ *daḥḥīl* "timorous", without giving also to words written with the
same consonants the under point proper to them, *viz:*—ܣܝܡܐ *sīmā* "set",
ܐܝܕܐ *īḏā* "a hand", ܕܚܝܠ *dēḥīl* "terrible". Here too we must note the
employment of ܗ almost without exception to signify the suffix of the
3ʳᵈ pers. fem. sing., e. g. ܒܗ *bāh* "in her" as set over against ܒܗ *bēh*

"in him"; ܩܶܛܰܠܬܳܗ qêṭaltāh "thou hast killed her"; and so also ܩܕ̇ܡܷܗ qêḏāmēh "before her"; ܢܶܩܛܠܺܗ neqṭēlīh "he is slaying her" (Impf.), &c.

In the latter case this system has already in part given up the exact, and relatively phonetic significance of the 'points'. That significance, however, came to be abandoned in many other cases besides, as when, for instance, one began to write ܣܳܡ sām "he placed", because it is a Perfect like ܩܛܰܠ qêṭal. Other considerations too mixed themselves up with the matter; thus it became the practice to write the 1ˢᵗ pers. sing. perf. with — over the first consonant, e. g. ܩܶܛܠܶܬ qeṭleth "I killed" (*interfeci*). The points, upper and under,—particularly the former,—are often wrongly placed; thus ܚܟ̣ܡ is found for ܚܟ̇ܡ 'āveḏ "does", and ܣܳܠܩ for ܣܳܠܩ sāleq "ascends".

§ 7. Farther, a second or third point was often added to distinguish more exactly between verbal forms in particular; for example, there was written ܥܶܒܕܬ̣ 'evdeth, ܥܶܒܕܰܬ̣ or (East-Syrian) ܥܶܒܕܰܬ̣ 'evdath "she did"; ܡܰܢܘ manū "who is?" compared with ܡܳܢܰܘ mānau "what is?"; ܒܶܪܶܐ bêrē "*creatus*" as distinguished from ܒܶܪܳܐ bêrā "*creavit*" and ܒܳܪܶܐ bārē "*creat*", &c. This complicated system, often fluctuating according to districts and schools, and seldom faithfully attended to by copyists, still maintained a footing in many forms, even alongside of the employment of a more exact indication of the vowels.

§ 8. Out of this punctuation then, there was formed, with the Nestorians first of all, *a complete system of Vowel-Signs*. To be sure it never attained to perfect consistency and universal acceptance: even the appellations of the vowels fluctuate a good deal. The system is used in Nestorian impressions, on the authority of good manuscripts, after the following scheme:—

     — ă *Pêthāḥā*, e. g. ܒ̇ bă.

     — ā *Zêqāfā* (or according to Nestorian pronunciation, *Zêqāpā*): ܒ̣ bā.

     — ĕ, ĭ *Rêvāṣā arrīkhā* or *Zêlāmā pêšīqā*: ܒ bĕ.

     — ē *Rêvāṣā karyā* or *Zêlāmā qašyā*: ܒ bē.

     ܒ ī *Ḥêvāṣā*: ܒܝ bī.

     ܘ u, ū *'Ệṣāṣā allīṣā*: ܒܘ bu.

     ܘ o, ō *'Ệṣāṣā rêwīḥā*: ܒܘ bo.

Combination of points.

System of vowel-marking by points.

Rem. This orthography,—which otherwise is tolerably consistent,— substitutes in certain cases —̤ for —̇ , for no reason that can be discovered, *e. g.* in Passive Participles like ܚܒܝܕ "built". In old manuscripts —̤ is largely interchangeable with —̇ or —̤̇. ܝ is also found in isolated cases for ܘ, particularly for an initial *ī*. —̇ is also written for —̤̇. For other variations, v. §§ 42. 46. 48.—On the representation of *ai* and *au* v. § 49 A.

<table>
<tr><td>System
of vowel-
marking
by Greek
letters.</td><td>

§ 9. Much clearer is the *system of vowel designation by small Greek letters* set above or below the line,—a system which grew up among the Jacobites about A. D. 700. Unfortunately, however, this system represents in many parts a later pronunciation of the vowels, which had become prevalent at that time, so that we cannot in the Grammar altogether dispense with the other system,—the Nestorian. The method practised is as follows:</td></tr>
</table>

— *a* *Pĕthōḥō.*

— *ō* (older *ā*) *Zĕqōfō.*

— *e* *Rĕvōṣō.*

— *ī* (partly for old *ē*) *Ḥĕvōṣō.*

— —*u* (partly for old *o*) *'Ĕṣōṣō.*

Rem. Sometimes *i* or *ι* is found for — *i. e.* H, γ, following later Greek pronunciation; for — or — there appears ε, and ω too for *o*. This ω has been in use with the interjection ܐܳ "O!" from very ancient times: a later and disfigured form is ܐܳ. The diphthongs *au* and *ai* are written ܐ—, ܘ—; ܐ— is an earlier form for ܐ—; and similar forms occur for other diphthongs.

<table>
<tr><td>Mixed
system.</td><td>

§ 10. *A combination of a modified point-system with the Greek system* is in favour among the later West-Syrians and in our own impressions. In this usage</td></tr>
</table>

—̤ = — .

—̤̇ = — .

—̤ and —̤̇ without distinction = — .

ܘ, ܘ— or merely —̇ = ܘ—, —.

ܐ or ܘ without any certain distinction = ܐ—.

§ 11. *Rem.* No one of these systems carries out a distinction Marking between long and short vowels. The designation of vowels by the Syrian vowels. Grammarians as "long" or "short" rests upon a misunderstanding of Greek terms and has nothing to do with the natural quantity. Thus the first and certainly short *e* in *neγlē* is directly designated as "long *Rĕvōṣō*", and the second and long *e* as "short". The original *o* is for the Jacobites a "short *'Ĕṣōṣō*"; for the Nestorians on the other hand it is "broad", while *u* is for the former "long", for the latter "compressed"; and in neither case is the quantity of the vowel considered, but merely the quality.

§ 12. No established sign has been formed to denote the want of Marking any vowel (*Sh^eva quiescens*), nor yet the absence of a full vowel (*Sh^eva* of vowel. *mobile*). Here and there the sign —̣ (§ 6) or —̇ (§ 17) serves this purpose.

§ 13. A. Examples: *Nestorian*: ܝܘܡ ܠܡܠܐ ܕܡܠܟܐ ܕܝܠܗܘܢ *ṣūth lêmillē* Examples: use of vow-*ḍemalkā ḍīlhōn. Greek*: ܪܘܐ ܠܡܠܐ ܕܡܠܟܘ *ṣūth lêmelē ḍêmalkō* el signs. *ḍīlhūn. Mixed*: ܪܘܐ ܠܡܠܐ ܕܝܠܗܘܢ. The blending might be contrived in many other ways besides, for instance, ܪܘܐ ܠܡܠܐ &c.

B. From practical considerations, we employ in this work the Greek vowel-signs almost always, using however,—in conformity with the practice of the East-Syrians, and in general of the West-Syrians also,—the sign —̣ for that vowel which is pronounced *ē* by the East-Syrians, and *ī* by the West-Syrians, and in most cases discriminating ȯ (original *o*, West-Syrian *u*) from o⸌— = o (original *u*).

C. Syriac manuscripts are commonly content with the indication of the vowels given in § 6: only occasionally do they give exact vowel signs. But Nestorian manuscripts, in particular, are often fully vocalised. Many Nestorian manuscripts of the Scriptures produce quite a bewildering impression by the large number of points of various kinds employed in them (cf. § 14 *sqq.*).

OTHER READING-SIGNS.

§ 14. Very ancient is the point which never fails in genuine Syriac Diacritic point in manuscripts,—that which distinguishes ܀ from ܂. ܀ and ܂.

Rukkākhā
and
Quššāyā.

§ 15. The *soft pronunciation* (*Rukkākhā*) of the letters ܒ ܓ ܕ ܟ ܦ ܬ (§ 2) can be expressed by a point placed under them, the *hard pronunciation* (*Quššāyā*) by one placed over them, e. g. ܢܣܒܬ *nĕsavt* "thou didst take", ܢܶܣܒܶܬ *nesbeth* "I took" &c. (For farther examples v. in particular § 23 *et sqq.*). In the case of ܦ the hard sound is commonly indicated by a point set within the letter, something like ܦ̇; and by ܦ is represented the sound of the Greek π (§ 25), which diverges from this, being completely unaspirated([1]) and peculiarly foreign to a Semite. Others set down ܦ = *f*, ܦ = *p*, and ܦ = π. We shall however denote the Syriac hard *p* also by ܦ.

This system, of which certain variations appear (such as ܟ, with two points, instead of ܟ) is only carried out in very careful writing. In Nestorian manuscripts, however, particularly those of later origin, and in Nestorian printed matter, the system is largely employed. At the same time these points are usually left out, when they would interfere with the vowel points, e. g. ܚܶܟܡܐ, not ܚܶܟܡܐ; ܡܶܢܝܐ, not ܡܶܢܝܐ.

Plural
points.

§ 16. A. From the oldest times, and regularly, *plural forms*, of substantives in the first place, have been *distinguished by two superscribed points* ̈, called *Sĕyāmē*([2]): thus ܡܠܟܐ, ܡܠܟܬܐ *malkē*, *malkāthā* "kings, queens" are distinguished from the singulars:—ܡܠܟܐ, ܡܠܟܬܐ *malkā, malkéthā*. And so also ܡܠܟܘܗܝ *malkau* "his kings" &c., although in such a case there was no possibility of mistaking the word for a singular.

B. Substantive plurals in ܐ commonly receive the sign ̈, but not those of the predicative adjective, thus, ܐܡܝܢ *ammīn* "cubits", but ܫܪܝܪܝܢ *šarrīrīn* "(are) true".

True collective nouns, which have no special plural, must take ̈, e. g. ܥܢܐ *'ānā* "a flock", but we have ܒܩܪܐ *baqrā* "herd (of cattle)", because a plural ܒܩܪܐ *baqrē* "herds" appears.

([1]) Answering to the representation of τ by ܬ (not by ܛ) and of κ by ܦ (not by ܩ).

([2]) The Hebrew appellation in vogue,—*Ribbūi* is naturally unknown to the Syrians. It was borrowed by a European scholar from the Hebrew Grammarians, and means "plural".

The feminine plural-forms of the finite verb and of the predicative adjective take ⁓, e. g. ܟܬ̈ܒܝ "they (fem.) wrote", ܝܟܬ̈ܒܢ "they (fem.) write" (Impf.), ܛܒ̈ܢ "are good (f.)". Only, these points are generally wanting, when the 3ʳᵈ pl. fem. in the perfect is written like the 3ʳᵈ sing. masc. (§ 50 B).

With the numerals there is a good deal of fluctuation. The rule that only feminine numbers of the second decade,—because they end in the plural in *ē*,—are to be supplied with ⁓, is seldom strictly followed. Numerals with ܝ generally take ⁓; farther, all which end in ܝ,—in particular ܬܪ̈ܝܢ, ܬܪ̈ܬܝܢ "two". The plural sign is the rule in numerals which have a possessive suffix (§ 149).

C. Generally speaking, a tolerable uniformity is found,—and that in old manuscripts,—only in cases under A; in cases under B, these manuscripts often omit the sign ⁓, where it should stand, and employ it instead in other cases, but without consistency, e. g. in the masc. of the finite verb, as ܐܫܟܚܘ "they (masc.) found"; ܘܢܬܩܕܫܘܢ "that they (masc.) may be sanctified".(¹)

D. The position of the points ⁓ was not thoroughly determined: most frequently they were permitted to rest upon the third or fourth letter from the end of the word. Much depends here on the fancy of the writer; the position most favoured is over those letters which do not rise high above the line. With the point of the letter ܝ the plural sign generally blends into ̈ܝ, e. g. ܡܪ̈ܝܐ "lords"; ܫܪ̈ܝܪܐ "true"; still there are found also ܝܩܝܪ̈ܐ "revered", ܥܣܪ̈ܝܢ "twenty", ܩܘܪ̈ܝܐ "villages", and many others.

§ 17. Here and there a line over the letter is found as a sign of the want of a vowel, e. g. ܦܠܓܘ *péleγ* "were divided", as contrasted with ܦܠܓܘ "distributed"; ܠܚܡܝ *laḥm* "my bread". Oftener this ⁓ stands as a sign that a consonant is to be omitted in the pronunciation, e. g. ܡܕܝ̣ܢ̱ܬܐ *mēḏītā* "town", ܒܪ̱ܬ *bath* "daughter", ܗ̱ܘܐ *wā* "was". The West-

Upper and under line.

(¹) The sign ⁓ is even set improperly over words, which are singular, but look like plural, e. g. over ܠܝܠܝ "night" (sing. abs. st.) and over Greek words in ܠ— η like ܗܘܠܐ *ύλη*.

Syrians employ in this case partly ‐, partly — especially in more recent times; and this use of the *linea occultans* is followed in the most of
our impressions. But commonly in MSS. such a sign is altogether
wanting. (¹)

In contrast with the use of the upper line ‐, the under line —
is made use of, especially with the Nestorians, to denote a fuller vocalisation, that is to say when a vowel is inserted in order to avoid harshness, *e. g.* ܐܠܡܟܡܐ = ܚܟܡܬܐ for ܚܟܡܬܐ "wisdom" (§ 52 C) &c. So also
ܢܫܐܠܘܢ = ܢܥܠܟܘܢ for ܢܥܠܟܘܢ they ask (§ 34).

INTERPUNCTUATION AND ACCENTS.

**Interpunct-
uation.**
§ 18. The oldest *interpunctuation*, which is frequently retained even
in later times, consists of a single strongly marked point . after larger or
smaller divisions of the sentence, for which, in the case of large paragraphs, a stronger sign ، or the like, appears. But even in very ancient
manuscripts a system of *interpunctuation* is found, of a more or less formed
character. Later, alongside of the chief point ܦܣܘܩܐ (.ܣܟܡܐ), the main
distinction made is between "the under point" ܐܣܓܝܪܐ (.ܣܟܡܐ), "the
upper point" ܚܓܝܪܐ (.ܣܟܡܐ), and "the equal points" ܩܘܡܐ (:ܣܟܡܐ),—to
indicate different clauses of the sentence of greater or less importance.
To some extent other signs also are used for this purpose. The tests
of the usage are not clear, and the practice is very fluctuating, at least
on the part of copyists.

Accents.
§ 19. In order to signify with accuracy, whether,—in the recitation
of the sacred text in worship,—the individual words of a sentence should
be associated with more or with less connection,—and also what relative
tone befits each word,—a complicated system of "Accents" was employed
in Syriac as well as in Hebrew. This system however appears only in
manuscripts of the Bible, and in a grammatical point of view it is of
very slender importance. In isolated cases, signs taken from this

---

(¹) Sometimes the under line is found in still wider employment as a sign of
the want of a vowel, in Western MSS., *e. g.* ܚܢܝܢܐ *ḥĕnīnō* "who has obtained favour",
as contrasted with ܚܢܝܢܐ "rancid".

system are found also in other uses: thus, for instance, we may meet with an upper point lending emphasis to the word in a summons, a command, an interrogation. Such a point is not distinguishable in all cases, so far as appearance goes, from the points treated of in § 6 *sq.*

II. PHONOLOGY.

1. CONSONANTS.

GENERAL STATEMENT.

§ 20. *Every word and every syllable commences with a consonant.* That no word can begin with a vowel sound is expressed clearly in Semitic writing by ‏ܐ‎ [preceding such sound], *e. g.* ‏ܐܬܐ‎ *āthē*, or rather *'āthē* "comes"; ‏ܐܘܪܚܐ‎ *'urḥā* "a way"; ‏ܐܝܕܐ‎ *'īðā* "hand", &c. In cases like ‏ܝܕܥ‎ "knew", the word is spoken as if it stood ‏ܐܝܕܥ‎ *'īða'*, and so it is even written at times (§ 40 C). Beginning of the syllable.

No Syriac word begins originally with a double consonant. Yet such a consonant seems to have been produced by the falling away of a very short vowel in ‏ܫܬܐ‎, ‏ܫܬܝܢ‎ *štā*, *štīn* (as well as ‏ܐܫܬܐ‎, ‏ܐܫܬܝܢ‎) "six", "sixty" (in East-Syriac also, ‏ܫܬܝܬܐ‎ "the sixth"; cf. the forms for *sixteen* § 148 B); in the later pronunciation still oftener, and even in other cases, as perhaps in ‏ܟܣܐ‎ *ksē* from *kėsē* "covered".

§ 21. The West-Syrians appear to have lost long ago the original *doubling of a consonant*; the East-Syrians seem generally to have retained it: the former, for example, pronounce ‏עַמָּא‎ "people", ‏ܥܡܐ‎ *'amō*, the latter ‏ܥܡܐ‎ *'ammā*. Nearly every consonant then is to be held as doubled, which is preceded by a short vowel and followed by any vowel, thus ‏ܩܛܠ‎ "murdered", ‏ܢܣܒ‎ "takes" are pronounced *qaṭṭel, nessav*. Doubling.

The absence of doubling may be relied on only when a softened consonant continues soft, *e. g.* ‏ܐܬܐ‎ *'ethā* "came", not *'eththā*, for this softening, or assibilation, is inadmissible in a doubled letter; while on the contrary the hard sound in such a consonant after a vowel is a sure token of doubling, *e. g.* ܢܦܝܩ *nappīq* "gone forth". How far the gutturals ܥ and ܗ underwent a real doubling is a matter of question; but the treatment of the vocalisation for the most part is the same as if such doubling had occurred (cf. Hebr. בֵּעֵר, מַהֵר). The case is similar with ܪ, which also the East-Syrians at a pretty early date had already ceased to double, but for which they occasionally at least turned a foregoing *a* into *ā*.

In many cases the doubling has entered in a secondary way, as in ܐܠܗܐ *allāhā* "God", ܐܕܒܚ *eddabbaḥ* "I sacrifice".

B. The doubling at all events very early fell away, when merely a *sh*[e]*va* followed the doubled consonant, *e. g.* in ܪܓܬܐ "desire", properly *reggĕthā*, then *regthā*, and even very early through assimilation (§ 22) *rekthā*; so ܒܙܬܐ *bezzĕthā* "booty", *bezthā*, *besthā*. Thus ܡܬܓܫܫܐ "it is touched", properly *methgaššĕšā*, was early pronounced like *methgaššā* or even *methgašā*.

C. A very ancient dissolving of the doubling in the case of *r*, with compensation in lengthening the vowel, appears to occur in ܓܐܪܐ *gērā*

☞ p. 341 "arrow" from *garrā*; ܚܐܪܐ *ḥērē* (*ḥērīn* &c.) "free", from *ḥarrē*; ܒܐܪܝܬܐ *bēryāthā* "streets" from *barryāthā*. Thus perhaps also ܨܐܕ (ܨܐܕܘܗܝ &c.) "with" from *ṣadd*.

D. Consonants written double were originally separated by a vowel, though very short, *e. g.* ܣܡܡܐ φάρμακα *samâmē*, later *sammē*; ܓܠܠܐ "waves" *galâlē*, later *gallē*; ܓܕܕܐ "wormwood" *gedâdē*, later *geddē*. By a false analogy even ܣܡܡܢܐ φάρμακα *sammānē* is accordingly often written instead of ܣܡܢܐ, and in fact ܣܡܡܢܐ for the singular instead of ܣܡܐ *sammā*; and similarly in like cases. An actual exception to that rule is furnished only by cases like ܐܬܬܣܝܡ or ܐܬܣܝܡ *ettĕsīm* "was set"; ܐܬܬܥܝܪ or ܐܬܥܝܪ *ettĕʿīr* "was awakened" &c. (§§ 36. 177 B).

In Greek words letters are sometimes written double, even when such doubling does not occur in the original, *e. g.* ܦܝܠܠܝܦܘܣ Φίλιππος often instead of ܦܝܠܝܦܘܣ or ܦܝܠܝܦܦܘܣ.

Assimilation.

§ 22. When two consonants came together in the living speech, and still more in the somewhat artificial recitation of the Bible in religious service, the first consonant was frequently modified by the second, so that a *media* before a *tenuis* was turned into a *tenuis*, a *tenuis* before a *media* into a *media*, and so forth. ܙܠ was pronounced like ܣܠ (*e. g.* ܪܓܝܙܠܐ "vehemently angry" like ܪܓܝܣܠܐ), for ܙ is a *media* and ܣ a *tenuis* like ܠ (in spite of the assibilation); ܙܒ like ܣܒ (*e. g.* ܙܳܒܶܢ "conquers" like ܣܳܒܶܢ; ܕܙܰܟܰܪܝܳܐ "of Zacharias" like ܕܣܟܪܝܐ); *vice versa* ܣܕ like ܙܕ (*e. g.* ܚܶܣܕܳܐ "disgrace" like ܚܙܕܐ). Farther ܓܠ was given like ܟܠ (*e. g.* ܪܓܘܓܠܬܐ "greedy" like ܪܓܘܟܠܬܐ), and even ܩܠ, with suppression of the emphasis before the unemphatic ܠ, like ܟܠ (*e. g.* ܥܩܘܠܬܐ "sorrowful" like ܥܟܘܠܬܐ). The East-Syrians went much farther in this process, for they prescribed *e. g.* ܠܡܶܕܒܰܪ even for ܠܡܶܬܒܰܪ "to break"; ܝܳܓܕܺܝܢ for ܝܳܩܕܺܝܢ "they burn"; and they gave to ܫ immediately before ܒ, ܓ, ܕ, the sound of the French *j*, *ge* (Pers. ژ), *e. g.* in ܚܽܘܫܒܳܢܳܐ "an account". This subject might be treated at great length. Notice that such assimilations take place even when the consonants affected were originally separated by a *sh^e^va* (*ê*).—The *written* language exhibits only a few traces of these changes. (1)

Rem. A very ancient reversed assimilation consists in ܩܬ always becoming ܩܛ in Aramaic roots (2) at the beginning of the word, as the emphatic ܛ corresponds more accurately to ܩ than does ܬ. Similar equalisations in all roots might farther be pointed out.

RUKKĀKHĀ AND QUŠŠĀYĀ.

Rukkākhā and Quššāyā. R. and Q. in individual words.

§ 23. A. The rules for *Rukkākhā*, i. e. the soft (assibilated, hissing, or aspirated) pronunciation and for *Quššāyā*, i. e. the hard (or unaspirated) pronunciation, originally affect all the letters ܒ ܓ ܕ ܟ ܦ ܬ [*Beghadhkephath*] in equal measure. But the East-Syrians for a very long time have nearly always given ܦ a hard sound; only in the end of a syllable have they sometimes given it a soft pronunciation. (3) The ☞ p. 341

(1) The proper name כזבי (Num. 25, 15) is written in Ceriani's Pesh. ܟܘܣܒܝ, where *sb* has the sound of *zb*. In Aphr. 111, 6, and Ephr. Nis. 71 v. 65 (in one Codex) it still stands ܟܘܙܒܝ.

(2) ܩܶܬܪܳܐ "stone" would form an exception, but this word is probably of foreign origin. ☞ p. 341

(3) And in that case, apparently, they always make it quiesce into *u*. Even the best Nestorian MSS. are, from these circumstances, of almost no value for an

following rules accordingly are not applicable to the East-Syrian pronunciation of ܦ.

B. These letters are hard in the beginning of words, e. g. ܒܲܝܬܵܐ "house", ܓܲܡܠܵܐ "camel", &c. (but notice § 24 and 25).

C. ܒ ܓ ܕ ܟ ܦ ܬ experience R.— (i. e. take the soft pronunciation) after any vowel, however short, when they do not happen to be doubled. Thus after a full vowel ܩܛܲܠ, ܩܛܲܠ, ܩܛܲܠ, ܩܛܲܠ, ܩܛܲܠ, &c.

On the other hand these letters undergo Q. (i. e. take the hard form) when they are doubled: ܩܛܲܠ ܩܛܲܠ (ܩܲܒܸܠ), ܩܛܲܠ (ܣܲܢܝ), ܩܛܲܠ ܩܛܲܠ, ܩܛܲܠ ܩܛܲܠ, &c., and even after long vowels ܪ݂ܓ݂ܝ݂ܢ (rāggīn "they desire"), ܒܵܬܹ݁ (bāttē "houses"), &c.

Farther they take Q. immediately after consonants: ܩܛܲܠ ܩܛܲܠ, ܩܛܲܠ, &c. Diphthongs too have the effect of a consonantal ending, thus ܩܛܲܠ, ܩܛܲܠ, ܩܛܲܠ, ܩܛܲܠ, &c.

Exceptions: ܐܲܟ݂ "as", which is pronounced akh.

Even the mere sheva mobile effects R. just as a vowel would: ܩܛܲܠ (qevol), ܩܛܲܠ, ܩܛܲܠ, &c. Thus is it also when one of the particles ܒ ܠ ܕ ܘ is prefixed: ܩܛܲܠ; but ܩܛܲܠ (lēvānē); ܩܛܲܠ, but ܩܛܲܠ, &c. So too is it when several of these words or particles are prefixed, e. g. ܩܛܲܠ : ܩܛܲܠ, ܩܛܲܠ, ܩܛܲܠ; ܩܛܲܠ : ܩܛܲܠ, &c. Except upon the first consonant, these prefixes however have no effect, thus, ܩܛܲܠ kethāvā, ܩܛܲܠ lakhthāvā, originally lakhethāvā, not lakhtāvā &c.

Regularly the sheva mobile has a softening effect after a consonant originally doubled, thus ܡܸܫܬܲܡܲܥ (ܡܸܬܚܲܫܒܝܼܢ), ܩܛܲܠ (ܪܲܒܬܵܐ), ܩܛܲܠ mahhethā = manhethā), &c. So also, of course, when the consonant furnished with sheva mobile is preceded by another which is quite vowelless, as in ܩܛܲܠ, ܩܛܲܠ, ܩܛܲܠ, &c.

D. But many a sheva mobile fell away (sheva mobile transmuted into sheva quiescens) at a time when the influence which it exercised upon the softening process (Rukkākhā) was still a living one, with the result that the influence of the hardening process (Quššāyā) in turn ap-

---

enquiry into R. and Q. of p. Besides even good MSS. and prints contain errors sometimes, as regards these 'points'.

peared. On the other hand such falling away occasionally came about at a time when the influence referred to was no longer in being, so that *Rukkākhā* remained effective even after the disappearance of *sh^eva*...

peared. On the other hand such falling away occasionally came about at a time when the influence referred to was no longer in being, so that *Rukkākhā* remained effective even after the disappearance of *sh^eva mobile*. Upon the whole R. has been abandoned more completely in the case of the falling away of an *ĕ* that had originated from *i* (*e*), than in that of an *ĕ* from *a*: compare ܓ݂ܰܪܒ݂ܳܐ "scabies" from *garăvā*, with ܓ݂ܰܪܒ݂ܳܐ "scabiosus" from *garĭvā*. It makes no difference whether the foregoing syllable,—now a closed one (ending in *sh^eva quiescens*),—has a long or a short vowel; cf. ܢܶܣܚܽܦ, ܦ݂ܳܐܟܶܡ, ܡܚܰܝܒܳܐ, and other derivatives from the act. part. Peal([1]); ܐܰܥܺܝܪܶܗ, ܡܰܥܰܡܗ "I awakened him", &c.

In the interior of words R., when it comes after an earlier *sh^eva mobile* unpreceded by two consonants without a full vowel or by a double consonant, is now kept up only here and there, and that particularly in the verb: cf. even cases like ܢܶܠܕܳܢ *nēldān* (*nīldōn*) "they bring forth children", from *nēliðān*. For the substantive,—cf. cases like ܡܰܠܟܳܐ, contrasted with the Hebr. מַלְכֵי from *malăkhai* (but v. § 93) and ܡܰܠܟܽܘܬܳܐ, contrasted with מַלְכוּת.

E. The usage in the case of Fem. ܐ is specially fluctuating, for the ܬ here is often hard after a consonant, and often on the other hand soft. This ܬ has nearly always Q. [*i. e.* it is pronounced hard, as if with *Dag. lene*] after syllables which have a long vowel, particularly *ī* or *ū*, *e. g.* ܡܶܢܙܰܠܬܳܐ, ܘܳܙܘܰܓܬܳܐ, ܡܰܪܒܥܬܳܐ, ܕܡܶܢܬܳܐ, ܩܶܢܙܬܳܐ, ܦܶܝܢܡܬܳܐ, ܘܰܐܚܕܬܳܐ, ܒܰܐܪܙܬܳܐ, ܕܰܥܠܡܬܳܐ, ܡܰܚܕܘܬܳܐ, ܚܠܡܘܬܳܐ, ܘܙܘܬܳܐ, &c. Exceptions:—ܩܶܣܡܬܳܐ, ܙܰܥܡܬܳܐ, ܓܺܝܬܳܐ([2]); ܕܽܐܢܫܬܳܐ, and some others. With *ā*: ܢܣܽܒܬܳܐ, ܗܶܡܰܥܬܳܐ, ܡܶܚܙܢܬܳܐ, ܫܰܚܬܳܐ, &c.; but ܘܡܰܪܬܳܐ, ܡܶܙܥܰܪܬܳܐ, ܡܰܕܪܬܳܐ, ܩܰܠܚܬܳܐ, ܡܰܚܕܬܳܐ, ܓܶܡܥܬܳܐ, and a few others. Always Q. (*i. e. Quššāyā,* or *Dag. lene*) after ܢ, *e. g.* ܙܰܢܡܬܳܐ, ܐܰܢܫܬܳܐ. After syllables with *ă*, perhaps R. of ܬ somewhat preponderates: ܘܶܡܰܕܬܳܐ, ܣܶܓܙܬܳܐ, ܡܶܥܣܬܳܐ, ܡܶܢܙܝܰܠ, ܡܶܙܡܘܓܬܳܐ, ܡܶܕܘܙܓܬܳܐ, ܒܡܶܥܕܬܳܐ, &c.; yet ܡܶܚܕܬܳܐ, ܥܶܡܥܬܳܐ, ܡܰܡܓܣܬܳܐ, ܐܰܠܣܝܬܳܐ, and many others. With *ĕ* Q. has the preponderance: ܢܶܓܓܕܬܳܐ, ܡܶܚܕܬܳܐ, ܠܰܚܕܡܬܳܐ, and many others; yet ܢܳܘܦܬܳܐ, and so too, forms

---

([1]) Contrary to the Hebrew כֹּתְבִים, &c. A few exceptions, like ܦܳܠܚܰܝ 1 Cor. 9, 13, are cited.

([2]) According to the best traditions.

like ܪܚܡܬܐ, ܦܩܕܬܐ (to which ܦܪܫܬܐ, ܓܡܪܬܐ also belong). So ܚܡܬܐ "anger", and the like. With *u* and *o* we have ܐܠܡܘܣܬܐ, ܡܠܟܘܬܐ, ܐܬܓܒܘܪܬܐ, &c., overagainst ܡܩܘܣܬܐ, ܐܡܦܘܦܬܐ. Individual peculiarities are very complicated here, and the tradition occasionally varies. On the whole Q. is preferred after *r*, *l*, and *š*, and R. after ʿ, *m* &c., in the ܬ of the termination ܬܐ [*i. e.* ܬ in that feminine termination, is generally sounded *hard* after *r*, *l*, and *š*, and *soft*, or with assibilation, after ʿ and *m*]. The analogy of words of similar form or meaning has exercised great influence here. Something will be said on this head afterwards in treating of the parts of speech.

F. The quite peculiar Q. of ܫܬܐ, ܫܬܝܢ (along with ܐܫܬܐ, ܐܫܬܝܢ) "six", "sixty" points to the loss of a *shᵉva* in remote times [v. D].

G. Like ܚܡܬܐ "anger" we also have ܚܡܬܝ, ܚܡܬܗܘܢ "my, their anger"; here farther, analogy in this way breaks through the old law, that Q. must stand immediately after a consonant [v. C]. Thus ܕܗܒܝ, ܕܗܒܗܘܢ "my, their gold", following ܕܗܒܐ "gold" (from *dahăvā*), and many others. Thus the ܬ of the 3. sing. fem. in the Perf. (at least according to the usual pronunciation) remains always soft: ܩܛܠܬܗ "she has killed him", ܩܛܠܬܢܝ "she has killed me" (as against ܩܛܠܬܗ "I have killed him", &c.). On the other hand the ܬ of the 2. pers. in the Perf. is kept hard in all circumstances, thus ܩܛܠܬ "thou hast killed" (and ܐܢܬ "thou"), as well as ܓܠܝܬ "thou hast revealed", ܓܠܝܬܝ "thou (f.) hast revealed"; ܓܠܝܬܘܢ, ܓܠܝܬܝܢ "Ye (m. and f.) have revealed" &c.

In other respects too we find remarkable deviations from the fundamental rules, *e. g.* in ܐܪܒܥܬܝܗܝܢ (§ 149) "they four (f.)" or "the four of them", where ܬ݂ might have been expected. Although the fundamental rules are still clear, they became practically ineffective even at an early stage; and thus it came about that entirely similar cases often received dissimilar treatment. Besides, fluctuations of all kinds in the dialects and in the school-tradition, manifest themselves in the matter of R. and Q.(1)

(1) Even the best MSS. are not entirely free from error in their use of these points.—And in one or two cases, a distinction, founded upon R. and Q., has been established between words consisting of the same letters,—just through arbitrary pre-

H. Original doubling in the termination preserves Q. in زؚڪ (like
اِخُرا) "great", ڪؚۏڝ "a pit", ڪؚڟ (ڪؚڟۏ from ڪؚڟۏ) "side", زۏ "place";
so too اِلَ at = att from ant "thou"; so also ڪؚڿ leb "my heart" (like
ڪؚخُرا lebbā), ڝؚڪ gad "my good fortune" (like زؚڿ) and the like. On
the other hand we have ڪؚڡ "six" (its doubling early disappeared), ڝؚجؚڪ
"side" (also ڝؚجؚڪ "my side") and verbal forms like ڡؚج "lowered",
زؚ "longed for" (and also in the plural ڡؚزؚ &c.).

I. Secondary doubling, which causes Q., we find regularly in the
1st sing. Impf. when the first radical has a vowel, as in اؚزؚڡ "I tread",
اؚخؚزؚج "I tell lies", اؚخؚزؚج "I bless thee", زؚڪؚ "I hunt", &c. Farther
in the Aphel in some verbs middle o: اؚڡؚ "made ready", اؚڡؚڡؚ "measured", as contrasted with اؚلَج "gave back", &c. (§ 177 D).

J. Words, which are otherwise like-sounding, are often distinguished
through R. and Q., as ڝؚڿؚ "thou hast revealed", and ڝؚڿؚ "I have
revealed"; ڡؚڟؚ qešthā from qeššéthā (f. of Hebr. קַשׁ) "stubble", and
ڡؚڟؚ (קֶשֶׁת) "a bow", &c.

§ 24. R. appears in the beginning of a word, when this word is R. and Q. in closely associated words.
closely associated with a preceding one which ends in a vowel, thus
اؚلؚ وؚڟؚ, John 16, 8; ۏ اؚۏ, John 16, 16; اؚجؚ ڝؚ ۏاؚلؚ ڝؚ, John 10, 38
(Bernstein) &c. The slightest pause, however, interrupts the softening.
Similarly, two closely-associated words, of which the first ends in the same
consonant as that with which the second begins, or a consonant like it,
are so pronounced together that a doubling appears, which is indicated
by the Q. of both of them: ڝؚڟؚ ڝؚجؚ خؚاؚڟؚ massabbappē (instead of ڝؚڡؚج
خؚاؚڟؚ) "playing the hypocrite"; ۏؚڡؚ ڝؚڡؚ خؚاؚڟؚ "hypocrite"; ڝؚ زؚڡؚاؚ
"ink-bottle".

§ 25. According to the prescriptions of the Schools, Greek words are Greek words.
not to be subjected to the rules for softening and hardening. Thus اؚڡؚزؚۏڡؚ
dêπarṣōπā (πρόσωπον); ڝؚ ڡؚجؚڡؚڝؚ "from Philippos", &c. (where ڡؚ is

---

scription on the part of the Schools. Thus against all rules, they would have us say
اؚزؚجؚڡؚ "I dye", but اؚزؚجؚڡؚ "I dip into"; farther اؚسؚج "shut", but اؚسؚج "hold", although
these words are identical. The distinction, besides, between ڡؚڝؚڡؚ "resurrection"
and ڡؚڝؚڡؚ "share" was hardly known to the living speech. In addition to these
examples there is a medley of cases resting upon the caprice of the Schools.

the Greek π, § 15). ܒ is made the equivalent of the Greek β, ܘ that of δ, ܟ of ϑ, ܟ of χ, ܦ of φ; ܓ generally that of γ. Thus for instance ܟܠܡܘܣ χλαμύς, ܬܐܘܪܝܐ ϑεωρία, ܒܣܝܠܝܘܣ Βασίλειος, ܓܪܡܛܝܩܝ γραμματική, &c. ξ has to be ܟܣ, e. g. ܐܟܣܘܪܝܐ ἐξορία; yet ܓܣ appears frequently, e. g. East-Syrian ܛܟܣܐ τάξις (West-Syrian ܛܟܣܐ)). Generally speaking we find here too,—especially in words early introduced, —transformations, of a genuine Syrian type, e. g. ܐܣܟܡܐ σχῆμα, ܙܘܦܪܐ φϑορά, ܣܘܡܒܠܐ συμβολή, &c.

Other foreign words too, in individual cases, vary from the rules, as regards R. and Q., e. g. ܡܓܠܬܐ "word" (Persian), where one would expect a hard ܓ.

DENTALS AND SIBILANTS.

§ 26. A. The ܬ of the Reflexive changes place, according to a common Semitic fashion, with the sibilant immediately following it (as first radical), and is altered into ܛ with ܙ, and into ܛ with ܨ, thus ܐܣܬܒܪ (for ܐܬܣܒܪ) "was thought", from ܣܒܪ "thought"; ܐܫܬܒܝ "was taken prisoner", from ܫܒܐ; ܐܙܕܩܦ "was crucified", from ܙܩܦ; ܐܙܕܕܩ "was justified" from ܙܕܩ.

B. This ܬ is assimilated to a following ܛ and ܬ, becoming hard in the process: ܐܛܛܫܝ (pronounce *eṭṭašše*) "was concealed"; ܐܬܬܒܪ (written also ܐܬܒܪ, ܐܬܬܒܪ) *ettabbar* "was broken in pieces"; so too, before a ܕ furnished with a full vowel, e. g. ܢܬܕܟܪܟ *neddakhrākh* "remembers thee". A ܕ without a full vowel, on the other hand, here falls away in pronunciation, after the ܬ that has likewise become hard: ܐܬܕܟܪ *ettēkhar* "remembered"[1]. A like assimilation takes place, when an initial ܕ or ܬ without a full vowel is pressed by a foregoing prefix upon a following ܕ, ܬ or ܛ. The ܕ or ܬ is then written hard; ܘܡܢܕܕܡܐ "and who is like", ܠܒܢܝܢܫܐ "to persons *or* things, however small"; ܘܬܕܘܨ "and thou dost skip"; ܘܡܢܕܩܘܐ "and who abides"; ܘܬܘܕܐ "and repentest", ܘܬܛܫܐ "and hidest": and the pronunciation must have been *waddāmē, wattūṣ*, &c.

---

[1] Thus there are found in MSS. sometimes, forms like ܡܬܕܚܐ for ܡܬܕܚܐ "is pushed" and even ܡܬܕܝܢܢܘܬܐ for ܡܬܕܝܢܢܘܬܐ, ܡܬܕܝܢܢܘܬܐ "capability of being judged".

An ـܘ or ـܝ falls away before the ܬ of a suffix in cases like ܟܲܬܝܼܬܵܐ
ʿabbītā (or ʿabbittā?; West-Syr. doubtless ʿabītō) "thick (f.)"; ܦܫܝܼܛܵܐ
"simple (f.)"; ܣܠܲܝܬܘܿܢ "ye despised"; ܠܵܛܬܝ "thou didst curse", ܐܫܠܛܬܵܢܝ
"gavest him power"; ܥܕܬܐ "Church"; ܡܨܝܕܬܐ "net"; ܥܒܕܬܐ "work"; ܐܒܕܬܝ
"ye (f.) perished"; ܦܩܕܬܟܘܿܢ "I commanded you"; ܗܘܲܝܬ "didst", and many
others. In just the same way a pair of ܬ 's coalesce, in words like ܐܒܗܬ
avhet for avhetht "madest ashamed"; ܐܒܗܬܢ "madest us ashamed" &c.
The marking with R. and Q. varies; in effect, in all these cases only hard
ܬ remains. For ܚܕܬܬܐ ḥĕḋattā "nova", one writes ܚܕܬܐ straight away, and
ܟܲܠܬܐ "bride" for ܟܲܠܬܬܐ.

Radical ـܝ falls away before ܬ in ܚܲܬܐ, ܢܒܝܬܐ, ܐܒܠܘܬܐ: pronounce
ḥathā &c., "novus" &c.

C. A final ܬ has early dropped off in the absolute state of
Feminines: ā coming from ath, ū from ūth, ī from īth, e. g. ܛܵܒܵܐ "bona";
ܛܵܒܘܿ "bonitas"; ܬܘܼܕܐ "confession"; in their construct state the ܬ remains: ܛܵܒܲܬ, ܛܵܒܘܿܬ, ܬܘܼܕܲܬ; and so also in the singular case of ܚܕܵܐ
"a certain (f.)", and in many adverbs (§ 155).

D. Unusual is the assimilation found in ܓܦܵܐ "wing" from geḋpā,
as also the falling out in ܗܵܐ "this" from hāḋĕnā, and in other pronouns
(§§ 67 Rem. 1; 68 Rem. 2).

LABIALS.

§ 27. ܦ and ܒ are sometimes interchangeable. Thus ܙܸܦܬܐ Labials.
frequently occurs for ܙܹܒܬܐ "pitch"; and occasionally on the other hand
e. g. ܐܦܣܘܿܠ is found for ܐܒܣܘܿܠ "happy", and ܚܙܘܦܐ for ܚܙܘܒܐ
"Friday". The East-Syrians have, from remote times, pronounced ܦ quite
like ܘ (w, u); av accordingly becomes au, and uv, ū, e. g. ܡܘܓܫܐ šūḥā.
They also pronounce ܦ like ܘ, in cases where they leave it unusually soft
and do not turn it into p (§ 23 A). Generally this transition is found in
ܙܵܘܪܒܹ᷄ "magni", ܙܵܘܪܒܵܢ "magnates"; ܙܵܘܪܒ "made great", for רַבְּרְבִין, רַבְרְבָנֵי,
רַבְרֵב (§ 146). Compare ܫܘܫܡܢܐ "an ant" from ܫܡܫܡܢܐ (§ 31).

Liquids.

LIQUIDS.

n. § 28. *N*, as first radical, is almost always assimilated to the consonant immediately following it: ܐܰܦܶܩ "brought out", from *anpeq*; ܢܶܦܽܘܩ "goes out", from *nenpoq*; ܡܰܚܶܬ "brings down", from *manḥeth*; ܬܶܨܒܽܘܬ "plantest", from *tenṣov*, &c. Exception is made when ܗ follows: ܢܶܢܗܽܘܡ "roars"; ܢܶܢܗܰܪ "grows clear"; ܡܰܢܗܰܪ "lights", &c. (yet ܢܶܗܽܘܙ "thrusts" from *nenhaz*), and in other very rare cases (§ 173 A).

As second radical, *n* is assimilated in some nouns: ܥܩܳܐ "necklace"; ܥܰܩܬܳܐ "oppression"; ܐܰܦܶܐ "face"; ܓܶܒܳܐ "side"; ܐܶܦܬܳܐ "occasion"; ܫܶܬܶܐ "foundation", from *ʿenqā* &c.,—as against ܟܢܽܘܫܬܳܐ "congregation"; ܕܽܘܢܒܳܐ, ܕܽܘܢܒܬܳܐ "tail", which originally must have had a short vowel after the *n*, &c. The *n* that falls away is still written in ܓܶܢܒܳܐ "side", and ܐܢ̄ܬܬܳܐ (pronounce *attā* § 26) "woman", construct state ܐܢ̄ܬܰܬ; so in ܐܢ̄ܬ, f. ܐܢ̄ܬܝ "thou", pl. ܐܢ̄ܬܽܘܢ, f. ܐܢ̄ܬܶܝܢ.

Farther, *n* loses its sound in many cases before ܬܳܐ of the feminine ending: ܓܽܘܦܬܳܐ *gĕfettā* from *gĕfentā* "vine"; ܓܒܶܬܳܐ "cheese"; ܠܒܶܬܳܐ "brick"; ܓܪܰܒܬܳܐ "a field-measure"; ܬܐܢܬܳܐ, ܬܐܬܳܐ ([1]) "fig"; and with *n* still written, in ܡܕܺܝܢ̄ܬܳܐ "town"; ܣܦܺܝܢ̄ܬܳܐ "ship"; ܙܒܢ̄ܬܳܐ "a time"; ܫܢ̄ܬܳܐ "year"; and in ܠܒܽܘܢ̄ܬܳܐ "incense", the *n* of which is still pronounced by others.

In ܓܢ̄ܒܳܪܳܐ *gabbārā* "hero", the nasal which serves as compensation for the doubling has been stroked out later.

On the dropping off of the *n* in the Imperative v. § 171 C, and in certain substantives, § 105.

l. § 29. *L* falls away when next to another *l*, in ܡܰܡܠܠܳܐ *mamlā* "speech", written also in fact ܡܰܡܠܳܐ; and in ܡܰܛܠܠܳܐ *maṭlā* "covering". Thus most Syrians say ܩܽܘܠܠܳܐ *qovlā* "countenance" (others *qovelā*).

It farther falls away in many forms which come from ܐܙܰܠ "to go" (v. § 183), as also in forms from ܣܠܶܩ (v. same section).

r. § 30. *R* falls out in ܒܪ̈ܰܬ "daughter", construct state—(but not in the emphatic state ܒܪܰܬܳܐ).

([1]) Thus, with hard ܬ according to the best tradition. Probably the sing. of ܟܣܝ̈ܬܐ "corals" was pronounced as ܟܣܝܬܳܐ (Talmudic כסיתא).

§ 31. We have unusual abbreviations in several nouns which are Unusual Abbreviations with Liquids. formed from the doubling of a short root ending in *r*, *l*, *n*, *m*: thus ܫܐܫܠܬܐ, ܫܫܠܬܐ "chain", from *šelšaltā* (cf. ܩܩܙܐ "tape-worms"); ܓܝܓܠܐ "wheel"; ܓܘܓܪܬܐ "throat" from *gargartā*; ܩܢܩܢܐ, ܩܢܩܢܐ "plough" from *qenqênā*; ܫܘܫܡܢܐ([1]) "an ant", probably from ܫܘܫܡܢܐ, and one or two others.

§ 31[b]. *n* beginning a word becomes *l* in several foreign words, like *n* becoming *l* in foreign words. ܠܘܡܐ, along with ܢܘܡܐ, from νοῦμμος, *nummus*; ܠܡܛܐ with ܢܡܛܐ, from the Persian *namat* "carpet".

GUTTURALS.

Gutturals.

§ 32. ܐ for the most part loses in Syriac its consonantal sound. Falling away of initial ܐ. As an initial sound it falls away along with its vowel in many words to which it belongs: ܐܢܫ or ܢܫ, ܐܢܫܐ, ܢܩܝ, ܢܩܝ "man", "men", &c.; ܐܚܪܝܢ or ܚܪܝܢ, ܐܚܪܝܐ, &c. "another"; ܐܚܪܝܐ or ܚܪܝܐ "last", ܐܚܪܝܗ "his last", &c.; ܐܣܝܪ "related"; ܐܢܐ or ܐܢ in certain cases for ܐܢܐ "I". Even in writing, this ܐ is without exception wanting in ܚܪܝܐ "end"; ܚܕ, ܚܕܐ "one" (m. and f.); ܚܬܐ "sister"; ܟܣܐ "pocket" (bag), and "bearing beam" (rafter) (v. אחד); ܬܐ, ܬܘ, &c. "come"; ܙܠ, ܙܠ, &c. "go"; ܘܙܐ, ܘܙܐ "goose", from אַוְזָא; ܐܢ (properly "there") = אֲדֵין.

§ 33. A. As a medial, ܐ disappears completely according to the Treatment of medial ܐ. usual pronunciation, when it immediately follows a consonant or a mere *sheva*; and the vowel of the ܐ is transferred to the preceding consonant. Thus (a) ܡܛܐܒ *maṭev* "makes good" for *maṭʾev*; ܢܫܐܠ "demands" for *nešʾal*; ܣܢܐܐ "hater"; ܛܡܐܐ "unclean" f. (constr. st.) &c. (b) ܛܐܒ "was good" *tev* for *ṭeʾev*; ܫܐܠܐ *šīlā* "demanded" (part.); ܫܦܐܪ "beautiful"; ܫܦܐܪ "beautiful" (pl.); ܛܠܐܒ "blaming", &c. So too after prefixes: ܕܐܒܐ "of the father", from ܐܒܐ + ܕ; ܠܐܘܡܢܐ "to the artificer" *lummānā*; ܘܐܟܠ "and ate"; "in what? (f.)" &c. In writing, such an ܐ is always left out in ܒܣ "bad", from בְּאִישׁ, in ܡܓܒ, ܠܓܒ "teaches", "teachest", &c. for מְאַלֵּף, &c; farther, generally in the compound ܐܦܢ for ܐܢ ܐܦ "although".

([1]) This vocalisation with *au* is much better supported than that with *u* (ܫܘܫܡܢܐ).

Although this falling away of the ܐ is very ancient, yet the East-Syrians frequently retain it as a consonant in such cases: thus *e. g.* they prefer to punctuate ܢܫܐܠ, ܒܐܬܐ, without pushing forward the vowel to the preceding consonant, as if it should still be read *neš'al, be'āthā*; but all this without consistency.

B. Between two vowels ܐ receives with many Syrians (always?) the pronunciation *y*, *e. g.* ܐܐܪ *ōyar* "air" (West-Syr.). This pronunciation, which occasionally finds expression even in writing, *e. g.* ܣܝܐ for ܣܐܐ "defiled" (§ 172 A B), has however not been general.

In the end of a syllable ܐ always loses its consonantal value: ܫܐܠܬ "I demanded", is in sound the same as ܫܠܬ; ܢܐܟܘܠ "eats" = ܢܟܘܠ; ܣܐܒܝܢ "are growing old" = ܣܒܝܢ, &c. Etymology alone can decide here, as in many other cases, whether ܐ is a mere vowel-letter or an original guttural (Arabic *Hemza*). Such an ܐ is now no longer written in cases like ܣܓܝ from *saggī'* (cf. ܣܓܝܐܐ, ܣܓܝܐܐܝܢ, &c.) "much". On the changes of vowels at the disappearance of such an ܐ v. § 53.

Auxiliary vowel of the ܐ. § 34. An ܐ, which in the beginning of the syllable ought to receive a vocal *sh*^e^*va*,—according to the analogy of other consonants,—retains a full vowel instead; but in the middle of a word it gives up this vowel to the foregoing consonant (by § 33 A) and loses its own consonantal value. The vowel is ◌ܶ or ◌ܳ, and the latter even in many cases where it was originally *a*. Thus ܐܡܪ "spoke", compared with ܩܛܠ "killed" 3. s. (originally *amar, qaṭal*); ܐܡܝܪ "spoken", compared with ܩܛܝܠ "killed" (from *qaṭīl*); ܐܟܘܠ "eat", like ܩܛܘܠ "kill",—ܡܬܐܟܠ "is being eaten" (like ܡܬܩܛܠ "is being killed"); ܡܠܐܟܐ "angel" = מַלְאֲכָא; ܡܟܐܒܐ "afflicted" *machevē* (East-Syrian ܡܟܐܒܐ) &c. The Nestorians occasionally write in these cases ◌ܱ (§ 17) *e. g.* ܡܬܐܟܠ, which is even improperly used for regular vowels, as in ܫܬܐܣܝܗ = ܫܬܐܣܝܗ (§ 45) "her foundations". An *o* (perhaps lengthened?) has been thus maintained in ܐܘܪܘܬܐ (Plural of ܐܘܪܝܐ "manger") from *ŏrawāthā*. Such an ܐ with a *sh*^e^*va* disappears without leaving a trace in ܣܘܓܐܗܘܢ, ܣܘܓܗܘܢ "their multitude" from ܣܘܓܐܐ for *soγ'ā*.

Orthographic Note on ܐ. § 35. Seeing that a radical ܐ frequently thus falls away in pronunciation, it is often left out also in writing, and that even in the oldest manuscripts, *e. g.* ܡܟܘܠܬܐ for ܡܐܟܘܠܬܐ "food"; ܢܟܘܠ for ܢܐܟܘܠ "eats"; ܦܬܐ for ܦܐܬܐ "face". On the other hand ܐ, even when a manifestly superfluous letter, is yet placed in words where it should not have appeared at all,—as in ܢܣܐܒ for ܢܣܒ "to take"; ܬܥܐܠܘܢ for ܬܥܠܘܢ "ye enter"; ܛܐܒܐ for ܛܒܐ "report"; ܩܐܝܡܝܢ for ܩܝܡܝܢ "stand" (pl.); ܫܘܚܐܪܐ for ܫܘܚܪܐ "delay"; ܪܘܘܐܚܐ, ܪܐܘܘܚܐ and even ܪܐܘܘܐܚܐ for ܪܘܘܚܐ or (West-S.) ܪܘܘܚܐ "pity", &c.; or it stands in the wrong place, like ܛܐܡܘܬܐ for ܛܡܐܘܬܐ "uncleanness"; ܫܘܐܠܐ for ܫܐܠܬܐ "question"; ܫܝܐܠܐ for ܫܐܝܠܐ "demanded" (part.) &c.; or it is doubled instead of being written once, as in ܒܝܐܐ for ܒܝܐ "comforts", and the like. The superfluous ܐ is a good deal in favour in certain causative forms, particularly in short ones, *e. g.* ܡܐܚܐ = ܡܚܐ "gives life"; ܐܐܙܩ "injures".

§ 36. In certain cases a vowel-less ܬ, followed by an ܐ, blends with that letter into a hard ܬ doubled and generally written ܬܬ (pointed ܬܬ, ܬܬ, ܬܬ, ܬܬ, which all express the same sound, § 26): in older days it was often signified by a single ܬ. Thus, regularly, in the reflexive of Aphel ܐܬܬܩܛܠ, ܐܬܬܩܛܠ, for *etḥ'aqṭal*; ܐܬܬܩܝܡ "was established" (ܐܬܐܩܝܡ) v. § 177 D &c. Thus, besides, in ܐܬܬܚܕ "was held" (ܐܬܐܚܕ) for *etḥ'eḥeḏ*, and occasionally in similar forms (§ 174 C). A single ܬ is almost always written for ܬܬ, if another ܬ precedes by way of prefix, *e. g.* ܬܬܩܝܡ, ܬܬܚܕ, instead of ܬܬܬܩܝܡ, ܬܬܬܚܕ. ܬܐ becoming ܬܬ. ☞ p. 341

§ 37. Even before the orthography was elaborated, a ܥ followed by another ܥ in the same root became ܐ (ܐܠܥܐ "rib", from ܥܠܥ; ܐܥܦܐ "doubled", from ܥܥܦ, and many others)[1]: In like manner, with the West-Syrians, a ܥ coming immediately before ܗ becomes ܐ and is treated like it in every respect. Thus ܥܗܕ "remembered",—pronounce ܐܗܕ, from ܥܗܕ; ܥܘܗܕܢܐ "recollection",—pronounce ܐܘܗܕܢܐ; ܡܬܥܗܕ *metheheḏ* for ܡܬܥܗܕ, &c. This change, which becomes noticeable even in the fourth century, and is occasionally indicated also in writing (ܐܗܘܪܝܢ, ܐܗܢ for ܥܗܘܪܝܢ, ܥܗܢ "to be in heat"), has however remained unknown to the East-Syrians. ܥ.

§ 38. ܗ, which as an initial letter had, even in ancient times, often ܗ.

---

(1) Cf. ܢܢܥܐ "mentha" ['mint'] from נַעְנְעָא.

passed into ܐ (*e. g.* in ܐܢܘܢ secondary form of ܗܢܘܢ "they", and in the Aphel ܐܩܛܠ from *haqṭel*, &c.), falls away in pronunciation in many forms of the suffix of the 3rd sing. masc., *e. g.* ܡܠܟܘܗܝ *malkau* from *malkauhī*, "his kings"; ܒܢܝܗܝ "built it" (m.); ܢܩܛܠܝܘܗܝ "kills him". The personal pronoun—ܗܘ "he" or ܗܝ "she"— loses the ܗ, when it is enclitic, *e. g.* ܩܛܠܘ ܗܘ *qĕṭalū*; ܠܗ ܗܘ or ܠܗܘ *lēhū*; ܡܢܐ ܗܝ *mānāi* from *mānā hī*; ܡܢܐ ܗܘ from *mānā hū*. In fact ܡܢܘ, ܗܢܘ, ܐܝܟܘ are often written for ܡܢܐ ܗܘ, ܗܢܐ ܗܘ, ܐܝܟܐ ܗܘ. So always ܠܘ "not", from ܠܐ ܗܘ. From ܗܘ ܗܘ, ܗܝ ܗܝ come ܗܘܝܘ, ܗܝܝ: but ܗܝ ܗܝ is occasionally written even yet, though we do not so often meet with ܗܘ ܗܘ.

The ܗ of ܗܘܐ "*fuit*", falls away when employed as an enclitic: ܩܛܠ ܗܘܐ, ܡܩܛܠܝܢ ܗܘܘ (§ 299), &c.

The ܗ of the very common verb ܝܗܒ "to give" falls away in the Perfect in all cases where it had a vowel; thus ܝܗܒ, ܝܗܒܬ, ܝܗܒܬܘܢ, ܝܗܒܬܗ, &c. The East-Syrians suppress the ܗ even in cases like ܝܗܒܬ, &c., and similarly in ܐܬܝܗܒܬ, ܝܗܒܬ, &c.

For ܝܗܘܕܐ "Judah", ܝܗܘܕܝܐ "a Jew", &c. (from יְהוּדָא, יְהוּדָיָא, &c.) one may say also ܝܘܕܐ, ܝܘܕܝܐ *Yūδā*, *Yūδāyā*. ܝܘܕܝܐ &c. are written even without ܗ.

Greek *rh.* § 39. In Greek words ܪܗ is often written to express the aspirated ῥ, *e. g.* ܪܗܘܡܐ Ῥώμη, ܦܪܗܣܝܐ, ܦܪܗܣܝܐ (along with ܦܪܪܣܝܐ, ܦܪܪܣܝܐ and other forms of transcription) παῤῥησία, &c. This ܗ has no consonantal value, and only in mistake is it treated occasionally as a true consonant.

Vowel-Letters ܘ & ܝ. Usual changes.

THE VOWEL-LETTERS ܘ AND ܝ.

§ 40. A. *W* beginning a root becomes *y* in Syriac, as in Hebrew, when it is not protected by certain prefixes. Root WLD thus yields ܝܠܕܐ "child"; ܝܠܕܬ "she bare"; but ܐܘܠܕ "he begat"; ܡܘܠܕܐ "birth", &c. The initial *w* is however kept in ܘ, ܘ "and"; ܘܐܐ "it is becoming" (and so ܘܐܝܐ f.; ܘܐܝܘܬ "decently" &c.); ܘܥܕܐ "an appointment" (and thus ܘܥܕ "to appoint", ܐܘܬܘܥܕ "to agree upon"); ܘܪܝܕܐ "vein"; add the interjection ܘܝ "woe!", whence ܘܝܐ "the woe"; so too ܘܪܘܪܐ "bee-eater", and ܘܘܐ "a kind of partridge", which two words evidently are meant to reproduce the natural calls of these birds. Other words beginning with ܘ like ܘܪܕܐ "rose" are foreign or uncertain.

B. ܘ and ܝ have both of them too much of the nature of vowels to be able to stand as true consonants in the end of a syllable; they always form in that case simple vowels or diphthongs, thus: ܫܘܕܝܐ "promise" (with ܫܘܕܝ *šaudī* "promised") *šūdāyā*, not *šuvdāyā*, for it was frequently even written with just one ܘ (1); ܠܘ *lau* "not", not *lav* (from *lā-ū*, *lāhū* § 38); ܩܪܘ (East-Syrian ܩܪܰܘ) "called" *qĕrau*; ܓܠܝܘ "revealed" (3 pl.) *gallīu* (not *gallīv*) (2); ܒܝܬܐ "house" *baitā*; ܩܝܡܝܢ "rise" *qāimīn*; ܐܘܪܗܝܬܐ "Edessena" *Orhāitā*, &c.

C. ܝ without a full vowel always becomes *ī* in the beginning of the syllable. In the beginning of a word ܐܝ is often written for it; thus ܝܬܒ, ܐܝܬܒ *īthev* "sat", from יְתֵב; ܝܕܥ, ܐܝܕܥ *īδa*ʿ "knew", from יְדַע; ܝܕܥܬܐ, ܐܝܕܥܬܐ "knowledge"; ܝܪܚ, ܐܝܪܚ "month" (emphatic state ܝܪܚܐ); farther, ܘܝܬܒ or ܘܐܝܬܒ, ܕܝܕܥܬܐ or ܕܐܝܕܥܬܐ &c. In later times the ܐ is not so often written in such cases as it was in earlier days. But still the ܐ is always found in ܐܝܩܪܐ "honour", ܐܝܕܐ "hand", ܐܝܡܡܐ "day", and thus in ܒܐܝܕܐ, ܠܐܝܡܡܐ &c. On ܫܘܘܕܝܐ along with ܫܘܕܝܐ, and ܢܗܘܐ instead of ܬܗܘܐ v. § 38.

So too, within the word, ܢܬܝܗܒ "is given", from נִתְיְהֵב; ܚܕܝܗܘܢ "their breast", from חַדְיְהוֹן (ܚܕܝܐ); ܟܘܣܝܬܐ "cap", from כּוֹסִיתָא; ܫܘܓܫܝܗܘܢ "their commotion", from ܫܘܓܫܐ, &c.

In a closed syllable *ye* or *yi* becomes *ī* in ܐܝܬ "exists", and in the foreign names ܐܝܣܪܝܠ or ܝܣܪܝܠ "Israel"; ܐܝܫܡܥܝܠ "Ismael" (both with orthographic variants); ܐܝܙܪܥܝܠ (for יִזְרְעֶאל); and ܐܝܣܚܩ. Quite exceptionally, other forms are found, v. § 175 A, *Rem.*

For ܝܫܘܥ "Jesus" the Nestorians say ܝܫܘܥ *Īšō*ʿ.

---

(1) *Vice versâ*,—because ܘܘ was pronounced like ܘ, the words pronounced *šukōnō*, *šudōlō* were in later times written ܫܘܘܟܢܐ, ܫܘܘܕܠܐ, where the doubled ܘ had no etymological foundation, since these words in their fundamental form are *šukkānā*, *šuddālā*, and belong to *šakken* "presented", and *šaddel* "enticed".

(2) The barbarous custom of pronouncing ו in the end of a syllable like a German *w* or indeed an *f*, instead of giving it a vowel sound (*e. g.* אביו *aβīu*, מלכיו *mĕlākhāu*), should be given up in Hebrew too.

D. In the middle of the word, *ya* becomes *ī* in the adverbial ending *āïth*, from and along with *āyath* (§ 155 A). ܘ, which appears as an initial letter without a full vowel only in ܘ "and" (A *supra*), is sometimes treated within a word just like ܝ. Thus from remote times there appear as alternative forms ܚܰܝܘ̈ܬܳܐ *ḥaiwĕthā* and ܚܰܝܽܘܬܳܐ *ḥayūthā* "animal"; ܚܰܕܘ̈ and ܚܰܕܽܘܬܳܐ "joy" (§§ 40 D; 101; 145 F)(¹): forms with *ū* in these cases have become more usual; while other forms,—for instance, ܠܐܘܝ along with ܠܐܘܬܐ (לְאוּתָא) "weariness", ܘܢܬܪܘܚ (East-Syrian) along with ܘܢܬܪܘܚ "that they may have room"—occur only in isolated cases.

E. A ܝ after *ā*, and before another vowel, is pronounced by the East-Syrians like ܐ, thus ܚܰܝ "lives", ܐ̱ܚܪܳܝܐ "at last", like *ḥāē, ḥĕrāath*, &c.(²) (thus the converse of § 33 B). Perhaps old modes of writing, like ܪܘܚܣ̈ for ܪܘܚܢ̈ܝܬܐ "spiritual"(pl.), are founded upon this. If the vowel succeeding ܝ, after *a* or *ā*, is *e* or *i*, then the difference between the highly vocal *y* and ܐ is hardly perceptible. Whence come the interchangeable forms ܡܝܬܐ and ܡܐܝܬܐ "dead"; ܩܬܡ "remaining" and ܩܐܡ (§ 118); ܐܫܩܝܢܝ and ܐܫܩܐܢܝ "give me to drink" (§ 196) &c.: Thus old MSS. have ܫܪܝܪܐ for ܫܪܝܪܐܝܬ "truly" (§ 155 A).

F. In the same way *awu* and *a'u* are scarcely distinguishable by the ear. Accordingly we find, for example, ܪܡܘ or even ܪܡܐܘ for ܪܡܝܘ "they threw" (§ 176 E), ܡܚܣܘܗܝ or ܡܚܣܐܘܗܝ for ܡܚܝܣܘܗܝ "they struck him" (§ 192), &c. Similarly, ܡܕܥܐ as well as ܡܕܥܝܐ "matter".

G. ܝ serves in rare cases as a mark of a vowel and a consonant at one and the same time; *e. g.* in ܢܒܝܐ *nĕvīyā* "prophet" (in which the conclusion must have a sound differing very little indeed from that in ܐܝܬܝ "come", &c.); ܨܝܘܬܐ *ṣīyūthā* "form"; and in the before-mentioned ܐܫܩܝܢ *ašqāyīn*. Similarly ܡܥܘܣ for ܩܘܪܝܝܢ *quryāyīn* "rustici" (to avoid the triple ܝ).

H. The Greek *ια*, *ιω*, &c. are sometimes treated as monosyllables, sometimes as dissyllables, for instance: ܗܕܝܘܛܐ *ïdiώtης*; ܐܟܣܢܝܐ *ξενία*,

(¹) With the old poets these words are sometimes dissyllabic, sometimes trisyllabic. The Nestorians prefer the dissyllabic pronunciation of ܚܝܘܬ at least.

(²) Accordingly they like to put a small ܐ over such a ܝ.

ܡܪܩܝܘܢ Μαρκίων, together with ܡܪܩܘܢ; ܕܝܬܝܩܐ διαθήκη (along with ܕܝܬܩܐ); ܦܪܛܘܪܝܢ πραιτόριον (and ܦܪܛܘܪܝܢ) &c.

§ 41. In Semitic inflection *ā* appears instead of a theoretical *aya*, or *awa*, *e.g.* *qām(a)* "stood", like *qaṭal(a)* "killed"; *galāt* (Syriac *gĕlāth*) "she revealed", like *qaṭalat*: *ī* instead of *awī*, *e. g.* *qīm* "stood (part.)" for *qawīm*, &c. ܘ and ܝ as representing the 2nd and 3rd radical.

But in these cases the question turns very little indeed upon actual sound-transitions. Of quite predominant importance here, are those ancient analogical modes of formation, which mount up to a time long before the separation of the several individual Semitic tongues.

2. VOWELS.

2. Vowels.

LONG AND SHORT VOWELS IN OPEN AND CLOSED SYLLABLES.

§ 42. Long vowels in open syllables remain unshortened. Syriac however has closed syllables with long vowels, even in the middle of the word, *e. g.* ܩܡܬܘܢ "ye stood" (2. m. pl.), ܐܩܝܡܬܘܢ "ye raised", and later formations like ܒܪܝܟܬܐ (first from *bĕrīkhĕthā*) "*benedicta*", ܝܬܒܝܢ "sit" (part.), ܐܝܬܥܝܪܬܗ "I awoke him", &c. The East-Syrians have a marked inclination to shorten long vowels in closed syllables, and accordingly they often write straight away ܥܠܡܝܢ "eternities", for ܥܠܡܝܢ, ܥܠܡܝܢ, &c., and so too in the final syllables of ܐܬܬ for ܐܬܬ "she came", (ܐܬܬ), &c. On the other hand they incline to lengthen short vowels in an open syllable, if these are exceptionally retained, and thus, *e.g.*, regularly write ܐܪܡܝܬܗ "she threw it (m.)" for ܐܪܡܝܬܗ. Long vowels.

Rem.—As they have ceased to notice that the ◌ܵ, which they perhaps write in ܩܛܠܬ but pronounce short, is a long vowel, they set down now and then ◌ܵ for short *a*, *e. g.* ܡܠܦܝܢ for ܡܠܦܝܢ, ܡܠܦܝܢ "they teach" (part.). ☞ p. 341

§ 43. A. Short vowels in closed syllables remain; but in open syllables short vowels have, in Aramaic, at a very early stage passed mostly into *sh*ᵉ*va mobile*. This occurrence is precisely what has given the language its characteristic stamp. Thus, for instance, ܩܛܠ *qĕṭal* from *qaṭal* "killed"; ܕܗܒ from *dahav* (cf. ܕܗܒܐ) "gold"; ܡܡܠܟܝܢ from *mamlikhīn* Short vowels.

"are kings" (sing. ܡܰܠܟ̈ܝܼܢ), &c. Then in Syriac even the *sh^eva mobile* has often quite disappeared, as we are able in part to establish, even for very early times, through the relations of Rukkākhā and Quššāyā (§ 23 D): compare also the treatment of originally doubled consonants (§ 21 B).

B. A sharpened syllable does not count for an open one, even when the double-consonant is itself simplified (§ 21 A, B). Thus the short vowel remains, with resulting hardness, in ܪܒܺܝ (*rabbī*, West-Syrian *rabī*) "brought up"; ܪܶܒܺܝܬ݂ܳܐ "interest"; ܡܰܚܶܡ (*maḥḥem*) "heats"; ܩܽܘܛܳܠܳܐ (*quṭṭālā*) "murder"; and so even ܫܰܐܶܠ "asked"; ܫܽܘܐܳܠܳܐ "question" (for theoretical *ša*"*el*, *šu*"*ālā*). Here and there the falling away of the doubling in the pronunciation is to be made up for by lengthening the vowel.

C. But still in certain cases a short vowel holds its ground even in an open syllable: thus with ܐ as the initial letter of a syllable (§ 34), e. g. ܡܰܠܰܐܟ݂ܳܐ for ܡܰܠܐܱܟ݂ܳܐ "angel"; in the secondary forms ܢܩܽܘܡ, ܢܩܺܝܡ for ܢܩܽܘܡ, ܢܩܺܝܡ "stands", "sets" (§ 177 C); in many later forms like ܡܰܗܟ̈ܡ, ܩܳܛܽܠ̈ܝ (§ 158 D); and in the forms of the Imperative with Object-suffixes like ܕܒܰܪܰܝܢܝ "lead me" (§ 190), &c. So also is it in forms like ܓܠܳܬ݂ܳܗ "she revealed it" (§ 152), a recent formation from ܗܿ— + ܓܠܳܬ݂. The Nestorians (always?) lengthen the *a* in such cases (§ 42).

D. Where there had been two open syllables with short vowels, one of these had of course to remain; thus ܕܰܗܒ݂ܳܐ from *dahavā* "gold"; ܕܶܟ݂ܪܳܐ from *dakharā* "a male"; ܩܶܛܠܰܬ݂ from *qaṭalath* "she killed", &c.

E. So too, when the prefixes ܒ ܠ ܕ ܘ come before a vowel-less consonant, their vowel remains as an *a*([1]), thus ܒܡܰܠܟܳܐ from ܡܰܠܟܳܐ + ܒ "in a king"; ܠܓܰܒ݂ܪܳܐ "to a man"; ܕܰܩܛܰܠ "who killed"; ܘܰܢܣܰܒ݂ "and took". With the words mentioned in § 51, which may assume an ܐ as their commencement, the prefix ܒ is given as ܒ, and so with the other prefixes, thus ܒܰܫܛܳܪܳܐ "in the written bond"; ܠܰܫܬܳܐ "to the six", &c.

Thus too, *a* appears in the corresponding case, when several such prefixes come together at the beginning of a word: ܘܰܕ݂ܡܰܠܟܳܐ "*et regis*",

---

([1]) With ܘ and ܠ, *a* is the original vowel; perhaps ܒ has just been adapted thereto by analogy, though originally it appears to have been *bi*; and certainly analogy explains the treatment of ܕ, which is shortened from *dī*.

from ܡܚܝܒ + ܕ + ܘ; ܘܠܕܡܚܝܒܩܛܠܐ "and to him that is involved in murder", from ܩܛܠܐ + ܒ + ܕ + ܠ + ܘ; ܘܒܕܩܛܠ from ܩܛܠ + ܕ + ܒ + ܘ, &c. (but of course ܠܕܡܚܝܒܩܛܠܐ, ܒܕܩܛܠ, &c.).

If the second consonant of such a word is an ܐ, then the prefix usually takes the vowel: ܘܡܐܐ "and a hundred" *wamā* from *wam'ā* = מְאָה + וְ; ܕܠܐܝ "who wearied" *dalī* from *dal'ī*; ܘܐܣܢ "and put on thy shoes" *wasan* from *was'an*, &c. And yet, along with these are also found, through ignoring the ܐ, forms like ܘܫܐܠ "and demanded" *wešel* = *wĕ* + *š'el* (along with ܘܫܐܠ); thus, in particular, we most frequently have ܘܡܐܣܝܐ, ܘܐܣܝܐ, ܘܠܡܐܣܝܘ, and other forms from ܐܣܝ "to heal". ☞ p. 342

When two such prefixes stand before initial ܐ, the ܐ is generally neglected, *e.g.* ܘܒܡܢܐ "and in whom *or* what?", from ܡܢܐ + ܒ + ܘ; ܘܠܐܡܟ "and to thy mother"; ܠܕܐܬܕܟܪܢ "to him who remembered us"; ܘܠܐܠܗܐ "*et Deo*", &c.—More rarely with ܲ: ܠܕܐܗܡܝ "to him who neglected", from ܐܗܡܝ + ܕ + ܠ; ܕܒܐܘܪܚܐ "he who is on the way", &c. The same fluctuation is found with ܐܝ, ܝ, from *ye*: ܕܒܐܝܕܐ "who *or* what is in hand"; ܘܒܐܝܕܝ̈ܗܘܢ, with ܕܒܐܝܕܝ̈ܗܘܢ, ܕܠܝܫܘܥ (East-Syrian § 40 C); ܕܒܐܝܕܗ, &c.

Rem. The old poets express themselves in all these cases either with or without the *a* according to the requirement of the verse.

An ܝ, originating according to § 40 C, yields with such a prefix the forms ܠܝ, ܘܝ, &c., *e. g.* ܘܝܕܥ or ܘܐܝܕܥ "and knew", from ܝܕܥ, ܐܝܕܥ (= יָדַע) + ܘ.

Rem. The Nestorians oddly give the vowel *a* to the prefixes before ܝܗܘܕܐ, ܝܗܘܕܝܐ, &c., "Judah, Jew", thus ܠܝܗܘܕܝܐ, ܕܝܗܘܕܐ, ܘܐܝܗܘܕܐ, &c.

SOME OF THE MOST IMPORTANT VOWEL-CHANGES.

Some of the most important vowel-changes.

ā.

§ 44. The *ā* is retained with the East-Syrians, but has become *ō* with the West-Syrians. The former also set down ܵ for the most part to represent the Greek *α*, particularly in an open syllable,—for which the West-Syrians prefer to keep ܲ. ☞ p. 342

Before *n* the transition from *ā* to *ō* is partly found even earlier; thus in the sporadically occurring ܬܡܘܢ, ܬܡܘܢܐ, ܒܣܡܘܢܐ, ܣܘܣܘܢܝܬܐ, &c., for ܬܡܢ "there", ܬܡܢܐ "eight", ܒܣܡܢܐ "spices", ܣܘܣܢܝܬܐ "*menstruans*"; in

ܐܘܦ = ܐܦ "also" (1); still more usual are ܢܣܝܘܢܐ "temptation" (from ܢܣܝܢܐ though somewhat different in signification ["test *or* trial" 2 Cor. 2. 9]); ܓܠܝܘܢܐ as well as ܓܠܝܢܐ "revelation"; ܙܪܥܘܢܐ "vegetables" &c. (§ 74).

a. § 45. *a* has frequently become *e*, *e. g.* ܩܛܠܬ "she killed", from *qaṭalath* (cf. ܩܛܠܬܗ "he killed him"); ܒܣܪܐ "flesh", from *basarā*, &c. Here and there the vocalisation fluctuates between *a* and *e*: the East-Syrians especially give preference, upon occasion, to the former; *e. g.* in ܐܠܨ *alaṣ* for ܐܠܝܨ "afflicted" (§ 174 A); ܫܬܐܣܬܐ for ܫܬܐܣܬܐ "foundation"; ܡܥܪܬܐ for ܡܥܪܬܐ "cavern"; ܪܗܛܐ for ܪܗܛܐ "course, run"; and in
☞ p. 342 several others that have a guttural for the middle letter.

A *š*, immediately followed by another consonant, sometimes occasions *e* instead of *a*: ܐܫܟܚ, ܡܫܟܚ instead of *aškaḥ*, *maškaḥ* "find" (§ 164); ܡܫܬܝܬܐ "texture", contrasted with ܡܪܕܝܬܐ "course"; ܡܫܬܘܬܐ "feast" (but ܡܫܬܝܐ the same) overagainst ܡܪܕܘܬܐ "chastisement"; ܬܫܘܝܬܐ "bed", ܬܫܡܫܬܐ "service", contrasted with ܬܟܣܝܬܐ "covering", ܬܟܫܦܬܐ "petition" (but ܬܫܥܝܬܐ "narration") (2): notice farther ܐܫܬܐ, ܐܫܬܝܢ, ܐܫܬܥܣܪ (§ 51). Similarly *s* in ܒܣܬܪ "behind", from ܣܬܪ + ܒ, where according to other analogies *ba* was to be expected.

☞ p. 342 *ē.* § 46. Within the word an *ē* has sometimes been produced through the quiescing of a consonantal ܐ, as in ܒܐܪܐ "well"; ܪܫܐ or ܪܝܫܐ "head"; ܐܡܪ "says" (§ 53): and sometimes it has been produced in other ways, as in ܟܐܦܐ "stone", ܟܐܢܐ, ܟܐܢ, or ܟܝܢ, "right, just" (§ 98 C). In an open syllable *ē* is, without regard for etymology, expressed freely by ܐ, or even not expressed at all (and in the same way the Greek *αι* and *ε* are dealt with: thus even ܩܐܪܣܐ *qērsā* = *καιρός*), while in a closed syllable ܝ (or even ܐܝ) is set down by preference: In later times ܝ is more prevalent; *e. g.* the old form ܢܐܦܫܐ, becomes later ܢܝܦܫܐ *nĕfēšā* "refreshment, recovery"; and ܠܡܐܢܐ *λιμένα* "harbour" takes later the form ܠܡܝܢܐ, &c.

---

(1) ܦܘܪܣܝܐ "Persians" is probably an intentional defacement of the other and still more usual form ܦܪܣܝܐ: The hostile nation was denoted by a word which means "pudenda".

(2) ܡܫܟܢܐ "a pledge" is a borrowed word from the Assyrian, and accordingly does not belong to this class.

This *ē* became to a large extent *ī* with the West-Syrians: They said ܢܺܐܡܰܪ *nīmar* "says", ܐ̱ܚܺܪܺܢܳܐ *ḥêrīnō* "*alius*", ܪܺܫܳܐ *rīšō*, ܟܺܐܦܳܐ *kīfō*, ܟܺܐܢ *kīn*, &c. Yet they keep the ܶ in ܢܶܐܟ݁ܽܘܠ "eats", ܡܶܐܟ݁ܽܘܠܬ݂ܳܐ "food", ܓܶܐܪܳܐ "arrow", &c.; and there are found still in isolated cases ܢܺܐܩܳܐ as well as ܢܶܐܩܳܐ, ܡܺܐܡܳܐ as well as ܡܶܐܡܳܐ (Inf.) "to swear", ܐܬ݂ܺܐܒܶܕܬ݁ܽܘܢ as well as ܐܬ݂ܶܐܒܶܕܬ݁ܽܘܢ "are lost" (2. m. pl.), &c. (§§ 174 A, 175 B). ܐ, ܐܝ—or the defective form of writing *i*,—are (even apart from etymology) in these cases almost invariably certain marks of an original *ē*. The style of writing of the East-Syrians separates ܹ *ē* with tolerable consistency from ܝ݂ *ī* ([1]).

In the end of a word the West-Syrian transition from *ē* to *ī*, except in ܢܶܐ (= Hebr. נֵא) appears only in Greek words in *η*, *e. g.* ܕܺܝܰܬ݂ܺܝܩܺܐ or even ܕܺܝܰܬ݂ܺܝܩܺܝ διαθήκη for ܕܺܝܰܬ݂ܺܝܩܹܐ of the East-Syrians. Otherwise ܶ remains here: ܓܠܶܐ "reveals", ܡ̈ܰܠܟܶܐ "kings", &c.

§ 47. The short ܶ seems to have been *ĕ* in the West, from ancient times; in the East it was pronounced sometimes as *ĕ*, sometimes as *ĭ*. This difference has no grammatical significance. *e.*

A short *ĕ* may often be lengthened in the concluding syllable through the (original) tone: thus ܕܳܚܶܠ "terrifies", ܩܶܛܠܶܬ݂ "I killed" (in which cases the second vowel is written by the East-Syrians with ܹ) should perhaps be pronounced *dāḥḗl*, *qeṭlḗth*: It is the same perhaps with the monosyllabic ܫܶܠܝ (ܫܶܠܝ) "suddenly" and ܫܶܬ݂ "six", for which ܫܝܠ and ܫܝܬ are found in very old MSS. Yet this is not certain; and still less certain is it whether such a lengthening was generally practised. But beyond all doubt ܒܶܪܝ "my son" (§ 146) has a long *ē*.

§ 48. The ܘܿ (*ō*) with the West-Syrians at an early date coincided with ܘܽ (ܘܽ, *ū*). It has been retained only in the interjections ܐܘܿ and ܐܘܿܝ "oi" (for which others say ܐܘܽܝ). Thus we have otherwise ܩܳܛܽܘܠܳܐ *qōṭūlō* for ܩܳܛܳܘܠܳܐ *qāṭōlā* "murder"; ܨܠܽܘܬ݂ܳܐ *ṣĕlūthō* for ܨܠܳܘܬ݂ܳܐ *ṣĕlōthā* "prayer", &c. Moreover such an East-Syrian ܘܿ appears not seldom to be only the result of toning down an original *ū*, especially in the neighbourhood *ō, o.*

([1]) Now-a-days the East-Syrians pronounce ܹ,—both in cases where it corresponds to the ܶ and in those where it corresponds to the ܺ of the West-Syrians,—for the most part very like *ī*, and yet in another way than the pointed ܝ݂.

of a guttural or an *r*, *e. g.* ܢܶܩܛܽܘܠ (§ 40 C), ܙܥܽܘܪܳܐ "small", ܚܽܘܪܳܐ "hole", ܫܽܘܥܝܳܬ݂ܳܐ "report", ܫܽܘܥܳܐ "rock", and many others: so too in the neighbourhood of an *n*, *e. g.* ܬܰܢܽܘܪܳܐ "oven", ܡܰܫܟ݁ܽܘܢܳܐ "tent". In many cases ܘܿ may denote an *o* originally short, but lengthened by the tone; so perhaps in ܢܶܩܛܽܘܠ "kills", ܡܩܽܘܕܫ "sanctuary" (§ 103), &c. Still, there is as little certainty about this as about the similar case in § 47.

The East-Syrians in particular distinguish also a short ܘܿ (*o*) from a short ܘܼ (*u*), but this distinction is of little importance. Here too a guttural or an *r* frequently seems to bring about the ܘܿ pronunciation, *e. g.*: ܬܶܫܒ݁ܽܘܚܬ݂ܳܐ "glory", ܐܽܘܪܝܳܐ "manger", &c.

It is curious that the West-Syrians have, besides the form ܟ݁ܽܠ "all", the form *kol*, which accordingly they have to write ܟ݁ܳܠ. Is it a lengthened *kōl?* So too ܟ݁ܽܠܗܽܘܢ, ܟ݁ܽܠܟ݁ܶܝܢ, &c.

While even with the East-Syrians the sound *o* began pretty early to pass into *u*, the tradition varies a good deal in the case of ܘܿ and ܘܼ; but with respect to cases of grammatical importance there is no doubt whatever.

Greek *o* and *ω* are with the West-Syrians either retained,—and then they are written ܘ—ܳ, —ܳ, *e. g.* ܬ݂ܪܳܘܢܳܘܣ, ܬ݂ܪܳܢܳܘܣ *ϑρόνος*—,or they become *u*. There is a good deal of variation in the usage, *e. g.* ܩܶܠܶܦܽܘܣ and ܩܶܠܶܦܳܘܣ, ܗܶܓ݂ܡܽܘܢܳܐ and ܗܶܓ݂ܡܳܘܢܳܐ *ἡγεμών* &c.

With the East-Syrians ܘܿ corresponds to the Greek *o* and *ω*, in so far as they keep from altering the words more decidedly.

As they cannot express an *o* without a vowel letter, they put —ܵ with defective-writing for the Greek *o*, *ω*, and pronounce it *ā*, *e. g.* ܬܐܵܕܵܪܘܿܣ *Theodāros* for ܬܐܳܕܳܘܪܳܘܣ *Θεόδωρος*.

ai and *au.* § 49. A. The diphthongs *ai* and *au* remain very steady, particularly in the beginning of a word, although in dialects the pronunciation *ē* and *ō* occurred. Commonly, however, simplification of the diphthong prevails in a closed syllable. The West-Syrians farther proceed (according to § 46) to turn the *ē* occasionally into *ī*, and the *ō* always into *ū* (§ 48): thus, along with ܒܰܝܬ݂ܳܐ, ܒܶܝܬ݂ "house"; with ܚܰܝܠܳܐ, ܚܶܝܠ "strength"; with ܥܰܝܢܳܐ, ܥܶܝܢ "eye"; ܡܓ݂ܰܠܶܝܢ from *mĕγallain*, "they reveal"; ܬ݁ܪܶܝܢ from *tĕrain*, "two"; ܣܰܘܦܳܐ, ܣܽܘܦ, ܣܳܘܦ "end", &c. So by analogy from ܒܶܝܬ݂ (*in oculo* = *coram*) even in an open syllable ܠܥܶܝܢܰܘ̈ܗܝ, ܠܥܶܝܢܰܘ̈ܗܝ &c. *coram eo*; but only in the prepositional use; for example, otherwise, ܠܥܰܝܢܰܘ̈ܗܝ "to his eyes".

ܡܰܘܬܗܽܘܢ, ܡܰܘܬܝ "their, my death", ܥܰܝܢܟܽܘܢ "your eye", &c. form no exception, for in these cases it was only in the last development that the syllable became a closed one. Thus also is explained perhaps the retention of the *ai* before suffixes, in forms like ܡܰܠܟܰܝ̈ܟ (from *malkaikā*), ܡܰܠܟܰܝ̈ܢ (from *malkainā*) "thy, our kings", and in verbal forms like ܓܠܰܝܬ and ܓܠܰܝܢ (from *gĕlaitā*, *gĕlainā*) "thou didst reveal", "we revealed". In ܠܰܝܬ "is not", from ܠܐ ܐܺܝܬ, the diphthong is of more recent origin. On the other hand we have simplification in ܬܰܘܪܬܐ, ܬܳܘܪܬܐ "cow", from *taurĕthā*, and in East-Syrian ܠܺܠܝܳܐ, ܠܶܠܝܳܐ *lēlyā*, *lelyā*, West-Syrian ܠܶܠܝܳܐ, usually ܠܺܠܝܳܐ from *lailĕyā* "night". So too in ܒܰܝܥܬܐ, ܒܶܥܬܐ "egg" from *bai'ĕthā*, pl. ܒܶܥܶܐ, ܒܰܝܥܶܐ.

B. The East-Syrians for the most part write ܘܼ for ܘܿ, and much more rarely ܘܹ. So also in cases where the *w* is virtually doubled, as in ܚܰܘܺܝ = ܚܰܘ̈ܝ חַוִּי "pointed out"; ܬܶܬܩܰܘܶܐ תִּקְוֵא "thou remainest"; ܟܰܘ̈ܐ = ܟܰܘ̈ܐ "windows", &c. Thus too in ܡܳܪ̈ܰܘܳܬܐ = ܡܳܪ̈ܘܳܬܐ "Lords", and other plurals of that kind; farther in cases like ܐܰܫܩܰܘܘܳܗܝ = ܐܰܫܩܰܘܳܗܝ "give ye him to drink"; ܪܡܰܘܢܝ = ܪܡܰܘܢܝ "they overthrew me" (§ 192).

Sometimes on the other hand they write ܝܼ for ܝܹ, *e. g.* ܚܦܺܝܢ for ܚܦܶܝܢ "barefooted", and always in the Imperative ܩܛܽܘܠܝܼܗܝ = ܩܛܽܘܠܶܝܗܝ "kill him".

The West-Syrians also write an *au* produced by *ā* and *u* coming together,—with the vowel-sign ܿ, *e. g.* ܡܰܠܟܳܐ ܗܘ *malkau* "is king", although the separate members are ܗܽܘ + ܡܰܠܟܳܐ. With them indeed ܡܰܠܟܳܐ ܗܘ would have the sound *malkōu*.

LOSS OF VOWELS.

Loss of vowels.

§ 50. A. Final vowels coming immediately after the original tone-syllable have all fallen away. This happened to *ā* even before the settlement of the orthography, thus ܠܰܢ from *lánā* "to us"; ܐܢ̱ܬ from *á(n)tā* "thou"; ܩܛܰܠܬ from *qĕṭáltā* "hast killed", &c. (but ܡܰܠܟܳܐ *malkā* "king", &c.). Other final vowels too have at quite an early date thus fallen away,

3*

without leaving a trace. On the other hand many vowels of this kind are still set down in consonantal character, although they had ceased to be pronounced even in the oldest literary epoch represented by documents (*circa* 200 A. D.) ([1]), and are ignored in punctuation. These are:—

(1) *ū* of the plural in the Perfect and Imperative after consonants: ܩܛܰܠܘ *qĕṭal* from *qĕṭálū*; ܩܛܘܠܘ, ܐܶܬܩܛܶܠܘ, ܩܰܛܶܠܘ; ܫܰܒܰܚܘ "they praised", &c. (but we have the full sound in ܓܠܰܘ *gĕlau*, ܓܰܠܺܝܘ *gallīu* "revealed", &c.).

(2) *ī* of the suffix of the 1st sing. after consonants, thus: ܡܰܠܟܝ *malk* "my king" from *malkī*; ܩܛܰܠܰܢܝ "killed me"; ܓܠܳܢܝ, ܓܰܠܝܰܢܝ "revealed me", &c. (but ܡܰܠܟܰܝ "my kings"; and also the monosyllables ܒܝ "in me", ܠܝ "to me", in which no falling away was possible: So too ܟܽܠܝ, ܟܽܠܰܢܝ "I wholly", "the whole of me" ["my totality"]).

(3) *ī* of the suffix of the 3rd sing. m. ܗܝ with the noun: ܡܰܠܟܰܘܗܝ *malkau* from *malkauhī* "his kings", and with the Verb in cases like ܓܠܳܘܗܝ, ܢܩܰܛܠܽܘܢܳܗܝ, ܩܰܛܠܽܘܢܳܗܝ, ܓܠܳܝܗܝ, no doubt from *gĕlāihī* &c.

(4) *ī* of the 2nd fem. sing. in ܐܰܢ̇ܬܝ *at* from *a(n)tī* "thou" (f.); ܡܰܠܟܶܟܝ *malkēkh* from *malkēkhī* (both with *ē?*); ܡܰܠܟܽܘܬܶܟܝ; ܠܶܟܝ; ܩܛܰܠܬܝ; ܫܡܰܥܬܝ, &c.

(5) In the following special cases: in ܡܶܢ ܫܶܠܝ "from quiet" = "suddenly", absolute state of ܫܶܠܝܳܐ from *šélī* (like פֶּרִי); in ܐܶܡܰܬܝ "when?" from *emmáthai*; ܐܶܬܡܳܠܝ "yesterday" from *ethmālē*; and the derived word ܡܶܢܬܡܳܠܝ "the day before yesterday"; lastly in the much maimed form ܐܶܫܬܩܕܝ (or ܐܶܫܬܰܩܕܝ) "last year".

B. Even in very ancient MSS. the unpronounced ܝ 's are often wanting: a similar ܘ is more rarely omitted. Conversely ܝ, which one was in the habit of so often writing,—apparently without cause,—was in some cases attached parasitically to words ending in a consonant; *e. g.* there occurs in old manuscripts ܐܠܗܝ for ܐܰܠܳܗ "God" (Construct State); ܐܒܝ for ܐܳܒ "August"; ܪܘܚܝ for ܪܽܘܚ "spirit". Occasionally it is

([1]) Even the hymns of Bardesanes seem to neglect them, as regards the number of syllables.

employed as a diacritic mark of the 3rd sing. fem. of the Perf. *e. g.* ܩܛܠܬܝ for ܩܛܠܬ "she killed". Such an employment of ܝ in the 3rd pl. fem. Perf. has gradually come into full use with the West-Syrians; ܩ̈ܛܠܝ "they (f.) killed", for the old ܩܛܠ̈ retained by the East-Syrians (from original *qĕṭálā*, not *qĕṭálī*). The employment of ܝ in the 3rd sing. fem. Imperf.,—coming into view in rather late times,—prevails among the West-Syrians, though not quite so universally; ܬܩܛܘܠܝ, ܬܩܛܠܝ "she kills", &c., in order to distinguish it from the 2nd sing. masc., ܬܩܛܘܠ, ܬܩܛܠ "thou killest": the Nestorians are completely unacquainted with the ܝ in this usage.

NEW VOWELS AND SYLLABLES.

New vowels and syllables. Vowel prefixed. (Alaf prosthetic).

§ 51. An ܐ with a vowel is sometimes prefixed to an initial consonant which has not a full vowel. Thus ܐ in ܐܫܬܐ "six", ܐܫܬܝܢ "sixty", alongside of ܫܬܐ, ܫܬܝܢ; ܐܫܛܪܐ "a written bond" along with ܫܛܪܐ, and always ܐܫܬܝ "drank"; farther ܐܟܒܪ "already" sometimes for ܟܒܪ. Frequently so in Greek words with στ, σπ, like ܐܣܛܪܛܝܐ or ܣܛܪܛܝܐ στρατεία, ܐܣܦܝܪܐ and ܣܦܝܪܐ σπεῖρα, &c.

The prefix, pretty frequently met with in ancient MSS. before ܪ, is probably to be pronounced ܐܶ; *e. g.* ܐܪܚܝܡܐ for ܪܚܝܡܐ "Beloved"; ܐܪܕܝܕܐ for ܪܕܝܕܐ "upper garment"; ܐܪܩܝܥܐ for ܪܩܝܥܐ (1) "firmament"; ܐܪܘܚܐ for ܪܘܚܐ "contented", and many others. So too ܐܫܪܘܬܐ for ܫܪܘܬܐ "a meal"; ܐܓܠܝܕܐ for ܓܠܝܕܐ "ice". In the frequently occurring ܐܘܪܫܠܡ the *u* of the rarer form ܪܘܫܠܡ, ܪܘܫܠܡ is brought to the front. The early adopted Persian word *rāzā* ܐܪܙܐ, more rarely ܪܙܐ, ܪܐܙܐ "a secret" seems to have been pronounced with a vowel-prefix, which however is ignored in the pointing.

Auxiliary vowels.

§ 52. A. The poets sometimes insert an *e* before ܒ ܠ ܕ after a word ending in a consonant, *e. g.* ܐܝܬ ܠܗܘܢ "is to them" *īth elhōn* (with three syllables) = ܐܝܬ ܠܗܘܢ.

(1) ܐܪܩܝܥܐ is measured as dissyllabic like ܪܩܝܥܐ in Moesinger's Monumenta Syriaca II, 86 v. 152 *et passim*, but ܐܪܕܝܕܐ, ܐܪܕܝܕܗ as trissyllabic in Jacob of Sarûg, Thamar v. 247, 251.

B. Essentially the same thing takes place frequently within the word. Especially when a consonant without a full vowel follows one that has no vowel, a short vowel is inserted often between the two to facilitate pronunciation. Thus ܡܰܕܢܚܳܐ = ܡܰܕܶܢܚܳܐ "sunrise"; ܕܶܚܠܬܳܐ = ܕܶܚܶܠܬܳܐ "fear"; ܬܶܫܒܩܘܢ = ܬܶܫܶܒܩܘܢ "you permit *or* remit"; ܬܶܕܚܠܝܢ = ܬܶܕܶܚܠܝܢ "thou fearest (f.)"; ܢܶܙܒܢܘܢ = ܢܶܙܶܒܢܘܢ "they buy"; also ܡܰܘܡܝܳܐ = ܡܰܘܡܝܳܐ "she swears"; ܙܘܥܬܳܐ = ܙܰܘܥܬܳܐ "quaking"; and ܫܶܐܶܠܬܳܐ (= ܫܶܐܶܠܬܳܐ v. *infra* C) "question". Particularly does this occur when one of the letters is a liquid or ܥ ܐ ܗ ܝ ܘ; on the other hand it is never found between sibilants and dentals. A marked amount of fluctuation however prevails in individual cases in the pronunciation of the various dialects and schools. With the old poets the longer forms, as indicated by the metre, are upon the whole rare; they abound in the vocalisation of the Bible, with both East- and West-Syrians.

C. The small stroke under the letter, called *mehagyānā* "the accentuator", serves as a sign of the fuller pronunciation particularly with the East-Syrians; the one above the letter, called *marhĕṭānā* "the hastener", as the sign of the shorter (§ 17). Yet often the full vowel is also written instead of the former, thus ܐܶܫܬܰܠܰܛܶܬ or ܐܶܫܬܰܠܛܶܬ = ܐܶܫܬܰܠܛܶܬ "I empowered".

The sign ̱ stands sometimes too in cases where the vowel which is supposed to be inserted is an original vowel, *e. g.* in ܩܘܠܩܠܬܳܐ = ܩܘܠܩܠܬܳܐ from *qalqaltā*. Sometimes it is not easy to say whether a vowel is original or inserted. Here and there such a vowel alters the original vocalisation more strongly; thus from ܥܩܰܪܒܳܐ "scorpion", has come the West-Syrian ܥܩܰܪܒܳܐ and then the East-Syrian ܥܰܩܪܒܳܐ.

The inserted vowel is mostly *e*, but often too it is *a*, especially before gutturals, and before *q* and *r*.

The relations of Rukkākhā and Quššāyā suffer no alteration through this insertion, as several of the foregoing examples show.

INFLUENCE OF THE CONSONANTS UPON THE VOWELS.

Influence of the consonants upon the vowels. Of ܐ.

§ 53. An ܐ originally a consonant and ending a syllable in the middle of a word becomes, in combination with a preceding *a* or *i*, an *ē*, which for the most part is farther developed with the West-Syrians into *ī*.

Thus ܪܺܫܳܐ from רֵאשָׁא "head"; ܐܳܡܰܪ "says"; ܐܳܟ݂ܶܠ "eats"; ܐܶܡܰܪ "I say"; ܕܺܐܒܳܐ "wolf", from דִּאְבָא; ܒܺܐܪܳܐ "a well" (also written ܒܺܝܪܳܐ § 46), and so forth.

On the other hand the ܐ becomes ā in ܥܳܢܳܐ "small cattle", through the influence of the neighbouring gutturals from עַאְנָא; ܥܳܕܢܳܬܳܐ "battlements" from עַאְעִיתָא; ܥܳܠܳܐ "a certain thorny shrub" from עַאְלָא; and similarly ܚܳܢܳܐ "bosom" from חַאְנָא for original חַעְנָא.

In the end of the word we have ܢܳܐ from na'. In other cases ܐ— is retained here according to the analogy of corresponding forms ending in other gutturals, *e. g.* ܛܰܡܐܳ "unclean" (§ 100); ܡܛܰܡܐܳ "polluted"; ܒܝܐܳ "consoled" (§ 172), &c.

§ 54. ܚ ܗ ܥ and ܪ as final radicals, especially when they close the syllable, transform an ĕ into an ă; thus, ܝܳܕܰܥ "knows" (compared with ܝܳܬܶܒ "sits"); ܕܒܰܚ "sacrificed", compared with ܩܛܰܠ; ܢܒܰܗ "arose", for nĕveh; ܡܕܰܒܰܪ "leads", for neδabber; ܐܰܘܕܰܥܢ "we made known"; ܢܒܰܗܬܘܢ "you arose"; ܦܪܰܚܬܳܐ "a bird"; ܕܒܰܪܬܘܢ "you led", &c. (§ 170). Of the other gutturals and of *r*.

In rare cases the transformation of an ܘ into *a*, before these final consonants, has been retained from very remote times, as for instance in ܢܶܦܬܰܚ "opens"; compare on the other hand ܢܶܟܣܽܘܣ "slaughters", &c. (§ 170). In certain cases they have the effect even of transforming a *following* *e* (or *o*?) into *a* (v. § 169).—On the exchange of *a* and *e* in words which have middle gutturals v. § 45.

On the shading off of an *a* into *e* through the influence of a sibilant, v. § 45; and of a *u* into *o*, effected by a guttural v. §§ 48, 49. In like manner the gutturals, as well as other consonants, particularly emphatic ones, must have brought about a special shading of the vowels in still other instances, without the writing giving much indication of such delicate turns.

3. STRONGER ALTERATIONS.

3. Stronger alterations.

§ 55. We find these, for instance, in the blending of Participles and Adjectives with the Subject-Pronouns: *e. g.* ܩܳܛܠܺܝܬܽܘܢ (ܩܳܛܠܺܝܢ ܐܰܢ̱ܬܽܘܢ) from *qātlīn a(n)tōn*; ܩܳܛܠܺܝܢܰܢ from ܩܳܛܠܺܝܢ ܚܢܰܢ; ܒܪܺܝܟ݂ܳܬܝ "*benedicta tu*", from ܒܪܺܝܟ݂ܳܐ ܐܰܢ̱ܬܝ; ܩܳܛܠܰܬ from ܩܳܛܠܳܐ ܐܰܢ̱ܬ (§ 64 A), &c. Blendings with ܐܰܢ̱ܬ appear in still other situations, *e. g.* ܕܰܗܒܳܐ ܐܰܢ̱ܬ *dahvat* "thou art gold";

ܐܰܢ݊ܬ ܐܝܟܐ "*ubi es?*"; ܐܰܢ݊ܬ ܒܪܘܝܐ ܒܪ *bar bārōyat* "thou art the son of the Creator"; ܐܰܢ݊ܬ ܕܚܝܬ *dĕḥayyēt* "*vitae es*", &c. Still in these cases the preservation of the separate portions is the more usual practice.

Amongst other instances we meet with extraordinary mutilations in the numerals of the second decade (§ 148 B); and farther in certain compounds (§ 141).

4. TONE.

§ 56. The Nestorians now put the tone on the penult throughout, and that very distinctly. The Maronites([1]), on the other hand, put the tone always, or almost always, on the last syllable, when it is a closed syllable, e. g. ܐܙܠ *ōzél*, ܩܛܠܬ *qeṭlát*, ܢܙܕܩܦ *nezdqéf*, ܝܘܡܝܢ *yaumín*, ܝܫܘܥ *Ješú*, and so also in endings with a diphthong, e. g. ܐܬܐܘ *etáu*, ܠܬܠܡܝܕܘ *talmīdáu*, ܫܒܩܘܝ *šabqúi*, ܐܒܢܘ *ebnéu*. On the other hand they always, or nearly always, put the tone on the penult, when the word ends in a simple vowel: ܐܬܐ *étō*, ܢܝܬܐ *nítē*, ܨܒܐ *ṣóbē*, ܢܗܘܐ *néhwē*, ܚܡܐ *ʿámō*, ܡܠܐ *mélē*, ܣܦܪܐ *sófrē*, ܗܢܐ *hónō* &c. Occasionally a secondary tone also becomes perceptible. At an earlier time the final syllable invariably had the principal accent.

([1]) I am indebted to my friend GUIDI, following the communications made by P. CARDAHI, for the data on the accentuation of the Maronites.

PART SECOND.

MORPHOLOGY.

§ 57. The large majority of all Semitic words, as is well known, Strong and weak roots. are derived from roots which for the most part have three, but occasionally even four or more 'Radicals'. If the *three* radicals are firm consonants, the roots are then called *Strong*: but if one of the radicals is o or ‿ (frequently appearing as a vowel), or if the due weight of the word is attained by the doubling of one of two firm radicals, then the roots are called *Weak*. On practical grounds we retain this method of treating roots, without insisting farther on the point that even with strong roots a radical is often demonstrably of quite recent origin, while on the other hand there is much variety in the origin of weak forms of the root, and while in many cases at least, the assumption of an original *Waw* or *Yod* as a radical, or that of a third radical with the same sound as the second, is a pure fiction. Thus we speak of roots *primae* o or ‿ (פֿ״, פֿ״י) [Pe Waw, Pe Yod] meaning those whose first radical is taken as *W* or *Y*; so of roots *mediae* o or ‿ (עֿו, עֿי) [Ayin Waw, Ayin Yod], and *tertiae* ‿ and *mediae geminatae* (עֿע) [Lamed Yod, and Ayin doubled]. In addition we have frequently to deal specially with words of which ן is a radical; for this sound (cf. § 33 *sqq.*) undergoes many modifications. In like manner we have to treat of words which have *n* as the first letter of the root. The forms too, which have a guttural or an *r* as second or third radical, are, by reason of certain properties, brought occasionally into special notice.

Variation of weak roots

§ 58. *Weak roots* vary a good deal in their weak letters. Thus חמם, חום, חמי, יחם (to which is added another secondary form חמת) are essentially modifications only of the same fundamental root, which means "hot". In particular, roots עו׳ and עע׳ are very closely related. Thus also in Syriac they very readily change into one another: the substantive belonging to פדר "to err" (Perf. ܦܕܰܪ, Impf. ܢܶܦܕܽܘܪ) is ܦܽܘܕܳܪܳܐ, as if from פוד; and along with the frequently occurring חנן "to pity" חון is found (Perf. ܚܳܢ, Impf. ܢܚܽܘܢ), and with כפף "to bend", כוף, &c.

Roots *med. gem.*

§ 59. Forms *med. gem.* in Syriac attain like weight with that of the strong forms, by doubling not the second radical, but the first, when it is possible, *i. e.* when a prefix ending in a vowel precedes it. Thus from גזז "to shear" ܐܶܓܰܙ *aggez* (answering to ܐܶܩܛܰܠ); ܐܶܓܽܘܙ *eggoz* (= ܐܶܩܛܽܘܠ); ܢܶܓܙܽܘܢ *negzūn*, properly *neggĕzūn* (= ܢܶܩܛܠܽܘܢ); ܬܶܚܒܶܢ "you (fem. pl.) love" (= ܬܶܩܛܠܶܢ from חבב); ܡܶܚܡܳܐ "boiler" (from חמם "to warm"); ܡܰܥܠܳܐ, ܡܰܥܠܬܳܐ, ܡܰܥܠܳܐ "entrance", &c.

Yet in some nouns we find the general Semitic method,—*i. e.* the method of either directly or virtually doubling the third radical, even
☞ p. 342 with the prefixes mentioned: thus ܡܚܰܛܳܐ "needle" (not ܡܚܛܳܐ); ܡܓܰܢܳܐ or ܡܓܶܢܳܐ (East-Syrian) "shield"; ܡܛܰܠܬܳܐ "a booth" (*mĕṭalthā*, properly *mĕṭallĕthā*), pl. ܡܛܰܠܶܐ (*mĕṭallē*); ܡܪܰܒܬܳܐ "sieve"; ܡܥܰܪܬܳܐ "a cave"; and ܡܬܰܡܰܡ, ܡܬܰܡܡܳܐܝܬ, &c., mostly used adverbially, "completion" (תמם), "continually".

Two *l* 's stand beside each other like two different consonants (1) in ܡܡܰܠܠܳܐ "speech"; ܡܛܰܠܠܳܐ "cover, shelter" (§ 46); and the quadriliteral form ܦܽܘܟܠܠܳܐ "face". In these formations, however, the *l* is again dropped in the usual pronunciation (§ 29), so that in point of fact the regular form makes its appearance. Add the peculiar form ܐܶܠܝܰܠ, ܐܶܠܝܠܶܬ &c. "to lament" (2). The following appear to be later formations: ܬܰܗܠܠܬܳܐ "mockery", from ܐܰܗܠܶܠ (הלל); and from ܐܶܨܛܰܠܺܝ, ܨܠܺܝܬܳܐ "a prayer". Thus, farther, regularly in the Ethpeel ܐܶܬܓܙܶܙ "was shorn" (as compared with ܓܙܳܐ "shore").

(1) ܡܰܪܩܠܳܐ, formed in this way Judges 3, 22 "a part of the abdomen" is pronounced *marqā*, but others read ܡܰܪܩܽܠܳܐ.

(2) ܫܰܟܠܶܠ "to finish" is a word borrowed from the Assyrian.

In Syriac too the second and third radicals, when identical, are always kept in separate existence, if a long vowel comes between them, in the course of the formation, *e. g.* ܣܢܝܼܩ "pardoned"; ܣܢܝܼܢܐ "favour", &c., as well as when the first of the two is itself doubled, *e. g.* ܐܬܚܢܢ *ethḥannan* "begged for pardon".

§ 60. With roots of four radicals we also rank such as are de- Quadriliter-al roots.
monstrably formed originally from roots of three radicals with well-known suffixes or prefixes, but which are treated in the language quite like quadriliteral forms, *e. g.* ܡܥܒܕ "to enslave", properly a causative form from ܥܒܕ; ܢܟܪܝ "to estrange", "to alienate", from ܢܘܟܪܝ "strange", from נכר, &c.

§ 61. Nouns, properly so called (Substantives and Adjectives), and Nouns and verbs.
verbs, have in all respects such a form that they are subject to the scheme of derivation from roots composed of three or more radicals, although sufficient traces survive to show that this condition was not, throughout and everywhere, the original one. The only marked divergences in formation, however, are found on the one hand with the Pronouns (which originate partly in the welding together of very short fragments of words), and on the other hand with many old Particles. To these two classes, the Pronouns and Particles,—we must therefore assign a separate place, although both in conception and usage they belong to the Noun. The same treatment must be extended to the Numerals, which, to be sure, stand in form much nearer to the usual tri-radical formations.

§ 62. Overagainst all true words, or words that express some Inter-jections
conception, stand the *expressions of feeling—*or *the Interjections*, which originally are not true words at all, but gradually enter,—at least in part,—into purely grammatical associations, and even serve to form notional words. Thus ܘܿܝ "woe!" is a mere exclamation of pain, and ܦܘܿܦ "fye!" one of detestation; but ܘܿܝ ܠܓܒܪܐ "woe to the man!" or ܦܘܿܦ ܥܡ ܓܒܪܐ "fye upon the man!" is already a grammatical association of words, and ܘܿܝܐ "the woe" is a regular noun. [1]

---

[1] This subject might be treated at great length.

Such Interjections are ܐܘ (§ 9), ܐܘܝ "O!" ܝܐ, ܝܐ "O!"; ܐܘܗ "Ah!"; ܐܗܐ "Ho! Ho!" (in mockery), &c. Also the demonstrative form ܗܐ "Here!" "Lo!", which is greatly employed in the formation of Pronouns and Adverbs, is to be regarded as originally an interjection.

Nouns.

I. NOUNS.

Pronouns.

1. PRONOUNS. (1)

Personal Pronouns. Subject-Forms.

PERSONAL PRONOUNS.

§ 63. (a) *Subject-Forms.*

			Separate Forms.	*Enclitic Forms.*
Singular.	1. pers. "I"		ܐܢܐ (ܐܢܐ)	ܢܐ (ܐܢܐ), ܢܐ
	2. pers. "Thou"	m.	ܐܢ̱ܬ	ܢ̱ܬ
		f.	ܐܢ̱ܬܝ	ܢ̱ܬܝ
	3. pers.	m. "He"	ܗ̇ܘ	ܗ̄ܘ, ܘ (§ 38)
		f. "She"	ܗ̇ܝ	ܗ̄ܝ
Plural.	1. pers. "We"		ܐܢܚܢܢ, ܚܢܢ	ܢܢ
	2. pers. "You"	m.	ܐܢ̱ܬܘܢ	ܬܘܢ
		f.	ܐܢ̱ܬܝܢ	ܬܝܢ
	3. pers. "They"	m.	ܗ̇ܢܘܢ	ܐܢܘܢ
		f.	ܗ̇ܢܝܢ	ܐܢܝܢ

On ܗ̄ܘܝܘ "he is", ܗ̄ܝܝ "she is" v. § 38.

Rem. The form ܐܢܚܢܢ,—(originally *anaḥnán*, but in our literature certainly no longer of three syllables, indeed seldom having two as *ånaḥnan*, and commonly being monosyllabic in speech, and merely a remnant of early orthography for ܚܢܢ, ܢܢ),—is found only in old manuscripts.

ܐܢܘܢ, ܐܢܝܢ, besides representing enclitic Subject-forms or Copula-forms (§ 311 *sq.*), represent also for the 3rd pers. pl. the Object, which is ex-

---

(1) Notice the points (§ 6), which with many of these words are set down almost without exception, even with the full vocalisation.

pressed by Suffixes for the other persons (§ 66). They also appear, though rarely, in other connections (§ 220 B).

§ 64. *Enclitic forms* of the 1ˢᵗ and 2ⁿᵈ pers. often coalesce with participles and,—though more rarely,—with adjectives; in such cases marked transformations occasionally occur. In particular in the plural, the first portion [*i. e.* the participle] loses its final *n*, while the second [the pronoun] loses its *ḥ* or *a(n)*. In the 2ⁿᵈ pers. singular, the first portion always loses a short vowel before the final consonant. Thus with ܩܳܛܶܠ "killing" (f. ܩܳܛܠܳܐ &c.); ܓܳܠܶܐ "revealing"; ܫܰܦܺܝܪ "beautiful": ܘܰܟܝ "clean":—

Enclitic forms with participles and adjectives.

Sing. 1. m. ܩܳܛܶܠ ܐܢܳܐ or ܩܳܛܶܠܢܳܐ "I kill"; ܓܳܠܶܐ ܐܢܳܐ, ܓܳܠܶܢܳܐ "I reveal"; ܫܰܦܺܝܪ ܐܢܳܐ "I am beautiful"; ܘܰܟܝ ܐܢܳܐ "I am clean".

1. f. ܩܳܛܠܳܐ ܐܢܳܐ; ܓܳܠܝܳܐ ܐܢܳܐ; ܫܰܦܺܝܪܳܐ ܐܢܳܐ; ܘܰܟܝܳܐ ܐܢܳܐ.

2. m. ܩܳܛܶܠܬ; ܓܳܠܶܬ; ܫܰܦܺܝܪܰܬ; ܘܰܟܝܰܬ; or without coalescing: ܩܳܛܶܠ ܐܰܢ̱ܬ; ܓܳܠܶܐ ܐܰܢ̱ܬ; ܫܰܦܺܝܪ ܐܰܢ̱ܬ; ܘܰܟܝ ܐܰܢ̱ܬ.

2. f. ܩܳܛܠܰܬܝ; ܓܳܠܝܰܬܝ; ܫܰܦܺܝܪܰܬܝ; ܘܰܟܝܰܬܝ; or separately ܩܳܛܠܳܐ ܐܰܢ̱ܬܝ; ܓܳܠܝܳܐ ܐܰܢ̱ܬܝ; ܫܰܦܺܝܪܳܐ ܐܰܢ̱ܬܝ; ܘܰܟܝܳܐ ܐܰܢ̱ܬܝ.

Plural 1. m. ܩܳܛܠܺܝܢܰܢ; ܓܳܠܶܝܢܰܢ; ܫܰܦܺܝܪܺܝܢܰܢ; ܘܰܟܝܺܝܢܰܢ; or written separately, though pronounced in exactly the same way: ܩܳܛܠܺܝܢ ܚܢܰܢ; ܓܳܠܶܝܢ ܚܢܰܢ; ܫܰܦܺܝܪܺܝܢ ܚܢܰܢ; ܘܰܟܝܺܝܢ ܚܢܰܢ; (ܩܳܛܠܺܝܢ ܐܢܰܢ).

☞ p. 343

1. f. ܩܳܛܠܳܢ ܚܢܰܢ; ܓܳܠܝܳܢ ܚܢܰܢ; ܫܰܦܺܝܪܳܢ ܚܢܰܢ; ܘܰܟܝܳܢ ܚܢܰܢ; (say *qāt-lānan*, &c.).(¹)

2. m. ܩܳܛܠܺܝܬܽܘܢ; ܓܳܠܶܝܬܽܘܢ; ܫܰܦܺܝܪܺܝܬܽܘܢ; ܘܰܟܝܺܝܬܽܘܢ; or written separately, though spoken in the same way:—ܩܳܛܠܺܝܢ ܐܰܢ̱ܬܽܘܢ; ܓܳܠܶܝܢ ܐܰܢ̱ܬܽܘܢ; ܫܰܦܺܝܪܺܝܢ ܐܰܢ̱ܬܽܘܢ; ܘܰܟܝܺܝܢ ܐܰܢ̱ܬܽܘܢ.

2. f. ܩܳܛܠܳܬܶܝܢ; ܫܰܦܺܝܪܳܬܶܝܢ(²) or written separately, ܩܳܛܠܳܢ ܐܰܢ̱ܬܶܝܢ; ܓܳܠܝܳܢ ܐܰܢ̱ܬܶܝܢ; ܫܰܦܺܝܪܳܢ ܐܰܢ̱ܬܶܝܢ; ܘܰܟܝܳܢ ܐܰܢ̱ܬܶܝܢ.

B. *Rem.* In more ancient times *en* or *n* appears also with the poets(³) as an enclitic form of the 1ˢᵗ sing., and in fact this is often

---

(¹) For the feminine form the masculine form ܩܳܛܠܺܝܢܰܢ, &c. sometimes appears.

(²) When the participle or adjective ends in ܝ—, the 2ⁿᵈ fem. pl. form of the enclitic, and the participle are written separately.

(³) In homely prose I find such a form in the Rules for Monks of Mᵗ Izlā, of the year 571 (Rendic. della Accad. dei Lincei 1898, 43, 10); ܚܕܶܢ *i. e.* ܚܕܶܝܢ "I beseech". Ebedjesu substitutes for it the usual ܚܕܶܐ ܐܢܳܐ.

☞ p. 343

written ܣ, through confusion between it and the object-suffix: *Masc.* after ܠ̣: ܡܰܓܝ = ܐܳ ܡܓܰܐ̈ "I call"; ܡܚܰܘܶܐ "I acknowledge", ܡܬܰܘܣܶܠ "I point out", &c. (¹): *Fem.* ܓܚܰܙܢܶܣ = ܐܳ ܓܚܰܙܢܳ "I pass over"; ܐܳܡܪܢܶܣ "I say"; ܡܬܬܙܝ̈ܥܢܣ "I am alarmed", ܨܳܒܝܐ "I wish", ܡܬܫܰܒܩܢܣ "I am forsaken".

☞ p. 343

Possessive suffixes.

§ 65. (b) *Suffixed personal pronouns.*

Possessive suffixes.

Singular.	1. pers.		ܝ (§ 50 A) "my"	
	2. pers.	m.	ܟ̊ and after vowels	ܟ̣ "thy"
		f.	ܟ̱ܝ ,, ,, ,,	ܟ̊ܝ "thy"
	3. pers.	m.	ܗ̱ ,, ,, ,,	ܗܝ "his"
		f.	ܗ̇ ,, ,, ,,	ܗ̇ "her"
Plural.	1. pers.		ܢ ,, ,, ,,	ܢ "our"
	2. pers.	m.	ܟ̊ܘܢ "your"	
		f.	ܟܶܝܢ "your"	
	3. pers.	m.	ܗܘܢ "their"	
		f.	ܗܶܝܢ "their"	

Object suffixes.

§ 66. *Object suffixes.*

Singular.	1. pers.		ܢܝ and after vowels ܢ "me"	
	2. pers.	m.	ܟ̊ ,, ,, ,,	ܟ̣ "thee"
		f.	ܟ̱ܝ ,, ,, ,,	ܟ̊ܝ "thee"
	3. pers.	m.	ܗ̱ ,, ,, ,,	ܗܝ, ܝܗܝ, and ܝܗܘ (§ 50 A) "him"
		f.	ܗ̇ ,, ,, ,,	ܗ̇ "her"
Plural.	1, pers.		ܢ ,, ,, ,,	ܢ "us"
	2. pers.	m.	ܟ̊ܘܢ "you"	
		f.	ܟܶܝܢ "you"	
	3. pers.	m.	The enclitics ܐܶܢܘܢ, ܐܶܢܶܝܢ serve instead of suffixes for the	
		f.	3ʳᵈ pers. pl. (§ 63).	

For the method of attachment of the Possessive Suffixes v. §§ 69, 145, 149, 157, 199; and for that of the Object- or Verbal-suffixes v. § 184 *sqq.*

(¹) Masculine forms from strong roots are very rare.

DEMONSTRATIVE PRONOUNS.

Demonstrative pronouns.

§ 67. (a) *For what is nearer*; "this": *masc.* ܗܳܢ, ܗܳܢܳܐ—*fem.* ܗܳܕܶܐ: Plural ܗܳܠܶܝܢ (m. and f.).

Rem. A rarer secondary form from ܗܳܕܶܐ is ܗܳܕ.

We get ܗܳܢܘ with ܗܘ (§ 38). For ܗܳܕܶܐ comes a ܗܳܕܳܐ before ܗܝ, thus ܗܳܕܳܐ ܗܝ *hāδāi* (*hōδōi*).

(b) *For what is more distant*; "that": masc. ܗܰܘ; fem. ܗܳܝ; Plural masc. ܗܳܢܽܘܢ, fem. ܗܳܢܶܝܢ.

Rem. 1. ܗܳܢܽܘܢ, ܗܳܢܶܝܢ "*illi, illae*" must not be too closely associated with ܗܳܢܳܐ "*hic*", merely because of a casual similarity of sound. The forms for "this" are compounded out of *den, dênā, dē, illēn* with *hā* (§ 62); those for "that", out of the personal pronouns *hū, hī, hennōn, hennēn* with *hā*.

Rem. 2. Only in very old writings there appear in isolated instances the farther forms ܗܳܠܽܘܟ "*illi*", ܗܳܠܶܟ "*illae*", and ܗܳܢܽܘܟ "*illi*" (a fem. form corresponding to the last is not known); the three forms given may be pronounced something like *hālōkh, hālēkh*; *hānōkh*. Very rarely indeed there appears also ܗܝ = *ܗܳܠܶܝܢ "*hi, hae*". ☞ p. 343

INTERROGATIVE PRONOUNS.

Interrogative pronouns.

§ 68. ܡܰܢ "who?". ܡܳܐ, ܡܶܢ, ܡܽܢ, ܡܳܢܳܐ "what?".

With ܗܘ, ܗܝ: ܡܰܢܽܘ, and fem. ܡܰܢ ܗܝ "who?, who is?". ܡܢܽܘ "what is?". Rarely ܡܽܘܢܳܐ for ܡܳܢܳܐ (§ 44).

ܐܰܝܢܳܐ "which?" *or* "what?" *m.*; ܐܰܝܕܳܐ "which?" *f.*; Pl. ܐܰܝܠܶܝܢ "which?".

Rem. 1. ܡܶܢ, ܡܽܢ, ܡܳܢܳܐ, ܡܽܘܢܳܐ have sprung from *mā* + *den, dênā*; ܐܰܝܢܳܐ, ܐܰܝܕܳܐ, ܐܰܝܠܶܝܢ from the interrogative *ai* with *dênā, dā, illēn*.

Rem. 2. ܐܰܝܢܳܐ, &c. is often improperly held as a demonstrative, because, like other interrogatives, it stands as correlative to the relative (§ 236).

THE RELATIVE PRONOUN.

The relative pronoun.

§ 69. The relative pronoun is ܕ, ܕ݁ (§ 43 E), which has a very wide range of use. The older form *dī* still shows itself in the *Separate possessive pronoun*, formed through its composition with the preposition ܠ

and the possessive suffixes (§ 65); ܝ݂ܟܶܠ "my"; ܝܟܶܠܺ "thy" *m.*; ܝܟܶܠܺ "thy" *f.*; ܗ݂ܟܶܠ "his"; ܗ݂ܟܶܠ "her" — ܝܟܶܠ "our"; ܦܟܶܠ "your" *m.*; ܝܟܶܠ "your" *f.*; ܢܘܗܟܶܠ "their" *m.*, ܢܝܗܟܶܠ "their" *f.*

2. *Nouns* in
the stricter
sense.
(Substantives and
adjectives.)
A. *Gender,
Number,
State.*
General
statement:
Paradigm
of the simplest forms.

2. NOUNS IN THE STRICTER SENSE.

(SUBSTANTIVES AND ADJECTIVES.)

A. GENDER, NUMBER, STATE.

§ 70. Every Syriac substantive or adjective has a gender, a number, and a state. The indications of all three conditions are very closely associated together, and almost interpenetrate one another. We shall therefore deal here with the three, at one and the same time.

Syriac has two *genders*, Masculine and Feminine, two *numbers*, Singular and Plural ([1]), and three *states*, Absolute, Construct, and Emphatic. The *Emphatic State* is formed by appending an *ā* (originally *hā?*) which possessed the significance of the Article (the Determination), but this meaning has for the most part been lost. The *Construct State* is the form of the noun immediately before a Genitive. A noun, which has neither of the States named, stands in the *Absolute State*. The Emphatic state is of by far the most frequent occurrence in Syriac substantives. Many are no longer met with in either of the other two states, or only in quite isolated cases: accordingly substantives at least are presented here throughout, in the Emphatic state, as being the form lying next to hand, even if not the most original. The other two states have no special ending for the singular of Masculines, nor for that of Feminines without the feminine sign. The termination of the Emphatic state (*ā*) combines with the masculine plural-ending to form *aiyā*, which again is generally farther blended into *ē*. The usual feminine ending in the Singular, was *at*, which has maintained itself as *ath* in the Construct state, but has become *ā* in the Absolute state. The plural-ending for Masculines in the Absolute state

---

([1]) Various traces of the Dual are still met with, but this Number has no longer a life of its own.

is $\bar{\imath}n$, and in the Construct state, *ai*: the corresponding endings for Feminines are *ān*, *āth*.

We give at this point, as an example of the most usual formations, the Adjective ܒܺܝܫ "wicked".

	Singular.			*Plural.*		
	St. abs.	St. constr.	St. emph.	St. abs.	St. constr.	St. emph.
m.	ܒܺܝܫ	ܒܺܝܫ	ܒܺܝܫܳܐ	ܒܺܝܫ̈ܺܝܢ	ܒܺܝܫ̈ܰܝ	ܒܺܝܫ̈ܶܐ
f.	ܒܺܝܫܳܐ	ܒܺܝܫܰܬ	ܒܺܝܫܬܳܐ	ܒܺܝܫ̈ܳܢ	ܒܺܝܫ̈ܳܬ	ܒܺܝܫ̈ܳܬܳܐ

Rem. Notice that the absolute state of the feminine singular and the emphatic state of the masculine singular for the most part sound alike.

On ܬ݂ܳܐ and ܬ݁ܳܐ v. § 23 E.

§ 71. Certain words insert a *y* (or *i*, v. § 40 C) before the feminine ending:— Insertion of ܝ before the feminine ending.

(1) First, those words (in all their forms) which terminate in the suffix *ān*, *ōn*, (*ūn*) : *e. g.* from ܡܩܰܛܠܳܢ "murdering", the feminine sing. abs. state is ܡܩܰܛܠܳܢܝܳܐ, the constr. state ´ـܢܝܰܬ, the emphatic state ´ـܳܢܺܝܬܳܐ; the feminine plural abs. state ´ـܢܝ̈ܳܢ, the constr. state ´ـܢܝ̈ܳܬ, the emph. state ´ـܢܝ̈ܳܬܳܐ. So from ܡܰܠܟܘܿܢܳܐ *regulus*, we have the feminine ܡܰܠܟܘܿܢܺܝܬܳܐ, &c. This analogy is followed in such old borrowed words as ܐܽܘܡܳܢܝܳܐ τεχνῖτις, and ܡܶܣܟܶܢܝܳܐ πτωχή, pl. ܡܶܣ̈ܟܶܢܝܳܢ, ܡܶܣ̈ܟܶܢܝܳܬܳܐ (but emphatic state fem. ܡܣܟܶܢܺܝܬܳܐ).—*Exceptions*, ܐܳܚܝܳܢܺܝܬܳܐ fem. from ܐܳܚܝܳܢܳܐ "related", and ܬܶܢܝܳܢܺܝܬܳܐ fem. from ܬܶܢܝܳܢܳܐ *secundus*. ☞ p. 343 ☞ p. 343

(2) Next, the adjective ܙܥܘܿܪ "little" in all its forms (fem.), except in the emphatic state sing.: ܙܥܘܿܪܝܳܐ, ܙܥܘܿܪܝܰܬ (but ܙܥܘܿܪܬܳܐ);—ܙܥܘܿܪ̈ܝܳܢ, ܙܥܘܿܪ̈ܝܳܬ (?), ܙܥܘܿܪ̈ܝܳܬܳܐ.

(3) Probably it is the same with Nomina agentis of the form ܦܳܥܘܿܠ. For the singular we have ܡܳܪܘܿܕܝܳܐ "rebellious", and the analogously-treated, although Greek, word ܐܣܘܿܛܝܳܐ ἀσώτη; for the plural of the absolute state, only ܐܣܘ̈ܛܝܳܢ. The abs. and construct states of these Nom. ag. almost never appear. In other cases [emph. st. pl.] there occur ܚܳܪܘܿܒܝ̈ܳܬܳܐ "destroying"; ܥܳܒܘܿܪ̈ܝܳܬܳܐ "transitory things"; ܩܳܛܘܿܠܳܝ̈ܳܬܳܐ "murderous", &c. Forms like ܡܳܝܘܿ̈ܬܳܬܳܐ "mortal" &c., without *y*, are of less frequent occurrence. ☞ p. 343

(4) So too, in the plural of feminine forms of Diminutives in ܘܿܣ (ܕܳܪܬܘܿܣܬܳܐ "yard [court]", pl. ܕ̈ܳܪܬܘܿܣܝܳܬܳܐ) ܝ is inserted, as also in the case of a number of other substantives, which before the feminine ending have

a consonant preceded by a long vowel, a doubled consonant, or two consonants. Thus ܡܥܨܪܬܐ "bundle", pl. ܡܥܨܪ̈ܝܬܐ; ܟܘܬܝܢܐ "tunic", pl. ܟܘܬܝ̈ܢܝܢ, ܟܘܬܝ̈ܢܬܐ; ܕܘܟܬܐ (דּוּכְתָּא) "place"; pl. ܕܘ̈ܟܝܢ, ܕܘ̈ܟܝܬܐ; ܕܘܢܒܐ "tail"; pl. ܕܘ̈ܢܒܬܐ, and many others. This formation is of more frequent occurrence in later times. Some have secondary forms, *e. g.* ܣܟܝܢܐ "knife"; pl. ܣܟܝ̈ܢܬܐ and ܣܟܝ̈ܢܝܬܐ (as well as ܣܟܝ̈ܢܐ).

Pl. emph. st. in *aiyā*.

§ 72. The plural-ending in the emphatic state was properly *aiyā* (from *ai* + *ā*): this ending ̈ܝܐ is still shown in the short words ܒܢ̈ܝܐ "sons"; ܫܢ̈ܝܐ "years"; ܙܢ̈ܝܐ "kinds"; ܬܕ̈ܝܐ "breasts"; ܐܕ̈ܝܐ (= יְדַיָּא § 40 C) as well as ܐܝ̈ܕܝܐ "hands"; ܐܦ̈ܝܐ "curtain" (= ܐܦ̈ܐ "face"). For all these words v. § 146.

Aiyā appears farther in the plural emphatic state,—through blending the final vowel of the root,—in adjectives and participles in *ē* and *ai* (*yā* in Emph. st. sing.), with the emphatic ending: ܩܫܐ "hard" (Emph. st. ܩܫܝܐ), ܩܫ̈ܝܐ; ܣܟܠܝܐ (st. abs. ܣܟܠܐ) "fool", ܣܟ̈ܠܝܐ; ܡܚܓܝ "lamed", ܡܚܓ̈ܝܐ, &c.

So with the substantives ܓܕܝܐ "kid", ܓܕ̈ܝܐ; ܟܟܪܐ "a talent (weight)", ܟܟ̈ܪܐ; ܩܢܝܐ "reed", ܩܢ̈ܝܐ; ܡܥܝܐ "bowels", ܡܥ̈ܝܐ; and so with the *Plur. tantum* ܡ̈ܝܐ "water" (and ܫܡܝܐ, ܫܡ̈ܝܐ "heaven" § 146); farther ܓܘܪܝܐ "young (of animal)", ܓܘܪ̈ܝܐ (later formation ܓܘܪ̈ܘܬܐ § 79 A); ܕܘܡܝܐ "image", ܕܡ̈ܝܐ "price" (later formation ܕܘܡܘ̈ܝܐ "images").—But not with the abstract nouns—ܨܪܝܐ "a rent", ܨܪ̈ܝܐ (as against ܨܪܝܐ "one who is torn", ܨܪ̈ܝܐ); ܓܪܝܐ "cold", ܓܪ̈ܝܐ.

Abs. and constr. states (corresponding).

§ 73. In the absolute state of the plural, such substantives have *īn*, so far as they appear in it at all: ܓܕ̈ܝܢ; ܟܟ̈ܪܝܢ; ܩܢ̈ܝܢ; ܕܡ̈ܝܢ; ܡ̈ܝܢ. Thus too the pronunciation of the very rare word ܫܡܝܢ must be *šĕmīn* and not *šĕmēn*. But the Adjectives have *ēn*: ܩܫܝܢ; ܣܟܠܝܢ; ܡܚܓܝܢ (from ܡܚܓܐ and from ܡܚܓܝ) &c.

In the construct state of the plural, such Substantives have *ai*: ܕܡ̈ܝ; ܟܟ̈ܪܝ; ܩܢ̈ܝ; ܫܡ̈ܝ; but the Adjectives, *yai*: ܩܫ̈ܝܝ; ܪ̈ܥܝܝ "herdsmen"; ܩܪ̈ܝܝ "criers"; ܡܚܘ̈ܝܝ "pointing out", &c. (cf. with this section § 145 K *infra*).

Plur. from enlarged forms in *ān*.

§ 74. The following Masculines form their plural from enlarged forms in *ān*. They are to some extent words of closely related meaning:—

ܐܒܐ "fruit"; ܐܒ̈ܐ (ܐܒܒܐ § 21 D), seldom ܐܒ̈ܐ.(1)

ܦܛܡܐ *φάρμακον*; ܦܛ̈ܡܐ (ܦܛܡܩܐ § 21 D).

ܒܣܡܐ "fragrance"; ܒܣ̈ܡܢܐ (also ܒܣܡܘܢܐ § 44) and ܒܣ̈ܡܐ.

ܪܝܚܐ "scent"; ܪ̈ܝܚܢܐ.

ܠܒܘܢܬܐ "frankincense"; ܠܒ̈ܘܢܬܐ and ܠܒ̈ܘܢܬܐ.(2)

ܡܫܚܐ "salve"; ܡܫ̈ܚܢܐ.

ܚܡܪܐ "wine"; ܚܡ̈ܪܐ (also ܚܡܪ̈ܘܬܐ § 44).(3)

ܓܘܢܐ "colour"; ܓ̈ܘܢܢܐ, usually ܓ̈ܘܢܐ.

ܨܒܥܐ "dyed stuff"; ܨܒ̈ܥܢܐ and ܨܒ̈ܥܐ.

ܥܡܪܐ "wool"; ܥܡ̈ܪܢܐ "woollen stuffs".

ܒܣܪܐ "flesh"; ܒܣ̈ܪܐ, together with ܒܣ̈ܪܐ.(4).

ܓܢܣܐ "race" (*γένος*); ܓ̈ܢܣܢܐ, also with ܓ̈ܢܣܐ.

ܛܪܦܐ "foliage"; ܛܪ̈ܦܢܐ.

ܫܠܝܛܐ "ruler"; ܫܠ̈ܝܛܢܐ and ܫܠ̈ܝܛܐ. From that form (ܫܠ̈ܝܛܢܐ) the singular ܫܠܝܛܢܐ has been derived anew.

ܟܘܡܪܐ "priest"; ܟܘ̈ܡܪܢܐ, usually ܟܘ̈ܡܪܐ.

ܪܒܐ "teacher"; ܪ̈ܒܢܐ (very rarely indeed a sing. from it occurs ܪܒܢܐ); ܪܘܪ̈ܒܢܐ "magnates" (v. § 146).(5)

§ 75. *Feminine substantives in* ܝܬܐ have ܝܬ in the absolute state of the singular (§ 26 C). Thus ܬܟܣܝܬܐ "garment", ܬܟܣܝ; ܡܪܕܝܬܐ "journey", ܡܪܕܝ; ܩܢܝܬܐ "beam", ܩܢܝ; ܪܒܝܬܐ "usury", ܪܒܝ. In the construct state ܝܬ: ܬܫܥܝܬܐ "narration", ܬܫܥܝܬ. But in adjectives, *e. g.* ܪܒܝܬܐ ☞ p. 343

Fem. in *ithā*.

(1) The East-Syrians say *abbā* (§ 45) &c., with *a*. The abs. state is ܐܒܒܝܢ: So far as such state appears in the case of the others, it is dealt with in a corresponding way.

(2) Singular ܠܒܘܬܐ is "tar".

(3) Thus the *Plurale tantum* ܗܪ̈ܘܦܢܐ "spices" clearly belongs to a sing. ܗܪܘܦܐ; and so ܝܪ̈ܩܢܐ "herbs", and ܙܪ̈ܥܢܐ "seeds, plants" must be plurals of ܝܪܩܐ and ܙܪܥܐ (also a pl. ܙܪ̈ܥܐ). The singular of ܒܣܡܢܐ "a certain wedding dainty" is probably ܒܣܡܐ. ☞ p. 343

(4) ܒܣܪ̈ܢܝܬܐ "fleshy layers", "membranes" is not however a plural from ܒܣܪܐ, since it is feminine. The singular would probably be ܒܣܪܢܝܬܐ.

(5) Some few are uncertain. Perhaps several others of those named have simple plurals.

"*pura*", the absolute state is ܦܘܪܐ, the construct, ܦܘܪܝ. In the plural all have the consonantal *y*: ܡܕܝܢܝ̈ܬܐ, ܦܘ̈ܪܝܢ, &c.

Fem. in *ūthā*. § 76. A. *Words in* ܘܬܐ (purely *feminine abstract nouns*) have ܘ in the absolute state of the singular (§ 26 C), and ܘܬ in the construct state, while in the plural they have for states abs., constr., emph.— ܘ̈ܬܢ, ܘ̈ܬ, ܘ̈ܬܐ. Thus for instance, ܡܠܟܘ "kingdom", ܡܠܟܘܬ, ܡܠܟܘܬܐ; and in plural ܡܠܟܘ̈ܬܢ, ܡܠܟܘ̈ܬ, ܡܠܟܘ̈ܬܐ.—ܒܥܘ "a request", ܒܥܘܬ, ܒܥܘܬܐ; ☞ p. 343 plural, ܒܥܘ̈ܬܢ, &c.—ܡܪܕܘܬܐ "chastisement"; ܡܪܕܘ̈ܬܐ, &c.

From ܐܣܝܘܬܐ "healing", there is formed (from an old ground-form ܐܣܘܬܐ) ܐܣܘ̈ܬܐ or (§ 40 C) ܐܣܝ̈ܘܬܐ. Even from ܦܠܓܘܬܐ "half", ܣܗܕܘܬܐ "testimony", ܝܪܬܘܬܐ "inheritance", the plural is ܦܠܓ̈ܘܬܐ, ܣܗܕ̈ܘܬܐ, ܝܪ̈ܬܘܬܐ: still there is also found, conformably to the original formation, ܦܠܓܘ̈ܬܐ, ܣܗܕܘ̈ܬܐ.

From ܓܢܒܪܘܬܐ "manliness" comes the plural ܓܢܒܪ̈ܘܬܐ "wonders".

B. Notice specially besides: ܨܘܪܬܐ "image" (ܨܘܪܬ, ܨܘܪܐ); pl. ܨܘ̈ܪܬܐ (ܨܘ̈ܪܢ). ܨܒܘܬܐ "thing" (ܨܒܘܬ, ܨܒܘ); pl. ܨܒܘ̈ܬܐ (ܨܒܘ̈ܢ). ܚܝܘܬܐ "animal" and ܚܕܘܬܐ "joy" (for and with ܚܝܘܬܐ([1]), ܚܕܝܘܬܐ § 40 D) form regularly ܚܝܘܬ, ܚܕܘܬ, ܚܕܘ; Plural being, of course, ܚܝ̈ܘܬܐ, ܚܕ̈ܘܬܐ.

Fem. in *ōthā*. § 77. *Feminines in ōthā*([2]): ܨܠܘܬܐ "prayer", constr. state, ܨܠܘܬ,— pl. ܨܠܘ̈ܬܐ, ܨܠܘ̈ܬܢ. So ܫܩܘܬܐ "thigh", ܫܩ̈ܘܬܐ; ܢܣܘܬܐ, ܢܣ̈ܘܬܐ "sawdust". On the other hand ܡܚܘܬܐ "stroke", abs. st. ܡܚܘ: in plural ܡܚ̈ܘܬܐ, ܡܚ̈ܘܢ (without *a* before ܘ).

Fem. in *āthā*. § 78. *Feminine forms in āthā*([3]) (in the singular occurring nearly always in the emphatic state) have in the plural *awāthā*: ܒܗܬܐ "thumb", ܒܗ̈ܘܬܐ; ܡܢܬܐ "portion", ܡܢ̈ܘܬܐ, ܡܢ̈ܘܢ, &c. Similarly ܡܐ̈ܘܬܐ (for מְאַוָתָא) from ܡܐܐ "a hundred". Some of these words in *āthā* form the plural

---

([1]) But of course the Abstract Noun ܚܝܘܬܐ = חַיּוּתָא "liveliness", which is formed by ܚܝ "living", combined with the suffix *ūth* (§ 138),—although in outward appearance it coincides with ܚܝܘܬܐ = חַיְוָתָא "animal"—has ܚܝܘ in the Abs. st. and ܚܝܘܬ in the Constr. st.

([2]) The Singular-forms not adduced (st. abs. or constr.) I cannot vouch for. The corresponding Plural-forms (in *ān* and *āth*) are easily supplied.

☞ p. 344 ([3]) ܡܢܬܐ, pl. ܡܢ̈ܘܬܐ, properly an Abstract noun, is masculine, when it means "associate".

as if the ܬ belonged to the stem and they were masculine: thus ܒܥܬܐ "seeking for", ܒܥܬܐ; ܨܐܬܐ "dirt" (for צְאָתָא § 33 A), ܨܐܬܐ.

ܡܘܡܬܐ "oath" (Abs. st. ܡܘܡܐ, constr. st. ܡܘܡܬ) remains unaltered in the plural, ܡܘܡܬܐ; or from a secondary form ܡܘܡܝܬܐ, it forms ܡܘܡܝܬܐ.

ܚܬܐ "sister",—plural, ܐܚܘܬܐ v. § 146.

§ 79. A. A number of *masculine substantives in* ܝܐ form their plural in ܘܬܐ—, instead of following § 72. (1) Pl. in *wāthā*.

Thus in particular:

ܐܘܪܝܐ "manger", ܐܘܪܘܬܐ (2) (§ 34); ܐܪܝܐ "lion", ܐܪܝܘܬܐ (§ 146); ܩܘܒܝܐ "pipe", ܩܘܒܘܬܐ; ܬܕܝܐ "breast", ܬܕܘܬܐ (and ܬܕܝܐ); ܚܘܝܐ "serpent", ܚܘܘܬܐ; ܟܘܪܟܝܐ "crane", ܟܘܪܟܘܬܐ; ܟܘܪܣܝܐ "throne", ܟܘܪܣܘܬܐ; ܓܒܝܐ "heap", ܓܒܘܬܐ; ܠܠܝܐ (for *lailĕyā* § 49 A) "night", ܠܠܘܬܐ; ܡܥܝܐ "bowels", ܡܥܘܬܐ, generally ܡܥܝܐ (§ 72); ܨܪܝܐ "rent", ܨܪܘܬܐ (as well as ܨܪܝܐ); ܡܫܠܝܐ "extracting-fork", ܡܫܠܘܬܐ; ܣܘܣܝܐ "horse", ܣܘܣܘܬܐ (3); the compound ܒܣܕܝܐ "pillow" (§ 141), with the irregular plural, ܒܣܕܘܬܐ (4); and the substantive participles: ܪܥܝܐ "shepherd", ܪܥܘܬܐ; ܐܣܝܐ "physician", ܐܣܘܬܐ; ܡܪܝܐ "Lord", ܡܪܘܬܐ (§ 146); ܫܩܝܐ "cup-bearer", ܫܩܘܬܐ. ☞ p. 344

So also the feminine ܢܩܝܐ "sheep", ܢܩܘܬܐ; and ܪܚܝܐ "mill", ܪܚܘܬܐ with ܪܚܝܐ.

Farther ܟܘܕܢܘܬܐ from ܟܘܕܢܝܐ "a mule", for which others give ܟܘܕܢܝܘܬܐ (not so well authenticated). (5)

Besides, it is common with Greek words,—particularly feminines: ܡܘܕܝܘܣ μόδιος, ܡܘܕܝܘܬܐ; ܦܠܛܝܐ πλατεῖα, ܦܠܛܝܘܬܐ; ܓܘܢܝܐ γωνία, ܓܘܢܝܘܬܐ, and many others. Also with other terminations: κῶλον, ܩܘܠܘܬܐ; ܐܣܛܕܝܘܢ στάδιον, ܐܣܛܕܘܬܐ; ܡܟܢܐ μηχανή, ܡܟܢܘܬܐ, and many others.

---

(1) I adduce those only which are well attested.

(2) So the later formation ܐܘܪܘܬܐ for ܐܘܪܝܐ (§ 72), where the short *u* is treated as long.

(3) A late formation is ܣܘܣܝܐ.

(4) This form appears to be the only correct one.

(5) Later formation,—ܟܘܕܢܝܐ. Along with it there is found (from the rare ܟܘܕܢܐ) the fem. ܟܘܕܢܬܐ, plural ܟܘܕܢܝܬܐ.

The vocalisation is not always certain in these cases: occasionally secondary forms are found besides, as from ܡܚܘܿܙܐ, ܬܚܘܿܡܐ (§ 72).

The peculiar ܐܘܿܝܠ "pot-stand, hearth", properly a plural-form, forms a new plural, ܐܘܿܝܠܬ̈ܐ: a secondary form is ܐܘܿܝܠܐ.

B. In addition the following words, not ending in *yā*, form plurals in ܘ̈ܬܐ:—

(1) Masculines, taking ⸗ before the ܘ: ܐܬܪ "place, ܐܬܪܘ̈ܬܐ; (¹) ܚܝܠ "strength", ܚܝܠܘ̈ܬܐ (and ܚܝܠܝ̈ܢ); ܠܒ "heart", ܠܒܘ̈ܬܐ (and ܠܒܝ̈ܢ); ܢܗܪ "river", ܢܗܪܘ̈ܬܐ; ܛܗܪ "midday", ܛܗܪܘ̈ܬܐ. In the later speech there are
☞ p. 344
a few additional examples.

(2) Feminines, not taking ⸗ before the ܘ: ܥܡܡܐ "folk", ܥܡܡܘ̈ܬܐ; ܐܫܬܐ "wall", ܐܫܬܘ̈ܬܐ (usually ܐܫ̈ܐ § 80); ܐܬܐ "sign", ܐܬܘ̈ܬܐ; ܩܪܝܬܐ "village", ܩܘܪܝ̈ܐ; ܐܫܬܐ "fever", ܐܫܬܘ̈ܬܐ (§ 114); ܢܘܪܐ "fire", ܢܘܪܘ̈ܬܐ (also ܢܘܪ̈ܐ); ܣܦܬܐ "lip", ܣܦܘ̈ܬܐ (§ 146). (²)

☞ p. 344

Feminine-ending treated as a radical.

§ 80. In §§ 78 and 79 B we have already had several feminines which treat their ܬ in the plural as if it belonged to the stem. So, farther, ܥܒܝܛܐ, ܥܒܝܛܬܐ "twig", ܥܒܝ̈ܛܐ, ܥܒܝ̈ܛܬܐ; ܕܘܥܬܐ "sweat", "exudation", ܕܘܥ̈ܬܐ: ܫܩܐ "bag", "beam", ܫܩ̈ܐ; ܡܕܬܐ "tribute", ܡܕ̈ܬܐ: perhaps too ܐܘܡܬܐ "sting, prick" (³) belongs to this class, with pl. ܐܘܡ̈ܬܐ: perhaps also ܓܘܡܕܐ "stem" with pl. ܓܘܡ̈ܕܐ. Several plurals of Abstracts like ܨܒܘܬܐ, as pl. of ܨܒܘܝ̈ܐ "care", are doubtful (ܨܘܬܐ "contention", "litigation" is regular: ܨܘܬܐ). ܡܬܩܠܐ "a balance" has, according to some, the pl. ܡܬܩ̈ܠܐ, but ܡܬܩ̈ܠܬܐ is better (for *masseāthā* √ܢܫܐ).

Falling away of fem.-ending in pl.

§ 81. A large number of feminines, particularly names of plants, have a feminine termination in the singular, but not in the plural. Thus *e. g.* ܐܡܬܐ "ell", ܐ̈ܡܐ, ܐ̈ܡܝܢ; ܐܫܬܐ "wall", ܐܫ̈ܐ; ܕܘܡܚܬܐ (commonly ܕܘܡ̈ܚܬܐ § 51) "a patch", ܕܘܡ̈ܚܐ; ܓܢܬܐ "garden", ܓܢ̈ܐ; ܓܕܝܐ "egg", ܓܕ̈ܐ (along with ܓܕ̈ܬܐ "vaults"); ܣܦܝܢܬܐ "ship", ܣܦܝ̈ܢܐ (with ܣܦܝ̈ܢܬܐ);

(¹) The simple pl. is given in ܐܬܪ̈ܝܢ ܚܟ̈ܐ "in all places",—"everywhere".

(²) Notice with regard to the foregoing sections that the East-Syrians write ܘܿܬܐ⸗ for ܘܿܬܐ⸗ (§ 49 B).

(³) This (with ܬ) seems to be the correct form. If, however, the *t* is hard, as another line of tradition represents it to be, then it belongs to the root.

ܫܳܥܬܳܐ "hour", ܫܳܥܶ̈ܐ; ܫܰܢ̱ܬܳܐ "year", ܫܢܰܝܳ̈ܐ (§§ 72, 146); ܡܶܠܬܳܐ "word", ܡܶܠܶ̈ܐ; ܡܰܫܟܢܳܐ "tent", "hut", ܡܰܫܟܢܶ̈ܐ (§ 59); ܡܓܕܠܳܐ "pit", ܡܓܕܠܶ̈ܐ; ܥܶܢܒܬܳܐ "grape", ܥܶܢܒܶ̈ܐ (§ 28); ܚܶܛܬܳܐ "wheat", ܚܶܛܶ̈ܐ; ܣܥܳܪܬܳܐ "barley", ܣܥܳܪܶ̈ܐ; ܬܺܐܢܬܳܐ (ܬܬܳܐ) "fig", ܬܺܐܢܶ̈ܐ (§ 28); ܫܶܢܬܳܐ "a kind of thorn", ܫܶܢܶ̈ܐ, &c., &c. ☞ p. 344

Notice — ܣܶܩܦܳܬܳܐ "vertebra" (and ܣܶܩܦܬܳܐ), ܣܶܩ̈ܦܶܐ (secondary form ܣܶܩ̈ܦܳܬܳܐ); ܓܽܘܡܪܳܬܳܐ "charcoal", ܓܽܘܡܪܶ̈ܐ (later additional forms ܓܽܘܡܪܳܬܳܐ and ܓܽܘܡܪܶ̈ܐ § 71); ܢܽܘܩܦܳܐ (secondary form ܢܽܘܩܦܳܐ) "vine-shoot", ܢܽܘܩ̈ܦܶܐ (§ 28); ܓܽܘܒܢܳܐ "cheese", ܓܽܘܒ̈ܢܶܐ; ܠܒܶܢܬܳܐ "brick", ܠܒܶ̈ܢܶܐ.

The foreign word ܡܶܚܫܒܳܐ (שַׁבָּת) "sabbath" (whose ܠ is properly a radical) is treated in this way: — ܩܕܳܫ, ܩܕܳܫ; in abs. st. sing. ܡܶܚܫܒ.

§ 82. Other feminines do not have a feminine termination in the singular, but take one in the plural. Thus, for instance ܐܽܘܪܚܳܐ "way", ܐܽܘܪ̈ܚܳܬܳܐ; ܐܰܪܥܳܐ "earth", ܐܰܪ̈ܥܳܬܳܐ; ܢܰܦܫܳܐ "soul", ܢܰܦ̈ܫܳܬܳܐ; ܪܽܘܚܳܐ "wind, spirit", ܪ̈ܽܘܚܳܬܳܐ and ܪ̈ܽܘܚܶܐ, &c. **Assumption of fem. ending in pl.**

Several separate the forms of the plural according to the signification, e. g. ܥܰܝܢܳܐ "eye, fountain", ܥܰܝ̈ܢܶܐ "eyes", — ܥܰܝ̈ܢܳܬܳܐ "fountains", &c. V. in §§ 84 and 87, the words concerned. (¹)

Of masculines, only ܫܡܳܐ forms its plural in this way, ܫܡܳܗܶ̈ܐ (rarely the constr. st. ܫܡܳܗܰܬ; — before suffixes ܫܡܳܗܰ̈ܝܗܽܘܢ, &c.) along with ܫܡܳܗܶ̈ܐ (but absolute st. only ܫܡܳܗܺ̈ܝܢ); similarly [with double forms] ܩܰܕܡܳܝܳܬܳܐ "names", together with ܫܡܳܗܳܬܳܐ, from ܫܡܳܐ; and ܐܰܒܳܗܳܬܳܐ "fathers", together with ܐܰܒܳܗܶ̈ܐ from ܐܰܒܳܐ (§ 146). ☞ p. 344

§ 83. *An old feminine ending ai* appears only in the following words, which are no longer capable of inflection and always stand in the absolute state of the singular: — **Feminine-ending: ai.**

ܣܰܠܘܰܝ "quails"; ܝܰܡܘܰܝ "a kind of bird"; ܒܰܪܘܰܝ "a kind of gnat"; ܓܘܳܓܰܝ "spider"; ܠܝܰܘ "condition (terms)"; ܛܳܥܘܰܝ "error"; ܛܳܡܘܰܝ "concealment" (only in ܒܛܳܡܘܰܝ "in secret"). ☞ p. 344 ☞ p. 344

§ 84. *A large number of feminines do not have a feminine termination in the singular.* I give here a list of ascertained words (²) of this **List of feminines not having a fem. ending.**

(¹) Very frequently a transferred meaning takes *āthā*; while the word in its proper meaning takes *ē*. The latter is properly a dual form in this case.

(²) Some doubtful words like ܓܶܕ̈ܫܶܐ = נדים I Kings 6, 9 — I have purposely

kind,—though of course not complete,—arranged alphabetically, keeping out Greek words, except a few that have been greatly altered. Those which always take the feminine-ending in the plural I mark with "*āthā*"; those which form the plural in both ways (§ 82), with "*āthā* and *ē*". The others form the plural only after a masculine type, *so far as a plural of theirs can be authenticated at all.*

ܐܰܓܳܢܳܐ bowl.
ܐܶܕܢܳܐ ear, *āthā* (handle &c.) and *ē*.
ܐܽܘܪܚܳܐ way, *āthā*.
ܐܺܝܕܳܐ hand (Plurals v. § 146).
ܐܶܠܥܳܐ rib.
ܐܶܠܦܳܐ ship.
ܐܶܡܳܐ mother (Plurals v. § 146).
ܐܶܣܛܠܳܐ cloak.
ܐܶܣܬܺܪܳܐ στατήρ.
ܐܰܦܶܐ (properly pl. or rather dual from אנף "nose") face.
ܐܶܦܥܳܐ hyena.
ܐܰܪܥܳܐ earth, *āthā*.
ܐܶܫܟܳܐ stone (1) (testic.).
ܐܶܫܟܳܪܳܐ field. (2)
ܐܰܬܳܢܳܐ she-ass.
☞ p. 344 ܒܺܐܪܳܐ spring.
ܒܽܘܪܟܳܐ knee.
ܒܶܩܪܳܐ herd. (3)
ܓܽܘܕܳܐ troop. (4)
ܓܽܘܪܙܳܐ stick. (4)
ܓܽܘܦܢܳܐ vine.
ܓܽܘܕܳܐ column in book. (4)
ܓܺܝܓܠܳܐ wheel.
ܓܶܠܠܳܐ wādy.
ܓܰܪܒܝܳܐ north.
ܕܽܘܢܒܳܐ tail.
ܕܰܦܢܳܐ side, rib, *āthā* and *ē*.
ܙܰܩܳܐ a skin, bottle.
ܚܽܘܦܢܳܐ handful.
ܚܰܨܺܝܢܳܐ axe.
ܚܶܨܪܳܐ little finger.
ܚܰܩܠܳܐ field, *āthā*.
ܛܰܪܦܳܐ bird of prey.
ܛܶܦܪܳܐ finger-nail, claw.
ܝܰܡܺܝܢܳܐ right hand.
ܝܰܪܽܘܪܳܐ jackal.
ܟܺܐܦܳܐ stone.

---

excluded.—The number of such Feminines may actually be a good deal larger than has come under observation up to the present time at least. The same remark holds good of the fluctuations in the matter of gender.

(1) Besides, ܐܶܫܟܬܳܐ, pl. ܐܶܫܟ̈ܬܳܐ.

(2) Besides, ܐܶܫܟܳܪܬܳܐ, pl. ܐܶܫܟܳܪ̈ܝܳܬܳܐ (§ 71). It is a foreign word.

(3) The feminine ܓܶܕ̈ܐ "wormwood" (§ 21 D) no doubt had a sing. ܓܶܕܝܳܐ and accordingly belongs to § 81. Exactly the same seems to be the case with ܥܩܶܪܳܐ "sedge-grass".

(4) Rare in the masc., and not so well supported.

ܟܒܕܐ liver.

ܩܐܘܠܐ (ܩܐܘܠܐ, &c.) ark (probably a foreign word).

ܟܘܪܐ bee-hive.

ܟܘܬܝܢܐ tunic (pl. v. § 71).

ܟܟܪܐ talent.

ܟܕܦܐ raft.

ܟܢܦܐ wing, *ātha* and *ē*.

ܟܦܐ handful, bowl.

ܟܪܣܐ body, belly, *ātha*.

ܟܪܥܐ shank.

ܟܬܦܐ shoulder, *ātha*.

ܠܘܚܐ tablet.

ܡܓܠܐ sickle. (¹)

ܡܓܢܐ shield.

ܡܕܢܚܐ rising (of the sun), east.

ܡܘܒܠܐ load.

ܥܓܠܐ calf.

ܡܚܛܐ needle.

ܡܠܚܐ salt.

ܡܥܐ copper-coin.

ܡܥܪܒܐ going-down (of the sun), west. (²)

ܢܘܪܐ fire (pl. § 79 B).

ܣܘܛܐ, ܣܘܛܐ thread (seemingly λίνέα).

ܢܦܫܐ soul, *ātha*.

ܥܢܐ sheep (pl. § 79 A).

ܣܟܝܢܐ knife, *ātha*, *ē* (and ܣܟܝܢܬܐ § 71, 4).

ܣܟܪܐ shield.

ܣܡܠܐ left-hand.

ܓܕܠܐ locks (of hair).

ܦܓܘܕܐ bit.

ܓܕܝܐ goat.

ܓܒܐ side, hip, *ātha*.

ܥܝܢܐ eye, *ātha*, (source, &c.) and *ē.*

ܓܠܓܠܐ storm.

ܓܙܪܐ small cattle.

ܥܢܢܐ cloud.

ܣܘܟܐ boughs. (³)

ܥܠܡܐ sprout.

ܥܩܒܐ heel, track. (⁴)

ܥܩܪܒܐ (v. § 52) scorpion.

ܓܘܒܐ trough.

ܥܪܣܐ bed, *ātha*.

ܥܪܦܠܐ mist.

ܢܝܪܐ yoke.

ܦܬܟܪܐ idolatrous altar (from the Assyrian).

ܨܒܥܐ finger, *ātha* and *ē*. [syrian].

ܨܚܪܐ dish.

ܨܦܪܐ a little bird.

ܩܕܪܐ pot.

ܩܘܦܕܐ hedgehog.

ܩܛܘ cat, pl. ܩܛܘܢܐ (foreign word of unknown origin).

ܩܠܡܐ louse, weevil.

ܩܣܛܐ a liquid measure. (⁵)

☞ p. 345

(¹) More rarely ܡܓܠܬܐ.

(²) The sing. of ܚܨܝܢ “loins” was probably ܚܨܐ.

(³) Sing. is probably ܣܘܟܐ “mane”; the plural ܣܘܟܐ also means “mane”; there is also a pl. ܣܘܟܐ.

(⁴) ܥܩܒܬܐ—“tracks”—belongs to the sing. ܥܩܒܐ.

(⁵) The ܠ here is altered from l: the word originally had the fem.-ending.

ܩܪܢܐ horn, *āthā* and *ē*.
ܩܪܩܠܐ grated cover. ([1])
ܪܓܠܐ foot, *āthā* (bases) and *ē*.
ܪܘܡܚܐ spear.
ܚܘܒܙܐ mallow.
ܪܚܝܐ mill (pl. § 79 A).
ܪܡܟܐ herd (especially of horses, word from the Persian).

ܩܘܒܥܬܐ an enveloping upper garment (word appears to be borrowed from the Assyrian).
ܫܠܕܐ corpse (from the Assyrian).
ܫܢܐ tooth *āϑā* (peaks) and *ē*.
ܫܪܐ navel.
ܬܘܠܥܐ worm.
ܬܝܡܢܐ south.

Add hereto all names of letters, like ܐܠܦ, ܒܝܬ, &c.

Farther, add feminine proper names, to which also the Hebrew words ܬܐܒܝܠ תֵּבֵל "earth", ܫܝܘܠ שְׁאוֹל "Hades", &c. belong.

Out of the above list certain groups of significations may be readily recognised as mostly feminine, *e. g.* limbs appearing in pairs (but ܕܪܥܐ "arm"; ܬܕܝܐ "breasts", &c. are masc.), as well as certain simple utensils and vessels, &c.

Fluctuation of gender in names of animals.

§ 85. *Names of animals*, which *for the most part* are *feminine*, appearing *sometimes* however as *masculine*, especially when they denote male individuals,—are:

ܐܘܪܥܕܐ frog.
ܐܪܢܒܐ hare.
ܕܒܐ bear.
ܩܩܒܐ partridge.
ܚܘܪܒܐ stork.
ܝܘܢܐ pigeon.

The correctness of using these words as masculines—is not quite established in every case. On the other hand, certain other names of animals, which have been noted above as being feminine, may occasionally be made use of in the masculine gender. ([2]) Conversely, the masculines ܓܡܠܐ "camel", ܚܡܪܐ "ass", when they have to denote females, are also employed as feminines. Also the word ܪܟܫܐ "horses" appears in the meaning "mares" as fem. (as well as ܪܟܫܬܐ).

Radical ܬ treated as fem.-ending.

§ 86. *Nouns formed with the sign of the feminine,* ܬܐ, *remain feminine*, even when this termination is not so readily recognisable as being such a sign. Thus, for example ܐܬܐ "sign"; ܐܫܬܐ "fever"; ܫܢܬܐ

☞ p. 345

([1]) From *cracli*, a vulgar form of *clatri* or *clathri*, which again is traceable to κλῇϑρα "bars".

([2]) Often we can by no means determine the gender by the name alone.

"sister"; ܩܶܫܬܳܐ "bow" (pl. ܩܶܫܬܳܬܳܐ); ܣܰܩܳܐ "bag" (§ 80). The feminine termination is doubtless also present in the feminine ܡܳܬܳܐ "home", "village" (Assyrian word); ܙܰܩܬܳܐ "sting", (§ 80); ܙܶܦܬܳܐ or ܙܶܦܬܳܐ "pitch". Cf. p. 57, Note (5). But ܨܳܐܬܳܐ "dirt", and ܕܽܘܥܬܳܐ "sweat", occur certainly as masculines, though very rarely.

On the other hand phonetic analogy attracts to the feminine gender the following words, which have a radical ܠ:—ܐܰܪܥܳܐ "ground"; ܢܳܐ "glue"; ܓܶܠܳܐ "mote (כתת?); ܒܶܣܳܐ "anise" (foreign word); ܒܪܽܘܬܳܐ "cypress"; ܩܶܛܥܳܐ "disposition" (שות); ܟܰܪܳܬܳܐ "leek"; ܟܰܦܳܐ "self-sown grain" (foreign word?); ܚܽܘܡܪܳܐ "rust"; ܚܽܘܡܳܠܳܐ "sediment", "lees". In isolated cases the otherwise masculine nouns which follow are employed in the feminine: ܬܗܽܘܡܳܐ (East-Syrian ܬܗܽܘܡܳܐ) "abyss"; ܩܽܘܫܬܳܐ "truth"; ܨܶܒܬܳܐ "adornment" (from which even appears a pl. ܨܶܒܬܶܐ, as if in accordance with § 75) (¹); ܕܶܚܠܬܳܐ "terror" (but only masculine ܕܶܚܠܳܐ, and many others). ܗܳܘܝܳܐ "being" is almost always fem.

☞ p. 345

§ 87. *Other words are common to both genders*:—ܐܶܬܪܽܘܢܓܳܐ, ܐܶܬܪܽܘܢܓܳܐ, "orange", m. and f., (foreign word).

Nouns of common gender.

ܒܥܺܝܪܳܐ "cattle", sing. f. and pl. f.; yet also pl. m.

ܓܠܽܘܣܩܡܳܐ "urn", "sarcophagus" (foreign word) m. and f.

ܕܰܝܪܳܐ "dwelling" (pl. ܕܰܝܪܶܐ, ܕܰܝܪܳܬܳܐ); in particular when meaning "convent", always f. (and then too, pl. always ܕܰܝܪܳܬܳܐ).

ܙܰܒܢܳܐ "time" (*Zeit*) m.; "time" (*Mal*) generally f. (as also ܐ̈ܚܪܳܢܳܬܳܐ, ܙܰܒ̈ܢܳܬܳܐ, "times").

ܚܽܘܛܪܳܐ "a rod" m., very rarely f.

ܚܶܟܳܐ (ܚܶܟܳܐ) "palate"; pl. ܚܶܟ̈ܶܐ m. and f.

ܚܰܪܒܳܐ "sword", "destruction", m. and f.

ܚܰܒܪܳܐ "companion" m. and f.

ܡܶܠܬܳܐ "word", f. (pl. § 81); only as a dogmatic expression, ὁ λόγος, (not in a natural sense), m.

ܡܰܒܽܘܥܳܐ "source", f. (pl. ܡܰܒܽܘܥ̈ܶܐ, more rarely ܡܰܒܽܘ̈ܥܳܬܳܐ); rarely m.

ܣܰܗܪܳܐ "moon", m. and f.

(¹) It is of course possible that on the other hand the root is צבי, and that the ת has only come from ܨܶܒܬܳܐ into the new root צבת.

ܠܡܩܩ "weevil", m. and f.

ܠܘܫܝ "copy (of a writing)" m. and f.

ܩܠܒܘܡ "quiver", m. and f. (foreign word).

☞ p. 345   ܪܘܚ "wind", "spirit", preponderatingly f., especially in the sense of "wind"; pl. ܪܘ̈ܚܐ and ܪ̈ܘܚܬܐ (this only f.).

ܪܩܝܥܐ "firmament" (Hebr.) m., rarely f.

ܩܠܚܐ "stalk", f. (like the more usual ܚ̈ܓܕܐ, pl. ܩܠܚ̈ܐ) seldom m.

ܩܥܪ "herd" (of swine and demons) m. and f.

ܫܡܝܐ "heaven", is employed as sing. m., sing. f., and pl. m. (in this last use almost confined to translations of the Bible).

ܫܡܫܐ "sun", m. and f.

ܫܒܠܐ "spike", "ear of corn", m. and f.

ܫܩܐ "leg", "stem" f., seldom m.

ܛܘܦܢܐ "flood" (Hebrew) m. and f.

ܬܐܠ "brook" m. and f.

Gender of
Greek
words.   § 88. Greek words keep their native gender in the large majority of cases. Thus for instance the following are fem.: ܩܪܛܣ "a letter" σάκρα; ܐܣܛܠܐ (constr. st. ܐܣܛܠܬ) "robe" στολή; ܐܘܪܩܐ "gastric disease" φθορά; ܣܡܫܝܪܐ "sword" σαμψήρα (this from Persian *šamšēr*); ܦܠܓܐ φάλαγγα (Acc.); and the numerous words in ܠ, ܐ (η § 46). Amongst others almost all those in ܘܣ are masc., as also ܛܘܡܣܐ τόμος; ܦܘܪܣܐ πόρος; ܩܕܘܣ κάδος; ܩܐܪܘܣ καιρός; ܐܓܪܘܣ ἀγρός. Yet many variations occur here too. Thus ܐܣܛܘܐ στοά is m.; ܩܪܩܘܪܐ ὁ κέρκουρος, is fem.; ܐܣܦܘܓܐ ὁ σπόγγος, is mostly f.; ܚܘܪܐ χώρα, (also ܚܘܪ) appears too as masc.; ܛܝܡܐ τιμή "price" is held as fem. in the sing. or as masc. in the pl. ܛܝܡ̈ܐ (like the Syriac word of the same meaning ܕܡܝܐ); ܐܐܪ ἀήρ is mostly f., yet m. also; ܚܪܛܣ ὁ χάρτης is m. and f.; ܣܘܪܘ "gallery" σύριγγα (f.) m. and f. &c.

Greek neuters are oftenest masc. in Syriac; yet sometimes they are also fem.: Thus is it with ܒܐܡܐ, ܒܡ βῆμα; ܬܐܛܪܘܢ (ܬܐܛܪ and other secondary forms) θέατρον; ܒܝܠܘ (ܒܠܐ, ܒܠܘ) βῆλον = *velum*, &c. ܩܠܕܪ "hot water boiler" καλδάριον *caldarium* occurs as m. and f.

Greek
plural-
endings.   § 89. Greek words pretty frequently form Syriac plurals (particularly when, in the Syriac fashion of their singular, they end in ܠܐ),

e. g. ܦܘܪܘܣ πόρος, pl. ܦܘܪ̈ܘܣ; ܛܟܢܐ m. τέχνη, pl. ܛܟ̈ܢܐ; ܛܟܣܐ (East-Syrian), ܛܟܣܐ (West-Syrian) m. τάξις, ܛܟ̈ܣܐ; ܩܠܝܪܝܩܐ κληρικός, ܩܠܝܪ̈ܝܩܐ; ܙܛܡܐ ζήτημα, ܙܛ̈ܡܐ; but often too they receive Greek plural terminations. Thus in particular:—

1. ܘ݂ = οι: ܡܬܘܕܘܣ μέθοδοι; ܣܘܢܗܕܘ σύνοδοι; ܐܘܪܬܘܕܘܟܣܘ ὀρθόδοξοι; ܣܛܘܝܩܘ Στοϊκοί; ܩܠܝܪܝܩܘ κληρικοί, and many others.
2. ܐ̈ = αι (accordingly not distinguishable from the Syriac masc. plural-ending): ܣܘܢܗܕܝܩ̈ܐ συνοδικαί (pl. of ܣܘܢܗܕܝܩܐ συνοδική "synodal letter"); ܕܝܐܬܝܩ̈ܐ διαθῆκαι (from ܕܝܐܬܝܩܐ, ܕܝܐܬܝܩܝ), &c.
3. ܐܣ, ܝܐܣ = ᾱς: ܕܝܐܬܝܩܐܣ διαθήκας; ܐܘܣܝܐܣ οὐσίας, &c. Very often ܘܣ is used for this (properly ους, but seldom answering exactly to this Greek termination): ܕܝܐܬܝܩܘܣ; ܡܐܟܢܘܣ μηχανάς, &c. So ܛܘܢܘܣ, ܛܘܢܝܣ as pl. from ܛܘܢܘܣ τόνος. This ܘܣ is customarily vocalised as ܘܣ (to amend the old error), which is to be read *as*. So also ܐܣ = ᾰς: ܦܠܐܩܐܣ πλάκας; ܩܣܪܐܣ Καίσαρας; ܐܐܪܐܣ ἀέρας; ܘܣ also appears for this, *e. g.* ܣܝܪܝܢܘܣ Σειρῆνας.
4. ܝܣ = εις: ܛܟܣܝܣ τάξεις (from ܛܟܣܝܣ τάξις); ܠܟܣܝܣ λέξεις (from ܠܟܣܝܣ); ܗܪܣܝܣ αἱρέσεις, &c. In rare cases only is ܐܣ, ܗܣ = ες employed.
5. ܐ = α: ܐܘܢܓܠܝܘܢ εὐαγγέλια; ܩܦܐܠܐܐ κεφάλαια, &c. Add ܛܐ, ܛܐ: ܕܘܓܡܛܐ δόγματα; ܙܛܡܛܐ ζητήματα, &c.

The Greek terminations are often wrongly applied, *e. g.* ܛܘܦܪܟܘ τοπάρχαι; ܒܝܠܣ βῆλα, &c.

Greek analogy is followed also in the formation of ܓܢܣ, ܓܢܝܣ (instead of ܓܢ̈ܐ § 81) from the Syriac ܓܢܬܐ "garden", and ܩܘܪܝܣ, ܩܘܪܝܣ (instead of ܩܘܪ̈ܝܐ § 146) from ܩܪܝܬܐ "a town".

§ 90. Proper names suffer no change in the plural in cases like ܬܪܝܢ ܐܕܡ "two Adam's"; ܐܪܒܥ ܡܪܝܡ "four Mary's"; ܠܘܛ ܣܓܝܐܐ "many Lot's" &c. So too for the most part is it with names of letters of the alphabet, *e. g.* ܬܪܝܢ ܢܘܢ "two Nūn's", although ܢܘ̈ܢܐ is also found, &c. Thus too ܚܡܫ ܓܝܪ "five *gēr's*", *i. e.* five times the particle *gēr*. Also ܬܪܝܢ ܘܝ "two woes", as well as ܬܪܝܢ ܘܝ; for which others have ܬܪܝܢ ܘܝ̈ܐ as well as ܬܪܝܢ ܘܝ̈ܐ. **Nouns undergoing no change in plural.**

§ 91. Many substantives appear only in the singular, others only in the plural. A good many,—particularly of those of the masculine form,—want the absolute and construct states, at least in the singular, or have these supplied only later and artificially, or at least they rarely appear in them. On the other hand a very few appear merely in the construct state or in the absolute state.

§ 91ᵇ. An Abstract expressed by the pl., is found in ܚ̈ܝܶܐ "life"; ܪ̈ܰܚܡܶܐ "compassion"; ܚܺܐܪ̈ܘܬ "emancipation"; ܡܶܫܟ̈ܚܳܐ "marriage"; ܡܶܟ݂ܪ̈ܐ (East-Syrian ܡܶܟ݂ܪ̈ܐ) "betrothal".

B. SURVEY OF THE NOMINAL FORMS.

§ 92. We deal here only with forms consisting of three or more radicals, and with bi-radicals which have become quite analogous to those forms;—as ܦܘܡܐ "mouth", ܩܶܫܬܐ "bow", &c. (to which many others are added, that can no longer be authenticated by us as such). For the other bi-radicals, or for words in other respects very irregularly formed,—ᴠ. under anomalous forms § 146. Besides, in instituting this survey, we are in no way aiming at completeness.

According to § 91,—in many substantives, particularly such as have not a feminine ending, we can only authenticate the Emphatic state in the singular. In most cases, however, this form is itself sufficient, particularly with words which have a feminine ending, to enable us to construct the other contingent State-forms.

Alterations are sustained by the ground-form, through the approach of the endings, but, as a rule, in cases only where vowels originally short take thereby a place in an open syllable. The Construct state (with which, in words that have no feminine ending, the Absolute state coincides) exhibits words in most instances as still in their relatively original form, cf. ܡܶܕܠܝܐ, ܡܶܓܡܘܓ, ܙܢܰܡ, &c., which in the Emphatic state become, according to § 43 A, ܡܶܕܠܝܐ, ܡܶܓܡܘܓ, ܙܢܰܡ. Many words of the simplest form are exceptions to this rule; and in these words it is only the Emphatic state which retains the vowel in its own place (ܡܶܕܠܝܐ; Absolute and Construct states, ܡܠܟ for malk § 93). In certain respects feminine formations also are exceptions, like ܐܠܝܨܐ; constr. st. ܐܠܝܨ, &c.

(AA) TRI-RADICAL NOUNS UN-AUGMENTED EXTERNALLY.

(AA) Tri-radical nouns un-augmented externally. Preliminary observations.

THE SHORTEST FORMS.

§ 93. Forms with short vowel of the first radical and absence of vowel of the second (originally *qaṭl, qiṭl, quṭl*) coincide so frequently in Syriac with those which had a short vowel both after the first and the second radical (*qaṭal, qaṭil, qiṭal,* &c.), that we can only in part keep them separate.

The monosyllabic ground-form *qaṭl*, &c., when no ending is attached, throws the vowel behind the 2nd radical, in the case of a strong root, *e. g.* ܡܠܶܟ for *malk,* ܩܘܽܕܶܫ for *quδš.*

The insertion of an *ă* after the 2nd radical in the plural (Hebrew *mĕlāchīm, malĕchē* from *malakīm, malakai* from *malk*) is still shown in a few traces. On this rests the double writing in ܥܰܡܡ̈ܶܐ, ܛܶܠ̈ܠܶܐ, &c. (§ 21 D), which springs from a time when the plural *ʿamămē* was still formed from the singular ܥܰܡܳܐ. Some few of these nouns, farther, 'soften' the 3rd radical in the plural as if it followed a vowel: thus ܥܶܣܒܳܐ "herb"; ܥܶܣ̈ܒܶܐ (East-Syrian) from *ʿesăvē*; ܓܢܽܒܬܳܐ "theft", ܓܢ̈ܽܒܳܬܳܐ (East-Syr. tradition); ܐܰܠܦܳܐ "thousand"; ܐܰܠ̈ܦܶܐ, ܐܰܠܦܺܝܢ; and ܥܶܩܰܪܬܳܐ "stock", ܥܶܩܳܪ̈ܳܬܳܐ, &c. The influence of the original vowel in these cases is evident in some examples; *e. g.* in ܗܽܘܠܳܟ̈ܳܬܳܐ "ways, journeys", from *halakhāthā* from ܗܶܠܟܬܳܐ out of original *halakhathā.* But the large majority fashion the plural forms directly according to those of the singular. ☞ p. 345

§ 94. A. With *a* and *e* of strong root: (a) ܡܰܠܟܳܐ "king", absolute and construct states ܡܠܶܟ; pl. ܡܰܠ̈ܟܶܐ, absol. st. ܡܰܠܟܺܝܢ, constr. st. ܡܰܠܟܰܝ, &c.

With *a* and *e* of strong root.

In the constr. and abs. states of the sing. an *e* appears in these cases throughout: ܓܰܪܡܳܐ "bone", ܓܪܶܡ; ܡܳܪܳܐ "lord", ܡܳܪܶܐ; ܢܰܦܫܳܐ "soul", ܢܦܶܫ. So ܟܪܶܣ "belly"; ܥܒܶܕ "servant"; ܪܡܶܫ "evening"; ܨܠܶܡ "image"; ܛܥܶܡ "taste"; ܚܒܶܠ "rope", and many others.

On the other hand, *a* appears before a final guttural and *r* (§ 54): ܬܰܪܥܳܐ "door", ܬܪܰܥ; ܦܓܰܪ "body"; ܨܦܰܪ "morning", &c.

With feminine ending: ܡܰܠܟܬܳܐ "queen", abs. state ܡܰܠܟܳܐ (does it occur?), constr. st. ܡܰܠܟܰܬ; pl. ܡܰܠܟ̈ܳܬܳܐ, abs. st. ܡܰܠܟܳܢ, constr. st. ܡܰܠܟܳܬ, &c.

B. (b) With *e*: ܦܠܓܐ "half", abs. and constr. st. ܦܠܓ; pl. ܦܠܓܐ (the East-Syrians ܦܠܓܐ § 93), ܦܠܓܝܢ, ܦܠܓܢ, &c.—In the abs. and constr. states of the sing., here also *e* appears throughout, *e. g.* ܪܓܠܐ "foot", ܪܓܠ; ܟܣܦ "silver"; ܥܣܒ "herb":—but of course ܒܣܪ "flesh", &c.

With feminine ending: ܢܨܒܬܐ "plant", ܕܚܠܬܐ (ܕܚܝܠܬܐ, ܕܚܠܬܐ § 52 B) "fear", &c. But also ܪܓܠܬܐ "brook" (others ܪܓܠܬܐ); ܥܓܠܬܐ "calf" (or ܥܓܠܬܐ § 52), constr. st. ܥܓܠܬ, pl. ܥܓܠܬܐ; ܓܦܬܐ for ܓܦܢܬܐ "vine" (§ 28), and some others,—belong to this class.

C. (c) Manifest traces of an originally short vowel after the second radical are farther shown by ܕܗܒܐ "gold" (from *dahăvā* § 23 D), abs. and constr. st. ܕܗܒ; ܚܠܒܐ "milk" (1); ܥܘܪܒܐ "raven"; ܟܪܟܐ "town"; ܠܚܡܐ "bread", &c.; and with transition to *e*: ܟܢܦܐ "wing" (from *kanafā*); ܪܛܒܐ "dampness" (West-Syrian ܪܛܒܐ), and many others. That words like ܣܒܪܐ "hope", ܣܒܪ; ܕܒܪܐ "*mas*", ܕܒܪ; ܒܣܪܐ "flesh", ܒܣܪ; ܩܠܦܐ "husk"; ܥܕܪܐ "prey"; ܥܦܪܐ "earth" (as a material) belong to this class, can no longer be recognised by the form: on the other hand the *a* of the abs. and constr. st. of ܕܩܢܐ "beard", ܕܩܢ; ܙܒܢܐ "time", ܙܒܢ; ܓܡܠܐ "camel", ܓܡܠ, manifestly refers them to this class.

D. The adjectives, which mostly had *ĕ* after the 2nd radical, do not show any clear trace of it (§ 23 D): ܓܪܒܐ "leprous", ܓܪܒ; ܕܡܟܐ "sleeping", ܕܡܟ; ܥܠܓܐ "stammering", ܥܠܓ; ܚܕܬܐ "new" (§ 26), ܚܕܬ; ܥܣܩܐ "difficult", ܥܣܩ, and many such. *a* is shown in this class not only by those which end in a guttural, like ܥܩܪܐ "unfruitful", ܥܩܪ, but also by those in *l*: ܫܦܠܐ "brought low", ܫܦܠ (West-Syrian ܫܦܠ); ܥܛܠܐ "difficult", ܥܛܠ (generally ܥܛܠ); ܣܟܠܐ "foolish", ܣܟܠ.

There was an original *e* also in ܟܬܦܐ "shoulder", ܟܬܦ, and in ܟܒܕܐ "liver"; probably also in ܥܩܒܐ "heel" (still with softening).

E. Various forms with feminine ending are yielded, agreeing in part with those under (a) and (b). Thus of words with originally two *a*'s: ܢܦܫܬܐ "soul", abs. st. ܢܦܫܐ, constr. st. ܢܦܫܬ, pl. ܢܦܫܬܐ; ܢܦܩܬܐ "expenditure", ܢܦܩܬܐ (also ܢܦܩܬܐ); ܦܩܥܬܐ "level place", ܦܩܥܬܐ; ܪܩܥܬܐ

(1) With the generality of these words the constr. and abs. st. of the singular cannot be authenticated.

"time", ܙܒ̈ܢܬܐ, &c. So of adjectives: ܡܟܝܟܬܐ "humble (f.)", ܟܦܢܬܐ "hungry (f.)", ܥܣܩܬܐ "difficult (f.)", ܚܕܬܐ "new (f.)" (§ 26); to which add ܚܒܪܬܐ "*socia*", &c.; all these have in the pl. ܡܟܝ̈ܟܬܐ, &c., with *a* of 1st radical. Other adjectives have always *a* with the 1st: ܛܢܦܬܐ "unclean (f.)"; ܚܪܒܬܐ "waste" (pl. ܚܪ̈ܒܬܐ, with soft ܒ); ܢܟܦܬܐ "modest"; ܒܛܢܬܐ or ܒܛܝܢܬܐ (§ 52 B) "pregnant", &c. So the East-Syrians have ܛܡܐܬܐ, the West-Syrians ܛܡܝܬܐ "unclean" (f.).

With *e*, ܙܕܩܬܐ "alms", ܙܕ̈ܩܬܐ; ܝܠܠܬܐ, ܝܠܝܠܬܐ (§ 52 B) "howling"; ܗܠܟܬܐ "course" (§ 52 B; the East-Syrians ܗܠܝܟܬܐ (1)), ܗܠ̈ܟܬܐ, &c. So the adjectival ܢܩܒܬܐ "a female", abs. st. ܢܩܒܐ, pl. ܢܩ̈ܒܬܐ.—Cf. ܥܢܒܬܐ "cluster of grapes", ܥܢܒ̈ܐ (§ 81).

§ 95. *With forms from roots primae* ܐ, section § 34 comes frequently into operation. To this class belong, amongst others, ܐܓܪܐ "hire", constr. st. ܐܓܪ; ܐܪܥܐ "earth", ܐܪܥ;—ܐܒܠܐ "mourning";—ܐܠܦܐ "ship", ܐܠܦ.

With *a* and *e* of roots *primae* ܐ.

Feminines: ܐܫܟܬܐ "testicle"—ܐܢܚܬܐ "groan" (pl. will be ܐܢ̈ܚܬܐ); ܐܒܕܬܐ "what is lost" (West-Syrian ܐܒܝܕܬܐ, constr. st. ܐܒܕܬ).

§ 96. *Primae* ܝ (ܘ): ܝܪܚܐ "month", constr. and abs. st. ܝܪܚ, ܐܝܪܚ (§ 40 C); ܝܠܕܐ "offspring", &c.—Feminines: ܝܕܥܬܐ "knowledge", "science", ܝܙܦܬܐ (West-Syrian ܝܘܙܦܬܐ) "loan", ܝܙܦܬ, ܝܙ̈ܦܬܐ; ܝܨܝܬܐ "excrement".—ܘ remains in ܘܥܕܐ "an agreement" (§ 40 A), constr. and abs. st. wanting.

With *a* and *e* of roots *primae* ܝ (ܘ).

§ 97. *Mediae* ܐ: ܪܫܐ, ܪܝܫܐ "head"; ܪܫ, ܪܝܫ (§ 53)—ܒܐܪܐ "well"; ܕܐܒܐ "wolf"; ܟܐܒܐ "pain", ܟܐܒ—ܬܐܬܐ, ܬܬܐ "fig" (§ 28)—ܠܐܘܬܐ "weariness", ܠܐܘܬ; ܦܐܘܬܐ "*luxus*" (only in pl.); ܚܐܘܬܐ, constr. st. ܚܐܘܬ "butter"—ܫܐܠܬܐ "question" (§ 52 B), ܫ̈ܐܠܬܐ.

With *a* and *e* of roots *mediae* ܐ.

§ 98. *Mediae* ܘ (*and* ܝ). To the simplest formations with *a*, there correspond forms like ܣܘܦܐ "end", ܣܘܦ (§ 49 A); ܝܘܡܐ "day", ܝܘܡ; ܡܘܬܐ "death"—ܒܝܬܐ "house", ܒܝܬ; ܥܝܢܐ "eye", ܥܝܢ; ܩܝܛܐ "summer".

With *a* and *e* of roots *mediae* ܘ (and ܝ).

With ܗܘܢܐ "understanding", and the foreign word ܨܘܥܐ "dye", the East-Syrians form the abs. and constr. st. ܗܘܢ, ܨܘܥ, the West-Syrians ܗܘܢ, ܨܘܥ.—Feminines: ܩܘܡܬܐ "stature"; ܣܘܟܬܐ "twig"; but ܬܘܪܬܐ "cow"—ܪܝܡܬܐ "wild goat" (fem.), but ܒܝܥܬܐ, ܒܝ̈ܥܬܐ "egg" (§ 49 A).

With *ī*: ܕܝܢܐ "judgment" (דין); ܢܝܪܐ "yoke", &c.

---

(1) Similar differences of form are farther met with.

B. To forms with two *a* 's from strong roots, correspond (§ 41) those with *ā*, like ܩܳܠܳܐ "voice"; ܣܳܒ, ܣܳܒܳܐ, f. ܣܳܒܬܳܐ "an old person"; ܥܳܩܬܳܐ (abs. st. ܥܳܩܳܐ, constr. st. ܥܳܩܰܬ) "distress", &c. But along with these appear relatively later forms having a consonantal *w*: ܪܰܘܚܬܳܐ "free space", and ܙܰܘܥܬܳܐ (East-Syrian ܙܽܘܥܬܳܐ §§ 52; 49 B) "a quaking"; ܬܰܘܗܳܝܳܐ (ܬܽܘܗܳܝܳܐ) "amazement".

C. A special class is formed by words with *ē* (*ī*) like ܟܺܐܦܳܐ "stone"; ܪܺܝܚܳܐ "fragrance"; ܫܺܐܕܳܐ "demon"; ܦܺܐܪܳܐ "fruit"; ܟܺܐܢ, ܟܺܐܢ, ܟܺܐܢܳܐ "just"; ܚܺܐܪܶܫ,
☞ p. 345 ܚܺܐܪܫܳܐ "deaf"; ܕܺܓܠܳܐ "falsehood", and some others, which in part at least spring from roots *med.* ܘ and follow their analogy.

With *a* and *e* of roots with middle *n*.

§ 99. *With middle n.* The shortest forms here in part assimilate the *n*, according to § 28; thus ܐܶܩܬܳܐ "oppression"; ܐܰܦܶܐ "countenance"; ܚܶܟܳܐ "palate" (1) &c. But otherwise ܟܶܢܫܳܐ "assembly". The constr. st. of ܥܶܙܳܐ "goat" is ܥܶܢܙ. From ܓܶܒܳܐ "side" with ܠܘܳܬ comes the expression ܠܘܳܬ ܓܶܢܒ (the throwing out of *n* being only a later alteration).

With *a* and *e* of roots *tertiae* ܐ.

§ 100. *Radical* ܐ *in the* 3rd *position* still leaves its traces in ܣܶܢܐܬܳܐ (ܣܢܶܐܬܳܐ for שִׂנְאֲתָא § 34) "hatred"; ܛܶܢܐܬܳܐ (ܛܢܶܐܬܳܐ) "zeal"; ܦܶܠܐܬܳܐ "simile", parable", ܦܠܶܐܬܳܐ; and in the adjective ܛܰܡܶܐ "unclean" (abs. and constr. st.), emph. st. ܛܰܡܐܳܐ, f. ܛܰܡܐܳܐ, ܛܰܡܐܬܳܐ, ܛܰܡܶܐܬܳܐ or ܛܡܺܐܬܳܐ (East-Syrian).—Otherwise the forms of *tert.* ܐ pass into those of *tert.* ܝ.

With *a* and *e* of roots *tert.* ܝ (ܘ).

§ 101. *Tert.* ܝ (ܘ) (2): ܓܰܕܝܳܐ "he-goat"; ܪܚܝܳܐ "mill"—ܪܶܢܝܳܐ "meditation"; ܟܶܣܝܳܐ "concealment", &c. all want the constr. and abs. st.; only ܫܶܠܝܳܐ "rest" still forms an abs. st. ܫܶܠܶܐ (§ 50 A).—With ܘ: ܫܰܠܘܳܐ "serenity"; ܣܚܘܳܐ "swimming"; ܫܶܠܘܳܐ "ceasing"; ܚܶܙܘܳܐ "look" (pl. ܚܶܙܘܶܐ, ܚܶܙܘܺܝܢ); and some few feminines ܚܰܕܘܬܳܐ, ܚܰܕܽܘܬܳܐ "joy"; ܚܰܝܘܬܳܐ, ܚܰܝܽܘܬܳܐ "beast" (§§ 40 D; 76 B); cf. ܐܰܚܘܬܳܐ and ܓܠܽܘܬܳܐ (§ 97). Perhaps also ܡܢܳܘܬܳܐ "share" (if it stands for מְנָוָתָה).

To those with short vowel after the 2nd radical, correspond several substantives like ܩܰܢܝܳܐ "reed"; ܫܡܰܝܳܐ (plural form) "heaven" (§ 146); and many adjectives like ܕܰܟܝܳܐ "pure"; ܩܫܶܐ "hard", &c. Feminines: ܕܰܟܝܬܳܐ

(1) The secondary form—ܚܶܢܟܳܐ, usually in the pl. ܚܶܢܟܶܐ, must belong to § 94 C: Probably also ܟܶܢܫܳܐ.

(2) On the plurals of these forms v. §§ 72 and 79 A.

(abs. st. ܪܡܐ, constr. st. ܪܡܝܐ; pl. ܪܡܬܐ); ܡܩܡܐ, &c. Similarly the substantives ܒܪܝܐ "creation", pl. ܒܪܝܐ; ܦܬܢܐ "direction", ܦܬܢܐ; ܐܠܝܐ
(East-Syrian ܐܠܝܐ) "fat-tail"; ܡܙܪܥܐ "village" (§ 146), and many others,
which however,—at least part of them,—belong to the simplest forms. ☞ p. 345

There are, farther, special forms of the second kind, in *āthā*: ܒܥܬܐ
"seeking"; ܣܘܦܐ "smell"; ܨܐܬܐ (for צֹאָתָה) "dirt", &c., as well as those
spoken of in § 77, like ܨܠܘܬܐ "prayer", &c.,—to which farther belong
ܓܘܦܬܐ "dung-cake" (ܓܦܬ(¹)) appears as its plural, with constr. st. ܓܦܬ),
ܡܣܘܦܬܐ (as well as ܡܣܘܦܐ) "rennet—calf's paunch—for curdling milk",
and ܩܕܘܦܐ "wax".

§ 102. Forms *mediae geminatae*. In those without fem.-ending, no With *a* and *e* of roots
distinction can be maintained between the first and second formations: *mediae geminatae.*
ܥܡܐ "folk" (§ 21 D); ܪܓܠܐ "brook"; ܛܠܐ "dew";
ܪܒܐ "great"; ܟܗܢܐ "priest"; ܚܝܐ "living":—ܠܒܐ "heart", ܚܕ;
ܕܒܐ "bear"; ܙܘܦܐ "wormwood" (pl.). With Fem.-ending ܟܠܬܐ "bride",
ܪܒܬܐ *magna*; ܚܝܬܐ *viva*—ܥܠܬܐ "cause", ܟܠ; ܟܠܬܐ, ܟܠܬܐ;
ܡܠܬܐ "word", ܡܠܠ (pl. ܡܠܐ § 81).—According to the second
formation ܥܠܠܬܐ "produce", ܥܠܠܬܐ; ܝܠܠܬܐ (West-Syrian ܝܠܠܬܐ)
"lamentation", ܝܠܠܬܐ.

§ 103. *With u.* The forms *quṭl* and *quṭul* were never so separated With *u* of strong root.
as, for instance, *qaṭl* and *qaṭal*. Certain traces of a vowel after the
2nd radical are shown (in the softening of the 3rd), which vowel however
can hardly be called original. The *u* frequently takes the second place
(or remains there only).

Of *strong roots*, and those similar to them: ܓܘܫܡܐ "body"
ܓܘܫܡܐ, &c.; ܩܘܕܫܐ "holiness"; ܪܘܚܩܐ "remoteness"; ܫܘܚܕܐ "bribery";
ܐܘܪܟܐ "length"; ܒܘܪܟܐ "knee"; ܨܘܕܝܐ "desolation"; ܥܘܫܢܐ "strength"; ☞ p. 345
ܙܘܥܐ "trembling" (without assimilation of the *n*), &c.: abs. and constr.
st. ܓܘܫܡ, ܪܘܚܩ, ܫܘܚܕ, ܐܘܪܟ. So also the adjectival ܥܘܪܠܐ
"uncircumcised" (originally formed differently, it would seem), ܥܘܪܠ;
as well as ܪܘܩܐ *ἀμφοτεροδέξιος*, and ܚܓܝܪ "limping", *"claudus"* (²).
But ܐܘܪܚܐ "way" and ܐܘܪܥܐ "meeting" have ܐܘܪܚ and ܐܘܪܥ.

(¹) Others read ܡܚܬܐ.
(²) If, however, this is ܚܓܝܪ with Quššāyā, then it belongs to § 114.

Feminines (to some extent at first formed differently): ܠܘܚܫܬܐ "whispering", ܠܘܚ̈ܫܬܐ; ܒܘܪܟܬܐ "blessing", ܒܘܪ̈ܟܬܐ; ܕܘܢܒܬܐ "tail", ܕܘܢ̈ܒܬܐ (and ܕܘܢܒ̈ܝܬܐ § 71); ܬܘܪܥܬܐ, ܬܘܪ̈ܥܬܐ (§ 52 B) "cleft"; ܢܘܫܩܬܐ, ܢܘܫܩܬܐ "kiss", ܢܘܫ̈ܩܬܐ; ܐܘܚܕܬܐ, ܐܘܚܕ̈ܬܐ "riddle", ܐܘܚ̈ܕܢܬܐ; ܪܘܩܥܬܐ (perhaps ܪܘܩܥܬܐ) or ܐܘܪܩܥܬܐ (§ 51) "patch", pl. ܪܘܩܥܐ and ܐܘܪ̈ܩܥܬܐ &c. But ܡܫܘܚܬܐ "measure", ܡܫܘܚܬܐ, ܡܫܘܚܬ, ܡܫܘ̈ܚܬܐ; ܓܘܡܪܬܐ "coal", ܓܘܡܪ̈ܐ; ܚܘܠܝܬܐ "vertebra", ܚܘܠ̈ܝܐ and ܚܘܠ̈ܝܬܐ (§ 81); ܕܘܢܒܬܐ = ܕܘܢܒܬܐ "tail".

With *u* of weak roots. § 104. *Mediae* ܘ: ܪܘܚܐ, ܪܘܚ "wind, spirit"; ܢܘܪܐ "fire", &c.—With ܘ: ܟܘܦܐ "owl".—Feminine ܨܘܪܬܐ "form".

Tert. ܐ: ܣܘܓܐܐ "multitude", constr. st. with feminine ending ܣܘܓܐܬ.

Tert. ܝ: ܐܘܪܝܐ "manger" (pl. § 79 A); ܓܘܪܝܐ "young animal", ܓܘܪ̈ܝܐ (§ 72); ܕܘܡܝܐ "likeness", ܕܘܡܝܐ (id.).—Feminines: ܨܘܚܝܬܐ "evil-speaking, abuse", ܨܘܚ̈ܝܬܐ; ܟܘܣܝܬܐ "cap"; ܐܘܠܝܬܐ "wailing", ܐܘܠ̈ܝܬܐ; ܟܘܠܝܬܐ "kidneys" (pl.), &c. (1).

Mediae gem.: ܟܘܠ, ܟܠ (ܟܠ, ܟܠ § 48) "all", emph. st. ܟܘܠܐ, ܟܠܐ; ܕܘܟܐ "place", ܕܘܟ; ܥܘܒܐ "bosom"; ܓܘܒܐ "pit"; ܥܘܙܐ "strength"; ܡܘܚܐ (or ܡܘܚܐ) "marrow"; ܚܘܪܫܐ "deaf person".—Feminines: ܕܘܟܬܐ "place", ܕܘܟܐ, ܕܘܟ, pl. ܕܘܟ̈ܝܬܐ (§ 71); ܐܘܠܬܐ "lamentation".

With falling away of 1st rad. § 105. We have the remains of a formation from *prim.* ܘ *with falling away of the 1st radical* in ܫܢܬܐ "sleep", from ישן, constr. st. ܫܢܬ, abs. st. ܫܢܐ, as if it were *med. gem.*, but East-Syrian still ܫܢܐ; farther ܨܦܬܐ "care" (also indeed ܝܨܦܬܐ, ܐܝܨܦܬܐ); ܚܡܬܐ "wrath"; ܥܒܬܐ "excrement" (as well as ܐܥܒܬܐ). Perhaps also ܫܬܐ (for ܫܬܬܐ) "stem" belongs to this class (pl. ܫܬ̈ܐ, ܫܬ̈ܝܢ as if from שתת). So ܕܘܬܐ "sweat".— Similarly from *prim.* ܢ: ܦܘܚܬܐ and ܦܚܬܐ "breath" from ܢܦܚ, ܢܦܘܚ; and perhaps ܦܣܐ "lot" and ܦܣܬܐ "lot" and "strip, rag" (it must have Greek π § 15); farther ܛܘܦܬܐ pl. ܛܘ̈ܦܐ "drop".—Of *prim.* ܐ in the same way: ܚܪܬܐ "end", constr. st. ܚܪܬ (as if from חרר); and ܚܬܐ "pocket" and "beam" (for ܐܚܬܐ from אחד), pl. ܚܬ̈ܐ. It is obvious that the speech itself takes over these words into other classes (2).

---

(1) Whether it is ܘ or ܘ here,—is not in every instance certain.

(2) ܥܕܬܐ (ܥܕܬܐ, ܥܕ̈ܬܐ) "church", which according to its formation belongs to this class, is borrowed from the Hebrew (עֵדָה).

WITH *Ā* AFTER THE FIRST RADICAL.

With ā after the 1st rad.: With short vowel after 2nd rad.

§ 106. (a) *a* after the 2nd radical is or was found in the case of: ܥܠܡ,(1) ܥܠܡܐ, ܥܠܡܐ, ܥܠܡܝܢ "eternity", world"; ܚܬܡܐ "seal" (2); and perhaps ܢܪܓܐ "axe" (East-Syrian ܢܪܓܐ). The usual form of the Act. Part. of the simple stem of the verb has *e* after the 2nd: ܪܚܡ "loving"; ܪܚܡܐ, ܪܚܡܐ, ܪܚܡܝܢ, &c.—ܦܪܚ "flying"; ܬܒܪ "breaking" (§ 54)—ܩܐܡ "standing", ܩܝܡܝܢ; ܣܢܐ "hating", ܣܢܝܐ "hater, enemy" (§§ 33 A; 172 C); ܓܠܐ "revealing", ܓܠܝܢ; ܝܐܐ "beautiful", ܝܐܝܢ.—ܥܐܠ "entering" (עלל), ܥܐܠܝܢ or ܥܠܝܢ &c. Sometimes the Participial form is purely substantive, thus ܩܨܪܐ "a fuller", ܬܪܥܐ "doorkeeper" (which have no verb supporting them).—Feminines: Abs. st. ܪܚܡܐ; ܩܝܡܐ; ܓܠܝܐ, ܓܠܝܢ; ܝܐܝܐ, ܝܐܝܢ; ܥܐܠܐ or ܥܠܐ, ܥܐܠܢ or ܥܠܢ. In the Emph. st. mostly substantive: ܐܟܠܬܐ "eating", "consuming"; ܩܝܡܬܐ "column", &c.—ܩܝܡܬܐ. With the 3rd rad. a guttural: ܦܪܚܬܐ "bird"; ܓܙܪܬܐ "island", &c. (§ 54); but so also with *a* ܦܩܕܬܐ "nape of the neck"; ܥܓܠܬܐ "waggon" (others ܥܓܠܬܐ).—ܙܢܝܬܐ "whore", ܙܢܝܬܐ; ܩܪܝܬܐ "beam", Abs. st. ܩܪܝ (§ 75), ܩܪܝܬܐ, &c.—ܣܢܝܬܐ.

With ō after 2nd rad.

§ 107. (b) With ܘ after the 2nd radical, *Nomina agentis* may be formed from every Part. act. of the simple verb stem (Peal): ܩܛܘܠܐ "murderer"; ܩܪܘܒܐ; ܓܠܘܝܐ, &c.—Feminines: ܩܛܘܠܬܐ; ܩܪܘܒܬܐ, &c. (on the plurals of the feminines v. § 71). We join to this class several other substantives, like ܝܪܘܪܐ "jackal"; ܦܬܘܪܐ (with ܘ according to exact tradition) "table".

With ī after 2nd rad.

§ 108. (c) Some few have *ī* after the 2nd radical, like ܩܪܝܡܐ "weaver's beam"; ܐܓܡܐ "a marsh"—ܩܪܝܬܐ "a weaver's beam"; ܩܛܝܢܬܐ "*brevia*"; ܙܪܝܦܬܐ "storm of rain"; ܚܘܛܪܬܐ "club", &c.

WITH SHORT VOWEL OF THE 1ST AND *Ā* OF THE 2ND RADICAL.

With short vowel of the 1st and ā of the 2nd rad.

§ 109. The short vowel must become throughout (except with ܐ) a mere *sh*ᵉ*va* (§ 43 A); it is in very many cases no longer possible to determine whether it was originally *a*, *i* or *u*. Many varieties have met together here.

---

(1) The Nestorians distinguish the Construct st.—hardly ever occurring in old times in the meaning "world"—artificially by the vocalisation ܥܠܡ.

(2) ܚܬܡܐ is a very ancient word borrowed from the Egyptian.

For example we have Abstract nouns, particularly numerous *Nomina actionis* from verbs of the simple stem: ܚܬܡܐ "confirming by seal"; ܦܣܩܐ "decision"; ܩܪܒܐ "war"; ܥܒܕܐ "deed"; ܒܠܥܐ "swallowing"; ܚܘܪܐ "looking at", "regard"; ܩܝܡܐ "covenant"; ܪܘܙܐ "exulting"; ܪܟܝܢܐ "inclination"; ܗܘܝܐ "becoming"; ܐܝܩܪܐ "honour" (§ 40 C); ܐܫܕܐ "pouring out"; ܐܣܘܪܐ (East-Syrian ܐܣܘܪܐ) "fetter"(1). Also ܥܘܕܪܐ "help" probably belongs to this class. Add ܫܥܠܐ "cough"; ܕܠܦܐ "weakness of the eyes", and several other names of bodily ailments.

☞ p. 345
☞ p. 345

Farther, ܚܡܪܐ "ass"; ܥܪܕܐ "wild-ass"; ܐܢܫ, ܢܫ &c. "man" (§§ 32; 146), and ܐܠܗܐ "god".—Add to these, adjectives like ܫܥܝܥ "smooth"; ܩܪܚ "bald"; ܓܒܚܐ "baldheaded"; ܣܥܪ "hairy"; ܓܡܠܐ "hook-nosed"; ܫܚܡ "swarthy"; ܒܠܝܐ "worn out"; ܫܢܐ "out of one's mind"; ܕܘܪܐ "impaired in mind" (2).—Feminines: ܩܝܡܬܐ "resurrection"; ܫܟܚܬܐ "discovery", "invention"; ܩܪܝܬܐ "appeal", &c. Farther, ܢܣܪܬܐ "sawdust"; and several other words for "parings", "filings".

☞ p. 345
☞ p. 345

With short vowel of the 1st and ī (ē, ai) of the 2nd rad: With ī of 2nd rad.

WITH SHORT VOWEL OF THE 1ST AND *Ī* (*Ē*, *AI*) OF THE 2ND RADICAL.

§ 110. All Passive participles belonging to the simple stem (excepting those of *tert.* ܝ) have ī after the 2nd radical (and originally *a* after the 1st); so also have many adjectives: thus—ܩܛܝܠ, ܩܛܝܠܐ, ܩܛܝܠܬܐ &c. "killed"; ܐܡܝܪ "said"; ܐܓܝܪܐ "day-labourer"; ܐܒܝܠܐ "sad", "an ascetic"; ܝܠܝܕ "born"; ܓܙܝܙ "shorn". From *med.* ܘ: ܨܝܕ "caught"; ܢܝܚ "mild"; ܣܝܡ "placed" (f. ܣܝܡܬܐ "treasure") &c.; but ܪܘܝܚ "wide"; ܥܘܝܪ "blind".—From *tert.* ܐ farther, the pl. ܣܢܝܐܝܢ, ܣܢܝܐܐ, fem. sing. ܣܢܝܬܐ "hated" (cf. § 172 C; the sing. abs. state would be ܣܢܐ). Thus also many substantives, like ܟܠܝܠܐ "crown"; ܣܦܝܢܬܐ "ship", &c.

With ē of 2nd rad.

§ 111. An ē, which generally becomes ī with the West-Syrians, is exhibited by ܪܬܝܬܐ "terror"; ܢܦܝܫܐ, West-Syrian ܢܦܝܫܐ or ܢܦܫܐ, ܢܦܫܐ "recovering breath", "recreation"; ܟܡܝܢܐ, ܟܡܢܐ "ambush". Probably one or two others are to be met with. (3)

---

(1) Perhaps belonging to § 116.

(2) I adduce adjectives here, without adhering to consistency, sometimes in the Abs. st., sometimes in the Emphatic.

☞ p. 345

(3) The East-Syrians read ܡܠܝܐ for ܡܠܝܐ "fulness" (ܡܒܘܠܐ "flood" is an Assyr.

§ 112. Diminutives were formed by a *u* after the 1st, and an *ai* after the 2nd radical. Whence we have in Syriac still ܥܠܝܡܐ "young man", and f. ܥܠܝܡܬܐ "young girl"; ܚܙܝܪܐ "sucking-pig"; and with *u* still ܥܘܙܠܐ "gazelle". ὅμηρος "hostage" has been turned into a like form: ܗܡܝܪܐ. **With *ai* of 2nd rad.**

WITH SHORT VOWEL OF THE 1ST AND $\bar{U}$ ($\bar{O}$) OF THE 2ND RADICAL.

§ 113. The short vowel was *a*,—predominating with the adjectives, or *u*,—predominating with the Abstract nouns. Here there seems to be no specific distinction between the *ū* and the *ō*; ܘ is in fact a derived shade from ܘ. **With short vowel of the 1st and ū (ō) of the 2nd rad.**

A few exhibit the signification of a Passive Participle (as in Hebrew): ܪܚܘܡܐ "loved", f. ܪܚܘܡܬܐ; ܣܢܘܐܐ "hated" m., ܣܢܘܐܬܐ, ܣܢܘܬܐ "an unloved woman"; ܕܘܫܬܐ "concubine" ("*quae calcatur*"), pl. ܕܘܫܝܬܐ; ܓܢܘܒܬܐ "thing stolen" (1); ܫܡܘܥܬܐ "report", pl. ܫܡܘܥܝܬܐ. Farther, ܠܒܘܫܐ "garment"; ܒܬܘܠܬܐ "virgin", ܒܬܘܠܢ, &c.; ܙܥܘܪ "little" (§ 71); ܟܢܘܫܬܐ "synagogue", ܟܢܘܫܢ, ܟܢ̈ܘܫܬܐ; ܩܒܘܪܬܐ "burial"; ܓܙܘܪܬܐ "circumcision"; ܟܠܬܐ (for ܟܠܠܬܐ § 26) "bride"—ܓܕܘܠܐ "ringlet"; ܫܦܘܠܐ "skirt"; ܣܓܘܠܐ "bunch of grapes"—ܬܘܒܐ "vomiting"; ܟܣܘܬܐ "name of a star-image". (2)

WITH DOUBLING OF THE MIDDLE RADICAL. **With doubling of the middle rad.: With two short vowels.**

§ 114. (1) With two short vowels. There are only a few cases; several can no longer be recognised by outward marks, and have passed over to other classes, probably at an early date. Some may have been originally quadriliteral, and the doubling may thus have been caused by the assimilation of an *n*: ܨܦܪܐ "small bird", abs. st. ܨܦܪ, pl. ܨܦܪܝܢ, ܨܦܪܐ;

---

borrowed-word). East-Syrian ܡܥܪܐ "chasm", "cave" instead of ܡܥܪܐ is no doubt just a way of writing ܡܥܪܐ—which also occurs—necessitated by leaving out the ܐ.

(1) Perhaps this word, which has no known plural, has a short *u*. In that case it stands for ܓܢܝܒܬܐ, and belongs to § 94 E.

(2) This seems more accurate than ܟܣܘܬܐ, for with the old poets the word is dissyllabic.—In addition to the forms given above, notice ܡܠܘܬܐ (ܡܠܘܬܐ) "matter", "mass", "sum" (properly "fulness").

ܐܕܪܐ "threshing-floor", ܐܕܪ; ܐܡܪܐ "wedder", ܐܡܪ; ܚܨܪܐ "little finger"; ܫܒܠܐ "stalk", ܫܒܠ with ܫܒܠܬܐ, pl. ܫܒܠܐ; ܣܒܠܬܐ "ladder"; ܩܘܦܕܐ "hedgehog"; ܣܟܪܐ "shield"; ܩܘܠܪܐ "bar"; ܢܓܘܕܐ "one who tows a vessel"; and no doubt several more. Perhaps ܥܘܪܒܐ "raven", and ܚܘܪܒܐ "stork" also belong to this class.

An old feminine form of this kind is also found in ܐܫܬܐ "fever" (f. from the Hebrew אֶשָּׁה), constr. st. ܐܫܬ, pl. ܐܫܬܘܬܐ.

With *a* after the 1st, and *ā* after the 2nd rad.

§ 115. (2) *With a after the 1st and ā after the 2nd radical.* Adjectives of degree, *Nomina agentis*, and names of occupations,—throughout: ܙܟܐ "pure", "victorious", ܙܟܝܐ, ܙܟܝܬܐ, &c., ܢܨܝ "contentious"; ܩܝܡ "firm", from קום, but with *w*, ܚܘܪܐ "keenly eyeing, greedy"; ܓܢܒܐ "thief"; ܛܒܚܐ "butcher"; ܚܝܛܐ "tailor" &c. As *nomina agentis* these forms belong to verbs of the simple stem (Peal); yet there are found with the double-letter stem (Pael) ܡܠܠܐ "speaking" (ܡܠܠ to speak); ܚܒܠܐ "destructive"; ܟܕܒܐ "liar"; ܕܓܠܐ "liar"; ܕܒܪܐ "leader"; ܦܩܩܐ "babbler". ☞ p. 345 —ܓܢܒܪܐ "hero" (§ 28).—So too ܚܦܪܐ "pit"; ܕܒܒܐ (others ܕܒܒܐ) "fly".

With *e* after the 1st and *ā* after the 2nd rad.

§ 116. (3) *With e after the 1st and ā after the 2nd radical* there are but a few: ܣܬܪܐ "covering"; ܛܠܠܐ "shadow"; ܬܢܢܐ "smoke"; ܥܩܪܐ "root"; ܐܓܪܐ "roof"; ܠܫܢܐ "tongue"; ܙܢܪܐ "hook" (pl. ܙܢܪܬܐ); and the adjective ܚܘܪ "white" (ܚܘܪܐ, ܚܘܪܬܐ, ܚܘܪܬܐ, &c.) (1).

With *u* after the 1st and *ā* after the 2nd rad.

§ 117. (4) With *u* after the 1st and *ā* after the 2nd radical, a *nomen actionis* can be formed from *any* verb in *Pael* or its reflexive, *Ethpaal*: thus ܩܘܛܠܐ "murdering", from ܩܛܠ (he) "murdered"; ܙܘܗܪܐ "warning"; ܙܘܘܓܐ "combining"; ܣܘܡܟܐ "supporting"; ܙܘܘܓܐ "pairing"; ܫܘܐܠܐ "question"; ܠܘܥܙܐ (abs. st. ܠܘܥܙ) "off-putting"; ܥܘܝܐ "howling" (from ܥܘܐ), &c. So also ܢܘܓܐ "shipwreck" from ܢܓܐ *ναυαγεῖν*.—Farther the adjectives of colour: ܐܘܟܡ "black"; ܣܘܡܩ "red"; ܝܘܪܩ "yellow"; ܙܘܗܪ "reddish"; ܐܘܓܐ "party-coloured (?)" (2) and ܙܘܗܡܐ "hard stone".—Perhaps also ܪܘܡܢܐ "pomegranate".

---

(1) ܣܡܠܐ "left hand" is quadriliteral (= שְׂמֹאלָא).

(2) So too is formed ܩܘܢܒܐ, ܩܘܢܐ, which, however, must be *κυάνεος*. To these names of colours, ܚܘܪ (§ 116) belongs. ܐܘܡܢ, ܐܘܡܢܐ (f. st. abs. ܐܘܡܢܝܐ § 71) "artistic", "artificer" is probably of Assyrian derivation.

§ 118. (5) *With a after the 1ˢᵗ and ī after the 2ⁿᵈ radical* a large number of adjectives are formed, especially such as are found with intransitive verbs as verbal adjectives or perf. participles (part of them being pretty recent formations). Thus ܝܦܝܩ "gone out"; ܐܙܝܠ "gone"; ܐܒܝܕ "lost"; ܝܬܝܒ "sitting" ("having set oneself, seated"); ܦܪܝܫ "parted, departed"; ܩܪܝܒ "near"; ܪܚܝܩ "far"; ܐܪܝܟ "long"; ܪܟܝܟ "soft"; ܥܫܝܢ "mighty"; ܣܓܝ "much", ܣܓܝܐܝܢ, ܣܓܝܐܝܢ, &c.; ܐܬܐ "come", ܐܬܐܝܢ, ܐܬܝܢ, ܗܘܐ "been"; ܗܘܐܬ, ܡܝܬܐ or ܡܝܬ (§ 40 E) "dead"; ܒܣܝܡ, ܒܣܝܡ "fragrant", &c. To distinguish these from the form ܩܛܝܠ they are commonly written with the upper point (§ 6), e. g. ܡܟܝܟ = ܡܟܝܟ "humble", compared with ܡܚܣܝ or ܡܚܣܝ = ܡܚܣܝ "spread under". The active signification is remarkable in ܡܗܕܝܢܐ, ܡܗܕܝܐ "guide".

§ 119. (6) *With a after the 1ˢᵗ and ū after the 2ⁿᵈ radical*, appear many adjectives like ܚܫܘܟ "dull, dark"; ܚܡܘܨ "sour"; ܟܚܝܫ "lean"; ܫܟܝܒ "lying still", and many others:—ܝܠܘܕܐ "child", f. ܝܠܘܕܬܐ; ܥܡܘܕ "pillar"; ܚܛܘܪܐ and ܚܛܘܪܬܐ "rod"; ܐܬܘܢܐ "oven", "furnace", &c. So also ܩܛܘܬܐ "cucumber" (for קטוּאתָא) § 146.

§ 120. (7) With *e* after the 1ˢᵗ and *ā, ō* after the 2ⁿᵈ radical there are a very few forms, as ܕܒܘܪܐ "wasp", ܕܒܘܪܬܐ "bee"; ܚܫܘܟ "dark", and ܚܫܘܟܐ "darkness". Thus some say ܫܪܘܬܐ "throat" (others ܫܪܘܬܐ). Also ܬܝܘܬܐ "disposition" (from שׁוּת "to place") belongs, one would say, to this class.

§ 121.   WITH DOUBLING OF THE 3ᴿᴰ RADICAL.

The following seem to be thus formed: ܦܝܩܠܐ "idol's-altar"; ܡܕܒܚܐ "stream"; ܦܢܝ "millet", of which however the first is certainly, the others probably, ancient borrowed-words. Possibly ܦܓܘܕܬܐ "bridle", pl. ܦܓܘܕܬܐ is of this class.

(BB) OF NOUNS OF FOUR OR MORE RADICALS WITHOUT EXTERNAL INCREASE.

§ 122. We class under this head also those nouns in which the multiliteral character is brought about either by the repetition of one, or two radicals, or by the insertion of a formative consonant in the root.

To the former belong *e. g.* ܩܘܒܠܠܐ from קבל; ܫܠܡܡ from שלם; ܒܘܠܒܠܐ from בלל: to the latter ܒܘܗܪܪܐ from בהר; ܚܘܡܚܡܐ from חמם, &c. In the last resort indeed all multiliteral roots are reducible to those of three or of two syllables.

Almost no adjectives are found among these forms.

The vowels vary considerably. The chief classes are represented by the following words: ܓܪܓܪܐ "threshing-sledge"; ܩܪܩܦܬܐ "skull"; ܐܪܡܠܬܐ "widow";—ܦܪܙܠܐ "iron" (originally with *e* of the *z*); ܦܪܕܬܐ "corn, kernel"—ܦܫܦܫܐ "bugs"—ܟܘܪܣܝܐ "throne", constr. st. ܟܘܪܣܐ (pl. ܟܘܪ̈ܣܘܬܐ); ܥܘܩܒܪܐ "mouse"; ܩܘܪܙܠܐ "knuckle, ankle"; ܦܘܪܨܘܦܐ, ܦܪܨܘܦܐ (§ 52 B) "countenance"—ܥܪܦܠܐ "mist"—ܦܘܓܥܐ "meeting" (from ܦܓܥ, ܐܬܦܓܥ)—ܐܝܕܐܝܕܐ "milliped" or "centiped" (lit. "hand-hand"); ܟܪܙܠܐ "hut", "tabernacle"; ܥܠܥܠܐ "storm"; ܦܪܢܣܬܐ "nourishment"—ܙܠܝܩܐ "ray of light"—ܨܪܨܘܪܐ "a kind of locust"; ܦܪܬܘܬܐ "crumb of bread"; ܕܚܠܘܠܐ "scarecrow"; ܚܠܚܠܬܐ "a slender thread" (forms of this kind have occasionally a diminutive signification)—ܛܠܘܦܚܐ "lentils", and many others.

To this class belong also the forms spoken of in § 31, like ܓܓܪܬܐ "throat" for *gargartā*; ܓܝܓܠܐ "wheel", from *gilgēlā*, &c.: as well as ܪܘܪܒܝܢ, &c. from רַבְרְבִין (§§ 27; 146), and perhaps ܟܘܟܒܐ "star".

Abstract nouns with *u—ā*. § 123. A special class, corresponding exactly to those treated of in § 117, is formed by the *Abstract nouns in u—ā*, which serve as *nomina actionis* to *all* verbs which are regarded as quadriliteral. As ܩܘܛܠܐ stands to ܩܛܠ, so stands ܟܘܪܒܠܐ "sifting" to ܟܪܒܠ, as well as ܫܘܥܒܕܐ "subjection" to ܫܥܒܕ, &c. Thus *e. g.* we have ܬܘܠܡܕܐ "instruction"; ܕܘܠܕܠܐ "perplexity"; ܪܘܡܪܡܐ "exaltation"; ܫܘܡܠܝܐ "constancy"; ܫܘܒܗܪܐ "haughtiness" (connected with reflexive ܐܫܬܒܗܪ); ܬܘܪܣܝܐ "nourishment, food" (with ܬܪܣܝ); ܫܘܘܕܝܐ or ܫܘܕܝܐ "promise" (with ܫܘܕܝ § 40 B, and retaining the 'hard' ܕ); ܫܘܘܕܥܐ "announcement" (exactly similar); ܓܘܙܠܐ "kindling, vehemence" (with ܓܙܠ); ܨܘܨܝܐ (for ܨܘܨܘܝܐ § 40 B) "twittering" (with ܨܨܝ) &c.

Similarly have been formed ܬܘܣܦܬܐ "addition" from ܐܬܬܘܣܦ, ܐܘܣܦ; ܬܘܟܘܝܐ "brand" from ܐܟܘܝ; and ܬܘܠܒܫܬܐ "clothing" from ܠܒܫ (cf. ܐܬܠܒܫ).

§ 124. *Five-lettered nouns* have mostly sprung from the repetition of the last two radicals. Thus the adjective ܫܰܡܠܡܰܠ (ܫܰܡܠܡܰܠܳܐ &c.) "complete"; ܚܰܒܠܒܠܳܐ "ivy"; ܚܰܘܪܘܪܳܐ "cataract", "*gutta serena*"; ܫܦܪܦܪܐ a kind of bird ("piper"); ܦܪܚܘܚܝܬܐ "spark". Five-lettered nouns.

§ 125. Among the multiliterals some old compounds may be hiding, as for instance ܦܰܪܚܕܽܘܕܳܐ "bat", and the much mutilated form ܐܽܘܪܕܥܳܐ "frog" (the Aramaic original form being עפרדע). Besides, some of these nouns may be suspected of being foreign words, *e. g.* ܫܪܕܘܕܐ "skeleton", "corpse". Presumptive compounds.

☞ p. 345

(CC) FORMATIONS WITH PREFIXES.

(CC) Formations with prefixes: With *m*.

WITH *M*.

§ 126. A. As in all Semitic tongues, so in Syriac *m* is extensively employed in Noun-formation. First fall to be considered here the Participles of all derived verbal stems (Conjugations), like ܡܩܰܛܶܠ, pass. ܡܩܰܛܰܠ; ܡܰܩܛܶܠ, ܡܰܩܛܰܠ; ܡܶܬܩܰܛܰܠ, &c. For these v. Verb *infra*. So too the Infinitives, like ܡܶܩܛܰܠ, ܡܩܰܛܳܠܽܘ, &c.

B. With *ma* are formed, besides, (1) words with short vowel after the 2nd radical ܡܰܫܟܢܳܐ, ܡܰܫܟܰܢ "tent"; ܡܰܚܬܳܐ and ܡܰܚܬܳܬܳܐ "descent" (נחת cf. § 26 B); ܡܰܣܒܳܐ, ܡܰܣܰܒ "taking" (נסב); ܡܰܣܩܳܐ, ܡܰܣܰܩ "mounting", and so ܡܰܣܩܬܳܐ (סלק § 183); ܡܰܪܟܰܒܬܳܐ "chariot", "boat"; ܡܰܪܒܥܳܐ, ܡܰܪܒܰܥ "womb", &c.—ܡܰܕܰܥ, ܡܰܕܥܳܐ "intelligence" (ידע cf. § 175 A); ܡܰܘܕܰܥܬܳܐ "a well-known person", "an acquaintance"; ܡܰܘܬܒܳܐ "sitting", "seat"; ܡܰܘܗܰܒܬܳܐ "gift".—ܡܰܫܬܝܳܐ "drink"; ܡܰܪܕܝܳܐ, constr. st. ܡܰܪܕܳܐ "journey", and so ܡܰܪܕܺܝܬܳܐ, abs. st. ܡܰܪܕܺܝ (§ 75)—ܡܰܘܡܳܬܳܐ "oath" (§ 78)—ܡܰܣܩܠܬܳܐ "hazard" (נשא § 80). To this section belong also ܡܶܐܟܽܠܳܐ "eating", ܡܐܟܠܐ, and ܡܐܬܝܬܐ "coming", ܡܐܙܠܐ and ܡܐܙܠܬܐ "going"; ܡܐܦܝܬܐ "cooking" (§ 53).—ܡܰܟܢܫܬܳܐ "besom" (East-Syrian ܡܶܟܢܰܫܬܳܐ).

From forms *med. gem.*, ܡܰܥܠܳܐ and ܡܰܥܠܬܳܐ "entrance"—ܡܡܰܠܠܳܐ "speech" (§ 29)—ܡܓܰܢܳܐ, ܡܓܰܢܳܐ "shield" (גנן); ܡܰܫܢܳܐ "hone" (שנן) (§ 59).

From middle ܘ are to be brought into this class forms like ܡܩܘܡܐ "station"; ܡܫܘܓܝܬܐ "washing-tub"; ܡܕܝܢܬܐ "city"; ܡܨܝܕܬܐ "net", &c. The last may have been originally a participle, as is certainly the case with ܡܶܝܢܰܩܬܳܐ "nurse" (for ܡܶܝܢܩܳܝܬܳܐ). (1)

(1) ܡܙܰܪܩܳܝܬܳܐ, ܡܙܪܩܬܐ "sacrificial bowl" is a borrowed Hebrew word.

A short *u* occurs in ܡܐܟܘܠܬܐ "food", abs. st. ܡܐܟܠܐ, pl. ܡܐܟܘܠܬܐ; ܡܩܘܡ "lasting", "ever" (§ 59); so too ܡܫܘܕܥܬܐ "an acquaintance", and several others. ܡܣܪܘܩܐ (according to others ܡܣܪܘܩܐ(1)) "comb", "crest", is a special, secondary form.

C. (2) Words with *ā* after the 2nd rad. ܡܬܩܠܐ "weight"; ܡܚܪܫܐ "magician"; ܡܟܚܠܐ "a pencil for staining the eyes"; ܡܣܪܐ "saw" (נשר); ܡܘܠܕܐ "birth"; ܡܕܢܚܐ "rising (of the sun)"—pl. from נגה; ܡܐܣܘܪܬܐ "bundle" and many others.

D. (3) Words with *ū* (*ō*): ܡܒܘܥܐ "fountain" (נבע); ܡܦܘܚܐ "bellows"; ܡܥܠܘܠܐ "storm"; ܡܟܫܘܠܐ "stumbling", "offence" (the last two also with ܘ); ܡܣܘܟܐ "gush", "torrent" (נסך); ܡܬܩܘܠܬܐ "weight", and many others.

E. *Me* appears (apart from the cases cited above of ܡܐ, ܡܐ from *ma'*) in ܡܥܙܠܬܐ "web"; ܡܕܝܪܐ "dwelling", "house-story".

H. With *mu*: ܡܘܙܠܐ (others say ܡܘܙܠܐ) "spindle".

G. With *mā*: ܡܐܙܘܢܐ "nourishment" (זון); ܡܐܡܘܪܐ "cistern": a few other doubtful cases might be added. (2)

WITH *T*.

With *t*. § 127. A number of Abstract nouns occur, which mostly belong to the Pael or its reflexive, in part also to the Aphel: Sometimes they bave taken a concrete meaning. Such formations, amongst others, are:

ܬܥܕܪܐ "help" (ܥܕܪ); ܬܛܠܝܠܐ "roof" (ܛܠܠ); ܬܨܒܝܬܐ "ornament" (ܨܒܬ); ܬܠܡܝܕܐ "disciple", f. ܬܠܡܝܕܬܐ "female disciple" (*ܠܡܕ); ܬܥܝܩܐ "vexation" (ܐܥܝܩ); ܬܘܣܦܬܐ "something added" (ܐܘܣܦ):—ܬܚܠܘܦܐ "compensation", "hostage" (ܚܠܦ); ܬܦܢܝܬܐ "flattery" (ܦܢܝ); ܬܟܬܘܫܐ "combat" (ܐܬܟܬܫ); ܬܘܫܒܬܐ "object of disdain" (ܐܫܬܒ):—ܬܘܬܒܐ "settler" (ܐܬܘܬܒ); ܬܘܬܪܐ "remnants" (ܝܬܪ).

With short vowel after 2nd rad., and feminine-ending: ܬܟܫܦܬܐ "beseeching" (ܐܬܟܫܦ); ܬܓܚܟܬܐ "mockery" (ܐܬܓܚܟ); ܬܛܢܦܬܐ "pollution" (ܛܢܦ); ܬܐܢܚܬܐ "groaning" (ܐܬܢܚ for ܐܬܐܢܚ § 174 C):—ܬܒܗܬܬܐ (East-Syrian ܬܒܗܬܬܐ) "shame" (ܐܬܒܗܬ); ܬܘܟܣܬܐ (East-Syrian ܬܘܟܣܬܐ) "ad-

(1) ܡܣܪܩܐ also appears (§ 52).

(2) ܡܚܘܙܐ "city" (חוז) seems to have been borrowed from the Assyrian.

dition" (ܐܘܒܕ);—ܬܫܡܫܬܐ "service" (ܫܡܫ);—ܬܫܒܘܚܬܐ "glory", "praise" (ܫܒܚ), pl. ܬܫ̈ܒܚܢ; ܬܕܡܘܪܬܐ "wonder", "miracle" (ܐܬܕܡܪ), ܬܕܡܪ̈ܬܐ; ܬܬܓܘܪܬܐ "trade" (ܐܬܬܓܪ), ܬܬܓܪ̈ܬܐ. To this section also belong probably ܬܦܫܘܪܬܐ "urine", and ܬܓܪܡܘܣܬܐ "skeleton":—With vowel originally short, also—ܬܟܣܝܬܐ "clothing" (ܟܣܝ); ܬܪܒܝܬܐ "education" (ܪܒܝ); ܬܫܥܝܬܐ "narrative" (ܐܫܬܥܝ), ܬܫ̈ܥܝܬܐ; ܬܘܕܝܬܐ "praising" (ܐܘܕܝ); ܬܫ̈ܪܝܬܐ "foundations" (ܫܪܝ), &c.—ܬܫܪܝܬܐ "camp" (ܫܪܐ).

So perhaps ܬܟܦܘܪܬܐ "atonement" (ܐܬܟܦܪ) and ܬܚܒܘܠܬܐ "corruption" (ܚܒܠ), if they stand for *ܬܟܦܘܪܘܬܐ, *ܬܚܒܘܠܘܬܐ and do not take the abstract termination *ūthā* (§ 138).

A few others too seem to be formed with a *t*, but of a different sort,—like ܬܘܠܥܐ, ܬܘܠܥܬܐ "worm".

§ 127*. OTHER PREFIXES.

Other prefixes.

Some of these are matter of doubt. We have:

(1) ܗ, ܐ in ܗܝܟܠܐ, ܗܰܝܟܠ "palace"—ܐܣܩܘܦܬܐ "threshold" (here ܐ is perhaps a mere starting sound, in accordance with § 51), ܐܣܟܘܦܬܐ; ܐܒܘܒܐ "flute" (נבב); ܐܨܚܬܐ "manuscript" (from ܨܚܐ, root צחח); ܐܢܩܦܬܐ *concentus* (ܢܩܦ, root נקף).

(2) *ya*, as it seems, we have in ܝܪܘܒܥܐ "jerboa"; ܝܚܡܘܪܐ "a kind of antelope"; ܝܒܪܘܚܐ "mandragora"; ܝܥܢܘܪܐ "smoke"; ܝܥܪܘܪܐ "toad"; ܝܩܘܣܪ "thorny rhubarb".

(DD) FORMATIONS WITH SUFFIXES.(1)

WITH *ĀN* (*ŌN*).

(DD) Formations with suffixes: With *ān* (*ōn*). Abstract nouns and nouns substantive.

§ 128. A. In this class appear many Abstract nouns and common nouns (a) with *a* after the 1st rad.: ܡܘܬܢܐ "plague"; ܫܪܟܢܐ "residue"; ܛܘܥܝܢܐ "error"(2); ܛܪܢܐ (טרר) "rock", &c. p. 345

(b) With *u*: ܥܘܠܨܢܐ "oppression"; ܝܘܬܪܢܐ "gain"; ܦܘܩܕܢܐ "command"; ܝܘܠܦܢܐ "doctrine"; ܛܘܠܢܐ "refuse" (*tert.* ܐ); and many other abstract

(1) In part with prefixes at the same time.

(2) ܐܒܕܢܐ, for which also occurs ܐܒܕܘܢ "perdition", "the nether world", is perhaps borrowed from the Hebrew.

nouns; but only a few forms from roots *tert.* ܝ, like ܕܘܡܝܢܐ "wedding-gift"; ܟܘܡܝܢܐ "swelling" (along with ܒܡܝܢܐ).

(c) With *e*: ܒܢܝܢܐ "building"; ܢܟܝܢܐ "harm"; ܪܢܝܢܐ "thought"; ܦܓܝܢܐ "pronouncing"; ܨܒܝܢܐ "will"; and many other abstract nouns from *tert.* ܝ.—So also ܚܘܪܢܐ "look". A few besides, like ܦܪܫܢܐ "distinction"; ܒܛܠܢܐ "sloth" (perhaps ܥܕܢܐ "time" for עִתְדָנָא?).

Rem. Of such doubling as we have in פִּקָּדוֹן, הִגָּיוֹן, no sure trace is any longer to be found. So far as we can settle it, the 2nd rad. is *always* soft, the 3rd hard.

B. Instead of *ān* we have an old ending *ōn* (*ūn*) in ܢܣܝܘܢܐ "temptation", "affliction" a secondary form to ܢܣܝܢܐ "experiment", "trial"; ܓܠܝܘܢܐ, ܓܠܝܢܐ "revelation"; and, according to East-Syrian pronounciation, ܕܘܢܐ (*dawōnā*) "pity", West-Syrian ܕܘܢܐ (*duwōnō* = *duwānā*); v. § 44.

C. Of substantives with prefixes in this class:—ܡܫܩܠܢܐ "decamping"; ܡܥܠܢܐ "entry"; ܡܣܩܢܐ (סלק § 183) "ascent", &c. So too, ܩܡܪܢܐ "girths". Perhaps also ܝܘܓܢܐ "alarm" (from יגי?) (1).

Adjectives. § 129. *ān* (f. *ānyā*, *ānīthā* &c. § 71) is attached to a great variety of words, to form *adjectives*. Thus ܐܪܥܢ "earthy, earthly"; ܢܘܪܢ "fiery"; ܡܠܠܢ "talkative"; ܫܐܕܢܐ "one who is possessed" (from ܫܐܕܐ "demon"); and so ܕܝܘܢܐ (from the Persian ܕܝܘܐ "demon"); ܫܡܝܢ "heavenly"; ܛܪܟܢ "slanderous" (from ταραχή?); ܕܫܬܢܝܬܐ "*menstruans*" (from ܕܫܬܐ "menstruation"); ܚܘܪܢ "whitish"; a feminine from it is ܚܘܪܢܝܬܐ "white poplar". So ܛܠܠܢܝܬܐ "shadow".

☞ p. 345 From ܓܪܓܪܬܐ "throat" is formed ܓܪܓܪܢ "gluttonous"; so ܦܘܟܢ "spotted" from ܦܘܟܘܟܬܐ "spot" (pl. ܦܘܟܟܐ); ܕܘܢܒܢܐ (ܟܘܟܒܐ) "comet" from ܕܘܢܒܬܐ "*fimbria*".—In other cases the ܬ of the feminine remains before *ān*, as in ܚܪܝܢܬܢ "quarrelsome"; ܚܡܬܢ "given to anger"; ܢܫܬܢ "womanly"; ܐܟܬܢ "angry", &c.; and even from substantives without this ending, similar forms in ܬܢ are derived, *e. g.* ܛܘܒܬܢ "happy" (along with ܛܘܒܢ) from ܛܘܒܬܐ "health", "happiness"; ܩܪܒܬܢ "warlike"; ܚܝܠܬܢ,

(1) The meaning of the word in Is. 16, 3 is not quite certain: later writers employ it according as they severally understood this passage.

ܫ̣ܝܚܝ݂ (§ 52 B) "strong"; ܟܐܓܝ "painful"; ܐܣܟܡܝ "indicating a σχῆμα"   ☞ p. 346
(ܐܣܟܡܐ), &c.

Specially in favour are adjectives of this form like ܡܣܟܠܝ "in-
telligent"; ܪܘܓܙܝ "angry"; ܚܪܥܡܝ "crafty" (from ܦܘܪܣܐ, πόρος, like
ܡܦܪܣ "to be cunning"); ܙܥܦܢܝ "anxious", and many others. In these
cases no Abstract noun like ܡܣܟܠܐ can any longer be pointed to as
the fundamental form; and with the most of them such an Abstract
noun has never existed.—So too, ܚܢܦܣܟܠܐ "flatterer" (ܚܢܦ "to
flatter") (¹).

§ 130. Farther, *Nomina agentis* may be formed by the suffix *ān*   *Nomina agentis.*
from *all* Participles which begin with *m*: and so participles from Peal
are alone excluded. Thus ܡܫܒܚܢܐ "one who praises" (from ܡܫܒܚ);
ܡܢܗܪܢܐ "enlightener" (ܡܢܗܪ); ܡܪܓܙܢܐ "one who provokes" (ܡܪܓܙ);
ܡܢܣܝܢܐ "tempter" (ܡܢܣܐ); ܫܒܝܚܢܐ "one worthy of praise" (ܡܫܬܒܚ);
ܡܬܬܣܪܚܢܐ "one who has to be ordained" (ܡܬܬܣܪܚ), &c.

In some quadriliterals the *m* thereupon falls away. The ascertained
cases of this sort are ܡܦܫܩܢܐ "interpreter" (along with ܡܬܪܓܡܢܐ);
ܫܓܘܫܢܐ "braggart"; ܕܡܝܢܐ "bloody" (together with ܕܡ)—(otherwise,
however, ܡܡܪܡܪܢܐ "refractory", &c.).

§ 130ᵇ. The following appear to be formed in *m*: ܡܫܘܦܢܐ "file"   With *m.*   ☞ p. 346
(from שׁוּף "to rub down"); ܡܫܘܦܢܐ "turtle-dove", f. ܡܫܘܦܢܝܬܐ;
"lark"; ܡܪܙܠܐ "hoar frost" (not quite certain; a secondary form is ܡܪܙܠܐ),
and a few others. Cf. § 132.

DIMINUTIVES.   *Diminutives.*

§ 131. Diminutives are formed at pleasure with *ōn*: e. g. ܡܠܟܘܢܐ   *With ōn.*
"*regulus*"; ܐܠܗܘܢܐ "minor god"; ܟܬܒܘܢܐ "little book"; ܛܠܝܘܢܐ "little
boy"; ܒܪܘܢܐ "little son", &c.—Feminines take ܐܝܬܐ (§ 71, 1), e. g. ܐܠܦܐ
"ship" (f.): ܐܠܦܘܢܝܬܐ; ܐܕܢܘܢܝܬܐ "little ear"; ܟܐܦܘܢܝܬܐ "small stone";
ܥܪܣܘܢܝܬܐ "a little bed". ܬ of the feminine termination is retained before this suffix: ܡܕܝܢܬܘܢܝܬܐ "small town"; ܥܕܬܘܢܝܬܐ "a small church";
ܐܓܪܬܘܢܝܬܐ "a short letter", &c. However, we have ܡܠܟܘܢܐ "ane-

---

(¹) On the termination ـܝ v. *infra* § 136.

mone" ("little bride" from ﻞﺑﺠﺩ) and ﺧﻨﺑ (to be pronounced no doubt as ﺧﻨﺑﻪ) "curricle" from ﺧﻨﺑﻪ. From the pl. ﺧﺩﻪ (sg. ﻞﺑﺠﺩ) appears in this way ﺧﺩﻪﻧﻞ "short words".

§ 132. *Rem. īn* may also be a Diminutive suffix: ﺮﻓﺰﻞ, secondary form to ﺮﻓﺰﻪ "small bird". Yet it is not to be held as altogether certain.

§ 133. *With ōs*. Not so frequently met with as *ōn*: thus *e. g.* ﻧﺰﻪﻣﻞ "hatchet"; ﻧﻮﺩﻪﻣﻞ "small fish"; ﺧﺠﻪﻣﻞ "little boy" (without any ground-form in use); ﻠﺧﻪﻣﻞ "little boy", &c.—Feminine forms have ﻣﻪﻞ, pl. ﻣﻪﻞ (§ 71). ܠ of the fem. termination falls away before the suffix: ﻣﻪﺟﻞ "small court" from ﻞﺟﺰ; ﻣﻪﺧﻞ "small garden" from ﺑﺠﻞ; ﺧﻔﻪﺧﻞ "small bowls", "cups" from ﺑﺠﻞ; ﺧﺠﻪﻣﻞ "little girl".

§ 134. *Rem.* ﻣﻪﺧﺟﻞ ὑδρίσκη from ﺧﻪﺧﻞ likewise appears to be a Diminutive. Besides these we still have traces of other diminutive-endings, notably in secondary forms of the more familiar names. Compare farther § 112, as well as Diminutives formed by reduplication of the 3rd rad. § 122. Add thereto, although not attested by very old authority, ﺧﺧﻔﻞ "a little hill", pl. ﺧﺧﻔﻞ, from ﻞﻞ "hill" ([1]), alongside of ﺧﺧﻔﻞ.

WITH *ĀI.*

☞ p. 346

§ 135. *With āi* (ﺧ, ﺧ, ﺧ, &c.) corresponding adjectives([2]) were formed at pleasure, from substantives, and more rarely from other nouns; notably national appellations. Thus *e. g.* ﻧﻮﺯﻞ "fiery" from ﻧﻮﺯ; ﻣﻠﺧﺩﻞ "kingly"; ﺟﻤﺟﻞ οἰκεῖος; ﺣﺰﻧﻞ, ﺧﻪﻧﻞ "foreign" from ﺟﻤﻞ "foreign country"; ﻧﻮﺟﻞ "foreign"; ﺧﺰﺟﻞ "naked" (from the adjective ﺧﺰﺟﻞ); ﺟﻤﻞ "external"; ﺧﻪﻧﻞ "internal"; ﺣﺴﻮﻧﻞ "alone" (from the adverb ﺣﺴﻮﻧ); ﺧﺠﺰﻞ "belonging to", "proper" (from ﺧﺩ § 69), &c.—

([1]) Is ﻞﻣﻪﻞ, ﺧﻣﻪﻞ (in Arabic dress ﻕﺎﻗ) "street" ῥύμη by any chance an old Diminutive from ﻞﻣﻪ "broad street" πλατεῖα?

([2]) This mode of formation for the derivation of appellatives was much less frequently employed in remoter times than it came to be in later days, in the scholastic style of learned translators and imitators of Greek writings.

ܝܘܢܝܐ "Greek" (noun and adj.); ܐܠܢܝܐ "Alan"; ܝܗܘܕܝܐ "Jew"; ܗܝܢܕܘܝܐ "Hindoo" from the Persian *Hindū*; ܩܪܕܘܝܐ "man of Kardū" from *Qardū*; ܦܪܬܘܝܐ "Parthian" from *Parthau*.

From the feminine ܣܒܬܐ "old woman", ܣܒܬܢܝܐ "old-womanish"; but from ܡܕܝܢܬܐ,—ܡܕܝܢܝܐ, πολιτικός; and thus appears ܐܚܣܢܝܐ ἱκέσιος from ܐܚܣܢܐ.

From ܠܠܝܐ "night" (§ 49 A); ܠܠܝܝܐ, but also ܠܠܝܝܐ.

From plurals are formed: ܢܩܒܝܐ "effeminate" (ܢܩܒܐ "women" § 146); ܐܡܗܝܐ "maidenly" (ܐܡܗܬܐ "maidens" § 146); ܐܒܗܝܐ "fatherly" (ܐܒܗܐ), together with ܐܒܗܝܐ "patrician"; ܐܡܗܝܐ "motherly" (ܐܡܗܬܐ § 146); ܫܡܗܝܐ "nominal" (ܫܡܗܐ). Cf. with these § 138 A. Similarly ܩܘܪܝܐ "rustic", from ܩܘܪܝܐ (§ 146).

From ܢܘܬܠܐ "booth", and ܓܠܘܬܐ "banishment", are formed ܢܘܬܠܝܐ "host", "innkeeper", ܓܠܘܝܐ "exile", "outlaw"; so ܗܦܘܟܝܐ (ܗܦܘܟܝܐ?) "beginner". From ܙܓܘܓܝܬܐ "glass", ܙܓܘܓܝܐ "glazier".

From name of month ܬܫܪܝܢ: ܬܫܪܝܢܝܐ "Teshrīn (as adj.)", or "autumnal". So ܡܩܘܒܝܐ "monk", especially "novice", from ܡܩܘܒܝܐ κοινόβιον.

Final *ē* or *ai* falls away throughout before the suffix. Thus ܪܗܘܡܝܐ "Roman", from ܪܗܘܡܐ Ρώμη; ܡܩܕܘܝܐ "clerk", "sacristan", from κόγχη ("choir"); ܡܘܫܝܐ "of Moses" from ܡܘܫܐ; ܢܝܢܘܝܐ "Ninevite" from ܢܝܢܘܐ; ܓܙܝܪܝܐ from ܓܙܝܪܐ (name of a place); ܡܕܝܐ "from the convent of St. Matthew" (ܕܝܪ ܡܬܝ). Similarly ܐܘܪܗܝܐ "of Edessa", from ܐܘܪܗܝ; ܐܦܡܝܐ from Ἀπάμεια; ܫܡܪܝܐ from ܫܡܪܝܢ "Samaria". But ܓܪܒܝܝܐ "northern" from ܓܪܒܝܐ.

Short vowels have fallen out originally at the approach of the suffix, to the extent required by § 43. Thus ܦܪܣܝܐ "Persian", from ܦܪܣ (which itself is of course nothing but a more convenient pronunciation of *Pārs*); ܒܒܠܝܐ "Babylonian", from ܒܒܠ; ܐܪܡܝܐ "Aramaic", "heathen", from the original *Arăm* (1); ܓܪܒܝܐ "Arabian", "Arab" (still with soft ܒ, v. § 23 D) from ʻ*Arav*; ܡܘܨܠܝܐ "from *Mauṣil*"; ܕܡܫܩܝܐ

_____

(1) The West-Syrian schools arbitrarily derived ܐܪܡܝܐ "Aramaic" from ܐܪܡ, which is a copy of the Hebrew אָרָם, and they left the genuine ܐܪܡܝܐ with the signification of "heathen".

"of *Garmaq*"; ܒܪܒܪܝܐ "barbarian" from *βάρβαρος*; ܐܪܫܟܝܐ (along with ܐܪܫܟܢܝܐ §§ 42 and 52 B) "royal" from the royal name ܐܪܫܟ *Arsaces*; ܓܫܘܡܝܐ "from ܓܫܘܡ" (locality-name); cf. ܕܪܡܣܘܩܝܐ "from Damascus" ☞ p. 346 ܕܪܡܣܘܩ; and ܩܦܕܘܩܝܐ "from Καππαδοκία". A like mode of formation will probably hold good also in other cases, which we can no longer settle: Thus the national appellation from ܐܟܕ is doubtless ܐܟܕܝܐ, not ܐܟܕܝܐ, &c. But in other cases, the need of having the primitive word clearly recognised may have had an influence here,—even at an early period,—in defiance of phonetic rules. Thus ܕܝܠܘܡܝܐ "from *Dēlŏm*". From ܡܘܩܢ come ܡܘܩܝܐ and ܡܘܩܢܝܐ.

☞ p. 346 More decided abbreviations we have in ܕܝܨܢܝܐ from ܕܝܨܢ (river at Edessa), as well as from ܒܪ ܕܝܨܢ (Bardesanes); ܨܝܕܢܝܐ from ܨܝܕܢ (Sidon); ܚܪܢܝܐ "from Ḥarrān", ܚܪܢ; ܢܨܝܒܢܝܐ (also ܢܨܝܒܝܢܝܐ), from ܢܨܝܒܝܢ; ܡܪܕܝܢܝܐ "from ܡܪܕܝܢ"; ܬܠܙܒܕܢܝܐ "from ܬܠ ܙܒܕܢ".

The following are also irregular: ܐܝܣܪܝܠܝܐ "Israelite" from ܐܝܣܪܝܠ; and ܐܝܫܡܥܝܠܝܐ "Ishmaelite" from ܐܝܫܡܥܝܠ.

As shown by several of the foregoing examples, the ending may be attached even to compounds: thus,—to give farther instances—ܓܪܡܦܝܠܝܐ (late formation) *ἐλεφάντινος*, from ܓܪܡ ܦܝܠܐ "bone of the elephant", *i. e.* "ivory"; ܕܪܫܥܝܢܝܐ "from ܕܪܫ ܥܝܢܐ", &c. Yet along with these we have ܢܗܪܝܐ "Mesopotamian", from ܒܝܬ ܢܗܪܝܢ; ܬܗܘܡܝܐ, from ܒܝܬ ܬܗܘܡܐ; ܡܟܠܝܐ "overseer of the refectory" (ܒܝܬ ܡܟܠܐ); ܕܝܨܢܝܐ "of Bardesanes"— ☞ p. 346 v. *supra*.

Many names of cities form their *gentilicium* first from a form with *n*. Probably the ending was originally *ānāi*, but pronounced *nāi* in certain words. Thus ܡܣܘܪܢܝܐ "from ܡܣܘܪܐ", and probably ܠܓܝܘܢܝܐ "from ܠܓܝܘܢ" (along with it, but occurring more rarely, ܠܓܝܘܢܝܐ).—From ܟܪܡܐ comes ܟܪܡܘܢܝܐ (probably *Karmōnāyē*).

In the *gentilicia* of foreign names of localities, the forms of the foreign language are sometimes made perceptible, *e. g.* ܡܪܘܙܝܐ "from ܡܪܘ", after the Persian form *Marwazī*; ܪܙܝܩܝܐ "from ܪܝ", after the more ancient Persian form *Rāǧīk*.—Many more transformations too, which cannot now be checked, appear assuredly in such *gentilicia*.

One Abstract noun in *āi*, which however is perhaps of different origin, is ܓܕܦܝ, more rarely ܓܘܕܦܐ, "blame" (constr. st. ܓܕܦ).

§ 136. The compound, made up of *ān* (§ 129) and *āi*, which we had even in the *gentilicia*, appears often, and especially in the more scientific diction, in derivatives from appellatives: the ܬ of the fem. is almost always retained before it: Thus ܢܘܪܢܝܐ "fiery"; ܢܦܫܢܝܐ ψυχικός; ܪܘܚܢܝܐ πνευματικός; ܥܕܬܢܝܐ "ecclesiastical"; ܫܢܬܢܝܐ "yearly"; ܒܘܪܟܬܢܝܐ "blessing"; ܟܘܕܪܬܢܝܐ "begging", &c.: With the falling away of the feminine ending, however, in ܫܫܠܢܝܐ "chain-formed", from ܫܫܠܬܐ. With *ānāi*.

As *ān* even by itself is used in this way,—which assumes a ܢ before the feminine ending,—it is not always certain whether, for instance, a form ending in ܢܝܬܐ is to be read ܢܳܝܬܳܐ or ܢܺܝܬܳܐ. There are actually found variants like ܐܪܥܢܝܬܐ and ܐܪܥܢܳܝܬܐ ἐπίγειος (f.) Jas. 3, 15.

WITH *Ī*, *Y*.

§ 137. These forms are, it may be, of much diversity of origin; in part of them at least the *ī* may have been originally identical with that which has coalesced with another ending into the *āi* of the preceding sections. With *ī*, *y*

To this section belongs the *i* of feminine forms like ܐܪܥܢܝܬܐ, ܠܒܘܪܝܐ, &c. (§ 71). So, farther, we have ܕܒܘܪܝܬܐ "bee", pl. ܕܒܘܪܝܬܐ; ܣܢܘܢܝܬܐ "swallow"; ܕܒܒܝܬܐ "dog-fly"; ܚܘܝܬܐ "female snake" (ܚܘܝܐ "snake", pl. ܚܘܘܬܐ § 79 A); ܚܫܡܝܬܐ "dinner"; ܫܘܩܝܬܐ "streets" (§ 21 C); ܣܪܛܢܝܬܐ "cancer"; ܥܒܥܒܝܬܐ "shivering fit in ague"; ܬܠܬܝܬܐ "a breaking out"; ܒܘܥܘܬܝܬܐ "a breaking out"; ܕܘܟܠܝܬܐ, ܐܕܘܟܠܝܬܐ "bubo (in the human body)"; ܐܪܓܘܢܝܬܐ "purple"; ܟܪܣܝܬܐ "stomach of ruminants"; ܚܙܘܝܬܐ "shivering fit in ague; ܫܠܗܒܝܬܐ "flame"; ܡܥܡܘܕܝܬܐ "baptism"; ܡܫܪܘܩܝܬܐ "flute" (and others of this form), &c.

Farther, many masculine abstract nouns, like ܚܛܘܦܝܐ "robbing"; ܠܥܘܨܝܐ "oppressing"; ܐܣܘܪܝܐ "fettering"; ܗܦܘܟܝܐ "overturning"; ܚܒܘܩܝܐ "embracing"; ܓܒܘܠܝܐ "formation"; ܕܘܘܝܐ "sadness" (1), &c.

Perhaps also words like ܓܪܒܝܐ "north" might belong to this class.

(1) Some of the Syrians have foolishly turned the form ܐܘܠܨܝܐ "affliction",—fashioned according to this section,—into a form ܐܘܠܨܢܝܐ, as if it had the Greek ending ία.

WITH *ŪTH.*

With *ŭth.* § 138. A. This suffix serves to form Abstract nouns from nouns of all kinds (for inflection v. § 76). Thus *e. g.* ܡܰܠܟܽܘܬܐ "kingdom"; ܓܰܢܒܳܪܘܬܐ "heroism"; ܝܳܪܬܘܬܐ "inheritance"; ܡܳܝܽܘܬܐ "mortality"; ܒܰܪܳܝܘܬܐ "externality", "exterior"; ܛܳܒܘܬܐ "goodness", "good"; ܩܶܢܝܳܢܘܬܐ "property, attribute"; ܡܶܫܬܰܒܩܳܢܘܬܐ "abandonment" (from ܡܶܫܬܰܒܩܳܢ *nomen agentis* from ܐܶܫܬܒܶܩ "was abandoned" § 130); ܓܶܠܝܳܢܘܬܐ "revelation"; ܡܦܳܣܘܬܐ "consent" (ܐܦܶܣ), &c. So even ܐܰܝܟܰܢܳܝܘܬܐ *οἰκονομία.* The extension of this mode of formation is unlimited: particularly in scientific diction new examples are constantly appearing. Many of these forms, however, are very old, such as ܛܰܝܒܘܬܐ *χάρις*; ܣܰܝܒܘܬܐ "extreme old age"; ܗܰܝܡܳܢܘܬܐ "belief", their primitive words being no longer extant. Infinitives in ܳܘ— also belong to this section (v.—'Verb'). From plurals are formed ܐܰܒܳܗܘܬܐ

☞ p. 346 "fatherhood", alongside of ܐܰܒܳܘܬܐ *"patrocinium"*, and ܡܒܰܬܘܠܘܬܐ "maiden-hood" (cf. herewith § 135).

B. From roots *tert.* ܘ there are formed ܫܰܘܝܘܬܐ "equality" (from ܫܘܐ, ܫܳܘܐ); ܕܰܟܝܘܬܐ "purity"; ܪܰܒܘܬܐ "magnificence"; ܙܰܢܳܝܘܬܐ "fornication" (from ܙܢܐ, ܙܳܢܶܐ); ܡܰܥܩܪܘܬܐ "childlessness", and many others. But, alongside of these, there are other forms also which follow a more ancient method,—that of omitting the last radical: ܙܰܟܘܬܐ "innocence" (from ܙܟܐ); ܓܳܠܘܬܐ "banishment"; ܫܳܩܘܬܐ "a meal"; ܒܳܥܘܬܐ "petition".—In ܕܡܘܬܐ "form", and ܨܒܘܬܐ "thing" (§ 76 B), and likewise in ܡܰܪܕܘܬܐ "correction" (ܡܰܪܕܘ, ܡܰܪܕܘܬܐ); ܡܟܰܣܢܘܬܐ "censure"; ܡܰܫܩܘܬܐ "watering"; ܡܰܩܪܘܬܐ "fight"; ܡܰܫܬܘܬܐ "banquet",—it is not quite certain whether or not the abstract-suffix belonged originally to these words: and the same question arises in the case of ܚܘܣܳܝܐ "atonement", and ܚܒܳܠܘܬܐ "corruption" (§ 127).

Traces of other word-forming suffixes. § 139. TRACES OF OTHER WORD-FORMING SUFFIXES.

Traces of suffixes, like *ām, el, n* (ܦܽܘܪܬܰܥܢܐ "flea") are still repeatedly met with, but the words concerned no longer form an established class, and they may be regarded as multiliterals.

FOREIGN SUFFIXES.

§ 140. The suffix αριος, current in later Greek, but originally Latin,—which appears in several words, like ܚܢܝ βανιάριος "bath-master", and some others,—has also been joined to the Persian but adopted word ܐܣܛܘܢܐ "pillar", the Persian ܒܙܐ "falcon", and the pure Syriac ܐܠܦܐ "ship", thus: ܐܣܛܘܢܪܝܐ στυλίτης; ܒܙܝܪܐ "falconer"; ܐܠܦܪܝܐ "ship-master". The Persian *kān* is added to the Syriac ܚܡܪܐ "ass"; ܚܡܪܟܢܐ (properly ܚܡܪܕܟܢܐ) "ass-driver", and to the Greek ܩܝܛܘܢܐ κοιτῶν: ܩܝܛܘܢܩܢܐ "chamberlain". So, in addition, we have ܒܛܪܘܩܣܠܝ βοτρυώδης from the Syriac ܣܓܘܠܐ "a bunch of grapes". From ܐܣܛܠܝ "played" is formed, after the fashion of Greek words like εὐθηνία or σαφήνεια, ܐܣܛܠܝܢܐ "a game". Cf. ܐܣܛܪܢܝܐ "luxury", "wantonness" [I Tim. 5, 6] στρῆνος (or rather a secondary form—not yet, it is true, otherwise authenticated—στρηνεία).

☞ p. 346

C. COMPOUNDS.

§ 141. Several words, regularly and closely associated in a genitive connection, are treated as a single word, and attach to their second member those endings, which the first (standing in the constr. st.) should have received. Thus ܐܪܥ (constr. st. of ܐܪܥܐ "ground" § 146) forms with ܐܫܝܐ (pl. ܐܫܝܐ) "wall" a firm compound ܫܬܐܣܬܐ "foundation", of which the plural is ܫܬܐܣܐ; from this quite a new verb then originates, ܫܬܐܣ (also written ܫܬܐܣ) "he founded". So too are treated several compounds of ܒܝܬ "house", e. g. ܒܝܬ ܩܒܘܪܐ "tombs", "graves built inside"; ܒܝܬ ܩܦܣܐ "storehouses"; ܒܝܬ ܝܠܕܐ "houses of nativity", i. e. "constellations of nativity" (γενέσεις), &c.; and also other compounds, such as ܒܥܠܕܒܒܐ ("lord of..."?) "enemy", ܒܥܠܕܒܒܐ "enemies", ܒܥܠܬܕܒܒܬܐ "female enemy", ܒܥܠܕܒܒܘܬܐ "enmity"; ܪܝܫ ܝܪܚܐ "beginnings of a month"; ܥܙܐ ܕܛܘܪܐ "capra montis", "steinbock", pl. ܥܙܐ ܕܛܘܪܐ "steinbocks"; "wild goats"; ܦܣܩ ܕܝܢܐ "sentence" ("judicial decision"), pl. ܦܣܩܝ ܕܝܢܐ; ܡܣܡ ܒܪܝܫܐ "punishments"; and thus also several others, though not a great number of them,—while, in cases quite analogous, the ordinary procedure is followed, e. g. ܒܪܬ ܩܠܐ "filia vocis", i. e. "word",

☞ p. 346

pl. ܒ̈ܢܝ ܡܠܟܐ, and so with all compounds of ܒܪ "son" and ܒܪܬ "daughter", however close the combination may sometimes be.

Some compounds show a more decided blending of sounds. Thus, for instance, ܒܣܬܪܟܐ "pillow" ["cushioned couch"—"*pulvinar*"], pl. ܒܣ̈ܬܪܟܘܬܐ (§ 79 A), of which the first portion is equivalent to ܒܝܬ, while the second is a form nearly related to ܐܣܬܪܐ "foundation". So ܓܝܕܢܫܝܐ 'name of a tendon' = גִּיד נְשִׁיָּא; ܫܘܬܐܣܝ̈ܢܐ, ܫܘܪܝ̈ܢܐ ([1]), pl. ܫܘܪ̈ܝܢܐ or even ܫܘܬܪ̈ܝܢܐ "navel" = ܫܬܐ ܕܫܪܐ "basis(?) of the navel", and some others. Cf. § 125.

p. 346 **Gender of such compounds.**

§ 142. The second member of such compounds determines even the gender and number. Thus ܒܝܬ ܫܒܬܐ "*domus* (m.) *sabbatis* (f.)" *i. e.* "refectory", and ܒܝܬ ܨܠܘܬܐ "chapel", "house of prayer" are feminine: ܦܠܓܘܬ ܝܘܡܐ "half of the day", "mid-day", is used as masculine: ܐܦ̈ܝ ܬܪܥܐ "face (f. pl.) of the door (m. sing.)" = "curtain" is always masc. sing.

Compounds with *lā*.

§ 143. A special class is formed by nouns compounded closely with ܠܐ "not", like ܠܐ ܡܝܘܬܐ "immortal", f. ܠܐ ܡܝܘܬܬܐ, pl. ܠܐ ܡܝܘ̈ܬܐ, ܠܐ ܡܝܘ̈ܬܬܐ, &c.; ܠܐ ܡܝܘܬܘܬܐ "immortality"; ܠܐ ܡܛܝܬܐ "non-arrival", &c.

Remark on the treatment of Greek proper-names.

D. REMARK ON THE TREATMENT OF GREEK PROPER-NAMES.

§ 144. *Greek proper-names* in ος and ας are used either in the nominative- or vocative-form: ܦܘܠܘܣ; ܦܛܪܘܣ; ܐܠܟܣܢܕܪܘܣ; ܬܐܘܕܐܣ (Θευδᾶς), &c.; or (used, however, also as subject &c.,) ܦܘܠܐ; ܦܛܪܐ; ܐܠܟܣܢܕܪܐ; ܬܐܘܕܘܪܐ; ܬܐܘܕܐ; ܐܪܣܛܘܒܠܐ; &c. The East-Syrians however write ܐ— for this ܐ— and ܐ—, or even ܐ— without any difference in the pronunciation.

The termination ιος, ειος very frequently falls completely away: sometimes there still remains of it a ܝ: ܡܘܪܝܩܝ alongside of ܡܘܪܝܩܝܘܣ Μαυρίκιος; ܐܝܓܢܛܝ Ἰγνάτιος; ܒܣܝܠ, ܒܣܝܠܝ, ܒܣܝܠܝܣ Βασίλειος; ܙܢܘܒ, ܐܙܢܘܒ, ܙܢܘܒܝ Ζηνόβιος (also ܐܙܢܘܒܝܘܣ); ܠܐܘܢܛܝ, ܠܐܘܢܛܝܣ Λεόντιος, &c. This happens too, though much more rarely, with the simple ος, *e. g.* ܦܛܪ, as

---

([1]) Vocalisation not settled.

well as ܒܣܘܣ, ܒܣܐ Βάσσος; ܐܢܛܘܢܝܣ Ἀντωνῖνος. Of course there are found, besides, many deviations from the accurate Greek forms, which are not limited to the terminations.

E. ATTACHMENT OF THE POSSESSIVE SUFFIXES.

Attachment of the possessive suffixes.

☞ p. 346

§ 145. A. The Suffixes enumerated in § 65 coalesce with the *ai* of the pl. m. into the following forms:

Suffixes of the Plural.

"my"	ـܝ̈		"our"	ـܝ̈ܢ
"thy (m.)"	ـܝ̈ܟ		"your (m.)"	ـܝ̈ܟܘܢ
"thy (f.)"	ـܝ̈ܟܝ		"your (f.)"	ـܝ̈ܟܝܢ
"his"	ـ̈ܘܗܝ	(ـܘܗܝ § 49 B)	"their (m.)"	ـܝ̈ܗܘܢ
"her"	ـܝ̈ܗ		"their (f.)"	ـܝ̈ܗܝܢ

Thus the same scheme holds throughout; only ـ̈ܘܗܝ from *auhī* constitutes a deviation. Notice that the otherwise constantly soft ܟܘ of the 2nd pers. becomes hard after *ai*.

Example: ܕܝܢܐ "judgment" (constr. and abs. st. ܕܝܢ; pl. ܕܝܢ̈ܐ, ܕܝܢܝܢ, ܕܝܢ̈ܝ).

Singular:

ܕܝܢܝ my judgment	ܕܝܢܢ our judgment
ܕܝܢܟ thy (m.) judgment	ܕܝܢܟܘܢ your (m.) judgment
ܕܝܢܟܝ thy (f.) ,,	ܕܝܢܟܝܢ your (f.) ,,
ܕܝܢܗ his ,,	ܕܝܢܗܘܢ their (m.) ,,
ܕܝܢܗ̇ her ,,	ܕܝܢܗܝܢ their (f.) ,,

Plural:

ܕܝܢ̈ܝ my judgments	ܕܝܢ̈ܝܢ our judgments
ܕܝܢ̈ܝܟ thy (m.) judgments	ܕܝܢ̈ܝܟܘܢ your (m.) judgments
ܕܝܢ̈ܝܟܝ thy (f.) ,,	ܕܝܢ̈ܝܟܝܢ your (f.) ,,
ܕܝܢ̈ܘܗܝ his ,,	ܕܝܢ̈ܝܗܘܢ their (m.) ,,
ܕܝܢ̈ܝܗ̇ her ,,	ܕܝܢ̈ܝܗܝܢ their (f.) ,,

B. No difficulty of any kind is occasioned in attaching the suffixes to any noun, of which the stem or ground-form (*i. e.* the form left after removal of the termination *ā*) has a long vowel—or another consonant

without a vowel—before the final letter, or ends in a double-consonant:
thus *e. g.*, like ܪܒܳܐ given above, ܚܰܒܪܳܐ "garment"; ܚܰܒܪܶܗ, ܚܰܒܪܳܢ,
ܚܰܒܪܰܝܟܽܘܢ; ܨܳܡܳܐ "silver": ܨܳܡܦܳܐ(¹), ܨܳܡܦܽܘܢ(²); ܐܶܡܳܐ "mother"; ܐܶܡܝ,
ܐܶܡܳܟ, ܐܶܡܗܽܘܢ(³), &c.
The vocalisation in these cases is, throughout, the same as in the
emphatic state.

Rem. No difference of treatment is exhibited here between words
of the simplest formation with originally one short vowel, and those
with originally two short vowels. Like ܕܰܗܒܳܐ (from *dahăvā*), we have not
merely ܕܰܗܒܝ, but also ܕܰܗܒܶܗ, ܕܰܗܒܽܘܢ(⁴). If,—besides ܐܰܬܪܝ, ܐܰܬܪܽܘܢ from
ܐܰܬܪܳܐ (for *atharā*) "place",—ܐܰܬܪܝ, ܐܰܬܪܽܘܢ are occasionally met with, it is
not the original vocalisation which is maintained therein, but one which is
to be understood as a method of facilitating pronunciation in accordance
with § 52 B, just as, with words of the simplest formation there is
written also upon occasion ܠܐܰܚܕ (= ܠܐܶܚܕ), ܐܶܚܕܶܗ, ܐܶܚܕܽܘܢ.

C. This method prevails also with all terminations of the pl. f.;
and suffixes are attached thereto in the same way as to the singular.
Like ܡܰܠܟܳܬܳܐ "queens" we read, for instance, ܡܰܠܟܳܬܟ, ܡܰܠܟܳܬܽܘܢ, ܡܰܠܟܳܬܶܗ, &c.
It is the same with those of the pl. m.,—with the exception of many
forms *tertiae* ܝ for which v. *infra*, K. Like ܡܰܠܟܶܐ "kings", ܣܳܗܕܶܐ "witnesses", we have ܡܰܠܟܰܝ, ܡܰܠܟܰܝܟܽܘܢ, ܡܰܠܟܰܝܗܽܘܢ; ܣܳܗܕܰܝ, ܣܳܗܕܰܝܟܽܘܢ,
ܣܳܗܕܰܝܗܽܘܢ, &c.

D. Even with forms which have a short vowel before the final
consonant, including the feminine termination *ath* (ܰܬ) the vocalisation
entirely resembles, for all suffixes, that of the emphatic state, with the
exception of the 1st sing. and 2nd and 3rd pl. Thus like ܡܶܣܒܳܐ "taking",
from ܡܶܣܒ, and ܡܰܠܟܳܐ, from ܡܰܠܟ, so too ܡܶܣܒܝ, ܡܶܣܒܰܟ, ܡܶܣܒܶܗ,
ܡܰܠܟܰܝ; ܡܰܠܟܟ, ܡܰܠܟܶܗ, ܡܰܠܟܟܽܘܢ, ܡܶܣܒܟ; ܡܶܣܒܶܗ, ܡܶܣܒܽܘܢ.

E. At the approach of the suffixes of the 1st sing. and 2nd and
3rd pl., the short vowels before the final consonant are frequently retained,

---

(¹) Thus ܟܶܣܦܝ, ܓܰܠܕܟ, ܐܶܙܕܗ, ܝܰܥܡܶܗ, ܥܰܡܟܽܘܢ; ܥܰܡܗܳܐ, ܥܰܡܟܽܘܢ; ܫܽܠܕ, ܟܶܣܦܽܘܢ, &c.

(²) Thus ܡܶܣܟܽܘܢ, ܝܰܥܡܶܗ, ܕܶܘܥܡܟ, ܐܶܚܕܽܘܢ, ܐܶܡܘܽܘܢ, &c.

(³) Thus ܫܶܡܗ, ܟܶܬܒ, ܟܶܬܒܝ, &.

(⁴) Thus ܫܶܠܕ. Cf. farther ܓܶܦܽܘܢ, ܐܶܓܕܽܘܢ, ܚܶܡܣܝ, ܚܶܡܣܘܽܘܢ, ܒܶܩܦܽܘܢ, &c.

although in other cases they disappear, no doubt from the analogy of the other forms. They are retained throughout, where there is no feminine ending, except in the instances given under J: Thus ܡܫܡܫ (ܡܫܡܫܢܐ, ܡܫܡܫܢܘ &c.); ܡܫܡܫܝ, ܡܫܡܫܟ, ܡܫܡܫܟܘܢ, ܡܫܡܫܗܘܢ, ܡܫܡܫܢ. So ܡܘܒܠܝ "my burden"; ܡܐܡܪܝ "my speech"; ܡܘܬܒܗܘܢ "their seat"; ܪܚܡܝ "my friend" &c.

F. *a* of the feminine-ending *ath* disappears before these suffixes [that is to say, the analogy of the emph. state is followed], when the middle consonant has a short vowel; thus like ܬܒܥܬܐ "vengeance", ܬܒܥܬܗ, and ܬܒܥܬܝ, ܬܒܥܬܗܘܢ; ܡܛܪܬܐ "watch", ܡܛܪܬܝ; ܡܚܫܒܬܐ "thought", ܡܚܫܒܬܗܘܢ; ܬܫܡܫܬܐ "service", ܬܫܡܫܬܝ, ܬܫܡܫܬܗܘܢ; ܬܫܒܘܚܬܐ "praise", ܬܫܒܘܚܬܝ, ܬܫܒܘܚܬܗܘܢ; ܝܠܕܬܐ "a mother", ܝܠܕܬܝ, ܝܠܕܬܟ; ܓܓܪܬܐ "throat", ܓܓܪܬܝ; ܡܐܟܘܠܬܐ "eating", ܡܐܟܘܠܬܝ, ܡܐܟܘܠܬܟ, &c. So ܓܦܬ "vine" (for ܓܦܢܬܐ), ܓܦܬܗܘܢ, &c.

Thus also with many, which have a long vowel in the syllable preceding the ܬܐ of the feminine: ܢܝܚܬܐ "rest, pleasure", ܢܝܚܬܝ; ܒܥܠܕܒܒܬܝ "my enemy (f.)"; ܣܥܪܬܗܘܢ "their hair"; ܩܪܝܒܬܝ "*proxima mea*"; ܟܢܘܫܬܗܘܢ "their synagogue"; ܪܫܝܬܗܘܢ "their first"; ܡܨܝܕܬܝ, ܡܨܝܕܬܗܘܢ "net"; ܒܝܫܬܝ, ܒܝܫܬܗܘܢ, ܒܝܫܬܟ "evil"; ܣܘܣܬܝ "my mare", ܡܝܬܝ (also written ܡܝܬܬܝ, ܡܝܬܬܝ, but all to be pronounced *mīt*) "my dead (f.)" (§ 26 B).

Where the long vowel represents a radical ܘ or ܝ, there is a good deal of fluctuation. Thus ܡܕܝܢܬܗܘܢ "their city", but ܡܕܝܢܬܝ; with reversed procedure in ܛܒܬܝ "my good", but ܛܒܬܗܘܢ; ܡܪܬܝ "my Lady, mistress", as well as ܚܘܒܬܝ "my necessity"; ܪܘܡܬܝ "height", ܕܪܬܝ "court"; ܫܥܬܝ, ܫܥܬܟ "hour". With falling away again, ܨܘܪܬܗܘܢ "their form", and with *a* ܓܘܕܬܗܘܢ, ܓܘܕܬܟ "troop". In some cases the usage has fluctuated. Thus ܣܝܡܬܗܘܢ "their treasure" with Ephraim, while in the Bible tradition we have ܣܝܡܬܗܘܢ. From ܥܕܬܐ "church" the East-Syrians have ܥܕܬܝ *ʿēðath*, the West-Syrians ܥܕܬܝ *ʿīt*.

G. Th *a* is retained, when the middle consonant wants the vowel. Thus ܡܠܟܬܐ, ܡܠܟܬܝ, ܡܠܟܬܗܘܢ; ܕܡܥܬܝ "tear"; ܒܘܪܟܬܝ, ܒܘܪܟܬܗܘܢ "blessing"; ܕܚܠܬܝ, ܕܚܠܬܟ "fright"; ܐܘܚܕܬܝ "riddle". So too ܫܐܠܬܝ, ܫܐܠܬܗܘܢ "question"; ܠܐܘܬܗܘܢ, ܠܐܘܬܟ "fatigue"; ܚܕܘܬܝ, ܚܕܘܬܗܘܢ,

ܚܰܕ݂ܘܳܬ݂ܳܐ "joy" (from *ḥaδwĕthā*, or *ḥaδūthā* § 40 D. 101), &c. Thus also with diphthongs, like ܩܘܡܬܝ, ܩܘܡܬܗܘܢ "stature"; ܪܘܬܬܟܘܢ "quaking"; ܚܘܒܬܝ "guilt", &c.—It is the same when the middle radical is doubled in cases like ܪܓܝܓܬܐ "pleasure"; ܪܓܝܓܬܝ, ܪܓܝܓܬܗܘܢ; ܡܠܬܝ, ܡܠܬܗܘܢ "word"; ܓܢܬܝ "garden"; ܫܬܬܝ "basis"; ܕܘܟܬܝ, ܕܘܟܬܗܘܢ "place", &c. ܫܢܬܐ "sleep" conforms to these examples: ܫܢܬܝ, ܫܢܬܗܘܢ; while from analogous formations (§ 105) we have ܪܢܝܬܝ, ܪܢܝܬܟܘܢ "care"; ܚܡܬܝ, ܚܡܬܗܘܢ (for which, however, the old poets have ܚܡܝܬܗܘܢ, ܚܡܝܬܟܘܢ). So ܐܡܬܝ "maid-servant"; ܚܪܬܝ, ܚܪܬܗܘܢ "end"; ܐܫܬܗܘܢ "basis".

H. The feminines of derivatives from *tertiae* ܝ present no difficulty. ܝܬܐ, ܘܬܐ are there retained unaltered: ܫܒܝܬܝ, ܫܒܝܬܗܘܢ "prisoner (f.)"; ܡܕܝܢܬܝ "city"; ܡܫܒܚܢܝܬܝ "praising"; ܡܡܠܠܝܬܝ "conversation"; ܠܘܝܬܗܘܢ "escort".—ܡܚܘܬܝ "stroke"; ܨܠܘܬܝ, ܨܠܘܬܟܘܢ "prayer".—Similarly, of course, with those in ܝܬܐ, and abstracts in ܘܬܐ.

☞ p. 347 J. Forms which end in ܝܐ in the abs. st. sing. preserve their vocalisation before the suffixes of the 2nd and 3rd sing. and the 1st pl. thus, ܚܣܝܐ, ܚܣܝܐ "pious"; ܟܘܪܣܝܐ "throne": ܚܣܝܗ, ܚܣܝܟ; ܟܘܪܣܝܟ, ܟܘܪܣܝܢ, &c.

ܟܘܪܣܝܐ (constr. st. ܟܘܪܣܐ), ܡܫܪܝܐ "camp", ܡܫܬܝܐ "drinking" form with the suffix of the 1st sing. ܟܘܪܣܝ, ܡܫܪܝ, ܡܫܬܝ. In other cases those which end in ܝܐ in the emphatic st. have ܝܝ, which is either not pronounced at all, as in East-Syrian, or, as in West-Syrian, pronounced as a simple *ī*: sometimes only one simple ܝ is written instead of the two: ܪܢܝܝ (ܪܢܝܝ § 17) or ܪܢܝ "my meditation"; ܛܠܝܝ or ܛܠܝ "my boy"; ܓܒܝܝ or ܓܒܝ "mine elect"; ܚܢܘܩܝ "my suffocation"; ܪܥܝܝ, ܪܥܝ "my shepherd". If the ܝܐ stands after a vowel, the suffix is then at all events silent; thus from ܒܪܘܝܐ "creator", ܒܪܘܝ; from ܩܪܝܐ "call", ܩܪܝ.

The ܝ of the suffix is in like manner silent after ܐ as final radical: ܒܘܝܐܝ "my consolation"; ܣܢܐܝ "mine enemy, [my hater]"; and so ܡܪܝ "my lord" (= ܡܪܐܝ).

Before the suffixes of the 2nd and 3rd pl. we have, in accordance with § 40 C, ܪܢܝܗܘܢ; ܫܓܘܫܝܗܘܢ "their confusion", &c. So too the West-Syrians have ܡܫܪܝܗܘܢ, ܡܫܬܝܟܘܢ, &c., while the East-Syrians have ܡܫܬܝܟܘܢ, ܡܫܪܝܗܘܢ, &c.

K. In the pl. short adjectives may treat the radical *y* as a strong consonant, but they may also fashion shorter forms: ܚܳܙܰܝܟ݂ܽܘܢ "those who see you", alongside of ܫܳܒ݂ܰܝܗܽܘܢ "their captors", ܫܳܒ݂ܰܝܢ "our captors"; ܫܳܬܰܝܢܳܝܗܝ "those who drink it"; ܚܰܣܰܝܳܘܗܝ and ܚܰܣܳܘܗܝ "his pious ones"; ܛܠܳܝܳܘܗܝ and ܛܠܳܘܗܝ "his young men". Pure substantives have always the shorter form: ܡܰܥܰܝ, ܡܰܥܰܝܟ݂ܽܘܢ, ܡܰܥܰܘܗܝ "bowels"; ܓܘܪܳܘܗܝ "*catuli ejus*", &c. So ܫܡܰܝܳܐ "heaven": ܫܡܰܝܟ݂ܽܘܢ, &c. Compare with all this § 73.

L. Greek words in ܘܣ ος, ܘܝ οι (pl.), ܐܣ ας, &c. do not take suffixes (§ 225).—ܕܺܝܰܬܺܝܩܺܐ διαθήκη takes suffixes, as if it were a plural, without however being construed as a plural: ܕܺܝܰܬܺܩܰܘܗܝ "his testament"; ܕܺܝܰܬܺܩܰܝܢ (sg. f.) &c. In the very same way occur ܛܺܝܡܰܝ, ܛܺܝܡܰܘܗܝ "my, his price" from ܛܺܝܡܺܐ τιμή as a sing. fem. Perhaps there are still other Greek words in η, which are thus treated. ☞ p. 347

F. LIST OF ANOMALOUS NOUNS.

F. List of anomalous nouns. Substantives and adjectives.

§ 146. ܐܰܒ݂ܳܐ "father", ܐܰܚܳܐ "brother", ܚܡܳܐ "father-in-law" — end properly in *ū*:

Accordingly we have ܐܰܒ݂ܽܘܗ݈ܝ, ܐܰܒ݂ܽܘܗܝ, ܐܰܒ݂ܽܘܟ݂, ܐܰܒ݂ܽܘܗ, ܐܰܒ݂ܽܘܟ݂ܽܘܢ, ܐܰܒ݂ܽܘܗܽܘܢ, ܐܰܒ݂ܽܘܟ݂ܶܝܢ, ܐܰܒ݂ܽܘܢ. So ܐܰܚܽܘܗܝ, ܐܰܚܽܘܟ݂; ܚܡܽܘܗܝ, ܚܡܽܘܟ݂, &c. But, ܐܰܒ݂ܝ "my father", ܐܰܚܝ "my brother", ܚܡܝ "my father-in-law". Abs. and constr. states are wanting.—Pl. ܐܰܚܶܐ (ܐܰܚܰܝ, ܐܰܚܰܝܟ݂ܽܘܢ, &c.), but ܐܰܒ݂ܳܗܳܬ݂ܳܐ or ܐܰܒ݂ܳܗܳܐ, ܚܡܳܗܳܬ݂ܳܐ.

ܚܳܬ݂ܳܐ "sister" (without constr. or abs. st.); ܚܳܬ݂ܝ, ܚܳܬ݂ܶܗ, &c.; pl. ܐܰܚܘܳܬ݂ܳܐ.—ܚܡܳܬ݂ܳܐ "mother-in-law" (plur.?):

ܐܶܡܳܐ "mother"; ܐܶܡܝ, ܐܶܡܶܗ, &c.; pl. ܐܶܡܳܗܳܬ݂ܳܐ.

ܒܰܪ "son"; emph. st. ܒܪܳܐ. With suff. ܒܪܳܟ݂, ܒܪܶܗ, ܒܪܳܢ, &c., but ܒܶܪܝ, ܒܶܪܗܽܘܢ, ܒܶܪܟ݂ܽܘܢ: pl. ܒܢܰܝܳܐ, ܒܢܰܝ, ܒܢܰܝ; with suff. ܒܢܰܝܟ݂ܽܘܢ, &c.

ܒܪܰܬ݂ܳܐ "daughter"; wanting abs. st.; constr. st. ܒܪܰܬ݂; ܒܪܰܬ݂ܳܟ݂, ܒܪܰܬ݂ܶܗ, ܒܪܰܬ݂ܟ݂ܽܘܢ, &c.; but ܒܶܪܬ݂ܝ; pl. ܒܢܳܬ݂ܳܐ, ܒܢܳܬ݂, ܒܢܳܬ݂ (ܒܢܳܬ݂ܗܽܘܢ, &c.).

ܫܶܡ, ܫܡܳܐ "name"; ܫܡܶܗ, ܫܡܳܟ݂, ܫܡܝ, ܫܡܟ݂ܽܘܢ, &c.; pl. ܫܡܳܗܶܐ, and ܫܡܳܗܳܬ݂ܳܐ.

ܕܡܳܐ, ܕܶܡ "blood"; ܕܡܶܗ, ܕܡܝ, ܕܡܗܽܘܢ; pl. ܕܡܶܐ. ☞ p. 347

ܙܢܐ "kind, species"; constr. st. ܙܢ (West-Syrian ܙܢ); pl. ܙܢܝܐ, ܙܢ̈ܝܢ, ܙܢ̈ܝ, ܙܢܝ̈ܗܘܢ, &c. An early naturalised Persian word.

ܐܡܐ "*mamma*"; ܐܡܗ; pl. ܐܡܗܬܐ, ܐܡܗ̈ܬ, ܐܡܗܬܗܘܢ.

ܐܝܕܐ "hand" (for יְדָא § 40 C); constr. st. ܝܕ, particularly in transferred application and adverbial use (ܒܝܕ "by means of", "owing to"; ܥܠ ܝܕ ܢܗܪܐ "by the side of the river", &c.), and ܐܝܕ (substantively); thus before suffixes:—ܐܝܕܗܘܢ, ܐܝܕܝ, ܐܝܕܟ, &c. (ܒܝܕܗܘܢ "through them": In West-Syrian appears indeed the artificial formation ܒܝܕܘܗܝ δι' αὐτοῦ). Pl. ܐܝ̈ܕܝܐ, ܐܝ̈ܕܐ; ܐܝ̈ܕܝܢ; ܐܝ̈ܕܝ: with suffix, ܐܝܕܝ̈ܗܘܢ, &c. ܐܝ̈ܕܝܬܐ (East-Syrian ܐܝ̈ܕܘܬܐ "handles").

ܫܡܝܐ "heaven"; ܫܡ̈ܝܢ (§ 73), ܫܡ̈ܝ, ܫܡܝ̈ܟ, &c.: In form always plural.

ܡܝܐ "water"; ܡ̈ܝܢ, ܡ̈ܝ. With suffixes, at pleasure either ܡ̈ܝ, ܡܝ̈ܟ, ܡ̈ܝܟܝ, ܡܝ̈ܗܝ, ܡ̈ܝܗ, ܡ̈ܝܢ, ܡ̈ܝܟܘܢ, ܡ̈ܝܗܘܢ, or ܡ̈ܝܟܝ, ܡܝ̈ܗܝ, ܡ̈ܝܗܘܢ &c.

ܐܫܬܐ "ground, bottom"; constr. st. ܫܬ, East-Syrian ܫܬ, (almost never occurring except in combinations like ܫܬ ܐܣܬܐ "foundation"; ܫܬ ܐܘܨܪ̈ܐ "waste from storehouses"). With suff. ܐܫܬܗ, ܐܫܬܗܘܢ; Pl. ܐܫ̈ܬܬܐ; and with suff. ܐܫ̈ܬܬܗܘܢ; and also ܐܫܬܝ̈ܬܗܘܢ "their seats", &c.

ܫܢܬܐ "year"; abs. st. ܫܢܐ; constr. st. ܫܢܬ (doubtful whether used with suffixes): pl. ܫܢܝܐ, ܫܢ̈ܝܢ, ܫܢ̈ܝ; with suff. ܫܢܝ̈ܟ, &c.

ܐܡܬܐ "maid-servant" (probably without abs. or constr. state); ܐܡܬܝ, ܐܡܬܗ, &c.—ܐܡ̈ܗܬܐ, ܐܡܗ̈ܬܗܘܢ.

ܣܦܬܐ "lip": abs. st. ܣܦܐ; constr. st. ܣܦܬ; ܣܦܬܗ, &c.—ܣܦܘ̈ܬܐ.

☞ p. 347 ܦܐܬܐ, ܦܬܐ "side, face"; ܦܐܬܗ. Defective parts supplied from ܐܦܐ "face", ܐܦ̈ܝܢ, ܐܦ̈ܝ; ܐܦܝ̈ܗܘܢ, &c.; (properly Dual of *anp* "nose" § 28).

ܪܐܬܐ, ܪܬܐ (better ܪܐܬܐ "lungs". Pl. ܪܐܘ̈ܬܐ: according to others (perhaps more correctly) ܪܐܘ̈ܬܐ, *i. e.* רְאוָתָא.

ܒܝܬܐ "house": abs. st. ܒܝܬ (§ 26 C); constr. st. ܒܝܬ; ܒܝܬܝ, &c.: *pl.* ܒ̈ܬܐ, ܒ̈ܬܝܢ, ܒ̈ܬܝ: ܒ̈ܬܝܗܘܢ, &c.

ܐܢ̈ܬܬܐ, ܐܢܬܬܐ (two different modes of writing down the same pronunciation of the word *attā*, *atō*) "woman": constr. st. ܐܢܬܬ; ܐܢܬܬܝ, &c.

Pl. ܝܩܪ, ܝܩܬܝ, ܒܝܬ; ܝܡܬܘܗܝ, &c.—As a diminutive, appears ܝܩܦܣܬܐ "little women". Sing. of this form is said to be ܐܬܩܣܠܐ.

ܐܢܫ, ܢܫ "one", τὶς ("man"); pl. ܐܢܫ̈ܝܢ, ܐܢܫܝܢ "several", "certain" τινὲς. The emph. st. ܐܢܫܐ signifies "man", "of human nature", but much more frequently it bears the original collective sense, "men" or "people". It is never found in the emph. st. in the plural; but in the constr. st. and with suff. it is found only in the pl.: ܐܢܫ̈ܝ ܡܕܝܢ̈ܬܐ "the people of the town", &c.; ܐܢܫܘܗܝ "his people", &c. "Man" is more accurately expressed by "son of man" or "a son of men" ܒܪ ܐܢܫ, ܒܪ ܐܢܫܐ; pl. ܒܢܝ ܐܢܫܐ; pl. ܒܢܝ ܐܢܫܐ, ܒܢܝܢܫܐ. Very rarely we meet with ܒܪ ܐܢܫܐ "man"; rarely with ܒܪܬ ܐܢܫܐ "woman".

ܠܠܝܐ, ܠܝܠܝܐ or ܠܠܝܐ, ܠܠܝܐ (§ 49 A); there is no constr. st., and it is almost never used with suff. Abs. st. is ܠܠܝ (for which ܠܠܝܐ is often improperly written, § 16 C. Rem.) and ܠܠܝ (ܠܠܝܐ not so good) in the combination ܐܝܡܡ ܘܠܠܝ "by night and day" (§ 243), also "the space of a night and a day". On rare occasions the words are found in reversed order ܠܠܝܐ ܘܐܝܡܡܐ. Pl. ܠܝ̈ܠܘܬܐ, ܠܝ̈ܠܘܢ.

☞ p. 347

ܐܪܝܐ "lion" (for אֲרִיָא); no constr. or abs. st. Pl. ܐܪ̈ܝܘܬܐ, ܐܪ̈ܝܘܢ.— Fem. ܐܪܝܬܐ "lioness"; pl. no doubt ܐܪ̈ܝܬܐ.

ܡܩܛܬܐ (for קִשּׁוּאָתָא) "cucumber"; pl. ܡܩ̈ܛܐ, ܡܩ̈ܛܐ, and later form (as if we had in this case the abstract-ending ܘܬܐ) ܡܩܛܘܬܐ.

ܡܪܝܐ (only used of God and of Christ), and ܡܪܐ (= מָרֵא) "master, lord" constr. st. ܡܪܐ. A secondary form of the constr. st. *mār* appears to present itself in ܡܪܐ ܐܠܗ̈ܐ Spic. 41, 15, and even ܡܪ ܐܠܗ̈ܐ in the ancient Inscription ZDMG XXXVI, tab. 1, 8 = ܡܪܐ ܐܠܗ̈ܐ "the lord of the gods", i. e., *Zeus* [1]. Abs. st. wanting; ܡܪܘܢ, ܡܪܝ, ܡܪܘܬܐ, &c.; pl. ܡܪ̈ܝܐ and more rarely ܡܪ̈ܝܢ, ܡܪ̈ܝ, ܡܪ̈ܝ; with suff. ܡܪ̈ܝܘܗܝ, &c.; or even ܡܪ̈ܘܬܐ, ܡܪ̈ܘܢ (but hardly a corresponding constr. st., or corresponding forms with suffixes).— Fem. ܡܪܬܐ, ܡܪܬܝ, ܡܪܬܢ; ܡܪ̈ܬܐ, &c.

ܡܕܝܢܬܐ "city, village"; abs. st. ܡܕܝܢ; constr. st. ܡܕܝܢܬ, also ܡܕܝܢܬ; with suff. ܡܕܝܢܬܟ, ܡܕܝܢܬܗ, &c.; pl. (the collective) ܡܕ̈ܝܢܬܐ; constr. st. ܡܕ̈ܝܢܬ;

---

[1] In ܡܪܘܗܝ Euseb. Church Hist. 395, 5 (but the manuscript is of the year 462) we have before us no doubt merely a short-hand mode of writing. The phrase intended must have been the common one, *mārē khol*.

no abs. st. Pl. with suff. (1) ܩܘܪ̈ܝܢܝ, ܩܘܪ̈ܝܢܗܘܢ, (2) more frequently ܩܘܪ̈ܝܝ, ܩܘܪ̈ܝܗ, ܩܘܪ̈ܝܟܘܢ, &c.—As secondary forms of the pl., ܡܕ̈ܝܢܬܐ and ܩܘܪ̈ܝܗܝ (§ 89, end).—Cf. besides the purely artificial imitation ܩܘܪ̈ܝܬ ܡܕ̈ܝܢܬܐ κωμοπόλεις ["village-towns", or "country towns"].

ܚܡܪܐ "ass"; pl. ܚܡ̈ܪܐ, but also (when a collective, like ܩܘܪ̈ܝܐ) ܚܡܝ̈ܪܐ. With suff. ܚܡܝ̈ܪܘܗܝ, ܚܡܝ̈ܪܝܗܘܢ, &c.

ܐܘܡܬܐ "folk"; pl. ܐܡ̈ܘܬܐ, ܐܡ̈ܘܬ; in isolated cases, ܐܘܡ̈ܘܬܐ, ܐܘܡ̈ܘܬ.

ܛܠܐ, ܛܠܝܐ, f. ܛܠܝܬܐ "young" forms, as an adjective and also in the meaning "servant", in accordance with rule, ܛܠܝ̈ܐ, ܛܠܝ̈ܢ, ܛܠܝ̈ܟ; ܛܠܝ̈ܘܗܝ ("his young men"), &c.; ܛܠܝ̈ܬܐ, ܛܠܝ̈ܬܢ, ܛܠܝ̈ܬܗ, &c.; but in the meaning "boy", "girl": ܛܠܝ̈ܐ, ܛܠܝ̈ܢ (it is a matter of question whether it has suffixes in this meaning); ܛܠܝ̈ܬܐ. In like manner ܦܬܝܐ "piece (of bread)"; pl. ܦܬ̈ܝܐ: and ܬܕܝܐ "breast", with ܬܕ̈ܝܬܐ (§ 79 A), as well as ܬܕ̈ܝܐ.

ܐܟܘܬ "like"; pl. f. emph. st. ܐܟ̈ܘܬܐ, pl. m. ܐܟ̈ܘܬܐ, ܐܟ̈ܘܬܢ. The other forms are doubtful.

ܐܚܪܝܢ "alius": ܐܚܪܢܐ; f. ܐܚܪܢܝܬܐ (East-Syrian: ܐܚܪܢܝܬܐ); ܐܚܪܢܝܬ; ܐܚܪ̈ܢܐ; ܐܚܪ̈ܢܝܢ, ܐܚܪ̈ܢܐ; ܐܚܪ̈ܢܝܢ, ܐܚܪ̈ܢܝܢ, ܐܚܪ̈ܢܝܬܐ.

ܪܒ "great", "master", &c.; ܪܒܐ, ܪܒܬܐ, &c. *Pl.* "great, tall, grown up", ܪܘܪ̈ܒܐ, ܪܘܪ̈ܒܝܢ, ܪܘܪ̈ܒܐ; ܪܘܪ̈ܒܢ, ܪܘܪ̈ܒܢ, ܪܘܪ̈ܒܬܐ—"great ones": ܪܘܪ̈ܒܢܐ, ܪܘܪ̈ܒܢܝܢ, ܪܘܪ̈ܒܢܝ; ܪܘܪ̈ܒܢܝܗܘܢ, &c.; f. ܪܘܪ̈ܒܢܝܬܗܘܢ, &c.—"teachers": ܪ̈ܒܢܐ, ܪ̈ܒܢܝ, &c. In close combinations, in pl. constr. st. we have, ܪ̈ܒܝ: ܪ̈ܒܝ ܒܬܐ "householders"; ܪ̈ܒܝ ܟܘܡܪ̈ܐ "high priests", &c.—In very rare instances we may even come upon a singular ܪܘܪܒܐ, (used as an Adjective): Probably the forms ܪ̈ܒܐ &c. never occurred as plurals in the earlier times.

So ܙܥܘܪ̈ܝܢ, ܙܥܘܪ̈ܐ "small" (pl.), of which the singular in use is ܙܥܘܪ. The sing. ܙܥܘܪ is very rarely used indeed.

From ܡܛܠܠܐ "roofing", the West-Syrians form ܡܛܠ̈ܠܐ, the East-Syrians ܡܛܠܠ̈ܐ, as if it stood ܡܛܠ̈ܠܐ: thus they treat the word exactly in the way which is usually adopted with forms *med. gem.* (§ 59).

Pronominals.

§ 147. We might mention here also one or two nouns of vague meaning:

ܡܕܡ "something" (exceedingly rare, ܡܕܡܕܡ), indeclinable: a later pl. however is ܡܕ̈ܡܐ "things".

ܦܘܿܢ "a certain one" f. ܦܘܿܢܝܼܬܐ.

ܐܘܿܢܝ (East-Syrian) and ܦܘܿܢܝ (West-Syrian) "a certain number", from ܝ (ܝ) (v. § 146) and the above-mentioned ܦܘܿܢ.

3. NUMERALS.

§ 148. CARDINAL NUMBERS.

First Decade.

	m.	f.		m.	f.
1.	ܚܰܕ	ܚܕܳܐ	6.	ܐܷܫܬܳܐ, ܐܷܫܬܐ	ܫܷܬ
2.	ܬܪܷܝܢ	ܬܰܪܬܷܝܢ	7.	ܫܰܒܥܳܐ	ܫܒܰܥ
3.	ܬܠܳܬܳܐ	ܬܠܳܬ	8.	ܬܡܳܢܝܳܐ	ܬܡܳܢܷܐ
4.	ܐܰܪܒܥܳܐ	ܐܰܪܒܰܥ	9.	ܬܷܫܥܳܐ	ܬܫܰܥ
5.	ܚܰܡܫܳܐ	ܚܡܷܫ	10.	ܥܷܣܪܳܐ	ܥܣܰܪ

Rem. ܐܢܳܫܝܼܢ "some"; f. ܐܢܳܫܝܳܬܐ, may be regarded as plural of ܐܢܳܫ.

B. The numerals 11—19 show secondary forms of many sorts, and fluctuate in their vocalisation. Various modes of expressing the vowels, which are occasionally found, are very doubtful or to be rejected altogether.

Second Decade.

	m.	f.
11.	ܚܕܰܥܣܰܪ	ܚܕܰܥܷܣܪܷܐ (ܚܕܰܥܷܣܪܐ).
12.	ܬܪܶܥܣܰܪ	ܬܰܪܬܰܥܷܣܪܷܐ (ܬܰܪܬܰܥܷܣܪܐ).
13.	ܬܠܳܬܰܥܣܰܪ	ܬܠܳܬܰܥܷܣܪܷܐ (ܬܠܳܬܰܥܷܣܪܐ).
14.	ܐܰܪܒܰܥܣܰܪ (¹)	ܐܰܪܒܰܥܕܰܥܣܰܪ, commonly	ܐܰܪܒܰܥܷܣܪܷܐ (ܐܰܪܒܰܥܷܣܪܐ) and
		(ܐܰܪܒܰܥ)ܐܰܪܒܰܥ ܣܰܪ	ܐܰܪܒܰܥܷܣܪܐ (rarely).
15.	ܚܡܶܫܰܥܣܰܪ (¹)	ܚܡܶܫܬܰܥܣܰܪ	ܚܡܶܫܰܥܷܣܪܐ, ܚܡܶܫܰܥܷܣܪܷܐ.
16.(²)	East-Syrian ܫܶܬܬܰܥܣܰܪ and ܫܶܬܰܥܣܰܪ West-Syrian ܫܶܬܰܥܣܰܪ	East-Syrian ܫܶܬܬܰܥܷܣܪܐ, ܫܶܬܰܥܷܣܪܐ. West-Syrian ܫܶܬܰܥܷܣܪܐ.

(¹) Known to the author only from grammatical tradition.

(²) In all expressions of the numeral 16 attested by ancient authorities (*šet-ta'sar, šetta'sērē; šetha'sar, šetha'sērē; (e)šta'sar*) only one ܬ is taken into account:

	m.	f.
17. ܫܒܥܣܪ (rarely)	ܫܒܥܬܥܣܪ, commonly ܫܒܬܥܣܪ	ܫܒܥܣܪܐ (ܫܒܥܣܪܐ) & ܫܒܬܥܣܪܐ (rarely).
18. ܬܡܢܣܪ (rarely)	ܬܡܢܬܥܣܪ	ܬܡܢܥܣܪܐ (ܬܡܢܥܣܪܐ).
19. ܬܫܥܣܪ (rarely).	ܬܫܥܬܥܣܪ, commonly ܬܫܬܥܣܪ	ܬܫܥܣܪܐ (ܬܫܥܣܪܐ).

C. *Tens*. The tens are:

20. ܥܣܪܝܢ	60. ܫܬܝܢ, ܐܫܬܝܢ
30. ܬܠܬܝܢ	70. ܫܒܥܝܢ
40. ܐܪܒܥܝܢ	80. ܬܡܢܝܢ, also written ܬܡܐܢܝܢ
50. ܚܡܫܝܢ	90. ܬܫܥܝܢ

100 is ܡܐܐ (ܡܐܬܐ, ܡܐܐ v. § 43 E).

☞ p. 347 200 is ܡܐܬܝܢ (others ܡܐܬܝܢ).

300 is ܬܠܬܡܐܐ, &c.

1000 is ܐܠܦ.

10,000 is ܪܒܘ (better perhaps ܪܒܘ).

☞ p. 347 From ܡܐܐ appears in the emph. st. ܡܐܬܐ "one hundred", pl. ܡܐܘܬܐ. So ܐܠܦܐ from ܐܠܦ, pl. ܐܠܦܝܢ, ܐܠܦܐ (1); and ܪܒܘܬܐ from ܪܒܘ; pl. ܪܒܘܢ, ܪܒܘܬܐ. The plurals of ܐܠܦ and ܪܒܘ are joined, exactly like other substantives, to the numerals from 2 to 9, which are placed before or after them, in order to form a multiple of 1000 or 10,000; *e. g.* ܐܪܒܥܐ ܐܠܦܝܢ 4000; ܐܠܦܐ ܚܡܫܐ 5000; ܪܒܘܬܐ ܚܡܫ 50,000.

☞ p. 347 E. With the larger numbers the higher order always comes first: ܐܪܒܥܡܐܐ ܘܥܣܪܝܢ ܘܚܕܐ, 421 (f.); ܬܠܬܡܐܐ ܘܬܡܢܝܢ ܘܫܬ, 386 (f.); ܫܒܥܐ ܐܠܦܝܢ ܘܬܠܬܡܐܐ ܘܬܠܬܝܢ ܘܫܒܥܐ, 7337 (Ezra 2, 65); ܐܠܦ ܘܫܒܥܬܥܣܪ, 1017 (2, 39); ܐܪܒܥܐ ܪܒܘܢ ܘܐܠܦܝܢ ܬܪܝܢ ܘܬܠܬܡܐܐ ܘܫܬܝܢ, 42,360 (2, 64); ܚܡܫܝܢ ܘܐܪܒܥܐ ܐܠܦܝܢ ܘܐܪܒܥ ܡܐܐ, 54,400 (Num. 2, 6), &c.

Forms with suffixes. § 149. The numbers from 2 to 10 yield special *forms with suffixes*, to indicate groups:

---

accordingly we meet sometimes also with ܫܬܥܣܪ, ܐܫܬܥܣܪ, ܐܫܬܥܣܪܐ, the last the f. of *ešta'sar* and certainly to be pronounced *ešta'serē* or *ešta'esrē*.—The form usual in print ܫܬܬܥܣܪ, ܫܬܬܥܣܪܐ (after the analogy of ܫܒܬܥܣܪ, &c.) appears to be met with only in pretty late manuscripts.

☞ p. 347 (1) The pronunciation of the secondary form ܐܠܦܝܐ is uncertain. Perhaps ܐܠܦܝܐ.

2. ܬܪ̈ܝܢ "we two"; ܬܪ̈ܝܟܘܢ "you two"; ܬܪ̈ܝܗܘܢ "they two". This number alone has in addition a feminine form used in this meaning ܬܪ̈ܬܝܗܝܢ, &c.

3. ܬܠܬܝܗܘܢ "they three"(1)	7. ܫܒܥܬܝܗܘܢ
4. ܐܪܒܥܬܝܗܘܢ	8. ܬܡܢܬܝܗܘܢ (?)
5. ܚܡܫܬܝܗܘܢ	9. ܬܫܥܬܝܗܘܢ (?)
6. ܫܬܬܝܗܘܢ	10. ܥܣܪܬܝܗܘܢ

§ 150. The abs. st. of the masc. numbers from 2 to 19(?) appears in the meaning of "the nth day of the month" (always, to be sure, with prep. ܒ): Days of the month.

2. ܒܬܪ̈ܝܢ (2) "on the 2nd day of the month".
3. ܒܬܠܬܐ "on the 3rd day of the month".

4. ܒܐܪܒܥܐ	9. ܒܬܫܥܐ	13. ܒܬܠܬܥܣܪ
5. ܒܚܡܫܐ	10. ܒܥܣܪܐ	14. ܒܐܪܒܥܣܪ
6. ܒܫܬܐ, ܒܫܬܬܐ	11. ܒܚܕܥܣܪ	15. ܒܚܡܫܬܥܣܪ
7. ܒܫܒܥܐ	12. ܒܬܪܥܣܪ	17. ܒܫܒܥܬܥܣܪ
8. ܒܬܡܢܝܐ		

§ 151. Another substantive-form is ܬܪ̈ܬܥܣܪܬܐ "the Twelve" (Apostles or a similar company); ܬܪ̈ܬܥܣܪܬܗ "his Twelve"; also—ܐܪܒܥܝܬܐ "quaternion", "four together", and ܥܣܪܝܬܐ "decade". Another substantive-form.

☞ p. 347

§ 152. Forms of the constr. st. in ܬ̄ appear occasionally for the purpose of denoting things which are closely associated: ܥܣܪܬ ܡܕ̈ܝܢܬܐ "the ten cities" (Δεκάπολις); ܫܒܥܬ ܡܓܕ̈ܠܝܢ ἑπτάπυργος; ܫܬܬ ܓܦ̈ܝܗܘܢ "their six wings"; ܐܪܒܥܬ ܪ̈ܘܚܐ "the four winds"; ܫܒܥܬ ܝܘ̈ܡܝܢ "a week"; ܐܪܒܥܬ ܦܢ̈ܝܬܗ "her four points"; ܐܪܒܥܬ ܙܘ̈ܝܬܗ "his four corners".— For ܐܫܬܬ ܝܘ̈ܡܝܢ "the Hexameron (of the Creation)" ܐܫܬܐ ܝܘ̈ܡܐ is doubtless better. From the somewhat forced formation ܐܪܒܥܬ ܪ̈ܓܠܘܗܝ τετράποδον there is current as pl. ܐܪܒܥܬ ܪ̈ܓܠܝܗܘܢ or ܐܪܒܥܬ ܪ̈ܓܠܐ. Numerals in compound expressions.

(1) I give only the forms of the 3rd m. pl. Notice the hardness of the ܬ, which, however strange it may seem, is quite certain.

(2) Also ܒܬܪ̈ܝܢ, like ܚܡܫ.—I give the vowels in those forms only in which they are certain.

Other formations, of an artificial character and modelled on the Greek, are ܡܬܬܐ (say ܕܗܦܟ) ὀυοφυσίται; ܘܪܐ ܘܪܐ ἀμφοτεροδέξιος, &c.

Ordinal numbers.

§ 153.   ORDINAL NUMBERS.

1ˢᵗ ܩܕܡܝܐ (also ܩܕܡܐ, abs. st. ܩܕܡ).
2ⁿᵈ ܬܪܝܢ, f. ܬܪܬܝܢ; more rarely ܬܪܝܢ,
f. ܬܪܬܝܢ (§ 71).
3ʳᵈ ܬܠܝܬܝܐ.
4ᵗʰ ܪܒܝܥܝܐ.
5ᵗʰ ܚܡܝܫܝܐ.

6ᵗʰ ܫܬܝܬܝܐ (W.-Syrian ܫܬܝܬܝܐ).
7ᵗʰ ܫܒܝܥܝܐ.
8ᵗʰ ܬܡܝܢܝܐ.
9ᵗʰ ܬܫܝܥܝܐ.
10ᵗʰ ܥܣܝܪܝܐ.

Sometimes this formation is carried still farther, and one says, for instance, ܚܡܫܬܥܣܪܝܐ "the 15ᵗʰ"; ܥܣܪܝܐ "the 20ᵗʰ". So even ܪܒܘܬܐ "the ten-thousandth"; but there are no such forms from ܡܐ 100 or ܐܠܦ 1000. Generally speaking, these forms are avoided in practice. These are true adjectives. In the constr. st. they mostly signify so-many-fold; e. g. ܪܒܝܥ ܓܦܐ "with four wings".

Other forms derived from numerals.

☞ p. 348

§ 154. *Rem.* From the simple numbers are formed, besides, derivatives of all sorts. Thus one or two fractional numbers, like ܬܘܠܬܐ "a third part" (but ܬܘܠܬܐ "three years old"); ܪܘܒܥܐ "a fourth"; ܚܘܡܫܐ "a fifth"; ܬܘܡܢܐ "an eighth"; ܬܘܣܥܐ "a ninth"; ܥܘܣܪܐ "a tenth"(¹).— We have also adverbs, like ܬܠܝܬܐܝܬ "in the third place" (§ 155 A), &c., and verbs like ܬܠܬ "to do three times", &c. A strange formation is given in ܬܪܝܢܘܬ "for the second time": the termination is Greek in form; no doubt it was originally ܬܪܝܢܘܬܐ, an emph. st. of ܬܪܝܢܘ

4. Particles.

4. PARTICLES.

ADVERBS AND CONJUNCTIONS.

Adverbs and conjunctions.

§ 155. A. Adverbs of quality are sometimes expressed by bare nominal forms (in the abs. st.), e. g. ܫܦܝܪ "beautifully"; ܒܝܫ "badly", "ill"; ܣܪܝܩ "in vain" (which does not occur as an adjective); ܣܘܦ (end)

___
(¹) In old authors I find only ܬܘܠܬܐ, ܪܘܒܥܐ, ܚܘܡܫܐ. For "a sixth" I find, but only late, ܫܬܘܬܐ. There is a quite recent form, after the Arabic *suds*, ܣܘܕܣܐ or plainly ܣܘܕܣ.

"completely", and a few more. To this class belong the Feminine forms, which in ancient fashion preserve the *th* in the abs. st. used adverbially, particularly ܟ݁ܪܺܝܬ݂ "barely"; ܪܳܒ݂ܰܬ݂ (others ܪܳܒ݂ܰܬ݂) "very"; ܚܺܝܰܬ݂ "actively"; ܠܳܐ ܠܥܺܝܣ "without eating"; ܚܕ݂ܐ and ܚܕ݂ܳܐܺܝܬ݂ "at the same time"; ܦܐܝܐܺܝܬ݂ "finely", "handsomely"; ܕ݁ܬ݂ܰܪܬܶܝܢ "for the second time"; ܠܬܺܠܬܝܗܝܢ "for the third time"; and in ܩܰܕ݂ܶܡ ܚܕ݂ܰܘܰܬ݂ "to make a present of", "to bestow" (χαρί-ζεσθαι). So too ܐܚܪܳܝܰܬ "at last", and ܩܰܕ݂ܡܳܝܰܬ "first". From the *āyath* of these forms (f. of *āi* § 135) has then sprung ܐܳܝܺ—, *the usual termination* by means of which Adverbs of Quality are formed from all adjectives and from many substantives: ܫܰܦܝܺܪܳܐܺܝܬ݂ "beautifully"; ܫܰܪܺܝܪܳܐܺܝܬ݂ "truly"; ܕ݁ܟ݂ܝܳܐܺܝܬ݂ "purely", "pure"; ܟ݁ܣܝܳܐܺܝܬ "hidden", "secretly"; ܐܰܠܳܗܳܐܺܝܬ "divinely", &c. Notice ܐ݇ܚܪܺܢܝܳܐܺܝܬ (East-Syrian ܐ݇ܚܪܺܢܳܐܺܝܬ) "another way", (§ 146), and ܪܰܚܦ݂ܙܳܐܺܝܬ "little" (adv.) (ܪܰܚܦ݂ܙܳܐܺܝܬ also seems correct) with the *y* of the f. (§ 71).—ܝܰܝ or even ܝ is sometimes written for ܐܺܝ (§ 40 E): ܫܰܪܺܝܪܳܐܝܬ; ܙܰܕ݁ܝܩܐܝܬ "justly" = ܙܰܕ݁ܺܝܩܳܐܺܝܬ. In a few cases, a form occurs with the preposition ܒ݁:—ܒ݁ܰܐܚܪܳܝܰܬ "lastly", "at last"; ܪ݂ܗܘܡܳܐܺܝܬ "in Latin fashion"; ܒ݁ܫܬ݂ܺܝܬ݂ܳܐܺܝܬ "six-fold".

Farther, many words compounded with prepositions are used as adverbs, *e. g.* ܚܬ݂ܺܝܬ݂ "thoroughly"; ܠܡܰܚܣܶܢ "scarcely"; ܒ݁ܰܩܕ݂ܳܡܳܝܐ(¹) "in truth", in rare instances ܚܣܳܡܺܝܬ݂ and ܒ݁ܚܳܣܶܡ; ܒ݁ܩܰܕ݂ܡܳܝܰܘ(¹) "first" (vowels not quite certain). ܚܕ݂ܐ, ܚܣܺܝܦ (§ 156) "all at once"; ܐܰܟ݂ܚܰܕ݂, ܐܰܟ݂ܚܰܕ݂ ܣܰܐܺܝܢ, ܐܰܟ݂ܚܰܕ ܐܰܝܢܐ "at the same time".

B. Some adverbs of place and time, most of them being compounds of prepositions, are as follows:—

ܠܥܶܠ "above".

ܠܬܰܚܬ, ܒ݁ܠܬܰܚܬ "below".

ܠܬܰܚܬܳܐ(¹), (ܠܬܰܚܬܳܐ ܕ݁ܓ݁ܒ݂) "downward".

☞ p. 348

ܠܩܕ݂ܡܰܝ (East-Syrian, as it seems, ܠܩܰܕ݂ܡܝ) "in earlier times", "of old".—

So ܒ݁ ܠܩܕ݂ܡܰܝ; and ܒ݁ ܠܩܰܕ݂ܡܳܝܬܐ, ܠܩܰܕ݂ܡܳܝܬܐ(¹).

ܒ݁ ܡܩ݂ܒ݂ܶܠ "overagainst".

ܗܳܫܐ, ܗܐ "now" (present time).

(¹) Notice the peculiar plural-ending.

7*

ܥܕܡܫܐ, ܥܕܡܫ (vocalisation not quite certain) "up till now, hitherto, still".

ܝܘܡܢܐ, ܝܘܡܢ "to-day"; ܡܚܪ "to-morrow"; ܐܬܡܠ "yesterday"; ܡܢܬܡܠ "two days ago".

☞ p. 348 ܐܫܬܩܕܝ "last year"; ܠܫܢܬܐ, ܠܫܢܬܗ, ܠܫܢܬ "next year". ܐܡܬܝ "when?"; ܗܝܕܝܢ, ܗܝܕܝܟ [1] "then".

☞ p. 348 ܐܝܟܐ "where?" (ܐܝܟܘ "why?"): ܗܪܟܐ "here"; ܡܟܐ (= ܡܢ ܟܐ), ܗܡܟܐ "from here", "hence"; ܐܝܡܟܐ "where...from", "whence?"; ܠܟܐ "hither", "this way", "on this side" (ܠܟܐ ܡܢ); ܡܢ ܗܐ ܡܟܐ "from this place"; ܐܠܟܐ "where?"; ܠܐܠܟܐ "whither, where...to?" (these two forms are found only in one old text); ܗܪܟܐ "here"; ܬܢܢ "here"; ܬܡܢ "there"; ܗܪܬܡܢ "yonder": ܠܗܠ "away there", "on that side" (ܠܗܠ ܡܢ).

ܡܟܝܠ "now"; ܥܕܡܟܝܠ, ܥܕܟܝܠ "up till now", "still", "yet"; ܗܟܝܠ "now", "thus".

ܡܬܘܡ, ܡܢ ܡܬܘܡ, ܡܟܡܬܘܡ "at all times".

ܟܒܪ "already", "perhaps", "possibly", &c.

ܟܕܘ "sufficiently", "already".

ܡܢ ܟܕܘ "already".

The phrases ܒܪ ܝܘܡܗ ("son of his day") "on the same day" ܒܪ ܫܥܬܗ "at the same hour" and ܒܪ ܒܣܬܪܐܝܬ "backward" (§ 321 B) are
☞ p. 348 used quite adverbially.

C. Adverbs of Quality of the most general kind; Connective Adverbs, of which some have more special significations of Space or of Locality; and pure *Conjunctions*:

ܐܝܟܢܐ, ܐܝܟܢ "how?"; ܐܝܟ "as" (and its combinations: cf. § 364); ܗܟܢܐ, ܗܟܢ "thus" (with Prepositions: ܒܬܪ ܗܟܢ "thereupon"; ܡܢ ܗܟܢ "thereof, therefrom", &c.). ܗܟܘܬ "thus"; ܟܢ "thereupon"; with ܘ, ܘܟܢ
☞ p. 348 or ܘܐܟܢ, ܘܟܢ (ܒܬܪ ܟܢ "thereupon"; ܡܛܠ ܟܢ "on this account").—ܟܝܢ
☞ p. 348 "thus". ܟܝܬ "namely". *ܕܝܢ [2] (on very rare occasions heading a

---

(1) Also, ܡܢ ܗܝܕܝܢ "thenceforward", &c. In the same way many more of the adverbs mentioned here may be combined with Prepositions.

(2) In what follows, an asterisk (*) marks those particles which never, or only exceptionally, stand at the beginning of the sentence.

clause) "thus"; *ܟܝܠ "thus". *ܗܟܘܪ "thus". ܐܪܐ ἄρα, ἆρα. *ܟܝܬ "to wit" (particularly in citing foreign remarks or thoughts). *ܓܝܪ(1) "for".— ܠܐ "not"; ܠܘ "not".

ܘ "and", "also"; ܐܦ "also"; ܬܘܒ "farther", "again"; ܐܘ "or"; ܐܘܟܝܬ "*sive*":—ܒܪܡ "but"; *ܕܝܢ (properly "thén") "but". *ܡܢ μέν.— *ܒܠ, ܬܘ "please!", "pray!".

ܐܢ "if"; ܐܠܘ "if"; ܐܠܐ = ܐܢ ܠܐ "but", "if not"; ܐܦܢ "although". ܥܕ "until", "so long as". ܠܘܝ, ܐܠܘܗܝ "*utinam*".

ܕ "that" (in the widest sense), and many prepositions combined therewith: ܟܕ "at the time, when", "when"; ܟܕ "whereas"; ܟܕܓܘܢ "thus" (from ܟܕ + γοῦν); ܡܢ ܕ "since", and so with other prepositions (§ 360).— ܟܐ ܕ "where"; ܐܝܟܐ ܕ "where"; ܐܝܟ ܕ, ܐܝܟܢܐ ܕ, ܐܝܟ ܡܐ ܕ, ܐܝܟܡܐ ܕ, ܐܟܙܢ ܕ (ܐܟܙܢ ܕ; even mere ܐܟܙܢ), and many others, "as", "just as". ܡܐ ܕ "when", "at the time, when"; ܥܕܡܐ ܕ "until", &c.

ܠܡܐ, ܕܠܡܐ, ܕܕܠܡܐ, ܕܪܡ, ܕܕܪܡ, "if perhaps; possibly; lest perhaps" (§ 373).

The following, amongst others, are pure Greek words: ܛܟܐ τάχα "perhaps"; ܐܝܛܐ εἶτα; ܛܘܣ, ܛܐܘܣ τέως; ܡܠܠܘܢ μᾶλλον; ܡܠܝܣܛܐ μάλιστα.

PREPOSITIONS.

Prepositions. List of prepositions.

§ 156. Prepositions,—or Nouns in the constr. st. used adverbially—, are either simple in origin, or have sprung from the combination of such forms with other short prepositions. Most of them may even take personal suffixes. Those below, marked with *pl.*, assume the plural form in *ai* before suffixes. Certain variations of form before suffixes are also met with here and there:—

ܒ "in" ܠ "to" ܡܢ "from"	The *n* of ܡܢ is assimilated in the adverbials ܡܚܕܐ, ܡܚܕܐܘ "all at once"; "suddenly"; "forthwith"; ܡܟܝܠ; ܡܟܝܠܘܡ; ܡܟܐ; ܡܪܝܫ; ܡܪܝܫ "anew,—in one's turn", which are also sometimes written ܡܢ ܚܕܐ &c. (2).

(1) ܓܝܪ and ܕܝܢ are genuine Syriac words, which, however, have been employed almost entirely to imitate γάρ and δέ.

(2) In pronunciation the *n* of *men* was frequently assimilated even at other times.

ܒܝܬ[1] (no suff.); ܒܝܢܬ; ܒܝܢܝ "between".

☞ p. 348 ܬܚܝܬ (not used with suff.); ܬܚܘܬ pl.; ܬܚܝܬܝ (before suff. too?) "under".

ܥܠ as pl. "upon" (ܥܠܝܟ, ܥܠܘܗܝ &c.; in poetry often ܥܠܝܟ, ܥܠܘܗܝ &c.); ܠܥܠ "over".

ܥܡ "with".

ܠܘܬ "with", "to".

ܓܒ (§ 21 C) pl. "with", "to".

ܩܕܡ pl. "before": ܩܘܕܡܬ "before" (not with suff.), *ܩܘܕܡܝ (only before suff.).

ܚܕܪ (not with suff.), ܚܕܪܝ "round", "about".

ܚܠܦ pl.; *ܚܘܠܦܝ (only before suff.) "instead of".

ܥܕ "until", "up to" (not with suff.).

*ܐܟܘܬ (only before suff.) "like".

ܡܛܠ (ܡܛܘܠ; not with suff.); *ܡܛܠܬ, *ܡܛܘܠܬ (only before suff.) "for the sake of", "on account of".

ܒܬܪ (from ܐܬܪ + ܒ "on the track of") "after".

ܒܣܬܪ (ܣܬܪ + ܒ "hiding from") "behind".

ܒܠܥܕ pl. "without".

ܠܘܩܒܠ "against": ܠܥܒܪ pl. (§ 49 A) "*coram*".

ܠܦܘܡ "in conformity with".

ܡܢ ܒܠܝ [*ex inopia*] "without" (not with suffix).[2]

Of these, some have already been formed by intimate blending with ܠ and ܒ. And so ܠ and ܡܢ are still set before many prepositions, in some cases without perceptible modification of the meaning, *e. g.* ܡܢ ܠܘܬ "παρά τινος"; ܡܢ ܒܣܬܪ "from behind, behind"; ܠܒܬܪ "after"; ܡܢ ܬܚܘܬ "below", &c. Cf. ܡܢ ܠܒܪ "from without" [ܠܒܪ being "*foris in campo*"]; ܡܢ ܠܓܘ "from within" [ܠܓܘ meaning "*in medio*"]; alongside of ܡܢ ܒܪ, ܡܢ ܓܘ.

---

(1) Not to be confounded with the like-sounding ܒܝܬ when used adverbially, meaning "in the house of, *i. e.* in the place of".

(2) The limits of the idea of a Preposition are not exactly determined. Several of the cases cited here might be excluded, such as ܠܦܘܡ "according to the mouth", ܠܥܝܢ "in the eye",—while others might be added, like ܒܝܕ "by the hand of", "by means of".

ܒܠܥܕ ܡܢ may be used for "without", just like ܒܠܥܕ alone.

ܠ must of necessity stand in ܥܕܡܐ ܠ "as far as, up to": rarely are found ܥܕܡܐ ܠܘܬ, ܥܕܡܐ ܒ "as far as in" ("even in"). Very rare is ܠܥܠ ܡܢ "over, above". ☞ p. 348

§ 157. With suffixes: (1) Singular Forms; ܥܡܟ, ܥܡܗ, ܥܡܗܘܢ, &c., according to § 145 A. So ܠܝ, ܠܟ, ܒܗ, ܠܗ, &c.; but ܒܝ and ܠܝ. (2) Plural Forms: ܩܕܡܝ, ܩܕܡܝܟ, ܩܕܡܝܗ̈ܝ, ܩܕܡܝܗܘܢ, &c., likewise according to § 145 A. Such is the procedure too with those forms which even without suffixes end in *ai* (pl.), (to which class also belongs ܥܠ for *ܥܠܝ, sg.): ܥܠܘܗܝ, ܥܠܝܟ, &c. (ܥܠܝܗ̈ܝ, &c.). — Preposition with suffixes. ☞ p. 348

ܒܬܪ and ܡܛܠܬ keep their *a* before the suff. of the 1st sing., and 2nd and 3rd pl.: ܒܬܪܝ, ܡܛܠܬܝ; ܒܬܪܟܘܢ, ܡܛܠܬܗܘܢ: but ܒܬܪܗ, ܡܛܠܬܗ, &c. So ܠܘܩܒܠܟ, ܠܘܩܒܠܗܘܢ, &c. (more rarely ܠܘܩܒܠܝܗܘܢ) but ܠܘܩܒܠܝܗ.

ܒܝܢܬ for the most part takes the suffixes at once, yet ܒܝܢܝܗܘܢ is found alongside of ܒܝܢܬܗܘܢ, ܒܝܢܬܟܘܢ.

II. VERBS.

II. Verbs.

§ 158. A. The Syriac verb appears, sometimes with *three* radicals, sometimes with *four* (§ 57). It makes no difference in the inflection, whether the verb is primitive, or has been derived from a noun. — Preliminary observations.

B. The *Tenses* are *two* in number: *Perfect* and *Imperfect* (called also Aorist and Future). The different Persons, Genders, and Numbers are indicated in the Perfect by terminations, and in the Imperfect by prefixes, or by prefixes together with terminations. Add to these the *Imperative*, which agrees for the most part with the Imperfect in vocalisation, but is inflected by terminations only. Several of the terminations in the Perfect and the Imperative are now silent (§ 50). Lastly fall to be considered the Verbal Nouns, closely related to the finite Verb, viz, the *Infinitive*, and the *Participles* (as well as *Nomina actionis*, and *Nomina agentis*). The inflectional marks in the finite verb are always the same, except that they occasionally undergo a slight alteration when ܝ is the final radical. They are as follows:—

C. *Perfect.*

☞ p. 348

Sg. 3 m. —	Pl. 3 m. ܘ (silent); ܘܢ
3 f. ܰܬ	3 f. — (or silent ܝ); ܶܝܢ (1)
2 m. ܬ݁	2 m. ܬܽܘܢ
2 f. ܬܝ (the ܝ silent)	2 f. ܬܶܝܢ
1. ܶܬ	1. ܢ, ܢܢ

Imperfect. (2)

Sg. 3 m. ܢ	Pl. 3 m. ܢ — ܘܢ
3 f. ܬ	3 f. ܢ — ܳܢ
2 m. ܬ	2 m. ܬ — ܘܢ
2 f. ܬ — ܺܝܢ	2 f. ܬ — ܳܢ
1. ܐ	1. ܢ (3)

Imperative.

Sg. m. —	Pl. m. ܘ (silent), ܘܢ
f. ܝ (silent)	f. ܶܝܢ (4), ܝ (silent).

D. Where longer and shorter endings appear together, the latter are in all cases nearer the original forms. Contrary to the general rule given in § 43 [v. § 43 C], the assumption of these longer [and later] endings occasions no falling-away of short vowels in the open syllable; compare cases like ܩܛܰܠܬܽܘܢ, ܩܛܰܠܬܽܘܢ (sg. ܩܛܰܠܬ, ܩܛܰܠܬ) with ܢܶܩܛܠܽܘܢ, ܢܶܩܛܠܽܘܢ (sg. ܢܶܩܛܽܘܠ, ܢܶܩܛܠ); ܚܶܙܘܽܢ with ܢܶܚܙܘܽܢ. ܝܢ ܝ is also found written for ܢ, *e. g.* ܩܛܠܝ ܢ = ܩܛܠܝܢ. In the Imperative pl. f. the longer form is far more usual than the shorter.

☞ p. 349

E. The 3. f. pl. Perf. is written with a ܝ (and ܶ) in later West-Syrian texts; but the old orthography is retained with the East-Syrians,

---

(1) In more ancient MSS. ܢ is also found written without ܝ, *e. g.* ܣܓܕܢ for ܣܓܶܕܝܢ "worshipped", &c. (§ 4 A).

(2) The vocalisation of the Prefixes is different in different cases.

(3) The 1st pl. of the Impf. invariably coincides with the 3rd m. sg.

(4) In the older MSS. also written with ܢ alone, *e. g.* ܫܡܥܢ for ܫܡܥܝܢ "hear ye".

according to which the form is exactly the same as the 3 sg. m., except
in the case of verbs that have ܘ for their last radical. The West-
Syrians frequently supply the 3 f. sg. Impf. too with a purely orthographic ܝ, to distinguish it from the 2 m. (§ 50 B). Also in the shorter
form of the Imperative pl. f. the ܝ might well be merely a later addition.

TRI-RADICAL VERBS.

Tri-radical
verbs.

§ 159. These form the following *Verbal Stems* [or Forms, sometimes called *Conjugations*]: the simple conjugation *Peal* (ܦܥܰܠ; Hebrew
Qal) with its reflexive *Ethpeel* (ܐܶܬܦܥܶܠ); the conjugation employed to
denote, first, intensity and then too the causative and other allied
meanings,—having the middle radical doubled, and called *Pael*, (ܦܰܥܶܠ,
Hebrew *Piel*) together with its reflexive *Ethpaal* (ܐܶܬܦܰܥܰܠ Hithpael); the
causative conjugation *Aphel* (ܐܰܦܥܶܠ Hiphil), with its reflexive, Ettaphal
(ܐܶܬܬܰܦܥܰܠ or ܐܶܬܬܰܦܥܰܠ § 36).

The reflexives have for the most part acquired a passive meaning.

Rem. Ettaphal is much the most rarely used of these Reflexives,
and is upon occasion replaced by Ethpeel and Ethpaal, *e. g.* ܐܶܬܟܪܶܙ "to
be preached", instead of ܐܶܬܬܰܟܪܰܙ from ܐܰܟܪܶܙ; ܐܶܬܒܰܙܰܚ "to be mocked",
instead of ܐܶܬܬܰܒܙܰܚ from ܐܰܒܙܰܚ.

☞ p. 349

Attention is called to § 26 A and § 26 B in dealing with the
Reflexives.

Forms seldomer used, like the Causative ܥܰܒܶܕ "to enslave" and
several others, we find it more to the purpose to take in with the Quadriliteral (§ 180 f.).

VERBS WITH THREE STRONG RADICALS.

Verbs with
three strong
radicals.
Peal.

§ 160. A. *Peal.* In this conjugation there is a specially *Transitive*
form, which in the Perfect has *a* as the fundamental vowel of the second
radical, and in the Imperfect and Imperative *o* (*u*) or it may be *e*; and
a specially *Intransitive* form with *e* in the Perfect, and *a* in the Imperfect and Imperative: (1) ܩܛܰܠ, ܢܶܩܛܽܘܠ, ܩܛܽܘܠ "to kill"; ܥܒܰܕ, ܢܶܥܒܶܕ,
ܥܒܶܕ "to do". (2) ܦܳܫ, ܢܶܦܽܘܫ, ܦܽܘܫ "to be left remaining".

Of strong verbs with *e* in the Impf. and Impt. the only examples are ܢܶܙܒܶܢ, and ܙܒܶܢ "to buy".(¹) A few verbs *primae n* also take *e* (§ 173 B), as well as a few weak verbs.

Several intransitive verbs have the *e* of the Perfect changed into *a*, and thus have a uniform *a* in both Perfect and Imperfect. Thus ܫܠܰܛ, ܢܶܫܠܰܛ "to rule"; ܠܐܶܐ, ܢܶܠܐܶܐ "to be tired out"; ܣܦܰܩ, ܢܶܣܦܰܩ "to be enough"; ܪܘܰܙ, ܢܶܪܘܰܙ "to exult", and the other verbs which treat *w* as a firm consonant; ܓܕܰܫ, ܢܶܓܕܰܫ "to happen"; and several others.(²) We exclude from this list verbs *secundae or tertiae gutturalis* (§ 169 *sq.*).

Several have secondary forms: thus ܚܣܶܢ, ܢܶܚܣܶܢ and ܚܣܰܢ, ܢܶܚܣܽܢ "to be strong", "to overpower", although ܚܣܶܢ in the Perf., and ܢܶܚܣܶܢ in the Impf. might be most in favour. Through an intermixture of transitive and intransitive expression, the following verbs have *e* in the Perf., and *o* in the Impf. and Impt.: ܣܓܶܕ, ܢܶܣܓܽܘܕ "to reverence"; ܫܬܶܩ, ܢܶܫܬܽܘܩ "to keep silence"; ܩܪܶܒ, ܢܶܩܪܽܘܒ "to be near" (cf. ܢܚܶܬ, ܢܶܚܽܘܬ "to descend", and, it is said, ܟܚܶܫ, ܢܶܟܚܽܘܫ "to be lean", § 175 B).(³)

☞ p. 349 B. The only certain remains of a Perfect in *o* are found in ܣܡܽܘܪ "bristled", "stood up" Job 7, 5; 30,3; Lamentations 4, 8; Ps. 119, 120; and ܐܶܟܡܽܘܪ "they (f.) grew black", Nahum 2, 10.

Hardness and softness of the radicals. § 161. The letters ܒ ܓ ܕ ܟ ܦ ܬ [Beghadhkephath] are, in conformity with general rules (§ 23), soft, as 1st Radical in the Impf. and Inf. of the *Peal*: they are hard as 2nd rad. in the Impf. and Inf., but soft elsewhere in that stem; as 3rd rad. they are soft, except after a closed syllable; accordingly they are hard in the 3rd f. sg. Perf., the 1st sg. Perf., and the lengthened forms of the Participle. Examples: (1) ܢܶܬܒܽܘܪ; ܡܶܬܒܰܪ. (2) (a) ܢܶܪܟܽܘܒ, ܢܶܪܟܒܽܘܢ; ܡܶܪܟܰܒ; (b) ܪܟܶܒ, ܪܟܺܝܒ, &c. (3) (a) ܪܕܰܦ, ܢܶܪܕܽܘܦ, &c.; (b) ܪܶܕܦܰܬ, ܪܶܕܦܶܬ, ܪܳܕܦܺܝܢ.

Ethpeel. § 162. In the *Ethpeel* notice the transposition of the vowel in the Imperative ܐܶܬܩܰܛܰܠ, also written ܐܶܬܩܰܛܰܠ or ܐܶܬܩܛܶܠ § 17 (as compared with Perf. ܐܶܬܩܛܶܠ; Impf. ܢܶܬܩܛܶܠ).

(¹) In very rare cases occurs also the Impt. ܙܒܽܘܢ.

(²) Some, which grammarians have cited, are uncertain or utterly incorrect.

(³) The forms of the Impf. of Peal verbs, cited by Payne-Smith in '*Thes. syr.*' are not all well attested; several are decidedly inaccurate.

Here the consonants that may be softened are always hard as 1ˢᵗ rad., soft as 2ⁿᵈ, and soft as 3ʳᵈ except after a closed syllable, and in the Imperative, thus— : ܒܐܦܟܓ, &c., but ܒܐܦܟܓܟ, ܒܐܦܟܟܓ, and ܕܐܡܓܟ.

§ 163. The characteristic of the *Pael* and *Ethpaal* is the doubling ⟨Pael and Ethpaal.⟩ of the 2ⁿᵈ radical. This letter is accordingly always hard, just as the 3ʳᵈ is always soft. In Ethpaal the 1ˢᵗ rad. is always hard; in Pael it is soft in the Impf., with the exception of the 1ˢᵗ pers., where hardening appears: ܐܦܟܝ, &c. (§ 23 F). ☞ p. 349

The Imperative Ethpaal—with the East-Syrians, and in older times even in the West,(¹)—coincided with the Perfect; but with the West-Syrians at a later date the form of the Ethpeel came into very general use in this case, although the 3ʳᵈ rad. could never be hard. Thus Imperative ܐܬܓܙܝ, West-Syrian ܐܬܓܙܝ (usually written ܐܬܓܙܝ or ܐܬܓܙܝ). Still even the West-Syrians retained in some cases the original form, e. g. always ܐܬܪܚܡ "take (thou) pity on"(²).

§ 164. The characteristic of the *Aphel* is a foregoing ܐ, of which ⟨Aphel and Ettaphal.⟩ the guttural sound [ʼ] falls away, however, after prefixes; on ܐܫܟܚ "to find" with e, v. §§ 45 and 183.

The 1ˢᵗ rad. is constantly soft after prefixes, the 2ⁿᵈ hard, and the 3ʳᵈ soft. It is the same with *Ettaphal*.

§ 165. *Participles.* The Participles undergo changes for Gender ⟨Participles.⟩ and Number, as adjectives. Peal, Pael and Aphel have an Active and a Passive Participle. The Part. act. Peal, has *ā* after the 1ˢᵗ rad., and *e* after the 2ⁿᵈ, which falls away without a trace, when it comes into an open syllable (§ 106): sg. m. ܩܛܠ; sg. f. ܩܛܠܐ; pl. m. ܩܛܠܝܢ; pl. f. ܩܛܠܢ. The Part. pass. has an *ī* after the 2ⁿᵈ rad. (§ 110): ܩܛܝܠ, ܩܛܝܠܝܢ, &c. All other participles have an *m* as a prefix. The participles of Ethpeel, Ethpaal, and Ettaphal, as well as the active participles of Pael and Aphel, agree completely in their vocalisation with the corresponding forms

---

(¹) The old poets always employ the trisyllabic forms.

(²) On the other hand several of the abbreviated forms have also penetrated into the East-Syrian traditional usage, such as ܐܬܙܝܥ "shake thyself" Is. 52, 2, for which Ephr. III, 537 B still has ܐܬܬܙܝܥ.

of the finite verb, *e. g.* ܡܶܬ݂ܩܛܶܠ, ܡܶܬ݂ܩܰܛܠܳܐ, like ܢܶܬ݂ܩܛܶܠ, ܢܶܬ݂ܩܰܛܠܽܘܢ; ܡܶܬ݂ܩܰܛܰܠ, ܡܶܬ݁ܬ݁ܰܩܛܰܠ; ܡܩܰܛܶܠ; ܡܰܩܛܶܠ, &c. The participles passive of Pael and Aphel have *a* in place of *e* after the 2nd rad.: ܡܩܰܛܰܠ, ܡܰܩܛܰܠ. When this *a* comes into an open syllable, it falls away exactly like the *e* of the Active form, and so ܡܩܰܛܠܳܐ, ܡܰܩܛܠܺܝܢ, for example, may as easily be active as passive.

On the joining of the Participles to the attached subject-pronouns, v. § 64 A.

Nomina agentis. § 166. *Nomina Agentis* are formed by the Peal in the form ܩܳܛܽܘܠܳܐ (ܩܳܛܽܘܠ, ܩܳܛܽܘܠܺܝܢ, &c., § 107); and by the other stems by attaching *ān* to the Participles: Ethpeel ܡܶܬ݂ܕܰܒܪܳܢܳܐ; Pael ܡܕܰܒܪܳܢܳܐ; Ethpaal ܡܶܬ݂ܕܰܒܪܳܢܳܐ; Aphel ܡܰܥܒܪܳܢܳܐ; Ettaphal ܡܶܬ݁ܬ݁ܰܥܒܪܳܢܳܐ (§ 130).

Infinitive. § 167. *Infinitive.* The Infinitive Peal has the form ܡܶܩܛܰܠ (also written ܡܩܛܘܠ [1], it is true, but incorrectly); the other Infinitives have $\bar{a}$ after the 2nd rad., and $\bar{u}$ for a termination, *i. e.* they take the form of the abs. st. of Abstract Nouns in *ūth*: the *th* re-appears before Pronominal suffixes.

Rem. On *Nomina actionis* v. § 117 (123); cf. also § 109.

---

(1) In Ex. 5, 17, the reading ܡܶܕܒܰܚ is well supported, alongside of the usual ܡܶܕܒܰܚ.

§ 168. REGULAR VERB.

	Peal.		Ethpeel.	Pael.
Perf. sg. 3 m.	ܩܛܠ	ܕܚܠ	ܐܬܩܛܠ	ܩܛܠ
3 f.	ܩܛܠܬ	ܕܚܠܬ	ܐܬܩܛܠܬ	ܩܛܠܬ
2 m.	ܩܛܠܬ	ܕܚܠܬ	ܐܬܩܛܠܬ	ܩܛܠܬ
2 f.	ܩܛܠܬܝ	ܕܚܠܬܝ	ܐܬܩܛܠܬܝ	ܩܛܠܬܝ
1	ܩܛܠܬ	ܕܚܠܬ	ܐܬܩܛܠܬ	ܩܛܠܬ
pl. 3 m.	ܩܛܠܘ	ܕܚܠܘ	ܐܬܩܛܠܘ	ܩܛܠܘ
	ܩܛܠܘܢ	ܕܚܠܘܢ	ܐܬܩܛܠܘܢ	ܩܛܠܘܢ
3 f.	ܩܛܠ, ܩ̈ܛܠܝ	ܕܚܠ, ܕ̈ܚܠܝ	ܐܬܩܛܠ, ܐܬܩ̈ܛܠܝ	ܩܛܠ, ܩ̈ܛܠܝ
	ܩܛܠ̈ܝܢ	ܕܚܠ̈ܝܢ	ܐܬܩܛܠ̈ܝܢ	ܩܛܠ̈ܝܢ
2 m.	ܩܛܠܬܘܢ	ܕܚܠܬܘܢ	ܐܬܩܛܠܬܘܢ	ܩܛܠܬܘܢ
2 f.	ܩܛܠܬܝܢ	ܕܚܠܬܝܢ	ܐܬܩܛܠܬܝܢ	ܩܛܠܬܝܢ
1	ܩܛܠܢ	ܕܚܠܢ	ܐܬܩܛܠܢ	ܩܛܠܢ
	ܩܛܠܢܢ	ܕܚܠܢܢ	ܐܬܩܛܠܢܢ	ܩܛܠܢܢ
Impf. sg. 3 m.	ܢܩܛܘܠ	ܢܕܚܠ	ܢܬܩܛܠ	ܢܩܛܠ
3 f.	ܬܩܛܘܠ (ܬܩܛܘܠܝ)	ܬܕܚܠ (ܬܕܚܠܝ)	ܬܬܩܛܠ (ܬܬܩܛܠܝ)	ܬܩܛܠ (ܬܩܛܠܝ)
2 m.	ܬܩܛܘܠ	ܬܕܚܠ	ܬܬܩܛܠ	ܬܩܛܠ
2 f.	ܬܩܛܠܝܢ	ܬܕܚܠܝܢ	ܬܬܩܛܠܝܢ	ܬܩܛܠܝܢ
1	ܐܩܛܘܠ	ܐܕܚܠ	ܐܬܩܛܠ	ܐܩܛܠ
pl. 3 m.	ܢܩܛܠܘܢ	ܢܕܚܠܘܢ	ܢܬܩܛܠܘܢ	ܢܩܛܠܘܢ
3 f.	ܢܩ̈ܛܠܢ	ܢܕ̈ܚܠܢ	ܢܬܩ̈ܛܠܢ	ܢܩ̈ܛܠܢ
2 m.	ܬܩܛܠܘܢ	ܬܕܚܠܘܢ	ܬܬܩܛܠܘܢ	ܬܩܛܠܘܢ
2 f.	ܬܩ̈ܛܠܢ	ܬܕ̈ܚܠܢ	ܬܬܩ̈ܛܠܢ	ܬܩ̈ܛܠܢ
1	ܢܩܛܘܠ	ܢܕܚܠ	ܢܬܩܛܠ	ܢܩܛܠ
Impt. sg. m.	ܩܛܘܠ	ܕܚܠ	ܐܬܩܛܠ	ܩܛܠ
f.	ܩܛܘܠܝ	ܕܚܠܝ	ܐܬܩܛܠܝ	ܩܛܠܝ
m.	ܩܛܘܠܘ	ܕܚܠܘ	ܐܬܩܛܠܘ	ܩܛܠܘ
	ܩܛܘܠܘܢ	ܕܚܠܘܢ	ܐܬܩܛܠܘܢ	ܩܛܠܘܢ
f.	ܩ̈ܛܘܠܝ	ܕ̈ܚܠܝ	ܐܬܩܛ̈ܠܝ	ܩ̈ܛܠܝ
	ܩܛܘܠ̈ܝܢ	ܕܚܠ̈ܝܢ	ܐܬܩܛܠ̈ܝܢ	ܩܛܠ̈ܝܢ
Part. act. m.	ܩܛܠ	ܕܚܠ	ܡܬܩܛܠ	ܡܩܛܠ
f.	ܩܛܠܐ	ܕܚܠܐ	ܡܬܩܛܠܐ	ܡܩܛܠܐ
pass. m.	ܩܛܝܠ	ܕܚܝܠ		ܡܩܛܠ
f.	ܩܛܝܠܐ	ܕܚܝܠܐ		ܡܩܛܠܐ
Inf.	ܡܩܛܠ	ܡܕܚܠ	ܡܬܩܛܠܘ	ܡܩܛܠܘ

	Ethpaal.	Aphel.	Ettaphal.
Perf. sg. 3 m.	ܐܬܩܛܠ	ܐܩܛܠ	ܐܬܬܩܛܠ
3 f.	ܐܬܩܛܠܬ	ܐܩܛܠܬ	ܐܬܬܩܛܠܬ
2 m.	ܐܬܩܛܠܬ	ܐܩܛܠܬ	ܐܬܬܩܛܠܬ
2 f.	ܐܬܩܛܠܬܝ	ܐܩܛܠܬܝ	ܐܬܬܩܛܠܬܝ
1	ܐܬܩܛܠܬ	ܐܩܛܠܬ	ܐܬܬܩܛܠܬ
pl. 3 m.	ܐܬܩܛܠܘ	ܐܩܛܠܘ	ܐܬܬܩܛܠܘ
	ܐܬܩܛܠܘܢ	ܐܩܛܠܘܢ	ܐܬܬܩܛܠܘܢ
3 f.	ܐܬܩܛܠ, ܐܬܩܛܠܝ	ܐܩܛܠ, ܐܩܛܠܝ	ܐܬܬܩܛܠ, ܐܬܬܩܛܠܝ
	ܐܬܩܛܠܝܢ	ܐܩܛܠܝܢ	ܐܬܬܩܛܠܝܢ
2 m.	ܐܬܩܛܠܬܘܢ	ܐܩܛܠܬܘܢ	ܐܬܬܩܛܠܬܘܢ
2 f.	ܐܬܩܛܠܬܝܢ	ܐܩܛܠܬܝܢ	ܐܬܬܩܛܠܬܝܢ
1	ܐܬܩܛܠܢ	ܐܩܛܠܢ	ܐܬܬܩܛܠܢ
	ܐܬܩܛܠܢܢ	ܐܩܛܠܢܢ	ܐܬܬܩܛܠܢܢ
Impf. sg. 3 m.	ܢܬܩܛܠ	ܢܩܛܠ	ܢܬܬܩܛܠ
3 f.	ܬܬܩܛܠ (ܬܬܩܛܠܝ)	ܬܩܛܠ (ܬܩܛܠܝ)	ܬܬܬܩܛܠ (ܬܬܬܩܛܠܝ)
2 m.	ܬܬܩܛܠ	ܬܩܛܠ	ܬܬܬܩܛܠ
2 f.	ܬܬܩܛܠܝܢ	ܬܩܛܠܝܢ	ܬܬܬܩܛܠܝܢ
1	ܐܬܩܛܠ	ܐܩܛܠ	ܐܬܬܩܛܠ
pl. 3 m.	ܢܬܩܛܠܘܢ	ܢܩܛܠܘܢ	ܢܬܬܩܛܠܘܢ
3 f.	ܢܬܩܛܠܢ	ܢܩܛܠܢ	ܢܬܬܩܛܠܢ
2 m.	ܬܬܩܛܠܘܢ	ܬܩܛܠܘܢ	ܬܬܬܩܛܠܘܢ
2 f.	ܬܬܩܛܠܢ	ܬܩܛܠܢ	ܬܬܬܩܛܠܢ
1	ܢܬܩܛܠ	ܢܩܛܠ	ܢܬܬܩܛܠ
Impt. sg. m.	ܐܬܩܛܠ (ܐܬܩܛܠ)	ܐܩܛܠ	ܐܬܬܩܛܠ
f.	ܐܬܩܛܠܝ (ܐܬܩܛܠܝ)	ܐܩܛܠܝ	ܐܬܬܩܛܠܝ
pl. m.	ܐܬܩܛܠܘ (ܐܬܩܛܠܘ)	ܐܩܛܠܘ	ܐܬܬܩܛܠܘ
	ܐܬܩܛܠܘܢ (ܐܬܩܛܠܘܢ)	ܐܩܛܠܘܢ	ܐܬܬܩܛܠܘܢ
f.	ܐܬܩܛܠܝ (ܐܬܩܛܠܝ)	ܐܩܛܠܝ	ܐܬܬܩܛܠܝ
	ܐܬܩܛܠܝܢ (ܐܬܩܛܠܝܢ)	ܐܩܛܠܝܢ	ܐܬܬܩܛܠܝܢ
Part. act. m.	ܡܬܩܛܠ	ܡܩܛܠ	ܡܬܬܩܛܠ
f.	ܡܬܩܛܠܐ	ܡܩܛܠܐ	ܡܬܬܩܛܠܐ
pass. m.		ܡܩܛܠ	
f.		ܡܩܛܠܐ	
Inf.	ܡܬܩܛܠܘ	ܡܩܛܠܘ	ܡܬܬܩܛܠܘ

VERBS WITH GUTTURALS.(1)

Verbs with gutturals. *Mediae gutturalis.*

§ 169. A guttural (ܗ, ܚ, ܥ) or *r*, as 2nd radical, sometimes causes *a* to appear after it in the Impf. and Impt. Peal, instead of *o*, or again,—a change which also happens in certain other cases (v. § 160),—it may cause *a* to appear in the Perf. Peal instead of *e*. Which of the two cases,—outwardly identical,—is before us, it is not always easy to say. (2) Thus we have ܕܥܰܛ, ܢܶܕܥܰܛ (as well as ܢܶܕܥܽܘܛ) "to step"; ܙܥܰܩ, ܢܶܙܥܰܩ "to cry out"; ܛܚܰܢ (West-Syrian ܛܚܶܢ (3)), ܢܶܛܚܰܢ "to grind"; ܡܪܰܕ, ܢܶܡܪܰܕ "to rebel"; ܥܪܰܒ, ܢܶܥܪܰܒ "to set (of heavenly bodies)", (but ܥܪܰܒ, ܢܶܥܪܽܘܒ "to sift" and "to give security"); ܥܗܰܕ, ܥܗܶܕ (§§ 37; 174 G), ܢܶܥܗܰܕ "to remember", and others besides, although several are rather doubtful. As the examples which have been given above indicate, some of these forms are fluctuating.

However, in most of these verbs *mediae guttur.* or *r*, no such effect appears, *e. g.* ܗܦܰܟ, ܢܶܗܦܽܘܟ "to overthrow"; ܥܪܰܩ, ܢܶܥܪܽܘܩ "to flee"; ܣܗܶܕ, ܢܶܣܗܶܕ "to testify", &c.

Tertiae gutturalis.

§ 170. A guttural (ܗ, ܚ, ܥ) or *r*, as 3rd radical, when it closes the syllable, always changes *e* into *a* (§ 54). Thus, for example, ܦܳܬܰܚ, ܡܦܰܬܰܚ, ܡܫܰܡܥܳܗ, ܐܶܫܡܰܥܬܽܘܢ, ܐܶܫܡܰܥ, ܐܰܫܡܰܥ, ܐܶܫܬܡܰܥ, which correspond respectively to the forms ܢܳܛܶܠ, ܡܩܰܛܶܠ, ܡܩܰܛܠܶܗ, ܐܶܩܛܠܬܽܘܢ, ܐܶܩܛܶܠ, ܐܰܩܛܶܠ, ܐܶܬܩܛܶܠ. The difference in sound between the Active and Passive Participles accordingly falls away in Pael and Aphel; *e. g.* ܡܦܰܬܰܚ is the Act. Part. Pael (equivalent to ܡܩܰܛܶܠ) as well as the Pass. (equivalent to ܡܩܰܛܰܠ).

This rule is illustrated also in the Peal of many Intransitives, which properly would have *e* in the Perfect. To this class belong the great majority of those verbs *tert. guttur.* and *r*, which have *a* in the Perf., Impf.,

---

(1) Exclusive of ܐ.

(2) *Translator's Note*: For instance, in the example ܡܪܰܕ, ܢܶܡܪܰܕ,—is this form a result of the influence of the guttural upon an original form ܡܪܶܕ, ܢܶܡܪܰܕ, or upon an original form ܡܪܰܕ, ܢܶܡܪܽܘܕ? If the former, the guttural has taken effect upon the *e* of the *Perf.*, changing it into *a*; if the latter, the guttural has taken effect upon the *u* or *o* of the *Impf.*, changing it into *a*.

(3) Seems less original.

and Impt. Peal throughout, *e. g.* ܫܡܰܥ (for *šeme'*), ܢܶܫܡܰܥ "to hear"; ܛܒܰܥ, ܢܶܛܒܰܥ "to sink in, to be immersed" (Trans. ܛܒܰܥ, ܢܶܛܒܽܘܥ "to set in, to immerse"); ܪܬܰܚ, ܢܶܪܬܰܚ "to seethe"; ܒܨܰܪ, ܢܶܒܨܰܪ "to be wanting", and *all* that have ܗ, *e. g.* ܬܡܰܗ, ܢܶܬܡܰܗ "to wonder".

Of course in some *few* cases descending from remote times such a guttural has changed even the *o* of the Impf. and Impt. into *a*; thus:—ܕܟܰܪ, ܢܶܕܟܰܪ
☞ p. 349 "to remember"; ܓܪܰܪ, ܢܶܓܪܰܪ "to drag away"; ܬܒܰܪ, ܢܶܬܒܰܪ and ܢܶܬܒܽܘܪ "to break";
☞ p. 349 ܦܬܰܚ, ܢܶܦܬܰܚ, rarely ܢܶܦܬܽܘܚ "to open"; ܦܠܰܚ, ܢܶܦܠܽܘܚ, rarely ܢܶܦܠܰܚ "to serve, to cultivate"; ܕܒܰܚ, ܢܶܕܒܰܚ and ܢܶܕܒܽܘܚ "to slaughter". In the *large majority*, however, *of transitive verbs tert. guttur.*, we have *o* alone (sometimes of original formation, sometimes of later analogous formation). This vowel has even penetrated to some extent into original Intransitives, as in ܢܶܫܠܽܘܚ, a secondary form to ܢܶܫܠܰܚ, "to strip off" (but only ܢܶܫܠܽܘܚ "to send"); ܢܶܬܒܽܘܥ (more rarely) alongside of ܢܶܬܒܰܥ "to seek"; ܢܶܒܠܽܘܥ alongside of ܢܶܒܠܰܥ "to devour"; ܢܶܒܨܽܘܪ, more rarely ܢܶܒܨܰܪ, "to grow less" (only ܢܶܒܨܽܘܪ "to remove").

Rem. The practice of treating as exceptions, cases of *o* in verbs *tert. guttur.* and *r* is accordingly incorrect: such verbs surpass in number not only (by a large majority) those transitives which have *a* in the Impf., but even those intransitives, of which the *a* of the Impf. is original.

Verba mediae ܐ.

VERBA MEDIAE ܐ.

§ 171. A. These verbs present no difficulty, if the rules given in § 33 are attended to. The ܐ falls away in pronunciation whenever it stands in the end of a syllable. The same thing happens, at least according to the usual pronunciation, when the ܐ comes after a consonant without a full vowel. The vowel of the ܐ in the latter case is transferred to the 1st radical. This applies also to the vowel which has to appear with ܐ in place of the mere *sh^e^va* [§ 34]. Thus:

In the Perf. Peal ܫܐܶܠ (= שְׁאֵל) "demanded", ܫܶܐܠܰܬ, ܫܶܐܠܶܬ, ܫܶܐܠܬܽܘܢ, ܫܶܐܠܘ, &c.—Impf. ܢܶܫܐܰܠ, ܢܶܫܐܠܽܘܢ (= נִשְׁאֲלוּן) &c.—Impt. ܫܐܰܠ, ܫܐܰܠܘ &c.—Part. act. ܫܳܐܶܠ, ܫܳܐܠܺܝܢ; Passive ܫܐܺܝܠ, ܫܐܺܝܠܺܝܢ.—Inf. ܡܶܫܐܰܠ.—

Ethpeel ܐܶܫܬܶܐܶܠ ([1]), ܐܶܫܬܶܐܠܰܬ—ܢܶܫܬܶܐܶܠ, ܢܶܫܬܰܐܠܽܘܢ; Impt. ܐܶܫܬܶܐܶܠ.—Inf. ܡܶܫܬܰܐܳܠܽܘ, &c.—Aphel ܐܰܫܶܠ, ܐܰܫܠܶܬ,—ܢܰܫܶܠ, ܢܰܫܠܽܘܢ,—ܡܰܫܳܠܽܘ, &c.

Rem. In the Ethpeel the West-Syrians read ܐܶܫܬܰܐܠܰܬ for ܐܶܫܬܶܐܠܰܬ.—Part. pass. of Aphel in the emph. st. ܡܰܒܐܫܳܐ; East-Syrian ܡܰܒܶܐܫܳܐ (§ 34). In the Peal is found ܟܶܐܒܬ, ܟܶܐܒܬ݁ܳ, ܟܶܐܒܬܽܘܢ with hard ܒ݁ (through blending with the otherwise like-sounding forms *mediae gem.* § 178); but the more original form with soft ܒ݂, ܟܶܐܒ݂ܬ &c. is met with, as well as the other.

B. In the Pael and Ethpaal the vocalisation is quite the same as in the case of strong radicals: ܫܰܐܶܠ ("to ask"), ܫܰܐܶܠܬ, ܫܰܐܶܠܬܽܘܢ, ܢܫܰܐܠܽܘܢ, ܡܫܰܐܠܽܘ; ܐܶܫܬܰܐܰܠ, ܢܶܫܬܰܐܠܽܘܢ.

Rem. For ܐܶܬܒܶܐܫ (Ethpeel) "to be evil", there occurs frequently with the West-Syrians, even at an early date, ܐܶܬܬܐܶܒܶܫ (with transition to *primae* ܐ).—In like manner, occasionally ܬܶܐܒܰܫ, ܬܐܒܰܫ "*displicet*" (3 f. sg. Impf.) for ܬܶܒܰܐܫ.

VERBA TERTIAE ܐ.

§ 172. A. In some few verbs a final radical ܐ in Pael and Ethpaal still operates as a guttural, by altering *e* into *a*. The ܐ itself must of course fall away in pronunciation, and must give up its vowel to the preceding consonant. Of these verbs, ܒܰܝܰܐ "to comfort" is of specially frequent occurrence. It has the following inflection, exactly like ܩܰܛܶܠ for instance, with the exception of the falling away of the ܐ in pronunciation:— *Verba tertiae* ܐ.

Pael: Perf. sg. 3 m.	ܒܰܝܰܐ	pl. 3 m.	ܒܰܝܰܐܘ
3 f.	ܒܰܝܰܐܬ	3 f.	ܒܰܝܰܐ (ܒܰܝܰܐܶܝܢ)
2 m.	ܒܰܝܰܐܬ	2 m.	ܒܰܝܰܐܬܽܘܢ
2 f.	ܒܰܝܰܐܬܝ	2 f.	ܒܰܝܰܐܬܶܝܢ
1	ܒܰܝܰܐܬ	1	ܒܰܝܰܐܢ

Impf. ܢܒܰܝܰܐ, ܬܒܰܝܐܺܝܢ, ܢܒܰܝܐܽܘܢ, ܢܒܰܝܐܳܢ.
Impt. ܒܰܝܰܐ, ܒܰܝܰܐܝ, ܒܰܝܰܐܘ, ܒܰܝܰܐܶܝܢ.
Part. act. and pass. ܡܒܰܝܰܐ, ܡܒܰܝܐܺܝܢ.—Inf. ܡܒܰܝܳܐܽܘ.
Ethpaal ܐܶܬܒܰܝܰܐ; ܢܶܬܒܰܝܰܐ; ܢܶܬܒܰܝܐܽܘܢ, &c.

([1]) "Was demanded", and "begged to be excused", or "declined" (παραιτεῖσθαι).

Rem. In these and similar verbs un-etymological modes of writing are frequently met with, e. g. ﺟﻴﺮﺍ (§ 35), ﻣﺠﻨﺎﺋﻪ (§ 33 B), &c.

B. In rare cases, however, there appear transitions to the inflection of verbs *tert.* ﻭ (§ 176) even in those verbs, which usually are still inflected after the above fashion. It is no doubt owing to this tendency, that forms like ﺣﻴﺎﻩ, ﻻﺣﻴﺎﻩ, equivalent to ﺣﺰﺍﻩ, ﻻﺣﺰﺍﻩ are occasionally pronounced with an audible ﻩ (like ﺣﻴﻪ; with the diphthong). Farther there appears ﻻﺣﻤﺎﺏ Impt. sg. f. instead of ﻻﺣﻤﺎﺏ (like ﻻﻳﺤﻤﻰ *tert.* ﻭ), ﻻﻏﻤﺎﺕ Perf. 3 pl. f. instead of ﻻﻏﻤﺪﺕ "were polluted" (like ﻻﻳﺤﺪﺕ), where, but for the mere retention of a written ﺍ, the form of *tert.* ﻭ is completely attained. Thus ﻻﻳﺨﻤﺎﺏ alternates directly with ﻻﻳﺨﻤﺎ (ﻻﻳﺨﻤﺎ) "to be proud"; ﺯﺍﺏ with ﺯﺍﺍ (also written ﺯﺍﺏ, § 33 B) "to pollute".

C. Quite isolated is an example of a similar formation for the *Peal* in the finite verb, viz.—ﻣﻜﻮ (like ﻭﺟﺰ) "were dark-coloured" (properly from κυάνεος § 117, Rem.); from this verb also there is an Ettaphal ﻻﻣﻜﻰ and what is like a Part. pass. Pael (pl. f.) ﺗﻜﻤﻞ.—Participles of Peal are found in the substantive forms ﺛﻮﺭﺍ "tutor", pl. ﺛﻮﺭﺍ (from θεωρία?)—to which belong the Pael ﺛﺎﺭ, and Ethpaal ﻻﺛﺎﺭ (also written ﺛﻮﺭ, ﻻﺛﻮﺭﺍ), with the *nomen agentis* ﻣﻬﺜﺮﺍ "tutor"—, and ﻣﻬﻴﻨﺎ "hater", "enemy", pl. ﻣﻬﻴﻨﻰ, f. ﻣﻬﺎﻧﻴﺎ, and the adjective Part. pass. ﻣﻨﻴﻼﺍ "hated (f.)", pl. m. ﻣﻨﺴﻼﺏ, ﻣﻨﺘﻼﺍ (verbal Part. ﻣﻬﻰ, ﻣﻬﻨﻰ, ﻣﻬﻴﺐ, constr. st. ﻣﻬﺘﻴﺐ(¹)). ﻻﻫﻤﺎ "I have been hated" appears also.

Rem. The verbs mentioned in this section might thus be held to be about the only ones, in which the ﺍ is still treated as a guttural. Otherwise Verbs, which originally were *tert.* ﺍ, pass completely over to the formation *tert.* ﻭ (as even ﻓﺎﻩ "to be beautiful", which is usually reckoned as belonging to this section).

(¹) In Aphr. 286, 5, for ﻗﻼﺍ ﻣﻬﺘﻴﺐ "who hate reproof" there is a variant ﻣﻬﻘﻼ ﻗﻼﺍ "haters (enemies) of reproof".—Cf. farther ﻣﻨﻴﺎ "hated" § 113 (and ﻣﻨﻴﺎ "hatred" § 100). The other derivatives look as if from *tert.* ﻭ.

VERBA PRIMAE ܢ.

§ 173. A. The *n* as 1ˢᵗ rad. is assimilated to the following one, if *Verba* it comes directly upon it (§ 28), which can happen only in the Peal, Aphel *primae ܢ* and Ettaphal,—thus from ܢܦܩ "to go out", ܐܦܶܩ = ܐܢܦܶܩ; ܢܶܦܽܩ = ܐܶܦܽܩ, &c. Several verbs are excepted, which have ܗ as 2ⁿᵈ rad.; *e. g.* from ܢܗܪ "to be bright", we have ܢܶܢܗܰܪ, ܐܰܢܗܰܪ; and from ܢܗܡ (the West-Syrians, it seems, have ܢܒܗܡ) "to roar", ܢܶܢܗܰܡ, ܐܶܢܗܽܘܡ. So from ܢܫܦ "to be barefooted", ܐܰܢܫܶܦ (but from ܢܚܬ "to descend", ܢܶܚܽܘܬ, ܐܰܚܶܬ, &c.).

Rem. Rare cases, like ܢܕܽܘܪܶ̈ for the usual ܢܶܕܪܶ̈ "vows"; ܡܢܟܣ = ܡܢܟܣܽܘ "to slaughter" (Inf.), &c. are probably rather graphical than gram- ☞ p. 349 matical deviations.

B. In the Peal, some verbs have, along with *a* in the Perf., *a* also in the Impf. (and Impt.). Thus in particular ܢܣܒ "to take", ܢܶܣܰܒ; ܢܦܚ "to blow", ܢܶܦܰܚ; and of course the intransitives *tert. gutt.* ܢܕܚ "to come forth", ܢܶܕܰܚ; ܢܒܥ "to well forth", ܢܶܒܰܥ; ܢܬܪ "to fall off", ܢܶܬܰܪ &c. Only a few preserve the intransitive pronunciation in the Perf., like ܢܩܦ "to adhere to", ܢܶܩܰܦ.

Of transitives ܢܛܪ "to keep" has *a* in the Impf., ܢܶܛܰܪ, but ܢܶܛܽܘܪ is met with also. *O* is found besides in the Impf. with *tert. gutt.* in ܢܕܪ "to vow", ܢܶܕܽܘܪ; ܢܩܒ "to dig *or* cut through"; ܢܩܽܘܒ; ܢܦܚ "to blow *or* sound", ܢܶܦܽܘܚ; ܢܒܚ "to bark", ܢܶܒܽܘܚ.

Many more of these verbs have *o* in the Impf. and Impt. (*v.* what follows).

In the Impf. (Impt.) the following have *e*:— ܢܦܠ "to fall"; ܢܶܦܶܠ; ܢܓܕ "to draw", ܢܶܓܶܕ; ܢܥܪ "to shake", ܢܶܥܶܪ; ܢܦܨ "to cast lots", ܢܶܦܶܨ; add to these ܢܬܠ "gives" (of which ܝܰܗܒ serves as the Perf. § 183).

Notice farther ܢܚܬ "to step down", "to descend", ܢܶܚܽܘܬ, and ܢܫܦ "to be lean", ܢܶܫܽܘܦ (not certain) § 160 A.

C. In many of these verbs the Impt. Peal loses the *n* altogether. Thus ܣܰܒ "take"; ܦܽܘܚ "blow"; ܩܽܘܦ "adhere to"; ܛܰܪ or ܛܽܘܪ "keep"; ܦܶܠ "fall"; ܓܶܕ "draw"; ܥܰܪ "shake"; ܚܽܘܬ "step down"; ܩܽܘܒ "perforate"; ܡܚܰܝ "strike"; ܫܽܘܦ "sift"; ܨܽܘܒ "plant"; ܟܽܘܣ "slay"; ܫܽܘܩ "kiss"; ܨܽܘܩ "pour"; ܛܽܘܠ "put away"; ܦܽܘܩ "go out".

8*

On the other hand the *n* is retained in the Impt. in *e. g.*, ܢܕܘܪ "vow", ܢܟܘܬ "bite", and perhaps in the most of those which have *a* in the Impf., (farther in those which are at the same time *tert.* ܝ, like ܢܨܝ, from ܢܨܐ "to quarrel") and in those which do not assimilate the *n*, like ܢܓܘܗ "become clear", "dawn"(¹).

The following synopsis shows the principal forms, which deviate from the usual type of the verb.

Peal.

Perf. ܢܦܩ, ܢܣܒ, ܢܚܬ.

Impf.			Impt.		
ܢܦܘܩ	ܢܣܒ	ܢܚܘܬ	ܦܘܩ	ܣܒ	ܚܘܬ
ܐܦܘܩ	ܐܣܒ	ܐܚܘܬ	ܦܘܩܝ	ܣܒܝ	ܚܘܬܝ
ܐܦܩܝܢ	ܐܣܒܝܢ	ܐܚܬܝܢ	ܦܘܩܘ	ܣܒܘ	ܚܘܬܘ
			ܦܘܩܘܢ	ܣܒܘܢ	ܚܘܬܘܢ
ܢܦܩܘܢ &c.	ܢܣܒܘܢ &c.	ܢܚܬܘܢ &c.	ܦܘܩܝܢ	ܣܒܝܢ	ܚܘܬܝܢ

Aphel ܐܦܩ, ܐܦܩܬ; ܢܦܩ, ܢܦܩܘܢ—ܡܦܩ; ܡܦܩܘ.
Ettaphal ܐܬܬܦܩ, ܐܬܬܦܩܬ &c.

E. *Rem.* In these verbs softness or hardness in the consonants depends in every case absolutely on the general rules given in § 23, and that which is noted in § 161 *et sqq.* A consonant to which *n* is assimilated has the value of a double consonant, and must accordingly be hard, while the one that follows can never be hard.

VERBA PRIMAE ܐ.

Verba primae ܐ.

§ 174. A. The ܐ must, in accordance with § 34 take a full vowel in place of a *sheva*, and this vowel is *e* in the Perf. Peal and in the whole of Ethpeel: ܐܡܪ, ܐܬܐܡܪ, while it is *a* in the Part. pass. Peal: ܐܡܝܪ.

Rem. The East-Syrians use *a* even in the Perf. Peal of some verbs: ܐܠܨ "oppressed"; ܐܟܪ "was angry"; ܐܪܥ "met";—farther, ܐܒܠ "mourned", and ܐܦܐ "baked", which are at the same time *tertiae* ܝ. But in other cases they too have ܐܡܪ, &c.

☞ p. 349

(¹) In many verbs *primae* ܢ the formation of the Impt. does not admit of being established with any certainty. The vowels too of the Perf. and Impf. in many verbs of this class are uncertain.

B. The prefix-vowel of the Impf. Peal and the Inf. Peal forms, with the radical ܐ, an *ē* (§ 53), which for the most part becomes ◌ܶ (1) with the West-Syrians in those verbs that have *a* in the Impf., as well as in those verbs that are at the same time *tert.* ܝ,—while in verbs with *o* it remains *ē*. With *a* in the Impf. and Impt. are ܐܒܰܕ "to perish", ܢܐܒܰܕ; ܐܡܰܪ "to say", ܢܐܡܰܪ; and perhaps two or three more: add thereto ܐܙܰܠ "to go", ܢܐܙܰܠ, but Impt. ܙܶܠ (§ 183). To this class belong also ܐܦܳܐ "to bake", ܢܐܦܶܐ; ☞ p. 349 ܐܠܳܐ "to mourn", ܢܐܠܶܐ; ܐܬܳܐ "to come", ܢܐܬܶܐ, but Impt. ܬܳܐ (§ 183). On the other hand with *o* are ܐܓܰܪ "to hire", ܢܐܓܽܘܪ; ܐܚܰܕ "to hold", ܢܐܚܽܘܕ; ܐܟܰܠ "to eat", ܢܐܟܽܘܠ, and many others. ☞ p. 349

Verbs with *o* take *a* as the vowel of the ܐ in the Imperative: ܐܰܟܽܘܠ, the others take *e*: ܐܶܡܰܪ.

C. In the Ethpeel notice the application of § 34, according to which, in certain forms the *e* which ܐ must take instead of the *sh*^e^*va* is thrown forward on the ܬ; the same thing is done with the regular *a* of the other forms of Ethpeel, as well as of all those of Ethpaal: ܐܶܬ݂ܶܐܟܶܪ and ܐܶܬ݂ܰܐܟܰܪ "to be oppressed"; ܐܶܬ݂ܶܐܡܰܪ (or ܐܶܬ݂ܶܐܡܰܪ §§ 17; 34 *Rem.*); f. ܬܶܬ݂ܶܐܡܪܺܝܢ, Impt. ܐܶܬ݂ܶܐܡܰܪ. In the Ethpeel of ܐܚܰܕ "to take", however, the ܐ is assimilated to ܬ instead, the ܬ becomes hard and the *e* falls away (§ 36): ܐܶܬܬܚܶܕ (written also ܐܬܚܕ merely), ܬܶܬܬܚܶܕ, &c. Others too have sometimes a like formation, *e. g.* ܐܬܣܪܬܘܢ "you are bound" (say ܐܶܬܬܣܰܪܬܘܢ). It is exactly the same with ܐܶܬܬܰܢܰܚ "to groan" (2).

D. For the Pael it has to be noted that the 1st sing. Impf. is not ܐܶܐܰܟܶܪ, like ܐܶܩܰܛܶܠ, but simply ܐܰܟܶܪ. Of course the *a* of the ܐ passes over to the prefixes in cases like ܬܰܐܟܶܪ, ܡܰܐܟܶܪ. In ܐܰܠܶܦ "to teach" this ܐ is almost always parted with, even in writing, *e. g.* ܢܰܠܶܦ = ܢܰܐܠܶܦ, ܡܰܠܶܦ &c. Individual cases of this kind are found also with other verbs, *e. g.* ܡܰܪܰܚ "goes away", instead of ܡܰܐܪܰܚ (= מְאָרֵחַ Denominative from ܐܽܘܪܚܳܐ "way").

(1) There are sporadic exceptions in accordance with § 46, like ܬܶܐܟܪܘܢ Sap. 14, 10 as variant for ܬܐܟܪܘܢ; ܬܶܐܒܕܘܢ Deut. 4, 26 as var. for ܬܐܒܕܘܢ; and various forms from ܐܙܠ (§ 183) (ܬܶܐܠܘܢ θρηνήσετε John 16, 20 Bernstein).

(2) The language takes ܬܢܚ as root and sometimes even forms derivatives from it, like ܬܘܢܚܐ "groaning".

E. In the Aphel and Ettaphal([1]) verbs *primae* ܝ pass over wholly to the formation of verbs *primae* ܘ (v. § 175 B). Thus from ܐܘܟܠ, ܐܘܟܠܐ, ܐܘܟܠܝܢ; ܝܘܟܠ; ܝܘܟܠ. (Only ܝܠܝ, which is at the same time *tertiae* ܝ, forms, in accordance with the analogy of the original *primae* ܝ, ܐܝܠܕ, ܐܝܠܝܕ. Cf. also the old Aphel ܗܝܡܢ "to believe", "to intrust to", ܡܗܝܡܢ.)

F. *Rem.* In other respects also indication is given of a certain effort in verbs *primae* ܝ to cross over to the class *primae* ܘ (ܝ). Thus with ܝܠܦ "to teach" the Peal is ܝܠܦ "to learn"; thus farther one says ܐܘܟܡ "to be black" and ܐܪܟ "to be long", for אכם, ארך. Similarly there is also found the verbal adjective (§ 118) ܝܒܝܕ for the usual ܐܒܝܕ "lost".

G. According to the West-Syrian pronunciation, even verbs beginning with ܕܟ (§ 37) share in the treatment of verbs *primae* ܝ, thus: ܝܕܟܪ "to remember", ܐܝܕܟܪ &c. (East-Syrian ܝܕܟܪ, ܐܝܕܟܪ). — Still more completely of course does this happen with those verbs whose initial ܥ has already become ܝ in writing, like ܝܦܥ "to meet" (from ערע), ܐܝܦܥ, Aphel ܐܘܦܥ.

H. The following survey shows the principal forms which deviate from the common type.

Peal.

Perf. ܐܘܟܕ, ܐܘܟܕܐ, ܐܘܟܕܬ, ܐܘܟܕܝ, ܐܘܟܕܝܢ.

Impf. { ܬܐܟܘܠ, ܐܟܘܟܡ, ܐܟܘܠܝ, ܐܟܘܠܝܢ, ܢܐܟܘܠ, — ܐܟܘܠ (1st sing.).
{ ܐܐܟܕ, ܢܐܟܕ, ܬܐܟܕ, ܝܐܟܕܝ, ܝܐܟܕܝܢ, — ܐܟܕ (1st sing.).

Impt. { ܐܟܘܟܬ, ܐܟܘܟ, ܐܟܘܟܡ, ܐܟܘܟܝ, ܐܟܘܟܝܢ.
{ ܐܟܕ, ܐܟܕܝ, ܐܟܕܝܢ, ܐܟܕܬ, ܐܟܕܝ.

Inf. ܡܐܟܕ; ܡܐܟܕ. Part. pass. ܐܟܝܕ.

Ethpeel.

Perf. ܐܬܐܟܕ, ܐܬܐܟܕܐ, ܐܬܐܟܕܬ. — Impf. ܝܬܐܟܕ, ܝܬܐܟܡ. — Impt. ܐܬܐܟܕ.([2])
— Part. ܡܬܐܟܕ, ܡܬܐܟܕ. — Inf. ܡܬܐܟܕ.

([1]) So too in the Shaphel ܡܘܟܬ, ܐܘܟܬ (§ 180).

([2]) There are several examples of this form. But ܐܬܠ as Impt., also occurs with three syllables; thus, no doubt, ܐܬܠܝ Ephr. II, 347 D, and repeatedly, (where Ethpaal is scarcely admissible).

Pael.

Perf. ܐܰܟ݁ܶܠ.—Impf. ܢܐܰܟ݁ܶܠ, ܢܐܰܟ݁ܠܽܘܢ.—ܐܰܟ݁ܶܠ (1st sing.).—Impt. ܐܰܟ݁ܶܠ.—Part. act. ܡܐܰܟ݁ܶܠ, ܡܐܰܟ݁ܠܳܐ; pass. ܡܐܰܟ݁ܰܠ, ܡܐܰܟ݁ܠܳܐ.—Inf. ܡܐܰܟ݁ܳܠܽܘ.

Ethpaal.

Perf. ܐܶܬ݂ܐܰܟ݁ܰܠ, ܐܶܬ݂ܐܰܟ݁ܠܰܬ݂, &c.—Impf. ܢܶܬ݂ܐܰܟ݁ܰܠ, ܢܶܬ݂ܐܰܟ݁ܠܽܘܢ.—Impt. ܐܶܬ݂ܐܰܟ݁ܰܠ (ܐܶܬ݂ܐܰܟ݁ܰܠ).— Part. ܡܶܬ݂ܐܰܟ݁ܰܠ, ܡܶܬ݂ܐܰܟ݁ܠܳܐ.—Inf. ܡܶܬ݂ܐܰܟ݁ܳܠܽܘ.

Aphel ܐܰܘܟ݁ܶܠ }
Ettaphal ܐܶܬ݁ܬ݁ܰܘܟ݁ܰܠ } v. Inflection of verbs *primae* ܘ.

VERBA PRIMAE ܘ AND ܝ.

§ 175. A. In verbs of this sort, which besides are not numerous, ܝ appears throughout, except in Aphel and Ettaphal, (and setting aside the exceptions mentioned in § 40 A, viz: Part. act. Peal ܘܳܠܶܐ "it is fitting", and the Pael ܘܰܥܶܕ "to appoint", along with Ethpaal ܐܶܬ݂ܘܰܥܰܕ) both for original ܝ and for original ܘ (and in part for ܐ, v. § 174 F). *Verba primae* ܘ *&* ܝ.

Instead of ܝ with *sh*[e]*va*, ܝܺ ī has to appear (§ 40 C) in Peal and Ethpeel, thus:—ܝܺܕܰܥ, ܝܺܠܶܕ, ܢܶܬ݂ܝܺܕܰܥ, ܡܶܬ݂ܝܺܠܶܕ, &c. ܐܝ is often written instead of it, in the beginning of the word, *e. g.* ܐܝܪܬܘ = ܝܺܪܬܘ "they inherited", &c.[1]

In the Perf. Peal, those verbs which do not end in a guttural or *r* (with the exception of ܝܗܰܒ §§ 38; 183) have *e*, thus ܝܺܪܶܬ݂ "inherited"; ܝܺܠܶܕ "bare"; ܝܺܬ݂ܶܒ "sat"; ܝܺܩܶܕ "burned"; but of course ܝܺܕܰܥ "knew"; ܝܺܩܰܪ "was heavy".

In the Impf. and Inf. Peal the two most frequently occurring verbs of this class, ܝܺܕܰܥ and ܝܺܬ݂ܶܒ, lose their ܝ, but instead double (and harden) their 2nd rad., and so become here like to verbs *primae* ܢ. They farther lose the ܝ in the Impt. Peal (as also does ܝܗܰܒ which does not appear in the Impf.), thus: ܢܶܕ݁ܰܥ, ܢܶܬ݁ܶܒ; ܡܶܕ݁ܰܥ, ܡܶܬ݁ܰܒ; ܕ݁ܰܥ, ܬ݁ܶܒ (ܗܰܒ), &c. (cf. ܡܶܕ݁ܰܥ, ܡܶܕ݁ܥܳܐ § 126 B). The rest pass over entirely, in the Impf. and Inf. Peal, to the analogy of those verbs *primae* ܐ, which have *a* in the Impf., *e. g.*

(1) An individual case is found even of ܐܝܬܪܬ "I have gained" = ܝܶܬ݂ܪܶܬ݂ Apost. Apocryph. 306, 7; also ܐܝܕܥܬ "she knew" = ܝܺܕܥܰܬ݂ Spicileg. Syr. 40, 8 (both cases after ܠܐ).

ܒܠܝܓ, ܒܠܝܕܘܢ (cf. § 23 D) from ܓܠܓ [1]. These have likewise *a* in the Impt. and preserve the 1ˢᵗ rad. as ـܒ.

B. In the *Aphel*, ܝܢܩ "to suck" still shows the radical ـܒ: ܐܝܢܩ; and so also runs ܐܝܠܠ "to wail", (if it is really an Aphel). All the rest have *au* in the *Aphel* and *Ettaphal*: ܐܘܬܒ, ܐܬܬܘܬܒ; ܐܘܕܥ, ܐܬܬܘܕܥ; ܐܘܒܫ "to dry up", &c. In this form ܐܘܒܫ occurs as well as ܝܒܫ. In the inflection this *au* or *ai* is treated exactly like *e. g.* the *aq* in ܐܩܝܡ.

C. In the Pael and Ethpaal these verbs are not discriminated from strong verbs: *e. g.* ܝܒܫ, ܐܬܝܒܫ; ܝܒܒ, ܝܒܒܠ, &c. are exactly like ܩܝܡ, &c.

D. The following tabular statement shows the principal forms which deviate from the general type:

Peal.

Perf. ܝܪܬ [2], ܝܪܦܝ, ܝܪܦܬ, ܝܪܦܬܘܢ, ܝܪܦܬ.

Impf. { ܐܪܬ—ܐܪܦܘܢ, ܐܪܦܝ, ܐܪܦܝ, ܐܪܦ (1ˢᵗ sing.).
 { ܐܕܥ—ܐܕܥܝ, ܐܕܥ, ܐܕܥ, ܐܕܥܘܢ.
 { ܐܪܬ—ܐܪܬܘܢ, ܐܪܬ, ܐܪܬܝ, ܐܪܬ.

Impt. { ܝܪܬ, ܝܪܦܘܢ, ܝܪܦܬܝ.
 { ܐܕܥ, ܐܕܥܝ, ܐܕܥܬ.
 { ܐܪܬ, ܐܪܬܝ, ܐܪܬܬ.

Inf. ܡܐܪܬ—ܡܐܕܥ, ܡܐܒܫ.—Part. pass. ܝܪܬ.

Ethpeel.

Perf. ܐܬܝܪܬ, ܐܬܝܪܦܝ, ܐܬܝܪܦܬ.—Impf. ܝܬܝܪܬ, ܝܬܝܪܦܘܢ.—Inf. ܡܬܝܪܦܘ.

Aphel.

ܐܘܕܥ, ܐܘܕܥܝ—ܐܘܪܬ, ܝܘܕܥ, ܝܘܕܥ—ܡܘܕܥ—ܡܘܕܥܘ.

Ettaphal.

ܐܬܬܘܕܥ, ܐܬܬܘܪܒܝ—ܐܬܬܘܕܥ, ܝܬܬܘܕܥ—ܝܬܬܘܕܥ—ܡܬܬܘܕܥ—ܡܬܬܘܕܥܘ.

Rem. Examples of the Impt. Ethpeel like ܐܬܝܪܬ and Impt. Ethpaal ܐܬܬܘܕܥ scarcely ever appear.

---

[1] Here too with the West-Syrians the ـܠ is occasionally still retained instead of the ـܠ, *e. g.* ܢܐܠܦ (Deut. 33, 19 according to Barh.), ܢܓܠܦ (Bernstein's Johannes S. VI), instead of the usual ܢܐܠܦ, ܢܓܠܦ (ܡܐܠܕ) variant of ܡܐܠܕ Matth. 26, 74).

[2] "to borrow", "to lend".

VERBA TERTIAE ܝ.

§ 176. A. Verbs *tertiae* ܝ deviate from the strong verb much more decidedly than the classes hitherto described. The radical i, y brings about a vowel-termination, and is fused with the endings in various ways. In the Perfect Peal a transitive form of pronunciation with $\bar{a}$ in the 3rd sing. m. (like ܪܡܐ "threw") and an intransitive with $\bar{\imath}$ are to be distinguished; but side by side with the latter form there appears and that widely, one with $\bar{a}$ (e. g. ܚܕܝ and ܚܕܝ "rejoiced" [1]). In the Impt. Peal the transitive form in $\bar{\imath}$ has almost completely supplanted the intransitive form in ai, v. *infra* D.

B. The *Perf.*, except in Peal, always has $\bar{\imath}$, which, like the $\bar{\imath}$ of the intransitive Peal, is retained even before endings, and with o forms the diphthong ܐܘ *īu*. The later West-Syrians often attach an additional ܝ, of course a silent one, to the 3rd pl. f. as a diacritic mark, e. g. ܐܬܓܠܝ̈ = ܐܬܓܠܝ "they (f.) are revealed".

Notice the difference between the 1st sing. ܝܬ with soft ܬ and the 2nd sing. m. ܝܬ with hard ܬ in all classes [2]; in the transitive Peal, at least with the East-Syrians, it farther happens that the 1st sing. has $\bar{e}$ (ܝܬ).

C. The *Impf.*, when without any of the endings, terminates in ܐ— in all classes; the same is the case with the active *Participles*. With that ܐ— the ending *ūn* blends into ܘܢ (West-Syrian *ūn*), and the ending *īn* into *ēn*.

D. The *Impt.* sing. m. ends in $\bar{a}$ in the Pael, Ethpaal, Aphel, (and Ettaphal?).—In the Impt. Ethpeel the ending with the West-Syrians is ai, e. g. ܐܬܓܠܝ "reveal thyself"; ܐܬܚܘܝ "show thyself"; the East-Syrians vocalise the 1st rad., after the analogy of the strong verb, and write a double, but silent ܝ, thus: ܐܬܓܠܝ, ܐܬܚܘܝ. The West-Syrians

---

[1] So ܝܡܐ "swore", alongside of the less frequent ܝܡܝ. As variants of the West- and East-Syrian tradition, without consistency on either side, ܝܡܝܘ and ܝܡܘ; along with ܝܡܬ is found ܝܡܬ &c.

[2] Transgressions against this rule in manuscripts and editions are due to oversight.

also often say ܐܬܬܘܝ as well as ܐܬܬܘܝ "repent", and even in very early times it is found written (1) plainly ܐܬܬܘ.

The intransitive form of the Impt. sing. m. Peal was properly *ai*. But this form is authenticated with certainty still only in ܝܡܝ "swear" (of the class *primae* ܝ at the same time), occurring alongside of ܝܡܝ, and in ܐܫܬܝ "drink" (with prefix ܐ, according to § 51) from ܐܫܬܝ. In other cases the form throughout is ܚܕܝ "rejoice", &c. (On ܬܐ "come", v. § 183).

E. The 3rd pl. m. Perf., at least in Peal, and in like manner the Impt. m. pl., and the 3rd pl. f. Perf. in all the verb-classes, [or Conjugations] have occasionally *lengthened* forms: ܪܡܝܘ (ܪܡܝܘܢ, ܪܡܐܘܢ) = ܪܡܘ; ܪܡܝܝܢ = ܪܡܝ; ܚܕܝܝܢ = ܚܕܝ; ܐܪܡܝܝܢ = ܐܪܡܝ; ܐܬܪܡܝܝܢ = ܐܬܪܡܝ, &c.; there is also written instead, ܪܡܝܢ, ܐܪܡܝܢ, ܐܬܪܡܝܢ &c. For ܝܢ of the Imperative pl. f. there is also found ܐܝ, *e. g.* ܨܠܐܝ *i. e.* ܨܠܐܝ "pray ye" (§ 40 E). More rarely we meet here with the short forms in ܝ (probably *āi*) like ܚܕܝ "rejoice ye" (f.); ܐܬܕܡܝ "be ye like" (f.). In the 1st pl. perf. we meet with ܪܡܝܢܢ, ܚܕܝܢܢ, ܐܪܡܝܢܢ &c. as well as ܪܡܝܢ &c.

F. The *Ettaphal* does not occur with sufficient frequency to call for its consideration in the Paradigm. Besides, the only form open to doubt is the Impt. sing. m.; all the other forms follow the analogy of the other reflexives.

On the blending of the Participles in *ē*, and pl. *ēn*, with affixed subject-pronouns v. § 64 A.

Rem. Verbal forms, which showed ܘ as 3rd rad. no longer appear.

---

(1) ܐܬܬܘܐ, as it is usually printed in Rev. 2, 5 and 15, is inaccurate. [Gutbir gives ܐܬܬܘܝ]. And yet this remarkable form of the Imperative ܐܬܬܘܐ will have to be recognised, for likewise in Euseb. Church Hist. 211, 1 the two manuscripts which belong to the 6th century have ܐܬܬܘܐ for μετανόησον. The other two,—tolerably ancient also, have ܐܬܘܐ. It looks like a regular Ethpaal form, but the verb appears to occur only in the Ethpeel.

PARADIGM OF VERB TERTIAE ܝ.

	Peal.		Ethpeel.	
Perf. sg. 3. m.	ܪܡܐ	ܚܕܝ	ܐܬܪܡܝ	
3. f.	ܪܡܬ	ܚܕܝܬ	ܐܬܪܡܝܬ	
2. m.	ܪܡܝܬ	ܚܕܝܬ	ܐܬܪܡܝܬ	
2. f.	ܪܡܝܬܝ	ܚܕܝܬܝ	ܐܬܪܡܝܬܝ	
1.	ܪܡܝܬ	ܚܕܝܬ	ܐܬܪܡܝܬ	
pl. 3. m.	ܪܡܘ	ܚܕܝܘ	ܐܬܪܡܝܘ	
3. f.	ܪ̈ܡܝ	ܚ̈ܕܝ	ܐܬܪ̈ܡܝ	
2. m.	ܪܡܝܬܘܢ	ܚܕܝܬܘܢ	ܐܬܪܡܝܬܘܢ	
2. f.	ܪܡܝܬܝܢ	ܚܕܝܬܝܢ	ܐܬܪܡܝܬܝܢ	
1.	ܪܡܝܢ	ܚܕܝܢ	ܐܬܪܡܝܢ	
Impf. sg. 3. m.	ܢܪܡܐ		ܢܬܪܡܐ	
3. f.	ܬܪܡܐ		ܬܬܪܡܐ	
2. m.	ܬܪܡܐ		ܬܬܪܡܐ	
2. f.	ܬܪܡܝܢ		ܬܬܪܡܝܢ	
1.	ܐܪܡܐ		ܐܬܪܡܐ	
pl. 3. m.	ܢܪܡܘܢ		ܢܬܪܡܘܢ	
3. f.	ܢܪ̈ܡܝܢ		ܢܬܪ̈ܡܝܢ	
2. m.	ܬܪܡܘܢ		ܬܬܪܡܘܢ	
2. f.	ܬܪ̈ܡܝܢ		ܬܬܪ̈ܡܝܢ	
1.	ܢܪܡܐ		ܢܬܪܡܐ	
Impt. sg. m.	ܪܡܝ		ܐܬܪܡܝ	(ܐܬܪܡܝܝ)
f.	ܪܡܝ		ܐܬܪܡܝ	
pl. m.	ܪܡܘ		ܐܬܪܡܘ	
f.	ܪ̈ܡܝܝܢ		ܐܬܪ̈ܡܝܝܢ	
Part. act. sg.	ܪܡܐ,	ܪܡܝܐ	ܡܬܪܡܐ,	ܡܬܪܡܝܐ
pl.	ܪܡܝܢ,	ܪ̈ܡܝܢ	ܡܬܪܡܝܢ,	ܡܬܪ̈ܡܝܢ
pass. sg.	ܪܡܐ,	ܪܡܝܐ		
pl.	ܪܡܝܢ,	ܪ̈ܡܝܢ		
Inf.	ܡܪܡܐ		ܡܬܪܡܝܘ	

	Pael.	Ethpaal.	Aphel.
Perf. sg. 3. m.	ܪܡܝ	ܐܬܪܡܝ	ܐܪܡܝ
3. f.	ܪܡܝܬ	ܐܬܪܡܝܬ	ܐܪܡܝܬ
2. m.	ܪܡܝܬ	ܐܬܪܡܝܬ	ܐܪܡܝܬ
2. f.	ܪܡܝܬܝ	ܐܬܪܡܝܬܝ	ܐܪܡܝܬܝ
1.	ܪܡܝܬ	ܐܬܪܡܝܬ	ܐܪܡܝܬ
pl. 3. m.	ܪܡܝܘ	ܐܬܪܡܝܘ	ܐܪܡܝܘ
3. f.	ܪ̈ܡܝ	ܐܬܪ̈ܡܝ	ܐܪ̈ܡܝ
2. m.	ܪܡܝܬܘܢ	ܐܬܪܡܝܬܘܢ	ܐܪܡܝܬܘܢ
2. f.	ܪܡܝܬܝܢ	ܐܬܪܡܝܬܝܢ	ܐܪܡܝܬܝܢ
1.	ܪܡܝܢ	ܐܬܪܡܝܢ	ܐܪܡܝܢ
Impf. sg. 3. m.	ܢܪܡܐ	ܢܬܪܡܐ	ܢܪܡܐ
3. f.	ܬܪܡܐ	ܬܬܪܡܐ	ܬܪܡܐ
2. m.	ܬܪܡܐ	ܬܬܪܡܐ	ܬܪܡܐ
2. f.	ܬܪܡܝܢ	ܬܬܪܡܝܢ	ܬܪܡܝܢ
1.	ܐܪܡܐ	ܐܬܪܡܐ	ܐܪܡܐ
pl. 3. m.	ܢܪܡܘܢ	ܢܬܪܡܘܢ	ܢܪܡܘܢ
3. f.	ܢܪ̈ܡܝܢ	ܢܬܪ̈ܡܝܢ	ܢܪ̈ܡܝܢ
2. m.	ܬܪܡܘܢ	ܬܬܪܡܘܢ	ܬܪܡܘܢ
2. f.	ܬܪ̈ܡܝܢ	ܬܬܪ̈ܡܝܢ	ܬܪ̈ܡܝܢ
1.	ܢܪܡܐ	ܢܬܪܡܐ	ܢܪܡܐ
Impt. sg. m.	ܪܡܐ	ܐܬܪܡܐ	ܐܪܡܐ
f.	ܪܡܝ	ܐܬܪܡܝ	ܐܪܡܝ
pl. m.	ܪܡܘ	ܐܬܪܡܘ	ܐܪܡܘ
f.	ܪ̈ܡܝܝܢ	ܐܬܪ̈ܡܝܝܢ	ܐܪ̈ܡܝܝܢ
Part. act. sg.	ܡܪܡܐ, ܡܪܡܝܐ	ܡܬܪܡܐ, ܡܬܪܡܝܐ	ܡܪܡܐ, ܡܪܡܝܐ
pl.	ܡܪܡܝܢ, ܡܪ̈ܡܝܢ	ܡܬܪܡܝܢ, ܡܬܪ̈ܡܝܢ	ܡܪܡܝܢ, ܡܪ̈ܡܝܢ
pass. sg.	ܡܪܡܝ, ܡܪܡܝܐ		ܡܪܡܝ, ܡܪܡܝܐ
pl.	ܡܪܡܝܢ, ܡܪ̈ܡܝܢ		ܡܪܡܝܢ, ܡܪ̈ܡܝܢ
Inf.	ܡܪܡܝܘ	ܡܬܪܡܝܘ	ܡܪܡܝܘ

VERBA MEDIAE ܘ AND ܝ.

§ 177. A. Verbs, whose 2ⁿᵈ rad. is looked upon as a ܘ, or rather *Verba* verbs which replace the 2ⁿᵈ rad. by a long vowel, are still farther re- *mediae* ܘ *&* ܝ. moved from the general type, in Peal, Aphel, Ethpeel and Ettaphal, than the preceding class.

In *Peal* they have *ā* in the Perf. between the two firm radicals (ܩܳܡ "stood"), and *ū* in the Impf. and Impt. (ܢܩܽܘܡ, ܩܽܘܡ). The intransitive מות "to die" alone has *ī* in the Perf. (ܡܺܝܬ).(¹) In the Part. act. they have *ā-e*, and with lengthening, *āi-* (ܩܳܐܡ, ܩܳܝܡܺܝܢ): in the Part. pass. *ī* (ܩܺܝܡ), and in the Inf. *ā* (ܡܩܳܡ). The Inf. is sometimes written inaccurately ܡܩܳܡܘ. The only verb which still exhibits middle ܝ, has *ī* in the Impf. and Impt. (ܢܣܺܝܡ, ܣܺܝܡ)(²); in other respects it is exactly like those with middle ܘ.

B. In the *Aphel ī* appears throughout (ܐܩܺܝܡ, ܢܩܺܝܡ), except in the Part. pass. and the Inf. (ܡܩܳܡ, ܡܩܳܡܘ).—It is the very same in *Ettaphal*, where only the Inf. has *ā* (ܐܬܬܩܳܡ, ܢܬܬܩܺܝܡ—ܡܬܬܩܳܡܘ). *The Ethpeel agrees completely with the Ettaphal*, or rather the Ethpeel in these verbs is quite supplanted by the Ettaphal. In the reflexives even a single ܠ may be written for the double ܠ (§ 36). The frequently occurring ☞ p. 349 reflexive of ܐܦܺܝܣ "to persuade" (with Greek π § 15, from πεῖσαι) is written ܐܬܦܺܝܣ, ܐܬܦܺܝܣ, and oftenest ܐܬܦܺܝܣ (*etpīs*), by assimilation of the ܠ to the π. So by a wrong use, in a few rare cases even ܐܬܦܺܝܣ "to burst out in anger" ("to boil").

C. The prefixes ܢ ܬ ܡ are applied in the Peal and Aphel without a vowel. And yet forms of the prefix with a vowel are not infrequently found, particularly in the poets, like ܢܩܽܘܡ, ܐܩܺܝܡ, ܢܥܺܝܪ "wakens up", ܡܕܺܝܢ; rarely we have Infinitives like ܡܩܳܘ "to remain". Whether forms of three syllables like ܢܩܳܘܡܘܢ occurred also, is not certain.

(¹) Very rarely indeed ܡܳܬ is said to appear.

(²) But not in the Perf., where only *sām* occurs, not *sīm*. In verbs *med.* ܘ no trace has been retained of an intransitive mode in the Impf. and Impt. Peal.

D. In the Aphel, hardening occurs according to tradition after the vowel *a* in ܐܰܛܺܝܒ "made ready", and in ܐܰܟܺܝܠ (1) "measured", while the softness of the 1st rad. may be held certain in ܐܰܬܺܝܒ "gave back", ܐܰܕܺܝܩ "beheld", ܐܒܺܝܬܶܬ "I spent the night", and many others.

E. *Pael* and *Ethpaal* make use of a double ܝ (*aiy*) in place of the 2nd rad., as ܩܰܝܶܡ "to maintain", ܐܶܬܩܰܝܰܡ; ܦܰܝܶܣ "to charge", &c., but sometimes a double ܘ (*auw*), as ܛܰܘܶܫ "to bedaub" (East-Syrian manner of writing is ܛܰܘܘܶܫ § 49 B); ܬܰܘܶܨ "to set right", "to admonish" (alongside of ܬܰܝܶܢ "to set or attach on the right side" &c.). The inflection of these verbs is exactly that of the strong verbs.

F. Those verbs also are declined like strong verbs, which have an altogether consonantal *w*, *e. g.* ܪܘܰܙ "to exult", ܪܘܳܙܳܐ, ܢܶܪܘܰܙ, ܪܘܽܙ, &c.; ܠܰܘܺܝ "to add to" (Denominative from ܠܘܳܬ "by, on to"), ܠܰܘܳܝܳܐ, ܡܠܰܘܝܳܢ, &c.; ܐܰܥܘܶܠ "to act wickedly" (from ܥܰܘܠܳܐ "iniquity"); ܪܘܰܚ "to be wide", ܐܰܪܘܰܚ, ܪܰܘܰܚ "to widen" (contrasted with ܐܰܪܺܝܚ "to smell", ܪܰܝܰܚ "to soften, to appease"); ܚܘܰܪ "to be white" (ܚܶܘܳܪ § 116,—contrasted with ܚܳܪ "glanced"). They are mostly Denominatives, and by no means the remains of a formation more original than that of verbs properly *med.* ܘ.

G. The following synopsis gives a view of the deviations from the general type, which occur in these verbs.

Peal.

Perf.		Impf.	
ܩܳܡ (ܩܳܡ)	ܣܳܡܶܬ	ܢܩܽܘܡ (ܢܩܽܘܠ)	ܢܣܺܝܡ
ܩܳܡܰܬ	ܣܳܡܬܳܐ	ܐܩܽܘܡ	ܐܣܺܝܡ
ܩܳܡܰܬ̈	ܣܳܡܬ̈	ܢܩܽܘܡܽܘܢ	ܢܣܺܝܡܽܘܢ
ܩܳܡܘ	ܣܳܡܬܘ	Impt.	
ܩܳܡܬܶܝܢ	ܣܳܡܬܶܝܢ	ܩܽܘܡ, ܩܽܘܡܝ	ܣܺܝܡ, ܣܺܝܡܝ
ܩܳܡܝ	ܣܳܡܢ	ܩܽܘܡܶܝܢ	ܣܺܝܡܶܝܢ
Part. act. ܩܳܐܶܡ (ܩܳܝܶܡ, ܩܳܝܡܳܐ), ܩܳܝܡܳܐ,		Inf.	
pass. ܩܺܝܡ (ܣܺܝܡ).		ܡܩܳܡ (ܡܩܳܝܰܡ, ܡܩܳܡܬ).	

☞ p. 349

(1) In certain modifications of meaning, however, the former of these two words is said to be given as ܐܰܛܺܝܒ: and the whole matter is thereby made a subject of considerable doubt. ܐܰܟܺܝܠ in particular owes its hardness expressly to the silly

Aphel.

Perf.	Impf.	Impt.
ܐܩܝܡ	ܢܩܝܡ	ܐܩܝܡ
ܐܩܝܡܬ	ܐܩܝܡ	ܐܩܝܡܝ
ܐܩܝܡܬ	ܢܩܝܡܘܢ	ܐܩܝܡܝܢ
ܐܩܝܡܘ	Part. act. ܡܩܝܡ	
ܐܩܝܡܬܘܢ	pass. ܡܩܡ	
ܐܩܝܡܢ	Inf. ܡܩܡܘ	

Ettaphal and Ethpeel.

ܡܩܝܡ ܐܬܬܩܝܡ, ܐܬܬܩܝܡܬ—ܐܬܬܩܝܡ ܒܝܐܩܝܡ, ܡܩܝܡ ܐܬܬܩܝܡ—ܡܩܡ ܐܬܬܩܡ.ܗ.

VERBA MEDIAE GEMINATAE.

§ 178. A. Verbs which restore the 3rd rad. by doubling the 2nd are in their origin closely related to verbs *med.* o, and they still repeatedly give and take to and from them (§ 58). They double the 1st rad. after prefixes, otherwise the 2nd if it is preceded and followed by a short vowel. When there is no ending, and immediately before consonants, the 2nd consonant remains without doubling. Only Peal, Aphel, and Ettaphal fall to be considered here.

Verba mediae geminatae.

In the Perf. Peal all these verbs of course have *a*, and in the Impf. and the Impt. sometimes *o*, sometimes *a*: *e. g.* ܥܠ "to enter", ܢܥܘܠ, ܥܘܠ; ܓܙ "to shear", ܢܓܘܙ; ܓܫ "to grope", ܢܓܘܫ, &c.—ܚܡ "to be hot", ܢܚܡ; ܣܐܒ "to be old", ܢܣܐܒ; ܒܐܫ "to be abominable", ܢܒܐܫ; ܪܓ "to covet", ܢܪܓ, and many others. The latter set are plainly intransitives. Only ܛܥܐ "to err" has ܢܛܥܐ with *e*.

B. The Part. act. is like that in verbs *mediae* o: ܩܐܡ, ܣܐܒ; but doubling makes its appearance whenever the Participle is lengthened: ܩܝܡܝ, ܣܝܒܝ, &c. Also in these forms, particularly in ܥܠ "to enter", an ܐ is usually written, which however has no significance for pronunciation: ܥܐܠܝܢ or ܥܠܝܢ; ܣܝܐܒ or ܣܝܒ. A superfluous ܐ is also sometimes written in the Aphel (§ 35) *e. g.* ܠܡܚܒܐܠܘ "to love" for ܠܡܚܒܘ (Inf.).

---

desire to distinguish it from ܐܟܝܠ "eaten" (§ 23 G. *Rem.*). At the same time it is stated that, "in the land of Ḥarrān", that is, in the very home of the dialect, they say ܐܟܝܠ. Thus always ܡܚܝܒ &c.

C. In forms furnished with prefixes (Impf. and Inf. Peal, and the whole of Aphel and Ettaphal), hardening always appears: thus ܢܒܘܙ "robs"; ܐܦܩ "hatched", &c. In this, as also in other respects, these forms (and the Impt. Peal likewise) agree entirely with the formations of verbs *primae* ܢ, so that sometimes a doubt may actually exist as to whether a verbal form belongs to the one or to the other.

In the Perf. Peal the 2nd rad. becomes hard, only when an original vowel following it has been retained: thus like ܕܩ "dashed in pieces", ܕܩܬ, ܕܩܬܘܢ, also ܕܩܘ and even in the later formations ܕܩܘܢ, ܕܩܬܝܢ; but ܕܩܬ, ܕܩܬ. In the Impt. it is always correspondingly soft: ܕܘܩ, ܕܘܩܝܢ, ܕܘܩܘ.

D. In the *Ethpeel* the 2nd and 3rd rads. (contrary to the fundamental rule) are kept separate, and the inflection is quite the same as in the strong verb. Only,—when the two come together, the mode of writing is sometimes simplified, *e. g.* ܢܬܒܙܘܢ for ܢܬܒܙܙܘܢ (like ܢܬܩܛܠܘܢ); ܡܬܡܨܐ for ܡܬܡܨܨܐ (like ܡܬܩܛܠܐ) from ܐܬܒܙܙ "to be robbed", ܐܬܡܨܨ "to be imputed".—In the *Pael* and *Ethpaal* these verbs exactly resemble the strong verbs, although the pronunciation, at least in later times, in cases like ܦܩܩܬ (properly *paqqĕqath*) allowed of a simplification (to *paqqath* or even *paqath*).

E. We give in what follows a complete paradigm of the *Peal* (short only of the secondary forms).

	Perf.	*Impf.*		*Impt.*
sg. 3. m.	ܒܙ	ܢܒܘܙ	sg. m.	ܒܘܙ
3. f.	ܒܙܬ	ܬܒܘܙ	f.	ܒܘܙܝ
2. m.	ܒܙܬ	ܬܒܘܙ	pl. m.	ܒܘܙܘ
2. f.	ܒܙܬܝ	ܬܒܙܝܢ	f.	ܒܘܙܝܢ
1.	ܒܙܬ	ܐܒܘܙ		
pl. 3. m.	ܒܙܘ	ܢܒܙܘܢ	Part. act.	ܒܐܙ, ܒܐܙܐ
3. f.	ܒܙܝ, ܒܙ	ܢܒܙܢ	pass.	ܒܙܝܙ
2. m.	ܒܙܬܘܢ	ܬܒܙܘܢ		
2. f.	ܒܙܬܝܢ	ܬܒܙܢ	Inf.	ܡܒܙ
1.	ܒܙܢ	ܢܒܘܙ		

For the *Aphel* the following abstract may suffice: Perf. اَخֹר, اَخֹרַت;
اَخֹרֶه, اֶخַּרֶלֶף;—Impf. يֹخֹר, يֹخֹרֶهֹ—Impt. اَخֹר, اَخֹרֶת;—Part. act. مُخֹר,
مُخֹרֶه.—Part. pass. مُخֹר,—مُخֹרַה.—Inf. مُخֹרֶه.
The Ettaphal would run اֶתֹّاَخֹر, &c.

VERBS WEAK IN MORE THAN ONE RADICAL.

§ 179. A. Verbs, which contain two weak radicals, present almost Verbs weak in more than one radical.
no peculiar difficulties. Verbs *primae* נ, which are at the same time
tert. ى, show the peculiarities of both classes, *e. g.* from نֹכֹا "to damage"
يֹבֹا; Aphel اֶכֹّר, مُכֹّا; Impt. Aphel اَכֹّا "cause to forget"; اֹهֹم "put to
the proof", &c. They retain the *n* in the Impt. Peal: نֹבֹם, &c.

Verbs *primae* נ, which are at the same time *med.* o or *med. gem.*,
retain their *n* in all circumstances, thus *e. g.* نֹבֹم (*med.* o) "sleeps"; يֹבֹب
(*med. gem.*) "is abominable".

B. Verbs *primae* اֹ, which are at the same time *tert.* ى, correspond:
اֶלֹا "to wail"; اֶפֹا "to bake" (East-Syrian اֹלֹا, اֹפֹا); بֹבֹاֹلֹا; بֹلֹاֹלֹا; لֹمֹاֹلֹا
(also اֹלֹמֹכֹ § 174 B, *Rem.*); Impt. اֶפֹם; f. لֹاֹمֹ (East-Syrian لֹاֹמֹ); Ethpeel
نֹלֹمֹاֹلֹا, &c. (For a third verb of this kind, which appears in the Peal, اֹלֹا,
v. § 183). Pael اֶמֹ "to heal", نֹاֹהֹم &c.

It is the same with verbs which are at once *primae* and *tertiae* ى
[*i. e.* they show the variations associated with both types of weakness in
the radical]: يֹמֹا "to swear"; يֹגֹا "to sprout": يֹهֹם or (intr.) نֹمֹם
(§ 176 D, *Rem.*);—بֹاֹمֹخֹا; بֹاֹגֹا; مֹاֹגֹم (also مֹכֹאֹمֹכֹ § 175 A, *Rem.*); Aphel
اֹمֹכֹם, اֹهֹגֹم, to which add اֹهֹفֹ "to confess" and a few others which
do not occur in the Peal: اֹהֹפֹم, بֹهֹפֹם, بֹمֹהֹפֹ, &c.

C. Verbs *tert.* ى, which have a *w* as 2nd rad., *e. g.* لֹهֹمֹ "to accompany"; لֹהֹمֹ "to be equal", keep it always as a consonant, and accordingly do not diverge at all from the usual type of verbs *tert.* ى: *e. g.*
لֹהֹمֹ; بֹيֹهֹا; اֹلֹهֹمֹ; اֹهֹمֹ; نֹגֹهֹمֹ, &c.

D. Even in verbs *secundae* اֹ, which are at the same time *tert.* ى,
the procedure is in accordance with the rules elsewhere given. What
effect these rules have is shown in the following forms: Perf. اֹלֹא "to find

fault with", f. ܩܳܠܺܝ, pl. ܩܳܠܽܘ; Impt. ܩܳܠ, f. ܩܳܠܳܝ; Inf. ܡܶܩܒܳܠ. Ethpeel ܐܶܬܩܒܶܠ.—
Intrans. Perf. ܠܺܐܝ "to grow tired", ܠܺܐܝܰܬ, ܠܐܶܬ, ܠܐܺܝܬ, ܠܐܶܝܢ, ܠܺܐܝ and ܠܐܺܝܢ,
Impf. ܢܶܠܐܶܐ, ܬܶܠܐܶܝܢ, ܬܶܠܐܶܐ; Part. ܠܐܶܐ, ܠܐܶܐ; Inf. ܡܶܠܐܰܐ. Aphel ܐܰܠܐܺܝ; Part. f.

☞ p. 349 ܡܰܠܐܝܳܐ, &c.

E. Several other combinations, which however occur very seldom
indeed,—such as *primae ܐ* and *med. gem.* in ܐܳܢܬܝ (ܐܳܢܬܝ) "thou art
groaning", or *prim. ܐ* and *med.* ܘ in ܐܶܬܐܰܘܚܰܬ(¹) "she longed for", or
primae ܚ and *secundae ܐ* as in ܚܳܐܒܳܐ "she longs for", ܐܶܬܚܳܐܒ (improperly written ܐܶܬܚܰܐܰܒ § 33 B) "he longed for", and the triple weakness
in ܐܰܘܳܐ (Pael) "to restore to harmony", Ethpaal ܐܶܬܐܰܘܺܝ (also written, to
be sure, ܐܶܬܐܰܘܠܝ)—need no special explanation. ܐܶܠܳܐ "to lament" (§ 175 B)
has its two *l*'s always separated: ܐܶܠܰܠܘ, &c.

QUADRILITERAL AND MULTILITERAL VERBS.

Quadriliteral and multiliteral verbs. Formation of quadriliterals.

§ 180. As Quadriliterals we reckon here both those verbs which
cannot readily be traced back to shorter stems, such as *e. g.* ܒܰܕܰܪ "to
scatter", and those, in which this is easily done. To the latter class belong, amongst other:—

(1) Causatives formed with *ša*, like ܫܰܥܒܶܕ "to enslave"; ܫܰܢܙܶܒ "to
suspend"; ܫܰܟܠܶܠ "to complete"; and (from *primae* ܘ or ܐ) ܫܰܘܕܰܥ "to
proclaim"; ܫܰܘܫܶܛ "to stretch forth"; ܫܰܘܕܺܝ "to promise"; ܫܰܘܚܰܪ "to
delay" (אחר).

(2) The few quadriliterals formed with *sa* ܣܰܪܗܶܒ "to hasten";
ܣܰܩܒܶܠ "to bring against"; ܣܰܥܡܶܡ "to tend or nurse" (probably
from אסי).

(3) Denominatives in *n*, like ܐܶܬܢܰܫܝ "to be possessed", from
ܢܰܫ "demoniac" (adj. from ܫܐܕܳܐ "demon"); ܢܰܣܡܶܟ "to sustain", "to
hold out".

(4) Denominatives in *ī*: ܒܰܓܢܺܝ from ܢܘܟܪܳܝ "foreign"; ܓܰܝܠ οἰκειοῦν
from ܓܰܝܠ οἰκεῖος (from ܚܰܝܠܳܐ "house").

(¹) This form is at an early date disfigured in many ways.

(5) Denominatives formed by reduplication of the 3rd radical, like ܥܰܒܕܶܕ "to make a slave of" (ܥܰܒܕܳܐ); ܥܰܙܪܶܪ "to wrap in swaddling clothes" (ܥܙܳܪܽܘܪܶܐ).

(6) Reduplicated forms like ܐܶܬܓܰܘܪܰܪ "to chew the cud" from גרר; ܐܶܬܒܰܘܪܰܪ "to become stupid" from בור.

(7) Reduplicated forms like ܒܰܠܒܶܠ "to complicate", and ܓܰܪܓܰܪ "to drag", from בלל, גרר; ܙܰܥܙܰܥ "to shake"; and ܪܰܡܪܶܡ "to raise up" from זוע, רום.

(8) Forms like ܣܰܘܒܰܪ "to maintain", "to nourish", from סבר; ܐܶܬܥܰܘܩܰܦ "to be wreathed", from עקף; ܐܶܬܬܰܘܟܰܙ "to lean upon a staff" (ܬܽܘܟܙܳܐ). And so too, others of all sorts.

To these may be added simple Denominatives like ܬܰܠܡܶܕ "to teach" from ܬܰܠܡܺܝܕܳܐ "disciple"; ܡܰܫܟܶܢ "to pledge", from the Assyrian borrowed-word ܡܰܫܟ݁ܽܘܢܳܐ "pledge"; ܐܶܬܓܰܝܰܪ "to become a proselyte", from the Jewish word ܓܺܝܽܘܪܳܐ; ܨܰܘܪܶܬ "to give form" (ܨܽܘܪܬ݂ܳܐ), &c.; and, along with these, even compounds like ܐܶܬܒܰܪܢܰܫ "to become man", from ܒܰܪ ܐ݁ܢܳܫܳܐ; ܒܥܶܠܕܒܶܒ "to be an adversary", from ܒܥܶܠܕܒ݂ܳܒ݂ܳܐ (from ܕܒ݂ܳܒ݂ܳܐ + ܠ + ܒ), &c. Along with these Quadriliterals there are many also from Greek words, like ܩܰܛܪܶܓ "to accuse", from κατήγορος; ܩܰܬܪܶܣ "to remove", "to depose", from καθαίρεσις, &c.; ܠܰܣܛܶܣ "to rob" from ܠܶܣܛܳܝܳܐ λῃστής.

The Quadriliterals have an Active form, and a Reflexive form: ܥܰܪܓܶܠ "to roll" (trans.), ܐܶܬܥܰܪܓܰܠ "to roll" (intrans.); ܬܰܠܡܶܕ "to teach", ܐܶܬܬܰܠܡܰܕ "to be taught"; ܢܰܟܪܝ "to estrange", ܐܶܬܢܰܟܪܝ "to become estranged"; ܫܰܘܕܰܥ "to notify", ܐܶܫܬܰܘܕܰܥ "to understand, *or* know", &c. Many appear in the reflexive form only.

§ 181. *The inflection is exactly that of the Pael and corresponding* **Inflection.** *Ethpaal*, except that in this case the two middle consonants take the place of the one double consonant, thus: ܥܰܪܓܶܠ like ܩܰܛܶܠ, ܥܰܪܓܠܰܬ, ܥܰܪܓܶܠܘ; Impf. ܢܥܰܪܓܶܠ, ܢܥܰܪܓܠܽܘܢ; Impt. ܥܰܪܓܶܠ, ܥܰܪܓܶܠܘ; Part. act. ܡܥܰܪܓܶܠ, ܡܥܰܪܓܠܳܐ; pass. ܡܥܰܪܓܰܠ, ܡܥܰܪܓܠܳܐ; Inf. ܡܥܰܪܓܳܠܽܘ (*Nomen actionis* ܥܽܘܪܓܳܠܳܐ § 123).—Reflexive ܐܶܬܥܰܪܓܰܠ, ܐܶܬܥܰܪܓܠܰܬ; Impf. ܢܶܬܥܰܪܓܰܠ, ܢܶܬܥܰܪܓܠܽܘܢ; Impt. ܐܶܬܥܰܪܓܰܠ; Part. ܡܶܬܥܰܪܓܰܠ, ܡܶܬܥܰܪܓܠܳܐ; Inf. ܡܶܬܥܰܪܓܳܠܽܘ.

It makes no difference whether the 2nd letter be a ܘ or a ܝ, as, for instance, in ܣܰܝܒܰܪ "to support"; ܣܰܘܒܰܪ "to announce".

Those which end in *ī* follow entirely the analogy of the Pael of *tert.* ܝ, *e. g.* ܫܰܡܠܺܝ "to complete", ܫܰܡܠܺܝܬ݁, ܫܰܡܠܺܝܬ݂ (2nd sing. m.), ܫܰܡܠܺܝܬ݂ (1st sing.), ܫܰܡܠܺܝܘ; Impf. ܢܫܰܡܠܶܐ, ܢܫܰܡܠܽܘܢ; Impt. ܫܰܡܠܳܐ.—Reflexive ܐܶܫܬ݁ܰܡܠܺܝ, ܐܶܫܬ݁ܰܡܠܺܝܬ݂, &c. Of an Impt. of the Reflexive of such verbs I know only the forms ܐܶܬ݂ܦܰܪܢܰܣܝ (1) (ܐܶܬ݂ܦܰܪܢܰܣܝ?) and ܐܶܬ݂ܟ݁ܰܠܕ݁ܺܝ (2); and these

☞ p. 350 do not end in *ā*, as one would have expected.

Multiliteral verbs. § 182. In like manner several Quinqueliterals also appear. To this class belong first, verbs which repeat the two last radicals, like ܐܶܬ݂ܚܰܠܡܰܡ "to have bad dreams", from ܚܶܠܡܳܐ "a dream", and ܫܰܪܓܰܪܓ݁ "to stir up fancies", the reflexive of which, ܐܶܫܬ݁ܰܪܓܰܪܓ݁ "to have fancies", (from ܫܪܳܓ݂ܳܐ "a little lamp", a borrowed-word from the Persian) occurs frequently. Farther, words occur like ܐܶܫܬ݁ܰܚܪܰܪ (ܚܪܐ) "to show one's self off", "to swagger". The inflection of these verbs is quite like that of the Quadriliterals, except that here it is generally the first consonant which is without the vowel.

Rem. Detached words like ܐܶܬ݂ܒ݁ܰܥܠܕ݁ܺܝܢ "to be at law" (ܒ݁ܥܶܠ ܕ݁ܺܝܢܳܐ); ܐܶܬ݂ܩܽܘܒ݁ܰܪܢܰܛ "to be a κυβερνήτης", and even ܐܶܬ݂ܒ݁ܰܥܠܕ݁ܒ݂ܳܒ݂ "to be an enemy" (ܒ݁ܥܶܠ ܕ݁ܒ݂ܳܒ݂ܳܐ), and ܐܶܬ݂ܟ݁ܪܺܣܛܝܰܢ "to be a χριστιανός" are to be regarded as

☞ p. 350 affected malformations, which in no way belong to the language.

LIST OF ANOMALOUS VERBS.

List of anomalous verbs. § 183. (1) ܐܶܫܟ݁ܰܚ "to find" (Aphel) instead of ܐܰܫܟ݁ܰܚ; so ܢܶܫܟ݁ܰܚ, ܡܶܫܟ݁ܰܚ (Part.), ܡܶܫܟ݁ܚܳܢܽܘܬ݂ܳܐ. Only the Part. passive is transferred to the Peal: ܫܟ݂ܺܝܚ (3). A new Aphel, certified only in later times, appears perhaps in ܐܰܫܟ݁ܰܚ "to cause to find" Job 7, 2 Hex.

---

(1) LAGARDE, Anal. 20, 28 (6 Codd.).

(2) Gregor. Naz. Carm. II, 23, 21; but ܐܬܟܠܕܘ in Testam. Jesu Christi 104, 12.

(3) So ܫܟ݂ܺܝܪ "*foedus*" (adj.) from ܫܰܟ݁ܰܪ "*foedare*" &c. A Peal ܫܟ݂ܰܪ in this or in a similar meaning does not otherwise occur. The forms given by PAYNE-SMITH 4158 all belong to the Pael. ܫܰܟ݁ܰܪ is properly, perhaps, a Shaphel of נכר.

(2) ܐܬܐ "to come". Impt. ܬܐ (with loss of the ܐ and with *ā*), f. ܬܝ; pl. ܬܘ, f. ܬܝܢ (ܬܐܝܢ).—Aphel ܐܝܬܝ. Ettaphal ܐܬܬܝܬܝ. ☞ p. 350

(3) ܪܗܛ "to run". Impt. ܗܪܘܛ (1).

(4) ܐܙܠ "to go". The ܠ falls out (§ 29), as often as it would otherwise have to follow a vowel-less ܙ, and take a vowel itself, thus ܐܙܠܬ (1st sg.): ܐܙܠܬ (3 f. sing.); ܢܐܙܠܘܢ; ܐܙܠ; ܐܙܠܝܢ, &c., but ܐܙܠܬ, ܐܙܠܬܘܢ (2) &c. Impt. ܙܠ (with falling away of the ܐ and with *e*), ܙܠܝ, ܙܠܘ, ܙܠܝܢ. Only the Peal occurs. ☞ p. 350

(5) ܣܠܩ "to ascend". The ܠ is assimilated to the ܣ, whenever the latter stands in the end of a syllable and the former comes first in the one immediately following. These forms, namely Impf. and Inf. Peal, Aphel and Ettaphal, look just as if they had been derived from נסק, thus: ܢܣܩ, ܢܣܩܘܢ, ܬܣܩܝܢ, ܡܣܩ; ܐܣܩ, ܐܣܩܬ, ܡܣܩ, ܡܣܩܐ, ܡܣܩܘ, ܢܬܬܣܩ,, &c. (Pael and Ethpaal are regular ܣܠܩ, ܐܣܬܠܩ.) The Impt. too runs as if from נסק (§ 173 C): ܣܩ, ܣܩܝ, ܣܩܘ (ܣܩܘܢ), ܣܩܝܢ.

(6) ܝܗܒ "to give" (with poets also dissyllabic, thus ܝܗܒ doubtless) loses its ܗ in the forms ܝܗܒ, ܝܗܒܬ, ܝܗܒܬ, ܝܗܒܘ, ܝܗܒ (ܝܗܒܢ), ܝܗܒܬܘܢ, ܝܗܒܬܝܢ, ܝܗܒܝܢ; but ܝܗܒܬ, ܝܗܒܬ (the East-Syrians throw it out in these forms also, § 38). Impt. ܗܒ, ܗܒܝ, ܗܒܝܢ (the *a* occurring on account of the guttural, by § 169). Part. act. ܝܗܒ, ܝܗܒܐ;—pass. ܝܗܝܒ. For the Inf. (only as Inf. absol., along with forms from ܝܗܒ) ܡܝܗܒ; but usually a ܡܬܠ, from נתל appears instead, which also supplies the Impf.; one says only ܢܬܠ, ܢܬܠܘܢ, &c.—Ethpeel is regular, ܐܬܝܗܒ, ܐܬܝܗܒܬ, &c. No other conjugations from ܝܗܒ or ܢܬܠ are in use.

(7) ܚܝܐ "to live". The Perf. is regular: ܚܝܐ, ܚܝܬ, ܚܝܬ, ܚܝܬ, ܚܝܘ, ܚܝܝ, ܚܝܬܘܢ, ܚܝܝܢ.—So too the Impt.: ܚܝܝ, ܚܝܝ, ܚܝܘ. But the Impf. is formed as if from a verb *med. gem.*: ܢܚܐ, ܐܚܐ, ܢܚܘܢ, ܐܚܘܢ (and no

(1) The pronunciation *hat* with the falling away of the *r* appears to be known neither to the ancient tradition of the East-Syrians, nor to that of the West-Syrians.

(2) In BERNSTEIN's Johannes are varying forms like ܠܡܐܙܠ, ܐܙܠܬܘܢ, &c. which have *ē*, alongside of those like ܠܡܐܙܠ &c. which have ܐ— (§ 174 B. *Rem.*).

doubt نَتُبْ, إِنْتُبْ). Now this readily passes into the form of verbs *primae* {: even at a pretty early date there is found written لابْ, and the later West-Syrians at least have نَابْ, نَائِبْ, &c. The Inf. too is مَنَاب (قَانْشَا, قَشْنَا).—Part. نَيَاب, f. نَاشُب; pl. نَيِيب or نَيَاب, f. نَنُب (¹). The Aphel too is formed as if from *med. gem.*: أَتَب, أَسِيَب, أَتَسَب; يَسَب; مَشَب; مَسَب (Part. pass.); مَحَشَب (*Nomen agentis* مَحَسَب). The mode of writing which is preferred for these Aphel forms is نَابْ, مَابْ, &c. (§ 35). So with the Ettaphal أَتَّتَب.

(8) هَوَا "to be". The Perf. هَوَا, هَوَيْ, &c. is quite regular: as an enclitic, however, it loses (v. §§ 38; 299) its و: هَوَا, هَوَا, &c. The Impf. also is usually quite regular: نَهْوَا, نَهْوَا, نَهْوُون, &c.; still, the following secondary forms occur, in which the o has fallen out, and with no difference of meaning: نَهْو, نَهْوَا, نَهْوُون, نَهْوُون, نَهْوِن (2 sing f.). Even the first two forms are far less frequently employed than the full forms, and the others still less frequently, in particular the last one. Notice alongside of the Part. هَوَا, هَوَا "being, becoming", the Part. pass. هَوَا, هَوَا, pl. هَوَيْن (Emph. st. هَوَيْ) "existing" (or "created") and the verbal adjective هَوَا, هَوَيْ "been" (§ 118).

VERBS WITH OBJECT-SUFFIXES.

§ 184. V. *supra* § 66.

The 1st person of the verb cannot have the suffixes of the 1st joined to it, nor the 2nd those of the 2nd.(²) There is no suffix of the 3rd pl.; the separate أَنُون, or أَنِين supplies its place.

هَو,—which comes in room of هَ after a vowel-ending,—becomes, with *ā*, هَوَهِ; with *ī* it becomes هَوَهِ; with *ē*, هَوَهِ (§ 50 A. (3)).

Before Suffixes, تَ of the 2nd sg. m. Perf. is modified into تَ;

تَ of the 2nd sg. f. Perf. into تَ;

تَ of the 1st pl. Perf. into تَ;

Verbs with object-suffixes.
(a) With strong termination.
Leading rules.

(¹) Not to be confounded with the adjective حَي, حَيَا, &c. "living", "active".

(²) The only exception known to me is the poetical expression أَحْزِينِي "that I might see myself", Ephr. II, 506 C.

the ending ٯ, ڡ (ٯٮ) into ڧڢ, ڢ (ٯٮ̱ڢ);

the ending ؎ into ـلٮـ (more rarely ـلٮـ);

the ending ؎ into ـلٮ;

the ending ؎ (ؠٮ) into ـلٮـ (ـلٮٮ);

and the 3 pl. f. Perf. is made to end in *ā*.

The *ā* of these forms is wanting, however, before the suffix of the 2nd sing. f. ـڥٮ, which here preserves its *e*, (probably also in the 3rd pl. f. before the suffix of the 2nd pl.).—Secondary forms also occur in which the suffix of the 3rd sing. m. (ـٯٮ) retains the *e*.

The forms of the Impf. which end in the 3rd consonantal rad. (3 sg. m. and f.; 2 sg. m.; 1. sg. and pl.) assume an *ī* before the suffixes of the 3rd sing.; the Impt. sing. m. takes an *ā* or an *ai* before all suffixes, when it ends in a consonant.

Attention should be paid to the distinction between ط and ؟ in the different persons of the verb. Only the East-Syrians, however, are consistent in this matter; the West-Syrians frequently give a *hard* sound even to the ط of the 3rd sing. fem.

The verbal forms are least altered before the suffixes of the 2nd pl. (ٯٮ and ؎).

Seeing that these suffixes ٯٮ and ؎ are treated entirely alike, and that, besides, very few vouchers are found for the latter, I leave it out of the Paradigm. For the forms of the Impf. which end in the 3rd rad., the 3rd sing. m. may suffice as their representative; for those in *ūn*, the 3rd pl. m.; for those in *ān*, the 3rd pl. f.

I mark with an asterisk (*) those forms, of which the accuracy does not appear to be fully established.

§ 185.   REGULAR VERB

Perfect Peal.	Sg. 1st.	Sg. 2. m.	Sg. 2. f.
Sg. 3. m.	ܩܛܰܠܬ݁	ܩܛܰܠܟ݂	ܩܛܰܠܟ݂ܝ
3. f.	ܩܛܰܠܬ݂ܶܢܝ	ܩܛܰܠܟ݂	ܩܛܰܠܬ݂ܶܟ݂
2. m.	ܩܛܰܠܬ݁ܳܢܝ	—	—
2. f.	ܩܛܰܠܬ݁ܝܼܢܝ	—	—
1.	—	ܩܛܰܠܬ݂ܳܟ݂	ܩܛܰܠܬ݂ܶܟ݂
Pl. 3. m.	ܩܛܰܠܽܘܢܝ	ܩܛܰܠܽܘܟ݂	ܩܛܰܠܽܘܟ݂
3. f.	ܩܛܰܠܶܢ	ܩܛܰܠܶܟ݂	ܩܛܰܠܶܟ݂*
2. m.	ܩܛܰܠܬ݁ܽܘܢܳܢܝ	—	—
2. f.	ܩܛܰܠܬ݁ܶܝܢܳܢܝ	—	—
1.	—	ܩܛܰܠܢܳܟ݂	ܩܛܰܠܢܶܟ݂*

Impf. Peal.

Sg. 3. m.	ܢܶܩܛܠܰܢܝ	ܢܶܩܛܠܳܟ݂	ܢܶܩܛܠܶܟ݂
2. m.	{ ܬ݁ܶܩܛܠܰܢܝ ܬ݁ܶܩܛܠܺܝܢܳܢܝ	—	—
2. f.	ܬ݁ܶܩܛܠܺܝܢܳܢܝ	—	—
Pl. 3. m.	ܢܶܩܛܠܽܘܢܳܢܝ	ܢܶܩܛܠܽܘܢܳܟ݂	ܢܶܩܛܠܽܘܢܶܟ݂
3. f.	ܢܶܩܛܠܳܢܝ	ܢܶܩܛܠܳܟ݂	ܢܶܩܛܠܳܢܶܟ݂*

Impt. Peal.

Sg. m.	ܩܛܽܘܠܰܝܢܝ	—	—
f.	ܩܛܽܘܠܺܝܢܝ	—	—
Pl. m.	{ ܩܽܘܛܠܽܘܢܝ ܩܽܘܛܠܽܘܢܳܢܝ	—	—
f.	{ ܩܛܽܘܠܳܢܝ* ܩܛܽܘܠܺܢܳܢܝ	—	—

Inf. Peal.	ܩܶܛܠܰܢܝ	ܩܶܛܠܳܟ݂	ܩܶܛܠܶܟ݂
Pael.	ܩܰܛܳܠܽܘܬ݂ܳܢܝ	ܩܰܛܳܠܽܘܬ݂ܳܟ݂	ܩܰܛܳܠܽܘܬ݂ܶܟ݂

WITH SUFFIXES. (Peal.)

Sg. 3. m.	Sg. 3. f.	Pl. 1.	Pl. 2. m.

Observations on the Perfect.

§ 186. *On the Perfect*: For the 3 pl. m. there appears also before suffixes, although rarely, the lengthened form in *ūn(ā)*, as ܣܳܡܽܘܢܳܘܗܝ "they laid him"; ܚܕܳܪܽܘܢܳܢܝ (no doubt ܚܕܰܪܽܘܢܳܢܝ) "they encompassed me":— Overbeck's 'Ephraim Syr. &c.' 137, 9; ܐܰܓܥܠܽܘܢܳܟ "they entrusted thee".— Julianus 90, 25; ܐܰܝܢܩܽܘܢܳܟ "they gave thee suck" Jac. Sar., Constantin v. 402 Var. (cf. § 197).—In the same way there occur for the 3 pl. f. forms with *ēn(ā)*, like ܟܒܰܫܶܢܳܗ (also written ܟܒܫܢܗ, which has been inaccurately understood as ܟܒܰܫܢܳܗ; hardly perhaps to be pronounced ܟܒܰܫܶܢܳܗ).

☞ p. 350

For the 3rd sg. f., with suffix of the 2nd pl. there is found as a variant for ܒܶܛܢܰܬܟܽܘܢ "conceived you" Is. 51, 2, the doubtless more original ܒܛܶܢܬܟܽܘܢ (from the intrans. ܒܛܶܢ).

The 3rd pl. m. sometimes remains without ending before the suff. of the 2nd pl.: ܐܰܠܨܟܽܘܢ (East-Syrian ܐܰܠܨܳܟܽܘܢ § 174 A) Judges 10, 12 "they oppressed you"; and ܕܰܠܚܟܽܘܢ ἐτάραξαν ὑμᾶς, Acts 15, 24 (also Hark.).

Examples of variations.

§ 187. The trifling *variations* from the Paradigm, which are called for in Intransitives, in certain weak roots, and in the Pael and Aphel, are shown by the following examples, to the analogy of which the other forms also give way: *Intransitives*; ܪܚܶܡܬܳܗ̇ "she loved her"; ܒܛܶܢܬܰܢܝ "she conceived me".— *Weak*; ܐܚܰܕܳܗ̇ "he held her"; ܐܶܪܰܥܟܽܘܢ "he met you"; ܐܶܚܕܰܬܢܝ "she held me"; ܝܰܠܕܰܢ "begat us"; ܝܶܠܕܰܬܳܟ "she brought thee forth"; ܝܶܕܥܶܬܟܽܘܢ "I knew you"; ܝܰܕܥܽܘܟ "they knew thee"; ܝܰܗܒܳܗ̇ "he gave her"; ܝܰܗܒܬܳܟ "I gave thee" (§ 183); ܫܰܐܠܳܟ "he begged thee"; ܫܰܐܠܽܘܟ "they begged thee" (others—ܫܶܐܠܳܟ, ܫܶܐܠܽܘܟ, cf. § 171); ܫܡܰܥܟܽܘܢ "he heard you"; ܣܳܡܬܳܗ̇ (others—ܣܳܡܰܬܳܗ̇ § 184) "she set her"; ܣܳܡܬܰܢܝ "thou didst set me"; ܣܳܡܬܳܟ "I set thee"; ܣܳܡܬܟܽܘܢ "I set you"; ܣܳܡܽܘܗܝ, ܣܳܡܽܘܢܳܘܗܝ "they set him"; ܟܪܳܗ̇ "he dug it (f.)"; ܦܶܫܚܰܬܶܗ "she dashed it (m.) in pieces"; ܪܓܶܬܳܗ̇ "I desired her"; ܓܪܽܘܗܝ "they dragged him forth".

Pael and *Aphel*: ܒܰܪܟܶܗ "he blessed him"; ܩܰܒܠܰܢ "he received us"; ܦܰܩܕܟܽܘܢ "he ordered you"; ܐܰܕܪܟܶܗ "he reached him, *or* came up with him"; ܩܰܒܠܰܬܶܗ "she received him"; ܨܰܒܥܰܬܢܝ "she dipped me"; ܚܰܝܠܶܬܳܟ "I strengthened thee"; ܐܰܪܓܶܙܬܺܝܢܝ "thou (f.) didst make me angry";

ﺇﻭﺯﺣﺪﻭﺟﻦ "I made known to you"; ﺣﺰﺑﻠﺠﻦ "we blessed you"; ﺇﻭﺯﺣﺪﻭﺟﻦ "we made known to you"; ﺇﺎﻋﺤﺪﻣﺄﻭﻧﺴﻪ "you delivered him up"; ﺟﻤﺄﻛﺪﻭﻩ "they deflowered her"; ﻣﺤﺸﺴﻮﻩ "they (f.) praised him"; ﺇﺎﻗﺪﺭﻓﻦ "made (3 pl. f.) us astonished": ﺇﺎﻋﺘﻘﺴﺒﻮﻩ "found (3 pl. f.) him"; ﺇﺎﻫﻤﻤﻪ "he made him ascend" (§ 183); ﺇﺎﻗﻤﺄﻭﺟﻦ "I led you forth"; — ﺣﺒﺎﺯﺄﻟﺲ "thou comfortedst me" (§ 172 A); ﺍﺯﻗﺪﺍﻭﻩ "polluted (3 pl.) him"; ﺟﺎﺭﻛﻢ "they asked us"; — ﺇﺎﻗﺴﺠﺪﻭ "he raised him up"; ﺇﺎﺯﺪﺣﺄﺭﻩ "thou didst disturb her"; ﺯﻯﺄﺳﺤﺄﻩ "she disturbed thee"; ﺇﺎﻗﺴﺪﺣﺪﻭﻩ "they raised him up", "established him"; ﺇﻓﻴﺴﺼﻪﻋﺴﺒﻮﻩ "they persuaded him". — ﺇﺎﺳﺠﺒﺲ "he loved me"; ﺇﺎﺷﺠﺪﺄﺳ "thou lovedst me"; ﺇﺎﺷﺠﺪﻭﺟﻦ "I loved you"; ﺇﺎﻗﻠﻮﻩ "they made him eager"; ﺇﺎﺣﺠﻪ "he introduced him"; ﺇﺎﺣﺪﻛﻮﺑﺲ "they introduced thee (f.)"; ﺇﺎﺟﺤﺄﺩﻭﺟﻦ "I introduced you (pl.)".

§ 188. *On the Imperfect*: The 2nd form of the 2nd sg. m. accomodates itself entirely to the Impt. sg. m. (§ 190). It serves properly to denote prohibition (with ﻻ "not"), but it stands also in other uses, just as the original form stands also in prohibition.

The 2nd sg. f. also takes before suffixes the form ﻣﯩﻦ: thus, ﻣﻠﺴﻠﻴﻮﺯﺟﻞ "thou (f.) dost hunt me"; ﻣﻘﺴﻠﻮﺯﻭﺳﻮﻩ "thou art justifying him"; ﺇﺎﺳﻘﺴﻴﺮﻩ "thou art choking her".

The forms of the suff. of the 3rd sg. m. ﻩﻮ and ﻣﻮﻫﻰ alternate without distinction in the cases concerned. With f. suff., forms like ﻳﻤﻠﺤﺬﻩ in place of ﺗﻤﻠﺤﺬﻩ, &c. occur more rarely.

For ﻣﻮﻩ there occurs in the Codex Sinaiticus ﻣﻮﻩ (how pronounced?), interchanging with the usual forms, e. g. ﻣﻮﻛﻠﺴﺠﻰ "I take him" (= ﻣﻮﻫﻰﻛﻤﺠﻰ); ﻣﻮﻳﺴﺤﻤﺪ "finds him"; ﻣﻮﻣﺪﻋﻤﻰ "I place him"; ﺯﻭﻧﺴﻌﺪﻭﻩ "I pity him", &c. So ﺑﻤﻮﻩﻮﻩ "judges him" Isaac I, 242 v. 397. Isolated cases of ﻣﻮﻩ used instead, occur in the Cod. Sin., e. g. ﺑﻌﻤﻠﺪﻟﻮﻩ "gives him power" (= ﺑﻤﻠﺪﻯﻫﻮﻩ); so ﺑﺎﻛﺰﻭﻩﻮﻩ "we constrain him" Vita St. Antonii ed. Schulthess 11 paen.(¹)

☞ p. 350

_____

(¹) There is an additional example there 'of such a form. The editor draws attention,—in the Introduction p. ٥, *Rem.* 3—, to several others in the cod. D of the Vita Alexis.

On the Imperfect.

The very rare forms in ܗ instead of ܘܗ before suffixes are hardly certain, like ܢܣܡܟܘܢܝ "they support me" Apost. Apocr. 316, 4 *ab. inf.* and ܢܩܘܡܘܢܝ according to Martin in a *Karkafish* gloss of a Parisian Codex of Jer.

☞ p. 350

☞ p. 350

Examples of variations.

§ 189. *Examples of variations*(¹): With *a*: ܢܓܙܘܟܘܢ "he takes you away"; ܐܓܙܘܟ "I break you"; ܐܓܒܟܘܢ "I take you"; ܐܣܒܗ "I take her"; ܐܢܫܩܝܘܗܝ "I kiss him"; ܢܛܪܘܢܝ "keep (3 pl.) him"; ܬܨܒܬܝܗ "thou (f.) plantest her";—ܐܬܠܟܝ "I give thee (f.)"; ܐܬܠܟܘܢ "I give you (f.)";—ܐܟܠܐܟܝ "she eats you"; ܐܣܪܝܘܗܝ "I hold him"; ܢܣܪܘܢܝܗܝ "they hold him"; ܢܐܪܬܘܢܗ "they inherit it (f.)"; ܬܕܥܝܗ "you know her";—ܐܒܥܝܘܗܝ (ܐܒܥܝܘܗܝ § 34) "I beg him"; ܬܒܥܢܢܝ "you beg me, *or* ask me";—ܐܕܘܢܟܝ "I judge thee (f.)"; ܢܕܘܢܝܘܗܝ "we judge him"; ܐܕܘܢܟܘܢ "I judge you"; ܢܕܘܢܢܟܝ "they judge thee (f.)"; ܢܨܘܬܢܝܗܝ "they (f.) listen to him"; ܢܣܝܡܘܢܝܗܝ "they place him";— ܢܪܓܝܗ "lusts after her".

Pael and *Aphel*: ܢܒܪܟܢ "blesses us"; ܬܫܪܝܢܝ "thou causest me to dwell"; ܐܟܢܫܟܝ "I gather thee (f.)"; ܢܬܠܘܢܟܝ "they give thee (f.) gain"; ܢܫܒܚܘܢܝܗܝ, ܢܫܒܚܘܢܝܗܝ "they glorify him"; ܢܫܒܚܢܟܝ "they (f.) glorify thee"; ܐܪܓܙܝܢܝ "thou (f.) provokest me to anger"; ܢܣܒܪܟܘܢ "he brings tidings of good to you"; ܢܥܡܕܟܘܢ "baptises you";—ܐܦܩܗ "I cast him out"; ܢܦܩܘܢܟܘܢ "they cast you out"; ܢܒܝܐܘܢܟܘܢ "they comfort you";— ܢܫܐܠܟ "he asks thee"; ܢܫܐܠܘܢܝܗܝ "they ask him"; ܐܫܐܠܟܘܢ "I ask you";—ܐܠܦܟ "I teach thee"; ܐܠܦܟܘܢ "I teach you";—ܢܩܝܡܘܢܝܗܝ "I establish him";—ܢܥܝܪܝܘܗܝ "he awakens him"; ܢܥܝܪܢ "they (f.) awaken us"; ܢܩܝܡܟܘܢ "he establishes you"; ܢܩܝܡܘܢܗ "they establish him";— ܐܩܝܡܢܝ "thou directest me aright"; ܢܣܝܒܗ "he profanes it (her)"; ܐܣܚܒܝܘܗܝ "thou (f.) lovest him"; ܐܠܐܨܝܢܝ "thou (f.) vexest me"; ܢܪܡܘܢܗ "they shatter him (*or* it) in pieces".

On the Imperative and the 2nd Sing. m. Impf.

§ 190. A. *On the Imperative*: Besides the two forms of the pl. m. noted in the Paradigm, there are other two secondary forms occurring here and there, as, for instance, ܫܒܩܘܗܝ "leave him", and ܫܩܠܘܢܝ

(¹) For 2ⁿᵈ form of the 2ⁿᵈ sg. m. v. on the Impt. § 190 C.

"sacrifice him" (v. under F). There are some traces found of a form of the sg. f. like ܩܛܘܠܝܢܝ or even ܩܛܘܠܝܢܢܝ.

B. The sg. m. *always* retains the vowel immediately before the 3rd rad., thus not merely in ܩܛܘܠܝܗܝ; ܫܡܥܝܢܝ "hear me"; ܕܟܘܪܝܢܝ (East-Syrian ܕܟܘܪܝܢܝ § 174 G) "think on me", "remember me"; ܪܚܡܝܗ "love her"; ܙܒܢܝܗ "buy her"; ܥܒܕܝܗܝ "make him":—ܝܠܦܝܗܝ "learn it" (and of course ܣܝܡܝܗ "place her"; ܠܘܛܝܗܝ "curse him"), &c., but also in the *Pael* and *Ethpaal*, as ܬܚܘܡܝܗܝ "fix his bounds": ܢܛܪܝܗ "observe her"; ܐܠܦܝܢܝ "teach me"; ܒܝܐܝܢܝ "comfort me"; ܪܒܝܗ "cherish her"; ܐܫܠܡܝܗܝ "deliver him up"; ܐܘܕܥܝܢܝ "make known to me"; ܐܘܕܥܝܗ "make known to her"; ܐܥܠܝܢܝ "lead me in".

So too verbs *primae* ܢ and ܘ, with falling away of the 1st rad.: ܢܫܘܩܝܗܝ, ܢܫܘܩܝܢܝ "kiss him", "kiss me"; ܩܦܝܢܝ "follow me"; ܣܒܝܗ "take her"; ܓܕܝܢܝ "draw me"; ܗܒܝܗ "give her"; ܗܒܝܗܝ "give him"(1); ܕܥܝܗܝ "acknowledge him".

C. Exactly the same vocalisation holds good also in the 2nd form of the *2nd sg. m. Impf.* ܬܦܪܩܝܢܝ "thou deliverest me"; ܬܚܢܩܝܗ "thou art choking her"; ܬܪܚܡܝܗܝ "thou lovest him";—ܬܬܓܕܝܗ "thou art drawing her"; ܬܬܠܝܗܝ "thou givest him";—ܬܪܣܝܢܝ "thou sprinklest me";—ܬܫܠܡܝܢܝ "thou deliverest me up"; ܬܐܠܦܝܢܝ "thou teachest me"; ܬܘܒܕܝܢܝ "thou destroyest me"; ܬܥܠܝܢ "thou leadest us in", &c.

D. Such a vowel, however, is not found in the shorter form of the pl. m. Notice that the vowel *u* stands here, in the Peal, even with verbs which have *a* or *e* in the Impf. and Impt.: *e. g.* ܕܒܪܘܗܝ "take ye him away"; ܥܒܕܘܗܝ "make him"; ܫܡܥܘܢܝ "hear ye me"; ܐܡܪܘܗܝ "say ye of him" (and of course ܕܘܢܘܗܝ "judge ye him"; ܠܘܛܘܗ "curse ye her"), &c.—*Pael* and *Aphel*: ܦܨܘܢܝ "save me"; ܐܫܪܘܗܝ "make him secure"; ܩܒܠܘܗܝ "take him"; ܐܘܒܠܘܢ "lead us away"; ܐܘܒܠܘܗܝ "lead him away"; ܐܦܩܘܗܝ "cast him out"; ܒܝܐܘܗܝ "comfort ye him", &c. But in ܐܣܐܢܘܗܝ "put shoes upon him", a vowel is of course needed for

(1) Barh., for Ex. 22, 26 and 1 Sam. 21, 9, would have ܗܒܝܗܝ, but that is hardly correct. ☞ p. 350

the ܐ (§ 34). This is the formation adopted by some writers even in the case of very short forms ܗܰܒܘܽܗܝ, ܗܰܒܘܽܗ̇ "give ye him", "give her"; ܣܰܒܘܽܗ̇ "take ye her"; while others say ܗܳܒܘܽܗܝ, ܗܳܒܘܽܗ̇; and even ܣܘܒܘܗ̇ (= ܣܰܒܘܽܗ̇) occurs.

So too in the sg. f. of Pael and Aphel there should be no vowel before the 3rd rad., thus: ܫܰܒܚܺܝܢܝ "praise me"; ܦܰܬܓܶܝܘܗܝ "entice him"; ☞ p. 350 ܐܰܝܢܶܩܺܝܘܗܝ "suckle him"; ܐܰܫܡܥܺܝܢܝ "cause me to hear"; still we find also ܫܰܒܰܚܺܝܢܝ; ܐܰܫܡܰܥܺܝܢܝ; ܩܰܒܰܠܺܝܘܗܝ "take him"; and in fact this corresponds to the vocalisation of the Peal (as ܐܶܚܽܘܕܺܝܘܗܝ "hold him"). Cf. the fluctuation between ܗܰܝܡܢܺܝܢܝ and ܗܰܝܡܶܢܺܝܢܝ "believe me" (§ 197). Thus ܗܰܒܶܝܘܗܝ (others ܗܰܒܝܘܗܝ), and ܢܰܛܪܺܝܗ̇ "preserve her".—For a longer form in *īnā* as in the Impf. v. § 198 A.

E. Altogether, only a few examples occur of the pl. f., as ܫܰܒܚܶܝܢܳܝܗܝ "praise him" (without any vowel before the 3rd rad.), or of the longer form ܫܡܰܥܶܝܢܳܢܝ "listen to me".

☞ p. 350 F. In the pl. m. in *ūn(ā)* two forms stand overagainst each other in the Peal,—the more usual one, like ܩܒܽܘܪܽܘܢܝ "bury me"; ܐܶܚܽܘܕܽܘܢܳܝܗܝ "take him"; ܫܡܰܥܽܘܢܝ "hear me",—and the less common one, with the vowel before the 3rd rad., like ܡܚܳܒܽܘܢܝ; ܩܛܽܘܠܽܘܢܳܝܗܝ "slay him"; ܛܥܽܘܡܽܘܢܝ "taste me". The forms *primae* ܢ follow the second of these two modes, like ܣܒܽܘܢܝ, ܣܒܽܘܢܳܝܗܝ "take me", "take him"; ܛܪܽܘܢܳܝܗܝ, ܛܪܽܘܢܳܗ̇ "preserve him", "preserve her" (cf. in addition ܫܡܳܥܽܘܢܝ "listen to me"; ܕܽܘܢܽܘܢܳܝܗܝ "judge him", &c.). The vowel is always retained in the Pael and Aphel: ܩܰܒܶܠܽܘܢܝ "receive me"; ܢܰܛܰܪܽܘܢܳܗ̇ "guard her"; ܐܰܘܕܥܽܘܢܝ "make known to me"; ܐܰܠܒܶܫܽܘܢܳܝܗܝ "clothe him"; ܐܰܦܶܩܽܘܢܳܝܗܝ "cast ye him out".

☞ p. 350 G. For ܚܳܙܶܝܗܝ (sg. m.) the East-Syrians write ܚܙܺܝܗܝ (§ 84 B).

On the Infinitive. § 191. *On the Infinitive*: In the Peal cf. farther ܡܶܬܠܳܗ̇, ܡܶܬܠܳܟ݂ "to give her", "to give thee"; ܡܕܳܢܳܗ̇ "to judge her".

Occasionally forms are met with, which, following the analogy of the Impf., insert an *ī* before the suff. of the 3rd sg. m.:—ܡܶܣܰܒܠܺܝܘܗܝ "to take him" (in place of ܡܥܡܠܟܘ); ܡܕܝܟܘܗܝ "to pay him"; ܡܕܩܝܗ "to set her free"; ܡܚܩܥܘܗܝ "to enchant([1]) him".

The forms of the Aphel, as ܡܘܠܟܘܐܝ, &c. correspond to those of the Pael; in verbs *mediae* ܘ, we have ܡܗܦܟܘܝ "to lead thee back", &c.

§ 192. *Verbs tertiae* ܝ require special treatment. The $\bar{a}$ of the 3ʳᵈ sg. m. Perf. is retained before suffixes; and it is the same with the vowel endings of the root in the Impf. and Impt. On the other hand, the $\bar{\imath}$ of the Perf. and the $\bar{a}$ of the Inf. pass into y, except before ܩܝ, and ܩܝ. Notice the transmutations of the diphthongs peculiar to each: *au* into *a(w)ū* ܐܘ— (also written ܘܐ—, ܘܐܐ—: East-Syrian ܐܘ—, &c. § 49 B): *iu* into *yū*; *āi* (Impt. sg. f.) into $\bar{a}(y)\bar{\imath}$ ܐ— (or written ܐ—). For orthographic differences also with $\bar{e}$ in these cases, v. *infra*.

§ 193. We give the forms of the Perf. complete in the *Paradigm*, for Peal and Pael, and from the latter the corresponding forms of the Aphel are easy to construct. Only we omit the 2ⁿᵈ pl. f. (in ܝ) which can hardly be authenticated, but which at any rate follows exactly the analogy of the 2ⁿᵈ sg. m. (*i. e.* of the strong verb). In the Impt. we require to cite the Pael forms for the sg. m. only. It is not necessary to cite them at all in the Impf. It may suffice generally for this section of the Paradigm to note down one single personal form ending in ܠ, seeing that the forms with other endings follow the analogy of the strong verb.

Verba tert. ܝ *with Suffixes. Leading rules.*

Paradigm.

([1]) Geop. 95, 22; Clemens 136, 18; Is. 37, 34, Hex.; Clemens 140, 13, 14 (twice); three examples from the Codex of 411 A. D.

PARADIGM OF VERB TERT. ܝ

(Peal and

Perfect.		Sg. 1.	Sg. 2. m.	Sg. 2. f.
Sg. 3. m.	Peal	ܓܠܢܝ	ܓܠܟ	ܓܠܟܝ
	Pael	ܓܠܝܢܝ	ܓܠܝܟ	ܓܠܝܟܝ
3. f.	Peal	ܓܠܬܢܝ	ܓܠܬܟ	ܓܠܬܟܝ
	Pael	ܓܠܝܬܢܝ	ܓܠܝܬܟ	ܓܠܝܬܟܝ
2. m.	Peal	ܓܠܝܬܢܝ	—	—
	Pael	ܓܠܝܬܢܝ	—	—
2. f.	Peal	ܓܠܝܬܝܢܝ	—	—
	Pael	ܓܠܝܬܝܢܝ	—	—
1.	Peal	—	ܓܠܝܬܟ	ܓܠܝܬܟܝ
	Pael	—	ܓܠܝܬܟ	ܓܠܝܬܟܝ
Pl. 3. m.	Peal	ܓܠܐܘܢܝ	ܓܠܐܘܟ	ܓܠܐܘܟܝ
	Pael	ܓܠܝܘܢܝ	ܓܠܝܘܟ	ܓܠܝܘܟܝ
3. f.	Peal	ܓܠܝܢܢܝ	ܓܠܝܢܟ	ܓܠܝܢܟܝ
	Pael	ܓܠܝܢܢܝ	ܓܠܝܢܟ	ܓܠܝܢܟܝ
2. m.	Peal	ܓܠܝܬܘܢܢܝ	—	—
	Pael	ܓܠܝܬܘܢܢܝ	—	—
1.	Peal	—	ܓܠܝܢܟ	ܓܠܝܢܟܝ
	Pael	—	ܓܠܝܢܟ	ܓܠܝܢܟܝ
Impf.	Peal	ܢܓܠܝܢܝ	ܢܓܠܝܟ	ܢܓܠܝܟܝ
Impt. sg. m.	Peal	ܓܠܝܢܝ	—	—
	Pael	ܓܠܢܝ	—	—
sg. f.	Peal	ܓܠܐܝܢܝ	—	—
pl. m.	Peal	ܓܠܐܘܢܝ	—	—
pl. f.	Peal	ܓܠܝܢܢܝ	—	—
Inf.	Peal	ܡܓܠܝܢܝ	ܡܓܠܝܟ	ܡܓܠܝܟܝ
	Pael	ܡܓܠܝܘܬܢܝ	ܡܓܠܝܘܬܟ	ܡܓܠܝܘܬܟܝ

☞ p. 350

WITH PRONOMINAL SUFFIXES.

Pael).

Sg. 3. m.	Sg. 3. f.	Pl. 1.	Pl. 2. m.
ܢܰܓܶܒܗ	ܢܰܓܒܳܗ	ܢܰܓܒܰܢ	ܢܰܓܶܒܟܘܢ
ܢܰܓܒܗ	ܢܰܓܒܳܗ	ܢܰܓܒܰܢ	ܢܰܓܒܟܘܢ
ܢܰܓܒܝܗܝ	ܢܰܓܒܝܳܗ	ܢܰܓܒܝܰܢ	ܢܰܓܒܝܟܘܢ
ܢܰܓܒܝܘܗܝ	ܢܰܓܒܝܳܗ	ܢܰܓܒܝܰܢ	ܢܰܓܒܝܟܘܢ
ܢܰܓܒܝܢܗܝ	ܢܰܓܒܝܳܗ	ܢܰܓܒܝܰܢ	—
ܢܰܓܒܝܢܗܝ	ܢܰܓܒܝܳܗ	ܢܰܓܒܝܰܢ	—
ܢܰܓܒܢܗܝ	ܢܰܓܒܝܳܗ	ܢܰܓܒܝܰܢ	—
ܢܰܓܒܢܗܝ	ܢܰܓܒܝܳܗ	ܢܰܓܒܝܰܢ	—
ܢܰܓܒܝܗ	ܢܰܓܒܝܳܗ	—	ܢܰܓܒܝܟܘܢ
ܢܰܓܒܝܗ	ܢܰܓܒܝܳܗ	—	ܢܰܓܒܝܟܘܢ
ܢܰܓܠܘܗܝ	ܢܰܓܠܳܗ	ܢܰܓܠܢ	ܢܰܓܠܟܘܢ
ܢܰܟܣܘܗܝ	ܢܰܟܣܳܗ	ܢܰܟܣܢ	ܢܰܟܣܘܟܘܢ *
ܢܰܟܣܬܘܗܝ	ܢܰܟܣܳܗ	ܢܰܟܣܬܝ	?
ܢܰܟܣܬܘܗܝ	ܢܰܟܣܳܗ	ܢܰܟܣܬܝ	?
ܢܰܓܒܐܦܘܗܝ	ܢܰܓܒܐܦܳܗ	ܢܰܓܒܐܦܰܢ	—
ܢܰܓܒܐܦܘܗܝ	ܢܰܓܒܐܦܳܗ	ܢܰܓܒܐܦܰܢ	—
ܢܰܓܒܢܘܗܝ	ܢܰܓܒܢܳܗ	—	ܢܰܓܒܢܟܘܢ
ܢܰܓܒܢܘܗܝ	ܢܰܓܒܢܳܗ	—	ܢܰܓܒܢܟܘܢ
ܢܶܓܒܘܗܝ	ܢܶܓܒܳܗ	ܢܶܓܒܰܢ	ܢܶܓܒܟܘܢ
ܢܰܓܒܘܗܝ	ܢܰܓܒܳܗ	ܢܰܓܒܰܢ	—
ܢܰܓܒܘܗܝ	ܢܰܓܒܳܗ	ܢܰܓܒܰܢ	—
ܢܰܓܠܘܗܝ	ܢܰܓܠܳܗ	ܢܰܓܠܰܢ	—
ܢܰܓܠܘܗܝ	ܢܰܓܠܳܗ	ܢܰܓܠܰܢ	—
ܢܰܓܒܬܘܗܝ	ܢܰܓܒܢܳܗ	ܢܰܓܒܢ	—
ܡܰܓܒܝܗ	ܡܰܓܒܣܳܗ	ܡܰܓܒܝܒ	ܡܰܓܒܝܓܶܦ
ܡܰܓܒܐܦܗ	ܡܰܓܒܐܦܳܗ	ܡܰܓܒܐܦܢ	ܡܰܓܒܐܦܓܦ

10

On the Perfect.

§ 194. *On the Perfect*: The ܬ of the 2nd pers. always remains hard; the East-Syrians usually extend this process to the 1st sg. also, except in the Peal,—contrary to the ancient practice—while the genuine West-Syrian tradition leaves the ܬ soft in this position. Notice the forms of the 3rd f. sg. in the Pael and Aphel, which preserve the *a*, for which the East-Syrians put *ā* (*e. g.* ܐܪܡܝܬܗ "she threw him", § 43 C).

Forms from these verbs of the 3rd m. pl. in *ūn(ā)* before suffixes ☞ p. 351 are very rare, the only cases known to me being the following two: ܚܙܘܢܝܗܝ "they saw him" Mark 6, 49 S.; and ܡܚܘܢܝܗܝ "they scourged him" Land II, 26, 11: on the other hand individual cases of the 3rd f. pl. in *ēn(ā)* are somewhat oftener met with, like ܚܙܝܢܝܗܝ "they (f.) saw him" = ܚܙܝܢܗܝ.

Forms of Aphel: ܐܪܡܝܗ "he threw him"; ܐܣܓܝܟܘܢ "he increased you"; ܐܘܡܝܬܟܝ "I adjured you (f.)"; ܐܣܠܝܘܗ "they rejected her";—ܐܚܝܢܝ "he enlivened me"; ܐܚܝܬܢܝ "she enlivened me"; ܐܚܝܬܢܝ "thou didst enliven me".

On the Imperfect.

§ 195. *On the Imperfect*: The *ē* before the suff. of the 2nd pl. is often not expressed through ܝ: ܐܚܘܟܘܢ = ܐܚܘܝܟܘܢ "I show you", &c. The forms which do not end in ܐ follow closely the analogy of the strong verb; cf. ܢܩܪܘܢܝܗܝ "they call upon him", alongside of ܢܫܬܘܢܗ "they drink it (m.)"; ܢܩܪܘܢܟ "they call thee"; ܢܫܠܡܘܢܟܝ "they deliver thee (f.)"; ܢܚܙܝܢܝܗܝ "they (f.) see him", alongside of ܢܨܚܝܢܗ "they (f.) revile him"; ܬܩܪܝܢܢܝ "you (f.) call me"; ܢܒܟܝܢܗ "they (f.) bewail her";—ܬܩܪܝܢܝ "thou (f.) callest me"; ܬܣܩܝܢܝܗܝ "thou (f.) bringest him up", and even ܬܚܙܝܢܝܗ "thou (f.) seest her", which can only be ܬܚܙܝܢܗ (§ 188).

Answering to the forms cited above (§ 188) there are found, without ܘ, in Cod. Sin. a few like ܐܚܙܝܗܝ "I see him" (= ܐܚܙܝܘܗܝ); ܐܚܘܝܗܝ "I show him". And answering on the other hand to the forms referred to in the end of that section there occurs in Cod. D of Alexis (Var. to 18, 17), as well as in the Sinai Codex of the Acts of Thomas (Burkitt ☞ p. 351 10, 11) = Wright's Apost. Apocr. 315, 3, ܐܚܙܝܘܗ "I see him".

Rem. A poet (in Barh. gr. I, 151, 19) says once ܠܐ ܬܫܪܝܝܗܝ (instead of ܬܫܪܝܘܗܝ) "do not loose him", following the analogy of the 2nd form of the 2nd sg. m. in the strong verb (§ 190 G).

§ 196. *On the Imperative*: Longer forms of the pl. m. are found, like ܫܪܐܘܘܢܢܝ, alongside of ܫܪܐܘܘܢܝ "loose me"; ܠܘܐܘܢܢܝ (ܠܘܘܢܢܝ for proper ܠܘܘܢܢܝ) "accompany me"; ܐܣܐܘܢܗܝ "heal him". Forms of the 2nd pl. f. without *n* before the suffix hardly ever occur. Modes of writing are found like ܟܣܐܝܢܢ = ܟܣܝܢܢ "cover (f.) us"; ܩܪܐܝܢܗܝ "call ye (f.) upon him".—For the 2nd sg. f. a shorter style of writing is found, as ܐܫܩܝܢܝ "give (f.) me to drink" = ܐܫܩܐܝܢܝ. **On the Imperative.**

As in the Impf., so here also, forms occur without ܘ, though very rarely indeed: ܫܕܝܗܝ "throw him" (Lagarde, Anal. 11, 11), and ܥܢܝܗܝ (Wright, Catal. 897 *b*, 19) "answer him" (for ܫܕܝܘܗܝ, ܥܢܝܘܗܝ). Farther, there occurs in the refrain of an ancient Church Hymn (¹) ܥܢܝܗ "answer her", a dissyllable, thus doubtless ܥܢܝܗ according to the analogy of ܦܩܘܕܝܗ. ☞ p. 351 ☞ p. 351

§ 196*. *A transition of verbs tert.* ܐ *to the formation of verbs tert.* ܝ is indicated by the expressions ܒܝܐܘܗܝ "they comforted him" (Perf.), and "comfort ye him" (Impt.); ܒܝܐܘܢܝ "comfort ye me",—which occur as secondary forms of ܒܝܐܘܗܝ, ܒܝܐܘܢܝ (cf. § 172 B). **Transition of Verbs *tertiae* ܐ to Verbs *tertiae* ܝ before Suffixes.**

§ 197. *The Quadriliterals* (taken in the wide sense of the term adopted above, § 180) bear themselves before suffixes also, exactly like the Pael forms. A few examples will suffice: Perf. ܫܥܒܕܗ "he reduced her to slavery"; ܪܘܪܒܘܟ (or ܐܪܘܪܒܘܟ § 52 B) "they exalted thee"; ܡܪܡܪܘܗܝ "were stubborn against him"; ܗܝܡܢܬܘܢܝܗܝ "ye believed in him". With *ūn* ܦܫܦܫܘܢܝܗܝ "they tore him in pieces". (²) **Quadriliterals before Suffixes.** ☞ p. 351

Impf. ܬܪܘܪܒܟ (ܬܐܪܘܪܒܟ § 52 B) "she raises thee up"; ܢܣܡܟܝܘܗܝ "he supports him"; ܐܣܡܟܟܘܢ "I support you"; ܢܫܥܒܕܘܢܝܗܝ "they enslave him", &c.

Impt. (with retention of the vowel before the last radical) ܐܦܩܣܝܗܝ "set him *or* it forth"; ܫܘܙܒܝܢܝ "save me"; and thus too the 2nd form of the 2nd sg. m. Impf. ܬܫܥܒܕܝܘܗܝ "thou enslavest him".—Plural ܫܥܒܕܘܢܝ

(¹) Said to be by Ephraim; in the *Officium Feriale* of the Maronites, for Thursday, Noon, at the end (Roman edition of 1863, p. 355 *sq.*; Kesruân ed. of 1876, p. 414 *sq.*). The refrain is repeated eight times.

(²) Overbeck 292, 25 (in four syllables).

"suffer me", of course without the vowel; but the usage fluctuates between ܗܰܝܡܢܺܝܢܝ and ܗܰܝܡܶܢܺܝܢܝ "believe (f.) me".

The Quadriliterals which end in ܝ correspond to the Pael forms of verbs *tert.* ܝ; cf. ܫܰܡܠܝܶܗ "perfected him *or* it (m.)"; ܐܰܪܣܝܟܽܘܢ "he nourished you"; ܡܪܰܣܝܳܟ "nourishes thee"; ܡܫܰܡܠܶܝܢܝ "perfects me"; ܣܰܘܣܶܝܢܝ "tend me" (Impt.), &c.

☞ p. 351

Reflexive Verbs before Suffixes.

§ 198. A. *Of Reflexive verbs*, only a few, that have become transitive, appear with suffixes: Of those ending in a strong rad., there occur in particular ܐܶܬܕܰܟܰܪ "to remember"; ܐܶܬܥܗܶܕ "to remember"; ܐܶܬܟܪܶܟ "to surround"; ܐܶܬܥܛܶܦ "to put on"; ܐܶܬܗܓܺܝ "to meditate on";—and the Quadriliteral ܐܶܫܬܰܘܕܰܥ "to recognise". Examples: Perf. ܐܶܬܗܰܓܝܳܗ̇; ܐܶܬܕܰܟܪܳܟ; ܐܶܫܬܰܘܕܥܳܗ̇; ܐܶܬܕܰܟܪܬܳܗ̇ "thou didst remember her"; ܐܶܬܕܰܟܪܬܳܟ "I remembered thee"; ܐܶܬܕܰܟܪܽܘܢܳܗ̇; ܐܶܙܕܰܘܰܕܢܳܝܗܝ "we provided ourselves therewith"; ܐܶܬܕܰܟܪܬܳܢܝ; ܐܶܬܟܰܪܟܽܘܢܝ; ܐܶܬܕܰܟܪܽܘܟ; ܐܶܫܬܰܘܕܥܽܘܗܝ; ܐܶܬܟܰܪܟܳܗ̇ (3 pl. f.), &c. *Impf.* ܢܶܬܕܰܟܪܳܟ; ܐܶܬܕܰܟܪܰܢܝ; ܢܶܬܥܰܛܦܺܝܗ̇; ܢܶܬܕܰܟܪܽܘܢܳܟ; ܢܶܫܬܰܘܕܥܽܘܢܳܟܽܘܢ, &c. *Impt. sg. m.* ܐܶܬܕܰܟܪܳܝܗ̇; ܐܶܬܕܰܟܪܰܝܢܝ; *sg. f.* ܐܶܫܬܰܘܕܥܺܝܗ̇; ܐܶܬܕܰܟܪܺܝܢܝ and also ܐܶܬܕܰܟܪܺܝܢܳܢܝ from the lengthened form (§ 190 D) (1); *pl.* ܐܶܬܕܰܟܪܽܘܢܝ. There occur also, however, with a strange imitation of the vocalisation of the Peal, ܐܶܬܟܪܽܘܟܽܘܗܝ and ܐܶܬܟܪܽܘܟܳܗ̇ (2), alongside of ܐܶܬܟܰܪܟܽܘܗܝ and ܐܶܬܟܰܪܟܳܗ̇.

Inf.: ܡܶܬܟܰܪܟܽܘܬܳܗ̇.

B. Of reflexives *tertiae* ܝ we have ܐܶܫܬܥܝܶܗ, ܐܶܫܬܥܝܳܗ̇ "he told of him, of her"; ܐܶܬܛܥܝܽܘܢܝ "they forgot me"; ܐܶܫܬܥܶܝܗ̇ "I tell of her".

ܐܝܬ.

ܐܝܬ.

§ 199. ܐܺܝܬ "*is*",—properly something like "existence" (ground-form אִיתַי,—of which the emph. st. ܐܺܝܬܝܳܐ "the being" τὸ ὄν is still quite current as a substantive)—in practice passes completely over to the class of verbs. It combines with itself possessive suffixes, which are attached

---

(1) Jacob of Sarûg in Mart. II, 242 middle.

(2) These forms are well authenticated by both East- and West-Syrians—Josh. 6, 3 *sq.*; 2 Kings 11, 8; Ps. 48, 12 (in Hex. also), although the other form has likewise good authority (Ceriani's Text).

to the original ending *ai*, in the very same way as to the *ai* of the pl. (§ 145 A). Thus:

ܐܝܬܰܝ — I am.		ܐܝܬܰܝܢ — We are.
ܐܝܬܰܝܟ — Thou art.		ܐܝܬܰܝܟܘܢ — You are.
ܐܝܬܰܝܟܝ — Thou (f.) art.		ܐܝܬܰܝܟܝܢ — You (f.) are.
ܐܝܬܰܘܗܝ — He is.		ܐܝܬܰܝܗܘܢ — They are.
ܐܝܬܶܝܗ — She is.		ܐܝܬܰܝܗܝܢ — They (f.) are.

Besides this usage, ܐܝܬ may be combined with the separate Personal pronouns. — v. § 302.

With a foregoing ܠܐ we have ܠܐ ܐܝܬ or ܠܰܝܬ "is not". The contracted form also takes suffixes, *e. g.* ܠܰܝܬܘܗܝ "he is not", &c.

PART THIRD.
SYNTAX.

I. THE SEPARATE PARTS OF SPEECH.

§ 200. In this branch of the subject we adhere to the division, which has already been adopted in the "Morphology", of all the words of the language into *Nouns* and *Verbs*. This is a division, however, in which there cannot be any sharp line of demarcation. Participles, for instance, which in origin belong to the Noun, must on account of their essentially Verbal treatment be taken with the Verb; and it appears a proper course farther, to associate with them in certain cases even the Predicative Adjective (§§ 254 D; 314).—With the Noun we again reckon Adverbs and Prepositions; and the treatment of Copulative Conjunctions will come up farther on in dealing with combinations of two or more sentences.

1. NOUNS.

A. GENDER.

§ 201. A real distinction betwixt *Neuter* (what is inanimate) and what has gender, is known to Syriac, only in the interrogative pronouns "what?" ܡܐ, ܡܘ, ܡܢܐ, ܡܢܘ, and "who?" ܡܢ. In the short-hand use of the adjective or pronoun standing alone, the Feminine usually takes the place of our Neuter: Thus, *e. g.* ܐܚܪܬܐ "something else" Jos. St. 5, 7;

ܗܘ ܕ "*id quod*"; ܗܳܕܶܐ "*hoc*"; ܥܰܡ ܗܳܕܶܐ "therewith, in addition to this" Ov. 176, 5; ܗܽܘ ܕܶܝܢ ܗܳܕܶܐ "this however" Jos. St. 12, 11; ܐܰܝܕܳܐ ܕܗܘܳܬ "that which happened" Moes. II, 68, 25; ܚܕܳܐ ܗܝ ܕܶܝܢ ܕܡܶܬܒܰܥܝܳܐ ἑνὸς δέ ἐστι χρεία Luke 10, 42; cf. Aphr. 250, 19; ܛܳܒܬܳܐ "the good"; ܒܺܝܫܬܳܐ "the evil" Gen. 2, 9 and frequently; ܦܳܐܝܳܬܳܐ "properly", "in a fitting manner" Aphr. 460, 5, &c. Cf. cases like ܘܕܝܰܬܺܝܪ .... ܡܫܟܚܐ "and that which still more .... can &c." Spic. 19, 10 (where the relative ܕ is construed as feminine), and many instances in accordance with § 254.

But that the Masc. also is permissible in this case is shown, first by the adverbial use of words like ܫܰܦܺܝܪ "finely"; ܛܳܒ "well"; ܒܺܝܫ "ill" &c. (§ 155 A). This is farther shown by instances like ܠܳܐ ܦܳܪܫܺܝܢ ܛܳܒ ܡܶܢ ܒܺܝܫ Aphr. 424, 22 or ܘܠܳܐ ܦܳܪܫܺܝܢ ܛܳܒ ܡܶܢ ܒܺܝܫ Aphr. 170, 13 "they discern not good from evil"; and farther ܐܰܘ ܠܛܳܒ ܐܰܘ ܠܒܺܝܫ "either to good or to evil" Spic. 3, 6; ܢܟܺܝܠܺܝܢ ܠܛܳܒ "crafty for what is good" Aphr. 190, 4; in the Emph. st. ܠܳܐ ܢܳܣܶܒ ܒܨܺܝܪܳܐ ܐܳܘ ܝܰܬܺܝܪܳܐ "takes neither too little nor too much" Ephr. II, 485 B; ܘܕܽܘܢ ܣܰܢܝܳܐ ܘܫܰܦܺܝܪܳܐ "and judge what is hateful and what is beautiful" Ephr. II, 316 C. Thus frequently ܕܒܺܝܫ "what is bad"; ܕܛܳܒ "what is good", &c. = "the bad", "the good". With the Pronoun, cases like ܗܳܝ ܕ "this is what" are not abundant (Aphr. 211, 8; 396, 3); but they occur often after prepositions, as in ܡܶܛܽܠ ܗܳܝ "on that account"; ܒܰܠ ܗܳܘ "therefore". And ܗܳܝܢܽܘ "that is"; ܗܳܝܢܽܘ ܕܶܝܢ "but that is" = "namely" are of very frequent occurrence.

In the Plur. however the Fem. is exclusively employed: ܛܳܒܳܬܳܐ "goods", "*bona*"; ܗܳܠܶܝܢ ταῦτα (only construed as fem.); ܗܳܠܶܝܢ ܟܽܠܗܶܝܢ "all this"; ܗܳܠܶܝܢ ܓܶܝܪ ܠܬܪܰܬܰܝܗܶܝܢ "for, both of these" Aphr. 9, 16 and various other examples.

B. ABSOLUTE STATE; EMPHATIC STATE.

§ 202. A. Originally the Emph. St. denoted the Determination [as did the prefix הַ in Hebrew]: מלך was "*a* king", מַלְכָּא "*the* king". But the use of the emph. st. became so prevalent in Syriac, that very scanty traces now remain of its original and proper signification. This is clearly shown by cases like ܝܰܘܡܳܬܳܐ "a few days" Spic. 1, 1, and by the circumstance that a

B. Absolute State: Emphatic State. Abs. St. in the Substantive.

very large number of substantives appear now only in the emph. st. Add to this, that the Abs. St., even where it still survives, may almost always have the emph. st. substituted for it in the Substantive, and that it appears repeatedly even in determined words. But if the difference of meaning in the two states is in this way as good as lost completely for the language, there are still many cases[1] in which the abs. st. appears in the substantive often, or indeed preponderatingly, on the ground of its original signification. It occurs in the following cases:

B. (1) In several genuine Syriac Proper-names, which being determined in themselves required no determining sign. Thus names of localities like ܚܡܘܪܝܢ, ܢܨܝܒܝܢ "Pillars"; ܩܢܫܪܝܢ (also ܩܢܫܪܐ) = *qen nešrīn* "Eagles'-nest"; ܛܘܪ ܥܒܕܝܢ "Mountain of the Servants (of God?)"; ܟܦܪ ܨܠܡ "Image-town" (near Edessa, Jos. St. 58, 2); ܬܠܨܗܝܐ "Thirsty Hill" Anc. Doc. 73, 13, and many others; but, along with these, many appear in the emph. st. like ܫܘܪܐ "Wall"; ܚܣܢܐ "Fortress", &c. Names of Persons: ☞ p. 351 ܚܒܝܒ "Beloved"; ܐܕܣ "Patricius" (together with ܐܕܣܐ); ܩܫܝܫ "Senior"; ܡܙܕܩܬܐ "Justificata" (f.) &c.; but here too the emph. st. preponderates, as in ܙܥܘܪܐ "Little"; ܡܟܝܟܐ "Humble"; ܐܚܐ "Brother" &c. Thus the poets make use even of ܫܡܝܢ "The Heavens" as a proper name, as in Isaac II, 4 v. 32; 344 v. 1753 and in several other instances. Of course foreign proper-names like ܦܛܪܘܣ &c. receive no mark of the emph. st.

Rem. Constant epithets of proper-names were retained in the Abs. st. in earlier times: thus in the names of the Months still ܬܫܪܝ ܩܕܝܡ or ܬ' ܩܕܝܡ "Tešrī First" (= October); ܟܢܘܢ ܐܚܪܝܢ "Kānōn Second (= January) &c.

C. (2) In distributive repetition: ܟܠ ܫܢܐ ܫܢܐ "every year" Sirach 47, 10; Jos. St. 26, 18; ܝܘܡ ܡܢ ܝܘܡ "from day to day" frequently; ܙܒܢ ܙܒܢ "from time to time" frequently; ܙܒ̈ܢܝܢ ܙܒ̈ܢܝܢ "at times" Aphr. 45, 5; ܣܓܝܐܝܢ ܐܢܘܢ ܢܡܘܣܐ ܒܡܠܟܘ ܡܠܟܘ ܘܒܐܬܪ ܐܬܪ ܘܒܦܢܝܢ ܦܢܝܢ "numerous are the laws in all kinds of kingdoms, lands, and districts" Spic. 18, 16;

---

[1] In the Plural and in the Abstract form in *ūth* the Abs. st. occurs much more frequently than elsewhere; the characteristic forms (in *īn*, *ān*; *ū*) may still be fashioned here in every case.

ܒܪܟܗ ܪܟܗ "with any thing" Aphr. 308, 18; ܕܪܓ ܡܢ ܕܪܓ "step by step" Ephr. Nis. p. 77 v. 98; ܒܡܕܝܢܐ ܡܕܝܢܐ "city by city" repeatedly; ܡܢ ܡܕܝܢܐ ܠܡܕܝܢܐ "ἀπὸ πόλεως εἰς πόλιν" Matt. 23, 34; ܗܕܡ ܗܕܡ ܢܬܦܣܩ "he shall be cut to pieces, limb by limb" Jul. 87, 17; ܒܥܠܠܢ ܥܠܠܢ "on any pretext whatsoever" Ov. 221, 6; ܒܐܘܠܨܢܐ ܕܥܩܐ ܥܩܐ "in vexation from all sorts of straits" Mart. I, 185, 12; ܕܙܢܝܢ ܙܢܝܢ "of all manner of kinds" Aphr. 267, 2, and repeatedly; ܩܝܡܝܢ ܗܘܘ ܓܘܩܝܢ ܓܘܩܝܢ "they stood in crowds" Addai 2, 12 &c. Yet the emph. st. occurs here also: ܡܢ ܙܒܢܐ ܠܙܒܢܐ "from time to time" Sim. 301 mid.; ܡܕܝܢܬܐ ܥܡ ܡܕܝܢܬܐ "city with city" Is. 19, 2; ܟܣܪܝܬܐ ܟܣܪܝܬܐ "a loaf of bread a-piece" Judges 8, 5; cf. Matt. 24, 7; Ps. 19, 3 &c. Matt. 24, 2 has in P. ܟܐܦ ܥܠ ܟܐܦ λίθος ἐπὶ λίθον, and thus Aphr. 412, 17; but in S. the reading is ܟܐܦܐ ܥܠ ܟܐܦܐ.

D. (3) After ܟܠ, with Numerals and in similar connections: ܟܠ ܙܢܝܢ ܛܒܝܢ ܘܫܦܝܪܝܢ ܘܡܝܬܪܝܢ "all good, beautiful and excellent kinds" Aphr. 297, 8; ܒܟܠ ܚܦܝܛܘܬܗ "with all zeal" Ov. 178, 7; ܟܠ ܩܢܝܢܝܢ "all possessions" Ov. 166, 24; ܒܟܠ ܙܘܗܪ "with all caution" Prov. 4, 23; ܒܟܠ ܒܝܫܢ "with all evils" Prov. 5, 14; ܟܠ ܟܬܦ ܫܠܝܚܐ "every shoulder (f.) has been stripped" Ezek. 29, 18; ܟܠ ܐܣܘܢ ܒܟܠ ܐܬܪ "all remedies in every place" Ephr. III, 251 A; ܒܟܠ ܙܒܢ ܕܐܘܠܨܢܐ "in every time of distress" Sirach 2, 11; ܟܠ ܥܠܐ πᾶσαν αἰτίαν Matt. 19, 3—and very often thus. More rarely the emph. st. occurs here, and particularly in the pl., *e. g.* ܟܠ ܢܚܠܐ "all the streams" Eccl. 1, 7; ܠܟܠ ܡܗܝܡܢܐ "to all believers" Aphr. 202, 1 &c. For ܠܟܠ ܟܐܒܐ "to all pains" Aphr. 135, 3 there is a variant ܒܟܠ ܟܐܒܝܢ. ☞ p. 351

Along with numerals; (a) when the numeral precedes: ܚܕܐ ܢܦܫ ܘܠܒ ܚܕ καρδία καὶ ψυχὴ μία Acts 4, 32; ܡܢ ܚܕ ܕܡ ἐξ ἑνὸς αἵματος Acts 17, 26; ܬܪܝܢ ܥܠܡܝܢ "two worlds" Ephr. III, 111 C; Ov. 135, 7, 8; ܝܘܡܝܢ ܬܪܬܝܢ ܘܥܣܪܝܢ ܡܠܟܘܢ ܕܒܝܬ ܝܗܘܕܐ "the days of the twenty-two reigns of Judah" Aphr. 84 *ult.* and very often thus;—(b) When the numeral follows: ܫܢܝܢ ܬܡܢܐ ἐτῶν ὀκτώ Acts 9, 33; ܝܘܡܝܢ ܡܐܐ "a hundred days" Aphr. 483, 4; ܫܢܝܢ ܫܒܥܡܐܐ "seven hundred years" Land II, 277, 3 &c. In like manner also ܒܥܠܬܐ ܡܢ ܥܠܠܢ "on any pretext" Ov. 187, 10; ܒܚܕ ܡܢ ܝܘܡܝܢ "on a day" Ov. 167, 26 &c. Even when strict determination is ☞ p. 351

present, the Abs. st. may be retained alongside of the numeral: ܗܠܝܢ ܐܪܒܥܐ ܝܪܚܝܢ "these four months" Sim. 276, 5; ܒܗܠܝܢ ܬܪܬܝܢ ܦܘܩܕܢܝܢ ἐν ταύταις ταῖς δυσὶν ἐντολαῖς Matt. 22, 40 (Aphr. 24, 4, 9); ܡܢ ܗܠܝܢ ܠܬܠܬ ܡܚܘܢ ἀπὸ τῶν τριῶν πληγῶν [τούτων] Rev. 9, 18 (Gwynn); ܗܠܝܢ ܠܬܠܬܐ ܙܕܝܩܝܢ "these three righteous ones" Aphr. 453, 12; ܗܠܝܢ ܬܪܬܝܢ ܡܠܟܘܢ ܬܩܝܦܢ "these two powerful kingdoms" Jul. 106, 27 &c.

But in all these cases the Emph. st. is permissible also, and in several of them it is much more usual, cf. ܚܕܐ ܢܦܫ ܘܚܕܐ ܬܪܥܝܬܐ "one soul (abs.) and one mind (emph.)" Moes. II, 72, 12; ܒܚܕ ܩܠܐ "with one voice" Acts 19, 34; ܚܕ ܓܒܪܐ ܚܟܝܡܐ "one wise man" Aphr. 394, 12; ܫܒܥ ܬܘܪܬܐ "seven kine" Gen. 41, 3 (v. 2 ܫܒܥ ܬܘܪܢ); ܪܒܘ ܫܡܗܐ ܒܝܫܐ "ten thousand wicked names" Jul. 76, 24 (together with ܪܒܘ ܒܝܫܢ ܘܣܘܪܚܢܝܢ "ten thousand villanies and crimes" *ibid.* 34, 4) and countless others.—ܝܘܡܐ ܠܬܠܬܐ Ephr. III, 303 B; cf. Aphr. 481 *sqq.* where ܫܢܝܐ appears oftenest with the numeral following, but sometimes ܫܢܝܢ; so too ܥܕܡܐ ܠܫܥܐ ܬܫܥ ἕως ὥρας ἐνάτης Matt. 27, 45 P. S., alongside of ܠܘܬ ܬܫܥ ܫܥܝܢ περὶ τὴν ἐνάτην ὥραν *ibid.* 46.—ܚܕ ܡܢ ܟܘܟܒܐ "one of the stars" Spic. 3, 18.—For ܡܢ ܗܢܘܢ ܠܬܠܬܐ ܓܒܪܝܢ "of those three men" Aphr. 16, 19 there is a variant ܓܒܪܐ, and the emph. st. in itself suits the passage better.

☞ p. 351 E. Similarly, with ܟܡܐ "how much?" and "some": ܟܡܐ ܙܒܢܝܢ "how many times?" and "several times"—frequently; ܟܡܐ ܐܣܦܪܝܕܝܢ πόσας σπυρίδας Matt. 16, 10; ܟܡܐ ܫܢܝܢ τοσαῦτα ἔτη Luke 15, 29; so Sim. 348 mid.; but ܟܡܐ ܢܦܩܬܐ "how much expense?" Jos. St. 15, 17; ܟܡܐ ܙܢܝܐ "how many wantons?" Sim. 344, where there are farther examples. ܟܡܐ ܐܓܝܪܐ πόσοι μίσθιοι Luke 15, 17 P. C., but S. ܐܓܝܪܝܢ.

Sometimes also with ܐܝܢܐ: ܐܝܢܐ ܟܐܒܐ "what pain?" Spic. 40, 20; ܥܠ ܐܝܕܐ ܨܒܘ "on what thing?" Zingerle, Chrest. 407 v. 33 (Isaac); ܒܐܝܠܝܢ ܨܒܘܢ "in what things?" Aphr. 8, 14 &c.; but ܐܝܢܐ ܦܘܩܕܢܐ ποία ἐντολή Matt. 22, 36 &c.; and ܒܐܝܢܐ ܫܘܠܛܢ ἐν ποίᾳ ἐξουσίᾳ alternates with ܒܐܝܢܐ ܫܘܠܛܢܐ Matt. 21, 23, 24 and 27; Luke 20, 2 (cf. C. and S.) (1).

(1) Similarly ܡܢܐ ܢܘܬܪ ܘܝܘܬܪܢܐ "what sort of use (abs.) and advantage (emph.)?" Aphr. 204. 20, if the text is quite accurate.

F. (4) Often, in negative expressions; ܕܠܐ ܚܘܣܝܢ "without sparing" Ov. 170, 8; ܕܠܐ ܚܛܗܝܢ "without sin (pl.)" frequently; ܕܠܐ ܡܢܝܢ "without number" frequently; ܕܠܐ ܟܣܦ "without money" Ex. 21, 11; and often in this way with ܕܠܐ; But ܕܠܐ ܟܣܦܐ ܘܕܠܐ ܕܡܝܢ "without money (emph.) and without price (abs.)" Is. 55, 1; ܕܠܐ ܢܣܝܢܐ ܘܕܠܐ ܡܪܬܝܢܘ "without trial (emph.) and without admonition (abs.)" Aphr. 252, 2; ܕܠܐ ܗܝܡܢܘܬܐ "without faith" Aphr. 214, 1, together with ܕܠܐ ܗܝܡܢܘ *ibid.* 206, 21, and frequently; and thus the emph. st. is not unfrequently found with ܕܠܐ. For ܕܠܐ ܒܢܝܐ *ἄτεκνος* Luke 20, 29 *sq.*, C. and S. have ܕܠܐ ܒܢܝܢ.—ܝܘܬܪܢ ܠܝܬ "there is no profit" Prov. 10, 2; ܝܘܬܪܢ ܠܝܬ Hebr. 7, 18; ܘܠܐ ܢܗܘܐ ܠܗ ܥܘܗܕܢ ܠܝܪܒܥܡ "and let there be no remembrance of Jeroboam" Sirach 47, 23 (Var. ܕܘܟܪܢܐ); ܠܝܬ ܬܟܣܝܬܐ ܠܐܒܕܢܐ "the world of death [*or* the abode of destruction] has no covering" Job 26, 26; ܕܪ̈ܚܡܝܢ ܠܝܬ ܠܗ "who has no pity" Prov, 17, 11 (and often with ܠܝܬ); ܘܠܐܝܟܐ ܠܐ ܢܦܩܝܢ "and to no place do they go out" Ov. 212, 14; ܘܦܬܓܡ ܠܡ ܠܐ ܝܗܒ ܠܕܝ̈ܢܘܗܝ "and he answered never a word to his judges" Aphr. 222, 8. Cf. Luke 1, 33 and many a like example. Thus farther ܡܪܐ ܩܢܝܢ ܠܐ ܐܬܩܪܝ "was not called the possessor of riches" Spic. 46, 7. But the Emph. st. is still more used even in such cases. ☞ p. 351

Similarly in a conditional clause ܐܢ ܓܝܪ ܢܦܓܘܥ ܒܢ ܓܒܪ ܥܘܠ "for if a wicked man happen to meet us" Aphr. 297, 1; this however is unusual. ☞ p. 351

G. (5) In certain adverbial expressions like ܒܪܓܠ "on foot"; ܡܢ ܪܝܫ ܠܪܝܫ "from one end to the other"; ܒܙܒܢ "once"; ܠܥܠܡ and ܠܥܠܡܝܢ "for ever"; ܡܢ ܫܠܝ "out of quiet", *i. e.* "unexpectedly, suddenly" (also ܡܢ ܫܠܝܐ) and many others. So ܒܪܘܚ *ἐν πνεύματι* in various uses Matt. 5, 3 P. (C. and S. different); 22, 43 P. (C. ܒܪܘܚܐ); Philox. 106, 9; Rev. (Gwynn) 1, 10; 4, 2; 17, 3; 21, 10 (the later version has always ܒܪܘܚܐ).

H. (6) In some combinations the Abs. St. is always retained. Thus ܨܘܪܬ ܡܠܬܐ "the image of the word", "the written text" (definite); ܠܠܝ ܐܝܡܡ "a *νυχθήμερον*" (§ 146) (1); ܐܠܗ ܒܪܢܫܐ *θεάνθρωπος*; ܩܘܪܝܐ ܡܕܝܢܬܐ = *κωμόπολις* ☞ p. 352

(1) Indeclinable: ܠܬܠܬ ܠܠܝܢ ܐܝܡܡ May, *Nova Coll.* X, 341 a = Land III, 208, 23, for which line 20 has ܠܬܠܬ ܐܝܡܡܝܢ ܘܬܠܬ ܠܠܝܢ.

Mart. I, 100, 24 &c.; and after these patterns later writers have formed more of the same kind, as ܟܠܒ ܒܪ̈ܢܫܐ κυνάνθρωποι (as pl.) &c. ܒܝܬ ܒܟܝܐ "*domus plorantis*" sg. abs. st., *i. e.,* "house of mourning", is assumed by the usage of the language to be a compound of a pl. emph. st., and takes suffixes accordingly, thus: ܒܝܬ ܒܟܝ̈ܘܗܝ &c.

I. (7) The Absolute State is farther found pretty frequently in other scattered instances, particularly in fixed phrases. Forms in ܘܬܐ— (§ 138) especially incline to stand in it. And yet even in these the Emph. St. is almost always the one which is found in actual use. Examples: ܐ̄ܢܫ, ܢܫ; ܐ̄ܢܫ̈ܝܢ, ܢܫ̈ܝܢ τὶς, τινὲς (§ 146); ܫܠܡ, ܫܠܡ ܠܟ "Peace!", "Peace be to thee!", frequently; ܒܛܝܒܘ "in kindness" Aphr. 448, 15; ܡܢ ܛܠܝܘ ܠܡܥܠܐ ܠܩܒܘܪܐ "from youth to the grave" (emph. st.) Ephr. III, 225 B;
☞ p. 352
ܒܙܒܢ ܐ̄ܚܪܝܢ "at another time" Aphr. 461, 10, for which *ibid.* 458, 15 ܒܙܒܢܐ ܐ̄ܚܪܢܐ; ܦܪ̈ܝܩܝܢ ܒܕܡ ܝܩܝܪ "redeemed by precious blood" Aphr. 260, 10; ܛܪ ܒܙܗܝܪܘ ܗܝܡܢܘܬܐ ܕܒܪ ܐܠܗܐ ܘܒܕܟܝܘܬܐ ܡܥܡܘܕܝܬܐ "keep thou with care faith in the Son of God, and with purity (emph.) baptism" Jac. Sar.,
☞ p. 352
Thamar v. 407; ܠܝܘܡ ܐ̄ܚܪܝܢ "for another day" Ov. 136, 2; and thus ܐ̄ܚܪܝܢ frequently as a substantive "another" [ein Anderer] *e. g.* Matt. 11, 3;
☞ p. 352
John 4, 37; 5, 7; 21, 18; ܢܗܘܐ ܕܘܟܪܢ ܛܒ ܠ′ "a good remembrance be to . . ." Aphr. 305, 2; ܫܘܒܚ ܠ′ "glory [be] to . . ." frequently, (along with ܬܫܒܘܚܬܐ ܠ′ "glory [be] to . . ."); ܥܬܝܪܐ ܒܛܝܠ ܒܫܢ̈ܝܢ ܕܠܐ ܚܝ "the rich man is anxious about years in which he is no longer to be alive" Aphr. 268, 1 &c.[1] Philox. has frequently ܪܘܚܢ "spiritual" (like ܒܪܘܚ v. sub section G, 5), *e. g.*
☞ p. 352
29, 8; 500, 5. Much more frequently than elsewhere, the abs. st. is used in the Old Testament, especially in certain books, *under the influence of the Hebrew text and the Targum tradition.* Cases like עבד עבדים ܥܒܕ ܥܒ̈ܕܝܢ Gen. 9, 25; אֵל אלהים ܐܠܗ ܐܠܗ̈ܝܢ Ps. 50, 1; 84, 7; 136, 2; אש להט, ܢܘܪ ܝܩܕܐ Ps. 104, 4 אלהין קדישין ܐܠܗ̈ܝܢ ܩܕ̈ܝܫܝܢ Dan. 4, 8, 9, 18; 5, 11 hardly conform to the genuine Syriac usage. On the other hand the rather more frequent use of the abs. st. in so ancient a writing as the letter of Mārā bar Serapion (Spic. 43 *sqq.*) must be regarded as a genuine record of antiquity.

K. But when the realisation of the difference in meaning between

---

(1) For ܒܚܝܠܐ ܦܓܪܢ "with bodily strength" Spic. 5, 14, the MS. has ܒ′ ܦܓܪܢܝܐ.

the emph. st. and the abs. in the Substantive had disappeared, even ancient poets ventured to set the latter state alongside of ܗܳܢ "this", which is formed like an abs. st.: ܒܗܳܢ ܢܰܦܫ Ephr. II, 424 D (but ܗܳܢ ܢܰܦܫܳܐ III, 263 D); ܒܗܳܢ ܕܳܪ "in this generation" Ephr. III, 3 C; ܒܗܳܢ ܙܒܰܢ "during this time" Isaac II, 80 v. 169.(1) Thus even in prose and verse ܒܗܳܘ ܙܒܰܢ Ephr. Nis. p. 4 v. 7; 100 v. 189; Ephr. (Lamy) I, 245, 16; 261, 21; II, 411, 11, 14 (ܒܗܳܘ ܙܒܢܳܐ I, 391 *ult.*); Jul. 119, 6; Philox. 518, 13, 20 and frequently (519, 12 var. ܒܗܳܘ ܙܒܢܳܐ); like ܗܰܘ ܙܒܰܢ Jul. 89, 3 "in that time". Later poets, especially of the Nestorian order, go much farther in the arbitrary employment of the abs. st. for the emph. ☞ p. 352

L. (8) Many foreign words do not form any emph. st. at all; thus the Greek ܐܐܰܪ ἀήρ, ܦܪܰܛܘܪܺܝܢ πραιτώριον, ܕܝܰܬܺܝܩܺܐ διαθήκη; the Persian ܫܰܓܳܠ "jackal", ܕܰܠܶܩ "weasel" &c., as well as the Greek plurals § 89. Some Greek words often lose even their final *α*, *e. g.* ܟܘܪ χώρα, alongside of ܟܘܪܳܐ (ܟܘܪܳܐ); ܒܶܡ βῆμα, alongside of ܒܝܡܐ, ܒܶܡܳܐ (ܒܶܡܳܐ) &c.

M. (9) Syriac Feminines in *ai* (§ 83) stand always in the abs. st.; thus ܛܘܥܝܝ "error", "the error".

§ 203. Several of the above examples already show that the *attributive Adjective* to a noun in the abs. st. stands also in the abs. st.; cf. farther ܟܽܠ ܡܶܠܳܐ ܒܺܝܫܳܐ πᾶν πονηρὸν ῥῆμα Matt. 5, 11; ܓܰܒܪܺܝܢ ܫܰܪܺܝܪܺܝܢ "true men" Ex. 18, 21; ܠܥܰܡ ܢܽܘܟܪܳܝ "to a foreign people" Ex. 21, 8; ܓܒܰܪ ܥܰܬܺܝܪ, ܓܒܰܪ ܡܶܣܟܺܝܢ "rich man, poor man" Aphr. 302, 20, 21 (303, 8, 9 in the same connection ܓܰܒܪܳܐ ܥܰܬܺܝܪܳܐ, ܓܰܒܪܳܐ ܡܶܣܟܺܢܳܐ); ܡܰܚܫܒܳܢ ܒܺܝܫܳܢ "wicked thoughts" Aphr. 296, 13; ܒܪܶܥܝܳܢ ܚܰܟܺܝܡ "with wise reflection" Spic. 48, 20; ܐܰܝܟ ܚܰܝܘܬܳܐ ܒܺܝܫܬܳܐ "like an evil beast" Ephr. (Lamy) I, 369, 17 &c. State of the Attributive Adjective.

Yet there are also cases like ܠܗܳܠܶܝܢ ܠܬܠܳܬܳܐ ܣܳܗܕܺܝܢ ܫܰܪܺܝܪܳܐ "to these three true witnesses" Aphr. 461, 3 (where variant is ܣܳܗܕܶܐ), cf. Eus. Ch. Hist. 146, 1; ܗܳܢܽܘܢ (ܗܳܠܶܝܢ) ܬܠܳܬܳܐ ܓܰܒܪܺܝܢ ܙܰܕܺܝܩܳܐ "those (these) three righteous men" Aphr. 16, 19; 454, 3 (in both passages a variant ܙܰܕܺܝܩܺܝܢ); ܗܳܠܶܝܢ ܟܬܳܒܶܐ ܥܣܰܪ ܙܥܘܪܶܐ "these ten small books" Aphr. 200, 15, where the

(1) These are all the undoubted examples which I have been able to collect. In Ephr. also the emph. st. with ܗܳܢ is far more frequent.

signification is determined; ܘܰܠܟܽܠܗܘܢ ܡ̈ܰܘܬܺܝܢ ܦܰܓܪ̈ܳܢܳܝܶܐ "and to all modes of bodily death" Anc. Doc. 101, 3. Cf. farther Philox. 367, 6; Jos. Styl. 70, 10; John v. Tella (Kleyn) 28, 5. *Vice versâ*, with a word standing in the emph. st., but indefinite in meaning, and in form exchangeable with the abs. st., the attributive adjective occasionally assumes the abs. st., as in ܫܰܒܥܳܐ ܪ̈ܽܘܚܳܐ ܐ̱ܚܪ̈ܳܢܝܳܢ ἕπτα ἕτερα πνεύματα Matt. 12, 45 (C. ܪ̈ܽܘܚܺܝܢ; S. without ܐ̱ܚܪ̈ܳܢܝܳܢ); ܫܰܒܥ ܬܰܘ̈ܪܳܬܳܐ ܫܰܡ̈ܺܝܢܳܢ ܒܒܶܣܪܗܶܝܢ "seven kine fat in their flesh" Gen. 41, 18 (otherwise in v. 2 and v. 19); and in very loose connection ܝܰܘ̈ܡܳܬܳܐ ܠܳܐ ܙܥܽܘܪ̈ܝܳܢ "ἡμέρας ἱκανάς" Acts 9, 43; ܘܳܐܦ ܢܶܫ̈ܶܐ ܪ̈ܰܘܪ̈ܒܳܬܳܐ ܠܳܐ ܙܥܽܘܪ̈ܝܳܢ "γυναικῶν τε τῶν πρώτων οὐκ ὀλίγαι" Acts 17, 4; and oftener still in the singular: ܟܶܣܦܳܐ ܠܳܐ ܙܥܽܘܪ "ἀργύρια ἱκανά" Matt. 28, 12; ܕܰܗܒܳܐ ܠܳܐ ܙܥܽܘܪ "not a little gold" Jos. St. 37, 5; ܙܒܰܢܳܐ ܠܳܐ ܙܥܽܘܪ "not a short time" Aphr. 165, 13; Sim. 363 *inf.* Thus often ܐ̱ܚܪܺܢ when standing before the noun:

☞ p. 352 ܐ̱ܚܪܺܢ ܦܰܓܪܳܐ "another body" Ephr. Nis. p. 96 v. 54 &c. (§ 211 B); and even when standing after it ܐܰܠܳܗܳܐ ܐ̱ܚܪܺܢ "another god" Jac. Sar., Constantin v. 28. 632.—The peculiar substantives ܐܝܘܬ, ܬܘܟܝܬ (§§ 83; 202 M) always indeed take their adjectives in the emph. st., *e. g.* ܒܰܐܝܽܘܬ ܚܰܣܺܝܢܬܳܐ "on the rigorous condition" Moes. II, 74, 3. An incongruity, no longer felt, exists in rare cases like ܓܰܒܪܳܐ ܥܳܒܶܕ ܢܺܝ̈ܫܺܝܢ ܘܫܳܪܶܐ ܩܶܛܪ̈ܺܝܢ "a man that is a worker of miracles, a solver of difficulties [knots]" Land III, 213, 14 (the 2nd epithet is from the passage in Dan. 5, 12, unskilfully translated);— ܟܽܠܗܽܘܢ ܐ̱ܢܳܫ̈ܳܐ ܦܳܪܽܘܫ̈ܶܐ ܝܳܕ̈ܥܰܝ ܛܳܒ ܡܶܢ ܒܺܝܫ "all discerning people who know good from evil" Bedjan, Mart. II, 572, 10. In these cases the undetermined genitives occasion the proper indeterminateness of the constr. st. In the immensely preponderating mass of cases, a substantive, furnished with an adjective, stands like the adjective itself in the emphatic state.

State of the Predicative Adjective. § 204. A. The Abs. St. however, in the *adjective* is the proper form of the *predicate*. Thus *e. g.* ܠܰܚܡܳܐ ܡܛܰܫܝܳܐ ܒܰܣܺܝܡ "bread hidden is pleasant" Prov. 9, 17; ܠܳܐ ܦܰܝܫ ܚܛܳܗܘܗܝ "his sin is not great" Aphr. 45, 8; ܚܽܘܒܳܐ ܪܳܡ ܡܶܢ ܦܠܽܘܓܬܳܐ "love is high above dissension" Aphr. 256, 15; ܡܰܝ̈ܳܐ ܓܢܺܝ̈ܒܳܐ ܚܠܶܝܢ "stolen waters are sweet" Prov. 9, 17; ܐܳܘ ܥܰܝܢܳܟ ܒܺܝܫܳܐ ὀφθαλμός σου πονηρός ἐστιν Matt. 20, 15 (a question); ܚܕܳܐ ܚܣܺܝܪܳܐ ܠܳܟ ἕν σοι λείπει Luke 18, 22; ܩܰܪܺܝܪܳܐ ܒܶܗ ܐܳܦ ܢܽܘܪܳܐ ܟܝܳܢܳܝܬܳܐ "even the fire of nature in him is cold" Philox. 355, 1 &c. A favourite proceeding is the alteration

of an attributive adjective, standing in the emph. st., into a predicative
one in the abs. st. and attached by the relative ܕ: cf. e. g. ܠܬܪܥܐ ܐܠܝܨܐ
ܘܐܘܪܚܐ ܕܩܛܝܢܐ "by the strait gate and the way which is narrow" Aphr.
447, 2, where ܕܐܠܝܨ ܠܬܪܥܐ or ܠܐܘܪܚܐ ܩܛܝܢܬܐ might stand as well.

Very seldom indeed in good texts are there cases like ܐܚܪܝܢ ܗܘ ܦܘܪܥܢ
ܥܒܕܐ ܘܐܚܪܝܢ ܗܘ ܦܘܪܥܢܐ ܕܡܠܐ "for the reward of deeds is one thing (adj.
in abs. st.) and the reward of words is another thing (adj. in the emph.
st.)" in the Testament of Ephr., Ov. 141, 14. (¹)

B. On the other hand the emph. st. sometimes stands along with
the Personal Pronoun, both when the latter is the direct subject, and
when it is merely the copula. This usage proceeds perhaps from a substantive conception of the adjectives, e. g. ܕܒܝܫܐ ܐܢܬܘܢ "[you] who are
evil persons" Matt. 7, 11; 12, 34; ܣܓܝܐܐ ܚܢܢ πολλοί ἐσμεν Mark 5, 9;
ܟܕ ܚܝܒܐ ܐܢܬܘܢ "while you are guilty (guilty persons)" Aphr. 144, 7;
ܟܐܢܐ ܚܢܢ "we are honest men" Gen. 42, 11, 31; ܚܟܝܡܐ ܐܢܬܘܢ
"you are wise persons" Aphr. 293, 16; ܪܒܐ ܐܢܐ "am I a great man?"
Joseph 26, 14 [Ov. 282, 1]; ܐܦ ܗܘ ܡܝܘܬܐ ܗܘ "he also is a mortal" Ov.
67, 9; ܓܙܝܪܝ ܐܢܘܢ ܡܨܪܝܐ "the Egyptians are circumcised persons" Aphr.
210, 10; ܕܗܠܝܢ ܫܪܝܪܢ "that these things are true (or that this is the truth)"
Spic. 18, 7; ܠܐ ܡܬܚܙܝܢܐ ܗܘ ܟܝܢܐ ܕܐܠܗܘܬܐ "invisible is the nature of the
Godhead" Ov. 84, 18; ܘܗܠܝܢ ܡܢܘܬܐ ..... ܐܢܝܢ ܫܬܝܩܬܐ .... ܘܡܚܪܫܬܐ "these
parts are dumb and silent" Ov. 63, 12, and many other like instances.
But the abs. st. would be permissible in all these cases, and it is the
more usual form in such cases, e. g. ܥܪܛܠ ܐܢܐ, ܥܪܛܠ ܐܢܬ "I am naked,
thou art naked" Gen. 3, 10 and 11; ܚܝܠܬܢ ܐܢܐ "I am powerful" Aphr.
269, 12; ܚܢܢ ܕܡܣܟܢܝܢ ܚܢܢ "we, who are poor" Aphr. 119, 22; ܠܡܢ
ܥܪܛܠܝܢ ܐܢܘܢ "there, with him (Death) are they naked" Aphr. 426, 1;
ܚܠܫܝܢ ܗܘ ܡܢ ܕܝܠܢ "his weapons are weaker than ours" Aphr. 137,
21 &c. Cf. cases like ܚܛܝܐ ܟܕ ܚܝ ܡܝܬܐ ܗܘ ܠܐܠܗܐ ܐܘ ܕܝܢ
ܢܚܐ ܗܘ "the sinner, even while he is alive, is a dead man (²) for God, but

---

(¹) The reading is certain; even the Roman edition does not note any variants.
There can hardly be any suggestion of metrical exigency in this case, for the deficient
syllable might easily have been made up otherwise, e. g. by a ܗܘ.

(²) Thus pretty often ܚܝܐ and ܡܝܬܐ in the Predicate. Cf. C.

the righteous man, even when he is dead, is a living man for God" Aphr. 168, 17. For ܡܒܪܟܬܐ ܐܢܬܝ ܒܢܫ̈ܐ εὐλογημένη σὺ ἐν γυναιξίν Luke 1, 42 P., S. has 'ܒܪܝܟܬ ܒ = ܒܪܝܟܐ ܐܢܬܝ.

In like manner pure Participles are always in the abs. st.; v. § 269 *sqq*.

C. With ܗܘܐ the Adj. stands throughout in the Abs. St. where Persons are not concerned, *e. g.* ܕܚܝܠܐ ܗܘܬ ܕܝܢ ܡܠܬܗ "but dreadful was his word" Ov. 178, 25; ܬܪܥܝܬܗܘܢ ܗܘܬ ܚܪܝܦܐ ܘܡܣܬܟܠܢܝܬܐ "their intelligence was alert and attentive" Ov. 100, 1; ܘܗܘܝܐ ܚܪܬܗ (ܐܚܪܝܬܗ) ܒܝܫܐ καὶ γίνεται τὰ ἔσχατα αὐτοῦ χείρονα Matt. 12, 45 &c. With persons sometimes the abs. st. is employed, and sometimes the emph. st. Thus ܒܪܗܛܗ ܡܩܠܝܠ ܗܘܐ "in his course he was fleet" Sim. 269 mid.; ܢܗܘܐ ܓܝܪ ܪܒ ἔσται γὰρ μέγας Luke 1, 15; ܕܗܢܘܢ ܓܠܝܠܝ̈ܐ ܚܛܝ̈ܐ ܗܘܘ ὅτι οἱ Γαλιλαῖοι οὗτοι ἁμαρτωλοὶ .... ἐγένοντο Luke 13, 2. But ܕܣܡܝܐ ܗܘܐ "who had been blind (a blind man)" John 9, 13; ܡܝܬܐ ܗܘܐ "was dead" Luke 15, 24 and 32; ܘܗܫܐ ܡܛܠ ܗܕܐ ܙܗܝܪ̈ܐ ܢܗܘܘܢ "and now let them through this be cautious" Ov. 85, 7; ܢܫ̈ܐ .... ܕܗܘ̈ܝ ܡܨܥܪ̈ܢ ܡܢ ܒܥ̈ܠܝܗܝܢ "women who had been ill-treated by their husbands" Isaac I, 244 v. 407. So with animals ܟܠܒ̈ܐ .... ܠܐ ܗܘܘ ܥܠܘ̈ܒܐ "the dogs were not greedy (greedy ones)" Aphr. 383, 2; cf. farther Matt. 5, 48; 6, 16. In the most of these cases also a substantive conception attaches to the adjective. Clearly thus in ܐܡܗ ܕܝܢ ܡܗܝܡܢܬܐ ܗܘܬ "but his mother was a believer" Ov. 160, 16; ܡܗܝܡܢܐ ܗܘܬ would mean only "believed". How the two states shift about here is shown by ܘܬܗܘܐ ܠܟ ܣܢܝܩܐ ܠܬܝܒܘܬܐ "and thou be in need of conversion" Aphr. 144, 15, contrasted with ܠܬܝܒܘܬܐ ܠܐ ܬܗܘܐ ܣܢܝܩ *ibid.*, line 17. This is farther shown by the fact that for ܟܐܢܐ ܗܘܐ δίκαιος ὤν Matt. 1, 19 P., or ܗܘܐ ܟܐܢܐ C., there stands in S. ܟܐܢ ܗܘܐ. So for Matt. 10, 16 P. has the emph. st. and S. the abs. st.

D. On the other hand the Predicative Adjective with ܐܝܬ stands quite regularly in the emph. st.: ܟܠܗܘܢ ܐܝܟ ܕܐܝܬܝܗܘܢ ܡܘܬܪ̈ܢܝܬܐ "everything which is useful" Ov. 84, 17; ܝܬܝܪܬܐ ܐܝܬܝܗ̇ ܗܘܬ ܡܠܬܐ ܐܠܘ "had the word been redundant" Ov. 75, 23; ܫܝܛܐ ܐܝܬܝ ܘܡܨܥܪܐ "I (m.) am despised and insignificant" Ov. 281, 26; ܘܠܐ ܡܥܕܪܢܝܬܐ ܠܗܘܢ ܐܝܬܝܗ̇ "and, besides, it (f.) is immortal" Aphr. 125, 10; ܡܢܝ̈ܚܐ ܐܝܬܝܗܘܢ ܡܕܒܪ̈ܢܐ ܕܪ̈ܗܘܡܝܐ "the leaders of the Romans are gentle" Jos. St. 89, 13.

E. With verbs like "to show one's self as", "to be found", "to be called" &c., the emph. st. of the Adjective occurs perhaps rather more frequently than the abs.: ܐܬܚܘܝ ܚܓܝܪܐ "showed himself brave" Ov. 159, 9; ܐܫܬܟܚ ܙܟܝܐ "was found victorious" *ibid.* line 10; ܕܡܬܩܪܝܢ ܚܟܝ̈ܡܐ "who are called wise men" Aphr. 506, 17 &c., but ܐܫܬܟܚܬ ܒܛܢܐ εὑρέϑη ἐν γαστρὶ ἔχουσα Matt. 1, 18; ܡܫܬܟܚܝܢ ܣܪܝܩܝܢ ܡܢ ܟܠܗ ܝܕܥܬܐ "are found devoid of all knowledge" Spic. 2, 18; ܢܦܩܘ ܡ̈ܠܝܟܘܢ ܕܓܠܐ "your words proved false" Joseph 38 *ult.* [Ov. 288, 7]. For ܡܬܚܙܝܢ ܫܦܝܪ̈ܐ "φαίνονται ὡραῖοι" Matt. 23, 27 P., Aphr. 307, 5 has 'ܡ ܫܦܝܪܝܢ; the reading is different in S.

F. The Predicative Adjective, however, stands of necessity in the emph. st. when it is quite definitely determined: ܝܥܩܘܒ ܪܕܝܦܐ ܘܥܣܘ ܪܕܘܦܐ "Jacob is the persecuted, and Esau the persecutor" Aphr. 403, 14 (v. *ibid.* 403 *sqq.* for several other such sentences); ܐܢܐ ܐܢܐ ܩܕܡܝܐ ܘܐܢܐ ܐܢܐ ܐܚܪܝܐ "I am the first, and I am the last" Is. 48, 12; ܕܗܘ ܡܝܬܪܐ ܗܘܐ ܕܟܠܗ ܡܠܟܘܬܐ "for he was certainly the most distinguished person in all the kingdom" Aphr. 55, 3; ܕܝܬܩܐ ܐܚܪܝܬܐ ܕܗܝ ܩܕܡܝܬܐ "the last testament, which is the first" Aphr. 28, 9; ܕܐܝܢܘ ܚܝܒܐ ܘܐܝܢܘ ܙܟܝܐ "who may be the guilty one, and who the innocent" Ov. 191, 9.

C. GENITIVE AND CONSTRUCT STATE.

§ 205. A. The Genitive relation is still frequently expressed in various forms of reference by the Construct State: ܡܠܟ ܒܒܠ "king of Babylon" Aphr. 468, 18 (along with ܡܠܟܐ ܕܒܒܠ *ibid.* 471, 16 as well as 2 Kings 20, 12, and frequently); ܚܝܘܬ ܫܢܐ "*belua dentis*" *i. e.* "rending animal" ["carnivorous animal", "wild beast"] frequently; ܥܘܗܕܢ ܡܪܗ "remembrance of his master" Ov. 185, 12; ܒܡܘܙܓ ܡܟܝܠܬ ܚܘ̈ܒܐ "in the overflowing of the measure of debts" Aphr. 462, 3; ܒܛܢܦܘܬ ܪܓܬ ܚܬܗ "by reason of the uncleanness of the lust after his sister" (*i. e.* "his unclean lust after &c.") Aphr. 354, 6; ܩܠ ܙܡܝܪ̈ܬܐ "the sound of songs" Aphr. 229, 18; &c. In all these cases the emph. st. with ܕ might likewise

C. Genitive and Construct State. Genitive Connection by the Constr. St. and by ܕ.

be used. But this is not permissible in specially close combinations, like
ܚܕܪܕܒܒܐ "enemy"; ܡܦܩ ܝܘܩܪܐ "taking up the burden", *i. e.* "zeal"; ܛܢܢܐ
ܒܝܬ ܕܝܢܐ "judgment"; ܒܝܬ ܡܐܟܠܐ "refectorium" (and in other combinations with
ܒܝܬ); ܒܪ ܟܝܢܗ "son of his nature" *i. e.* "of the same nature as he is"; ܒܪ
ܚܐܪܐ "a freeman" ["son of the free"] (and others with ܒܪ, ܒܪܬ, ܒܝܬ, ܒܢܝ) &c.
The constr. st. also prevails in those combinations, in which the first half
is an adjective, whose relation to the Genitive may be of various kinds:
ܚܣܝܪ ܪܥܝܢܐ or ܡܣܟܠ ܡܢ ܪܥܝܢܐ "taken *or* bereft of understanding" *i. e.*
"without understanding" Aphr. 53, 13; Jul. 47, 10, and frequently;
ܡܩܠܥ ܠܒܐ "whose heart has been torn out", *i. e.* "without understanding" Mart. I, 35 mid.; ܠܒܝܫ ܙܝܘܬܗܘܢ "clothed in splendour" Joseph
196, 6 [Ov. 296, 10]; ܠܝܛ ܚܝܘܗܝ "whose life is accursed" Aphr. 110 *ult.*;
ܣܓܝ ܕܡܘܬܐ "of many forms" Ov. 168, 23; ܝܩܝܪ ܒܕܡܝܐ "πολύτιμον" Matt.
13, 46 [lit. "heavy *or* costly in price (pl.)] &c. With affixed (reflexive)
Personal pronoun, ܡܩܛܠ ܪܘܓܙܗ "he of murderous anger" Ephr. Nis.
1, 149 &c.; ܡܢ ܟܠ ܕܩܪܝܒ ܒܕܡܗܘܢ "from any that is close to them in
blood" Aphr. 232, 15 (cf. § 224*). And thus even ܡܟܝܠ ܟܠܗ "the completely pure man" ('the man whose totality is pure') Ephr. Nis. 31, 122,
and ܕܟܝܣ ܟܠܗ "the completely troubled one" *ibid.* 123. Cases like
ܚܣܝܢܝ ܗܘܘ ܗܘ ܒܦܓܪܐ "strong in body (pl.)" Spic. 5, 19 are rare; the emph.
st. in that instance was occasioned by ܗܘ coming between,—a particle
inserted here for the sake of emphasis (§ 221).

B. But otherwise the connection by ܕ predominates throughout.
Particular examples are not required here. Both methods occur too in
those cases in which the Genitive of an abstract noun denotes a
quality or property, *e. g.* ܪܘܚ ܩܘܕܫܐ and ܪܘܚܐ ܕܩܘܕܫܐ "the spirit of
holiness" *i. e.* "the Holy Spirit"; ܡܕܝܢܬ ܩܘܕܫܐ and ܡܕܝܢܬܐ ܕܩ'; ܩܘܕܫܐ
ܡܕܝܢܬܐ and ܡܕ' ܕܩ' "the holy city"; ܒܥܠܡܐ ܢܟܝܠܐ "in the deceitful
world" Aphr. 462, 6; ܦܐܪܐ ܡܪܝܪܐ "bitter fruits" Aphr. 473, 11; ܚܐܪܘܬܐ
ܕܠܥܠܡ "everlasting liberty" Ephr. III, 250 B; ܓܦܬܐ ܡܒܪܟܬܐ "the
blessed vine" Aphr. 446, 3; ܟܣܦܐ ܣܚܝܦܐ and ܟܣܦܐ ܕܙܐܦܐ "counterfeit
money" Aphr. 301 *ult.*, 285 *ult.*; ܚܘܒܐ ܫܪܝܪܐ "true love" Spic. 7, 1;
ܒܝܬ ܩܘܦܣܐ ܣܓܝܐܐ "considerable store-chambers" Land III, 215, 13;
and many like cases. So too in cases like ܛܘܪ ܕܣܝܢܝ "Mt. Sinai" Ephr.

☞ p. 352

II, 488 B, and elsewhere, alongside of ܛܘܪܐ ܕܩܘܕܫ Ephr. II, 433 F; ܒܐܪܥ ܡܨܪܝܢ "in the land of Egypt" Aphr. 313, 5, together with the more usual ܒܐܪܥܐ ܕܡܨܪܝܢ *ibid.* line 4, &c. (where even the relation of Apposition would be allowable). But the Construct State can never stand before the ܕ of the Genitive. ([1]).

C. When the two parts are determined in *pure Genitive relation*, then the reference to the genitive is very commonly indicated by the appropriate possessive suffix, *e. g.* ܒܪܗ ܕܐܠܗܐ "the Son of God" frequently, as well as ܒܪܐ ܕܐܠܗܐ; ܡܠܚܗ ܕܐܪܥܐ τὸ ἅλας τῆς γῆς Matt. 5, 13 P. C. Aphr. 457, 7 (S. ܡܠܚܐ); ܐܠܗܗܘܢ ܕܟܪܣܛܝܢܐ "the God of the Christians" Ov. 161, 13; ܒܢܝܗ ܕܥܕܬܐ "the children (adherents) of the Church" Ov, 221, 2 = ܒܢܝ ܥܕܬܐ *id.* 216, 16 and often; as well as innumerable other instances. But the following would hardly be admissible—ܐܪܥܗ ܕܡܨܪܝܢ "the land of Egypt" (Genitive of identity); ܪܘܚܗ ܕܩܘܕܫܐ "the Holy Spirit" (Genitive of quality). ܐܒܗܬܗ ܕܡܨܪܝܢ could only mean "the fathers of Egypt" (the latter being thought of as their child); "the Egyptian fathers" is ܐܒܗܬܐ ܕܡܨܪܝܢ Jul. 56, 23. It is true there is no sharp line of demarcation here. Thus we have even ܐܣܝܪ̈ܘܗܝ ܕܡܕܝܢܬܐ "the prisoners from the city" Jul. 58, 18.

D. Examples, in which several forms of Genitive connection are associated, are ܡܘܠܕܗ ܕܐܢܫܘܬܗ ܕܒܪܗ ܕܐܠܗܐ "the birth of the human nature of the Son of God" Jul. 155, 15; ܙܒܢ ܫܘܠܡ ܡܕܒܪܢܘܬܗܘܢ ܕܒܢܝ ܫܡ "the time of the end of the administration of the sons of Shem" Aphr. 88, 13; ܩܝܢܝܐ ܕܒܝܬ ܚܡܘܗܝ ܕܡܘܫܐ "the Kenites of the house of Moses' father-in-law" Aphr. 254, 15; ܦܠܓܗ ܐܫܬܐ ܓܪܒܝܝܬܐ ܕܗܝܟܠܐ ܕܥܕܬܐ ܕܡܕܝܢܬܗ "the northern half of the wall of the sanctuary in the Church of his town" Ov. 190, 13; ܘܒܡܕܢܚܐ ܕܢܘܗܪܐ ܕܣܘܟܠܐ ܘܒܡܥܒܕܢܘܬܐ ܦܐܪ̈ܘܗܝ ܕܙܝܬܐ ܡܢܗܪܢܐ "and through the rising of the light of understanding, and through the fruit-bearing of the olive tree, the enlightener" Aphr. 449, 11 &c.

([1]) Any such instances in our editions rest on textual errors. ܒܫܡ ܫܡ ܕܒܝܬ ܝܥܩܘܒ Aphr. 323, 4 is only an apparent exception; it means "by the name—'those of the house of Jacob'" (§ 209 A): So ܒܝܘܡܝ ܕܒܝܬ ܕܝܩܠܛܝܢܘܣ "in the days of those of the house of Diocletian" Jul. 24, 9.

E. Two nouns may thus stand in different Genitive relationship to the same noun, cf. ܫܘܒܗܪܗ ܕܐܝܣܪܝܠ ܕܦܘܪܫ ܡܐܟܘܠܬܐ "Israel's boasting about the distinction of meats" Aphr. 313, 12; ܥܒܪ ܦܘܩܕܢܐ ܕܐܕܡ "the transgression of the ordinance by Adam" Aphr. 419, 13; ܥܝܕܗ ܓܝܪ ܗܘܐ ܕܐܒܪܗܡ ܕܟܠ ܝܘܡ "for it was Abraham's daily custom" Aphr. 391, 8; ܪܘܚܐ ܕܩܘܕܫܐ ܕܐܒܘܟܘܢ "the Holy Spirit of your Father" Aphr. 415, 8; ܐܝܕܗ ܕܣܡܠܐ "his hand of the left" *i. e.* "his left hand", and thus frequently with ܕܝܡܝܢܐ and ܕܣܡܠܐ "right" and "left"; ܣܦܪܟ ܕܚܝܐ "thy book of life" Ps. 69, 28; ܟܝܢܢ ܕܥܦܪܐ "our nature which is of dust" Aphr. 41, 17 &c. A different construction, and one of a Hebrew type, is found in ܦܓܪܐ ܕܚܙܝܢܗܘܢ "their visible body" Aphr. 179, 1.

Constr. St. before Prepositions. § 206. Adjectives often stand in the Constr. St. before prepositions, especially when that which is governed by the prepositions is closely connected in thought with the adjectives. Thus ܫܦܝܪܬ ܚܙܘܐ (1) "beautiful in appearance" Gen. 12, 11; ܐܣܝܐ ܪܒܐ ܝܬܝܪ ܒܟܠ "the great physician, excelling in everything" Ov. 193, 21; ܢܣܒܝ ܒܐܦܐ "*accipientes vultum*", *i. e.* "hypocrites", frequently; ܡܫܠܛ ܒܢܦܫܗ "master of himself", "free" Spic. 19, 8; ܐܠܗܘܬܗܘܢ ܟܣܝܬܐ ܡܢ ܟܠ "their divine nature concealed from all" Jul. 41, 10; ܐܝܟ ܐܚܪܢܐ ܫܝܛܝ ܡܢ ܫܡܘܥܝܗܘܢ "like others, despised by their hearers" Ov. 179, 11; ܙܒܢܐ ܚܬܝܡ ܒܢܒܝܐ "the time determined by the prophets" Mart. I, 11, 2; ܚܝܪܝ ܠܗܒ ܠܝ "who look keenly to 'give me'" Aphr. 286, 8; ܠܒܝܫ ܒܡܫܝܚܐ "who has put on Christ" Ov. 397, 12; ܘܪܓܡܬ ܠܐܝܠܝܢ ܕܫܠܝܚܝܢ ܠܘܬܗ καὶ λιϑοβολοῦσα τοὺς ἀπεσταλμένους πρὸς αὐτήν Matt. 23, 37; Luke 13, 34, and a great many other instances. A very large number, *e. g.* occur in Philox. 366. Notice farther ܡܠܬܐ ܡܚܝܠܬ ܐܝܟܘܬܗ "a word of potency like it" Ov. 21, 18; and so even ܝܠܝܕܐ ܕܠܐ ܙܘܘܓܐ "born without connection" Ov. 91, 21. This construction in the case of the substantive is limited to one or two constant combinations like ܡܣܒ ܒܐܦܐ "*acceptatio vultus*" *i. e.* "hypocrisy"; ܡܦܩ ܒܪܘܚܐ (or ܡܦܩ ܪܘܚܐ) "going forth into the wind (?)" "defence, excuse"; cf. ܡܣܡ ܒܪܝܫܐ "the laying upon the head" (Inf.) *i. e.* "punishment"; ܡܣܡ ܒܪܥܝܢܐ "thought".

☞ p. 353

---

(1) Var. ܚܙܘܗ.

Constr. St. before Adverbs.

§ 207. In rare cases Adjectives stand thus in the Constr. St. before adverbs also, which in fact resemble a combination of preposition and substantive: ܡ̈ܝܘܬܝ ܡܥܓܠܐܝܬ "who die quickly" Mart. I, 79, 10; ܦܘ̈ܙܝ ܪܘܙܐܝܬ ܥܠ ܢܚ̈ܠܘܗܝ "that leap nimbly over its valleys" Mart. I, 47, 1; ܚ̈ܝܝ ܕܘܝܐܝܬ "leading a miserable life" (κακόβιοι) Jul. 112, 13; ܡܢܣ̈ܝܝ ܛܒ ܒܟܠ ܨܒ̈ܘܢ "persons well-experienced in all things" Jul. 162, 10; ܩܛ̈ܝܠܝ ܦܓܪܢܐܝܬ .... ܡܢܚ̈ܡܝ ܪܘܚܢܐܝܬ "slain in the body .... risen in the spirit" Sim. 305, 24. Such combinations are specially made use of to translate Greek words compounded with adverbs, *e. g.* ܚ̈ܫܝ ܛܒ *εὐπαθοῦντες* Ps. 91, 15 Hex.; and indeed the whole of this construction is modelled upon the Greek. Similarly occur the circumlocutions for "self", like ܪ̈ܚܡܝ ܢܦܫܗܘܢ ܠܗܘܢ *φίλαυτοι* 2 Tim. 3, 2, Hark. Even Cyrillona ZDMG XXVII, 573 v. 267 has thus ܚܘܝܐ ܡܫܚܩܗ ܗܘ ܠܗ "the serpent that has crushed himself".

☞ p. 353

Separation of Genitive from Governing-word.

§ 208. A. The Construct State must stand *immediately* before the Genitive. Only short words like the postpositive particles ܡܶܢ, ܓܶܝܪ, ܟܺܝܬ &c., as well as ܗܘܳܐ and such like, may sometimes interrupt the succession: ܒܢ̈ܝ ܓܝܪ ܒܠܗܐ "*filii vero Balae*" Land III, 39, 16; ܐܠܗܐ ܟܝܬ ܫܡܝܐ "*deus enim coeli*" Jul. 54, 28; ܥܠܬ ܡܢ ܒܛܘܠܐ "now the cause of the abolishing" Ephr. II, 124 B; ܥܠܬ ܕܝܢ ܟܐܒܐ "the cause, to wit, of the pain" Ephr. II, 108 A; ܘܣܪ̈ܝܩܝ ܬܘܒ ܚܪܝܢܘܬܗܘܢ "and farther those who are vain of their litigiousness" Statuti della Scuola di Nisibi (Guidi) 15, 10; ܕܒܢ̈ܝ ܐܢܘܢ ܙܕܝ̈ܩܐ "that they are the sons of the righteous" Ephr. II, 384 D; ܓܢܒܪ ܗܘܐ ܚܝܠܐ "he was a mighty man of strength" Judges 11, 1 &c. More remarkable is ܥܠ ܡܕܪܐ ܬܪܝܢ ܐܣܛܕܘܬܐ ܠܘܬܗ "for a distance of two stadia from it" Jul. 229, 4.

Cf. farther § 327.

As a somewhat isolated instance stands ܟܬ̈ܒܝ ܘܩܪ̈ܝ ܫܡܗ̈ܝܗܘܢ "writers and readers of their ṇames" Land III, 136, 14, where two words in the Constr. St. refer to one Genitive.

B. The separation of the Genitive from the governing word presents no difficulty, however, when ܕ is employed. Not only may the latter have an attributive word with it, as in ܢܩܠܬܗ ܚܠܝܬܐ ܕܚܛܝܬܐ "the sweet allurements of sin" Ov. 159, 15 (which might also stand thus: ܢܩܠ'

ܕܝܠܗ̇′ ܢܬܠ), but additional words are also allowed to intervene. Cf. ܘܫܘܬܦܐ ܗܘܐ ܬܘܒ ܕܐܒܠܐ "and he was, again, a companion of the mourning" Ov. 207, 21; ܡܛܠ ܕܒܕܡܘܬܐ ܥܒܝܕ ܕܐܠܗܐ ܗܘܢܐ ܡܪܢܝܐ "because after the image of God the lordly reason has been made" Moes. II, 94 v. 296; ܐܬܐܟܠܘ ܩܪ̈ܨܐ ܩܕܡ ܢܪܣܝ ܬܡܫܒܘܪ ܕܓܒܪܐ ܚܕ "accusations were brought against a man before Narsi Tamšābōr" Mart. I, 123; ܫܡ̈ܗܝܗܘܢ ܩܕܡ ܥܕܬܐ ܟܠܗ̇ ܡܟܪܙ ܗܘܐ ܕܟܠ ܐܝܠܝܢ ܕ "he proclaimed before the whole Church the names of all those who . . . " Ov. 176, 2.—In stray cases the Genitive stands even before the governing-word; ܗܟܢܐ ܐܦ ܕܟܠܗ̇ ܗܝܡܢܘܬܢ ܫܬܐܣܬܗ̇ ܟܐܦܐ ܗܝ ܫܪܝܪܬܐ "thus also of all our faith the foundation is that firm stone" Aphr. 6, 16; ܐܦܢ ܕܚܕܐ ܫܢܬܐ ܣܘܦܩܢܐ "supplies even for only one year" Sim. 346 mid.

Nouns with ܕ, when Governing-noun is not expressed.

§ 209. A. In these cases already the superior independence of ܕ, properly a Demonstrative-(Relative-)Pronoun ("that of"), is shown. This becomes still more conspicuous when no governing word is expressed; ܥܡ ܕܒܝܬ ܗܪܘܕܣ μετὰ τῶν Ἡρωδιανῶν Matt. 22, 16 P. (ܥܡ ܥܒ̈ܕܐ ܕܗܘ′ C. S.); ܕܒܝܬ ܝܥܩܘܒ "those of the house of Jacob" frequently; ܥܠ ܕܒܝܬ ܡܪܩܝܘܢ "on the adherents of Marcion" Ov. 193, 17; ܕܐܪܒܥܝܢ "the season of the forty-days' fast" Sim. 376, *sq.*; ܡܢ ܕܒܝܬ ܡܪܥܫܝܐ "from the district of the Marʿashenes" Sim. 356, 1; ܢܚܕܘܢ ܕܢܘܪܐ ܘܕܪܘܚܐ "those rejoice who are of the fire and the spirit" Ephr. (Lamy) I, 57 Str. 7; ܕܙܘܥܬܐ ܗܘܬ ܓܝܪ ܘܕܬܕܡܘܪܬܐ "for it was a matter of terror and amazement" Sim. 355, 3; ܕܓܢܝܐ ܗܘ "is worthy of blame" Philox. 544, 9; ܟܠ ܕܐܝܬܘܗܝ ܕܡܪܢ "every one who is the Lord's" Ov. 168, 19; ܕܝܡܝܢܐ ܡܬܩܪܝܢ "are called those of the right hand (= 'the just')" Spic. 12, 4; ܗܢܘܢ ܕܣܡܠܐ "those on the left" *ibid.* 12, 6; ܕܫܘܬܦܐ ܗܘܐ "was common" Ov. 167, 24; ܗܒܘ ܗܟܝܠ ܕܩܣܪ ܠܩܣܪ ἀπόδοτε οὖν τὰ Καίσαρος Καίσαρι Matt. 22, 21; ܡܢ ܕܡܣܟܢܐ "from that which belongs to the poor" Ov. 190, 16; ܕܐܢܣ ܕܚܒܪܗ "who has robbed the property of his companion" Aphr. 423, 19; ܕܩܝܣܐ "made of wood" Jac. Sar. in ZDMG XXIX, 109 v. 30; ܕܙܒܢܐ ܐܢܘܢ πρόσκαιροί εἰσιν Mark 4, 17; ܥܡܠܗܘܢ ܕܗܘܐ ܗܘܐ ܕܐܚܪ̈ܢܐ "their toil, which had become (the property) of others" Aphr. 506, 3, and frequently ܗܘܐ ܕ, and many like instances. To this place belongs also ܘܢܣܒܗ̇ ܕܬܪܝܢ ܠܐܢܬܬܗ καὶ ἔλαβεν ὁ δεύτερος τὴν γυναῖκα Luke 20, 30 P. S. (where C. reads differently,

ܠܐܬܬܐ ܗܘܐ); cf. v. 31, and 19, 18 (§ 239). Somewhat different are cases like ܘܠܐ ܐܬܕܡܝ ܨܘܡܗܘܢ ܠܕܒܝܬ ܐܝܙܪܥܝܠ "and their fast did not resemble that of the inhabitants of Jezreel" Aphr. 50, 11; ܐܬܩܒܠ ܩܘܪܒܢܗ ܕܗܒܝܠ ܘܐܣܬܠܝ ܕܩܐܝܢ "Abel's offering was accepted and Cain's rejected" Aphr. 60, *ult.*; ܐܟܠܘ ܗܘܘ ܩܪܨܝܢ ܘܕܫܡܥܘܢ "they raised accusations against us and Simeon" Mart. I, 19 *inf.*

B. To this section may be joined certain adverbial applications of ܕ, such as the following: ܕܗܫܐ "for the moment", "for the nonce", "now"; ܕܡܚܕܐ "immediately" (both occurring frequently); ܕܝܘܡܢܐ σήμερον Matt. 6, 11 C.; ܕܬܪܬܝܢ ܙܒܢܝܢ "twice", or "a second time" Gen. 43, 10; Eccl. 6, 6; Matt. 26, 42; John 3, 4; Sim. 300, 2; 317 mid.; ܕܬܢܝܢ "for the second time" Bedjan, Mart. II, 562, 6; 605, 17. Farther we have the favourite construction of ܒܛܠ with ܕ "to be concerned for that which is of . ." *i. e.* "to be concerned about": ܠܐ ܬܬܒܛܠܘܢ ܕܢܦܫܟܘܢ μὴ μεριμνᾶτε τῇ ψύχῃ ὑμῶν Luke 12, 22 C. (ܕܢܦܫܐ S.); ܒܛܠ ܕܐܬܠܘܬܐ "cared for the combat" Ephr. in Wright's Cat. 689 *a*, 3; ܘܗܘܘ ܒܛܠܝܢ ܠܗܘܢ ܐܝܟ ܕܗܕܡܝܗܘܢ "and they must care for them as for their own members" Ov. 216, *ult.*; ܒܛܠܝܢ ܕܟܠܗܝܢ "care for everything" Jos. St. 3, 11, and frequently thus, with ܕ (and ܕܥܠ § 225). Thus too ܪܢܐ is used sometimes: ܕܒܝܬܗ ܗܘ ܪܢܐ ܟܠܢܫ ܘܕܡܪܥܝܬܗ ܠܐ ܒܛܠ "every man is concerned for his house, but for his flock he cares nothing" Isaac I, 288 v. 267; cf. Ephr. in Zingerle's Chrest. 278, 6 *sq.*; Philox. 361, 18; Bedjan, Mart. II, 428, 7. Thus also ☞ p. 353 ܡܪܢܐ ܕܝܘܡܐ φρονῶν ἡμέραν Rom. 14, 6; ܕܠܐ ܡܪܢܐ ܐܢܬ ܕܐܠܗܐ ὅτι οὐ φρονεῖς τὰ τοῦ ϑεοῦ Matt. 16, 23. All these combinations with ܕ may, ☞ p. 353 for the rest, have been suggested by Greek Genitive constructions.

Determination of Governing Word.

§ 210. The substantive which stands before the genitive is generally determined; yet among the foregoing examples some of those substantives occur without any determination; thus particularly with the Abs. St., like ܟܠܗ ܒܣܪ ܕܚܝܘܬܐ "any flesh of beast" [*i. e.* the flesh of any animal] Spic. 7, 26.

Even the Constr. St. before the Emph. St. is not necessarily determined: ܒܪ ܫܢܬܐ "*filius anni*" "a (person, animal or thing, which is) one-year old" (often); ܬܪܬܝܢ ܒܢܬ ܡܠܟܐ "two king's-daughters" Aphr. 408, 3, 4; ܒܪ ܥܠܡܐ "a son of the world" *i. e.* "a layman" Sim. 286, 6;

نَـْ حَدَكُمْ حَجِ *τὶς βασιλικός* John 4, 46 (v. 49 حَدَكُمْ حَجِ ههٔ ὁ *βασιλικός*;
C. merely مَدَكُمْ); (حَدمِ نَـْ جِ مِنْ إِلُمْ "a brother's son" Mart. I, 149 mid.,
and of course quite properly in words like حَجِدَخُدُّ "the enemy" or "an
enemy".

D. CO-ORDINATION.

tributive
ljective.

§ 211. A. The *Attribute* as an Adjective stands in the same Gender
and Number as the Substantive, and throughout in the corresponding
State; for a few exceptions v. § 203. It comes after the substantive:
مِدَكُمْ حَدُّ, مِدَكُمْ حَدَهِمَا؟ مِدَهَمَا؟ حَجَا؟, مِدَكُمْ حَجَا؟ حَجَا؟ مِدَكُمَا؟ &c.

B. أُسَـَم and هَـٍـ, however, often come in before the substantive,
e. g. أُسـَٰـِا؟ حَجَا؟ "*ἄλλην παραβολήν*" Matt. 13, 24 P. or أُسـَٰـِا؟ حَجَا؟ C.
(S. هَـا؟ أَـا؟); 13, 31 and 33 P. (in both passages in C. and S. هَـا؟ أَـا؟);
لإِسـَٰـِا؟ حَجِتَبَا؟ *ἄλλοις γεωργοῖς* Matt. 21, 41 P. (C. and S. حَـدً؟ أَـا؟); أُسـَٰـِا؟
هَـمَـٰحَا؟ "*ἕτερον λογισμόν*" Sap. 19, 3; أُسـَٰـرَٰـَا؟ حَجَنَـٰكَا؟ "other reasons"
John Eph. 395, 12; and in the Abs. St. (§ 203) أُسـَٰـم مَـهٔ "another master"
Mart. I, 235 *inf.*; جَاسـَٰـم حَمهُا؟ "in another name" Ephr. II, 555 A;
أُسـَٰـم إِ؟ "another secret" Ephr. (Lamy) II, 739, 14; cf. line 20, and 741, 7;
جَاسـَٰـم حَجِهٔ "at his other side" *ibid.* 765, 2 and many others.—هَـٍـتَـٰلِ؟
هَـٍـتَـٰلِ؟ دَحَتَـٰلِ؟ هٔزَّتَـمَـهُا *πολλοὶ προφῆται καὶ δίκαιοι* Matt. 13, 7; إِنَـهُا؟ حَبِ؟
"many men" Aphr. 505, 7; هَـٍـتَـٰلِ؟ أَحَتَـٍـ "many times" Ephr. I, 398 F;
هَـٍـتَـٰلِ؟ إِمهٔ؟ يَحَفَكَا؟ "many souls, farther" Land II, 326, 2 &c. But
both these words are far oftener placed after the substantive. حَجِ too
is often put first: حَجِ حَمُـُـٰكَا؟ "such and such a thing" John Eph.
192, 21; حَجِهـٍتَـٰلَ مَـٍزَـٰكَا؟ "in a certain town" *ibid.* 1, 20; حَجِ إِهٔزَٰكَا
هَـمحَـرَهٔ "on this appointed business" Ephr. II, 179 A; but *ibid.* also the
usual order: حَزِحَـُـٰشَا؟ حَجِ "on such and such a sacrifice".

In rare instances the adjective when emphatic also precedes, especially
with the poets, e. g. حَمـٍرَـٰشَا؟ حَكَاهٔمَـٰكَا؟ "the first foundation" Spic. 49, 20;
إِحَفَا؟ وَحَرَـٰمـَٰهِكَا؟ "of the cleansed soul" Ov. 261, 14; إِحَعَا؟ حَكَاهٔكَاهٔحِ "thy
chaste virginity" *ibid.* line 16; إِحَكَا؟ حَمهٔكَا؟ "greedy death" Ephr. Nis. p. 57 v. 67.
Certain adjectives of praise or dispraise are frequently placed first, like
حَمـٍعَا؟ "the holy (sg.)"; حَمهٔدَكُّ؟, f. حَمهٔدَنَـُـٰكَا؟ "the (m. or f. sg.) happy (or
blessed)"; مَحَزَحَا؟ "the blessed (sg.)"; مَـٍحَـٰكَا؟إِ؟ "the excellent (sg.)"; إِحَمـٍحَا

"the wicked (sg.)"; ܠܝܛܐ "the accursed (sg.)" &c., *e. g.* ܢܨܝܚܐ ܐܩܩܝܣ "the splendid Akakios" Ov. 162, 21; ܡܝܬܪܐ ܕܝܢ ܣܪܓܝܣ "but the excellent Sergius" Jos. Styl. 84, 6; ܛܘܒܢܝܬܐ ܡܪܝܡ "the Blessed Mary" Aphr. 180, 2; ܗܢܐ ܠܝܛܐ ܬܡܫܒܘܪ "this accursed Tamšābōr" Mart. I, 124, 2; ܪܫܝܥܐ ܝܘܠܝܢܘܣ "the godless Julian" Ov. 160, 14 &c.; also in accumulations of adjectives like ܩܕܝܫܐ ܘܓ[ܒ]ܝܐ ܘܪܒܐ ܒܣܝܠܝܘܣ "the holy, elect, and great Basil" Ephr. III, XLIII *ad inf.*, and many like instances. But here too it is always allowable to put the adjective after the substantive; and with some it is oftener done. The two positions appear even in the same phrase: ܛܘܒܢܐ ܡܪܝ ܫܡܥܘܢ ܩܕܝܫܐ "the blessed Mār Simeon, the holy" Sim. 269 *supr.*

The attributive Adjective may be separated from its substantive: ܥܒܕܐ ܗܘ ܓܝܪ ܫܦܝܪܐ ܗܢܐ "*opus est enim pulchrum hoc*" Spic. 1, 20; ܘܟܠܗܝܢ ܨܒܘ̈ܬܐ ܒܐܝ̈ܕܝܗܘܢ ܗܘ ܕܒ̈ܢܝܢܫܐ ܣܝ̈ܡܢ ܪ̈ܘܪܒܬܐ ܘܙܥܘܪ̈ܬܐ "for all things, great and small, lie in the hands of men" Spic. 9, 9 &c.

§ 212. *The Apposition* may be either before or after the principal **Apposition**
word: ܡܠܟܐ ܐܢܣܛܣܝܣ "the emperor Anastasius" Jos. Styl. 28, 2; 42, 3; 90, 10; ܐܢܣܛܣܝܣ ܡܠܟܐ "Anastasius the emperor" *ibid.* 26, 7; ܡܠܟܐ ܡܗܝܡܢܐ ܐܢܣܛܣܝܣ "the believing emperor Anastasius" *ibid.* 8, 8; 16, 18. Upon the whole, additional forms indicating respect incline to precede the leading word (thus always ܡܪܝ "my Lord, Master"); explanatory or descriptive forms come after it: yet this is not to be regarded as a fast rule. As one example of the prior and posterior order in one and the same phrase, take ܡܝܬܪܐ ܘܪܚܡ ܡܫܝܚܐ ܡܪܝ ܛܝܡܬܐܘܣ ܐܦܝܣܩܘܦܐ "the excellent, Christ-loving, Mār Timotheus the Bishop" Aphr. Pref. 12, and many such.

§ 213. The Apposition may be loose, and may become a mere sub- **Loose**
stitution or parallelism. Examples like ܘܣܒܥ ܟܦܢܐ ܕܡܫܬܪܚܝܢ ܡܢ ܚܡܫܐ ܠܚܡܝܢ ܘܬܪܝܢ ܢܘܢܝܢ ܠܚܡܫܐ ܐܠܦܝܢ ܓܒܪܝܢ "and he satisfied distressed, hungering people with five loaves and two fishes—five thousand men" Aphr. 42, 17; ܒܐܪܥܐ ܕܒܥܠܕܒܒܘܗܝ ܒܐܪܥܐ ܕܡܘܐܒ "in the land of his enemies, in the land of Moab" (notice the repetition of the prep.) Aphr. 161, 12; ܦܨܚܐ ܓܝܪ ܕܝܗܘܕܝܐ ܝܘܡܐ ܗܘ ܕܐܪܒܥܣܪ ܒܝܪܚܐ ܠܠܝܗ ܘܐܝܡܡܗ "for the Passover of the Jews is the fourteenth day of the month,—in fact its night and **Apposition.**

day" Aphr. 223, 11; ‏ﻵﻴﻠﺤ ﻢﺠﺘﯩ ﺎﻫﻤ ﺷﻤﻫﺎ ﻩﻫﺍ ﻰﺟﺭﺪﺧ‎ "the wine was sold at a denarius for six measures" Jos. St. 36, 13—may suffice to illustrate several of the most important cases.

Rem. On the Person (grammatical) in apposition v. § 350 C.

Apposition in Words denoting Measure. § 214. Apposition is generally made use of in the case of words denoting measure, like ‏ﻰﺗﺎﺨﻣ ﻼﻫﻣ‎ ἕκατον βάτους ἐλαίου Luke 16, 6, cf. v. 7; ‏ﻢﯩﻘﻨﺍﻭ ﺰﻤﯨﺣ‎ "for with three ounces of bread" Ov. 182, 10; ‏ﻞﻫﻨﯩ ﻢﯨﻗ ﻰﺤﺠﺎﺘﻟ‎ thirty measures of wheat" Jos. St. 21, 20; ‏ﺎﻫﺍﺯ ﻰﻨﺘﺨﺍ ﻰﺒﻤﺠﺣ‎ "ten loads of silver-pieces" Jos. St. 10, 21; ‏ﻰﻓﺪﺤﻣ‎ ‏ﻼﻣﺯﻩ ﻰﻠﯩﻬﻋﻩ ﻼﻣﺯﻩ‎ "a measure and a-half of pulse" Sim. 360 *inf.*; ‏ﻼﻣﻫ ﺍﺯﻩﺍ‎ ‏ﺤﺠﯩﺍ‎ "a handful of dust" Aphr. 154, 5, and many similar cases. The genitive connection with ‏ﯨ‎ would also be allowable here.

Apposition of "much", "little"; "many", "few". § 215. ‏ﻰﻬﻤ‎ and ‏ﻼﻠﺠﻣ‎ often remain, unaltered in form, like adverbs, and standing either before or after the qualified word: ‏ﻼﻘﻧ ﻰﻬﻣ‎ "many fishes" Sim. 273, 14; ‏ﻰﻬﻣ ﻰﺤﻤﯩ‎ "many leopards" Land III, 335, 17; ‏ﻰﻬﻣ ﻰﻠﻨﺴﺨﺟ ﻰﻬﻣ‎ "many pearls" *ibid.* line 21; ‏ﻼﻫﻓﺯ ﻰﻬﻣ‎ "many things" Spic. 6, 6; ‏ﻼﻴﺠﻣ ﻰﻬﻣ‎ "many wars" Sim. 282 mid.; ‏ﻼﺨﺨﺨﺣ‎ ‏ﻼﻠﺠﻣ‎ "a little consolation" Jos. St. 32, 10; ‏ﻼﻤﻫﺍﺯﺍ ﻼﻠﺠﻣ‎ ‏ﻼﻫﺍ‎ "this brief exhortation" Aphr. 331, 2; ‏ﻼﻤﺒﻤﻗﺯ ﻼﻨﻤﻧ ﻼﻠﺠﻣ‎ ὀλίγα ἰχθύδια Matt. 15, 34 P. (S. merely ‏ﻼﻠﺴﻣ‎ (ﻼﻘﻧ)); ‏ﻼﻠﺠﻣ ﻼﻫﻤﻤﻗ‎ οὐ πολλὰς ἡμέρας John 2, 12 (for the same in Luke 15, 13, ‏ﻼﻠﺠﻣ‎ (ﻼﻫﻤﻤﻗ)); ‏ﻼﻤﻫﻨﻗ ﻼﻠﺠﻣ ﻼﻫﺍ‎ "this short demonstration" Aphr. 244, 7; ‏ﻼﻨﺴﻣ ﺪﺨﺘ ﻼﻠﺠﻣ ﻰﺠﻫﺍ‎ "these few words of peace" Aphr. 298, 19; ‏ﻼﻤﺤﻤﻫ ﻼﻠﺠﻣ‎ "a little sun" Aphr. 130, 18; cf. ‏ﻼﻨﻄﻫﻣ ﻢﻓ ﻼﻠﺠﻣ‎ "a little of Satan" Aphr. 130, 19; and ‏ﻼﻠﺠﻣ ﻰﺠﻫﺍ‎ ‏ﻰﻬﻣ ﻢﻓ‎ "these few things out of many" Jos. St. 91, 15; Jul. 98, 13; and similar instances. The abstract word ‏ﻼﯨﺨ ﻪﻤﻫ‎ is also employed in this way: ‏ﻼﻐﻨﺍ ﻼﯨﺨ ﻪﻤﻫ‎ "many men" Ephr. I, 520 *ult.*—521, 1; ‏ﻼﯨﺨ ﻪﻤﻫ ﻼﺘﻔﺤﺟ‎ "many Levites" *ibid.* 544 F.; עבדה הרבה מאד—‏ﻼﺒﺨﺤ ﻼﯨﺨ ﻪﻤﻫ‎ ﺪﻋ ‏ﻰﯨﻻﺯ‎ Job 1, 3; ‏ﺪﻔﻤﺯ‎—‏ﻼﯨﺨ ﻪﻤﻫ ﻼﺤﺟ ﻼﻣﻜﺯﻩ ﻼﻣﻫﺎﻫﺨﺤﺨﻤﻤﻣﻩ ﻰﯩﺤ ﺍﻤﺤﻤﺨﺘ‎ "for, wisdom and understanding and insight in much abundance" Ov. 191, 13;—‏ﻼﯨﺨ ﻪﻤﻫ ﻼﺤﺨﻤﺟﺯﻤﻣﻩ‎ ‏ﻼﯨﺨﺯ‎ "horses and chariots in very great number" Land III, 331, 8. (¹)

(¹) On ‏ﻼﯨﺨ ﻪﻤﻫ‎ "very", "much" v. § 243.

§ 216. A mode of Apposition is formed also by cases like ܘܥܠ ܗܘ ܠܓܘܗ ܩܕܡܝܐ "and he first (as the first) entered" Ephr. (Lamy) I, 535, 15; ܗܘ ܢܩܒ ܩܕܡܝܐ ܪܥܝܢܐ ܫܦܝܪܐ "he was the first to show good will" Jos. St. 23, 17; ܐܝܣܚܩ ܐܘܠܕ ܠܝܥܩܘܒ ܒܪ ܫܬܝܢ ܫܢܝܢ "Isaac, when sixty years of age, begat Jacob" Aphr. 464, 10; ܐܫܬܚܪ ܗܘܐ ܗܡܢ ܡܦܠܛܐ "Haman had been left remaining as one who had escaped" Aphr. 52, 15; ܘܐܬܝܗܒ ܡܐܟܘܠܬܐ ܠܡܗܝܡܢܐ "and has been given as nutriment to believers" Aphr. 114, 2; ܝܦܬܚ ܪܕܝܦܐ ܩܡ ܪܫܐ ܠܥܡܗ "Jephthah, the persecuted, came forward as the head of his people" Aphr. 407, 14, and many others.

Expressions of condition or state ("as").

E. ܟܠ.

E. ܟܠ.

§ 217. ܟܠ (ܟܘܠ) may be used in the Abs. St. as a substantive for "everything", "everybody". Thus, in particular, expressions like ܦܪܘܩ ܟܠ "the Redeemer of all" Ov. 208, 24; ܐܚܝܕ ܟܠ "παντοκράτωρ" frequently; ܡܪܐ ܟܠ "the Lord of all" Aphr. 22, 12; for the same we have ܡܪܐ ܕܟܠ Spic. 27, 24; ܡܪܝܐ ܗܘ ܕܟܠ Aphr. 63, 10; farther ܐܫܠܡ ܟܠ ܒܐܝܕܘܗܝ "put all things into his hands" Aphr. 123, 2 (from John 3, 35, where P. and C. have the more usual ܟܠ ܡܕܡ); ܕܬܗܘܐ ܟܠ ܟܠ ܠܐܢܫܐ "that thou mayest be all things to all men" Ov. 266, 15; ܗܘܝܢ ܟܠ "we would be everything" Spic. 20, 22; ܟܕ ܟܠ ܒܒܝܬܗ ܡܬܒܣܡ "while every one rejoices in his own house" Ephr. III, 651 A; ܐܬܒܥܝܢ ܡܢ ܟܠ ܕ "we demand of every man, that ..." Jul. 15, 5 &c. On rare occasions it appears as an adverb "quite", "thoroughly": ܘܟܠ ܡܬܢܗܡ ܢܗܡ ܗܘܐ "and roared on continually" Sim. 393, 12; ܕܟܠ ܒܫܡܝܐ ܬܠܝܠܐ ܥܝܢܗ "whose eye was wholly lifted up to heaven" Ephr. II, 415 F.

In Abs. and Emph. St.

☞ p. 353

In this way the Emph. St. ܟܠܐ (ܟܘܠܐ) is used for "the whole", "the universe": ܘܗܟܠ ܠܐ ܗܘܐ ܚܕ ܐܬܪܐ ܐܙܠ ܟܘܠܐ "does not everything (הַכֹּל) go to one place?" Eccl. 6, 6 Ceriani; ܡܣܬܓܕ ܡܢ ܟܘܠܐ "worshipped by all" Ephr. III, 532 C; f. ܡܣܬܓܕܢܐ ܡܢ ܟܘܠܐ *ibid.* 530 F; ܐܪܕܝܟܠܐ ܕܟܠܐ "the Architect of the universe" Ephr. Nis. p. 97 v. 110; ܒܫܝܢܐ ܬܠܐ ܟܘܠܐ "everything depends on peace" Ephr. Nis. p. 4 v. 46 &c.

☞ p. 353

§ 218. Much oftener ܟܠ stands in the Constr. St. We saw it before substantives both sg. and pl., § 202 D; cf. ܒܟܠ ܚܕ ܦܘܪܥܢ "for

In Constr. St. and with Suff.

in every way" Jul. 69, 12 (§ 208 A). With undetermined words ܟܠ means "every", "all" ("all" pl.). It may even stand before determined substantives: ܟܠܗܘܢ ܝܘ̈ܡܝ ܚܝ̈ܝܟ (ܚܝ̈ܘܗܝ) "all the days of thy (his) life" Jul. 14, 14, (Eccl. 8, 15).

In its favourite connection with the relative pronoun ܕ it means "every one, who", "all who", "all which": ܟܠ ܕܨܒܐ "every one, who pleased . . . " Aphr. 328, 14; ܟܠ ܕܒܥܝܢ ܠܗ "all, who seek him" Aphr. 198, 10; ܟܠ ܕܩܢܐ ܗܘܐ "all that he had acquired" Ov. 165, 25 &c.

So also ܟܠ ܐܢܫ ܕ, ܟܠ ܡܢ ܕ "every one who" [whoever], and similar combinations (§ 236 D). Farther, as adverbially used: ܟܠ ܩܪܝܒ "quite near to" Cyrillona ZDMG XXVII, 578 v. 81 *sq.*; ܟܠ ܐܝܟ ܕ "precisely as" Jul. 92, 7; ܟܠ ܟܡܐ ܕ "just as much as"; ܟܠ ܐܡܬܝ ܕ "as often as", and the like.

Very often a substantive has ܟܠ in apposition with it, and placed either before or after it, and furnished with a pronominal suffix of its own, referring to the substantive. *Sing.*: ܟܠܗ̇ ܡܕܝܢܬܐ "the whole town" Jer. 4, 29; ܟܠܗ ܟܢܫܐ πᾶς ὁ ὄχλος Mark 2, 13; ܟܠܗ̇ ܡܕܝܢ̄ܬܐ "the whole town" Ov. 207, 3, for which lin. 6 gives ܡܕܝܢܬܐ ܟܠܗ̇; ܢܦܫܝ ܟܠܗ̇ "my whole soul" Ov. 164, 21; ܟܠܗ̇ ܐܘܪܚܐ "the whole way" Joseph 192, 12; 214, 5 (in both passages Var. 'ܐ 'ܟ); ܠܥܠ ܡܢ ܟܠܗ ܐܢܘܢ ܢܡܘܣܐ "they are above the whole law" Aphr. 30, 12.—*Plur.*: ܟܠܗܘܢ ܚܛܗ̈ܐ πάντα . . . τὰ ἁμαρτήματα Mark 2, 28; ܟܠܗܘܢ ܢܚ̈ܠܐ "every valley" Is. 40, 3; Luke 3, 5 (Eccl. 1, 3 ܟܠ ܢܚܠܐ); ܗܠܝܢ ܟܠܗܝܢ ܨܒ̈ܘܬܐ "all these things" Aphr. 9, 10; ܠܩܠܝܪ̈ܝܩܘܣ ܟܠܗܘܢ "to all Clerics" Ov. 206, 11 &c. In other uses also the word has the pronominal suffixes attached: ܟܠܢ, ܟܠܟܘܢ, "we all", "you all"; ܒܟܠܗ "in him wholly, in him everywhere" Ov. 165, 9; ܠܘܬܝ ܐܝܬܘܗܝ ܟܠܗ "it remains entire with me" Aphr. 200, 1; ܐܝܠܢܐ ܕܟܠܗ ܚܝ̈ܐ ܗܘ "a tree, which is all life" Ov. 399, 22; ܗܢܘܢ ܕܝܢ . . . . ܥܢܘ ܟܠܗܘܢ "but they all answered" Sim. 321 mid., and many such. Also before relative-clauses ܟܠܗܝܢ ܕܐܡܪ "*omnia, quae dixit*" Joseph 256 *paen.* [Ov. 328, 7]; ܒܟܠܗܝܢ ܕܫܘ̈ܝܢ ܠܐܠܗܐ "in all things which are worthy of God" Ov. 173, 18 &c.

Notice, besides, the adverbial phrases: ܟܠ ܟܠܗ "entirely", which appears often; ܗܟܢܐ ܟܠܗ ("completely so") "very much so", "to that extent", for which on stray occasions appear also ܟܡܐ ܗܢܐ, ܗܕܐ ܟܡܐ, ܗܘ ܟܡܐ. So also ܟܠ with relative-clause following: ܒܟܠ ܡܕܡ ܕܥܒܕܘ ܒܗܝܡܢܘܬܐ ܐܬܝܬܪܘ "in all that they did, they distinguished themselves by faith" Aphr. 20, 8; ܘܒܥܓܠ ܟܠ ܕܦܩܕ ܨܒܝܢܗ ܥܒܕܝܢ ܗܘܘ "and speedily they carried out his wish in all that he commanded" Sim. 344, 22.

Cf. farther §§ 205 A; 347; 349; 358 B; 360 B.

F. ܡܕܡ.

F. ܡܕܡ.

§ 219. ܡܕܡ "something" is very often employed as a substantive; also in distributive repetition ܡܕܡ ܡܕܡ "all sorts of things". Thus it may even stand in the Genitive: ܟܠ ܡܕܡ "everything"—frequently; ܕܚܠܬܐ ܕܡܕܡ "fear of any thing" Jul. 39, 9; ܒܪܓܬܐ ܡܕܡ ܡܕܡ "in greed for all manner of things" Aphr. 289, 17; ܒܥܠܬܐ ܡܕܡ ܡܕܡ "on any pretext whatever" Aphr. 292, 2; or it may be followed by a genitive with ܕ: ܡܕܡ ܕܡܬܐܟܠܢܐ "something eatable" Ov. 221, 9. It has often an attributive adjective along with it: ܡܕܡ ܒܝܫ "something evil"; ܡܕܡ ܝܬܝܪ "something more" Spic. 2, 20. Sometimes the adjective has the ending *ā*, and it is a matter of uncertainty whether it is then the Abs. St. f. (according to § 201) or the Emph. St. m.: ܡܕܡ ܝܬܝܪܐ Ov. 210 *ult.* = 214, 21; ܡܕܡ ܪܒܐ "something great" Moes. II, 104, v. 428; 156 v. 1241. But the relative construction is more usual in that case ܡܕܡ ܕܒܝܫ &c.

Not seldom ܡܕܡ stands in apposition to a substantive, and with the meaning "any one *or* thing whatever", or qualified by the negation "no, none": ܕܡܕܡ ܝܘܬܪܢ ܠܝܬ ܒܗܘܢ "in which lies no advantage" Aphr. 230, 6; ܠܐ ܛܘܫܐ ܠܘܬ ܪܥܝܢܗܘܢ ܡܕܡ ܡܬܩܪܒܐ "no pollution whatever approaches their mind" Aphr. 428, 4; ܩܠܝܠ ܡܕܡ "a little" often; ܒܥܠܕܒܒܘܬܐ ܡܕܡ "a certain enmity" Jos. St. 45, 5;—ܕܢܫܐܠ ܡܘܗܒܬܐ ܡܕܡ "that he demand a gift" Jos. St. 78, 10; ܣܓܝܐܬܐ ܡܕܡ ܕܠܐ ܟܬܝܒܢ ܗܘܝ "many a thing that was not written" Aphr. 343, 17; ܕܡܕܡ ܐܬܐ ܢܚܙܐ τὶ σημεῖον ἰδεῖν Luke 23, 8; ܡܕܡ ܦܬܓܡܐ "a word" Matt. 27, 12 (there S. ܡܕ' ܦܬܓܡ); Luke 23, 9; ܕܚܙܘܐ ܡܕܡ ܐܝܬ ܠܗܘܢ "that they had a vision of some sort" Isaac II, 218 v. 318; ܐܢܫܐ ܡܕܡ "several men" Ephr. I, 549 F; ܒܝܬ ܦܓܪܐ ܡܕܡ ܕ "among some dead bodies which . . . " Ephr. I, 161 E &c.

مْدّم ؟, meaning "something which", and then directly "that which" —
is very common in an attributive relative-clause (§ 236 C).
مْدّم also stands in negative sentences adverbially: اِنَم اِقَّم لِا مْدّم
"did not injure them at all" Jos. St. 89, 13; لِا اَنْم اِوَزِه مْدّم "no man
hurt him at all" Sim. 357 mid.; اَنْم مْدّم لِا جِزِّه "no man whatever
helped him" Sim. 312 *ad inf.*; لِا وَوْ هَ مْدّم هْتَّم تَوْهَ حَلّ فَتَشَا "he was
not in the least in need of sacrifices" Aphr. 315, 9 and the like. So in
the interrogative sentence حَمْدُا اِمَلْسِجَك جِوْ مْدّم طّ مَّهَقْشُلَي "were
the windows altered at all from thy measurements?" ZDMG XXV,
339 v. 361.

Cf. farther §§ 169, 236.

G. PRONOUNS.

PERSONAL PRONOUNS.

§ 220. A. The separate Personal Pronouns are often still con-
joined with the finite verb: سِي هَعِدِح "we (with no special emphasis)
have heard" Aphr. 354, 8; سِي اِحِجِح وهِجْدِنُو اِنَّك شَهْهُ "if *we*
have done wickedly and have provoked thee, be *thou* merciful" Aphr.
491, 5; اِنَّ اِتَكُف اَزِحُف "if only *you* are willing" Ov. 117, 15; اِشَهِمِر وَاِلّ
"and *I* am to show it to thee" Aphr. 7, 9; سِي جَسْنِبِر لِا يَهْحُهَمِر "let
us not be unthankful towards [do wrong to] his mercy" Isaac I, 22 v. 462;
اِمِر وَوْه جِ هَوْه مَجْلِا وَوْه "as he used to tell us" Ov. 162, 8; وَثُحه هَنَف
"they were asleep" Ov. 168, 8; اِنَبِل\\ نَّلـهِلا هَنَف نَهوَزِ سِزْه "that because of Daniel they saw the light" Aphr. 67, 9, and many such instances. Necessarily of course the pronoun becomes specially conspicuous
through adverbial adjuncts, as in وِه وِمُه جِلسَه هَنَف "they alone remained"
Sim. 269, 1, and thus, frequently, اِلّ اِف, اِلّ اِف, اِف وْه &c.

B. Un-emphatically even اِنَف may be placed after the verb in place
of هَنَف: اِنَف دِحِاهِجِا وِاِلّلامِجِه "that they have stumbled against a stone"
Ephr. I, 404 F; اِنَف وَهِبِده اِزِحُدُا "whether haply they had dealt in
subtlety" Ephr. I, 496 F; اِمِر وَنِبِكُه اِنَف "that they should recognise"
Ephr. I, 498 E; اِنَف وَهِسُه "and they flew" Ephr. in Zingerle's Chrest.
279, 5; اِلِبِ اِنَف "they are coming" Jac. Sar. in Bedjan, Mart. V, 619, 3.

Cf., with position before the verb, ܬܪ̈ܬܝܗܝܢ ܐܝܟ ܡܩܒ̈ܠܢܟܝ "both of them (f.) came upon thee (f.)" Is. 51, 19.

C. On the Personal Pronoun in a Nominal sentence (§ 309) as subject and copula, v. § 311 *sq.*

On placing ܗܘ̇, ܗ̄ܝ &c. first, for the sake of emphasis, v. § 227.

§ 221. An enclitic ܗܘ often gives prominence only to the word, whether noun or verb, which it follows: ܠܚܕ ܗܘ ܐܠܗܐ ܣܓܕܝܢܢ "we adore *one* God" Mart. I, 227 *paen.*; ܠܒܢܝܢܐ ܗܘ ܓܝܪ ܕܡܝܐ "for it (f.) resembles a *building*" Aphr. 6, 12; ܪ̈ܓܠܝܗܘܢ ܠܒܝܫܬܐ ܗܘ ܪ̈ܗܛܢ "their feet run to *evil*" Prov. 1, 16; ܡܛܠ ܗܕܐ ܗܘ ܚܛܐ ܫܠܝܡܘܢ "on *that* account it was that Solomon sinned" Neh. 13, 26; ܐܢ ܐܢ̱ܬ ܨܒܐ ܗܘ ܠܡܐܠܦ "if thou art willing to *learn*" Spic. 1, 15; ܙܠ ܗܘ "go!" Ephr. III, XLV (twice) &c. It stands in this way as a strengthening particle after Demonstratives and Personal Pronouns: ܠܟܘܢ ܗܘ ܝܗܝܒ ὑμῖν δέδοται Matt. 13, 11; ܠܝ ܗܘ ܥܒܕܬܘܢ ἐμοὶ ἐποιήσατε Matt. 25, 40; ܗܢܘ ܓܒܪܐ ܕܡܫܘ̈ܒܚܘܬܗ "this (= ܗܢܐ ܗܘ) highly celebrated person" Ov. 204, 20; ܗܘܝܘ ܡܡܠܠ "*he* has spoken" Aphr. 5, 1; and thus repeatedly ܠܗ ܗܘ or ܠܗܘ̇ܘ "to him"; ܡܛܠ ܗܘ ܗܘ "therefore"; ܗܘ ܗܘ "thát" &c. (m. and n.).

§ 222. A favourite mode of accentuating a *determined* noun is by applying a Personal suffix. These suffixes are found applied as follows:—

(1) With the Genitive reference, v. § 205 C.

(2) Along with prepositions, the attachment being contrived thus:—

(a) As in the Genitive reference by means of ܕ, *e. g.* ܥܡܗ ܕܗܘ ܒܝܫܘܬܐ "with that wickedness" Ov. 200, 8. This construction has been ascertained in the case of ܥܠ, ܠܘܬ, ܚܕܪ, ܡܢ, ܥܡ, ܒܝܬ (also ܠܒܝܬ), ܡܛܠ, ܩܕܡ (ܩܕܡܘܗܝ), ܒܪ, ܒܝܢܝ, ܚܠܦ, 'ܐܝܟܘܬ, 'ܠܘܩܒܠ; it is completely excluded only in the case of ܒ and ܠ, apart from those prepositions which never assume suffixes at all.

(b) Through repetition of the prep., *e. g.* ܥܠܝܗ̇ ܥܠ ܟܐܦܐ "upon that stone" Aphr. 6 *ult.*, or by placing the prep. which has the suffix after the other, ܘܥܠ ܝܫܘܥ ܬܘܒ ܗܟܢܐ ܟܬܝܒ ܥܠܘܗܝ "and of Jesus [*or* Joshua] it is farther thus written" Aphr. 112, 9. Thus are construed ܥܡ, ܥܠ, ܩܕܡ, ܒ, ܠ (also to mark the Object; v. § 287 *sqq.*). Repetition is used also in cases like ܠܗܘܢ ܗܘܐ ܠܗܘܢ ܩܘܡܐ ܡܫܪܪܐ ܘܡܢ ܗܘܐ ܡܢ ܝܫܘܥ ܗܪܝܐ

Enclitic ܗܘ for Emphasising purposes.

Pronominal Suffixes for emphasising Determined Nouns.

ܘܦܪܘܩܐ "Moses was a leader to *them*, and Jesus was Guide and Redeemer to *us*" Aphr. 223, 25. We have even ܐܬܚܙܝ ܠܗ ܗܘ ܚܙܘܐ ܒܝܢܝ ܥܢܐ ܠܗ ܠܛܘܒܢܐ "there appeared to him, the blessed one, a vision amidst the flock" Sim. 270, 7 (where there is no special emphasis at all; the London manuscript has merely ܐܬܚ' ܠܗ ܠܛܘ' ܚܙܘܐ); ܕܥܒܕ ܗܘ ܐܠܗܐ ܒܗ ܒܩܢܘܡܗ "which God in his own person did" Ov. 164, 2 &c.

(3) With an Object-reference by means of Object-suffixes to the verb (§§ 288 *sq.*; 293).

Reflexive Pronouns.

§ 223. Personal Pronouns must also be employed to express the *reflexive* meaning, when the Verbal form does not already serve for that purpose. In cases like ܠܗܘܢ ܩܪܒ ܠܘܬܗ "he led them to himself" Ov. 193, 14; ܡܥܗܕܝܢ ܠܗܘܢ ܚܛܗܝܗܘܢ "they call up their sins to mind" Aphr. 223, 19, the simple Personal Pronoun is sufficient. In the case of a reflex Object the Subject-pronoun is often placed alongside of the prep. ܠ with the suffix of that pronoun attached thereto: ܘܐܥܠ ܗܘ ܠܗ "and he introduced himself" Anc. Doc. 90, 18; ܗܝ ܠܗ̇ ܐܥܘܠܬ "she wronged herself" Ephr. III, 2 C (and so, frequently ܗܘ ܠܗ, ܗܝ ܠܗ̇); ܐܢܬ ܠܟ ܐܥܡܕ "baptise thyself" Ephr. (Lamy) I, 126, 10; ܐܢܐ ܠܝ ܐܫܠܡܬ ܠܐܝ̈ܕܘܗܝ "I have let myself be caught by his hands" Ephr. III, 382 A &c. Compare farther ܗܘ ܠܗ ܒܗ ܡܛܫܐ "he hides in himself" Ephr. III, 10 C. In the last case the clearer phraseology ܒܢܦܫܗ would probably have been used in prose. In fact, ܢܦܫܐ "soul" and,—though more rarely—ܩܢܘܡܐ "person" are very often employed with personal suffixes to express the reflexive relation with accuracy, *e. g.* ܠܢܦܫܝ "to myself"; ܒܢܦܫܗ "in himself" &c.; ܫܕܝ ܢܦܫܟ ܠܬܚܬ βάλε σεαυτὸν κάτω Matt. 4, 6; ܦܪܫܘ ܢܦܫܗܘܢ "they separated (refl.)" Ov. 194, 10; ܥܠ ܩܢܘܡܗ ܡܬܦܠܓܐ "is divided against itself" Luke 11, 17 P. (C. is different); ܐܩܝܡܘ ܠܩܢܘܡܗܘܢ ܟܘܡܪܘܬܐ "they procured for themselves a priesthood"
☞ p. 353
Ov. 194, 11;—ܠܩܢܘܡܗ ܐܡܪ ܗܘܐ "spoke to himself" Ov. 281, 23. Thus also ܩܢܘܡܝܗܘܢ and ܢܦܫܬܗܘܢ "themselves" stand in parallel clauses in Ov.
☞ p. 353
207, 25 *sq.*; but such plurals are rare. Cf. too ܕܡܐ ܕܩܢܘܡܝ "my own blood" Joseph 26, 9 [Ov. 281, 23], and even ܠܩܢܘܡܐ ܕܢܦܫܗ "*sibimet ipsi*" Aphr. 455, 2. Even ܝܬܐ "essence" is similarly employed; ܣܦܩܐ ܠܝܬܗ̇ "she suffices for herself" Ephr. I, 428 E; ܣܦܘܩܐ ܠܝܬܗ "self-

contradiction" Ov. 60, 15; ܕܗ̄ܝ ܡܕܒܪܢܐ ܢܦܫܗ̇ ܘܡܫܠܛܢܝܬܐ ܟܝܢܗ̇ "who guides and rules herself" Ephr. II, 451 B; ܥܡ ܟܝܢܗ parallel with ܥܡ ܢܦܫܗ and ܥܡ ܩܢܘܡܗ Ov. 59, 4; ܦܠܓ ܥܡ ܟܝܢܗ "is at variance with himself" Ov. 45, 6 &c. ܢܦܫ' and ܩܢܘܡ' stand also in apposition with the Subject, *e. g.* ܗܘ̣ ܢܦܫܗ, ܗ̣ܢܘܢ ܢܦܫܗܘܢ "he himself", "they themselves"; ܗ̣ܢܘܢ ܩܢܘܡܗܘܢ "they themselves" Jul. 30, 3. ܩܢܘܡ' is sometimes much the same as "quite", "at all", "altogether": ܕܩܢܘܡܝܟܘܢ ܠܐ ܬܐܡܘܢ μὴ ὀμόσαι ὅλως Matt. 5, 34 C. S. (P. ܣܟ); ܐܢܬ ܩܢܘܡܟ ܒܚܛܗ̈ܐ ܐܬܝܠܕܬ ἐν ἁμαρτίαις σὺ ἐγεννήθης ὅλως John 9, 34 S. (P. ܟܠܟ); ܚܠܩܐ ܩܢܘܡܗ ܠܐ ܐܝܬܘܗܝ "Fate has no existence at all" Spic. 9, 9; ܕܒܢ̈ܫܐ ܩܢܘܡܗܘܢ ܠܐ ܡܬܩܪܒܝܢ "who do not at all approach women" Spic. 8, 1. Cf. farther ܐܝܢܐ ܒܝܬܐ ܩܢܘܡܗ ܗܘܐ ܠܗܘܢ "what sort of house had they at all?" Aphr. 352, 16.

§ 224. The preposition ܠ with reflexive personal pronoun often stands alongside of a verb, without essentially modifying its meaning (*Dativus ethicus*); ܢܦܩ ܠܗ "he went away" Acts 12, 19; ܩܘܡ ܠܟ ἀνάστηθι Acts 10, 26; ܘܪܗܛܬ ܠܗ̇ "she ran" Ov. 161, 15, and thus very frequently with verbs of motion; ܡܝܬܘ ܠܗܘܢ "they are dead" Matt. 2, 20; Ov. 170, 8; ܫܢܝܬܝ ܠܟܝ μαίνῃ Acts 12, 15; ܗܘܐ ܠܗ ܡܢ ܩܕܡܝ ἔμπροσθέν μου γέγονε John 1, 15 and 30; ܗܘܘ ܠܗܘܢ ܐܠܗ̈ܐ ܣܓܝܐܐ "there were many Gods" Aphr. 121, 1, and thus frequently with ܗܘܐ and ܐܝܬ; ܐܬܡܠܠܬ ܠܗ ܥܒܕܘܬܐ ܥܠ ܙܪܥܗ "servitude was foretold for his seed" Aphr. 27, 10, and thus in Aphr. often directly used with passive verbs &c.

Pleonastic ܠ with Pronominal Suffixes.

§ 224*. The mode of placing a reflex Possessive-Suffix in Genitive connections is peculiar, as in the frequently occurring ܡܪܝ ܫܡܥܘܢ ܕܐܣܛܘܢܗ "St. Simon Stylites" ("St. Simon of his pillar"), for which also often stands ܕܐܣܛܘܢܐ ("of the pillar"). So ܠܬܡܘܙ ܕܚܡܝܡܘܬܗ "the hot July" Ephr. III, 593 F; ܡܫܡܗܐ ܕܫܡܗ "the renowned", pl. ܡܫܡܗ̈ܐ ܕܫܡܗܝܗܘܢ Ov. 160, 4, 9; ܗܘ̣ ܕܫܐܕܘܗܝ ὁ δαιμονιζόμενος Mark 5, 15, 16, 18; ܗܝ ܕܕܡܗ̇ "she that had the issue of blood" Ephr. III, 554 E; ܒܪ̈ܒܪܝܐ ܣܥܝܪܝ ܕܦܪܨܘܦܗܘܢ "the shaggy barbarians" John Eph. 117, 13 (cf. 398, 16) and many similar instances (cf. § 205 A).

Reflexive Pronominal Suffix with the Genitive. ☞ p. 353

§ 225. A. The *Separate Possessive-Pronouns* with ܕܝܠ stand both as substantives and adjectives. ܢܬܠ ܠܙܒܢܐ ܕܝܠܗ "let us give to time

ܕܝܠ.

what is its own" Jul. 109 *ult.*; ܠܕܝܠܗ ܐܬܐ ܘܕܝܠܗ ܠܐ ܩܒܠܘܗܝ εἰς τὰ ἴδια ἦλθε καὶ οἱ ἴδιοι αὐτὸν οὐ παρέλαβον John 1, 11; ܕܠܐ ܕܝܠܟܘܢ τὸ ἀλλότριον (lit. "not your own"), and ܕܝܠܟܘܢ τὸ ὑμέτερον Luke 16, 12; ܠܐܢܫ ܡܢ ܕܝܠܗ "to one of his own people" Ov. 184, 15; ܦܫܘ ܕܝܢ ܚܕ ܚܕ ܡܢܗܘܢ ܒܕܝܠܗ "but they remained every one of them in his own (his own belief)" Ov. 160, 21; ܕܝܠܢ ܕܝܠܗ ܐܝܬܘܗܝ ܗܘܐ "ours was his" Aphr. 119, 10; ܕܝܠܝ ܐܢܬܘܢ "mine are ye" Isaac I, 22, v. 446; ܕܗܘ ܕܝܠܟ ܚܢܢ "for we are indeed thine" Aphr. 489, 9; ܘܝܗܒ ܠܢ ܕܝܠܗ ܢܝܚܐ ܘܒܣܝܡܐ "and gave us his own mild and pleasant one (yoke ܢܝܪܐ)" Aphr. 319, 10; ܗܢܐ ܕܝܠܟ "this of thine (thy distress ܐܘܠܨܢܐ)" Sim. 331 *ad inf.* &c.—With substantives, to give more prominence to the possessor: ܠܡܘܬܪܢܐ ܕܝܠܢ "for our advantage" Aphr. 459, 3; ܝܘܡܐ ܕܝܠܗ "his day" Aphr. 36, 5 &c.; and in particular with those Greek words which cannot take any suffix (§ 145 L); ܩܠܝܪܘܣ ܕܝܠܗ "his clergy" frequently; ܕܡܘܣܝܢ ܕܝܠܗ "its (f.) public bath (δημόσιον)" Jos. St. 70, 20; ܙܘܢܐ ܕܝܠܗ "his girdle" Sim. 317 *inf.*; ܐܘܣܝܣ ܕܝܠܗܘܢ "their resources" (οὐσίας) Jul. 37, 5, and many others. Very rarely the Constr. St. occurs here, as in ܠܢܣܝܢ ܕܝܠܟ "for thy trial" Ephr. III, 302 D; ܩܢܘܡ ܕܝܠܗܘܢ "their own person" Isaac I, 22 v. 454; ܒܠܚܘܕ ܕܝܠܗ "beside him" Ov. 273, 11; ܒܝܕ ܕܝܠܗ "by his means" Ephr. Nis. p. 60 v. 261. But ܕܝܠ, besides, often stands after the Possessive-suffix: ܡܐܟܘܠܬܝ ܕܝܠܝ ἐμὸν βρῶμα John 4, 34; ܛܢܢܗ ܕܝܠܗ "his zeal" Ov. 187, 17; ܨܠܘܬܝ ܕܝܠܝ "my prayer" Aphr. 454, 11; ܦܘܩܕܢܢ ܕܝܠܢ "our command" Ov. 219, 1 &c.; compare ܒܥܝܢܝܗܘܢ ܕܝܠܗܘܢ ܘܕܟܠ ܐܢܫ "in their sight and every man's" Ov. 184, 8.—Sometimes ܕܝܠ stands first, with the effect of emphasis: ܕܝܠܟ ܡܥܡܪܟ "*thy* dwelling" Aphr. 494, 13; ܕܝܠܢ ܣܝܡܬܢ "*our* treasure" Aphr. 506, 14; ܕܝܠܢ ܕܝܢ ܪܒ ܡܫܪܝܬܢ "but the general of *our* camp" Aphr. 59, 7 &c. Compare ܕܝܠܗ ܡܬܐܠܨܐ ܢܦܫܗ "*his* soul is distressed" Ephr. III, 651 A.

☞ p. 354

Thus it stands also with Genitive combinations, (§ 205 C) and that too sometimes without, sometimes with, a suffix attached to the governing member: ܐܣܛܐ ܕܝܠܗ ܕܡܕܒܚܐ "the partition-wall of the (said) altar" Jos. St. 29, 7; ܐܚܐ ܕܝܠܗ ܕܕܝܪܐ "the Brothers of the very convent" Ov. 210, 10 = 213, 4 &c. Cf. ܫܪܒܬܐ ܚܕܬܐ ܕܝܠܢ ܕܟܪܣܛܝܢܐ "the new race formed by us Christians" Spic. 20, 4.—ܒܝܘܡܘܗܝ ܕܝܢ ܕܝܠܗ ܕܚܙܩܝܐ "but in the days of the (said) Pērōz" Jos. St. 11, 9; ܩܕܡ ܬܪܥܗ ܕܝܠܗ ܕܗܝܟܠܐ "before the court of the (fore-mentioned) Temple" Sim. 271 mid.; ܒܐܝܕܘܗܝ ܕܝܠܗ ܕܗܢܐ "in the hands of this man" Ov. 160, 14 &c. For the most part a special emphasis, or at least a reference to something already mentioned, lies in this prolix construction. Compare farther ܛܒܬܐ ܕܝܠܗ ܗܝ ܕܒܪܢܫܐ "the good is man's own" Spic. 6, 11.

B. Farther ܕܝܠ also occurs frequently after prepositions with the suffix, to add emphasis to the latter: ܠܝ ܗܘ ܕܝܠܝ *ἐμοί* Matt. 25, 40 in Aphr. 381, 2 (in P. merely ܠܝ ܗܘ); ܡܢܝ ܕܝܠܝ "from me" Jos. St. 3, 14; ܠܒܝܬܗ ܕܝܠܗ "at his house" Ov. 208, 19; ܠܗ ܕܝܠܗ "to him" often; ܒܠܥܕܝܢ ܕܝܠܢ "without us" Aphr. 172, 7 &c. We have even ܠܢ ܕܝܠܢ ܝܗܒ ܠܢ "to *us* he gave" Aphr. 181, 5. Farther it occurs with substantives: ܬܚܝܬܘܗܝ ܕܝܠܗ ܕܡܕܒܚܐ "under the (fore-mentioned) altar" Sim. 272, 9; ܠܘܬܗ ܕܝܠܗ ܕܩܕܝܫܐ "with the saint" Sim. 274, 13; ܩܕܡܘܗܝ ܕܝܠܗ ܕܗܢܐ ܡܘܦܛܐ "before this Mōpet" Mart. I, 181 *inf.*, &c.

Just as ܒܨܦ is construed with ܕ (§ 209 B), so is it also with ܕܝܠ: ܕܝܠܗ ܒܨܦ or ܒܨܦ ܕܝܠܗ *μεριμνήσει τὰ ἑαυτῆς* Matt. 6, 34; ܒܨܦ ܕܝܠܗ *ἐπιμελήτηθι αὐτοῦ* Luke 10, 35; ܒܨܦ ܗܘܐ ܕܝܠܗܘܢ ܕܗܢܘܢ . . . "he was concerned for those, who . . ." Sim. 333 mid.; ܒܨܦܬ ܗܘܝܬ ܕܝܠܝ "thou didst care for me" Jos. St. 3, 10 &c.

DEMONSTRATIVE PRONOUNS.

§ 226. All the Demonstratives are used both as Substantives and as Adjectives. In the latter case they stand sometimes before, sometimes after, the substantive: ܡܠܟܐ ܗܢܐ or ܗܢܐ ܡܠܟܐ "this king"; ܐܪܥܐ ܗܝ and ܗܝ ܐܪܥܐ "that country"; ܗܢܐ ܡܘܠܟܢܢ "this counsel of ours" Aphr. 293, 2; ܡܠܝܢ ܗܠܝܢ "these our words" Aphr. 299, 2 &c. The majority of the ancient authors (like Aphr.) usually put the demonstrative first; others, however, prefer to place it after the substantive; but there is no consistent practice. (1)

Demonstrative Pronouns. Adjective- and Substantive-use.

(1) With the Edessan Joshua St. the method of putting the demonstrative second preponderates; with Rabbûlâ's biographer, on the contrary,—also an Edessan of a date not much earlier,—the prior position prevails.

§ 227. The Personal Pronoun of the 3rd person, which is always substantive, serves often to give greater prominence to a substantive by being placed before it: e. g. ܗ̇ܘ ܘܗܘܐ ܢܡܘܣܐ ܠ̣ܩܐ "thus it,—the law—was the guardian" Aphr. 26, 5; ܐܡܪ ܗܘ ܐܙܠ "again he,—Jeremiah—said" Aphr. 34, 1; ܗ̣ܘܐ "while even his nourishment itself was a complete fast" Ov. 182, 5 &c. Also before farther demonstratives: ܗ̇ܘ "he" $\tilde{\eta}\nu$ $\delta\grave{\epsilon}$ $\sigma\acute{\alpha}\beta\beta\alpha\tau o\nu$ $\dot{\epsilon}\nu$ $\dot{\epsilon}\kappa\epsilon\acute{\iota}\nu\eta$ $\tau\tilde{\eta}$ $\dot{\eta}\mu\acute{\epsilon}\rho\alpha$ John 5, 9; ܘܗܘ "and when this evildoer saw him" Sim. 331, 3 (Cod. Lond., without ܘܗܘ);— "but when these blessed ones went away" Sim. 332, mid. (Cod. Lond., otherwise); ܗ̇ܘ "this benediction" Aphr. 465, 13 &c. This pronoun may even stand here as Object: ܗ̇ܘ $o\dot{\upsilon}\chi\grave{\iota}$ $\kappa\alpha\grave{\iota}$ $o\dot{\iota}$ $\tau\epsilon\lambda\tilde{\omega}\nu\alpha\iota$ $\tau\grave{o}$ $\alpha\dot{\upsilon}\tau\grave{o}$ $\pi o\iota o\tilde{\upsilon}\sigma\iota\nu$; Matt. 5, 46 sq. (C. S. quite different); "the Church holds fast to this number" ZDMG XXXI, 377 ult. (Jac. Sar.); ܗ̇ܘ "informed him of this" Sim. 311 mid.; ܗ̇ܘ "David also has said this" Ov. 123, 19; ܗ̇ܘ "to do this" Jos. St. 3, 22; "but when he learned this (haec)" Sim. 312, 1 &c. Compare in addition "it, the truth, makes itself known to thee" Ov. 163, 16.

§ 228. The distinction between the nearer and the more remote is observed with greater strictness in the sing. than in the pl. This is shown by ܗ̇ܘ being very often employed as correlative: ܗ̇ܘ ܕ "those, who", exactly like ܗ̇ܘ ܕ "he, who", ܗ̇ܝ ܕ "she who", while ܗܢܐ ܕ, ܗܕܐ ܕ mean "this one (m.), who", "this one (f.), who", and only on very rare occasions does the sing. demonstr. pron. appear as a mere antecedent (as in ܗܢܐ ܕ "the chief Mōpet Adharphar, who ... " Mart. I, 134 ult., cf. I, 234, 3; Simeon of Bēth Arshām (Guidi) 7, 13; 1, 3 = Land III, 235, 15. So Jul. 4, 4; Euseb. Ch. Hist. 274, 8. ܗ̇ܝ ܕ, ܗ̇ܘ ܕ do not occur so often as ܗ̇ܘ ܕ.—In other respects also ܗ̇ܘ shares with ܗܘ &c., the tendency to weaken its demonstrative signification. Compare the cases ܗ̇ܘ, ܗ̇ܘ cited above (§ 224*); farther ܗ̇ܘ "yours" Mart. I, 182, 8; ܗ̇ܘ "to the first" Sim. 340 mid.; ܗ̇ܘ ܕ "but the adherents of Illus" Jos.

 mark: ☞ p. 354

Personal Pronoun of 3rd pers. placed with demonstratives before Substantives and before other Demonstratives.

Weakening of the demonstrative force.

St. 14, 1, like ܗܳܢܽܘܢ ܕܒܶܝܬ ܐܰܣܺܝܪ̈ܶܐ "the prisoners" Moes. II, 69, 26 &c.; whereas ܗܳܕܶܐ ܕܟܳܣܳܐ Ov. 314, 17 is "*this* affair of the cup". It is apparent that ܗܰܘ, ܗܳܝ, ܗܳܢܽܘܢ, ܗܳܢܶܝܢ and ܗܳܠܶܝܢ are gradually approximating to the meaning of the definite article, for which in fact they are directly used by certain translators from the Greek.

§ 229. In rhetorical antithesis "this—that" (= "the one"—"the other") we find ܗܳܕܶܐ—ܠܗܳܕܶܐ Ov. 119 *ult.*; Jul. 223, 24 *sq.*; Moes. II, 100 v. 371; ܗܳܝ ܕܠܳܐ ܗܳܝ *ibid.* v. 383, like ܗܰܘ ܡܶܢ ܗܰܘ Ov. 119, 14; ܗܳܕܶܐ ܡܶܢ ܗܰܘ Moes. II, 84 v. 117; ܕܗܳܠܶܝܢ ܕܒܳܬܰܪ ܗܳܠܶܝܢ Aphr. 450, 16 &c. "This"— "That".

§ 230. "*The very same*" is expressed by repetition of the Personal Pronoun with ܐܺܝܟ interposed, which here has still the meaning "as": ܚܰܕ ܗܽܘ ܘܗܽܘ ܐܺܝܟ ܗܽܘ ܟܝܳܢܳܐ "one and the same nature is there" Ov. 80, 4; ܗܺܝ ܗܺܝ (ܗܺܝܳܐ) ܐܺܝܟ ܗܺܝ "she is the same" Moes. II, 90 v. 237; Ov. 67, 7; ܗܶܢܽܘܢ ܐܶܢܽܘܢ ܐܺܝܟ ܗܶܢܽܘܢ "they are the same" Mart. I, 11, 9; ܐܰܠܳܗܳܐ ܕܗܽܘ ܗܘܳܐ ܐܺܝܟ ܗܽܘ "God, who is (always) the same" Moes. II, 106, v. 482; ܠܶܗ ܐܺܝܟ ܠܶܗ ܠܚܰܒ݂ܪܶܗ "to this very companion of his" Sim. 370, 4 (*Cod. Lond.* ܠܗ ܠܗܘ ܚܒܪܗ); ܒܳܗ̇ ܐܺܝܟ ܒܳܗ̇ ܒܗܳܝ ܡܪܰܟܰܒ݂ܬܳܐ "in that very chariot" Sim. 301, 11 (*Cod. Lond.* merely ܒܗ̇ ܒܗܝ); ܕܺܝܠܶܗ ܐܺܝܟ ܕܺܝܠܶܗ "belonging to the same" frequently, &c. With additional emphasis we have ܗܽܘܝܽܘ ܐܺܝܟ ܗܽܘܝܽܘ ܥܰܡܳܐ "it is exactly the same people" Ephr. (Lamy) I, 467, 11. "The very same".

INTERROGATIVE PRONOUNS.

§ 231. ܡܰܢ, ܡܰܢܽܘ (= ܡܰܢ ܗܽܘ) "who?"; ܡܳܐ, ܡܰܢ, ܡܳܢܳܐ, ܡܢܽܘܢ "what?" have a substantive character. Yet sometimes we have ܡܳܢܳܐ &c. placed beside a substantive, and signifying "what sort of?": ܡܳܢܳܐ ܝܽܘܬܪܳܢܳܐ = מה יתרון "what sort of advantage?", "what profit?" Eccl. 1, 3; ܡܳܢܳܐ ܦܽܘܪܥܳܢܳܐ "what kind of penalty?" Aphr. 261, 6; ܡܳܢܳܐ ܛܳܒ ܗܳܫܳܐ "what sort of good now?" Aphr. 468, 16; ܡܢܽܘܢ ܦܽܘܪ̈ܫܳܢܶܐ ܐܺܝܬ "what kind of distinctions exist?" Assemani I, 449 (Isaac Ninivita) &c. Such a use of ܡܰܢ is quite exceptional, as in ܠܡܰܢ ܥܰܬܺܝܪܳܐ ܦܫܺܝܩ ܗܘܳܐ "to what rich man would it be easy?" Jac. Sar. in Zingerle's Chrest. 374. Interrogative Pronouns. Substantive- and Adjective-use. ☞ p. 354

§ 232. A. The simple ܡܳܐ is considerably circumscribed in use, through the forms which have *n*. It stands (1) in short questions like ܡܳܐ ܠܳܟ݂, ܡܳܐ ܠܶܗ, ܡܳܐ ܠܗܽܘ, ܡܳܐ ܠܟ݂ܽܘܢ &c. "how stands it with him, with thee?" &c. "What?"

(properly: "what is the news of him?" &c.) Ruth 2, 5; 3, 10; Ephr. II, 505 D; Mart. I, 112, 2 &c.; ܡܐ ܠܟ ܕ "what aileth thee, that . . .?" Gen. 21, 17; ܠܢ ܡܐ ܠܢ τί πρὸς ἡμᾶς; "what is that to us?" Matt. 27, 4: similarly (2) as a Correlative, ܡܐ ܕ "that, which"; also in the meaning "when" "if" (§ 258, &c.): (3) As an adverb,—like ܡܐ ܥܩܝܩ ܬܪܥܐ τί στενὴ ἡ πύλη; Matt. 7, 14; ܡܐ ܝܩܝܪܝܢ ܡܠܝܟ "how noble are thy words!" Ov. 155, 22 (Var. ܟܡܐ); ܡܐ ܣܟܠ ܣܦܪܗ "how foolish his book is!" Ephr. II, 456 D &c.: (4) In compounds like ܟܡܐ "how much?"; ܠܡܐ "why?" (also ܠܡܢܐ, frequently ܥܠ ܡܢܐ) and, like ܕܠܡܐ, "if haply", "perhaps", "lest perchance" (§ 373) and several like compounds.

B. ܡܢܐ too is used adverbially in various ways, *e. g.* ܡܢܐ ܡܟܝܠ ܦܪܝܫ ܗܘܐ ܒܪܢܫܐ "how then would man be different . . .?" Spic. 3, 7; ܡܢܐ ܐܠܨܐ ܗܘܐ ܕ "why should it be necessary, that . . .?" Aphr. 350 *ult.*; cf. Ov. 67, 12; ܡܢܐ ܩܐܡ ܐܢܬ "why standest thou?" Moes. II, 70, 10; ܡܢܐ ܥܒܕܝܢ πῶς ἔχουσι Acts 15, 36; ܡܢܐ ܓܝܪ ܥܕܪܬ ܒܘܪܟܬܐ "for in what way did the blessing help?" Aphr. 347, 11, for which 346, 19 gives ܡܢܘ ܥܕܪܬܗ ܒܘܪܟܬܗ, like ܡܢܘ ܡܪܚܝܢ ܐܦܝܟ "why is thy face without shame?" Aphr. 318, 9; ܡܢܘ ܐܡܪ ܗܘܐ ܒܗܢܐ ܐܣܟܡܐ ܡܣܠܝܐ ܐܬܚܙܝܬܘܢ "why, said he, do you appear in this sordid dress?" Jul. 42, 12.

ܡܢܘ. § 233. ܡܢܘ signifies "who?" like ܡܢ: ܡܢܘ ܢܩܝܡ "who will maintain" Jul. 15 *ult.*; ܗܠܝܢ ܟܬܒܐ ܕܡܢܘ ܐܢܘܢ "whose books are these?" Sim. 269 *inf.*; ܡܢܘ ܓܝܪ ܢܡܢܐ "for who counts up?" Sim. 368 *inf.* &c.

But the ܗܘ, which is involved in ܡܢܘ, may also serve as copula: then ܡܢܘ is "who is?" *e. g.* Jul. 43, 5; 56, 2 &c.

ܐܝܢܐ. § 234. A. ܐܝܢܐ, ܐܝܕܐ, ܐܝܠܝܢ may be used substantively, *e. g.* ܐܝܢܘ (= ܐܝܢܐ ܗܘ) "who is?" often (amongst others Ephr. III, 359 A) exactly = ܡܢܘ (but differently in ܐܝܢܘ ܗܝ ܦܘܡܐ ܕ "which (mouth) then is the mouth, which . . .?" Ephr. III, 593 D); ܕܐܝܢܐ ܙܕܝܩ ܘܐܝܢܐ ܛܠܘܡ ܘܐܝܢܐ ܚܛܝ "who may be just, who violent, who sinful" Ephr. III, 310 F; ܥܡ ܐܝܠܝܢ ܐܬܟܪܝ ܠܗ τίσι δὲ προσώχθισε . . .; "with whom had he vexation?" Hebr. 3, 17.

More frequently however the word is used adjectively, v. § 202 E; see, as farther examples, ܐܝܕܐ ܕܚܠܬܐ ܫܪܝܪܬܐ "which religion is true?"

Mart. I, 182, 6; ܐܝܠܝܢ ܣܦܪ̈ܐ "which writers?" Sim. 368 mid.; ܐܝܢܐ ܓܝܪ ܦܘܡܐ "for, what mouth?" *ibid.*;—ܥܠ ܐܝܠܝܢ ܕܝܢ ܦܘܩܕ̈ܢܐ "of what commandments then?" Aphr. 318, 11 &c. The separation of the interrogative from the substantive is more marked in ܘܡܢ ܐܝܢܐ ܐܢܬ ܥܘܡܪܐ "and from what convent art thou?" Land II, 141 *paen.*; ܡܢ ܐܝܢܐ ܐܢܬ ܙܪܥܐ "of what seed art thou?" Apost. Apocr. 198, 1; ܕܐܝܕܐ ܐܢܬܘܢ ܪܘܚܐ *οἵου πνεύματός ἐστε ὑμεῖς* Luke 9, 55; ܐܝܕܐ ܗܘܐ ܐܝܦ ܥܠܬܐ ܠܢܡܘ̈ܣܐ "what cause produced the laws?" Ephr. II, 453 E.

B. All the Interrogative Pronouns may be employed as Correlatives also (§ 236 A).

THE RELATIVE PRONOUN.

§ 235. The general Relative ܕ betokens of itself the attributive relative-clause: ܡܠܟܐ ܕ "the king, who" ("whom" &c., according to the internal construction of the relative-clause, v. § 341 *sqq.*),—and so also ܕ "he, who" or "one, who"; ܐܝܬ ܕ "*est, qui*", "*sunt, qui*" often; ܕܫܠܝܛ ܓܝܪ ܥܠ ܟܠ ܚܕ ܗܘ "for He who is almighty is one only" Spic. 9, 22; ܕܥܡܠ ܚܕܐ "he who has exerted himself, is glad" Aphr. 114, 15; ܘܕܨܒܝܢ "and those who so wish" Aphr. 496, 12; ܠܕܡܝܩܪ ܠܗ̇ "him, who honours her" Aphr. 497, 3; ܠܡܥܒܕ ܕܫܦܝܪ "to do what is good" Spic. 5, 1;—ܕܠܐ ܫܡܥ ܐܕܢܘ̈ܗܝ ܗܘ ܚܙܐ "what his ears have not heard, he sees" Aphr. 281, 5; ܡܢ ܕܒܝܫ "from that which is evil" Aphr. 497, 2; ܥܠ ܕܡܝܬܪܢ "*super ea (talia), quae praestant*" Ov. 179, 6 &c. In particular this shorthand mode of expression is a favourite one with Aphraates.

The Relative Pronoun. By itself.

☞ p. 354

§ 236. A. Very often, however, in cases where there is no substantive antecedent, a Correlative takes its place. Thus with demonstratives, ܗܘ ܕ, ܗܝ ܕ, ܗܢܘܢ ܕ, ܗܢܝܢ ܕ; ܗܠܝܢ ܕ; with interrogatives ܡܢ ܕ; ܐܝܢܐ ܕ, ܐܝܕܐ ܕ, ܐܝܠܝܢ ܕ; and ܡܐ ܕ "that which". So for instance ܐܝܢܐ ܕ and ܗܘ ܕ "he who" interchange without any difference in meaning: Spic. 5, 1, 2, and frequently. But indeed these words are often heaped together before ܕ. Thus for example, ܗܘ ܡܢ ܕ "he who"; "one who" Aphr. 138, 2; Spic. 3, 6, 11 &c., for which in Spic. 4, 7, appears even ܗܘ̇ ܗܘ ܡܢ ܕ "he who" = "one who" (universal statement)—ܗܘ ܐܝܢܐ ܕ "he who" (de-

With Correlative.

☞ p. 354

☞ p. 354

finite) Spic. 12, 19; (general) Spic. 2, 2 &c. Plur. ܗܢܘܢ ܐܝܠܝܢ ܕ "those who" Aphr. 132, 15; 136, 19, 22 &c.; Ov. 78, 5 (*ea, quae* f.); rarely ܗܢܝܢ ܐܝܠܝܢ ܕ "those who" Ov. 200, 14. Apart from gender and number no decided difference in the use of these expressions of the Relative is visible, seeing that different forms are frequently found in juxtaposition, with like meaning. For the expression ܕܒܟܠ cited above, one might also say ܗܘ ܐܢܫ ܕܒ݀, ܗܘ ܡܢ ܕܒ݀, ܐܢܫ ܕܒ݀, ܡܢ ܕܒ݀, ܗܘ ܕܒܟܠ; similarly with the Pl.—Thus too ܗܘ ܡܐ ܕ *e. g.* Ephr. in Zingerle's Chrest. 327 v. 177 (var. ܗܘ ܡܢ ܕ).

B. The Demonstratives and ܐܢܫ, followed by ܕ, also appear often alongside of substantives, *e. g.* ܒܡܕܥܗ ܗܘ ܕܠܐ ܛܥܐ "by means of his knowledge, which is unerring" Jos. St. 6, 9; ܪ̈ܫܐ ܘܡܕܒܪ̈ܢܐ ܗܢܘܢ ܕ "the chiefs and leaders, who" Spic. 12, 2; ܠܗܢܘܢ ܟܠܗܘܢ ܕܟܪ̈ܐ ܕ "to all the male children, who" Spic. 16, 23; ܕܝܪ̈ܬܐ ܗܠܝܢ ܕ "the convents, which" Sim. 277 *ad inf.*; ܛܒ̈ܬܐ ܐܝܠܝܢ ܕ "the good, which" Spic. 4, 5; ܡܪ̈ܕܘܬܐ ܐܝܠܝܢ ܕ "the chastisements, which" Jos. St. 2, 6; ܐܝܠܝܢ ܟܘܟ̈ܒܐ ܕ "the stars, which" Spic. 14, 14 &c. Cf. farther ܡܢ ܐܚܪܢܐ ܗܘ ܐܢܫ ܕ "from another one, who" Spic. 19, 9. The Correlative is conveniently introduced when the substantive is more distant from the relative, as, for instance in ܝܬܝܪܐܝܬ ܥܠ ܡܣܟ̈ܢܐ ܡܟܝ̈ܟܐ ܡܚܘܐ ܗܘܐ ܚܦܝܛܘܬܗ ܪܒܬܐ ܗܢܘܢ ܕ "especially for the poor, afflicted ones, he showed great zeal,—those who" Ov. 203, 25; ܡܟܬܒ̈ܢܘܬܐ . . . ܗܢܘܢ ܕ "the writings . . . which" Jos. St. 1, 1 &c.

C. For the pure Neuter there comes in very often ܡܕܡ ܕ "something which", "that which", *e. g.* ܡܕܡ ܕܢܘܟܪܝ ܠܐܠܗܘܬܐ "something which would be foreign to God" Ov. 176, 5. Instead of this, there appears also ܗܘ ܡܕܡ ܕ, *e. g.* 1 Cor. 15, 37 (Aphr. 155, 8); Spic. 10 *ult.*; thus too ܒܗܘ ܗܘ ܡܕܡ ܕ Ov. 121, 20. ܗܢܐ and ܗܢܘܢ may also come before ܡܕܡ ܕ: ܫܡܥ ܗܢܐ ܡܕܡ ܕܟܬܒܢܐ ܠܟ "hear this, which I write to thee" Aphr. 79, 14;—ܨܒܐ ܒܗܢܐ ܡܕܡ ܕ "has pleasure in that, which" Spic. 1, 7; ܗܢܘܢ ܡܕܡ ܕܟܬܒܬ ܠܟ "*haec, quae scripsi tibi*" Aphr. 200, 12; ܗܢܘܢ ܡܕܡ ܕܝܐܝܢ "*ea, quae decent*" Aphr. 116, 11.

D. The variety of expression becomes still greater here from the possibility of adding, in many cases, a ܟܠ. Cf. *e. g.* ܟܠ ܐܢܫ ܕ "every one, "who" Ov. 164, 11; ܟܠܗܘܢ ܐܝܠܝܢ ܕ "all those, who" Aphr. 133, 17; ܟܠܗܘܢ ܕܝܢ ܐܝܠܝܢ ܕܡܘܬܪܢ "*omnia vero, quae prosunt*" Ov. 78, 5 &c.

H. NUMERALS.

§ 237. The numeral stands, by way of apposition, either before or after that which is numbered. Thus the variants in Aphr. 467, 1 ܡܠܟܐ ܬܡܢܬܥܣܪ; and ܡܠܟܝܢ ܬܡܢܬܥܣܪ; "18 kings" are equally correct grammatically; and thus ܡܐܐ ܫܢܝܢ Jul. 220, 23; 223, 4; 244, 24; ܡܐܐ ܫܢܝܐ Jul. 247, 2, 22; 248, 3; and ܫܢܝܐ ܡܐܐ Jul. 222, 5; 223, 6 are interchangeable expressions for "100 years". Placing the numeral first is the more usual practice. The numbered object takes either the Abs. or the Emph. State, as these examples also indicate. For farther instances v. § 202 D. Except with ܚܕ, ܚܕܐ the noun is always in the plural. Notice however ܥܣܪܝܢ ܘܚܕ ܝܘܡ Aphr. 56, 21; 57, 1; ܥܣܪܝܢ ܘܚܕ ܝܘܡܐ Sim. 272 *ult.*, "twenty-one days", where ܚܕ calls forth the sing.; but of course the plural is retained when the numbered object comes first: ܫܢܝܢ ܐܪܒܥܝܢ ܘܚܕܐ Aphr. 466, 17.

Numeral and Numbered Object.

The pl. of ܐܠܦ sometimes governs a Genitive with ܕ: ܫܬܐ ܐܠܦܝܢ ܕܫܢܝܐ "six thousands of years" = "6000 years" Aphr. 36, 20, and frequently thus with ܫܢܝܐ; ܬܪܝܢ ܐܠܦܝܢ ܕܓܒܪܐ "2000 men" Edessan Chron. ed. Hallier 146, 6 (Doc. of 201). In the same fashion ܥܣܪܝܢ ܪܒܘܢ ܕܟܪܣܛܝܢܐ "20 myriads of Christians" Jul. 83, 8.

Between the numeral and the numbered object a short word may intervene: thus frequently in the O. T. and elsewhere the word ܗܘܐ, in the phrase "*filius n erat annorum*", *e. g.* ܒܪ ܡܐܐ ܗܘܐ ܫܢܝܢ "he was a hundred years old" Aphr. 235, 18; farther ܗܐ ܥܣܪܝܢ ܠܝ ܫܢܝܢ ܒܒܝܬܟ "twenty years have I been in thy house" Gen. 31, 41; ܐܪܒܥܡܐܐ ܐܢܘܢ ܡܬܩܠܝܢ "it is 400 shekels" Gen. 23, 15; ܡܛܠ ܕܚܕ ܗܘܘ ܥܡܐ "for they were one people" Aphr. 207, 22 &c. A particle comes into the midst of the statement of number itself in ܬܠܬܡܐܐ ܐܝܬ ܐܢܝܢ ܘܬܫܥܝܢ ܘܚܡܫ ܫܢܝܢ "it is 395 years" (or lit. "three hundred there are and ninety and five years") Aphr. 399 *ult.* Rarely is the numbered object left to be understood, as in ܠܫܘܡܠܝ ܬܫܥܐ ܕܝܠܗ "at the completion of his nine" = "when he was nine years old" Jesussabran (Chabot) 509 *ult.*

Determination of that which is numbered.

§ 238. The simple numbers may always be used even in "determination", *e. g.* ܟ݇ܚܣܘ̈ܗܝ ܪܝܢ "his two cloaks" Aphr. 404, 21; ܠܬܠܬܐ ܠܬܠܡܝ̈ܕܘܗܝ "to his three disciples" Aphr. 460 *ult.* &c. Cf. the examples in §§ 202 D; 203. But the forms set forth in § 149, for numbers up to 10 inclusive may appear also in this use, *e. g.* ܥܡ ܚܕܥܣ̈ܪ ܬܪܝܢ ἐκ τῶν τεσσάρων ἀνέμων Mark 13, 27; ܗܠܝܢ ܬܠܬ ܦܘܪ̈ܫܢܐ "these three views (opinions)" Spic. 9, 14; ܬܠܬ ܗܠܝܢ "these three things" Aphr. 319, 15 (by the side of which, line 13 ܒܗܠܝܢ ܬܠܬ "for in these three things"); ܬܪܝܢ ܥܠܡ̈ܐ "the two worlds" Aphr. 493, 2; ܬܫ̈ܥܬ ܡܠ̈ܟܐ "the five kings" Josh. 10, 22; ܘܩܛܠ ܠܚܡܫ "smote the five (women)" Mart. I, 126, mid.

Cardinal numbers used for Ordinal numbers.

§ 239. The *Cardinal numbers* in the genitive are often employed for the *Ordinal numbers*: ܝܘܡܐ ܕܬܪܝܢ = ܝܘܡܐ ܬܪܝܢܐ "the second day" &c. Thus for ܒܕܪܐ ܕܬܡܢܝܐ "in the eighth generation" Aphr. 474, 21 the var. is ܕܬܡܢܝܐ. In numbers above 10 the genitive association either quite preponderates (according to § 153), or alone is in use, *e. g.* ܠܫܢܬ ܐܪܒܥܡܐܐ ܘܥܣܪܝܢ ܘܚܕ "to the year (of) 421" Aphr. 475, 2 &c. The repetition of the numbered object at the end of the clause, as in ܥܕܡܐ ܠܫܢܬ ܫܬܡ̈ܐܐ ܫܢܝܐ "up to the six-hundredth year" Aphr. 476, 2 &c. is a Hebraism.

Distributive Expression.

§ 240. A. *Doubling* the word to convey the idea of *distribution* (or *Distributive Repetition*) is a favourite practice in the case of numerals, *e. g.* ܫܒܥ ܫܒܥ "by sevens" or "every seven" (f.); ܫܒܥܝܢ ܫܒܥܝܢ "by seventies".

Grouping.

B. By means of the preposition ܒܝܬ "between", *numbers* are sometimes *taken together as a group*: ܒܝܬ ܫܒܥ ܢܫ̈ܐ "seven women together shall take hold of one man" Ephr. II, 26 A; ܟܕ ܒܝܬ ܐܪܒܥܐ "while four persons together carried him" Mark 2, 3; ܠܒܝܬ ܬܪܝܢ ܡܢܗܘܢ "for two of them together" Jos. St. 85, 10.

Approximate numbers.

C. *Approximate numbers* are indicated by two numbers following each other without being otherwise connected: ܬܪܝܢ ܠܬܠܬܐ ܡܗܝܡ̈ܢܐ "two or three eunuchs" 2 Kings 9, 32; ܬܠܬܝܢ ܐܘ ܐܪܒܥܝܢ ܡܢܗܘܢ "thirty or forty of them" Land II, 48, 13.

§ 241. The Cardinal numbers in the feminine, even without an accompanying ܙܒܢܐ, ܪ̈ܓܠܐ, denote the numeral adverbs of time: ܚܕܐ "once"; ܬܪ̈ܬܝܢ "twice". Thus ܪ̈ܓܠܐ ܘܬܪ̈ܬܝܢ "once or twice" Mart. I, 135, 9, and often; although ܩܕܡܝܬܐ ܘܬܪ̈ܬܝܢ ܘܬܠܬ "for the first, second, and third time" appears. So too ܚܕܐ ܚܕܐ "again and again" Land II, 356, 7. "For the nth time" may be signified also by means of ܕ (§ 209 B): ܕܬܪ̈ܬܝܢ Aphr. 19, 16: 31, 15. The *time within which* something regularly recurs, is expressed by means of ܠ: ܚܕܐ ܠܐܪܒܥ ܫܢ̈ܝܢ "once in the four years" Jos. St. 26, 8; ܚܕܐ ܠܫܒܥܐ ܝܘܡ̈ܝܢ "once in the seven days", *or* "every seven days" Spic. 19, 19; cf. ܚܕܐ ܠܪ̈ܒܘ σπανίως (literally, "one in ten thousand [times]") Lagarde Anal. 145, 14; ܚܕܐ ܠܢܘܓܪܐ ἐκ διαλειμμάτων ("once in a long time", "at long intervals") Sachau, Ined. 90 *ult.*; ܚܕܐ ܒܙܒܢܐ "sometimes" Joh. van Tella (Kleyn) 23, 16 (var. ܙܒܢܐ merely): 61, 2, and frequently.(1) Instead of this (*i. e.* ܠ to express recurrence) we have ܒ similarly used in ܚܕܐ ܒܫܢܬܐ "once a-year" Ephr. I, 223 E.

Multiplicity is expressed by means of ܥܦ̈ set before the number concerned, with or without ܒ: ܥܦ̈ ܒܬܪ̈ܬܝܢ "double" Ex. 22, 3, (6 ܥܦ̈ ܬܪ̈ܬܝܢ); ܥܦ̈ ܒܡܐܐ ἑκατονταπλασίονα Matt. 19, 29; Mark 10, 30; Luke 8, 8; ܥܦ̈ ܒܥܣܪܐ "tenfold" Jul. 115 *ult.*; ܥܦ̈ ܒܪ̈ܒܘ ܡܢ ܫܡܫܐ μυριοπλασίως ἡλίου Sir. 23, 19; ܥܦ̈ ܠܬܠܬܐ ܫܡܫܐ τριπλασίως Sir. 43, 4; ܥܦ̈ ܬܪ̈ܬܝܢ ܥܠ ܗܘ ܕ "twice as much as that which" Ex. 16, 5 &c. Thus, often ܥܦ̈ ܟܡܐ "how much more".

Rem. In Ephr. II, 227 C, ܥܦ̈ ܬܪ̈ܬܝܢ stands for "for the 2nd time".

Manifoldness may also be expressly denoted by means of ܐܥܦܐ (ܥܦܐ) "doubling": ܣܓܝ ܗܘܐ . . . ܒܥܣܪܐ ܥܘܦ̈ܝܢ "was ten times greater" Sim. 373 mid. Cf. *ibid.* 301 mid.; 325 mid.

Adverbial Expressions.

§ 242. The method most in favour, at least in the older writings, of expressing the *reciprocal relation* is by means of a doubled ܚܕ: ܣܢܝܢ ܚܕ ܠܚܕ μισήσουσιν ἀλλήλους Matt. 24, 10; cf. Matt. 25, 32; Mark 1, 27 &c.;

"One another"

☞ p. 354

(1) For the more ancient period however, the expression is hardly ever found, except in translations from the Greek. Generally speaking we are obliged for obvious reasons to have recourse to translations, oftener than is desirable, in dealing with these numerical expressions.

ܚܕ ܒܬܪ ܚܕ "one behind the other" Aphr. 507 *ult.* and frequently: ܡܣܬܩܘܒܠܝܢ ܐܢܘܢ ܚܕ ܕܚܕ "they are opposed to one another" Spic. 12, 3; ܒܚܘܠܛܢܐ ܕܚܕ ܥܡ ܚܕ "through mutual intermixture" Spic. 4, 23; ܘܩܪ̈ܨܐ ܚܕ ܕܚܕ ܠܐ ܢܐܟܘܠ "and let not one calumniate the other" Sim. 396 mid. &c. Cf. §§ 319; 351. Or else the words are run together into the single word ܚ̈ܕܕܐ, as if the foregoing expressions might be read ܒܬܪ ܚ̈ܕܕܐ, ܠܘܩܒܠ ܚ̈ܕܕܐ &c. Thus we find ܥܡ ܚ̈ܕܕܐ Luke 4, 36 P., where S. has ܚܕ ܥܡ ܚܕ like Luke 2, 15 P., and thus too ܚ̈ܕܕܐ often with prepositions; farther compare ܒܡܟܡܟܘܬܐ ܥܡܪܝܢ ܕܚ̈ܕܕܐ "they reside in the neighbourhood of one another" or "they are neighbours" Moes. II, 84 v. 115; ܐܢ ܐܝܩܪܐ ܕܝܠܢ ܗܘ ܐܦ ܨܥܪܐ ܠܘܬ ܕܚ̈ܕܕܐ "if there is honour, it is ours, and if there is disgrace, it again is on both sides" Ov. 151, 17 &c. Notice ܘܫܘܚܠܦܝ ܦܪ̈ܝܫܝܢ ܡܚ̈ܘܬܗܘܢ ܡܢ ܕܚ̈ܕܕܐ "and their strokes differ from one another" Sim. 296 mid., and ܡܫܚܠܦܝܢ ܪ̈ܝܚܝܗܘܢ ܡܢ ܕܚ̈ܕܕܐ "their odours are different from each other" Sim. 382, 8; ܐܝܟ ܕܡܢ ܪܓܠܐ ܕܚ̈ܕܕܐ "as on a common footing" Philox. 154, 7, where the genitive relation is expressly denoted.

☞ p. 355

Rem. The somewhat childlike method too of denoting the second member, even when both are impersonal, by ܚܒܪܐ, f. ܚܒܪܬܐ "fellow, mate (m. and f.)" has been greatly in use in Syriac even from ancient times, *e. g.* ܕܪܓܐ ܡܢ ܚܒܪܗ ܡܥܠܝ "one step is higher than the other" Aphr. 434, 17; ܡܢ ܕܘܟܬܐ ܠܚܒܪܬܗ "from one place to the other" John 5, 13 C. S.; Land II, 349, 2 &c.—Or the word itself is repeated: ܐܓܪܐ ܡܝܬܪ ܡܢ ܐܓܪܐ "one reward is higher than another" Aphr. 434, 17 &c.

J. ADVERBIAL EXPRESSION.

Substantives as Adverbs.

§ 243. Some few Nouns of Place serve, just as they stand, for adverbs of place. Thus in particular ܒܝܬ with Genitive following—"*in the house of, in the place of*" (completely to be distinguished from the like-sounding word which means "between" § 251), *e. g.* ܒܝܬ ܡܟܣܐ ἐπὶ τὸ τελώνιον "at the receipt of custom" (E. v.) Matt. 9, 9; ܒܝܬ ܐܒܝ P. S. or ܒܝܬ ܐܒܐ C. ἐν τοῖς τοῦ πατρός μου Luke 2, 49; ܒܝܬ ܠܚܡ ἐν Βηθλεέμ Matt. 2, 1 C. S. (P. ܒܒܝܬ); 2, 16 C. S. (P. otherwise); ܒܝܬ ܣܗܕ̈ܐ ܢܨܝ̈ܚܐ "in the sanctuary of the noble martyrs" Ov. 163, 25; ܒܝܬ ܡܥܪ̈ܒܐ "in the country of the Samaritans" Jul. 100 *ult.* &c. Also "*into the place* of": ܐܪܡܝܗ ܒܝܬ ܐܣܝܪܐ "threw him into prison" Jul. 129, 7 &c. Farther ܐܶܣܳܕܰܘܗ̱ܝ "at his head" 1 Sam. 26, 7; ZDMG XXV, 342, 453 and frequently (also ܡܶܢ ܐ' John 20, 12)—ܡܨܰܥܬ ܫܡܰܝܳܐ "in the midst of heaven" Spic. 13, 24 (15, 18 ܒܡܨܰܥܬ ܫ', and in this way ܡܨܥܬ and ܒܡܨܥܬ are frequently interchanged)—ܐܰܬܰܪ ܕ "in the place where" (§ 359) and several others.

Much more frequently there occurs an analogous use of Nouns of Time: ܫܰܦܪܳܐ ܒܶܝܬ ὑπὸ τὸν ὄρθρον Acts 5, 21; ܒܶܝܬ ܦܶܠܓܶܗ ܕܠܺܠܝܳܐ "at midnight" Jos. St. 28, 19; ܟܽܠܝܘܡ "every day" often; ܡܶܥܪܳܒ ܫܶܡܫܳܐ "at sunset" Matt. 8, 16 C.; Mark 1, 32 S.; Ov. 168, 1; ܡܶܥܠܰܝ̈ ܨܰܘܡܳܐ "at the beginning of the fast" Sim. 282 mid. (*Cod. Lond.* otherwise; cf. ܡܥ̈' ܫ' 2 Kings 11, 5, 9); ܙܰܒܢ̈ܐ ܣܰܓܺܝ̈ܐܬܳܐ "many times" Ov. 167, 24 and frequently (and similar cases); ܐܺܝܡܳܡܳܐ ܟܽܠܝܘܡ "during the day time always" Ov. 183, 8; ܠܺܠܝ ܐܺܝܡܳܡ "by night and by day" (§ 146) Sim. 372 *inf.* and often; "throughout both night and day" Ephr. I, 14 C; III, 253 C and frequently; ܒܠܺܠܝܳܐ ܘܐܺܝܡܳܡܳܐ "throughout both night and day" Sim. 275, 3 (not in the *Lond. Cod.*); ܙܰܒܢܳܐ ܬܚܺܝܡܳܐ "for a definite time" Ov. 167, 15; ܢܰܓܺܝܪܳܐ "for a long time" Ephr. II, 127 A; III, 423 B; ܢܰܓܺܝܪܳܐ ܣܰܓܺܝܐܳܐ "a very long time" Spic. 22, 5; ܢܰܓܺܝܪܳܐ ܕܫܢܝܐ "for long years" Sim. 390, 8 (*Lond. Cod.* different); ܡܶܢ ܕܗܘܳܐ ܒܗ ܚܕܳܐ ܫܢܬܳܐ ܘܬܰܪܬܶܝܢ ܒܗܳܢܳܐ ܒܥܒܳܕܳܐ "but after he had been at this work for one or two years" Sim. 279 mid. (wanting in *Lond. Cod.*); ܟܽܠܗ ܨܰܘܡܳܐ "during the whole fast" Sim. 282 mid., and many like instances. Compare besides ܐܰܪܒܥܺܝܢ ܝܰܘܡܺܝܢ "for forty days" Ov. 186, 1; ܙܒܢܐ ܙܥܘܪܐ βραχύ τι "for a short time" Acts 5, 34.

So too with other expressions of Measure of various kinds: ܚܕܺܝܘ ܗܘܰܘ ܐܘܪܚܐ ܟܽܠܗ̇ "they rejoiced the whole way" Joseph 192, 11, cf. 214, 5 [Ov. 294, 6; 305, 16]; ܛܘܪܳܐ ܡܪܰܗܛܳܐ ܪܘܚܩܳܐ ܪܳܒܳܐ "the stone runs a long distance" Moes. II, 88 v. 197; ܕܪܰܚܺܝܩܳܐ ܡܶܢ ܚܽܘܛܪܶܗ ܕܛܽܘܒܳܢܳܐ ܐܰܪܒܥܳܐ ܡ̈ܺܝܠܺܝܢ "which was four miles distant from the enclosure of the blessed one" Sim. 391 *inf.* (*Cod. Lond.* ܐܝܟ ܠܐܠܦܐ) and similar cases. So too ܛܳܒܳܐ "in large quantity", "very", "very much", *e. g.* ܛܳܒܳܐ ܡܰܟܐܶܒ ܠܳܟ "hurts thee much" Ov. 87, 21; ܕܛܳܒܳܐ ܚܰܛܳܝܺܢ "who are very sinful" Ov. 102, 22 &c. In the very same way are used the adjectives ܣܰܓܺܝ "much", "very"; ܩܰܠܺܝܠ "little"; ܒܨܺܝܪ "little", "less" (*e. g.* ܚܛܰܝܢ ܠܰܐܠܳܗܽܘܬܳܐ ܒܨܺܝܪ

ܝܘ̈ܡܝܢ ܐܪܒܥܝܢ "thirteen years less forty days" John Eph. 320, 21; ܒܪ ܡܢ
☞ p. 355 ܩܠܝܠ "with very little exception", "nearly" often); ܝܬܝܪ "more" &c. An expression of measure is also implied in ܢܦܩ ܡܛܪܬܐ "he went out for a night's watch", *i. e.* "he kept a vigil" *v.* Ov. 167, 25; Wright Cat. 664*b*, 18 and frequently.

In fact even the *Object*, when it is not formally indicated, might be brought under this category (*i. e.* of adverbial expressions), *e. g.* in ܚܦܪ ܒܐܪܐ "he dug a well", and, in like manner, cases like ܢܦܩ ܪܘܚܐ "he went into the wind(?)" *i. e.* "he sought to excuse himself". Farther, to this section belongs the construction of words like ܫܘܐ "worth", ܚܝܒ "guilty", and several others, used with a Noun: ܫܘܝܐ (read thus) ܕܡܥܐ "which is worth an obolus" Spic. 15, 23; ܚܝ̈ܒܝܢ ܡܘܬܐ "deserving of death" frequently; ܚܕܐ ܓܝܪ ܛܒܬܐ ܚܣܝܪ ܐܢܐ "for, one good thing I am lacking in" Jesussabran (Chabot) 568, 5 &c.

Adjectives as Adverbs of Quality. § 244. Adverbs of Quality of the following kind occur, but they are not numerous: ܥܪܛܠܝܐܝܬ ܗܠܟܘ "they went naked" Job 24, 10; ܢܫܒܩܘܢܟܝ ܥܪܛܠܝܐܝܬ "they leave thee (f.) naked" Ezek. 16, 39; ܢܕܒܪ ... ܫܒܝܬܐ ... ܛܠܝ̈ܐ ܘܣܒ̈ܐ ... ܥܪܛܠܝܐܝܬ ܘܚܦܝܐܝܬ "he shall lead away the captives ... young and old ... naked and barefooted" Is. 20, 4 &c. In cases like ܚܕ ܕܝܢ ܡܫܪܝ ܐܬܝܠܕ "but one had been born paralytic" Sim. 291, 11; ܘܣܠܩ ܢܨܝܚ ܡܢ ܓܘ ܡܝܐ "and he came up glorious out of the midst of the water" Ov. 360, 7 = Jac. Sar., Constantin v. 656 there is an actual adjective, for in the pl. it would be ܡܫܪ̈ܝܢ ܐܬܝܠܕܘ &c.; v. § 216. But usually there is a special clause, with ܟܕ "while", for such indications of condition; thus *Lond. Cod.* has in that passage ܟܕ ܡܫܪܝ ܗܘܐ.

Adverbs belonging to an Adjective or another Adverb. § 245. An adverb belonging specially to an adjective or another adverb may stand either before or after it: ܛܘܪܐ ܕܪܡ ܛܒ ὄρος ὑψηλὸν λίαν Matt. 4, 8; ܛܒ ܚܣܝܢ "very strong" Sim. 269 mid. (*Cod. Lond.* without ܛܒ); ܕܡܫܥܥ ܛܒ "which was much polished" Sim. 271, 8; ܝܬܝܪ ܢܗܝܪ "more bright" = "brighter" Ov. 150, 18, for which there is a variant (Roman edition) ܢܗܝܪ ܝܬܝܪ.

K. PREPOSITIONS.

§ 246. The relation of Prepositions to what is governed by them is, in Syriac, as in Semitic speech generally, that of the Constr. St. to the Genitive. In both cases the governed word must immediately follow the governing; although in both cases short words may, by way of exception, come between (§ 208 A). Thus ܚܠܦ ܕܝܢ ܟܘܙܒܝ "but instead of Kosbi" Ephr. Nis. p. 71 v. 65; ܒܠܥܕ ܓܝܪ ܒܘܟܪܐ "for without the First-born" Ephr. II, 411 E; ܥܠ ܟܡ ܦܣܬܐ ܐܝܕܝ "on the palms of my hands, as the saying goes" Ephr. II, 267 B; ܒܝܬ ܓܝܪ ܗܘ "for in the interval between" Ephr. II, 3 B; farther ܡܛܠ ܡܪܝ ܫܒܝܗ ܕܐܕܡ "because of the captivity of Adam, O Lord" Ephr. III, 383 E; ܒܬܪ ܡܪܝ ܐܘܠܨܢܝ "after my affliction, O Lord" Ephr. Nis. p. 18 v. 72 (cf. § 327). Such a separation however is impossible with ܒ and ܠ.—Compare besides, on the Construction of Prepositions, § 222, 1 *a* and *b*. *Separation of the Preposition from its Regimen.* ☞ p. 355

§ 247. In what follows we mean to say something about the use of the most important of the Prepositions, viz—ܠ, ܒ, ܥܠ, ܥܡ, as well as about ܒܝܬ &c. "between". *ܠ.*

ܠ, the Preposition of *direction towards*, employed in manifold fashion both with reference to space, and as marking the Dative, serves also to designate the Object (§ 287 *sqq.*). Cases like ܘܗܘܐ ܐܕܡ ܠܢܦܫܐ ܚܝܐ "and Adam became a living soul" Gen. 2, 7 are to be regarded as Hebraisms.(1) But we have relevant examples in ܕܙܒܢ ܚܡܨܐ ܠܡܪܓܢܝܬܐ "who has bought a pea [bright Indian seed] for a (instead of a) pearl" Isaac II, 12, 135, and ܐܢ ܢܙܒܢ ܐܢܫ ܥܒܕܐ ܠܥܒܕܐ ܛܒܐ "if one buys a slave as a good slave" Land I, 40, 5. As ܠ repeatedly indicates *the end*, so does it in certain cases indicate *the cause*: ܡܐܬ ܠܟܦܢܐ "is dying of hunger" Jer. 38, 9; ܡܝܬܬ ܠܨܗܝܐ "thou art dying of thirst" Aphr. 74, 12; ܠܩܪܝܟ ܡܝܬܬ "thou art dying because of thy cold, *or* of cold &c." *ibid.* line 17; ܠܩܪܝܟ ܐܝܬܝܟ ܡܬܐܘܠܨܐ "thou art in distress through thy cold" *ibid.* line 15.—With considerable frequency ܠ serves to denote *time*:

---

(1) Notice how the Pesh. employs circumlocutions to express "to anoint (him) king [לְמֶלֶךְ]" and the like.

ܠܝܘܡܐ ܘܡܚܪ "on the 7th day" Judges 14, 17; ܠܚܪܬܐ "at last" often; ܠܩܝܛܐ "in summer" Land III, 210, 10; ܠܙܒܢܐ "in process of time", "late" Land III, 106, 25 and in other passages: also "after a long time" Ephr. I, 55 F = 152 B; ܠܚܕܒܫܒܐ ܐܚܪܢܐ "on the second Sunday" Sim. 269 inf.;—ܠܬܠܬܐ ܝܘܡܝܢ "after three days", "on the third day" in the Credo; ܠܚܩܠܬܐ ܒܝ ܗ̈ܝ δι᾿ ἐτῶν δὲ πλειόνων Acts 24, 17; ܫܢ ܐܝܪܚܐ ܠܒܬܪ ܡܛܘ "they arrived a year and a month after" Sim. 351, 12 &c.

Direction in space or time is farther denoted in expressions like ܡܢ ܓܪܒܝܐ ܠܣܝܓܐ "to the north of the enclosure" Sim. 290 mid.; ܡܢ ܒܬܪ ܬܠܬܝܢ ܝܪ̈ܚܐ ܡܢ ܡܦܩܢܗ "thirty months after his departure" Mart. I, 70 mid.; ܝܘܡܐ ܕܬܠܬܐ ܠܒܬܪ ܡܠܟܘܬܗܘܢ "the third day after their coronation" Moes. II, 72, 5 &c. Cases like ܒܫܢܬ ܡܐܐ ܘܚܕ ܕܚܝܘܗܝ "in the hundred-and-first year of Abraham's life" Aphr. 479, 4, and those of the same nature,—probably arise out of the Hebrew idiom.

With the Passive participle ܠ very often denotes the agent,—the logical Subject (§ 279). In the connection of this preposition with certain reflexive verbs the same conception suggests itself, but in reality ܠ signifies in that case a direction, or a dative relation. The common ܐܬܚܙܝ ܠ is properly, not "to be seen by", but "to appear to one" (like ל נראה—near it in meaning is ܡܛܐ ܠ). So ܡܢ ܐܝܟܐ ܡܣܬܟܠܐ ܠܟ ܡܠܬܐ "how is the word intelligible for thee?" Aphr. 209, 4; ܘܕܡܘܬܗܘܢ ܐܦ ܠܣܡܝܐ ܡܬܚܙܝܐ "and their form is perceptible even to the blind" Jos. St. 66,13; ܐܝܟ ܕܠܚܡ ܠܗ ܕܡܐ "how she liked the blood" ("how the blood tasted to her") Simeon of Bēth Arshām 6, 5 ab inf.; ܕܢܬܝܩܪܘܢ ἵνα φανερωθῇ τῷ Ἰσραήλ John 1, 31; ܠܟ ܢܣܬܒܪܘܢ "may they (f.) be thus esteemed by thee" Spic. 26, 2; ܕܠܐ ܐܣܬܒܪ ܠܟ "that it may not appear to thee (as if . . .)" Jos. St. 34, 18; . . . ܠܐ ܡܣܬܝܡ ܠܟ "let it not be put for thee in place &c." Spic. 26, 3; ܢܫܬܟܚܘܢ ܠܫܪܪܐ "let them be found for the truth" Philoxenus, Epistola (Guidi) fol. 29 a, 2 mid.; ܡܛܠ ܕܫܠܡܝܢ ܒܢ̈ܝܢܫܐ ܕܢܬܠܦܘܢ "because that men surrender themselves prisoners to the longing for it" [i. e. "are made captive by their lust for it"] Spic. 46, 7; ܐܝܠܝܢ ܕܢܦܠܘ ܠܫܠܝ̈ܚܘܗܝ "they fell to the share of his apostles as their catch" Aphr. 284, 2; ܡܫܬܥܒܕ ܐܢܐ ܠܟ "I yield to thy persuasion", "I give way to thee" Spic. 13, 6; ܐܬܠܚܡܘ ܠܟ "they

☞ p. 355

became his disciples" Ephr. III, XXXIX, 3; ܕܢܬܚܙܐ ܠܫܒܘܪ ܕ "that it may appear to Sapor, that" Jul. 181, 13. And similarly is it with several other verbs. Of those which have been adduced, ܐܬܚܙܝ ܠ, ܐܬܚܫܒ ܠ, ܐܫܬܠܡ ܠ, for instance, occur frequently. Also ܘܢܬܠܛ ܠܡܪܐܠܗܐ, in the ancient inscription ZDMG XXXVI tab. 1 nr. 8, belongs to this class: "and let him be brought before the Master of the Gods as an accursed one", or of like tenor; compare ארור האיש לפני יהוה Josh. 6, 26. ☞ p. 355

§ 248. ܒ is the proper preposition to indicate locality and time, and farther, to express instrumentality, for which often the clearer ܒܝܕ, "by means of", "through",—appears. Thus also it indicates the medium of exchange, the price, and farther it signifies absolute equivalence of value: ܕܢܙܕܒܢ . . . ܒܣܓܝܐܐ πραθῆναι πολλοῦ Matt. 26, 9; ܐܙܕܒܢܘ ܗܘܘ . . . ܒܕܝܢܪܐ "were sold for a denarius" Jos. St. 33, 18; ܚܝܝ ܕܒܡܫܝܚܐ ܒܡܘܬܗܘܢ ܠܐ ܝܗܒ ܐܢܐ ܠܟ "my life in Christ I do not give up to thee for their death (*i. e.*—in order to prevent their death)" Mart. I, 23 mid. ܒ. ☞ p. 355

ܒ, like ܠ, is employed in intellectual references of most varied character, and it is associated with verbs of many kinds. A peculiar use, and, what is more, a very rare one in Syriac, is met with in ܘܩܪܐ ܐܢܘܢ ܒܥܬܝܪܐ "and denominated them (*or* designated them) rich persons" Aphr. 382, 7; ܒܝܥܠܐ . . . ܐܬܩܪܝܘ "they were called wild goats" Isaac II, 326 v. 1513.

Notice farther: ܘܟܠܗܝܢ ܨܒܘܬܐ ܕܓܕܫܢ ܠܗܘܢ ܒܥܘܬܪܐ ܘܒܡܣܟܢܘܬܐ ܘܒܟܘܪܗܢܐ ܘܒܚܘܠܡܢܐ ܘܒܫܘܚܢܐ ܕܦܓܪܐ "and all the things which happen to them, (made up of)—riches and poverty, and diseases and sound health, and bodily injuries (are . . .)" Spic. 9, 5. ☞ p. 355

§ 249. A. ܡܢ is "from", "out of", in the most diverse uses, both as regards space and otherwise. In certain connections it loses altogether its meaning as denoting the starting point of a movement in space or time: thus, ܡܢ ܝܡܝܢܗ "on his right hand"; ܡܢ ܐܣܕܘܗܝ πρὸς τῇ κεφαλῇ "at his head" John 20, 12; ܡܢ ܒܬܪ "after"; and in a great many combinations with adverbs and prepositions.—The starting point of the direction is denoted by ܡܢ when associated with ܘܠ, like ܡܢ ܥܒܪܐ ܕܦܪܬ ܘܠܡܕܢܚܐ "from the other side of the Euphrates and to the East", *i. e.* "eastward from the Euphrates" Spic. 15, 25; ܡܢ ܐܕܡ ܘܥܕܡܐ "from Adam and up till ܡܢ.

now", *i. e.* "from Adam onward" Aphr. 496, 5; ܡܢܗ ܘܠܗܠ "on the other side of him", "beyond him" Ephr. III, 136 B, and frequently: ܡܢܗ ܘܠܗܠܐ "on this side of him" *ibid.*; ܡܢܗ ܘܠܒܪ "besides him" Jac. Sar. in Moes. I, 31 v. 296.

B. Another application of these two prepositions in combination is the favourite one of ܡܢܗ ܘܒܗ "by himself", "alone"; ܡܢܗ̇ ܘܒܗ̇ κατὰ μόνας 1 Macc. 12, 36; ܕܢܐܟܠܘܢ ܥܡܝ ܓܒܖ̈ܐ ܗܠܝܢ ܡܢܗܘܢ ܘܒܗܘܢ ܡܨܖ̈ܝܐ ܘܥܒܖ̈ܝܐ ܡܢܗܘܢ ܘܒܗܘܢ "that these men eat with me,—the Egyptians by themselves, and the Hebrews by themselves" Joseph 203, 12 [Ov. 300, 6]; ܡܢܝ ܘܒܝ ܗܘܝܬ "I was alone" Land III, 73, 1.

Rem. From the Jewish idiom is borrowed the favourite phrase in Ephr. ܡܢܗ ܘܒܗ "in and by itself".

C. The partitive use of ܡܢ is pretty extensive, cf. ܠܝܬ ܡܢ ܛܒ̈ܐ ܕܩܐܡ ܒܗ "there is no one of the good who stands therein" Aphr. 451, 2; ܟܕ ܩܝܡܝܢ ܡܢ ܬܠܡܝܕܘ̈ܗܝ ܠܘܬܗ "while some of his disciples stood beside him" Sim. 381 mid.; ܡܢ ܪܘܚܟ ܒܢ "[a portion] of thy spirit is in us" Aphr. 488, 11;—ܐܟܬܘܒ ܡܢ ܐܝܠܝܢ ܕܐܬܥܒܕ̈ "*scribam* (*aliqua*) *ex iis, quae facta sunt*" Jos. St. 80, 1; ܠܐ ܡܢܬܗ ܗܘ ܐܘܠܕ ܐܒܐ ܘܡܢܬܗ ܡܪܝܡ "the Father did not procreate one part of him, and Mary another" Assemani I, 310 *b inf.* (Jac. Sar.); ܐܢ ܬܚܠܛ ܒܗ̇ ܡܢ ܥܘܠܐ "if thou mingle any iniquity in it" (f.) Ephr. III, 678 A; ܗܘܐ ܒܗ ܡܢ ܕܚܠܬܐ ܕܢܨܖ̈ܝܐ "he became (an adherent) of the religion of the Nazarenes" Qardagh (Feige) 58, 2 (= Abbeloos 68, 11); ܘܗܠܝܢ ܟܢܘ̈ܢܐ ܢܩܦܢܢ ܡܢܢ ܒܩܛܝܪܐ ܕܐܢܢܩܐ ܘܡܢܢ ܒܨܒܝܢܐ ܚܐܪܐ "and these Canons we have followed,—some of us by constraint of necessity, some of us of free will" Statuti della Scuola di Nisibi (Guidi) 10 *ult.* &c. So, frequently ܡܢܗܘܢ—ܡܢܗܘܢ "some—some". ܒ and ܠ may be put before such a double ܡܢ with suffix: ܘܠܡܢܗܘܢ ܡܢ ܩܕ̈ܝܫܐ ܩܛܠܘ ܒܣܝܦܐ ܘܠܡܢܗܘܢ ܐܫܠܡܘ ܠܝܩܕܢܐ ܕܢܘܪܐ "and some of the saints they killed with the sword, and others they consigned to burning by fire" Moes. II, 72, 14; ܠܡܢܢ—ܠܡܢܢ "some of us—others" Clemens 56, 25; ܒܡܢܬܗܘܢ ܡܬܛܦܝܣܝܢ ܚܢܢ ܘܒܡܢܬܗܘܢ ܠܐ "with one part of them we are satisfied, with another, not" Spic. 10, 19, 20. To this use of ܡܢ belongs, not merely ܡܚܝܗܝ . . . ܡܢ ܟܒܕܗ "struck him on (a part of) the liver, *or* (somewhere) in the liver" John Eph. 81, 18, but probably expressions also of time like ܡܢ ܨܦܪܐ, ܡܢ ܪܡܫܐ "in (a portion of) the morning,—*or* evening", frequently occurring; ܡܢ ܩܝܛܐ "in summer-time"; ܡܢ ܫܢܝ̈ܘܗܝ, ܡܢ ܝܘܡ̈ܘܗܝ, ܡܢ ܝܘܡ̈ܝ "at any time in his, *or* in my life" frequently.

D. Farther ܡܢ denotes, generally, the starting point of the action, ☞ p. 355 *i. e.* the *agent*, with the passive construction ([1]) as in ܐܬܩܛܠ ܡܢܗ "he was killed by him" &c.; but with the Part. pass. ܠ is oftener used for this purpose, v. §§ 247; 279.

E. As being the preposition of 'removal from', ܡܢ in a comparison denotes that which is surpassed, whether the relation of comparison is, or is not (which is the commoner case), distinctly expressed by means of ܝܬܝܪ "excelling", or ܛܒ 'much'; ܚܣܝܢܐ ܗܘܬ ܝܬܝܪ ܨܒܝܢܗ ܛܒ ܡܢ ܚܝܠܐ ܕܟܝܢܗ "for his goodwill was stronger than the vigour of his nature" Ov. 181, 25; ܕܡܪܚ ܛܒ ܡܢܗ "who is more insolent than he" Ephr. III, 658 B; ܕܫܦܝܪܐ ܗܘܐ ܝܬܝܪ ܡܢ ܫܡܫܐ "who was fairer than the sun" Sim. 272, 11; ܘܕܚܫܝܚ̈ܝܢ ܡܢܗܘܢ and ܛܒ, ܘܝܬܝܪ' ܡܢܗܘܢ "and more than they" frequently in Sim.; ܝܬܝܪ ܡܢ ܟܠܗܘܢ ܚܒܪ̈ܘܗܝ ܗܘ ܡܩܪܒ ܗܘܐ "he was nearer than all his companions" Anc. Doc. 42, 13; ܒܝܫܐ ܗܕܐ ܣܟܠܘܬܐ ܡܢ ܕܪܚܒܥܡ "this folly is worse than Rehoboam's" Aphr. 251, 19; ܘܝܬܪ ܢܘܚ ܒܙܥܘܪܘܬܗ ܡܢ ܟܠܗ "and Noah was better in his trifling number than the whole race" Aphr. 347, 4; ܝܬܝܪ ܡܢ ܢܦܫܟ ܐܚܒܬܢܝ "thou hast loved me more than thyself" Jos. St. 2, 17; ܘܪܚܡ ܗܘܐ ܐܝܩܪܐ . . . ܛܒ ܡܢ ܫܘܒܚܐ "and he loved honour . . . rather than glory" Mart. I, 166 *inf.*; ܚܣܝܢ ܡܢ "was stronger than" Jul. 170, 4 &c.—So also ܛܠܐ ܗܘܐ ܡܢ ܚܛܗ̈ܐ "he was too young for sins" Aphr. 221, 12; ܪܒܐ ܗܘ ܡܢ ܡ̈ܡܠܠܐ "is too great for tellers (of it)", *i. e.* "is greater than one can tell" Ephr. III, 42 B; and many instances of a similar kind (in which usually a relative clause stands with an Inf. and ܠ, *e. g.* ܣܒܘ ܡܢ ܕܢܘܠܕܘܢ "become too old to procreate" Spic. 11, 8). The correspondence of the two members, in sentences which convey comparison, is not always quite clearly expressed; compare cases like ܚܕܐ ܒܗ ܝܬܝܪ ܡܢ ☞ p. 355 ܠܬܫܥܝܢ ܘܬܫܥܐ χαίρει ἐπ' αὐτῷ μᾶλλον ἢ ἐπὶ τοῖς ἐνενήκοντα καὶ ἐννέα Matt.

([1]) My attention has been directed by Siegm. Fraenkel to the fact that ܡܢ stands even with intransitives used in passive meaning, *e. g.* ܫܠܡ . . . ܡܢܟܝ "was consumed by thee" Simeon of Bēth Arshām 10, 13.

18, 13; ܘܪܘܚܐ ܐܘܦ ܐܝܬܝܗ ܡܢ ܒܨܘܡܐ ܗܘܝܐ ܠܗ "moreover she pleased him more by fasting than *by* perfume" Ephr. III, 668 A; ܐܬܝܩܪܬ ܠܘܬܗ ܝܬܝܪ ܡܢ ܟܠܗ ܐܝܣܪܝܠ "it (the ark) was honoured with him more highly than *with* all Israel" Aphr. 329, 5 &c. But in such cases a relative period usually occurs with a more precise form of expression, like ܝܬܝܪ ܡܢ ܕܒܝ "more than me" Matt. 10, 37; ܝܬܝܪ ܡܢ ܕܒܟܠܡܕܡ ܐܚܪܢ ܗܘ ܫܘܠܛܢܐ ܕܒܪܢܫܐ ܒܗܠܝܢ ܦܘܩܕܢܐ "man has more power in the case of these commandments than in anything else" Spic. 5, 16 &c.([1])

ܥܠ § 250. Of the manifold uses also of the preposition ܥܠ "upon" we only bring forward a few. It means in the intellectual sense "resting upon". Thus, often ܥܠ ܣܒܪܐ ܕ, ܥܠ ܣܒܪܗ "upon hope of", *i. e.* "in the hope of"; ܥܠ ܬܘܟܠܢܐ ܕܡܪܚܡܢܘܬܟ "in reliance upon thy benignity" Aphr. 492, 10; ܥܠ ܗܢܐ ܬܘܟܠܢܐ "in this confidence" John Eph. 359, 3. Similarly ܥܠ ܡܢܐ "why?"; ܥܠ ܗܢܐ "therefore" &c. Farther it denotes often the being that has been affected by anything pleasant or unpleasant: ܕܥܠ ܐܝܟܐ ܕܠܐ ܡܬܚܪܝܢܢ ܥܠܝܗ ὅτι πανταχοῦ ἀντιλέγεται Acts 28, 22; ܐܫܬܦܪ ܥܠ ܡܪܗ "was acceptable to his master" [Ov. 287, 23] Joseph 38, 1; ܐܬܪܚܡܘ ܥܠ ܒܥܠܝܗܝܢ "were beloved by their husbands" Isaac I, 244 v. 414; ܝܩܝܪ ܥܠܝܟܘܢ "is burdensome to you" Ov. 173, 27; ܪܚܝܡ ܥܠ, ܚܒܝܒ ܥܠ "beloved by" often;—ܕܚܝܠ ܥܠ ܟܠܐ "dreadful to the universe" Moes. II, 98 v. 336, and in like usage,—frequently; ܕܒܥܠܕܒܒܘܬܐ ܣܢܐ ܗܘܐ "who was odious to him" Ov. 161, 20; similarly ܕܥܠ ܐܢܫܐ ܡܬܚܫܒܝܢ ܟܐܢܐ "who were considered by men as righteous" Isaac II, 192 v. 633.— ܥܠ denotes the subject of speech or thinking &c.—"about" (= Latin "*de*"); ܡܛܠ is often similarly used. It occurs in data of measurement, in cases like ܥܠ ܐܬܪ ܡܝܠܝܢ ܬܪܝܢ ܕܢܒܝܐ "at a place, 2 miles from the prophet" Land II, 345, 9; ܕܐܫܟܚܘܗܝ ܥܠ ܐܬܪܐ ܡܪܚܩ ܡܢ ܡܕܝܢܬܐ "who found him-

---

([1]) ܐܘ, in imitation of the Greek ἤ, sometimes takes the place of this phrase of comparison ܡܢ ܕ. Thus Matt. 11, 22 P. C. S.; 11, 24 P. C. S.; Mark 6, 11 P.; 10, 25 P. S.; Luke 10, 12 P. (C. S. ܡܢ ܕ); 10, 14 P. (C. S. ܡܢ ܕ); 15, 7 P. S. (C. and Aphr. 142, 9 ܡܢ without ܕ); 18, 25 P. C. S. So with a complete sentence ܐܘ instead of ܡܢ ܕ is found in Luke 16, 17 P. S.; 17, 2 S. (P. C. ܐܘ ܕ). Thus too in rare cases even in ancient original writings, *e. g.* Ov. 175, 22. Servile versions accordingly use this ܐܘ = ἤ even for the simple comparative ܡܢ, *e. g.* John 5, 1 Hark.; Is. 13, 12 Hex.

☞ p. 356

self three miles distant from the monastery" Sim. 359, 10; ܛܘܪܐ ܡܪܚܩ ܗܘܐ ܡܢ ܡܕܝܢܬܗܘܢ ܥܠ ܬܪܝܢ ܡ̈ܝܠܝܢ "the mountain was two miles distant from their town" Sim. 354 *inf.* (where ܥܠ might even have been wanting, § 243) &c.—ܥܠ ܚܕܐ ܙܒܢ "once" Bedjan, Mart. II, 609, 3; ܥܠ ܙܒ̈ܢܝܢ ܣܓܝ̈ܐܢ "many times" Jos. St. 50, 6.—ܐܝܬ ܥܠܝܗ̇ ܫܛܝܦܬܐ ἔχουσα ἀλάβαστρον Matt. 26, 4; ܐܝܬ ܥܠܘܗܝ ܚܡܫ ܓܪ̈ܝܨܢ ἔχει πέντε ἄρτους John 6, 9; ܐܝܬ ܗܘܐ ܥܠܘܗܝ ܚܢܢܐ "he had grace in himself" Sim. 334, 4 &c.; ܕܝܘܐ ܐܝܬ ܥܠܝܟ δαιμόνιον ἔχεις John 8, 48, 52 S. (P. ܒܟ);—ܫܪܝܢ ܗܘܘ ܥܠܝܗܘܢ "upon whom (as a burden) they were quartered" Jos. St. 87, 16.—ܥܠ scarcely ever indicates the mere direction "to", but often on the other hand the hostile sense "against". (On ܥܠ ܕ "within" v. § 360.) ☞ p. 356

"Between".

§ 251. The construction of the words ܒܝܬ, ܒܝܢܬ, ܒܝܢܝ has considerable variety. They may have a simple noun following, as in ܒܝܬ ܒ̈ܬܐ "between the houses" Ov. 212, 9; ܒܝܢܬ ܓܦ̈ܐ "between the wings" Moes. II, 146 v. 1081; ܒܝܢܬܗܘܢ, ܡܢ ܒܝܢܬܗܘܢ "among them" often; ܡܢ ܒܝܢܬ ܡܚܫܒܬܗ "in his thought" Aphr. 338, 2; ܒܝܢܝ ܚܝ̈ܠܘܬܐ "amongst the Powers" Spic. 12, 10 &c. But when various members are concerned, these may be connected by a ܘ merely, as in the Testament of Ephr. ܒܝܬ ܐܒܐ ܘܒܪܐ ܘܪܘܚܐ "between the Father, the Son, and the Spirit" (where Overbeck's text 147 *ult.* has ܠܒܪܐ ܠܪܘܚܐ); and thus frequently in the O. T., but no doubt a Hebraism. The usual practice is to mark the second member by ܠ, with or without ܘ. Moreover in this method there are several modifications, in which it is to be noticed that the most usual of the three forms of the prep. viz ܒܝܬ, cannot take a suffix directly but only through the interposition of ܠ. (1) ܒܝܬ ܪ̈ܗܘܡܝܐ ܠܦܪ̈ܣܝܐ "between the Romans and the Persians" Jos. St. 9, 4; ܒܝܬ ܡܘܬܐ ܠܚܝ̈ܐ "between life and death" ἡμιθανής Luke 10, 30 C. S.; ܒܝܢܝ ܓܒܪܐ ܠܐܢܬܬܐ "between the man and the woman" Matt. 19, 10; ܒܝܢܝ ܠܟ "between me and thee" Zingerle's Chrest. 411 v. 46 (Jac. Sar.); ܒܝܢܘܗܝ ܠܐܝܠܢܐ "between him and the tree" Aphr. 448, 6 &c.—ܒܝܬ ܠܗ ܠܐܒܘܗܝ "between him and his father" Ov. 400, 19; ܒܝܬ ܠܟ ܠܐܡܟ ܘܠܐܚܘܟ (Var. ܘܠܐܚܘܟ) "between thee, thy mother, and thy brother" Joseph 225 *ult.* (= Ov. 311, 21) &c. (2) ܒܝܬ ܥ̈ܠܝܐ ܘܠܬܚ̈ܬܝܐ "between the higher and the lower" Moes. II, 122, v. 724; ܒܝܬ ܫܢܬܐ ܘܠܡܥܝܪܘܬܐ "between sleeping and waking" Zingerle's

Chrest. 396 v. 7; ܒܝܢ ܐܪܝܣ ܘܟܐܘܢ "between Mars and Saturn" Spic. 17, 17; ܒܝܢܝ ܘܒܟ "between me and thee" 1 Kings 15, 19, and frequently; ܒܝܢܘܗܝ ܘܒܗ "by himself alone" Ov. 122, 26; ܒܝܢܝܗܘܢ ܘܒܝܬ ܩܒܘܬܐ "between them and the ark" Ephr. I, 294 F.—ܒܝܬ ܠܗ ܘܠܪܗܘܡܝܐ "between him and the Romans" Sim. 327 mid.; ܒܝܬ ܠܗ ܘܠܗܘܢ "between him and them" Ephr. I, 101 F &c. A modification of this method is met with in ܒܝܬ ܠܟ ܐܦ ܠܗ "between thee and him" ZDMG XXV, 339 v. 348 (with "also" for "and"). (3) More rarely with ܠܒܝܬ: ܒܝܬ ܪܚܒܥܡ ܠܒܝܬ ܝܪܘܒܥܡ "between Rehoboam and Jeroboam" 1 Kings 14, 30; ܒܝܬ ܡܝ̈ܐ ܕܠܥܠ ܡܢ ܪܩܝܥܐ ܠܒܝܬ ܡܝ̈ܐ ܕܠܬܚܬ "between the water above the firmament and the water under it" Aphr. 282, 13. (4) With repetition of ܒܝܬ: ܒܝܬ ܐܒܝܐ . . . ܘܒܝܬ ܝܪܘܒܥܡ "between Abia . . . and Jeroboam" 1 Kings 15, 6, and frequently in the O. T. (Hebraism).—Several other variations are not quite settled.

With regard to *meaning*, notice ܒܝܢܝܗܘܢ ܘܒܗ κατ' ἰδίαν "they with him apart" Matt. 17, 19 C. S.;(1) ܒܝܢܘܗܝ ܘܒܗ ἐν ἑαυτῷ John 11, 38; so Ov. 122 v. 26 quoted above; ܒܝܢܘܗܝ ܠܒܝܢܘܗܝ "by himself" Mart. I, 243 mid.;—farther, ܥܣܪܝܢ ܕܝܢ ܘܚܡܫܐ ܒܝܬ ܓܒܪ̈ܐ ܠܢܫ̈ܐ "twenty five, however, between men and women" Mart. I, 137 *inf.*; ܡܢܘ ܓܝܪ ܚܪܫܐ ܒܝܢܬܢ ܐܝܬ "for which of us two is a magician?" Bedjan, Mart. II, 612, 14. For the comprising or grouping sense, when used with numerals, v. § 240 B.

Prepositional Phrases treated like Substantives. § 252. ܒܝܬ ܥܝ̈ܢܐ "that which is between the eyes" [τὰ μέτωπα], ܒܝܬ ܢܗܪ̈ܝܢ Μεσοποταμία &c. are treated altogether like substantives, *e. g.* ܥܠ ܒܝܬ ܥܝ̈ܢܘܗܝ "on his brow" Sim. 282 *inf.*; ܥܠ ܒܝܬ ܨܘܪܘܗܝ "on his neck" Bedjan, Mart. II, 229, 10 &c.—The expression ܡܣܬ ܠܒܝܬ ܪܫܗ in Ov. 185, 3 is of the very same character, and means "something sufficient under his head", or "something large enough for being under his head", *i. e.* "as a support for his head".

☞ p. 356

---

(1) In Matt. 18, 15, even the Greek text has the Aramaic idiom μεταξὺ σοῦ καὶ αὐτοῦ; Syr. ܒܝܢܝܟ ܘܒܗ.

2. VERBS.

A. PERSON AND GENDER.

§ 253. Participles are connected with the finite Verb by this cir- *Subject of the 3rd* cumstance amongst others, that they may include the subject of the 3rd *Pers. not* person within themselves: cf. ܘܟܠ ܕܥܒܕ "and all, that *he* does" (יעשה) *expressed.* Ps. 1, 3; ܗܘ ܡܢܥ ܕܟܠ "that which *he* withholds" Aphr. 6, 4; ܗܘ ܐܬܒܢܝ ܠܒܢܝܢܐ "for *it* is like a building" Aphr. 6, 12; ܕܡܩܒܠ ܗܘ "*it* is adopted" Aphr. 8 *paen.*; ܕܠܐ ܓܝܪ ܒܗ ... "for not in confidence that *they* would come back in life did they proceed thither, but in the expectation that *people* would torture them and kill them, and that *they* would die the death of Martyrs, were they emboldened to do this" Ov. 170, 2 (where special persons, Eusebius and Rabbūlā, form the subject of some of these participles, and the indefinite body "people" forms the subject of the others), and so is it frequently. A similar use is found in the case of the predicative adjective, § 314.

§ 254. A. From cases like ܓܥܬ ... "our soul is weary of the bread" Num. 21, 5; נקעה נפשי *Impersonal Expression* مم27 "my soul turns in loathing from thee" Jer. 6, 8 (= Aphr. 402, 18); *"It".* ܬܬܦܫ ܪܥܝܢܟ "thy mind despairs" Sim. 301, 5,—there are fashioned the so-called *Impersonal Forms*, by leaving out the Subject, at first obvious to thought, but afterwards growing obscure. In Syriac the Fem. predominates in these forms. Thus we have frequently ܟܪܝܐ ܠܝ, ܟܪܝܐ ܠܝ "I was grieved, I was distressed"; ܒܐܫ ܠܝ ܥܡ or ܒܐܫ ܠܝ ܥܡ ܒ "I was disgusted with (this or that)"; ܛܢܬ ܠܝ ܥܠ "I was zealous for"; ܐܬܦܪܩ "he was out of his mind"; ܐܠܨ ܠܝ ܡܕܡ "something was a necessity for me"; ܩܠܝܐ ܠܝ ܒ "I was vexed with", and many others. With Participles and other verbal Adjectives: ܕܡܬܦܪܩܝܢ "who is in despair" Aphr. 108, 12; ܠܐ ܗܘܐ ܩܠܝܠ ܠܢ "we had no vexation" Aphr. 392, 20; περὶ τῶν κεκοιμημένων ἵνα μὴ λυπῆσθε 1 Thess. 4, 13; ܣܢܝܐ ܗܘܐ ܠܗ ܘܡܥܝܩ ܗܘܐ ܠܗ "he was pained and grieved" Aphr. 161, 8; ܐܬܬܥܝܩ ܗܘܐ ܠܝ "I was sorry" (§ 118) frequently; ܠܐ ܐܬܬܩܛܕ ܠܟ "thou hast not been provoked to anger" Joseph

258, 4 (= Ov. 328, 25); ܪ̈ܥܡܬܐ ܡܠܝܐ "she was full of complaints" Ov. 155, 10, and thus frequently (as ܪ̈ܥܡܬ ܡܠܝ Joseph 206, 4 *ab inf.*) &c. Cf. farther ܠܐ ܬܐܬܐ ܠܟ ܡܥܩܢܘܬܐ ܠܡܥܛܝܘ "let it not come to thee (as an annoyance) to blot out" = "and be not concerned about blotting out" Isaac II, 348 v. 1858 (sprung from cases like ܠܐ ܬܐܬܐ ܠܟ ܡܠܬ ܗܕܐ ܒܠܒܟ "let not this thing come [as a vexation] into thy mind" = "take not this to heart" 2 Sam. 13, 20).—The original Subject is farther indicated by a personal pronoun in ܟܪܝܐ ܗܝ ܠܗ ܠܢܦܫܝ *περίλυπός ἐστιν ἡ ψυχή μου* Matt. 26, 38.

In other cases, however, the Masc. appears. Thus ܟܐܒ ܠܝ ܥܠ "something pained me"; ܟܐܒ ܗܘܐ ܠܗ ܒܩܘܫܬܐ ܥܠ ܐܝܠܝܢ ܕ "he mourned sincerely for those who" Ov. 180, 5; ܐܬܦܢܝ ܠܝ ܥܠ "I was eager for" (literally: "I had leisure for"); ܛܢܢ ܠܝ ܥܠ "I am zealous for"; ܪܘܝܚ ܠܝ "it is spacious for me", "I have freedom"; ܫܦܪ ܠܝ, ܒܐܫ ܠܝ, "it is pleasing to me",—"it is displeasing to me" &c. One says (ܥܩܐ?) ܥܩܐ ܠܝ and ܥܩܬ ܠܝ "I am offended", "I am vexed" (with ܒ and ܥܠ "about"), and along with these the personal form ܥܩܬ is also used.

B. In meteorological occurrences we have in the fem. ܢܗܪܬ, ܚܫܟܬ "it has become clear", "it has become dark", but also ܢܗܪ (m.) "it has become clear". So too ܥܕ ܠܐ ܕܢܓܗ ܗܘܐ "before it was yet making for daylight" Sim. 313 *inf.* (Lond. Cod. quite different), overagainst ܥܕ ܠܐ ܕܢܓܗ *ibid.* 306, 6 (Lond. Cod. merely ܥܕ ܢܓܗ) (cf. ܥܕ ܠܐ ܕܢܓܗܘܢ ܪܡܫܐ "before it was yet making for evening" *id.* 306, 4). Similarly ܩܪܝܒܐ ܗܘܬ ܠܡܚܫܟܘ "it is coming near the darkening", it is drawing toward nightfall" Luke 24, 29 C. S. Cases like ܐܡܛܪܬ "it rained" and ܠܡܡܛܪܘ "that it rain" James 5, 17 Hark. do not appear to occur in ancient original writings. Notice however ܐܝܟ ܗܘ ܕܛܠܐ ܫܡܝܢܐ ܢܛܦܬ ܗܘܬ(1) ܥܠܘܗܝ "as if it dropped heavenly dew upon him" Sim. 382, 3. Cf. farther ܩܪܝܫ ܗܘܐ *ψῦχος ἦν* "it was cold" John 18, 18; Aphr. 343, 10; ܥܕ ܚܫܘܟ *σκοτίας ἔτι οὔσης* John 20, 1.

C. When an indefinite "it" is comprised in a phrase it is generally expressed by the fem. sing.: ܐܢ ܕܝܢ ܡܫܟܚܐ ܘܠܐ ܩܫܝܐ ܠܟܘܢ "but if it is

(1) The correct reading in Lond. Cod.; the printed Ed. gives ܗܘܐ.

possible, and is not burdensome to you" Ov. 173, 26; ܐܝܟ ܕܐܬܝܐ "as it comes", "any way" frequently; ܐܠܘ ܡܫܟܚܐ ܗܘܬ "if it had been possible" Ov. 201, 1; ܠܐ ܝܐܐ ܡܠܟܘܬܐ ܥܠ ܫܐܘܠ "for it does not suit Saul" Aphr. 342, 4; ܣܦܩܐ ܒܐܝ̈ܕܘܗܝ "it was possible for him", "he could" (literally "there was room in his hands"), *e. g.* ܘܠܐ ܠܡܬܟܬܫܘ ܣܦܩܐ ܒܐܝ̈ܕܝܗܘܢ "and they could not fight" Ov. 89 *ult.*, and even ܡܕܡ ܕܣܦܩܐ ܒܐܝ̈ܕܘܗܝ "whatever he can provide" Lev. 14, 30; ܡܕܡ ܕܣܦܩܐ ܗܘܬ ܒܐܝ̈ܕܘܗܝ "whatever he could" Jos. St. 23, 16, Note 2; and also with the phrase enclosed, ܡܢ ܣܦܩܐ ܒܐܝ̈ܕܝ ܕܐܥܒܕ "what can I do?" Kalilag and Damnag, 52, 16, and many like cases. Along with ܡܛܝܐ ܠܐܝ̈ܕܘܗܝ "it comes as far as his hands", ["it is within his reach"] "he can do it" Ov. 217, 15 &c., the masc. is found in ܡܛܐ ܠܐܝ̈ܕܘܗܝ Spic. 5, 13. The masculine occurs also in passive forms of expression like ܐܫܬܒܩ ܠܗ "it has been forgiven him" Aphr. 40, 8; ܐܝܟܢܐ ܕܐܫܬܦܪ ܩܕܡ ܗܘ "as it seemed good to that being" Spic. 12, 19; ܢܬܝܗܒ ܠܟܘܢ δοθήσεται ὑμῖν Matt. 7, 7; ܡܬܟܝܠܐ ܠܟܘܢ μετρήσεται ὑμῖν Matt. 7, 2. Cf. farther ܐܝܟ ܡܐ ܕܐܝܬܘܗܝ "how it is" Aphr. 31, 6; ܗܟܢܐ ܐܝܬܘܗܝ "thus is it" Aphr. 154, 8; ܘܠܐ ܐܝܬܘܗܝ ܢܘܟܪܝܐ "and it is not of foreign sort" Ephr. III, XXXIII mid.

The gender fluctuates also in those Verbal expressions in which a complete sentence with ܕ "that" takes the place of the Subject: ܓܕܫܐ ܕ "it happens, that" Aphr. 505, 15, and ܓܕܫ ܕ Ov. 63, 21; ܢܓܕܘܫ ܕ Aphr. 68, 12, aud frequently; ܟܬܝܒ ܕ and ܟܬܝܒܐ ܕ "it stands written, that" frequently; ܠܐ ܐܫܬܦܪܬ ܠܗ ܕ "it did not seem to him, that" Jos. St. 57, 16, but ܗܟܢܐ ܐܫܬܦܪ ܠܢ ... ܕ "it thus appeared (good) to us, that" Aphr. 304, 14; ܕܠܐ ܬܣܬܒܪ ܠܟ ܕ "that thou mightest not think, that" Jos. St. 34, 18; ܐܝܕܝܥܐ ܕ "it is well known, that" Ov. 63, 12, but ܝܕܝܥ ܕ *ibid.* 73, 1 and 4; ܐܡܝܪ ܕ and ܐܡܝܪܐ ܕ "it is said, that"; ܠܐ ܡܫܟܚܐ ܕ "it is impossible, that" Luke 17, 1; ܕܬܬܝܩܢ ܠܟ ܕ "that it may be to thee certain, that" Aphr. 168, 7; and thus frequently ܢܬܝܩܢ ܕ, ܬܬܝܩܢ ܕ; ܐܦܢ ܡܬܣܒܪܐ ܕ "although it be thought, that" Jos. St. 8, 2. It is always masculine, however, in ܙܕܩ ܕ, ܘܠܐ ܕ "it is fitting, that".

The masculine prevails in the case of the Inf. with ܠ, *e. g.* ܘܠܐ ܦܩܝܕ ܠܟ ܠܡܫܡܠܝܘ "and it is not enjoined thee to tire thyself out" Aphr. 230, 5; except in established phrases, as in ܣܦܩܐ ܒܐܝ̈ܕܘܗܝ (v. *supra*).—

Thus too the fem. is retained in verbs like ܥܩܬ ܠܝ ܕ, ܥܩܬ ܠܝ ܠ "I am vexed, that ..." or "I am vexed to ..."; ܪܓܬ ܠܝ, ܪܓܝܓܐ ܠܝ "I desire" ܕ "that", ܠ "to" (cf. ܗܕܐ ܪܓܬ ܠܝ ܕܐܙܠ ܠܐܘܪܫܠܡ "this I desire,—

☞ p. 356

to go to Jerusalem" Ov. 164, 23).

D. In such cases pure Adjectives also are treated like Participles: ܠܐ ܦܝܣ ܠܗ ܕ "he is not convinced, that" Aphr. 498, 6, but ܠܐ ܦܝܣܐ ܠܗ ܕ *ibid.*, *ult.*, and frequently; ܫܦܝܪ ܠܡܐܠܦ "it is well to learn" Aphr. 446 *paen.*; ܦܘܩܕܢܘܗܝ ... ܣܓܝܐܐ ܗܝ ܠܡܐܡܪ "his commands ... to tell,—is too much" ("his injunctions ... are too numerous to mention") Ov. 178, 16; ܥܠ ܚܪܝܦܘܬܗ ... ܝܬܝܪܐ ܗܝ ܠܡܡܠܠܘ "to speak of the prudence ... would be too much" Ov. 190, 24. But the masc. preponderates in such cases.

Compare with this section, § 201 *supra*.

B. TENSES AND MOODS.

PERFECT.

Tempus Historicum.

§ 255. The Perfect denotes past action; accordingly it is the tense of *Narration*, the proper *Tempus historicum*: every narration from the first verse of Genesis onward supplies examples in abundance.

Pure Perfect.

§ 256. It farther denotes the *completed result* (the *pure Perfect*): ܐܓܪܬܟ ... ܩܒܠܬ "thy letter I have received" Aphr. 6, 1; ܘܬܘܒ ܐܡܪ ܡܪܢ ܗܟܢܐ ܠܬܠܡܝܕܘܗܝ "and so the Lord has farther said thus to his disciples" Aphr. 7 *ult.*; ܥܩܪܒܐ ܒܥܘܩܣܗ ܡܚܐ ܠܡܢ ܕܠܐ ܐܚܛܝܗ "the scorpion with its sting strikes him who has given it no offence" Spic. 7, 20 &c. Such a Perfect, expressing the result of a prior occurrence, has often for us the appearance of a Present: thus ܗܘܐ "has become" γέγονε often = "is" (but also "was"); ܠܐ ܗܘܐ "is not", *e. g.* Aphr. 84, 12, 19; 158, 20 &c.; ܪܓܬ ܠܝ "desire has come to me", "I desire"; ܥܩܬ ܠܝ ܚܝܝ "I am (become) weary of my life" Gen. 27, 46 (§ 254 A); ܝܕܥܢ "*novimus*, we know" Aphr. 497, 17; ܗܫܐ ܝܕܥܬ ܠܝ "now I know" Mart. I, 244, 8 &c. Yet upon the whole this use is not of frequent occurrence in Syriac; with ܝܕܥ in particular the more distinct active participle is employed in preference.

Pluperfect.

§ 257. The action which is expressed by the Perf. may have happened prior to an action already narrated (*Pluperfect*): ܥܒܶܕ ܗܘܳ ܨܶܒܝܳܢܶܗ ܒܟܽܠܡܶܕܶܡ ܕܦܰܩܶܕ ܗܘܳ "and he did according to his will in all that he had commanded him" Mart. I, 124, 9; ܗܿܝ ܕܢܣܰܒ "whom he had married" (ἐγάμησεν) Mark 6, 17 P. (S. ܕܢܣܰܒ ܗܘܳܐ); ܡܶܛܽܠ ܕܣܒܰܪ ܗܘܳܐ ܕܥܰܪܩܘ ܠܗܽܘܢ ܐܰܣܺܝܪ̈ܐ νομίζων ἐκπεφευγέναι τοὺς δεσμίους Acts 16, 27. And just as little is expression given to the relative distinction of the tenses in cases in which we put the pluperfect first, e. g. in ܠܰܐܝܠܶܝܢ ܕܗܰܘ ܐܰܛܥܺܝ ܐܰܦܢܺܝ ܗܰܘ ܠܫܪܳܪܳܐ "those whom that one had led astray, he turned to the truth" Ov. 159, 14, or after ܡܶܢ ܕ "since" and similar conjunctions.

Future-Perfect. Perfect in Conditional Clauses.

§ 258. The Perfect in certain cases stands also for the *Perfectum futuri*. This is specially common after the conditional conjunction of time—ܡܳܐ ܕ "when", "if",—where sometimes the principal clause is also furnished with a Perfect; ܡܳܐ ܕܓܙܰܪܢ "when we shall have circumcised ourselves" Gen. 34, 22; ܡܳܐ ܕܰܐܫܠܶܡ ܡܳܪܝܳܐ . . . ܐܕܽܘܫ "when the Lord shall have delivered up . . . I will thresh" Judges 8, 7; ܘܟܽܠ ܕܒܳܥܶܝܢ ܡܶܫܬܰܟܚܺܝܢ ܡܳܐ ܕܫܰܐܠܘ "and all who seek, find (at the last day), if they have asked" Aphr. 304, 9; ܡܳܐ ܕܩܳܡܘ ܗܳܦܟܺܝܢ ܠܗܽܘܢ ܠܫܝܽܘܠ "as soon as they have risen, they turn back (forthwith) to Sheol" Aphr. 433, 11. So is it with the statement of permanent conditions, or of actions continually repeated: ܡܳܐ ܕܗܰܝܡܶܢ ܡܚܶܒ "if he believes, he loves" Aphr. 7, 11; ܡܳܐ ܕܐܢܳܫ ܒܰܪܢܳܫ ܐܶܬܩܪܶܒ ܠܗܰܝܡܳܢܽܘܬܳܐ ܐܶܬܬܣܺܝܡ ܠܶܗ ܥܰܠ ܫܽܘܥܳܐ "when man draws near to faith, he establishes himself upon a rock" Aphr. 7, 2 &c. But in all these cases the Part. act. may stand after ܡܳܐ ܕ. In ܡܳܐ ܕܩܳܐܶܡ ܦܰܓܪܳܐ ܕܙܰܕܺܝܩܶܐ ܘܡܶܫܬܰܚܠܦ ܐܶܬܩܪܺܝ ܒܶܗ ܫܡܰܝܳܢܳܐ ܘܐܰܝܢܳܐ ܕܠܳܐ ܡܶܫܬܰܚܠܦ ܐܶܬܩܪܺܝ ܒܶܗ ܒܟܝܳܢܶܗ ܐܰܪܥܳܢܳܐ "when the body of the righteous rises and is changed, it is called heavenly, and that which is not changed, is called earthly, in accordance with its nature" Aphr. 157, 12, the Perfect is made choice of directly in the principal clause, and correspondingly in the parallel sentence, where ܐܰܝܢܳܐ ܕ appears for the temporal conjunction ܡܳܐ ܕ. Moreover ܡܳܐ ܕ may be used to introduce even the pure Past, e. g. ܡܳܐ ܕ . . . ܐܰܥܒܰܪܘ "when they had done away with" Aphr. 15, 1.

The Perfect is used as a future Perfect in true conditional clauses also, although more rarely than with ܡܳܐ ܕ: ܐܶܢ ܥܒܰܕ ܦܺܐܪ̈ܐ κἂν μὲν ποιήσῃ κάρπον Luke 13, 9; ܐܢ ܐܫܟܚܢ "*si potuerimus*", "if we can" Spic. 13, 2; ܐܠܐ ܥܠܬ ܠܐ ܫܒܩܐ ܐܢܐ ܠܟ "unless thou enter, I do not let thee go", that is, "thou must enter" Sim. 286 mid.; ܘܐܠܐ ܚܙܝܬܗ ܦܘܪܩܢܐ ܠܐ ܐܝܬ "unless I see him, there is no way out (of the difficulty)", that is, "nothing will do, ☞ p. 356 except my seeing him" Jac. Sar. Alexander (Zeitschrift für Assyriologie VI, 368 v. 155); ܐܠܐ ܐܢ ܐܬܦܝܣܬ ܠܘܩܕܡ "unless I am first convinced" Spic. 2, 14. Cf. also Matt. 18, 15—17, where however C. and S. (like Aphr. 298, 4 *sqq.*) have in part the Impf. In the apodosis we meet thus with ܘܐܠܐ ܐܗܦܟܬܝܗܝ "and if not, thou restorest him" Jul. 217, 26.

In the same way the Perf. stands in sentences with ܐܘ—ܐܘ "either ... or"; "whether ... or whether": ܕܠܐ ܬܗܘܐ ܠܐܝܐ ܒܡܒܥܝܗ ܐܘ ܐܫܟܚܬܝܗܝ ܐܘ ܠܐ "that thou mayest not again have to weary thyself in seeking him, whether thou find him or not" Aphr. 144, 22; ܐܘ ܡܪܝܡ ܐܪܝܡ ܚܘܫܒܢ ܐܘ ܐܡܟ ܠܢ ܠܥܘܡܩܐ "he either greatly exalts our consideration, or he humiliates us to the very depth" Joseph 196 *ult.* [Ov. 296, 17]; ܒܥܪܘܩܐ ܐܙܠ ܐܢܐ ܠܗ ܐܘ ܩܛܠܢܝ ܐܘ ܩܛܠܬܗ "I go to meet him as a foe, whether he kill me, or I him" John Eph. 349, 13 (cf. Jul. 88, 21; Simeon of Bēth Arshām, 9, 14, and many others).

In Hypothetical Clauses. § 259. The Perfect is very extensively employed in hypothetical sentences like ܐܠܘܠܐ ܐܬܡܗܡܗܢ ܟܒܪ ܗܘܝܢ ܗܦܟܢ "if we had not delayed, we should already have returned" Gen. 43, 10 &c. (§ 375 A). With these are ranked cases like ܡܢ ܗܘ ܢܥܓܠ τίς ἀποκυλίσει "O that one would roll away!" Mark 16, 3; ܡܢܘ ܢܐܡܪ ܠܝ "O that one would say to me!" Sim. 301 *inf.*; ܡܢ ܗܘ ܢܚܘܐ ܠܟܘܢ ܚܘܒܝ ܪܩܬܘܢ ܠܝ ܒܐܦܝ ܟܠܟܘܢ "O that one would show you my sins, then would all of you spit in my face!" Ov. 140, 19; cf. Num. 11, 4; 2 Sam. 18, 33; Job 11, 5; 13, 5; 14, 13; ܐܡܬܝ ܗܘ ܗܘܐ ܪܡܫܐ "when might it indeed be evening?" = "would that it were evening at last!" Deut. 28, 67; cf. Ps. 41, 6; ܡܢ ܗܘ ܢܬܠ = מִי יִתֵּן frequently in the O. T. To this class also belong ☞ p. 356 ܣܦܩ ܗܘ ܘܫܠܡܬ ܠܐ ܚܙܬܢܝ "then would I have been ended and no eye would have seen me" Job 10, 18; ܫܕܪܬܟ ܗܘ "then would I have sent thee" Gen. 31, 27; ܕܘܠܐ ܗܘ ... ܘܠܡܛܢ ܗܘܝܬܝ "then wouldest thou (f.) have been bound to be afraid ... and to be zealous" Aphr. 48, 10; thus even ܗܠܝܢ ܗܘ ܠܡܥܒܕܘ ܘܗܠܝܢ ܗܘ ܠܐ ܠܡܫܒܩܘ ταῦτα δὲ ἔδει ποιῆσαι κἀκεῖνα μὴ ἀφιέναι Matt.

23, 23 C; Luke 11, 42 C. (S. and P. express themselves more clearly in both passages).—Thus the Perf. is often used after (ܕܝ) ܠܘܝ and ܐܠܘܦ ܕܝ "O if only!" "*Utinam!*". ☞ p. 357

§ 260. The Perf. ܗܘܐ often stands before an Adj. or Part. to denote a Wish, an Advice, or a Command. Originally the Perf. was meant to indicate the accomplishment of the action as completely certain,—as good as already done. This occurs particularly in the 2nd pers. Thus often ܗܘܝܬ ܚܠܝܡ "farewell", ἔρρωσο; ܥܒܕ ܗܘܝܬ ܗܟܢ ποίει ὁμοίως Luke 10, 37; ܗܘܝܬܘܢ ܕܟܝܪܝܢ μνημονεύετε Hebr. 13, 7; ܗܘܝ ܛܥܢ ܛܥܢܐ ܘܗܘܝܬ ܠܐܛ ܐܢܬ ܠܝ "take pains (take thou the burden) and curse me" Sim. 316 *ult.*; ܐܠܐ ܚܠܦ ܗܠܝܢ ܗܘܝܬܘܢ ܐܡܝܢܝܢ ܒܨܘܡܐ "but instead of this, be ye assiduous in fasting" Ov. 174, 14; ܗܘܝܬ ܕܝܢ ܝܕܥ "but know" Philox. 570, 11; ܡܛܠ ܗܢܐ ܗܘܝܬ ܝܕܥ "know therefore" Aphr. 55, 18. So farther, Matt. 5, 25; Luke 13, 14; Mark 11, 25 S.; 13, 33 S.; 13, 35 S.; Eph. 6, 9 &c. In the 3rd pers.: ܠܐ ܗܘܘ ܓܙܪܝܢ ܩܫܝܫܐ "the priests are not to use force"; Ov. 215, 11 (where there are more cases, varied with ܢܗܘܘܢ); ܗܘܬ ܚܫܝܒܐ "let her be esteemed" Addai 44 *ult.*; ܠܐ ܗܘܬ ܡܐܢܐ ܒܢ μὴ ἐκκακῶμεν Gal. 6, 9; ܗܘܘ ܐܡܝܢܝܢ ܠܘܬܗܘܢ "they are to be constantly with them" Ov. 215, 11; ܗܘܘ ܡܩܒܠܝܢ ܡܪܢܘܬܐ "they must receive blame" Statuti della Scuola di Nisibi 25, 9. ܗܘܐ Optative.

§ 261. So also ܗܘܐ *with a participle following* is often placed in a dependent clause, to express an action merely purposed or aimed at: ܘܦܩܕ ܗܘܐ ... ܕܟܠܗܘܢ ܗܢܘܢ ... ܠܐ ܗܘܘ ܒܝܬܝܢ ܒܡܛܠܬܗܘܢ ܐܠܐ ܚܡܫܐ ... ܢܛܘܪܐ ܡܕܝܢܬܐ ܗܘܘ ܒܝܬܝܢ ܥܠ ܫܘܪܐ "and gave charge ... that all those who ..., should not pass the night in their booths, but that five police-officers should pass the night on the wall", in the Document of 201 A. D. in the Chron. Ed. (ed. Hallier 147, 16), and so, frequently after ܢܚܕܐ ܒܢ ܕܐܪܒܥܣܪܐ ܕܟܠ ܝܪܚ ܗܘܝܢ ܢܛܪܝܢ ܝܘܡ "let us take delight to observe the fourteenth day of every month" Aphr. 230, 1; ܨܒܝܢ ܗܘܘ ܕܗܘܘ ܫܩܠܝܢ ܠܗ "they wished to carry it [the Ark]" Aphr. 264, 6; ܠܐ ܢܫܒܩܘܢ ܠܒܢܬ ܩܝܡܐ ܕܚܕܐ ܚܕܐ ܗܘܝܢ ܐܬܝܢ ܠܥܕܬܐ "they shall not allow the deaconesses [daughters of the ordinance] to come singly to the church" Ov. 217, 9; ܕܗܘܘ ܡܬܬܣܝܡܝܢ ܒܗ "that they might be placed in it" Jos. St. 23, 14; ܘܡܦܝܣ ܠܗܘܢ ܕܗܘܘܢ ܡܬܢܚܡܝܢ "and induces them to ܗܘܐ Subjunctive. ☞ p. 357

stand" Moes. II, 90 v. 233, and thus, often. By reason of ‏‎‏‏‏‎‏ being put first in such cases as the following, these cases also may be referred to this class, viz: ‏‏‏‏‏‏‏‎‏ ‏‏‏‏‏? ... ‏‏‏‏‏ ‏‏‏‏ "it was his custom ... to receive" Aphr. 391, 8 &c. Cf. farther ‏‏‏‏ ‏‏‏ ‏‏ ‏‏ ‏‏‏‏ ‏‏‏‏ ‏‏‏‏‏‏‏ ‏‏‏‏ (πρὸς τὸ δεῖν) παντότε προσεύχεσθαι, καὶ μὴ ἐκκακεῖν Luke 18, 1 C. S., where P. has ‏‏‏‏‏ ‏‏‏‏ ‏‏;—‏‏‏‏ ‏‏‏ ‏‏‏‏ ‏‏ ἵνα μὴ διψῶ μηδὲ διέρχωμαι John 4, 15 C. S., where P. has ‏‏‏‏ ‏‏‏ ‏‏ ‏‏‏‏ ‏‏‏ ‏‏;—‏‏‏‏‏‏ ‏‏‏‏‏ ‏‏ μὴ προμελετᾶν Luke 21, 14 C. S., where P. has '‏‏‏ ‏‏‏‏ ‏‏. The last examples show that in these cases the Impf. is interchangeable with the Perf. And, in fact, the Impf. is the more usual form.

☞ p. 357

Other de-
pendent
Perfects.

§ 262. The Perfect of course often stands dependently in still other circumstances, e. g. ‏‏‏‏ ‏‏‏ ‏‏‏‏‏ ‏‏ "when he saw that God had spoken to him" Aphr. 236, 19 &c. Frequently in these dependent clauses either the Perfect or the Imperfect may be employed, according as it is the notion of the *past occurrence* of, or that rather of the *sequence* of, the relatively later event, that is being specially emphasised. Thus after ‏‏‏‏‏ ‏‏‏‏ ‏‏‏‎‏ ... ‏‏‏‏ ‏‏‏‏; ‏‏‏‏‏ ‏ "they struck them, ... until they thought" Ov. 170, 7; ‏‏‏‏ ‏‏‏‏ "till there came" Aphr. 26, 6 (cf. the Impf. § 267). So in ‏‏‏‏‏ ‏‏ ‏‏ ‏‏‏ ‏‏ ... ‏‏‏ ‏‏‏‏ ‏‏‏‏ ... ‏‏‏‏‏ ‏‏‏‏‏‏ "why was he vexed that he did not enter into the land of pro- mise?" Aphr. 161, 9, ‏‏‏‏ might also have been used. In ‏‏‏‏ ‏‏‏‏ ‏‏‏‏ ‏‏ "the judge gave orders to hang them" Anc. Doc. 102, 3, the Perfect plainly indicates that the order has been actually carried into execution; thus it is to some extent a compromise between the usual constructions ‏‏‏‏‏‏ ‏‏‏‏ (§ 261), and ‏‏‏‏‏‏ ‏‏‏ (§ 334).

Perfect with
‏‏‏‏.

§ 263. The strengthening of the Perfect by means of an enclitic ‏‏‏‏ brings into still greater prominence the force of 'time gone by'; so that we may often translate this combination by the Pluperfect: ‏‏‏‏‏? ‏‏‏‏ ‏‏‏‏ "that I have told you" Spic. 18, 18; ‏‏‏‏ ‏‏‏‏‏‏ ‏‏‏‏‏ "I have explained to thee" Aphr. 172 *ult.*; ‏‏‏‏ ‏‏‏‏ ‏‏ "when he was born" Aphr. 180, 7; ‏‏‏‏ ‏‏‏‏‏‏‏ ‏‏‏‏ "they had been taught together" Ov. 162, 23; ‏‏‏‏ ‏‏‏‏‏‏‏ "and had been delivered up" (f.) Jos. St. 10, 2 &c. The ‏‏‏‏ is not absolutely necessary in any such cases, and it is often wanting in cases exactly corresponding to those which have it and standing close beside them. It has become so much of an expletive that it is found not seldom in narrative proper: ܝܗܒܘ ܗܘܘ ܠܗ ܡܥܡܘܕܝܬܐ "they gave him baptism" Sim. 268; ܩܡ ܗܘܐ ܕܒܪܗ "he arose and took him with him" Ov. 169, 26, and thus often in the ancient document in the Chron. Edess., in Ephr., Jac. Sar. &c.

IMPERFECT.

§ 264. The Imperfect stands in complete contrast to the Perfect in cases like ܕܝܢܐ ܟܐܢܐ ܕܐܠܗܐ ܕܒܗ ܢܬܠ ܦܬܓܡܐ "the righteous judgment of God in which he will render account" Ov. 200, 13; ܠܐ ܢܗܘܐ ܬܘܒ ܛܘܦܢܐ "there will not again be a flood" Gen. 9, 11; "these three things I have explained to thee by letter" (ܟܬܒܬ ܘܐܦܫܩܬܟ): 'other matters' ܒܙܒܢ ܙܒܢ ܐܟܬܘܒ ܘܐܦܫܩܟ "I shall explain to thee by letter from time to time" Aphr. 319 concl. &c. Future.

§ 265. In conditional sentences the Impf. not seldom stands after ܐܢ, in which case it is the participle which appears for the most part in the apodosis: ܐܢ ܬܗܦܟ ܐܦܝܟ ܫܠܡܝܢ ܥܡܘܪܝܗ "if thou turnest away thy countenance, the inhabitants thereof come to an end" Aphr. 493 *ult.*; ܐܢ ܕܝܢ ܢܓܕܫ ܘܢܦܘܩ ܒܥܒܕܐ ܬܗܘܐ ܡܬܥܩܪܐ ܗܝ ܡܢ ܢܦܫܢ ܝܕܥܬܐ ܕܡܥܒܕܢܘܬܗ "but if it happens that it proceeds actually from us, the knowledge of its operation is uprooted from our soul" Philox. 552, 20 &c. The Impf. is found in both clauses in ܐܢ ܢܡܠܠ ܢܒܨܪ "if we speak, we come short" Aphr. 496, 8; ܐܢ ܬܬܛܦܝܣܘܢ ܠܝ ܘܬܫܬܡܥܘܢ ܠܝ ܠܐ ܒܠܚܘܕ ܫܘܡܢܗ ܕܐܪܥܐ ܬܐܟܠܘܢ ܐܠܐ ܐܦ ܛܘܒܗ ܕܫܡܝܐ ܬܐܪܬܘܢ "if ye will be persuaded by me and will hearken unto me, ye shall not only eat of the fat of the earth, but also inherit the blessedness of heaven" Ov. 174 *ult.* (paraphrased from Is. 1, 19) &c. In like manner with ܡܐ ܕ:— ܢܘܢܐ ܡܐ ܕܢܣܩܘܢ ܠܐܐܪ ܡܝܬܝܢ "fishes die, when they come up into the air" Aphr. 494, 9; ܘܐܦܠܐ ܡܐ ܕܢܩܘܡ ܐܢܫ ܥܠ ܛܘܪܐ ܪܡܐ ܡܛܝܐ ܥܝܢܗ ܠܟܠ ܪܚܝܩܐ ܘܩܪܝܒܐ "and not even when one stands on a high mountain, does his eye reach to everything far and near" Aphr. 199, 12 &c. But in these cases the Participle is, throughout, the more usual form (cf. § 271). Imperfect in Conditional Sentences. ☞ p. 357

Modal Colouring. § 266. For the simple statement of the momentary or the continuous Present the Impf. is not readily used: on the other hand it is common whenever any reference to the future, or the slightest modal colouring, appears, *e. g.* ܐܫܪܐ "I will begin" Spic. 13, 19; ܡܟܝܠ ܐܢܫ ܢܐܡܪ "now some one may say" Spic. 6, 21; ܐܝܟ ܐܢܫ ܢܐܡܪ "as one might say" "as if, for instance, one should say" frequently; ܡܢ ܠܐ ܢܬܕܡܪ "who would not wonder?" Anc. Doc. 103, 13; ܡܢܐ ܟܝ ܢܐܡܪ "what are we to say then?" Sim. 303 mid. (wanting in the London Cod.). The Impf. is precisely the proper form for a wish, request, summons, or command. Thus, for instance, ܬܐܡܪ ܠܝ "*dicas mihi*" Aphr. 313, 12 (mocking request); ܘܗܝܕܝܢ ܬܫܬܘܕܐ "and then may you promise" Aphr. 71, 21; ܢܣܟܐ "let us await" Aphr. 103, 4; ܢܡܟ ܗܟܝܠ ܢܦܫܢ "let us then humble ourselves" Aphr. 119, 5; ܢܩܒܠ "let him accept" Aphr. 86, 13; ܘܨܘܚܝܬܐ ܠܐ ܢܦܩܢ ܡܢ ܦܘܡܢ "and let not revilings come out of our mouth" Aphr. 105, 2; ܢܬܥܠܒ ܘܠܐ ܢܥܠܘܒ "let him suffer oppression, but not oppress" Aphr. 117, 9 &c.

The 2nd pers. of the Impf. with ܠܐ is the direct contrary of the Imperative: ܠܐ ܬܕܚܠ "fear thou not" &c. Without ܠܐ however the 2nd person of the Impf. is but seldom used with imperative force; the Impt. is the proper mood for this.

Dependent Imperfect. § 267. The Impf. is farther the tense of dependent, subordinate clauses pointing to the future, even though the principal clause may lie in the past: ܘܢܩܦܣܘܢܝܗܝ ܕܢܨܠܐ ܥܠܝܗܘܢ "and they will urge him to pray for them" Sim. 290 mid.; ܚܕܐ ܓܝܪ ܬܡܝܗܬܐ ܗܝ ܕܢܕܥ ܐܢܫ ܢܫܐܠ ܫܘܐܠܐ "for this is an admirable thing, that one should know how to ask questions" Spic. 1, 20; ܐܢ ܕܬܙܕܕܩ ܠܐ ܡܫܟܚ ܐܢܬ "if thou canst not justify thyself" Aphr. 270, 5; ܨܒܐ ܐܢܐ ܕܐܦܫܩܟ "I wish to explain to thee" Aphr. 345, 1; ܪܚܡܘ ܫܝܢܐ ܕܬܩܒܠܘܢ ܦܘܪܥܢܐ "love peace that ye may receive the reward" Aphr. 304, 17—ܨܒܐ ܕܢܩܛܘܠ ܢܦܫܗ ἤμελλεν ἑαυτὸν ἀναιρεῖν Acts 16, 27; ܡܪܕܟܝ ܡܠܟܗ ܠܐܣܬܪ ܕܬܨܘܡ "Mordecai advised that Esther should fast" Aphr. 414, 5; ܟܕ ܨܒܐ ܗܘܐ ܕܢܘܟܠ ܐܢܘܢ ܕܡܐ "while he wanted to give them blood to eat" Mart. I, 122, 6; ܫܪܝ ܕܢܩܪܘܒ "began to attack" Moes. II, 64, 1; ܠܐ ܓܝܪ ܦܩܝܕ ܠܗܘܢ . . . ܕܢܣܓܕܘܢ "for it is not commanded them . . . to worship" Anc. Doc. 43, 25; ܐܠܨܗ ܕܢܣܒ "he obliged him to take" Ov. 167, 17; ܣܛܠܠ ܕܢܫܬܦܪ ܠܗ ܦܢܡ "he set himself to become agreeable to him" Mart. I, 122, 16, and thus in many other instances. So too after the words which mean "until, before, ere": ܢܘܚ ܐܢ̈ܬܬܐ ܠܐ ܢܣܒ ܥܕ ܩܕܡ ܕܢܡܠܠ ܥܡܗ ܐܠܗܐ "Noah did not take a wife until God had spoken to him" Aphr. 235 *ult.*; ܢܛܪ ܟܐܢܘܬܐ ܕܒܢܡܘܣܐ ܥܕ ܠܐ ܢܬܝܗܒ ܢܡܘܣܐ "he kept the righteousness which is in the law, before the law had yet been given" Aphr. 25, 5; ܥܕ ܠܐ ܢܙܕܩܦ ܝܗܒ ܕܡܗ "gave his blood before he was crucified" Aphr. 222, 5; ܡܠܟܐ ܕܐܡܠܟܘ ܒܐܪܥܐ ܕܐܕܘܡ ܩܕܡ ܕܢܡܠܟ ܡܠܟܐ ܠܒܢܝ ܐܝܣܪܝܠ "who reigned in the land of Edom before there reigned a king over the children of Israel" Gen. 36, 31; ܐܝܟ ܕܐܝܬܘܗܝ ܗܘܐ . . . ܥܕ ܩܕܡ ܕܠܐ ܢܬܓܫܡ "as it was, before he had yet taken a body" Ov. 198, 1 &c. Here the Perf. might stand in every case (§ 262), but the Impf. is more usual. Similarly ܥܕ ܥܕ ܠܐ ܢܥܘܠ "before we entered" Jul. 45, 2.—Cf. farther ܥܕ ܡܛܐ ܙܒܢܐ ܕܢܡܘܬ ܡܘܫܐ "when the time came for Moses to die" Aphr. 161, 7.

The Impf. appears with this sense, even when the dependence is not plainly expressed: ܠܐ ܝܕܥ ܐܢܐ ܐܒܢܐ "I do not know how to build" Sim. 271, 4; ܐܢ ܦܩܕܐ ܠܝ ܩܕܝܫܘܬܟ ܐܚܘܬ ܠܝܡܐ "if thy holiness commands me to go down to the sea" Sim. 336, 13; ܢܫܒܩܢܝ ܐܒܗܬܐ "leaves me in shame" ZDMG XXIX, 116 *ult.*; ܗܒ ܠܝ (ܡܝܐ) ܐܫܬܐ δός μοι πιεῖν John 4, 7 and 10; ܫܒܘܩܝܢܝ ܐܫܕܪ "let me send" ("grant me that I send") Jos. St. 76, 5; ܐܦܩ ܒܪܟ ܢܡܘܬ "bring out thy son (that) he may die" Judges 6, 30 (similarly Judges 20, 13); ܫܪܝ ܟܢ̈ܫܐ ܗܢܘܢ ܢܐܙܠܘܢ ἀπόλυσον τοὺς ὄχλους, ἵνα ἀπελθόντες κ. τ. λ. Matt. 14, 15 C. (P. ܘܢܐܙܠܘܢ), and often similarly used in the Gospels, especially in S. (Cf. on the one hand § 272, and on the other § 368).

§ 268. A. The combination of the Impf. with the Perf. ܗܘܐ appears sometimes in conditional clauses, to denote an action frequently repeated: ܐܢ ܐܢܫ ܢܐܡܪ ܗܘܐ "*si quis dicebat*" Land II, 97 *ult.*; ܘܐܢ ܝܬܝܪ ܡܢ ܥܣܪܝܢ ܢܣܒ ܗܘܐ "*et si plus quam viginti sumebat*" *ib.* 93 *ult.*, and so ܟܕ ܟܡܐ ܠܟܠܗ ܡܢ ܐܬܪܘܬܐ ܢܐܙܠ ܗܘܐ "for as often as he came to any place" *ib.* 251, 14; ܟܕ ܢܬܚܡܬ ܗܘܐ "whenever he was angry" Ov. 186, 21 &c. Similarly ܒܟܠܡܕܡ ܕܝܢ . . . ܕܢܬܒܥܐ ܗܘܐ "in every thing . . . which was required" Land II, 201, 7. For such cases the Part. with ܗܘܐ is far more

Imperfect with ܗܘܐ.

usual (§ 277). This combination is met with rather more frequently in hypothetical clauses like ﺍﺟﻤﺍ ﻻ ﻳﻌﺒﺮ ﻩﻭﻩ "how should he not have been handsome?" Joseph 38, Note 5 (Ov. 287, 26); ﻳﺸﺪ ﻩﻭﻩ "he would have had to love" Ov. 278, 15 (incorrect reading in Joseph 19, 3 ﻣﻨﺒﻴﺪ); ﻣﺤﺰﻭﻣ ﻩﻭﻩ "why should he have fled?" Anc. Doc. 90, 22; ﻣ ﺍﺣﺠﺮ ﻩﻭﻣﻚ "what should I have done?" ZDMG XXIX, 117 v. 235; ﻣﻨﻮ ﻩﻭﻩ "who would see?" Ephr. Nis. p. 64 v. 203; ﺣﺲ ﻻ ﺍﻭﺯ ﻫﺴﺮ ﺗﻮﺍﻭﺯﺍ "is not then the light in one month stronger, in order that the loss of that day might be supplied?" Ov. 70, 17, and many like instances. Similarly ﻳﻤﻬﻮﻣ ﺣﺲ ﻣﻦ "who could (can) then be sufficient?" Ephr. (Lamy) I, 175, 19; ﻧﺒ ﺣﻔﺪ ﻳﺎﻣﺒﻔ ﻫﻮﺑ "how much more must they be sanctified" ib. paen.; ﻧﺒ ﺣﻔﺪﻟ....ﺑﺠﺍ ﻩﻭﻩ "how much more must ... injure" ib. 205, 16.

B. But this combination is particularly common, in place of the simple Impf., in dependent clauses after Perfects: ﻭﻻ ﺍﺟﻤﺍ {...ﻣﺤﻴﻤﻪ ﻳﻤﺤﺸﻪ ﻩﻭﻩ ﺟﺴﻔﺪ ﻟﺤﺠﺍﻭﺍﻻ συνέρχεται—ὥστε μὴ δύνασθαι αὐτοὺς μήτε ἄρτον φαγεῖν Mark 3, 20; ﻩﻭﺕ ﻭﺑﻴﺎﺗﺘﺤﻰ ﺍﺑﻰ ﺍﺗﺴﺍ "he gave them life that they might be moved" Moes. II, 104 v. 448; ﻭﺑﻴﺎﻣﺪﻛﻪ ﻩﻭﻭ ﻭﻣﻴﻌﺒﻌﺪ ﻗﺴﻮﺩﺧﻴﺒ "and thou besoughtest that thine offerings might be accepted" Ephr. III, 254 D; ﺍﻭﺯﻡ ﻩﻭﻩ ﻻ ﺍﻭﺯﻡ ﻩﻭﻩ ﻭﺍﻟﺒﺴﻮﺗ ﻩﻭﻩ ﻭﺑﻴﺪﺑﺴﺒﺪ "it ﻣﺤﺠﺪﻩ 'the sabbath'] would have had to be given to Adam, to keep it" Aphr. 234, 2; ﻩﻭﻩ ﻟﺒﻴﺠﻼ ... ﻭﻓﺪﻣﻪﺍ ﻗﺴﻮﺩﻓﻦ ﻗﻲ ﺳﻤﻴﺎﻟ ﻭﺟﻼ ﻩﻭﻭ ﻭﻣﻴﺤﺠﺒ ... ﺗﻪﻭﻣﺎﻩﻳﻨﺒ "his clothes they brought, in order that the blessing might be conveyed to a large number of them" Ov. 186, 26; ﻭﻳﺴﻮﺍﻟ ﻩﻭﻩ ﻣﺠﻢ ﻣﻴﺒ ... ﻭﺍﻓﻼ "nor even ... was he alarmed before he fell into sin and was fettered" Ov. 81, 10 (line 8 has merely ﻭﻳﺴﺘﺍﻟ ﺣﻤﺰ ﻣﺠﻢ(ﻣﺠﻢ); ﺍﻭﻡ ﻩﻭﻩ "he would have had to make it gush out for him" Aphr. 314, 4 (where one MS. leaves out ﻩﻭﺍ) (1); ﺣﺠﺮ ﺍﻣﺤﺮ ﻻ ﺑﺴﺘﻼﻻ ﻩﻭﻩ ﺍﺣﺠﻮﺩﻣﻪﺍﻟﺒ ﻩﻭﻩ ﻟﺒﻌﺴﻼ "should he not have been afraid (v. supra A) to reduce thee to slavery?" Joseph 15, Note 10 [Ov. 277, 2] &c. In all these cases the simple Impf. would be sufficient; and in fact it is much oftener met with, even in this application, than the construction with ﻩﻭﻩ.

---

(1) This tedious construction is rare with Aphraates.

PARTICIPLES.

§ 269. The *Active Participle*, when it forms the predicate, denotes, Active
Participle.
as a Nominal form, first of all a condition, without reference to a de- Present.
finite time. Such a condition generally represents itself to us as a *present
condition*; and in this respect the Active Participle is not distinguishable
from any other predicative adjective: ﺃﻧﺎ ﻗﺎﻃﻞ "killing (am) I" is exactly
like ﺃﻧﺎ ﺯﺩﻕ "just (am) I". But its close connection with the finite verb
gives the Participle a more verbal character, which is specially shown
by the circumstance that the bare participial form can dispense altogether
with the expression of the 3rd person as a subject (§ 253); it farther
appears for the Impf. over a wide range, and becomes almost a tense,
without, however, losing completely its Nominal character. Although its
chief use is to express the Present, yet it is not a true Present; precisely
where it has the appearance of being so, it might for the most part be
taken as an Adjective proper.

The Active Participle thus denotes very frequently the continuing
as well as the momentary Present, and in this meaning it almost entirely
supplants the Impf. Examples abound: the following may illustrate the
transition from the representation of quite constant conditions to a statement of what is momentary: ﺍﻧﻠﺎ ﺣﻤﺮ ﺍﻭﻳﻞ ﻣﻢ ﻣﻠﻴﻪ "for the lion
by its nature eats flesh (always)" Spic. 7, 14; ﺍﺳﻠﺎ ﺍﻣﺤﺒﺎ ﻳﻌﻤﻪ ﺣﻤﺠﻢ
ﻗﻤﺴﺒﺎ ﻭﻭﻫﻤﻨﺎ ﻟﺤﻤﺠﻤﺪ ﻏﻤﺴﺒﺎ ﺳﻴﺎ "he ruins himself whoever accepts a
bribe, but he who hates to take a bribe lives (יחיה)" Prov. 15, 27; ﻣﺴﺒﺎ
ﺣﻤﺰ ﻭﻗﻤﻌﺪﻳﻦ ﺭﺳﻤﻌﻪﻩ ﻣﻌﻔﺎ ﺍﻭﻳﻜﻴﺎ ﻭﺯﺧﻮﺍﺍ ﻗﺎﻝ ﻣﻮﺍﻟﺎ ﺳﻤﻮﺟﻪ ﺣﺠﺠﻘﺎﺍﻭﻩﻩ
ﻭﺯﻟﻨﺴﻢ ﺭﺳﻤﻌﻤﻮﻩﻩ "for as soon as his friends hear the dear name of Rabbūlā, love for him is inflamed in their hearts and their bosoms glow"
Ov. 202, 12; ﺍﻥ ﻫﻤﻔﺎ ﻣﻤﺠﻤﻠﺎ ﺍﻧﻠﺎ ﻗﻤﻤﺒﻴﻪ "now also I receive his command" Ov. 172, 5; ﺯﺳﻤﺒﻢ ﺳﻴﺒﻢ ... ﺻﻤﺰﻟﻤﺎ "we figure (for you herewith) the
image" Ov. 159, 4 &c.

§ 270. The Participle stands plainly in direct antithesis to the past Future
in ﻟﺤﻤﺪﻟﻤﺠﻪ ﻭﻟﺎﺩﺑﺎ ﺍﻩ ﻣﻠﻪ ﺍﻧﻪ ﻟﺎ ﻣﻠﻪ ﺍﻩ ﻣﺤﺠﻤﻮﻩ "the word of God—no
man has come, or comes, to the end of" Aphr. 101, 17. Thus the Part.
often appears for *the Future*, whether it be that the condition is set be-

14*

fore us in a more lively fashion as a Present, or that the construction suffices to relegate the indefinite statement of the condition to the Future. The Impf. in these cases might be more obvious, but the very possibility of exchanging the two here shows that neither is the Part. a proper Present, nor the Impf. a genuine Future. Cf. ܓܠܐ ܗܘܐ φανερὸν γενήσεται 1 Cor. 3, 13; ܡܓܠܐ δηλώσει *ib.* (Harkl. ܡܬܓܠܝܐ ܬܗܘܐ and ܬܓܠܐ); ܫܒܚܬ ܘܬܘܒ ܡܫܒܚ ܐܢܐ ἐδόξασα καὶ πάλιν δοξάσω John 12, 28; ܠܥܠܡ ܠܐ ܡܐܬ οὐ μὴ ἀποθάνῃ εἰς τὸν αἰῶνα John 11, 26 S. (P. ܠܐ ܢܡܘܬ ܠܥ'); ܚܪܒܬ ܐܘܪܫܠܡ ܘܬܘܒ ܠܐ ܡܬܝܬܒܐ ܠܥܠܡ "Jerusalem has been destroyed, and will never again be inhabited" Aphr. 483, 18 (and frequently thus with ܠܐ . . . ܠܥܠܡ); ܒܥܓܠ ܡܕܪܟ ܠܟ ܕܝܢܐ ܟܐܢܐ ܕܐܠܗܐ "speedily the righteous judgment of God overtakes thee" Mart. I, 125 *ult.*; ܒܫܘܠܡ ܫܬܐ ܐܠܦܝ̈ܢ ܫܢܝ̈ܢ ܡܫܬܪܐ ܒܗ ܥܠܡܐ "on the completion of six thousand years the world is dissolved" Aphr. 36, 20; ܘܗܝܕܝܢ ܡܣܩ ܐܢܐ "and then I bring up" Aphr. 72, 15; ܚܪܝܢܐ . . . ܗܘܐ ܕܐܝܟܢܐ ܩܝܡܝܢ ܡܝ̈ܬܐ ܘܒܐܝܢܐ ܦܓܪܐ ܐܬܝܢ "controversy . . . continues as to how the dead rise and in what body they will come" (where the Impf. without more ado exchanges with the Part.) Aphr. 154, 1; ܡܚܪ ܚܙܐ ܐܢܬ ܠܗ "to-morrow thou seest him" Ephr. III, XLIII mid.; ܗܢܘܢ ܕܐܬܝܢ ܒܬܪܢ "those who shall come after us" Jos. St. 80, 2; ܘܒܬܘܩܢܗ ܕܥܠܡܐ ܚܕܬܐ ܗܘ ܫܠܝܢ ܟܠܗܘܢ ܙܘܥܐ ܒܝܫܐ ܘܡܫܬܠܡܝܢ ܟܠܗܘܢ ܣܘܪ̈ܚܢܐ "and on the establishment of that new world all bad movements cease, and all oppositions end" (farther participles follow) Spic. 21, 7 &c. With special frequency they occur in eschatological delineations, as in the 22nd chap. of Aphr. where the Impf. scarcely ever occurs.

In Conditional Clauses.

§ 271. Thus also the Part. appears very often in Conditional Sentences, both in the protasis and the apodosis: ܘܐܢ ܐܦ ܠܢ ܫܦܪ ܡܫܬܘܝܢܢ ܥܡܟ "and if it also pleases us, then we come to an agreement with thee" Spic. 2, 4; ܐܢ ܓܝܪ ܫܩܠ ܐܢܬ ܡܝܐ ܡܢ ܝܡܐ ܠܐ ܡܬܝܕܥܐ ܚܘܣܪܢܗ "for if thou takest water out of the sea, the loss of it is not noticed" Aphr. 101, 9, and many others. Similarly in quasi-conditional sentences with ܡܐ: ܡܐ ܕܣܓܝܐ ܥܘܬܪܐ ܪܒܐ ܪܚܡܬ ܟܣܦܐ "when riches increase, avarice becomes great" Aphr. 267, 21 (cf. § 265).

In all such cases the Part. is neither an actual Future, nor an actual Present. So too in sentences like ܡܓܪ ܕܝܢ ܐܡܪ ܐܢܬ "but perhaps some one may say" Jos. St. 5, 13; 42, 15, where the Impf. might stand quite as well.

§ 272. In a considerable number of instances the Part. stands for a Future action, instead of the Impf., even in dependent clauses: ܥܕ ܡܬܢܚܡ ܦܓܪܗ "till his body rise again" Ov. 208, 21; ܥܕܡܐ ܕܐܬܝܐ ܚܘܒܗ "until love for him come" Aphr. 39, 13; ܥܕܡܐ ܕܡܩܪܒܝܢ ܒܣܡܐ "till they should offer incense" Guidi, Sette Dormienti 24 v. 43; ܘܫܡܫ ܫܢܝܐ ܣܓܝܐܬܐ ܥܕ ܡܫܬܩܠ "and he ministered for many years till he was taken up" Aphr. 273, 2; ܣܡ ܠܘܬܗܘܢ ܡܫܟܢܐ ܘܡܗܝܡܢܘܬܐ ܩܘܐܕ ܒܪܗ ܥܕ ܡܫܕܪ ܠܗܘܢ "he placed with them as a pledge and hostage Kawādh his son till he should send (them) to them" Jos. St. 10, 17 and many like examples with ܥܕ, ܥܕܡܐ ܕ. — ܕܡܬܟܠܝܢܢ ܠܡܣܒܪ ܕܚܝܝܢ ܚܝܝܢܢ "that we confidently assume that we shall live" Aphr. 459, 18; ܗܒ ܠܝ ܡܗܝܡܢܐ ܕܠܐ ܢܦܩܝܢ ܐܢܬܘܢ ܒܬܪܝ "give me hostages that you will not come in pursuit of me" Jos. St. 61, 2: ܡܬܩܝܡ ܐܢܬ ܡܢܟ ܕܠܐ ܬܘܒ ܥܒܕ ܐܢܬ "dost thou engage, not again to do . . . ?" Sim. 292 *supr.*; ܟܕ ܣܒܪ ܕܡܗܦܟܝܢ ܠܗ ܩܢܝܢܗ ܕܥܘܠܐ "while he thought that they would restore to him his iniquitous possession" Mart. I, 127, 11; ܕܣܒܪܝܢ ܗܘܘ ܕܐܦ ܥܠ ܐܘܪܗܝ ܡܬܚܝܠܝܢ ܒܥܠܕܒܒܐ "who thought that the enemy would also seize upon Edessa (Orhāi)" Jos. St. 7, 18; ܘܠܐ ܝܕܥܘ ܘܐܪܓܫܘ ܣܟܠܐ ܕܒܥܓܠ ܥܩܬܐ ܘܬܘܝܬܐ ܡܕܪܟܐ ܠܗܘܢ "and the fools did not know and did not perceive that sorrow and regret would soon overtake them" Sim. 388 mid.; ܡܛܠ ܕܩܕܡ ܐܣܬܟܠ . . . ܐܝܠܐ ܕܒܝܫܬܐ ܩܫܝܬܐ ܓܕܫܐ "for he had come to understand beforehand, what grievous harm would befall" Ov. 197, 6; ܓܒܝܗ ܠܗ ܪܘܚܐ ܕܩܘܕܫܐ ܕܐܦ ܡܫܝܚܐ . . . ܡܢ ܙܪܥܗ ܡܬܝܠܕ "the Holy Spirit made choice of him (Noah) that from his seed even the Messiah should be born" Aphr. 236 *paen.*; ܕܐܫܬܘܕܝܘ ܕܡܬܦܢܝܢ ܠܘܬ ܐܠܗܐ "that they had promised to turn again unto God" Sim. 321 mid.; ܡܢ ܦܘܡܟ ܣܪܝܩܘܬܐ ܠܐ ܬܦܘܩ ܕܠܐ ܢܫܩܘܠ ܢܦܫܗ ܡܢܟ ܘܠܐ ܥܡܪ ܒܟ "let not vanity issue from thy mouth, lest He withdraw from thee and cease to dwell in thee" Aphr. 185, 20; ܕܠܡܐ ܟܕ ܐܬܐ ܪܫܐ ܠܝ "lest perhaps he find fault with me when he comes" Aphr. 340, 19; ܕܠܡܐ ܚܙܐ ܐܢܫ "whether perchance he saw any one"—Guidi, Sette Dormienti 27 v. 158, and many like cases. But still, the Impf. is far more usual in these cases.

In Dependent Clauses.

☞ p. 357

The Part. stands in like manner loosely as a consequence of a verb,
☞ p. 357 especially an Imperative: ܫܒܘܩܘ ܠܛܠܝܐ ܐܬܝܢ ܠܘܬܝ ἄφετε τὰ παιδία ἔρχεσθαι πρός με Mark 10, 14: Matt. 19, 14; ܫܒܘܩ ܡܝܬܐ ܩܒܪܝܢ ܡܝܬܝܗܘܢ ἄφετε τοὺς νέκρους θάψαι τοὺς ἑαυτῶν νέκρους Matt. 8, 22, and frequently so in the N. T. with ܫܒܘܩ, ܫܒܘܩܘ; ܫܒܘܩ ܐܙܠ "let him go" Sim. 283 *inf.*; ܦܩܘܕ ܡܙܕܗܪܝܢ (S. ܢܛܪܝܢ) κέλευσον ἀσφαλισθῆναι Matt. 27, 64; ܦܩܘܕ ܩܛܠܝܢ ܠܝ "bid them kill me" Mart. I, 25 mid.; ܦܩܘܕ ܠܗ ܝܬܒ "bid him sit down" John van Tella (Kleyn) 51, 3; ܐܡܪ ܠܐܚܝ ܦܠܓ ܥܡܝ ܝܪܬܘܬܐ εἶπε τῷ ἀδελφῷ μου μερίσασθαι μετ' ἐμοῦ τὴν κληρονομίαν Luke 12, 13; ܩܪܘ ܠܫܡܫܘܢ ܪܩܕ ܩܕܡܝܢ "call Samson, that he may dance before us" Judges 16, 25; ܩܘܡ ܢܦܘܩ ܒܝܬܝܢ "rise, that we may go forth and pass the night" Jos. St. 29, 11; ܒܚܕ ܡܢ ܓܘܒܐ ܕܒܡܕܒܪܐ ܫܕܘܗܝ ܛܒܥ ܒܚܡܝܬܐ "into one of the pits which are in the desert cast ye him, that he may sink in the mire" Joseph 29, 7 (Ov. 283, 11); ܕܒܪܘܗܝ ܠܘܬ ܐܒܘܗܝ ܐܬܐ ܘܚܙܐ "take him to his father, that he may come and see" Joseph 280, 13 &c. With other forms of the verb: ܠܐ ܬܫܒܘܩܝܗ ܢܦܩܐ "suffer her not to go out" Sir. 42, 11; ܕܠܐ ܬܫܒܘܩ ܠܦܓܪܐ ܡܬܚܒܠ "that it (f.) do not allow the body to be corrupted" Philox. 524, 11; ܢܫܒܘܩ ܚܛܬܐ ܪܒܝܐ "permit (subj.) the wheat to increase" Ov. 192, 20; ܫܒܩܬ ܐܢܘܢ ܐܙܠܝܢ "I allowed them to go" Sim. 328, 4; ܢܬܠ ܠܗܘܢ ܠܡܐܟܠ (S. ܢܬܠ) δώσωμεν αὐτοῖς φαγεῖν Mark 6, 37. (Cf. *supra* § 267).

Farther, notice ܐܣܝܐ ܕܝܕܥ ܗܘܐ ܡܐܣܐ ܟܐܒܐ "the physician, who was skilful in healing pains" Anc. Doc. 90, 23; ܠܐ ܪܓܝܐ ܛܝܒܘܬܐ ܡܩܒܠܐ ܠܬܝܒܐ "grace will not accept the penitent ..." Aphr. 153, 15 (cf. 187, 10); ܡܕܡ ܝܗܒ "is accustomed to give" Philox. 473, 23, and frequently thus with ܡܕܡ; ܕܐܡܝܢܝܢ ܡܣܩܝܢ ܠܢ "who constantly injure us" Statuti della
☞ p. 357 Scuola di Nisibi 13, 8, and frequently so with ܐܡܝܢ. With special fre-
☞ p. 357 quency, however, the Part. is found with "can" and "begin"; ܠܐ ܡܫܟܚ ܒܪܐ ܥܒܕ οὐ δύναται ὁ υἱὸς ποιεῖν John 5, 19 (C. ܠܡܥܒܕ); ܡܫܟܚ ܩܛܪ "can constrain" Aphr. 491, 13; ܠܐ ܡܨܝܢ ܡܒܛܠܝܢ "(they) cannot bring to nought" Ov. 62, 21; ܫܪܝܘ ܡܠܩܛܝܢ ἤρξαντο τίλλειν Matt. 12, 1; ܫܪܝܘ ܓܙܪܝܢ "they began circumcising" Aphr. 210, 4; ܫܪܝܘ ܥܪܩܝܢ "they commenced fleeing away" Sim. 342 mid. &c. Compare also ܫܪܝܘ ܣܦܪܐ ܘܦܪܝܫܐ ܡܬܚܬܝܢ ܠܗܘܢ ἤρξαντο οἱ γραμματεῖς καὶ οἱ Φαρισαῖοι δεινῶς

ἐνέχειν, Luke 11, 53 P., for which C. S. have ܚܢܩ ܡܬܚܪܝܢ ܗܘܘ ܠܗ' (cf. § 277 Concl.).

In like manner the Part. appears, connected however with ܘ, in ܚܘܝܢܝ ܗܕܐ ܘܡܬܛܦܝܣ ܐܢܐ ܡܢܟ "show me this, and then I shall be convinced by thee" Spic. 13, 6; ܢܐܙܠ ܐܢܫ ܡܢ ܡܝ̈ܬܐ ܠܘܬܗܘܢ ܘܬܝܒܝܢ "let one go to them from the dead, and they repent [= then they would repent]" Aphr. 384, 3; ܡܛܠ ܕܐܡܪܘ ܕܢܬܦܠܓܘܢ ܦܓܪ̈ܝܗܘܢ ܘܥܒܪܐ ܡܠܟܬܐ ܒܝܬ ܦܓܪ̈ܝܗܘܢ ܘܡܬܚܠܡܐ "because they had said that their bodies should be divided and that the queen should pass through the midst of their bodies, and then she would become well" Mart. I, 57 mid.

Use of Part. in denoting what was on the point of happening in the Past.

§ 273. Exceptionally the Part. denotes something on the point of happening in the past, in sentences like ܟܕ ܡܛܝ ܙܒܢܐ ܕܢܡܘܬ "when the time came for him to die" Aphr. 312, 6; ܠܐܬܪܐ ܕܡܩܒܠ ܗܘܐ ܒܫܢܩܐ ܐܘܒܠܘܗܝ "they led him away to where he was to suffer punishment" Mart. I, 246 mid. (a like case *ib. inf.*); ܝܘܡܐ ܕܡܬܦܬܚ ܒܗ ܬܪܥܐ ܪܚܝܩ ܗܘܐ "the day on which the door was to be opened was still distant" Sim. 363 mid. But the addition of ܗܘܐ is more usual in this case (§ 277).

Historical Present.

§ 274. Narration scarcely ever employs the Active Participle (as historical present) except in the case of ܐܡܪ; but this ܐܡܪ, ܐܡܪܐ, ܐܡܪܝܢ, or ܐܡܪܢ, "he or she said"; "they (m. or f.) said"—is very common. Thus ܥܢܘ ܘܐܡܪܝܢ καὶ ἀποκριθέντες εἶπαν Matt. 21, 27, and frequently; accordingly the form ܥܢܐ ܘܐܡܪ common in the N. T. must properly have been ܥܢܐ ܘܐܡܪ. Something different is the Part. in lively description of dreams, as in ܘܡܢ ܐܡܪܬ . . . ܒܦܠܓܗ ܕܠܠܝܐ ܟܕ ܕܡܟ ܐܢܐ ܒܡܫܟܢܐ ܚܙܐ ܐܢܐ ܓܒܪܐ "and after I had said . . . about midnight while I am sleeping in the tent, I see a man" Sim. 328 *supr.*, and thus frequently.

Contemporary Condition in the Past.

§ 275. In brief subordinate clauses the Part. often stands (like adjectives of another kind), to denote a contemporary condition in the past, especially after ܟܕ: ܥܢܐ . . . ܟܕ ܡܬܚܡܬ ἀποκριθεὶς . . . ἀγανακτῶν Luke 13, 14; ܟܕ ܢܚܬܝܢ . . . ܦܩܕ καταβαινόντων αὐτῶν . . . ἐνετείλατο Matt. 17, 9; ܕܒܚ ܗܘ ܢܦܫܗ ܠܫܐܕܐ ܟܕ ܢܚܬ "he sacrificed himself to the demons, to wit, when he descended" Ov. 160, 15; ܘܟܕ ܩܐܡ ܒܗܝܟܠܐ ܚܙܐ "and while he stood in the temple, he saw" Ov. 163 *ult.*; ܠܘܩܒܠ ܡܘܬܐ ܪܗܛ ܗܘܐ ܟܕ ܚܕܐ "to meet death he ran with joy" Anc. Doc. 90 *paen.*; ܐܬܐܡܪܘ

ܡܶܬܬܪܶܐ . . . ܕܰܐܟ̈ܠܰܩܰܪܨܶܐ . . . ܓܰܒܪ . . . ܟܰܕ ܐܳܡܪܺܝܢ "accusations were brought against a man, while they said" Mart. I, 123; ܟܰܕ ܗܽܘ ܡܡܰܠܶܠ "while he yet spake" Gen. 29, 9; Matt. 26, 47, and frequently thus, after ܟܰܕ "while yet". Cf. ܚܙܳܐ ܠܠܶܘܺܝ . . . ܕܝܳܬܶܒ εἶδε Λευῒν ... καθήμενον Mark 2, 14; ܘܟܰܕ ܫܡܰܥ ܕܶܐܓܰܪ̈ܳܬܳܐ ܡܶܬܩܰܪ̈ܝܳܢ "and when he heard that the epistles were read" Sim. 269 *ad inf.* (*Cod. Lond.* ܘܟܕ ܫܡܥ ܟܕ ܡܩ' ܐܓ'); ܫܰܪܺܝܘ ܢܳܛܪܺܝܢ ܗܘܰܘ . . . ܕܢܶܚܙܽܘܢ ܐܶܢ ܡܢܺܝܕ ܪ̈ܶܓܠܰܘܗܝ "they began to watch that they might see if he moved his feet" Sim. 275, 15 &c. Notice the contrast with the Perf. in ܟܰܕ ܚܙܳܬ ܠܝܺܗܽܘ ܕܰܐܡܠܶܟ ܘܳܐܬܶܐ "when she saw that Jehu had become king, and was coming" Aphr. 273, 9. In all these instances ܗܘܳܐ might have been added to the Part.

Modal Colouring. § 276. In several of the foregoing examples a beginning has been made in employing the Part. in room of the Impf., even in optative and other moods. Compare on this point rare cases like ܡܣܰܟܶܝܢܰܢ προσδοκῶμεν "have we to look for?" Matt. 11, 3; Luke 7, 19, 20; ܠܡܳܢܳܐ ܡܳܐܶܬ "why is he to die?" 1 Sam. 20, 32; ܠܡܳܢܳܐ ܡܳܐܶܬ ܐܰܢ̱ܬ "why wilt thou die?" Guidi, Sette Dorm. 22 v. 142 = 28 v. 168; ܐܰܝܟܰܢܳܐ ܫܳܒܩܺܝܢ ܠܟܽܘܢ "how are they to forgive you?" Aphr. 37, 12. Of course it is at the most merely the first approaches to a modal use of the Part. that can be discovered in these instances: modality itself still remains entirely with the Impf.

☞ p. 357

Active Participle with ܗܘܐ. § 277. The Part., properly expressing only a condition, is distinctly referred to the past by subjoining ܗܘܳܐ or, though not so frequently, by placing that word before it. Thus there arises a form expressing continuance or repetition in past time; ܥܳܒܶܕ ܗܘܳܐ is nearly = *faciebat.* The ܗܘܳܐ does not require to be repeated, when it refers to several participles: it may be altogether omitted, when the connection clearly attests the sphere of the past (§ 275). Farther, even the simple tense of past time, viz the Perfect, may appear instead of this combination, whenever the impression of continuance or repetition is not specially conveyed. Thus, in particular, we have almost invariably ܗܘܳܐ alone, instead of ܗܳܘܶܐ ܗܘܳܐ as *erat.* The combination is very common: ܡܩܰܪܒܺܝܢ ܗܘܰܘ προσέφερον Mark 10, 13 (S. ܩܰܪܶܒܘ); ܡܙܰܒܢܺܝܢ ܗܘܰܘ ἐπίπρασκον Acts 2, 45 (and in v. 47, farther instances); ܠܥܽܘܕܪܳܢܳܐ ܡܶܢܶܗ ܫܳܐܠܺܝܢ ܗܘܰܘ "*auxilium ab eo rogabant*" Mart. I, 122, 10; ܗܘܰܘ ܓܶܝܪ ܐܳܟܠܺܝܢ "*edebant enim*" Sim. 274 mid.; ܘܡܘܕܝܢ

ܗܘܳܐ ܢܽܘܪܳܐ ܘܣܳܐܶܡ "used to light a fire and place on it (incense)" Sim. 269, 9; ܟܰܕ ܡܰܦܩܺܝܢ ܗܘܰܘ ܠܩܰܕܡܳܝܳܐ ܕܡܺܝܬ ܗܘܳܐ ܐܰܟ̣ܡܳܐ ܕܗܳܦܟܺܝܢ ܗܘܰܘ ܡܶܫܟܚܺܝܢ ܗܘܰܘ ܐ̱ܚܪ̈ܳܢܶܐ "while they were bringing out the first who had died,—as soon as they turned round, they found others" Jos. St. 37, 17. Notice that the Part. here, along with ܟܰܕ, takes ܗܘܳܐ, though the simple Part. would have been sufficient (§ 275). It is somewhat different when a condition is entered upon suddenly: ܟܰܕ ܗ̄ܘ . . . ܡܦܺܝܣ ܗܘܳܐ ܠܶܗ . . . ܘܕܰܗܒܳܐ . . . ܐܶܫܬܰܕܰܪ "while he was still seeking to persuade him, the gold was (suddenly) sent" Jos. St. 35, 9. Similarly ܘܟܰܕ ܫܪܺܝܘ ܠܡܶܬܩܰܛܳܠܽܘ ܡܰܓܽܘܫܳܐ ܚܰܕ ܢܦܰܩ ܗܘܳܐ ܡܶܢ ܡܕܺܝܢ̱ܬܳܐ ܘܥܳܒܰܪ ܗܘܳܐ ܒܽܐܘܪܚܳܐ "and when they began to be put to death, a magician came (just then) from the city and passed by on the road" Mart. I, 94, 14.—The notion of continuance is more strongly impressed in ܘܗܘܰܘ ܟܰܕ ܡܶܬܚܪܺܝܢ ܥܰܡܶܗ ܡܶܢ ܨܰܦܪܳܐ ܘܰܥܕܰܡܳܐ ܠܫܳܥܬܳܐ ܬܫܰܥ "and they kept wrangling with him from daybreak till the ninth hour" Jos. St. 58, 20.

This combination farther denotes something on the point of happening in the past (without ܗܘܳܐ § 273): ܠܕܽܘܟܬܳܐ ܗܳܝ ܕܒܳܗ̇ ܡܶܬܩܰܛܠܺܝܢ ܗܘܰܘ "to the place where they were to be put to death" Mart. I, 91, 3; 99, 1; ܟܰܕ ܡܛܳܐ ܝܰܘܡܳܐ ܕܗܘܳܐ ܗܘܳܐ ܒܶܗ ܡܰܦܩܳܢܶܗ ܕܡܰܠܟܳܐ "when the day arrived on which the departure of the king was to take place" Mart. I, 106 *inf.*; ܕܰܠܡܳܢܳܐ ܟܪܺܝܬ ܠܶܗ ܒܟܽܘܪܗܳܢܶܗ ܕܡܳܐܶܬ ܗܘܳܐ "why he grieved in his sickness that he was to die" Aphr. 468, 14 &c.—ܠܦܳܪܣ ܡܒܰܗܬܳܐ ܗܘܳܐ ܠܫܺܝܓܰܪ ܡܒܰܢܝܳܐ ܗܘܳܐ "he wanted to put Persia to shame and build up Singara" Ov. 9, 25.

It stands also hypothetically in ܠܡܳܢܳܐ ܥܳܪܶܩ ܗܘܳܐ ܐܳܣܝܳܐ "why should the physician flee?" Anc. Doc. 90, 23 (close beside ܢܶܥܪܽܘܩ ܗܘܳܐ § 268 A); ܨܳܒܶܐ ܗܘܺܝܬ "*vellem*" Mart, I, 167 mid.; ܠܘܰܝ ܕܳܚܶܠܰܬ ܗܘܰܝܬ "would that thou didst reverence" Mart. I, 26 *inf.*; ܘܐܰܝܠܳܐ ܪܟܽܘܒܳܐ ܣܳܦܶܩ ܗܘܳܐ "and what means of conveyance would be sufficient?" Moes. II, 112 v. 550; ܐܰܝܟܰܢ ܛܶܥ̈ܢܶܐ ܫܳܪܶܐ ܗܘܺܝܬ "how could I have undone the loads?" Joseph 229, 14 (Ov. 313, 24); ܠܳܐ ܡܫܰܟܰܚ ܗܘܳܐ "could he not have &c.?" Sim. 374, 7; ܐܰܝܟ ܕܡܕܰܒܪܳܢܽܘܢ ܒܟܒܝ ܗܘܳܐ ܠܗܽܘܢ "as if he were carrying them (his wars) on, in their interest" Jos. St. 9, 18; ܒܳܗ̇ ܓܶܝܪ ܡܶܫܬܰܡܠܝܳܐ ܗܘܳܬ ܨܶܒܝܳܢܶܗ "for thereby his will would be fulfilled" Spic. 1, 9, and like cases. Thus too in clauses with ܐܶܠܘ "if" (§ 375 A).

Similarly also ܙܒܢܝܢ ܒܗܬ ܘܠܐ ܡܩܛܠ ܘܡܫܩܠ ܗܘܐ "perhaps he will be ashamed and will not put to death, and he (another subject) will take away" Mart. I, 124 mid., where at first the ܗܘܐ is wanting.

This combination stands in a dependent position,—amongst other instances,—in: ܟܕ ܡܬܟܪܝܢ ܗܘܘ ܟܠܗܘܢ ܥܠܘܗܝ ܕܡܐܬ ܗܘܐ "while all were grieved for him, that he was dying" Anc. Doc. 20, 14 = Addai 48, 8; ܘܪܡܙܘ ܩܕܝܫ̈ܐ ܕܠܐ ܡܕܒܚܝܢ ܗܘܘ "the holy men made a sign that they would not offer sacrifice" Anc. Doc. 103, 20 (line 25 has merely ܕܠܐ ܡܕܒܚܝܢ). And thus it sometimes stands, even when the dependence is not given expression to by ܕ (§ 272): ܘܫܪܝܘ ܗܘܘ ܒܥܝܢ ܗܘܘ ܡܢܗ "and they commenced to beg of him" Luke 24, 29 C. S. and even ܠܐ ܡܫܟܚܝܢ ܗܘܘ ܢܛܪܝܢ ܗܘܘ "they were not able to keep" Aphr. 15, 2; ܕܡܥܝܕܝܢ ܗܘܘ ܣܓܕܝܢ ܗܘܘ ܠܗ "which they had been accustomed to worship" Aphr. 312, 21; ܘܐܝܟܢܐ ܡܨܐ ܗܘܐ ܦܠܚ ܗܘܐ ܠܗ ܟܕ ܠܐ ܡܨܐ ܗܘܐ ܣܦܩ ܗܘܐ ܠܗ "and how could he have cultivated it when he could not summon up the needful strength" [*lit.* "when he could not suffice for it"] Ephr. I, 23 D &c. Here the tedious ܗܘܐ beside the dependent verb might throughout have been dispensed with.

Passive Participle. For the Perfect. § 278. A. *The Passive Participle* expresses the completion of an action, and stands as a predicate instead of the Perfect, just as the Active Participle does instead of the Imperfect: ܟܬܝܒ γέγραπται Matt. 2, 5, and often in the N. T. and elsewhere; ܒܗܝ ܚܐܪܘܬܐ ܕܝܗܝܒܐ ܠܗܘܢ ܡܢ ܐܠܗܐ "in that liberty which has been given them by God (= ܐܬܝܗܒܬ)" Spic. 13, 17; ܗܫܐ ܕܝܢ ܒܡܐܬܝܬܗ ܕܒܪܗ ܕܡܪܝܡ ܒܪܝܟܬܐ ܥܩܝܪܝܢ ܟܘ̈ܒܐ ܘܕܘܥܬܐ ܥܒܝܪܐ ܘܬܐܬܐ ܠܝܛܐ ܘܫ' "but now, through the coming of the son of the blessed Mary, the thorns have been uprooted, the sweat removed, the fig-tree cursed &c." Aphr. 113, 19; ܕܠܐ ܚܬܝܡܢ ܡ̈ܠܐ ܗܠܝܢ . . . ܘܠܐ ܡܬܚܬܡܢ "that these words have not been sealed and are not to be sealed" Aphr. 101, 5 (where the difference between the Passive Participle and the Reflexive Participle with the effect of the Active very clearly appears), and so in many instances. But what we have in all such cases is the true, result-announcing *Perfect*:—as a *narrative* tense this participle hardly ever appears.

B. With ‎ܗܘܐ‎ there is thus formed a kind of Pluperfect, *i. e.* the statement of a result reached already in the Past: ‎ܣܠܝܩ ܗܘܐ‎ "had been got ready" Ov. 172, 22; ‎ܒܝ ܠܐ ܗܘܐ ܗ ܘܐܬܚܬܡ ܘܐܬܪܫܡ‎ "for this testament had not been completed [lit. 'signed and sealed'] Aphr. 28, 8; ‎ܘܒܗ ‎ "in which the blessing had been hidden" Aphr. 464, 15 &c.

§ 279. A. A favourite mode of employing this Part. includes mention of the agent introduced by ‎ܠ‎ (§ 247): ‎ܥܒܝܕ ܠܝ‎ "(has been) done by me" = "I have done". A logical object may stand with it as grammatical subject; but such may also be wanting, so that the form of the verb may be impersonal; thus it may be formed even with intransitive verbs: ‎ܡܝܢ ܠܝ ܠܐ ܡܩܣ ܠܝ‎ ἄνδρα οὐ γινώσκω Luke 1, 34; "hast thou read the books?" Spic. 13, 8; ‎ܠܝ‎ "whom I have prepared for thee" Mart. I, 182 *inf.*; ‎ܐܠܢ ‎ "if by him the mountains have been searched, the rivers plundered, and the depths of the seas fathomed, and he has examined and searched the recesses of the thickets and of the caves" Ephr. II, 319 D (where the Active form continues what was expressed by the Passive); ‎ܐܝܟ ‎ "as we have heard" Spic. 16, 22; ‎ܠܐ ܩܡ ܠܝ‎ "it has not been stood by me (= I have not stood) before great ones" Kalilag and Damnag 88, 8; ‎ܩܡ ܠܗ‎ "he stood" Hoffmann, Märtyrer 108, 973; ‎ܗܠܟܬ ܠܝ‎ "I have walked" Spic. 43, 7; ‎ܠܐ ‎ "and I have had no experience of domestic ties" [lit. 'with marriage I have not met'] Ephr. (Lamy) II, 599, 8; ‎ܠܐ ܗܘܐ ܠܢ‎ "we have been engaged in no treacherous dealing with the Romans" ('it has been engaged by us in no treachery with &c.') Mart. I, 152, 9; ‎ܗܘܝܬ ܠܝ‎ "true and straightforward have I been" Mart. I, 27, 5. Cf. the troublesome sentence ‎ܡܢ ܗܢܘܢ ‎ "from those quarters where the people had contracted any of that relationship with one another which comes from baptism" (*or* "where, for the people, that relationship &c. had come into existence" *or*, still more literally, "where, for the people, existence had been assumed by that relationship &c.") Jac. Edess. in Lagarde's *Reliq. Juris Syr.* 144, 14 &c.

B. With ܗܘܐ we get also a Pluperfect of this type: ܕܒܢܐ ܗܘܐ ܡܢ ܦܪܣܝܐ "which had been built by the Persians" Jos. St. 17, 9; ܠܐ ܗܝܕܝܢ ܩܪܝܢܐ ܗܘܬ ܠܗ . . . ܐܘ ܫܡܝܥܐ ܗܘܬ ܠܗ ܗܕܐ "had he then not read . . . or had he not heard,—this?" Mart. I, 127 *supr.*; ܠܐ ܓܝܪ ܟܬܒܐ ܫܡܝܥܝܢ ܗܘܘ ܠܗ "for the books had not been heard of by him" Sim. 269, 9 &c.

Active Use. § 280. Several participles of the form ܫܩܝܠ are used with an Active signification. This arises partly from the circumstance that the verbs concerned may be doubly transitive, and partly from the influence of the analogy of forms allied in meaning. Thus ܛܥܝܢ "laden with" = "bearing"; ܚܕܝܪ, ܟܪܝܟ "thrown round (*circumdatus*)" = "encircling (*circumdans*)"; ܐܚܝܕ, ܠܒܝܟ, ܐܚܝܕ "holding"; ܢܣܝܒ "possessing"; ܣܝܡ "having placed"; ܫܩܝܠ "carrying"; ܓܪܝܪ "dragging away"; ܕܒܝܪ "leading away"; ܫܚܝܦ "pulling away"; ܓܦܝܦ "holding embraced"; ܕܟܝܪ "remembering" (according to others ܕܟܝܪ); ܠܒܝܫ "clothed with" = "wearing"; ܐܣܝܪ "girt with"; ܣܝܢ "shod with"; ܣܡܝܟ "leant upon (ܥܠ)" = "supporting", and some others. The pretty frequent ܩܢܐ [1] "having acquired" = "possessing" (as contrasted with ܩܢܐ "acquiring") deserves particular attention. Some examples: ܣܡܝܟܝܢ ܒܗ ܙܕܝܩܐ ܠܐܪܥܐ "the righteous support the earth" Aphr. 457, 8; ܢܫܐ ܕܝܢ ܛܥܝܢܢ ܗܘܝ ܡܝܐ "but women carried water" Jos. St. 60, 14; ܘܐܠܘ ܠܐ ܡܕܒܪܢܘܬܐ ܕܐܠܗܐ ܚܕܝܪܐ ܗܘܬ ܠܗ ܠܥܠܡܐ "and had not the protection of God embraced the world" Jos. St. 4, 14; ܣܡܝܐ ܕܐܬܘ ܟܕ ܕܒܝܪܝܢ ܠܗܘܢ "blind people who came, as they led them" Sim. 346 *ad inf.*; ܦܬܝܚܘܬ ܐܦܐ ܩܢܐ ܗܘܐ "candour [literally "openness of countenance"] he possessed" Anc. Doc. 90, 25; ܐܣܝܪ ܗܘܐ ܚܨܐ ܕܡܫܟܐ "he was girt with a girdle of a skin" Mark 1, 6, cf. Rev. 15, 6. Several examples are found in Philox., Epist. (Guidi) fol. 28*b* &c. Cf. also ܟܢܝܫ ܡܝܐ, pl. ܟܢܝܫܝ ܡܝܐ "having gathered water" = "dropsical" Luke 14, 2; Land IV, 87, 9; Geoponici 95, 2 &c.

---

(1) Just as this word is in a certain sense an Active Part. Peal, so also may the like be predicated of the Verbal Adjectives dealt with in § 118, *e. g.* ܐܬܐ "come", ܡܝܬ "dead, died"; ܝܬܝܒ "having seated oneself" = "sitting" &c. Similarly ܥܡܝܪ "dwelling", Part. Perf. of ܥܡܪ "to settle".

These words, however, may also be used in a true passive sense, *e. g.* ܢܣܝܼܒ "taken"; ܢܓܝܼܕ "pulled, torn away".

PARTICIPLES USED AS NOUNS.

§ 281. We disregard in this place such participles (Peal act.) as have become nouns completely, like ܪܳܚܡܳܐ "friend", ܪܳܥܝܳܐ "shepherd", ܘܓܳܕܘܿܫܬ and ܓܳܡܕܳܐ ἡ οἰκουμένη, ܩܝܳܡܬܳܐ "a pillar", ܦܳܪܚܬܳܐ "a bird", ܝܰܥܒܳܐ "herb", ܝܳܐܶܒ ὁ τὸ πρέπον &c. *As Pure Substantives.*

§ 282. A. The Part. Act. of the Peal may be employed in the Constr. State and with possessive suffixes, while the object is set in genitive connection, contrived sometimes by means of ܠ:—prepositions too may at times come after the Part. in the Constr. St. (§ 206): ܩܳܒܹܕ *Act. Participle of the Peal. Nomen agentis of the Peal.* ܡܥܩܕ "he who concludes the covenants" Aphr. 214, 14; ܣܳܐܶܡ ܢܳܡܘܿܣܳܐ "lawgiver" frequently; ܐܳܟܶܠ ܠܰܚܡܝ "he who eats my bread" Ps. 41, 9; ܐܳܘ ܗܳܝ ܕܡܳܝܬܳܐ ܡܘܿܬܳܐ ܣܢܹܐ "O thou who diest an evil death!" Mart. I, 180 *inf.*; ܬܳܒܰܥ ܡܚܝܼܒܘ ܕܝܼܢܳܐ "Justice which demanded doom" Aphr. 462, 5; ܡܳܠܟܬܳܐ ܡܰܢܩܬܐ "she who gave hateful advice" Aphr. 110, 10; ܕܳܚܠܰܝ ܫܡܳܟ "those who fear thy name" Ps. 61, 5; ܪܳܚܡܰܝ ܣܳܐܡܳܐ "lovers of money,—covetous persons" Ov. 190, 2; ܐܳܟܠܰܝ ܒܣܪܳܐ "are flesh-eaters" Spic. 7, 15; ܐܳܟܠܰܝ ܥܶܣܒܳܐ ܐܝܟ "are grass-eaters (f.)" *ibid.* 16.—ܪܳܚܡܰܝ ܡܫܝܼܚܳܐ φιλό-χριστος frequently; ܩܰܕܝܼܫܘܬܳܟ ܪܳܚܡܰܬ ܠܰܐܠܳܗܳܐ "thy God-loving holiness" Jos. St. 1, 1; ܡܳܩܪܝ ܩܰܪܢܳܬܳܐ "trumpeters" Aphr. 260, 4 = ܡܰܩܪܝܼ ܩܰܪܢܳܐ Aphr. 147, 13; ܢܳܓܒܰܝ ܠܰܐܒܕܳܢܳܐ "who lead to destruction" Aphr. 271 *ult.*; ܕܚܝܼܨܝ ܠܰܩܪܳܒܐ "those who rush into the fight" Aphr. 149, 18; ܒܳܢܝܼ ܝܰܠ ܚܳܠܳܐ "who build an edifice upon the sand" Aphr. 285, 9 (where the governing power continues notwithstanding the construct state, the object being placed at the end); ܪܳܚܡܰܝ ܠܰܡܫܝܼܚܳܐ "who love Christ in everything" John van Tella (Kleyn) 3, 8; 11, 9 (same form).— ܪܳܟܒܗ "his rider" Ps. 33, 17; ܕܳܚܠܰܘܗܝ "those who fear him" frequently; ܚܳܙܝܰܝܟ "those who see thee" Is. 14, 16 &c. The connection with suffixes is less frequent, it is true, and it is confined more to special words.

Only a few of these Active Participles can farther be used attributively, *e. g.* ܪܘܼܚܳܐ ܕܛܳܥܝܳܐ "an erring spirit" Is. 19, 14; ܗܘܰܬ ܗܳܘܝܳܐ ܡܰܛܥܝܳܐ

☞ p. 357

"is a devouring fire" Deut. 4, 24; 9, 3; Heb. 12, 29; ܢܽܘܪܳܐ ܝܳܩܶܕܬܳܐ "a burning fire" Daniel 3, several times; ܦܬܟܪ̈ܐ ܥܒ̈ܝܕܐ ܘܟܕ̈ܒܐ "idols fashioned and false" Anc. Doc. 42, 22. Thus too ܣܳܟܠܳܐ, f. ܣܳܟܠܬܳܐ "foolish"; ܡܣܰܦܩܳܐ "sufficient", "dexterous"; ܦܳܐܝܳܐ "fitting".[1]

B. For all those uses in which the Participle but rarely appears, the *Nomen agentis* comes in: ܦܳܪܽܘܩܳܟ "thy redeemer" Ps. 35, 3; ܡܥܰܕܪܳܢܶܗ "his helper" Ps. 10, 14; ܫܳܠܽܘܚܶܗ "he who sent him" Aphr. 289, 8; ܬܰܪܣܶܝܢ ܠܐܳܟܽܘܠܬܟܶܝܢ "nourish ye that (f.) which devours you"[2] Mart. I, 194, 10 &c. Thus in particular, as independent substantive, and as attribute ܢܳܛܽܘܪܳܐ "watchman" &c.

☞ p. 358

Other Active Participles, and *Nomina Ag.*

§ 283. **A.** The Part. Act. of the other Verbal classes [Conjugations] is also employed in the constr. st. On the other hand it seldom appears with possessive suffixes: ܡܰܘܠܶܕ ܟܽܠ "he who produces everything" Ephr. (Lamy) II, 247, 3; ܡܒܰܛܶܠ ܠܘܽܛܬܶܗ "who makes his cursing ineffective" Aphr. 236 *ult.*; ܡܩܰܪܶܒ ܨܠܰܘ̈ܳܬܳܐ "who offers prayers" Aphr. 66, 17; ܡܶܠܚܳܐ ܡܦܰܪܶܟ ܠܡܰܣܝܽܘܬܳܐ "salt, that breaks up rottenness" Aphr. 485, 16; ܬܰܪܣܳܐ ܡܩܰܒܶܠ ܓܶܐܪ̈ܶܐ "the shield which intercepts the arrows" Aphr. 44, 2;

☞ p. 358

ܡܩܰܒܠܺܝܢ ܟܣܳܦܳܐ "those who accept money" Aphr. 260, 16; ܡܚܰܘܶܝܢ ܝܽܘܬܪܳܢܳܐ "who exhibit a profit" Aphr. 287, 2; ܢܶܫ̈ܶܐ . . . ܡܫܰܥܒܕܳܢ ܠܒܰܥܠܰܝܗܶܝܢ "women, who subjugate their husbands" Spic. 15, 19; ܚܰܫ̈ܶܐ ܡܚܺܝܠܶܐ ܡܟܰܒܫܺܝܢ ܓܰܢܒܳܪ̈ܶܐ ܬܚܶܝܬ ܢܺܝܪܳܐ ܩܰܫܝܳܐ ܕܣܽܘܢܩܳܢܗܽܘܢ "weak passions that yet subdue heroes under the hard yoke of the need of them" Ov. 182, 18.—ܡܣܰܪܗܒܺܝܢ ܠܥܰܡܗܽܘܢ ܪܗܺܝܒܳܐܺܝܬ "who urge on their people hurriedly" Mart. I, 16, 6; ܡܬܟܰܬܫܺܝܢ ܒܚܰܝܠܗܽܘܢ "those who fight vigorously (with all their might)" Moes. II, 75, 5; Mart. I, 159 mid.; ܡܬܠܰܒܒܺܝܢ ܒܪܳܡܽܘܬܳܐ "who are strong in pride" Aphr. 430 *ult.* (cf. Is. 13, 3); ܡܶܫܚܳܐ ܡܰܚܶܐ ܠܠܰܐܝ̈ܶܐ "oil, that revives the wearied ones" Ephr. (Lamy) II, 179, 4 &c.

☞ p. 358

☞ p. 358

(1) Notice that Abstract Nouns in ܘܬܐ, Relative Adjectives in ܝ— and Adverbs in ܐܝܬ— can be formed from those Active Participles only which are also used as Adj. or Subst.

(2) Or ܠܐܟܽܘܠܬܟܶܝܢ without *a* (§ 145 F.)?

A very few of these Participles occur, besides, as attributive adjectives, and as substantives. Thus ܡܳܐܢ̈ܶܐ ܡܫܰܒ݂ܚ̈ܶܐ "splendid vestments", Anc. Doc. 42, 9, and elsewhere ܡܫܰܒ݂ܚ̈ܶܐ; frequently ܡܗܰܝܡܢܳܐ "faithful" (of which the fem. emph. state ܡܗܰܝܡܰܢܬܳܐ shows by the *a*, that it is no longer regarded as a Part. Act.; so is it too with ܡܶܝܢܰܩܬܳܐ "a wet nurse", and others which have become substantives). ☞ p. 358

Rem. Quite unique is the instance ܒ̈ܬܘܠܳܬܳܐ ܢܰܟ̈ܦܳܬܳܐ ܡܚܰܕ̈ܝܳܢܝܳܬܳܐ ܗ̱ܘ̈ܝ ܠܶܟ݂ܝ ܟܽܠ ܝܘܡ "the wise maidens gladdened thee daily" Ephr. III, 344 E, where in spite of the emph. st.,—in itself singular indeed in more respects than one, the power of governing remains. In prose it could be nothing but ܡܚܰܕ̈ܝܳܢ.

B. The *Nomen agentis* is, on the other hand, very extensively employed here: ܡܚܰܕ݁ܬ݂ܳܢܳܐ "the restorer" often; ܡܫܰܬ݂ܣܳܢ̈ܶܐ ܕܥܺܕ̈ܳܬ݂ܳܐ "founders of churches" Jul. 125, 27 (immediately beside ܘܡܣܰܡܟ݂ܳܢܰܝ̈ ܐܽܪܬܳܕ݁ܽܘܟ݂ܣܺܝܰܐ "and upholders of orthodoxy"); ܡܣܰܡܟ݂ܳܢܶܗ ܕܟ݂ܪܶܣܛܝܳܢܽܘܬ݂ܳܐ "upholder of Christianity" *ibid.* 126, 5; ܡܥܰܕ݂ܪ̈ܳܢܰܝ "my helpers" Ps. 3, 3; ܡܬܰܪܣܝܳܢܰܢ "who nourishes us" Ps. 84, 12; ܡܚܰܪܒ݂ܳܢܗܽܘܢ "he who destroys them" Aphr. 452, 13; ܡܚܰܪܒ݂ܳܢܺܝܬ݂ܶܗ "she who destroys him" Aphr. 47, 1; ܡܕܰܒ݁ܪ̈ܳܢܰܝܟ݂ܽܘܢ *τῶν ἡγουμένων ὑμῶν* Heb. 13, 7; ܡܫܬ݁ܰܡܥܳܢܰܝ̈ܗ̇ "those who are obedient to her" Aphr. 47, 2 &c. But the *Nomen Agentis* does not take the Constr. St. before the substantive expressing the object.(1) The *Nomina Ag.* of reflexives of passive meaning are on the whole used rather as adjectives in the sense of "capable of . . . ".

§ 284. Passive Participles are employed both as substantives and adjectives. They may be followed by a genitive as Subject or Object, and may even stand in the Construct State before prepositions; ܒܪ̈ܺܝܟ݂ܰܘܗ̱ܝ ܕܡܳܪܝܳܐ . . . ܠܝ̈ܺܛܰܘܗ̱ܝ "they that be blessed of the Lord . . . they that be cursed of him" Ps. 37, 22; ܡܠܰܦ̈ܝ ܩܪܳܒ݂ܳܐ "expert in war" Cantic. 3, 8; ܚܣܺܝ̈ܠܝ ܪ̈ܓ݂ܺܝܓ݂ܳܬ݂ܳܐ "who are weaned from pleasures" Aphr. 260, 8; ܡܐܰܣܪ̈ܝ ܒܽܘܨܳܐ ܘܡܨܰܒ̈ܬܝ ܒܐܰܪܓ݁ܘܳܢܳܐ "they who are girded about with byssus and adorned

Passive Participles.

(1) In ܡܫܰܬ݂ܣܳܢ̈ܶܐ ܕܥܺܕ̈ܳܬ݂ܳܐ ܘܡܣܰܡܟ݂ܳܢܰܝ̈ ܐܽܪܬܳܕ݁ܽܘܟ݂ܣܺܝܰܐ "founders of churches and upholders of orthodoxy" Jul. 125, 27 and ܡܣܰܡܟ݂ܳܢܶܗ ܕܟ݂ܪܶܣܛܝܳܢܽܘܬ݂ܳܐ "upholder of Christianity" *ibid.* 126, 5, the Constr. St. of the *nomen agentis* is plainly avoided.

with purple" Aphr. 261, 9; ܡܬܝܠܕܝܢ ܡܢ ܡܝܐ "those who are born of water" Aphr. 287, 16 &c. Farther ܡܠܦܝ ܕܐܠܗܐ "taught of God" Aphr. 293, 17; ܡܐܢܐ ܡܨܒܬܐ "garments adorned" Anc. Doc. 42, 9; ܨܠܘܬܗ ܡܫܡܥܬܐ "a prayer accepted (heard)" Aphr. 454, 19 &c. Other constructions, however, are preferred to this employment of the Pass. Part. as a Noun, except in the case of a few words.

Some of the participles mentioned in § 280 are of common occurrence in the Constr. St., *e. g.* ܫܩܝܠܝ ܢܝܪܐ "those, who bear the yoke" Aphr. 260, 20; ܐܚܝܕܝ ܩܠܝܕܐ "those who hold the keys" Aphr. 260, 7 &c.

IMPERATIVE.

Imperative. § 285. The Imperative mood cannot be used with a negative: ܩܛܘܠ "kill", but ܠܐ ܬܩܛܘܠ "do not kill" (§ 266).

We have one instance of a dependent Impt. in ܡܛܠ ܕܥ ܘܚܙܝ "for (properly "because") know and see" Mart. I, 160, 20. But this is at bottom an anacoluthon.

INFINITIVE.

Infinitive. § 286. Where the Inf. is not the Object Absolute (on this point v. § 295), it must always have ܠ before *it*. This preposition gives to the Inf. the sense of direction, of purpose, &c.; ܘܫܪܝܘ ܗܘܘ ܠܡܡܠܠܘ ἤρξαντο λαλεῖν Acts 2, 4; ܟܕ ܠܡܨܠܝܘ ܐܬܝܢ ܗܘܝ "while they (f.) came to pray" Aphr. 112, 12; ܘܟܕ ܣܦܣܪܐ ܠܡܚܪܒܘ ܦܘܩܕܢܐ "and while the sword receives the command to destroy" Aphr. 451, 4; ܠܐ ܫܗܝ ܠܗܘܢ ܠܡܬܦܪܢܣܘ "they did not fail to make provision for themselves" Aphr. 452, 9; ܕܚܣܝܪܐ ܠܗ ܡܝܐ ܠܡܫܬܐ "which is in want of water to drink" Aphr. 199, 1; ܥܬܝܕ ܠܡܥܒܕ "*dispositus ad faciendum*", "*facturus*";
☞ p. 358 ܡܙܥܩ ܗܘܐ . . . ܠܡܬܢܙܪܘ "he cried out . . ., that they should abstain" Ov. 179, 17; ܫܘܐ ܗܘ ܠܡܬܩܒܠܘܬܗ "it is worthy to be received" Aphr. 103, 1 &c. This signification gradually passes over to that of the Object; thus after verbs like "to wish", "to be able" &c.: ܒܥܘ ܠܡܐܚܕܗ ζητοῦντες αὐτὸν κρατῆσαι Matt. 21, 46 P. S. (C. ܒܥܘ ܗܘܘ ܕܢܐܚܕܘܢܗ); ܠܐ ܡܫܟܚܝܢ ܠܡܬܐܣܝܘ "cannot be healed" Aphr. 136, 4 (line 8 ܠܐ ܡܫܟܚܝܢ ܕܢܬܐܣܘܢ);

ܐܢܐ ܡܢ ܝܕܥ "how can I know?" Ov. 163, 2; ܡܓܡܠܦ "ye have neglected to go" Jul. 123, 5; ܡܢ ... ܠܡܒܢܐ "began to build" Jos. St. 24, 11; ܘܠܐ ܐܘܣܦ ܘܐܬ ܠ "and no longer continued to seek her" Jul. 98, 11 &c.

Thus too the Inf. with ܠ, as a kind of epexegesis which specifies direction, represents even the Subject. Compare "it still remains appointed for Israel, to be brought together" Aphr. 359, 3; 367, 5 (367, 11); "it is not possible for Israel yet to be brought together" Aphr. 359, 7; τί με δεῖ ποιεῖν Acts 16, 30, and many other instances. Cf. § 254 C.

In all these cases the Inf. with ܠ might be replaced by the finite verb with ܕ: Compare, besides the examples already given, "he is able to love, and to bless, and to speak the truth, and to pray for what is good" [last member of sentence being in finite form] Spic. 5, 11 &c. There are even rare instances of a blending of both constructions, namely ܕ and thereafter ܠ with the Inf.: ὅτι δύναται ὁ θεὸς ἐκ τῶν λίθων τούτων ἐγεῖραι τέκνα Luke 3, 8 C. (where P. merely has , and S. ...ܕ);

"if thou desirest to learn these things with diligence" Spic. 48, 16; "he dared to do this on the first day of the week" Apost. Apocr. 197 ult.(1)

Of necessity ܕ must be prefixed to ܠ when the Inf. depends on a ☞ p. 358 farther preposition (almost always ܡܢ; cf. § 249 E): "deliver me from seeing thee" Mart. I, 126, 10; "that one is saved from observing" Aphr, 22, 18; "it is easier to do good than to keep from evil" Spic. 6, 10 &c. More frequent is the form ... "he did not cease to teach" Ephr. III, XXXIII ult. (or the completely

(1) However little I am disposed to guarantee the integrity of the individual passages, the instances are so numerous, that the idiom must be recognised.

verbal form ܡܫܬܠܠ ܡܢ ܕܠܐ ܢܓܢܘܒ "too weak to keep from stealing" Spic. 5, 7).

With ܐܝܬ or ܗܘܐ the Inf. denotes an Obligation, Necessity, or even Ability: ܐܝܬ ܠܝ ܠܡܐܡܪ "I have to say" frequently; ܐܢ ܢܗܘܐ ܠܡܡܬ ܥܡܟ κἂν δέῃ με σὺν σοὶ ἀποθανεῖν Matt. 26, 35; ܐܝܬ ܠܡܐܠܦܘ "must be
☞ p. 358 learned" Ov. 63, 24; ܠܝܬ ܠܡܐܡܪ "cannot be told" Aphr. 496, 3 &c.
☞ p. 358 Sometimes the Inf. with ܠ is sufficient of itself in such cases: ܗܕܐ ܠܡܬܕܡܪܘ ܒܗ ἐν τούτῳ γὰρ τὸ θαυμαστόν ἐστιν John 9, 30 S. (P. ܗܕܐ ܗܘ ܕܝܢ ܠܡܬܕ'); ܠܐ ܠܡܬܕܡܪܘ ܥܠ ܓܢܒܐ ܕܡܬܐܚܕ "we need not wonder at him who is caught" Prov. 6, 30; ܠܡܬܗܪܘ ܕܝܢ ܘܠܡܬܕܡܪܘ ܒܗܢܐ ܣܒܐ "but we must feel amazement and wonder at this old man" Jul. 4, 10 (and frequently thus); ܠܡܚܕܐ ܗܟܝܠ ܘܠܡܪܘܙ "we must therefore rejoice and exult" Jul. 9, 7; ܐܝܟ ܚܠܡܐ ܠܡܫܬܪܝܘ ܠܗܘܢ "they must dissolve like a dream" Spic. 44, 1; ܠܐ ܠܡܡܛܐ ܓܝܪ ܪܘܡܗ "it is impossible to reach its height" Ephr. (Lamy) I, 645, Str. 15; ܟܡܐ ܠܝ ܠܡܟܬܒ ܦܘܩܕܢܐ "how many commands have I to write" *ibid.* 303, 11 &c.

In very rare instances a Subject is attached to the Inf. with ܠ, as if it were a finite verb, as in ܠܡܣܚܘ ܒܗܘܢ ܟܗܢܐ ܐܝܕܝܗܘܢ "that the priests may wash their hands therein" 2 Chr. 4, 6; cf. ܘܕܗܕܐ ܠܡܗܘܐ ܒܓܠܝܐ ܐܝܕܐ ܙܒܢܐ ܠܐ ܝܗܒ ܠܗ "and that this should happen publicly, fate did not grant him" Ov. 201, 2; ܐܚܐ ܠܡܣܓܕܘ ܠܟ ܩܫܝܐ ܗܝ "that the brethren should do homage to thee is a hard thing" Joseph 9, 6.

Rem. On the Inf. with Obj. v. § 293 *sq.*; on the Inf. Abs. § 295 *sqq.*

C. GOVERNMENT OF THE VERB.

Object expressed by the Personal Pronoun.

§ 287. Syriac has no thorough-going mode of designating the Object. (1) It is only in the case of the Personal Pronoun that the language possesses unequivocal Object-forms, and these are affixed to the finite

---

☞ p. 358 (1) For the Hebrew את, the Targum has the corresponding יָת. This ancient Objective mark ܝܬ is found in the O. T. about a dozen times. That the word was still known in some measure to the Edessans at the time of translating the O. T. we may conclude, from its employment in the ancient Gnostic (Bardesanic?) Hymn

verb. Occasionally, however, this method of indicating the Object is exchanged for another,—that, namely, which is contrived by ܠ, followed by the Pron. Suff.—It is true it is a less exact method than the former, because it serves other purposes besides. Examples: ܢܫܢܩ ܠܢ "he may torture us" Joseph 204, 4 [Ov. 300, 12]; ܩܒܠ ܠܢ "has received us" *ibid.* 194, 13 [Ov. 295, 15]; ܙܟܝܬ ܠܗܘܢ "I have conquered them" Mart. II, 233, 1 (Jac. Sar.); ܦܠܛܘ ܠܝ "have escaped (3 pl.) me" Ephr. Nis. p. 62 v. 83 &c. We have the form set before the verb in ܘܠܝ ܝܩܪܬܘܢ "and me ye have honoured" Ov. 141, 17 (var. ܘܝܩܪܬܘܢܢܝ); ܘܠܟܘܢ ܥܒܕܬ ܓܢܒܐ "and I made you thieves" Joseph 220, 4 [Ov. 308, 17]; ܘܠܝ ܙܘܚܘ "and accompany me (to the grave)" Ov. 142, 23 (var. otherwise) &c. With the Participle, however, which does not take Object Suffixes, the personal pronoun as Object, is of necessity denoted by ܠ, when the combination proper to Nouns is not preferred (§ 281).

Object designated by means of ܠ in the case of Determined Substantives.

§ 288. A. The ܠ serves besides as a means of indicating a Definite Object. The Determination is more emphatic when the Object Suffix, answering to the Substantive, is, besides, added to the verb. In the latter case the ܠ may even be omitted. The personal pronoun may be still more emphasised (§ 225 B); or it may be construed like an independent noun. Typical cases may be given thus:—

(a) Without Determination [Indefinite Object]: "he has built *a* house" ܒܢܐ ܒܝܬܐ or ܒܝܬܐ ܒܢܐ (there being no Object-sign).

(b) With Determination [Definite Object]: "he has built *the* house":

(1) ܒܢܐ ܒܝܬܐ or ܒܝܬܐ ܒܢܐ (without any Object-sign, just as in *a*).

(2) ܒܢܐ ܠܒܝܬܐ or ܠܒܝܬܐ ܒܢܐ.

(3) ܒܢܝܗܝ ܠܒܝܬܐ or ܠܒܝܬܐ ܒܢܝܗܝ.

(4) ܒܢܝܗܝ ܒܝܬܐ or ܒܝܬܐ ܒܢܝܗܝ.

In the case of the Part. taking the place of the finite Verb, ܠ with possessive suffix is used instead of the object-suffix; thus in our example ܒܢܐ ܠܗ is the regular equivalent of ܒܢܝܗܝ.

---

in the Apost. Apocr. 279, 7 (ܢܣܒ ܝܬܝ "he took me"). It was completely obsolete in the 4th century. The reflexive use of ܝܬ (§ 223) is quite distinct from this.

A few examples may suffice for all these cases:

(a) ܘܐܣܪܝܢ ܡܘܒܠܐ ܝܩܝܪܬܐ δεσμεύουσιν δὲ φορτία βαρέα Matt. 23, 4; ܐܚܝ ܠܬܠܬܐ ܡܝܬܐ "he raised three dead persons to life" Aphr. 165, 14; ܒܠܚܘܕ܆ ܢܓܝܪܘܬ ܪܘܚܐ ܘܡܣܝܒܪܢܘܬܐ ܩܢܝ "only acquire thou forbearance and patience" Sim. 270 *ad inf.*

(b) (1) ܕܠܐ ܝܕܥܝܢ ܐܢܬܘܢ ܟܬܒܐ ܘܠܐ ܚܝܠܗ ܕܐܠܗܐ μὴ εἰδότες τὰς γραφὰς μηδὲ τὴν δύναμιν τοῦ θεοῦ Matt. 22, 29; ܡܢ ܕܡܩܒܠ ܠܗ ܪܘܚܗ ܕܡܫܝܚܐ "he who receives the spirit of Christ" Aphr. 108, 3; ܠܐ ܚܙܘ ܢܘܗܪܗ "they have not seen his light" Aphr. 15, 13; ܢܨܒܬ ܒܪܢܫܗ ܓܘܝܐ "let him adorn his inner man" Aphr. 108, 4; ܠܢܨܝܒܝܢ ܠܝ ܡܗܦܟܬ "thou restorest Nisibis to me" Jos. St. 17, 3; ܩܘܪܝܗ ܙܒܢ ܐܢܘܢ "his villages he sold" Ov. 166, 14; ܐܓܪܬܟ ܚܒܝܒܝ ܩܒܠܬܗ "thy letter, (my) beloved, I have received" Aphr. 6, 1; ܗܠܝܢ ܗܘܐ ܠܬܠܬ ܪܘܚܐ ܐܚܝܕ ܗܘܐ "these three winds he held" Aphr. 93, 9.

(2) ܐܫܟܚܗ ܠܦܝܠܝܦܘܣ εὑρίσκει Φίλιππον John 1, 43; ܡܢ ܕܡܟܪܐ ܠܗ ܠܪܘܚܗ ܕܡܫܝܚܐ "he who grieves the spirit of Christ" Aphr. 108, 5; ܫܒܩܬܘܢ ܠܗ ܠܒܪܘܝܐ "ye have forsaken the Creator" Mart. I, 124 *inf.*; ܕܢܚܪܒܝܗ ܠܐܘܪܫܠܡ "that he may ruin Jerusalem" Aphr. 249, 16; ܘܝܘܚܢܢ ܚܙܐ ܠܫܡܝܐ ܟܕ ܦܬܝܚܝܢ "and John saw heaven opened" Aphr. 124, 2 (immediately after ܐܠܝܐ ܦܬܚ ܫܡܝܐ "Elijah opened heaven"); ܘܐܡܪܐ ܕܡܪܥܝܬܟ ܢܟܣ ܐܢܬ "and the lambs of thy flock thou slayest" Mart. I, 125 mid. (and parallel to it ܘܥܢܐ ܕܡܪܥܝܬܟ ܡܚܒܠ ܐܢܬ "and the sheep of thy flock thou destroyest"); ܠܥܠܡܐ ܐܫܒܩܝܘܗܝ "the world will I forsake" Ov. 164, 22 &c. Compare ܠܗܘܢ ܕܝܠܗܘܢ ܐܟܠܬ ܫܠܗܒܝܬܐ "*them* the flame devoured" Aphr. 183, 19.

(3) ܕܒܪܘܗܝ ܠܝܫܘܥ ܠܦܪܛܘܪܝܢ παραλαβόντες τὸν Ἰησοῦν εἰς τὸ πραιτόριον Matt. 27, 27; ܘܚܕܪܘܗܝ ܠܒܝܬܗ ܘܐܣܪܘܗܝ ܠܗ "and they surrounded his house and took him prisoner" Mart. I, 123 (and then ܘܒܙܘ ܒܝܬܗ "and plundered his house"); ܩܒܠܘܗ ܠܓܙܘܪܬܐ "have received circumcision" Aphr. 210, 1; ܡܚܐ ܐܢܝܢ ܠܚܡܫܬܝܗܝܢ "smote all the five (f.)" Mart. I, 126 mid.; ܗܘ ܕܡܩܕܫ ܠܗ ܠܕܗܒܐ ὁ ἁγιάσας τὸν χρυσόν Matt. 23, 17; ܡܚܢܦ ܗܘܐ ܠܗܘܢ ܛܪܘܢܐ ܠܒܢܝ ܩܘܣܛܢܛܝܢܘܦܘܠܝܣ "the tyrant flattered the inhabitants of Constantinople" Jul. 99, 21; ܟܕ ܐܚܝܕܝܢ ܗܘܘ ܠܗ ܠܐܓܪܬܐ ܗܕܐ ܐܘܪܗܝܐ "the people of Edessa held this letter

in very great regard" Jul. 125, 18; ܐܝܙܒܠ ܪܕܦܬܗ ܠܐܠܝܐ "Jezebel persecuted Elijah" Aphr. 123, 18; ܘܠܟܠܗܝܢ ܛܟ̈ܣܐ ܕܢܩ̈ܒܬܐ ܙܗܪ ܗܘܐ ܠܗܝܢ "and he warned the whole of the female orders" Ov. 177, 7; ܐܘܦ ܠܟܗ̈ܢܐ ܦܩܕ ܐܢܘܢ "and he likewise commanded the priests" Aphr. 112, 13 &c. Cf. farther ܚܙܐܘܗܝ ܠܗ ܠܗܘ ܡܫܡܫܢܐ "they saw that deacon" Sim. 294, 4; ܕܒܪ ܐܢܘܢ ܠܗܘܢ ܠܗܠܝܢ "he took these" Jul. 72, 21 (a similar construction occurs often); ܐܟܠܬ ܐܢܘܢ ܠܗܘܢ "it (f.) devoured them" Aphr. 62, 7; ܘܦܪܩܬܟܘܢ ܡܢ ܡܘܬܐ ܠܬܠܬܝܟܘܢ "and I rescue from death all three of you" Mart. I, 56, 13; ܐܘܦ ܠܗܘܢ ܐܦܩ ܐܢܘܢ "he also brought them out" Mart. I, 32 mid., as also ܘܠܝ ܦܩܕܢܝ ܡܪܝܐ "and the Lord commanded me" Deut. 4, 14.

(4) ܫܒܩܗ̇ ܐܢܬܬܗ ܠܐܚܘܗܝ *ἀφῆκεν τὴν γυναῖκα αὐτοῦ τῷ ἀδελφῷ αὐτοῦ* Matt. 22, 25 P. (different in C. and S.); ܫܕܝܗܝ ܟܣܦܐ *ῥίψας τὰ ἀργύρια* Matt. 27, 5; ܫܕܝܬܗ ܥܦܪܗ "I threw the dust of it (m.) away" Deut. 9, 21; ܫܚܠܦ ܐܢܝܢ ܐܝ̈ܕܘܗܝ "changed his hands" Gen. 48, 14; ܟܕ ܐܡܪܗ̇ ܗܕܐ ܡܠܬܐ "when he uttered this word" Aphr. 420, 18; ܣܟܪܗ ܦܘܡܝ "closed my mouth" Ephr. Nis. p. 57 v. 73; ܕܢܣܒ ܐܢܝܢ ܡ̈ܢܘܬܐ ܗܠܝܢ ܟܠܗܝܢ "that he take all these parts" Ov. 71, 10; ܡܚܐ ܐܢܝܢ ܐܦ̈ܘܗܝ ܥܠ ܐܪܥܐ "cast his face upon the earth" Jul. 131, 3; ܕܡܗ ܠܚܟܘܗܝ ܟܠ̈ܒܐ "the dogs licked his blood" Aphr. 183, 16; ܟܠܗܘܢ ܪ̈ܗܒܘܢܐ ܫܡܠܝܗܘܢ ܒܢܦܫܗ ܐܢܘܢ "all pledges he had fulfilled in himself" Aphr. 459, 19; ܩܫܝܘܬܐ ܠܐ ܝܕܥܝܢ ܠܗ̇ "stubbornness they know not" Aphr. 177 *ult.* &c. The fourth method, however, is far less frequently used than the others, at least when the object follows the verb, though it is still common enough.

The 3rd and 4th methods are combined in ܗܢܘܢ ܕܝܢ ܗܠܝܢ ܐܢܫ̈ܐ ܡܗܝܡ̈ܢܐ ܟܕ . . . ܠܗܘܢ ܠܗܢܘܢ ܚܛܦ ܐܢܘܢ ܛܢܢܐ ܐܠܗܝܐ "but when a godlike zeal . . . carried away these believing ones" Jul. 138, 1: we have here at the same time another instance of the drawling accumulation of demonstratives and personal pronouns, which occurs not seldom, though it is avoided by some writers.

B. In most cases complete uncertainty prevails as to the selection or rejection of a mark to indicate the object when definite, as several of the foregoing examples already show; cf. farther: ܐܫܟܚܘܗ̇ ܠܡܥܪܬܐ "they have profaned the sabbath" Aphr. 242, 16, 18, by the side of ﻣﻌﺰﻩ ﻣﺤﺠ﮺ "have put away the sabbath" *ibid.* 17 (twice); ὅτι κληρονομήσουσι τὴν γῆν Matt. 5, 5 ﻟﺍﺭﺧﺎ ﺑﻠﻓﻠﻮﺑﻨ S., ﻟﻧﺨﺎ ﻭﻣﺒﺲ C., ﺑﻠﺍﻭﻣﺒﺲ ﻟﻓﺤﻞ, ﻭﻩ 'ﺑﻠﺍﻟﻪ P. (like Is. 60, 21), cf. Aphr. 41, 10; ἀνασείει τὸν λαόν Luke 23, 5 ﺟﻔﻨﺍ ﻟﺭﺟﻪ C. S., ﻟﺤﺒﻲ ﻣﻪ ﺑﻲ P. Still, it is usual to have some mark when the object designates a named *Person*; and cases like ﻟﺨﺜﺪ ﺑﺴﻌﻔﺪ "shall I reckon Habib?" Anc. Doc. 87, 3 are comparatively rare. On the other hand, the object-mark is mostly omitted in the case of Common Nouns with reflex suffixes, *e. g.* ﻣﺤﻘﺴﻲ ﻟ ﺑﻤﺘﻨﺳﻲﻩ οὐ νίπτονται τὰς χεῖρας Matt. 15, 2; ﺩﻣﺤﻤﻪ ﻣﺮﺗﻨﻤﻲﻩ ἀφέντες τὰ δίκτυα Mark 1, 18; ﺟﺰﻣﻬﻲ ﺑﻤﻌﻮﻥ, ﻣﻠﺤﺠﻪ ﻭﻗﺘﻮﻣﻪ ﺑﻤﻌﻮﻥ ἆρον τὸν κράβατόν σου Mark 2, 9 *sq.*; "they spread out their wings and raised their heads" Sim. 272, 1; ﻣﻌﻞ ﺑﻤﺘﻮﺟﻪ "he stretched out his hands" Aphr. 18, 17 (and then ﻭﺭﻓﻞ ﻟﺤﻤﺨﺪﻡ "and conquered Amalek", with ﺑﺲ, as being a proper name) &c., and thus, frequently ﺑﻤﻌﻲﻩ ﻭﻣﺤﺎ "*se ipsum*" (compare ﻟﻠﺤﺠﻪ ﻭﻟﺜﺪ ﺑﻤﻌﻴﻪ "and hated himself and loved God" Ov. 168, 10), although cases like ﻟﺨﻤﻌﻴﻪ ﺣﺴﺰ ﻓﻠﻨﻪ "for he judged himself" Ov. 171, 24 do occur.

C. Demonstratives and Interrogatives in the Objective case are sometimes furnished with ﺑﺲ, and sometimes not: ﻓﺤﺩﻧﻲ ﻭﻓﺤﻲ ﺷﻠﻌﻠﺎﻥ βλέπετε ταῦτα πάντα Matt. 24, 2; ﻣﺤﺠﻲ ﻓﻘﻤﺰﻟﺎ ﻭﻓﺤﻲ "these commandments we have received" Aphr. 484, 14; ﺑﺴﺰﻩ . . . ﻭﻫﻮ ﻟﻠﺎ "saw (3rd pl.) this sign" Sim. 273 *inf.*; ﻭ ﻭﻫﻮ "*eum, qui*" Ov. 175, 26, but ﻭ ﻟﺤﺨﻮ Aphr. 48, 2; ﺟﻢ ﺑﻪﻭﻩ ﻣﻌﺠﻮ "when he heard this" Jos. St. 55, 14; ﺑﻤﺤﻘﺴﻪ ﻧﻘﺎﻝ ﻟﺤﻮﺟﻲ "these fishes they collect" Sim. 274, 1; ﻟﻠﺤﺠﻲ ﻭ "*eos, qui*" Ov. 211, 2 and elsewhere; ﻟﺤﺠﻲ ﻭ *ibid.* 214, 7 and elsewhere. So too ﻟﺤﺤﺠﻢ ﻭ "that which" Aphr. 126, 20, and even ﻭﻟﺘﺰﻟﻪ ﻟﻨﺖ ﻣﻪﻭﻣﺐ ﻟﺤﺤﺰﻡ ﺗﺴﻌﻤﺪﺍﻟﺴﺰﻩ "set before me, brethren, whatever ye have vowed" Ov. 141, 8, but ﻓﺤﺰﻡ ﻭ (Object) Aphr. 145, 13, and thus usually. With ﻟﻟﺎﻟﻪ (ﻓﺤﺪﻭﻥ, ﻭ ﻓﻠﺎ &c.)

☞ p. 358 ﺑﺲ preponderates, it is true, but on the other hand it may be wanting. It is peculiar that ﻟﻧﻪ, ﻟﻧﻘﺲ "τὶς, τινὲς" and ﻧﻢ "*one*" are conceived of as determined. The first two forms when standing as Object, have ﺑﺲ throughout: ﻟﻟﺎﻟﻪ ﻟﺍ ﺑﺴﺰﻩ οὐδένα εἶδον Matt. 17, 8; ﻭﻋﻠﺎ ﻟﻟﺎﻟﻪ ﻧﻤﺐ ﻭﻩﻟﻪ "he did not even know any one" Sim. 292, 1; and many like cases: ﻟﻠﻧﻘﺲ Ov. 189 *ult.*; and with still stronger determination: ﻣﺠﻤﻨﻲ ﺟﺪﻩ ﻟﻟﺎﻟﻪ "they awaken some one" Moes. I, 103, 28;[1] cf. *ibid.* 102, 12.—ܢܟܫܠ ܠܚܕ σκανδαλίσῃ ἕνα Matt. 18, 6; Luke 17, 2; ܟܕ ܚܙܐ ܠܚܕ ܡܢ ܒܢܝ ܓܢܣܗ "when he saw one of his fellow-countrymen" Mart. I, 12, 21; comp. Spic. 13, 26 and other passages (but Spic. 14, 25 ܡܢ ܕܩܛܠ ܚܕ ܡܢ ܗܠܝܢ "whoever kills one of these"); ܐܚܝܬ ܠܚܕܐ "revived the one (f.)" Mart. II, 237 *inf.* (Jac. Sar.); ܫܕܪ . . . ܠܡܪܙܒܢܐ ܚܕ "he sent a Marzbān (Satrap)" Jos. St. 17, 10; 65, 2 (but 64, 1 ܫܕܪ . . . ܡܪܙܒܢܐ ܚܕ); ܕܠܐ ܢܣܒܘܢ ܓܒܪܐ ܣܓܝܐܐ ܠܚܕܐ ܐܢܬܬܐ "that many men take not *one* wife" Spic. 17, 23 (but 16, 12 ܓܒܪܐ ܣܓܝܐܐ ܢܣܒܘܢ ܚܕܐ ܐܢܬܬܐ); ܐܩܝܡ ܠܚܕ ܚܕ ܡܢܗܘܢ "raised every single one of them" Aphr. 165, 16; ܠܟܦܠ ܚܕ ܚܕ ܡܢܗܘܢ ܙܘܕܗ "he endowed every single one of them" Ov. 166, 18. For ܚܙܘ ܓܒܪܐ ܐܘܟܡܐ "they saw a black man" Sim. 333, 6 *ab inf.* (the Lond. Cod. has ܚܙܘ ܠܓܒܪܐ ܚܕ ܐܘܟܡܐ ܗܘܐ). Thus ܠܟܠܢܫ "every one" John 2, 25; Ov. 179, 2 and frequently. ܐܚܪܢ too is treated like ܐܢܫ: ܠܐ ܓܒܐ ܠܐܚܪܢ "he nominated no other" Ephr. II, 554 F; cf. 555 B. So ܠܐܚܪܢܝܐ "*alios*" overagainst ܠܐܢܫܝܢ Ov. 190, 1.

ܣܓܝܐܐ (*οἱ πολλοί*), as an Object, also frequently takes ܠ, *e. g.* ܘܢܥܬܪ ܠܣܓܝܐܐ "and let us enrich many" Aphr. 105, 10, cf. 124, 17; 134, 12 &c.; also with substantive: ܘܠܣܓܝܐܐ ܦܪܣܝܐ ܩܛܠܘ "and they slew many Persians" Jos. St. 60, 13; still we find also ܚܪܒܘ ܡܢܗܘܢ ܣܓܝܐܐ "they destroyed many of them" Aphr. 242, 14.

§ 289. The ܠ of the Object may occur by the side of another ܠ [a true prep.]: ܫܕܪ ܐܠܗܐ ܠܒܪܗ ܠܥܠܡܐ ἀπέστειλεν ὁ θεὸς τὸν υἱὸν αὐτοῦ εἰς τὸν κόσμον John 3, 17; ܦܠܛܗ ܢܘܢܐ ܠܝܘܢܢ ܠܝܒܫܐ "the fish brought Jonah safe to dry land" Aphr. 66, 18; ܘܡܥܒܪܝܢ ܠܗ ܠܐܠܦܐ ܠܐܬܪܐ ܕܫܠܝܐ "and bring the ship to the place of quietness" Aphr. 458, 6; ܐܫܒܝ ܐܢܘܢ ܠܒܒܠ ܠܒܢܝ ܐܝܣܪܝܠ "led away the children of Israel captive to Babylon" Aphr. 36, 2; ܠܐ ܢܗܘܘܢ ܡܩܒܠܝܢ ܠܗܪܛܝܩܐ ܠܡܥܡܘܕܝܬܐ "they shall not admit heretics to baptism" Ov. 220, 19; ܕܢܥܒܕ ܠܥܠܡܐ ܕܐܠܗܘܬܐ ܡܫܥܒܕܐ ܐܦ ܠܐܪܝܢܐ "that he bring even the Arians into subjection to the

ܠ of the Object alongside of another ܠ.

(1) Cf. ܝܕܥܬܗ ܕܐܢܫ "one's knowledge" Ephr. (Lamy) I, 91, 9; ܕܚܒܝܒ ܠܗ ܠܐܢܫ "what is dear to one" Jul. 221, 6 (and thus frequently ܠܗ ܠܐܢܫ) where the determination by means of the personal suffix is clear.

☞ p. 359

truth of the exalted Trinity" Ov. 193, 13 &c. We have even as many as *three* ܠs, and these, besides, depending upon an Inf. with ܠ, in ܠܐ ܢܒܗܬ ܠܡܩܒܠܘ ܠܒܝܬ ܡܪܕܘܬܢ ܠܐܢܬܬܐ ܗܕܐ "we shall not be ashamed to take this woman under our instruction" Ov. 102, 15; cf. ܦܪܘܫܘ ܠܝ ܠܫܐܘܠ ܘܠܒܪܢܒܐ ܠܥܒܕܐ "ἀφορίσατε δή μοι τὸν Βαρνάβαν καὶ τὸν Σαῦλον εἰς τὸ ἔργον" Acts 13, 2; and ܐܠܐ ܐܓܪܘ ܠܗܘܢ ܠܒܠܥܡ ܒܪ ܒܥܘܪ ܠܡܠܛ ܐܢܘܢ "but they hired them Balaam, the son of Beor, to curse them" Aphr. 213, 7. In ܘܐܝܠܝܢ ܒܡܫܬܘܚܕܘܬܗܘܢ ܠܗ ܩܪܝܢ ܗܘܘ "and were wont to call on him for help in their loneliness" Mart. I, 122, 9, ܠܗ is indispensable on account of the participle; while in ܕܠܗܘܢ ܢܩܪܒ ܠܬܫܡܫܬܗ ܕܡܫܝܚܐ "that he may bring them to the service of Christ" Ov. 175, 19, in spite of the second ܠ, ܠܗܘܢ occurs in an unusual fashion in room of ܐܢܘܢ. But of course, alongside of another ܠ, the ܠ of the Object is often wanting, *e. g.* ܘܝܗܒ ܠܗ ܗܘ ܓܒܪܐ ܗܘ ܚܘܛܪܐ "and that man gave him that staff" Sim. 272 *inf.* &c.

Double transitive Construction.

§ 290. Examples of double transitive construction: ܕܢܫܐܠܝܘܗܝ ܒܪܗ ܠܚܡܐ ὃν αἰτήσει ὁ υἱὸς αὐτοῦ ἄρτον Matt. 7, 9; ܘܐܣܐܢܘܗܝ ܡܣܐܢܐ καὶ (δότε) αὐτῷ ὑποδήματα Luke 15, 22; ܢܚܫܐ ܚܦܝܗ "he overlaid it with brass" ZDMG XXIX, 109 v. 27 (but v. 26 with prep. ܚܦܐ ܣܐܡܐ ܠܐܠܗܗ "overlaid his god with silver"); ܫܐܠܬܗ ܡܠܐ "I asked him of the words" Aphr. 395, 2; ܚܘܝܗ ܥܬܝܕܬܐ "he showed him the future" Sim. 371 *inf.*; ܐܛܥܢܗ ܐܘܠܨܢܐ ܩܫܝܐ "laid severe afflictions upon him" Sim. 337, 9; ܚܘܝ ܐܢܘܢ ܡܕܡ ܕ "he showed them, what" Aphr. 160, 18; ܡܣܢܐ ܠܢ ܐܣܘܬܐ "makes physicians hateful to us" Ephr. III, 658 F; ܠܡܪܗ ܚܘܝܢܝ "show me his Lord" Ov. 296, 2; ܘܐܫܠܚܘܢܝ ܠܙܗܝܘܬܐ "and they stripped me of the splendid apparel" Apost. Apocr. 274, 16 (Gnostic Hymn); ܐܥܒܪ ܐܢܘܢ ܝܘܪܕܢܢ ܘܐܘܪܬܗ ܠܗܘܢ "caused them to cross the Jordan, and gave it (the land) to them for a heritage" Aphr. 357, 8; ܘܫܩܝܐ ܠܨܗܝܘܗܝ ܐܫܩܝܬ "and it (faith) gave water to drink to those who were athirst" Aphr. 22, 6; ܐܘܪܬ ܐܪܥܐ ܠܒܢܝ ܐܝܣܪܝܠ "he caused the children of Israel to inherit the land" Aphr. 20, 4 &c. In several of these examples it is only from the context that one can judge which is the first, and which the second Object; ܡܣܢܐ ܠܢ ܐܣܘܬܐ might, for instance, mean also "makes us hateful to the physicians"; and ܠܡܪܗ ܚܘܝܢܝ might even more readily suggest the conception "show me to his Lord". Moreover, keeping certain verbs out of view, we do not often, upon the whole, meet with such double transitive constructions, especially with two substantives. The theoretically possible employment of the Aphel as Causative of a transitive verb, which already has an object, is applied only within a limited range. It is doubtful whether both the Objects in a double transitive construction can receive ܠ.

§ 291. Apart from the participles treated of in § 280 (ܙܝܢܗ ܠܒܝܫܝܢ "they wear his armour" Aphr. 100, 17; ܫܘܒܚܐ ܠܒܝܫ ܐܢܬ "thou art clothed with glory" Aphr. 494, 12 &c.) the transitive construction of the Passive of a Double Transitive is very rare, and indeed wholly confined to certain verbs. Examples: ܢܬܟܣܘܢ ܣܩܐ "they shall cover themselves with sackcloth" Aphr. 49 *ult.*; ܐܬܦܪܥܬ ܒܝܫܘܬܟ "thou didst receive retribution for thy wickedness" 2 Sam. 16, 8, and, differently, ܐܬܦܪܥܘ ܕܝܢܐ ܟܐܢܐ "they received righteous judgment as a retribution" Aphr. 49, 3 (1) (but line 6 ܒܕܝܢܐ ܟܐܢܐ); ܪܘܓܙܐ ܪܒܐ ܐܬܡܠܝ "he was filled with great wrath" Mart. I, 18, 5; ܢܟܠܐ ܡܠܐ ܗܘܐ "he was full of cunning" Aphr. 61, 11 (and so, frequently, with ܐܬܡܠܝ and ܡܠܐ, but they are also often construed with ܒ). Cases like ܡܚܝܒ ܕܝܢܐ ܩܫܝܐ ܕܦܘܪܥܢܐ ܕܚܠܦܢܘܬܐ "he incurs [is condemned in] the severe punishment of retaliation" Spic. 14, 26 we have already noticed in § 243. (2)

Passive with Object.

§ 292. It must be kept in view here generally, that apart from the personal pronoun, Syriac has no clear mark or form for the Objective, nor even a clear notion of it, so that these Object-relations are at bottom treated always as mere adverbial adjuncts to the verb, whether with or without the preposition ܠ. This prep. as an objective sign, is of course distinguished from its other applications, by this circumstance amongst others, that it is bound to disappear, with transformation into the Passive. That the syntactical relation in ܡܛܠ ܫܡܥܘܢ ܠܐܒܪܗܡ is a different one

Character of Object-designation in Syriac.

(1) ܦܪܥ "to pay", "to requite" is doubly transitive, cf. Gen. 50, 15; 2 Sam. 16, 8, 12 &c.

(2) The subtle distinctions, which Arabic Grammar makes between these cases and the proper Object-relation, have no significance for Syriac.

from that in مرجّحيم‎ معدف‎ أمدـ‎ might not indeed be demonstrated by means of translation into other tongues, but would be so by means of transposition into the Passive of "Simeon killed Abraham", "Simeon said to Abraham": the former would then read ادּ‎ مَ‎ ٭ٮ‎ ٱٱمعلٰ‎, the latter ادּ‎ مع‎ ٭ܠٮ‎ أمدـ‎ ܗ. But in the case of many verbs undoubtedly transitive, the passive construction is quite unusual; and with several verbs there is a measure of uncertainty in distinguishing ܠ, as an objective sign, from ܠ, as a dative preposition.

INFINITIVE WITH OBJECT.

Verb-Con-
struction.

§ 293. The Infinitive, just like the finite verb, may have an object subordinated to it. Thus *e. g.* ܠمجّمقـ‎ "to kill me" Acts 26, 21, and frequently; ܠمجّخّةامٖ‎ "to put him to death" Anc. Doc. 89, 14; ܠܩّمُقّّماܠٮ‎ "to serve me" Ezek. 44, 13 &c. (cf. the forms with وهم‎, بّـ‎ § 191); besides cases like ܠمحّخّةه‎ ابّٮ‎ "to teach them" Ex. 24, 12; ܠܩّمعّمـ‎ ابّٮ‎ "to hear them" Ps. 34, 15 &c.

With other nouns, nearly all the cases noted in § 288 may be illustrated also by the Infinitive. It is rather a favourite practice to place the Object before the Inf. with ܠ.

(a) Without being determined: ܠبّمحّمَه‎ خّبّܠ‎ "ἐγεῖραι τέκνα" Matt. 3, 9; مجّـّزبّٱ‎ ܠمحّمَزّ‎ "to set in order many things" Jos. St. 81, 11 &c.

(b) Determined: (1) ܠبّمحّمܠ‎ خّجّه‎ جّزّٱ‎ وه‎ وبّخّمܠ‎ "to take the entire treasure of the king" Aphr. 199, 10; ܠمحّمَةه‎ وه‎ تبّخّمܠ‎ مزّبّگّ‎ "thou canst make good the dreams" Joseph 31, 11 [Ov. 284, 16]; ܠܩّمّمَجّـ‎ وزّٱ‎ وهـ‎ جّـ‎ ܠاهبّم‎ "I have been ordered to have this done" Jos. St. 3, 21; خّمَمَܠ‎ وقّܠا‎ مبّقّـ‎ خّمَاجّه‎ ومَܠقّمَهّقّگّه‎ "to learn and understand the investigation of words is an admirable thing" Aphr. 446, 15.—(2) ܠܩّمحّم‎ ٭٭مَمَܠ‎ بّمَقّع‎ "to kill myself" Ps. 40, 14; ܠخّقّبّزّ‎ ܠمحّخّهّܠ‎ اܠگّ‎ مَعّمَع‎ خّقّجّه‎ "to tend his people [as a flock]" Aphr. 193, 6; ܠمحّمَمَم‎ وقّبّٮ‎ "thou canst understand the saying of our Lord" Aphr. 71, 6; (= ܠمَجّازّܠٮ‎) خّمحّبّم‎ ܠاهّܠگّبّ‎ وهه‎ جّع‎ "they wanted to keep fast hold of the Astabedh" ["general"] Jos. St. 89, 8.—(3) ܠاابّخّه‎ ܠاابّجّه‎

"to curse the earth" Gen. 8, 21; ܠܡܣܬܠܒܘܬܗ ܠܓܒܪܐ "to despoil the man" Aphr. 130, 3; ܠܨܒܝܢܐ ܓܝܪ ܗܘ ܪܒܐ ܘܩܕܝܫܐ ܠܝܬ ܡܢ ܕܡܫܟܚ ܠܡܚܕܝܘܗܝ "*nam voluntatem illam magnam et sanctam non est quod possit retinere*" Spic. 20, 24.—(4) ܠܡܣܬܟܠܘ ܡܠܬܐ ܗܕܐ "to understand this word" Aphr. 70, 4.

§ 294. Together with these, there are cases in which the object clearly comes into genitive relation with the Inf. This can happen with personal pronouns only. Very rarely does it occur with the 1st sing.: ܠܡܕܟܝܘܬܝ "to make me clean" Matt. 8, 2 P.; Luke 5, 12 P.; in the former of which places C., and in the latter S., read ܠܡܕܟܝܘܬܢܝ. It is found rather more frequently with the 3rd pl.: ܠܡܘܩܕܘܬܗܘܢ "to burn them up" Ov. 126, 2 (instead of ܠܡܘܩܕܘ ܐܢܘܢ); ܠܡܫܠܡܘܬܗܘܢ "to deliver them up" Mart. I, 153, 15; ܠܡܒܛܠܘܬܗܝܢ "to render them (f.) ineffectual" John van Tella (Kleyn) 46, 12; ܠܡܥܒܕܗܝܢ "to make them (f.)" Aphr. 319, 5; ܠܡܛܪܗܝܢ "to preserve them (f.)" *ibid.* line 6. **Noun-Construction.**

INFINITIVE ABSOLUTE.

§ 295. The [indeterminate] general object,—the Inf. Abs.—is not of uncommon occurrence with Transitive and Intransitive, Active and Passive verbs. A definite object may also stand alongside of it. This Inf. serves to give more emphasis to the verb, by contrasting the action with some other one, or by giving expression to its intensity. Of course this emphasis has frequently become very trifling. Examples: ܕܡܒܢܐ ܒܢܐ "that he builds up" Aphr. 201, 5 (in antithesis to 'throwing down'); ܡܠܦܢܐ ܓܝܪ ܡܫܐܠܘ ܗܘ ܡܫܬܐܠܝܢ ܠܐ ܗܘܐ ܡܫܐܠܝܢ ܫܐܠܝܢ "for teachers are asked questions; they do not ask them" Spic. 1, 17; ܒܠܚܘܕ ܡܗܝܡܢܘ ܗܝܡܢ μόνον πίστευε Luke 8, 50 C. (= Aphr. 21, 1; P. S. without Inf.); ܐܦ ܟܕ ܡܙܟܐ ܙܟܝܢ "even when they are victorious" Jos. St. 15, 18; ܡܟܪܝܘ ܗܘܐ ܟܪܝܐ ܠܗ ܠܢܒܝܐ "the prophet was very sorry" Aphr. 453, 11; ܐܠܐ ܡܣܚܦܘ ܣܚܦܘܗܝ ܗܘܘ "but they destroyed (what he had built)" Aphr. 10, 20; ܡܗܦܟܘ ܗܦܘܟܝܗ "overthrow it" Aphr. 201, 6; ܘܟܕ ܡܙܕܪܙܐ ܙܪܝܙܝܢ "and while they are continually bestirring themselves" Aphr. 497, 7; ܘܡܚܙܐ ܠܐ ܚܙܐ ܗܘܐ ܠܐܢܫ "but *saw* no man" Sim. 304 mid.; ܡܚܝܠܘ ܠܚܡܐ ܚܝܠܬ **Placed before the Verb.**

"why hast thou then [so greatly] sinned?" Aphr. 270, 5; ܠܡܢܐ ܡܚܛܐ ܚܛܝܬ "was she then troublesome to him?" Joseph 293, 2. With the Part. pass.: ܩܛܝܠܐ ܩܛܝܠ "killed is he" Gen. 44, 28; ܡܛܪܦ ܐܛܪܦ ܝܘܣܦ "torn in pieces is Joseph" Gen. 37, 33; ܡܠܛܫ ܗܘ ܠܛܝܫ ܗܘܐ "was it (m.) then sharpened?" Mart. I, 126 mid.; ܠܐ ܡܚܙܐ ܚܙܝܐ ܗܘܬ ܠܗ ܡܡܬܘܡ ܠܨܘܪ οὐχ ἑωράκει ποτὲ τὴν Τῦρον Sachau, Ined. 2, 14 (§ 279) &c. Thus also with verbal Adjectives (§ 118) like ܕܡܥܪܩ ܥܪܝܩ "that he would have fled" Anc. Doc. 91, 3; ܕܡܫܬܩ ܫܬܝܩܝܢ ܗܘܝܬܘܢ "that you would altogether keep silence!" Job 13, 5. Similarly ܕܡܛܪ ܢܛܝܪܝܢ ܛܒ "that we keep good watch" Ephr. II, 401 B; ܘܡܟܪܗ ܠܐ ܟܪܝܗ "and is not sick" *Synodes* (Chabot) 28, 17, 22.

☞ p. 359

Placed after the Verb. § 296. Less frequently the Inf. Abs. stands *after* the verb, in which case the emphasis is even stronger: ܘܠܐ ܚܙܐ ܐܢܘܢ ܠܗܠܝܢ ܡܝ̈ܐ ܐܦܠܐ ܡܚܙܐ "and he did not see this water at all" Sim. 313, 12; ܠܟ ܕܬܐܡܪ ܡܐܡܪ "it is for thee to speak" Sim. 315 *ad inf.*; ܩܘܡ ܠܟ ܡܩܡ "arise!" Sim. 271, 6 (and such construction is frequently found in Sim.); ܦܪܚ ܡܦܪܚ "flew [swiftly]" Dan. 9, 21 (= Aphr. 370, 19); ܕܝܢ ܟܕ ܡܬܪܥܐ ܗܘܐ ܒܠܚܘܕ ܡܬܪܥܝܢܘܗܝ ܡܬܩܕܫܘܬܗ "then, as often as he merely *thought* on his sanctity" Ov.189, 14; ܗܝܡܢܝܢ ܠܟ ܡܗܝܡܢܘܬܗ "only *believe*" Spic. 2, 13; ܦܩܘܕ ܡܠܟܐ ܒܠܚܘܕ ܡܦܩܕ "only give command, O king!" Joseph 117, 11.

☞ p. 359

Without Finite Verb. § 297. In very rare cases with the Inf. abs. the finite verb is left out altogether: ܘܙܒܢܝܢ ܟܒܠܝܢ ܦܘܠܘܣ ܘܙܒܢܝܢ ܡܪܓܡ "and sometimes they put Paul in bonds, and at other times they stoned him" Aphr. 300, 20.

Abstracts, of another form, taking the part of General Object. § 298. The Inf. Abs. cannot take either attribute, or numeral, or attributive relative-clause nor can it stand in the plural or genitive, or govern a genitive. If the general object requires a measure of determination of that kind,(1) then an Abstract, of another form, answering to the verb, must be chosen. This however is sometimes done even where

---

(1) Syriac is commonly satisfied with a simple adverb of quality, *e. g.* ܠܐ ܩܫܝܐܝܬ ܟܘܢ ܐܟܣܢܐܝܬ "he did not find fault with them severely" Aphr. 261, 19, where also ܠܐ ܩܫܝܐ ܟܘܢ ܟܘܢܝܐ ܐܟܣܢܝܐ might have been used.

the Inf. Abs. might stand. Examples: ܐܬܬܙܝܥܬ ܐܢܛܝܘܟܝ ܙܘܥܐ ܪܒܐ "Antioch experienced a violent earthquake" Land III, 244, 18; ܡܝܬ ܡܘܬܐ ܒܝܫܐ ܘܡܪܝܪܐ "he died an evil and painful death" Sim. 333, 3 (a construction like this is common with ܡܝܬ); ܗܝܕܝܢ ܚܪܒܬ ܚܘܪܒܢܐ ܐܚܪܝܐ "then was it destroyed for the last time" Aphr. 399, 6; ܪܒܝܬܐ ܫܦܝܪܬܐ ܐܬܪܒܝ ܗܘܐ "he had been well brought up" Ephr. I, 110 E; ܗܐ ܒܘܪܟܬܐ ܒܪܟܬܟ "lo, I have blessed thee with a manifold blessing Joseph 297, 9; ܗܐ ܓܝܪ ܥܣܪܝܢ ܙܒܢܝܢ ܩܛܠܐ ܩܛܠܘܢܝ ܐܢܐ "for lo, I have twenty times been slain" Mart. I, 253 *ad inf.*; ܠܘ ܓܝܪ ܩܛܠܐ ܒܠܚܘܕ ܢܬܩܛܠ ܚܕܐ ܐܘ ܚܡܫܐ ܐܘ ܥܣܪܐ "for not once only shall he be put to death, or five times, or ten times" Mart. I, 246, 9; (¹) ܕܢܓܙܪܘܢ ܠܒܐ ܕܟܐܦܐ ܓܙܘܪܬܐ ܕܠܐ ܒܐܝܕܝܢ "that they circumcise the heart of stone with the circumcision which is not [made] with hands" Ov. 125, 26; ܠܡܩܛܠܘ ܩܛܠܐ "to put to death" Spic. 17, 20 (where the Abstract is employed to keep two infinitives from coming together). An Abstract occurs alongside of the Inf. Abs. in ܡܣܬܝܒܪܬ ܩܛܠܐ ܐܢܬܝ ܡܘܬܐ ܒܝܫܐ "thou art suffering a sad death" Simeon of Bēth Arshām (Guidi) 9, 10 = Knös, Chrest. 39. An abstract noun of allied meaning, but from a different root, appears in an exceptional way in ܡܐ ܕܫܟܒܝܢ ܒܢܝ ܐܢܫܐ ܗܢܐ ܫܢܬܐ "when men lie down in this sleep" Aphr. 170, 12; and ܕܡܟܘ ܫܢܬܐ "they fell asleep" Joseph 105, 11. ☞ p. 359

Such an Abstract noun may also be represented, where the connection is clear, by the relative ܕ referring thereto, or by a personal suffix: ܡܚܘܬܐ ܡܚܝܠܬܐ ܕܡܚܐ "the feeble reprimand which he employed" Aphr. 262, 5; ܩܛܠܐ ܕܒܝܫܐ ܕܩܛܠܝܢ ܐܢܫܐ ܠܐܚܝܗܘܢ "the wicked murders in which men destroy their brethren" Ov. 132, 14; ܒܘܪܟܬܐ ܕܒܪܟܬܢܝ "the blessings with which thou hast blessed me" Joseph 201 *ult.*—202, 1 [= Ov. 299, 9—10]; ܨܘܡܐ ܕܨܡܘ "the fast which they kept" Aphr. 49, 12, and frequently; and so ܨܡܘܗܝ "they kept it (the fast)" Aphr. 44, 5. Cf. farther—where the words are from different roots—ܣܟܠܘܬܐ ܕܐܣܟܠܘ ܒܟ "the offence, which they committed against thee" Sim. 295, 2.

(¹) A later recension for liturgical purposes substitutes a more convenient construction, with the preposition: ܠܘ ܚܕܐ ܩܛܠܐ ܒܠܚܘܕܝܗܘܢ *Offic. Sanctor. Maron. Hyemal.* (Romae 1656) p. 366*b* (cf. *Aestiv.* 74*b* *ult.*).

☞ p. 359 In ܐܠܩܝܘ ܐܪܒܥܝܢ ܐܪܒܥܝܢ "they received [were beaten with] forty each" Mart. I, 197 mid., the word "stripes" is left out, being understood. The instrument appears directly for the blow in ܘܡܚܝܢ ܠܗ ܡܐܐ ܫܒ̈ܛܝܢ "and they give him a hundred strokes" [*lit.* strike him (with) a hundred rods] Bedjan, Mart. II, 579, 8; ܡܚܝܗ̱ܝ ܠܬܡܢܬܥܣܪܐ ܡ̈ܚܘܢ ܣܝܦܐ "he gave ☞ p. 359 him eighteen strokes with the sword" Bedjan, Mart. IV, 179, 18; ܡܚܝܗ̱ܝ ܚܕ ܣܝܦܐ "gave him one stroke with the sword" Guria et Shamona 24, 8, 11.

D. ܗܘܐ.

Separate and Enclitic Forms.

§ 299. The enclitic form ܗ̱ܘܐ (ܗ̱ܘܐ with the West-Syrians, ܗ̱ܘܐ with the East-Syrians)—contrasted with ܗ̄ܘܐ having ܗ sounded (ܗ̄ܘܐ with the West-Syrians, ܗ̄ܘܐ with the East-Syrians) (1)—has the signification of "was" *after* a predicative Part., Adj., or Subst.: ܣܠܩ ܗ̱ܘܐ "ascended" Gen. 2, 6; ܚܕܝܐ ܗ̱ܘܝܬ "I rejoiced (f.)" Prov. 8, 30; ܚܪܝܡ ܗ̱ܘܐ "was cunning" Gen. 3, 1; ܗܘ ܟܘܡܪܐ ܗ̱ܘܐ ܕܐܠܗܐ ܡܪܝܡܐ "he was a priest of the most high God" Gen. 14, 18 &c. So too ܒܪ ܡܐܐ ܗ̱ܘܐ ܫܢܝܢ "he was an hundred years old" Gen. 21, 5 &c. It occurs farther after ܐܝܬ, and, by way of adding emphasis, after the finite verb (§§ 263; 268): ܐܝܬܘܗ̱ܝ ܗ̱ܘܐ; ܐܝܬ ܗ̱ܘܐ; ܐܝܬܝܘ ܗ̱ܘܘ ܥܠܘܗ̱ܝ "had afflicted him" Job 42, 11; ܗ̄ܘܐ ܗ̱ܘܐ "*fuerat*" frequently, &c. Thus also ܠܐ ܗ̱ܘܐ with the meaning "not", having nothing of the force of a verb.

ܗ̄ܘܐ, when the ܗ is pronounced, remains always *before* its own predicate: ܡܛܠ ܕܗܘ ܗ̄ܘܐ ܙܕܝܩ "for he was righteous" Job 32, 1; ܘܐܪܥܐ ܗ̄ܘܬ ܬܘܗ ܘܒܘܗ "and the earth was waste and empty" Gen. 1, 2; ܘܩܐܝܢ ܗ̄ܘܐ ܦܠܚ ܐܪܥܐ "and Cain was a tiller of the ground" Gen. 4, 2; ܘܝܘܣܦ ܗ̄ܘܐ ܒܡܨܪܝܢ "and Joseph was in Egypt" Ex. 1, 5; ܘܐܠܗܗ ܕܐܒܝ ܗ̄ܘܐ ܥܡܝ "and the God of my father was with me" Gen. 31, 5 &c. So with ܠܐ ܗ̄ܘܐ "is not" (verbal); ܡܛܠ ܕܠܒܟ ܠܐ ܗ̄ܘܐ ܬܪܝܨ ܩܕܡ ܐܠܗܐ ἡ γὰρ καρδία σου οὐκ ἔστιν εὐθεῖα ἐνώπιον τοῦ θεοῦ Acts 8, 21; ܠܐ ܗ̄ܘܝܬ ܪܚܡܗ ܕܩܣܪ οὐκ εἶ φίλος τοῦ Καίσαρος John 19, 12.—The ܗ is also pronounced when some other word comes in between the proper predicate and ܗ̄ܘܐ: ܠܟܘܢ ܓܝܪ ܗ̄ܘܐ

---

(1) For the determination of this distinction, which is not set forth in the old MSS. we are entirely dependent upon Biblical tradition.

ܡܘܠܟܢܐ ὑμῖν γάρ ἐστιν ἡ ἐπαγγελία Acts 2, 39; ܒܗ ܚܝ̈ܐ ܗܘܐ ἐν αὐτῷ ζωὴ ἦν John 1, 4.

ܗ̄ܘܐ seems also to stand after adverbs and adverbial qualifications, when these constitute the real predicate, *e. g.* ܕܥܡܟܘܢ ܗ̄ܘܝܬ "ὅτι μεθ' ὑμῶν ἤμην" John 16, 4; ܒܥܠܡܐ ܗ̄ܘܐ "ἐν τῷ κόσμῳ ἦν" John 1, 10; ܐܠܘ ܡܢ ܥܠܡܐ ܗ̄ܘܝܬܘܢ "εἰ ἐκ τοῦ κόσμου ἦτε" John 15, 19 (followed by ܐܠܐ ܠܐ ܗܘܝܬܘܢ ܡܢ ܥܠܡܐ with *h*, because it precedes the predicate) &c.:—but, throughout, ܗܘܐ with *h* has the meaning "became, happened" (ἐγένετο): ܥܠܡܐ ܒܐܝܕܗ ܗܘܐ "ὁ κόσμος δι' αὐτοῦ ἐγένετο" John 1, 10 (ܒܐܝܕܗ ܗ̄ܘܐ would mean "was in his hand"); ܚܢܢ ܡܢ ܙܢܝܘܬܐ ܠܐ ܗܘܝܢ "ἡμεῖς ἐκ πορνείας οὐ γεγεννήμεθα" John 8, 41; ܗܠܝܢ ܒܒܝܬ ܥܢܝܐ ܗܘܝ ταῦτα ἐν Βηθανίᾳ ἐγένετο John 1, 28; ܕܠܘܬܗܘܢ ܗܘܬ ܡܠܬܗ ܕܐܠܗܐ πρὸς οὓς ὁ λόγος τοῦ θεοῦ ἐγένετο John 10, 35; ܘܚܫܘܟܐ ܗܘܐ "and there was darkness" Gen. 15, 17 &c.

After adverbs and adverbial expressions, a diverse understanding of the ܗܘܐ is often possible, and accordingly variations occasionally occur in such cases, either among analogous forms in the same tradition, or among different traditions.

Forms of ܗܘܐ used for Emphasis and Modification.

§ 300. The Impf. ܢܗܘܐ is commonly placed before the Participle, to convey the sense of the Impf.,—either independently or dependently (after ܕ). This collocation is employed particularly to express *continued*, or *repeated actions*, or *actions determined by ordinance*: ܘܫܘܠܛܢܐ ܝܗܒ ܠܗ ܕܢܗܘܐ ܥܒܕ ܕܝܢܐ καὶ ἐξουσίαν ἔδωκεν αὐτῷ κρίσιν ποιεῖν John 5, 27; ܦܪܝܕܘܛܐ ܐܘ ܩܫܝܫܐ ܘܡܫܡܫܢܐ ܕܢܦܩ ܡܢ ܥܠܡܐ ܡܕܡ ܕܐܝܬ ܠܗ ܠܥܕܬܐ ܢܗܘܐ ܫܒܩ "a Visitor or Presbyter or Deacon, who quits the world, shall leave whatever he has to the church" Ov. 219, 24; ܦܩܕ ܓܝܪ ܠܝܗܘܕܝܐ ܕܠܐ ܢܗܘܘܢ ܓܙܪܝܢ "for he commanded the Jews that they should not circumcise themselves" Aphr. 95, 14; ܟܡܐ ܕܠܐ ܠܟܘܢ ܘܐܦ ܐܢܬܘܢ ܠܗܘܘܢ ܡܫܝܓܝܢ "how much the rather it befits you that you wash" John 13, 14 S., and essentially the same in Aphr. 227, 9 ὀφείλετε νίπτειν (where P. has ܘܠܡܫܝܓܘ); ܕܢܫܐ ܒܫܘܡ ܠܐ ܢܗܘܝܢ ܥܐܠܢ ܠܕܝܪܝܗܘܢ "that on no account should women enter into their convents" Ov. 210, 4 = 212, 4; and many instances to the like effect in these Canons, though alternating with the simple Impf. More rarely without ܕ: ܠܐ ܬܗܘܐ ܣܒܪ "think not" Mart. I, 218, 1; ܐܢ ܕܝܢ ܢܐܡܪ . . . ܘܢܗܘܐ ܐܟܠ ܘܫܬܐ ἐὰν δὲ εἴπῃ . . . ἐσθίῃ δὲ καὶ πίνῃ Matt. 24, 48—49; and quite independently ـمثكـٰـ لمحمُّ محمُّه, literally following the text ἔσονται ἀληθουσαι Matt. 24, 41. With the subject-pronoun attached to the participle, thus محمُّ لمحمُّه؟ مُّ مُّه محمُّمَّـمُّـمُّـ "if only we may enter and be blessed by thee" Sim. 308, 1; لمحمُّه محمُّه لمُّمُّه "thou shalt remember the oath" ibid. 323, 2. So too with Part. Pass.: محمُّ لمُّمُّه محمُّمُّه ـمُّمُّ لمُّمُّه ὑμᾶς δὲ [ὄψεσθε] ἐκβαλλομένους ἔξω Luke 13, 28; لمُّمُّمُّه محمُّمُّه "that they are continually taken up with fasting" Ov. 177, 2; محمُّمُّه لمُّمُّه "stand" Spic. 17, 17; لمُّمُّمُّ محمُّمُّه محمُّمُّه محمُّمُّه لمُّمُّه "it shall be made and prepared and placed at the door" Sim. 377, 8.

☞ p. 359

Rem. On لمُّه with other verbal forms v. §§ 261; 263; 268; 277; 278 B.; 279 B.; cf. farther §§ 260; 324 E.; 338 C. On لمُّه with the Inf. v. § 286, and with adverbs § 308.

E. لمُّ.

Preliminary Observations. § 301. لمُّ and its negative لمُّ لُّ or محمُّ (§ 199) are, in their syntax, essentially alike. In the matter of Tense, لمُّ (as Noun) resembles the Part.; when it is strengthened by an enclitic لمُّه, the resulting combination then answers to that of the Part. with لمُّه; thus لمُّه لمُّ is nearly equal to "erat". This لمُّه does not necessarily require to be inflected according to gender and number, seeing that لمُّ is properly a masculine substantive in the sg.

With separate Personal Pronouns. § 302. Sometimes محمُّ, and more rarely لمُّ, is found with the independent personal pronoun following: لُّ محمُّه "and I am no longer in being" Job 7, 21; محمُّ لمُّ "they are not there", "they are not in

☞ p. 359

being" Jer. 10, 20; Ephr. II, 554 C.; III, 419 A.; Ephr. Nis. p. 62 v. 88; Jul. 177,15; varied by محمُّ لمُّ لُّ οὐκ εἰσί Matt. 2, 18 C. (P. S. لمُّه محمُّه لُّ); محمُّ محمُّه لمُّه "non sunt qui veniant" Ephr. III, 418 E; محمُّ محمُّه لمُّه "those who are not in being" (set overagainst محمُّمُّه لمُّه) Aphr. 274, 6; محمُّ محمُّه لمُّه محمُّه لمُّه "and if for the moon they do not exist" Ov. 70, 3 (for which l. 1 محمُّه محمُّه لمُّه لمُّه لمُّه); محمُّه محمُّه لمُّه لمُّه لمُّه "in the trouble of man they are not [involved]" Ps. 73, 5. لمُّ is a mere copula in the original passage لمُّه محمُّه محمُّه لمُّه "who are Христ Christians" Land III, 258, 17 (so in محمُّه محمُّه محمُّه لمُّه "they are his agents" Land

III, 53, 26; and ܐܝ݂ܬ ܐܦ, ܐܝ݂ܬ ܐܝ݂ Land III, 91, 17; 140, 17; 141, 12; 142, 1; but all these passages are translations from the Greek; and in the very same way we have ܐܝ݂ܬ ܐܢ݂ܐ ܡܕܡ "I am nothing" Land III, 281, 13; ܐܝ݂ܟ݂ܐ ܕ݁ܐܝܬ݂ ܐܢ݂ "where I am" *ibid.* 285, 7).

§ 303. Far more common is the combination of ܐܝ݂ܬ with possessive suffixes for the 1st and 2nd persons; while for the 3rd person ܐܝ݂ܬ is used either alone, or with the possessive suffix. The usage here, in some meanings, is made to follow strict rules; in others it varies. **With Suffixes; and alone.**

ܐܝ݂ܬ in the sense of "exists", "is extant *or* at hand" appears most frequently by far without any suffix: ܒ݁ܟ݂ܽܠ ܥܺܕ݁ܬ݁ܳܐ ܕ݁ܺܐܝܬ݂ "in every church that there is" Ov. 217, 4; ܘܰܗܘܳܐ ܐܰܝܟ݁ܳܐ (var. ܗ݈ܘܳܐ) ܡܰܝܳܐ "and there was no water there" Ex. 17, 1; ܐܶܢ ܠܰܝܬ݁ ܙܰܕ݁ܺܝܩܶܐ "if there are no righteous persons" Aphr. 458, 9, ܕ݁ܺܐܝܬ݂ "*est, qui*", "*sunt, qui*" frequently; ܐܰܝܟ݁ܳܐ ܕ݁ܺܐܝܬ݂ "*est, ubi*" frequently; ܐ݈ܚܪܢܳܐ ܗ݈ܘ ܐܰܝܟ݁ܳܐ ܕ݁ܺܐܝܬ݂ "it is long, till" Aphr. 33, 2 &c. But it occurs with the suffix also: ܥܽܘܩܣܶܗ ܬ݁ܽܘܒ݂ ܐܺܝܬ݂ܰܘܗ݈ܝ "its sting still exists" Aphr. 135, 2; ܒ݁ܰܪ ܡܶܕ݁ܶܡ ܕ݁ܠܳܐ ܐܺܝܬ݂ܰܘܗ݈ܝ ܗ݈ܘܳܐ "he created what was not in being" Ephr. Nis. p. 55 v. 144; ܐܰܘ ܥܶܕ݁ܠܳܝܳܐ ܠܳܐ ܐܺܝܬ݂ܰܘܗ݈ܝ "or fate has no existence at all" Spic. 9, 9; ܕ݁ܳܐܦ݂ ܠܳܐ ܗ݈ܘܳܐ ܐܺܝܬ݂ܶܝܗ ܡܶܢ ܩܕ݂ܺܝܡ "she, who did not even exist at all before" Ov. 203, 16; ܟ݁ܰܕ݂ ܠܳܐ ܐܺܝܬ݂ܰܘܗ݈ܝ ܗ݈ܘܳܐ ܐܳܕ݂ܳܡ "when Adam did not yet exist" Aphr. 158, 11; ܡܶܛܽܠ ܟ݁ܽܠ ܕ݁ܺܐܝܬ݂ܰܘܗ݈ܝ "for every one who exists" Spic. 4, 15 &c.

The bare form predominates also with ܠ in the signification "belongs to", "is the property of": ܟ݁ܰܕ݂ ܐܺܝܬ݂ ܠܳܟ݂ "when thou hast something" Prov. 3, 28; ܡܶܢ ܟ݁ܽܠ ܕ݁ܺܐܝܬ݂ ܠܶܗ παντὶ τῷ ἔχοντι ("unto every one which hath") Luke 19, 26; ܟ݁ܽܠ ܕ݁ܺܐܝܬ݂ ܠܶܗ ܟ݁ܳܦ݂ܰܪ ܘܰܕ݂ܠܰܝܬ݁ ܠܶܗ ܡܶܬ݂ܟ݁ܰܬ݁ܰܫ ܠܡܶܩܢܳܐ "whoever has anything denies it, and whoever has nothing, struggles to get possession of something" Spic. 47, 2. In none of these three examples is there any definite subject. Compare ܕ݁ܺܐܝܬ݂ ܠܶܗ ܕ݁ܢܶܥܒ݁ܶܕ݂ ܠܳܟ݂ "he has to do with the judge" Isaac II, 42, 104. Farther, ܗܰܘ ܕ݁ܺܐܝܬ݂ ܠܶܗ ܘܡܰܘܒ݁ܶܕ݂ ܡܶܢܶܗ ܘܰܕ݂ܠܳܐ ܐܺܝܬ݂ ܠܶܗ ܘܪܳܗܶܛ ܒ݁ܳܬ݂ܪܶܗ "he, who has it (ܡܶܢܶܗ the possession) and loses it, does not find it again, and he, who has it not and runs after it, does not overtake it" Aphr. 356, 2; ܩܕ݂ܳܫܶܐ ܕ݁ܕ݂ܰܗܒ݂ܳܐ ܐܺܝܬ݂ ܗ݈ܘܳܐ ܠܗܽܘܢ "they had golden ear-rings" Judges 8, 24; ܐܶܠܳܐ ܕ݁ܺܐܝܬ݂ ܗ݈ܘܳܐ ܠܶܗ ܐܰܒ݂ܳܗܶܐ ܡܗܰܝܡܢܶܐ "but he had believing parents" Sim. 268; ܘܰܒ݂ܩܰܢܝܽܘܢܶܗ ܕ݁ܺܐܝܬ݂ ܗ݈ܘܳܐ "and his beauty was unbounded" Sim. 272, 13; ܕܐܝܬ ܗܘܳܬ ܠܗ ܒܪܰܬܳܐ "who had a daughter" Sim. 273, 12; ܠܟܽܠܗܶܝܢ ܐܽܘܠܨܳܢܶܐ ܐܺܝܬ ܚܽܘܠܡܳܢ̈ܶܐ "for all distresses there are remedies" Aphr. 135, 3 &c.

Very rarely occur cases like ܐܶܠܳܐ ܐܺܝܬܶܝܗ ܠܰܢ ܚܺܐܪܽܘܬܳܐ ܒܢܰܦܫܰܢ "but we have liberty in ourselves" Spic. 13, 4.

With other prepositions or adverbs likewise, the bare form ܐܝܬ appears freely, although ܐܝܬ with suffixes often occurs too, especially when it comes after the prepositional phrase. In such combinations the signification is indeed gradually passing into that of the pure copula: ܒܪܺܫܺܝܬ ܐܺܝܬܰܘܗܝ ܗܘܳܐ ܡܶܠܬܳܐ ἐν ἀρχῇ ἦν ὁ λόγος John 1, 1; ܒܟܽܠ ܐܰܬܪܳܐ ܓܶܝܪ ܘܰܒܟܽܠ ܥܰܡ ܐܺܝܬ ܥܰܬܺܝܪ̈ܶܐ ܘܡܶܣܟܺܢ̈ܶܐ "for in every land and among every people there are rich and poor" Spic. 18, 4; ܕܐܝܬ ܒܶܗ ܝܺܕܰܥܬܳܐ "in whom is knowledge" Spic. 3, 11; ܠܳܐ ܐܺܝܬ ܚܰܝܠܳܐ ܒܪܰܫܺܝܥܳܐ ܠܡܶܩܰܡ ܠܽܘܩܒܰܠ ܛܳܒܳܐ "there is no strength in the wicked man to stand against the good" Aphr. 182, 4; ܠܰܝܬ ܥܰܡܗܽܘܢ ܝܺܗܽܘܕܳܐ "Judas is not with them" Aphr. 65, 2; ܟܽܠ ܡܶܕܶܡ ܕܐܝܬ ܠܥܶܠ ܡܶܢܝ "all that is upon me" Spic. 3, 21; ܘܥܰܡ ܕܫܪܳܪܳܐ ܠܰܝܬ ܠܘܳܬܶܗ "and with whom is no truth" Aphr. 182, 13; ܐܝܬ ܠܬܰܡܳܢ "are there" Spic. 14, 1 &c.—ܛܶܢܦܳܐ ܕܚܰܛܺܝܬܳܐ ܕܰܒܩܽܘܪ̈ܝܳܐ ܐܺܝܬܶܝܗ "the filth of sin which is in the villages" Ov. 116, 7 (parallel to ܚܰܛܺܝܬܳܐ ܕܐܝܬ ܒܫܽܘܩܶܐ ܕܡܕܺܝܢ̈ܳܬܳܐ "the sin which is in the streets of the towns" line 6); ܟܽܠ (1) ܣܽܘܪ̈ܚܳܢܶܐ . . . ܐܺܝܬܰܝܗܽܘܢ ܒܝ "all faults . . . are in me" Ov. 141, 4; ܐܰܠܳܗܳܐ ܒܗܽܘܢ ܐܺܝܬܰܘܗܝ ܗܘܳܐ "God was in them" Aphr. 70, 6; ܐܰܚ̈ܶܐ ܐܳܝܠܶܝܢ ܕܐܺܝܬܰܝܗܽܘܢ ܒܕܰܝܪ̈ܳܬܳܐ "the brethren who are in the convents" Ov. 213, 11 (alongside of ܕܰܝܪ̈ܳܝܶܐ ܕܐܝܬ ܒܰܐܬܪ̈ܰܘܳܬܗܽܘܢ "the monks who are in their districts" Ov. 216 *ult.*); ܗܝ ܕܐܺܝܬܶܝܗ ܒܓܰܘܶܗ ܕܝܰܡܳܐ "she, who is in the midst of the sea" Apost. Apocr. 274 *paen.* (Gnostic Hymn); ܥܰܠ ܪܺܫ ܪ̈ܳܡܳܬܳܐ ܓܶܝܪ ܐܺܝܬܶܝܗ ܚܶܟܡܬܳܐ "for upon the top of high places is Wisdom" Prov. 8, 2; ܡܶܢ ܐܳܝܠܶܝܢ ܕܥܰܡܶܗ ܐܺܝܬܰܝܗܽܘܢ ܗܘܰܘ "from those who were with him" Ov. 162, 14; ܐܶܠܘ ܒܟܽܠܙܒܰܢ ܠܘܳܬܶܗ ܐܺܝܬܰܘܗܝ ܗܘܳܐ "if it had been always with him" Aphr. 128, 3; ܕܫܪܳܝܶܗ ܠܰܝܬܰܘܗܝ ܠܘܳܬܰܢ "the solution of which is not with us" Ephr. III, 687 C. &c.

ܐܝܬ occurs constantly with the suffix, when it is merely the copula; thus in cases like ܠܳܐ ܐܺܝܬܶܝܗ ܗܳܕܶܐ ܐܶܠܳܐ ܐܶܢ ܫܽܘܪܳܝܶܗ ܕܒܶܪܺܝܬܳܐ "this is nothing else

(1) Read thus.

save the sword of Gideon" Judges 7, 14; ܝܘܣܦ ܕܝܢ ܒܪ ܚܡܫܝܢ ܘܫܬ ܫܢܝܢ ܐܝܬܘܗܝ ܗܘܐ "Joseph was fifty-six years old" Aphr. 465, 11 (in the parallel passages merely ܗܘܐ); ܐܝܬܘܗܝ ܗܘܐ ܕܝܢ ܗܢܐ ܛܘܒܢܐ ܪܒܘܠܐ ܡܢ ܛܠܝܘܬܗ ܚܢܦܐ "but this blessed Rabbūlā was from his childhood a heathen [had been brought up as a heathen]" Ov. 160, 11; ܥܒܕܗ ܕܝܢ ܬܡܢ ܗܢܐ ܒܠܚܘܕ ܐܝܬܘܗܝ ܗܘܐ "his work there, however, was only this" Ov. 168, 15; ܘܓܘܗ̇ ܕܚܪܝܒ ܐܝܬܘܗ̇ ܐܘܪܫܠܡ "and her inward part, which is wasted, is Jerusalem" Aphr. 98, 9; ܘܒܢܝ ܫܠܡܐ ܐܝܬܝܗܘܢ ܐܚܘܗܝ ܕܡܫܝܚܐ "and the sons of peace are the brethren of Christ" Aphr. 305, 5 &c.

With suff. of the 1st and 2nd person: ܐܢܬܘܢ ܡܢ ܐܒܐ ܐܟܠܩܪܨܐ ܐܝܬܝܟܘܢ *ὑμεῖς ἐκ τοῦ πατρὸς τοῦ διαβόλου ἐστέ* John 8, 44; ܐܢ ܨܒܬ ܐܝܬܝܢ "if thou art willing, so are we" Aphr. 493, 18; ܥܕ ܐܝܬܝܢ ܒܥܠܡܐ "as long as we are still in the world" Ov. 195, 19; ܐܢܐ ܟܪܣܛܝܢܐ ܐܝܬܝ "I am a Christian" Moes. II, 73, 18; ܐܝܟ ܕܐܝܬܝ ܗܘܝܬ "as I was" ZDMG XXIX, 116 *paen.*; ܓܝ̈ܣܐ ܐܝܬܝܢ "we are robbers" Sim. 365 mid.; ܐܚܢܢ ܠܐ ܐܝܬܝܢ ܚܪ̈ܫܐ "we are no magicians" Mart. I, 182, 3; ܐܝܟ ܕܐܝܬܝܟ ܐܦ ܗܫܐ ܪܫܐ "as thou art now also the head" Jul. 18, 3; ܒܐܝܢܐ ܨܐܦܘܬܐ ܘܕܚܠܬܐ ܐܝܬܝܟܘܢ ܗܘܝܬܘܢ "in what anxiety and fear you were" Jul. 21, 15.

§ 304. Examples of the uninflected state of ܗܘܐ with ܐܝܬ: ܐܝܬ ܗܘܐ ܠܗ̇ ܐܡܬܐ "she had an handmaid" Gen. 16, 1 (Ceriani ܐܝܬ ܗܘܬ); ܐܚ̈ܐ ܕܝܢ ܠܐ ܐܝܬ ܗܘܐ ܕܥܡܪܝܢ ܬܡܢ "but there were no brethren, who dwelt there" Sim. 286 mid.; ܨܒܘ̈ܬܐ ܐܚܪ̈ܢܝܬܐ ܕܐܝܬ ܗܘܐ ܠܗ "other things which he had" Sim. 276, 7; ܘܒܓܘ ܢܘܪܐ ܐܝܬ ܗܘܐ ܕܡܘܬܐ ܕܐܪܒܥ ܚܝ̈ܘܢ ܘܐܪܒܥܐ ܐܦ̈ܐ ܐܝܬ ܗܘܐ ܠܚܕ ܚܕ "and in the midst of the fire was the form of four beasts, and every one had four faces" Moes. II, 98 v. 358; ܠܝܬ ܗܘܐ ܡܝ̈ܐ "there was no water" Aphr. 452, 13 (var. ܠܝܬ ܗܘܘ); ܡܠܩܛ̈ܐ ܘܡܣܟܢ̈ܐ ܘܐܟܣܢܝ̈ܐ ܕܐܝܬ ܗܘܐ ܬܡܢ "the gleaners, the poor and the strangers, who were there" Sim. 276 *inf.* Often too in translations from the Greek ܐܝܬܝܗܘܢ ܗܘܐ, ܐܝܬܝܗܝܢ ܗܘܐ alongside of ܐܝܬܝܗܘܢ ܗܘܘ, ܐܝܬܝܗܝܢ ܗܘ̈ܝ.

ܐܝܬ ܗܘܐ with Feminine and with Plural.

☞ p. 359

§ 305. That ܐܝܬ answers, as regards syntax, to the Part. (of ܗܘܐ), is shown also in constructions like ܥܕ ܠܐ ܐܝܬܝ ܓܒܠܬܢܝ "before I was in existence, thou didst fashion me" Ephr. III, 342 E; ܙܒܢ ܟܠܡܕܡ ܕܐܝܬ ܠܗ "he sold all that he had" Ov. 165, 24; ܝܠܦܘ . . . ܕܐܝܟܐ ܘܐܝܟܢ ܐܝܬܘܗܝ "they learned where and how he was" Ov. 169, 23; ܥܕ ܐܝܬܝ ܡܠܟܐ . . .

ܐܝܬ employed like a Participle; and with Forms of ܗܘܐ.

ܛܠܝ ܗܘܝܬ "when I was a boy, . . . I saw" Ov. 154, 10 (cf. § 275). Accordingly the word has been combined, like a participle, even with the Impf. of ܗܘܐ (§ 300): ܝܗܒ ܠܗ ܕܢܗܘܘܢ ܐܝܬ ܒܗ ܚܝ̈ܐ ἔδωκεν ζωὴν ἔχειν John 5, 26 C.; ܐܝܟ ܕܢܗܘܐ ܐܝܬܘܗܝ ܠܢ . . . ܛܘܦܣܐ "in order that he may be an en-sample for us" Ov. 159, 7; ܕܠܐ ܢܗܘܐ ܐܝܬܘܗܝ "that he may not be" Ov. 62, 22; ܕܥܠ ܫܘܚܠܦܐ ܪܒܐ . . . ܢܗܘܐ ܐܝܬܘܗܝ ܡܡܠܠܐ "that the discourse may be about a great change" Jos. St. 92, 4; ܕܒܟܠܗܝܢ ܥܕ̈ܬܐ ܐܘܢܓܠܝܘܢ ܕܡܦܪ̈ܫܢܐ ܢܗܘܐ ܐܝܬ ܘܡܬܩܪܐ "that in all the churches there may be a Gospel in separate parts [*i. e.* a book of the Gospel arranged in the original order], and that it be read" Ov. 220, 4; ܝܗܒ ܠܢ ܕܢܗܘܐ ܐܝܬܝܢ . . . ܐܝܟ ܕܡܢܗ "gave to us that we should be, as it were, of him" Regulae Monasticae ed. Chabot (Accad. dei Lincei, Rend. 1898, 41, 15), and thus, frequently,—particularly in translations from the Greek. Jacob of Edessa has the word with a purely future signification (Epist. 13 ed. Wright p. 11, 7): ܐܠܗܐ ܕܐܝܬܘܗܝ ܗܘܐ ܘܐܝܬܘܗܝ ܘܢܗܘܐ ܐܝܬܘܗܝ ܠܥܠܡܝܢ "God, who was, and is, and shall be for ever." So even ܕܢܗܘܘܢ ܐܝܬ ܗܘܐ ܠܗܘܢ ܚܝ̈ܐ ܘܗܘܢܐ ܪܒܐ "so that they even had life and great reasoning power" Moes. II, 104 v. 444. With the Part.: ܠܝܛ ܗܘ ܪܥܝܢܐ ܕܗܘܐ ܐܝܬ "cursed is the opinion which exists" Ephr. III, LIII *ad inf.* One translator ventures even upon ܗܘܝ ܐܝܬܝܟ ἴσθι Lagarde, Reliq. 21, 23, 24.

☞ p. 359

ܐܝܬ with Infinitive and complete Clauses.

§ 306. On ܐܝܬ with the Inf. v. § 286. So too ܕܡܫܟܚ ܗܘܐ ܐܝܬ ܠܗ ܕܢܪܓܫ "which could feel without the soul" Moes. II, 92 v. 242; ܡܐܢܐ ܓܒܝܐ . . . ܐܝܬ ܠܗ ܕܢܗܘܐ ܡܢܗ "a chosen vessel shall he become [*lit.* is it to him that there be of him]" Sim. 278 *ad inf.*, where *Cod. Lond.* has merely ܗܘܐ ܡܢܗ; and thus frequently.

ܐܝܬ ܠ "to have".

§ 307. When translators put ܐܝܬ ܠ for ἔχειν (also ܐܝܬ ܠܗ for ἔχει "he is" [of circumstance or condition]), they sometimes furnish the object of ἔχειν in the Syriac with ܠ also: thus even ܠܝ ܕܝܢ ܠܐ ܒܟܠܙܒܢ ܐܝܬ ܠܟܘܢ ἐμὲ δὲ οὐ πάντοτε ἔχετε Matt. 26, 11 (S. is different); John 12, 8.

☞ p. 359

ܐܝܬ and ܗܘܐ with Adverbs of Quality.

§ 308. Sometimes ܐܝܬ,—and even ܗܘܐ,—is combined with adverbs of quality instead of adjectives: ܐܢ ܫܪܝܪܐܝܬ ܐܝܬܘܗܝ ܦܬܓܡܐ "if the word is true" Deut. 13, 14; and frequently in translations such as ܒܝܫܐܝܬ ܐܝܬܝܗܘܢ "they are in an evil case" Euseb. Theoph. 2, 84 (towards the end), &c.—ܦܩܝܚܐܝܬ ܗܘܐ ܠܗ "it would be better for him" Ephr. in Zingerle's Chrest. 257, 8; ܘܠܐ ܗܘܐ ܣܪܝܩܐܝܬ ܗܘܬ ܡܐܬܝܬܗ "and his coming was not in vain" Aphr. 150, 15; ܘܣܘܦܗܘܢ ܗܘܐ ܒܝܫܐܝܬ ܠܚܪܬܐ "and it went badly with them in the end" Aphr. 293, 5; ܣܓܝܐܐܝܬ ܡܪ̈ܕܘܬܢ ܗܘܝ "our chastenings were manifold" Jos. St. 4, 14. ☞ p. 360

§ 308b. A very rare construction and one pronounced by BA no. 650 to be old and rude, is ܐܝܬ ܠ' = simple ܐܝܬ: ܘܐܝܬܝܗ ܠܟܬܒܢܘܬܐ ܗܟܢܐ "and the writing is thus" Land III, 327, 24; ܐܢ ܡܢ ܙܒܢܐ ܕܫ̈ܠܝܚܐ ܐܝܬ ܠܗ̇ ܠܗܕܐ ܢܛܘܪܬܐ "whether this observance comes from the time of the Apostles" Jac. Ed. in Lagarde, *Rel. Jur. Syr.* 144, 4. Cf. BB p. 151, 4. ܐܝܬ ܠ = simple ܐܝܬ.

II. THE SENTENCE.

1. THE SIMPLE SENTENCE.

A. THE SIMPLE SENTENCE IN GENERAL.

§ 309. The Nominal sentence,—that is, the sentence which has a Substantive, an Adjective, or an Adverbial expression as a predicate,—is not very sharply distinguished in Syriac from the Verbal sentence. The Participle,—becoming a pure Verbal form, but yet betraying its Nominal origin—, which is widely employed as a predicate, and ܐܝܬ which in like manner comes near to the Verb, mark stages of transition from the Nominal sentence to the Verbal sentence; while on the other hand sentences with the Substantive verb ܗܘܐ can scarcely be regarded as truly Verbal sentences. Farther the inner constructions severally of Nominal and Verbal sentences in Syriac do not greatly differ. **Nominal Sentence. Verbal Sentence.**

§ 310. A Nominal predicate, when set beside a Subject—without a copula—may form a sentence, just like a verb: ܚܘܒܐ ܪܚܝܩ ܡܢ ܫܘܒܗܪܐ "love (is) far removed from vainglory" Aphr. 256, 14 (v. farther examples, with Predicative Adjective § 204 A, and with Participle § 269 *sqq.*); ܚܘܒܐ ܢܘܗܪܐ "love is light" Aphr. 257, 22; ܗܠܝܢ ܡܛܠ ܒܪܢܫܐ **Copula wanting.**

ﻻﻮﻮﻮﺟﻼ ﺗﻮﻮﻮﺟﻼ, "this is the Apology against the Jews" Aphr. 331, 14; ﻣﻌﻤﺮ ﻳﺨﻞ "the Good Being is thy name" Aphr. 493, 10; ﺷﻮﻣﺪﺍ ﺟﺐ "in it is love" Aphr. 297, 7; ﻳﻤﻤﺔﺍ ﺍﻋﻼ ﺍﻫﻮﺍ ﻟﻞ ﺳﻤﻴﺔﺍ ﻳﺤﺪﻓﺤﻢ "and in this there is neither sin nor righteousness" Aphr. 308, 3; ﺟﺐ ﻗﻮﻣﺸﺮ ﻗﻢ "there is in us of thy spirit" Aphr. 488, 11 &c. It is but rarely that a copula is wanting, in longer sentences, as in ﻳﺎﻣﺪ ﺗﺤﺪﺍ ﺍﻓﺰﻣﻬﺎ ﻓﺤﺪﻣﻲ ﻗﺰﻓﻤﻲ ﻳﻤﻬﺪ ﻳﻔﺰﻧﻬﺎ ﺍﻟﺤﻨﺎ ﻳﺤﺪﻑ ﻓﺮﻫﻮ ﻣﺎﻳﻨﺎ ﻳﺨﻞ ﻳﻘﻤﺒﻬﺎ ﻳﺘﺨﻴﺎ "and farther this utterance,—of the which our Redeemer declared that upon it hang the Law and the Prophets,—is beautiful, good and excellent" Aphr. 30, 1 &c. But the omission, not merely of every copula, but even of the tense-marking ﻫﻮﺍ, is very common in short subordinate sentences, like ﻳﺘﻨﻬﺎ ﺟﻴﺘﻮﻣﻪ ﺟﺐ "while there are just persons within it" Aphr. 457, 16; ﻓﻠﺴﻮﻑ ﻳﻤﻘﻤﻬﺎ ﻣﻘﻤﺒﻼ ﺟﺐ ﻳﻔﻬﻻ "while the vine was torn out and taken from them" Aphr. 463, 5; ﺟﺐ ﺯﺩ ﺟﻮﺟﺢ ﻣﺆﻣﺴﺮ "while our wickedness before thee was great" Aphr. 488 *ult.*; ﻳﻘﻤﺒﻬﺎ ﻣﻌﻘﻤﺪ ﺣﺪ ﻳﺠﻬﻮﺍ ﻓﻲ ﺍﺣﺪﺍ ﺳﺮﺍ ﻳﺤﺪﻣﺠﺎ ﻓﻘﺼﻤﺤﺪﻩ ﻭﺍﻣﻬﺢ "and brought one great hewn stone, which was well polished and beautiful" Sim. 271, 7; ﺟﺐ ﻳﺪﺟﺢ ﻗﺼﻘﻤﺠﻼ ﺣﻤﻤﻲ ﻳﻔﻬﻻ "while these poor people were still in the Mandra" Sim. 312 mid. &c. (cf. §§ 275; 305). Wherever the past is involved, ﻫﻮﺍ (ﻻﻫﻮﺍ, ﻭﻫﻮﺍ) might also stand here. Thus in ﻟﻤﺎ ﻫﻮﺍ ﺟﺒﺮ ﻗﺪﻣﻪ ﻳﺤﺼﺪﻩ ﺍﺳﺮﻳﻞ ﺍﻳﻨﻞ "but he had another brother, whose name was Shemshai" Sim. 268 *ult.*, the *Cod. Lond.* has ﻭﺣﺼﻤﺪﻩ ﺣﺼﻤﺪﻩ ﻫﻮﺍ ﻣﺪﺯﺕ ﺍ.

§ 311. Apart from sentences of the last kind [§ 310], the employ- ment of a copula is far more usual. First of all, the 3rd pers. pron. serves as such, being really a reference indicating or recalling the subject. For ﺯﻳﻤﻒ ﻳﺤﺪﻓﻮﺍ "God is righteous", there is often said ﻳﺤﺪﻓﻮﺍ ﻫﻮﺍ ﺯﻳﻤﻒ or ﺯﻳﻤﻒ. ﻫﻮﺍ ﻳﺤﺪﻓﻮﺍ. Thus ﺯﻳﻤﻒ. ﺯﺩ ﻫﻮﺍ ﺳﻤﻴﻬﻮﻩ "great is his sin" Aphr. 45, 10 (l. 8 ﺳﻤﻴﻬﻮﻩ, without ﻫﻮﺍ); ﺯﻳﺒﺮ ﻣﻌﻘﻼ ﻫﻮﺍ ﻗﻢ ﻳﺤﺠﻲ ﻻ, ﻣﻲ "his weapon is weaker than ours" Aphr. 137, 21; ﻓﺰﻫﻮﻫﺎ ﻫﻮﺍ ﻓﺨﺪﻩ ﻳﺤﺠﺪﻩ "his whole heart is with him" Ov. 278, 26; ﻗﺼﺨﻤﺒﻼ ﻫﻮﺍ ﻗﺪﻩ ﻣﺒﺰﻧﺎ "older is the promise", and ﻣﺒﺰﻣﻨﺎ ﻗﺪ ﺗﺤﺪﺍ "older is the word" Aphr. 27, more than once; ﺟﺮﻧﻼ ﻫﻮﺍ ﻳﻞ ﺟﺮ ﻳ "if it is a disgrace to thee, that" Ov. 162, 8; ﺍﻛﻢ ﻳﺤﺞ; ﺍﺣﺰﻣﻬﺢ ﻫﻮﺍ ὁ πατὴρ ἡμῶν Ἀβραάμ ἐστι John 8, 39; ﺍﻧﻒ ﻳﺤﺰﻧﺎ ﻳﺤﺞ ﻳﻔﻬﻢ ﺟﺘﺤﻮﻗﻨﻒ "that his creators are many" Aphr. 51, 7; ﺟﻤﻦ ﺍﻧﻒ ﻣﺤﺼﺸﻒ; ﻭﻧﻔﺎ "these are the men and women" Sim. 271 *ad inf.*;

ﺀ‏‏ﻟﻤﺠ ﻟﻤﺘﻬﺎ ﺁ؟ﺗﻨﻬﺎ ﺀ‏‏ﻟﻤﺠ؟ "for the just and the upright are the salt of the earth" Aphr. 457, 5; ﻟﻤﺠ‏ﻮﺣ ﻟﻨﻒ ﻣﻊ "who are these?" Sim. 271 mid.; ﻟﻨﺎ ﻫﻦ ﻫﻨﺎ ‏‏ﺟﺪ ﻫﻮ؟ "what then is this?" Aphr. 13, 12; and frequently ﻣﻨﻮ "who is?"; ﻣﻴﻮ "what is?"; ﻫﺎﻳﻮ "this is" &c. It occurs, though rarely, with the Part., as in ﺀ‏‏ﻟﻤﺠ؟ ﻣﺤﻼ ﻟﻤﺘﻬﺎ ﺁ؟ﺗﻨﻬﺎ ﻟﻨﻒ ﻣﺘﺸﻤﺘﺸ ﺣﺪﺟﻜﺤ "the just and the upright are always found on the earth" Aphr. 455, 11; 457, 2; ﺀ‏‏ﻟﻮ؟‏ﺟﻴﻢ ﻟﻤﺠ‏ﻮﺣ ﺀ‏‏ﻳﺲ ﻣﻬﻘﻒ "these chastenings are sufficient" Jos. 5, 16.

§ 312. A. When the subject is a personal pronoun, it is sufficient **Personal Pronoun** to set it down once; and in fact it stands oftenest as an enclitic after the **as Subject.** most important word in the predicate: ﺀ‏‏ﻟﻨﺎ ﺀ‏‏ﺟﻒ "I am innocent" Job 33, 9; ﺳﻴﺐ ﺣﺠﻤﺪﺟ "we are thy people" Aphr. 488, 9; ﻟﻴﺲ ﺀ‏‏ﻟﺴﻮ؟ ﺀ‏‏ﻧﺎ ﻟﻮﻓﺰﻳﻦ ﻟﻮﻫﻔﺰﻳﻦ "am I then my brother's keeper?" Gen. 4, 9; ﺀ‏‏ﻟﻨﺎ ﻣﺘﻘﻤﺸ ﺀ‏‏ﻟﻮ "if thou art wise" Prov. 9, 12; ﺀ‏‏ﻟﻤﺠﺪﺣ؟ ﺀ‏‏ﻟﻨﺎ ﺀ‏‏ﻟﻮ؟ ... ﺀ‏‏ﻟﻨﺎ ﺀ‏‏ﻟﻤﺠﺪﺣﺎ ﻫﺎﻓﻮ "that thou art either God, or the son of God" Addai 3 *ult.*; ﺀ‏‏ﻟﻨﺎﺣ؟ ﻫﻮﻣﻼﻳﺐ ﺣﻴﺔ؟ﻫﺎﻓﻮ "ye are the sons of Cain" Aphr. 331, 9; ﻟﻤﺞ؟ ﺀ‏‏ﻳﺶ ﻫﻮ "he is my brother" Gen. 20, 5; ﺀ‏‏ﻟﻤﺞ؟ ﺀ‏‏ﻟﻤﺠﺪﺣ؟ "that he is the Son of God" Ov. 163, 12; ﻳﻘﻤﻴ؟ ﻫﻦ "she is precious" Prov. 3, 15; ﺀ‏‏ﻟﻤﺤﺠ؟ ﻫﻦ ﺀ‏‏ﻟﻤﺠﻼ ﺀ‏‏ﻟﻤﻨﺸﺎ "she is a tree of life" Prov. 3, 18; ﺀ‏‏ﻟﻤﺤﻘﺘﻨﺎ؟ ﻟﻨﻒ ﺀ‏‏؟ﻣﺪﻣﺘﺸﻼ "that they are the disciples of Christ" Ov. 177, 4 &c. For 1st and 2nd Pers. cf. the Participial forms, § 64.

In the case of two Participles, the Subject pronoun does not need to be repeated, *e. g.* ﺀ‏‏ﻳﺤﺠ؟ ﻣﻬﻌﺠﻴﻢ ﺀ‏‏ﻟﻤﺠﺪﺣﺎ ﻣﺘﺸﻤﻴ ἃ ἀκούετε καὶ βλέπετε Matt. 11, 4 P. (C. ﺀ‏‏ﻟﻤﺠﺪﺣ؟); (ﻣﺪﻳﻢ ﻳﺴﻠﻴﺐ ﺀ‏‏ﻟﻤﺠﺪﺣ؟ ﻣﺪﻳﻢ ﻳﻤﻼﻳﻨﺎﻳﺪ؛ ﺀ‏‏ﻟﻨﺎ ﻫﻤﺪﻳﺤ؟) ﻣﻬﺪﻟﻤﺎﻗﻒ "thou art exceeding angry and wrathful" Jesussabran (Chabot) 554, 11; ﺀ‏‏ﻟﻤﺠﺪﺣﻢ؟ ﻫﺎﺀﻟﻤﺠﺪﺣﻢ ﺀ‏‏ﻟﻤﺠﺪﺣ؟ ﻟﺞ ﻣﻬﻌﺠﻴﻢ ﻣﺪﻳﻢ ﻫﻦ "from me you receive nothing, and depart" John. Eph. 399, 15.

☞ p. 360

B. It is far less common for the pronoun of the 1st and 2nd person to stand alone at the commencement. A certain emphasis is usually conveyed in that arrangement: ﺀ‏‏ﻟﻨﺎﻟﻮ؟ ﻳﻜﺪﻫ؟ ﻣﻌﺠﺪﺣﺒ ﺀ‏‏ﻟﻨﺎ ﺣﻴﺠ "when I was still but a little boy" Apost. Apocr. 274, 9 (Gnostic Hymn); ﻟﺤﻴﺠ؟ ﺀ‏‏ﻟﻨﺎ ﺀﻣﺪ ﻣﻬﻤﺤﻴﻨﻠﻮ؟ "whilst thou art uplifted, vainglorious and proud" Aphr. 270, 8; similarly ll. 10, 11; ﺀ‏‏ﻟﻨﺎ؟ ﻣﻴﺮ؟ ﻣﺤﻤﺤﻴﺞ ﻣﻬﻤﺤﻴﻼ "for thou art waiting and hoping" Aphr. 341, 6; ﺀ‏‏ﻟﻤﺠﺪﺣ؟ﺀ ﻣﺪﻳﻢ ﻣﻬﻌﺠﻴﻢ ἃ ἀκούετε Luke 10, 24 P. S. (C. ﺀ‏‏ﻟﻤﺠﺪﺣ؟ ﻣﻴ) immediately after ﻣﻴﺮﻳﻤ ﻳﻨﺸﻠﻴ ﺀ‏‏ﻟﻤﺠﺪﺣ؟ ﺟﺬﻫﻮ ἃ ὑμεῖς βλέπετε; ﺀ‏‏ﻟﻤﺠﺪﺣ؟ ﻣﺤﻤﺤﻴﺞ ﺟﻤﻴﺢ؟ ﻣﺤﻤﻼﻟﻴﻦ οὐ γὰρ ὑμεῖς ἐστε οἱ λαλοῦντες Matt. 10, 20 P. S.;

ܠܐ ܐܢ̱ܬܘܢ ܐܡܪܝܢ οὐχ ὑμεῖς λέγετε (a question) John 4, 35 P. S. (C. ܐܢܬܘܢ ܐܡܪܝܢ ܐܢܬܘܢ); ܠܐ ܓܝܪ ܐܢ̱ܬܘܢ ܥܐܠܝܢ ὑμεῖς γὰρ οὐκ εἰσέρχεσθε Matt. 23, 14 C. S. (P. ܥܐܠܝܬܘܢ ܐܢ̱ܬܘܢ); ܐܝܬ ܕܐܢ̱ܬܘܢ ܠܐ ܝܕܥܝܢ ܠܗ̇ ἣν ὑμεῖς οὐκ οἴδατε John 4, 32 C. (P. S. ܐܝܬ ܕܐܢܬܘܢ ܠܐ ܝܕܥܝܢ ܐܢܬܘܢ); ܘܝܕܥܬܐ ܘܡܣܬܟܠܢܘܬܐ ܐܢܐ ܩܢܐ ܐܢܐ "and I acquire knowledge and understanding" Prov. 8, 12 &c. So in S. farther, Matt. 13, 17; Luke 22, 29 and 70; Luke 10, 24. With the 3rd pers. this is more frequent: ܘܗ̄ܝ ܡܫܘܪܐ "and she leaped" Sim. 273 *inf*. (*Cod. Lond.* adds ܗܘܬ) &c.

C. The personal pronoun as Subject is very commonly placed at the beginning, and then repeated enclitically before or after the leading word in the predicate, so that this second form constitutes the copula: ܐܢܐ ܐܢܐ ܡܪܝܐ "I am the Lord", occurring often; ܘܐܢܐ ܥܦܪܐ ܐܢܐ ܘܩܛܡܐ "and I am dust and ashes" Gen. 18, 27; ܐܢܐ ܐܟܘܬܟ ܐܢܐ "I am as thou" Job 33, 6; ܐܢܐ ܐܢܐ ܡܫܝܚܐ ἐγώ εἰμι ὁ Χριστός Matt. 24, 5; ܚܢܢ ܚܢܢ ܒܢܝ̈ ܐܒܪܗܡ "we are the sons of Abraham" Aphr. 331, 5 (l. 15 ܚܢܢ ܐܦ ܒܢܝ̈ ܐܒܪܗܡ); ܐܢ̱ܬ ܓܝܪ ܣܢܚܪܝܒ ܢܪܓܐ ܐܢ̱ܬ ܒܐܝ̈ܕܝ ܕܦܣܩ ܘܡܣܪܐ ܒܐܝ̈ܕܝ ܕܢܣܪ ܒܗ "surely thou, Sennacherib, art an axe in the hands of him who hews, and a saw in the hands of him who saws therewith" Aphr. 82, 2 (l. 4 ܘܫܒܛܐ ܐܢ̱ܬ ܠܡܡܚܐ ܒܗ "and art a rod for striking with"); ܐܢ̱ܬ ܡܢ ܐܢ̱ܬ "σὺ τίς εἶ" John 1, 19; ܠܡܐ ܐܢ̱ܬ ܪܒ ܐܢ̱ܬ ܡܢ ܐܒܘܢ "μὴ σὺ μείζων εἶ τοῦ πατρὸς ἡμῶν" John 8, 53 &c. In particular this use is often found with the Part. as in ܐܢܐ ܟܬܒ ܐܢܐ &c. So ܐܢܐ ܐܢܐ ἐγώ εἰμι "it is I" Matt. 14, 27, and elsewhere. So too when the pronoun of the 3rd person stands for the subject, the same word is frequently subjoined as the copula, and in fact the two are often directly combined: ܗ̄ܘܝܘ ܪܝܫ ܟܠܗܘܢ ܒܪ̈ܝܬܐ "he is the chief of all created things" Job 40, 19; ܗ̄ܝ ܗܝ (or ܗ̄ܝܝ) ܐܢ̱ܬܬܐ "she is the woman" Gen. 24, 44; ܕܗ̄ܘܝܘ ܡܫܝܚܐ ὅτι αὐτός ἐστιν ὁ Χριστός Matt. 16, 20; cf. John 4, 29.

D. But the pronoun of the 3rd person often appears too in the enclitic form as a copula with the 1st and 2nd persons as Subject: ܐܢܐ ܗܘ ܒܪܟ "I am thy son" Gen. 27, 18; ܐܢ̱ܬ ܗܘ ܣܒܪܝ "thou art my hope" Job 31, 24; ܐܢ̱ܬܝ ܗܝ ܬܘܟܠܢܝ "thou (f.) art my confidence" *ibid.*; ܐܢ̱ܬ ܗܘ ܡܫܝܚܐ σὺ εἶ ὁ Χριστός Matt. 16, 16 (cf. 26, 63); ܚܢܢ ܐܦ ܥܡܗ ܕܐܠܗܐ "we are the people of God" Aphr. 331, 4 and 15 (cf. *supra* C);

ﭏﮐﻒ، ﭏﻧﻜﻒ ﭏﻧﻜﻒ ὑμεῖς ἐστε τὸ ἅλας τῆς γῆς Matt. 5, 13; ﭏﻜﻒ، ﭏﻧﻒ ﺟﺎﻗﻞ ﺭّﺟﺰﻷ "ye are the stones of the field" Ov. 115, 12, and thus frequently ﭏﻧﺒﻒ ﭏﻧﻒ Aphr. 286 *sq.*

§ 313. The Copula may farther be expressed by ﭏﻟ with suffix ﭏﻟ as Copula. (§ 303), while ﻟﻬﻮﻯ does not represent a proper copula, seeing that it is Wide always an actual Tense form. But in all these cases the language has choice in a wide choice among various modes of expression. Instead of the two the Copula. forms cited in § 312 C for "we are the sons of Abraham", viz:— ﺳﻨﺒ ﺳﻨﺒ ﺗﻠﺲ ﭏﺣﺰﻧﻬﻢ and ﺳﻨﺒ ﭏﻧﻒ ﺩ' ﺩ' ﭏ, the sentence might also have run thus: ﺩ' ﭏ ﺩ' ﭏﺒﻤﻲ ﺳﻨﺒ or ﺳﻨﺒ ﺩ' ﭏ ﺩ' ﺳﻨﺒ or merely ﺳﻨﺒ ﺩ' ﺩ' ﭏ or,— slightly emphasing the subject,— ﺳﻨﺒ ﭏﺩ' ﺗﺪ.

§ 314. The omission of the subject, when it may be understood Subject from the connection, takes place not only with Participles, which pass wanting. over to the category of verbs (§ 253), but in certain cases also with Adjectives Thus in particular, in short accessory clauses, *e. g.*: ﺣﺪﻭﻑ، ﻭﻟﺴﻘﻤﺰ "who are in need" ("to whom it is insufficient") Ov. 217, 14; ﻣﺪﻝ ﻭﻟﻨﺖ "what he was due" Matt. 18, 30; ﻣﻘﺐ ﺟﻲ ﺳﻨﻬﺎ διέμενε κωφός Luke 1, 22; ﻟﻬﻞ ﺟﻲ οὔσῃ ἐγκύῳ Luke 2, 5; ﺣﺪﻭﻑ، ﺭّﻭﺩﺣﻔﻞ ﻣﻨﺖ ﺟﻲ ﻭﻣﻒ ﻟﻤ "and when he was on the point of entering, he saw" Sim. 271 mid. (and frequently thus with ﺟﻲ) &c. Farther in short sentences, rhetorically pointed with ﻭ: ﻭﻣﺤﺪﻗﺴﻌﺪﻷ ﺟﺮ ﻣﻌﺠﺪ ﺭّﻣﻌﺠﺰﻷ ﺭّﻷ ﺳﻘﺴﻤﻲ ﺟﺮ ﻣﻌﺠﺪﻷ ﺟﻤﺤﺪﻷ ﻭﻣﺤﺪﺟﻲ "of those who were killed I have written to thee, and (it is) true [on the Fem. v. § 254 C]; those who were stoned I have signified to thee, and (it is) to be relied upon" Mart. I, 120, 9; ﻭﻣﻌﺰﺳﻲ ﻭﻣﻌﻬﻮﻥ ﻣﺪﻻﻫﻮﻥ ﻭﻣﻌﻨﺲ ﻭﺳﻠﻤﺰ ﻫﺰﻣﻬﻮﻥ ﻭﺳﻠﻤﺰ "they struck him, and (he was) cheerful, lashed him, and (he was) proud, lacerated him and (he was) pleased" Moes. II, 56 v. 124; ﺣﺪﻩ ﻫﺰﻣﻬﻞ ﺣﻨﻬﺰ ﺭّ ﺣﺪﻭﻫﻮﻥ ﺣﺸﺰﻩ ﻭﺭﺣﻔﻨﻲ ﺣﺪﻩ "lacerating combs (were) in his sides, lashes on his back, and (they were) trifling to him" *ibid.* 57 v. 175; ﻭﻣﺴﻤﺪ ﺟﻼ ﺭّﻭﻗﻬﻞ "and (he is) in need of alms" Aphr. 8 *ult.*; ﻭﺭﺣﻔﺪ ﺣﺠﺪﻧﻬﻒ "and for avarice (that is) but little" Aphr. 268, 5 (where there are additional examples). Farther ﺣﺪﻧﻲ ﻭﺟﺤﻮﺩﺣﻲ ﺣﺴﻤﺪ ﻧﻲ "for they are circumcised and uncircumcised" Aphr. 204, 4 (where the Part. influences the Adj.);— ﭏﻷ ﺣﻘﺪﻡ ﺟﺤﻤﻠﻲ ﻭﺣﻘﺪﻡ ﭏﻷ ﺟﺤﻤﻠﻲ "but over some things they have power, and over others none" Spic. 9, 23; cf. 10, 22.

Time-range of the Nominal Sentence.

§ 315. The Nominal sentence in itself denotes a state of being, and accordingly, first of all, it represents the continuous present (§ 269). By the context, however, it may often become plain that the state or condition concerns the past, *i. e.*, is contemporaneous with the time of the principal clause. Thus *e. g.* ܡܠܝܨ ܗܘܐ ܠܗܘܢ ܕܒܟܠܡܕܡ ... ܢܚܘܘܢ ... ܕܬܠܡ̈ܝܕܐ ܐܢܘܢ ܕܡܫܝܚܐ "he urged them to show in every thing that they were (*are*) disciples of Christ" Ov. 177, 3; ܟܠ ܡܐ ܕܐܝܬ ܠܗ *πάντα ὅσα εἶχεν* Matt. 13, 46; ܚܙܐ ... ܠܥܡܐ ... ܕܣܟܐ ܠܝܬ ܠܗ "he saw the people, that had no limit" Sim. 271; ܟܕ ܬܡܢ ܐܢܘܢ ܐܬܡܠܝܘ *ἐν τῷ εἶναι αὐτοὺς ἐκεῖ, ἐπλήσθησαν* ... Luke 2, 6. Cf. on this use in the case of the Part. § 275, in which case, however, it occurs far oftener. In particular, the indication of past time is often wanting in short Relative clauses, of which the predicate is an Adverbial qualification (§ 355).—Sometimes, though but rarely, a Nominal clause is employed to delineate in a lively manner a past condition, just as in the example given in the foregoing section ܗܕܪܐ ܒܥܝܢܘܗܝ ܘܟܘ' &c.

Separation of the Subj. from the Pred. by means of ܘ.

§ 316. The separation of the Subject from the Predicate by means of ܘ, in short successive clauses, is a purely rhetorical device, exemplified in ܚܕܘܬܐ ܥܪܩܬ ܠܗ̇ ܦܨܝܚܘܬܐ ܐܬܥܛܠܝܬ ܘܫܠܡܐ ܐܬܛܪܕ ܘܫܠܝܐ ܐܬܕܪܝ ܥܘܕܪܢܐ ܠܝܬ ܘܡܥܕܪܢܘܬܐ ܘܠܐ ܩܪܝܒܐ ܗܘܬ ܘܟܘ' "Joy, it was fled; cheerfulness, it was removed; peace, it was chased away; quietness, it was driven off; help, there was none; assistance, it was not near &c." (eight more clauses of the same kind follow) Mart. I, 12 *ult.*, and in ܪ̈ܓܠܐ ܘܡܦܣܩ̈ܢ ܒܘܪ̈ܟܐ ܘܡܬܓܕ̈ܡܢ ܕܪ̈ܥܐ ܘܡܬܥܩܪ̈ܢ ܚܠܨ̈ܐ ܘܡܦܣܩ̈ܢ "the feet, they are struck off; knees, they are cut away; arms, they are torn out; haunches, they are struck off" Mart. I, 255 mid.

NOMINATIVE ABSOLUTE.

Nominative Absolute.

§ 317. It is not uncommon by way of emphasis to place a noun first, and leave its proper grammatical reference to be cleared up by a personal pronoun which comes after, and which answers to it. Of this class are constructions like ܒܝܬܐ ܒܢܝܗܝ "the house, he built it" (§ 288); on this also rests the employment of ܗܘ as copula together with other devices described in § 311 *sq.* In particular, we have in this class cases like ܢܘܗܪܐ ܢܗܝܪܐ ܗܿܘܝܘ ܡܫܝܚܐ "the clear light,—*that* is Christ" Aphr. 14, 10; ܫܬܐܣܬܐ ܕܝܢ ܗܿܝ ܗܝ ܫܘܪܝܐ ܕܟܠܗ ܒܢܝܢܐ "the foundation,—*that* is the beginning of the whole building" Aphr. 7, 2 &c. But a like course is followed also in the most diverse grammatical relations (1): ܠܟܠܗܘܢ ܗܠܝܢ ܕܟܝܘܬܗܘܢ ܗܘܬ ܠܗܘܢ ܨܘܡܐ ܓܡܝܪܐ "to all these their purity was a complete fast" Aphr. 45, 17; ܠܗܕܐ ܡܕܝܢܬܐ ܪܒܬܐ ܣܡ ܫܬܐܣܘܗܝ ܡܠܟܐ ܕܐܬܘܪ "of this great city the king of Assyria laid the foundations" Moes. II, 63 *inf.*; ܕܟܪܐ ܕܝܢ ܩܪ̈ܢܬܗ (2) ܡܬܬܒܪ̈ܢ ܐܢܝܢ "now the ram's horns are broken" Aphr. 83, 20; ܒܨܠܘܬܗ ܓܝܪ ܕܝܥܩܘܒ ܨܝܪ ܐܬܬܨܝܪ ܗܘܐ ܐܪܙܐ ܕ "for in Jacob's prayer the mystery was prefigured, of . . . " Aphr. 63, 17; ܗܒܝܠ ܓܝܪ ܡܛܠ ܗܝܡܢܘܬܗ ܐܬܩܒܠ ܩܘܪܒܢܗ "for Abel's offering was accepted for the sake of his faith" Aphr. 18, 4; ܘܡܢ ܕܠܐ ܒܗܬ ܡܚܘܬܗ ܡܬܐܣܝܐ "and whoever is not ashamed,—his wound is healed (= 'ܘܡܚܘܬܗ ܡܬܐܣܝܐ ܕܡܢ ܕܠܐ ܒܗܬ) Aphr. 136, 3; ܘܐܝܠܝܢ ܕܚܒܨܝܢ ܘܡܬܩܪܒܝܢ ܠܘܬܗ ܢܛܦ ܪܝܚܗ ܒܐܕܢܝܗܘܢ ܟܣܝܬܐ "and those who press on and approach him, into their secret ears his savour distills" Aphr. 449, 15; ܗܘ ܟܠܗ ܠܒܘܫܐ ܕ ܥܛܝܦ ܗܘܐ . . . ܐܬܚܙܝ ܒܦܓܪܗ . . . ܨܒܥܐ ܝܚܝܕܝܐ "on all that garment, which was wrapped about his body . . . appeared . . . only one single colour" Ov. 165, 7, and frequently thus with longer or shorter relative sentences: ܐܢܐ ܗܕܐ ܐܝܬ ܠܝ ܠܡܐܡܪ "I have this to say" Aphr. 486, 5; ܟܕ ܩܝܡܝܢܢ ܠܥܠ ܕܠܥܠ . . . ܡܩܕܡ ܟܕ ܗܘ ܚܙܐ ܘܡܬܕܒܪ ܟܠܗ ܥܡܐ ܒܢ "since we stand high, the whole people look to us, and let themselves be guided by us" Ov. 173, 11 &c. With Demonstrative pronoun: ܥܪܒܐ ܕܐܒܕ ܡܢ ܟܠܗ ܥܢܐ ܥܠ ܗܘ ܗܘ ܝܨܦ ܒܗ ܠܪܥܝܐ "the sheep which has been lost out of all the flock,—about it the shepherd has anxiety" Aphr. 142, 10.

CONCORDANCE OF THE PARTS OF THE SENTENCE.

§ 318. The words ܩܘܪ̈ܝܐ "villages", ܚܡܪ̈ܐ "asses", and ܐܢܫܐ when it signifies "men", are regarded as true plurals and are always construed with plural forms. The collective nouns denoting animals vary. Thus

Collectives as Sing. and Plur.

(1) In short sentences, however, it is comparatively rare.

(2) Read thus.

جْنَا "small cattle" is sometimes sing., sometimes plur., cf. إِلَاجْزَلِ جْتَسَ "my sheep were scattered" Mart. I, 47, 9 (followed by a number of other verbs in the sing.), along with مِحْدَهُم ةَوْأ جْتِهُ وبِمِحَنِ "put his sheep in heat, that they might multiply" *ibid.* 46, 5 &c. It is exactly the same with حَجِيْأ "larger cattle": sing. in Ov. 93, 19; pl. in Ov. 79, 18 *sq.* Others, like جِمْزَأ "a herd", زُسْمَأ "vermin" are wholly or preponderatingly singular.

The collective nouns which denote persons, are at first construed as singular; yet they may also be treated as plural, and so may other words which only in a transferred meaning denote a collection of persons, like إِلَزْأ "a land", مَزِيْتَأ "a city": their attributive adjuncts remain, however, in the sing. Examples:—سْرٍ جْمْفَأ "the people saw" Ex. 32, 1; وبِيْلِمِلْمَهُم مَفْجِهِ إِلَجْزَا ἀπογράφεσθαι πᾶσαν τὴν οἰκουμένην Luke 2, 1 S. (P. جْمْفَا إِلَجَزْأ); سَجِبْزِ جِهِ مِمِمِلْمَحِزَوْزَبِ جِه جْمْفَا زِبْهَوْزَبِلَ(وبِيْلِمِلْمَحْد فَجِه جْمْفَا) "the people of the Jews are proud of it, and glory in it" Aphr. 231, 12 [pl.], along with وَزَلَ مِمِمْلَمْحَدَوْزَ حَدَ خَنَ جْمْفَا وَزَلَمِزَلَ "in which in vain the people of Israel glory" [sg.] *id.* 242, 4; جْمْفَا مِمِلَلَ وَلَ مِجْدَه . . . حَمِزَ وَجِزَأ زَلَنَ; "the foolish [sg.] people, who had not received [pl.] . . . he uprooted and dispersed" Aphr. 184, 3 (and construed frequently thus, as sing. and as pl. [in the same sentence]); مِسْزَبِ جْهِ مَلِيْزَفَمِم "and the clergy surrounded him" Ephr. III, XLIII *inf.* [pl.] (usually sing.); إِلَه سْجِمِزَ فَجِهِ مَجِه فَجِهِ إِزَأ ةَه جْحْفَا وَةَه إِلَزْأ "for all that land came" Sim. 322, 12; مَلَأ ةَه جْحْفَا فَجِهِ أُمْلَ ةَةَأ "all the people ('tout le monde'), who were there, cried out" Sim. 383, 13 (*Cod. Lond.* حَمَا مَلَدَه مَجِيْتَلَأ . . . مَلَحَم); ةَةَه "when the whole city . . . was sitting there" Land II, 55, 18; مَزَةْفَا ؤَجِمِزَأ إِلَلِجَلَأ لَلَقْتِسَ إِلَزَجَيْدَه "what were left [*reliquiae*] of the blessed band of the three thousand were crowned (suffered martyrdom)" Moes. II, 71, 30; and many other instances. Even سَزَأ مِه لَجَدَا قَزِيْمَلِأ وَجِمَدَزِّبِمَد "a third part (f. sg.) of her inhabitants" Jul. 38, 25—is treated as a pl. masc. In the greater number of such cases, a plural, following in the Genitive, or a مَحِزَه, مَحِزَه, placed in apposition, tends to effect a plural construction, but yet the influence is not quite obligatory, cf. ةَه إِلَ فَجِهِ سَلَلَ وَلَ مِحِنَلَا سَزِّةَه "all this host without number surrounded it [Edessa]" Jos. St. 60, 6 (contrasted with سَلَلَ وَزَةَةَمْبَلَ

ܘܕܦܩ ܠܘܗ ܗܘܐ ܕܦܘܪ̈ܩܝܐ ܦܩܕܡܘ ,ܘܚܡܘܗ "the army of the Romans, which was with them, had dispersed themselves" Jos. St. 47, 20).

☞ p. 360

ܗܘܘ ܣܓܝ̈ܐ with a plural genitive is perhaps always construed as plural, e. g. ܣܓܝ̈ܐ ܗܘܘ ܪ̈ܗܘܡܝܐ ܕܝܬܒܝܢ ܬܡܢ ܐܡܪ "a large number of Romans (i. e. soldiers) lived there" Sim. 273 mid. (contrasted with ܣܓܝ̈ܐ ܘܚܕ ܥܡ ܘܕܚܠ ܐܬܬܙܝܥ "the great mass of the people [Sing. Gen.] was alarmed and terrified" Sim. 357 mid., and ܐܫܬ ܠܗ ܣܓܝ̈ܐ ܥܡܐ ܘܐܙܠܝܢ ܥܡܗ "the great body of the town marched along" Land II, 388, 6, where the Genitive determines the number and gender). Similarly ܘܡ̈ܝܬܝܢ ... ܗܘܘ ܣܓܝ̈ܐ ܡܢ ܬܪ̈ܝܢ ܐܠܦ̈ܝܢ ܓܒܪ̈ܝܢ "more than two thousand men perished" Chron. Edess. (Hallier) 146, 5 (Document of 201); ܣܓܝ̈ܐ ܗܘܘ ܘܐܝܠܝܢ ܕܦܫ ܥܡܗ ܓܒܪ̈ܐ ܡܢ ܕܚܠܝܐ "the most of the people of the town remained with him" Addai 31, 8.— ܟܠ with plural is construed as pl. only. With these are joined cases like ܟܠ ܡܝ̈ܐ Assemani I, 357 (Simeon of Bēth Arshām); ܟܠ ܡܝ̈ܐ ܘܐܝܠܝܢ ܕܐܬܘ "all who have come" ibid., and frequently thus; but the sing. is more usual here, and it occurs even in that passage.

§ 319. Even when the plural subject is resolved into its parts by means of ܣܒܪ ܣܒܪ (§ 242, cf. § 351), it may be construed as pl., and that even when it is itself omitted: ܗܠܝܢ ܟܬܒ̈ܐ ܥܣܪܐ ܘܡ̈ܟܬܒܐ ܙܥܘܪ̈ܐ ܓܝܪ ܫܒܪ ܡܢ ܚܕ ܫܒܪ ܢܣܒܬܝ "these ten little books which I have written thee take from one another" [i. e. "are written in continuation"—"form a series"] Aphr. 200, 15; ܫܒܪ ܚܕ ܫܒܪ ܟܠܝ "they plunder each other" Ov. 119, 16; ܐܘܕܥܬܢܝ ܫܒܪ ܡܢ ܫܒܪ "which are different from one another" Spic. 17, 19; ܝܩܣܬ ܘܗܘܬ ܫܟܠܚ̈ܕܝ ܫܒܪ ἄτινα ἐὰν γράφηται καθ᾽ ἕν John 21, 25: ܥܩܝܢ ܫܒܪ ܫܒܪ ܒܐܘܪ̈ܚܬܗܘܢ "but they adhered to their several ways" Ov. 160, 21; ܗܘܐ ܡܟܝ̈ܟܝܢ ܡܬܦܫ̈ܝܐ ܐܒ̈ܗܝܢ ܟܠ ܫܒܪ ܡܢ "all our ancestors were humble" Aphr. 188, 17; ܘ̈ܚܝܠܐ ܠܗܘܢ ܐܝܬ ܚܕ ܚܕ ܡܢ ܟܠ ܫܒܪ ܡܢ ܫܒܥܐ ܗܠܝܢ ܘܡܫܠܛ̈ܝܢ "and these seven [planets] have each of them power [severally] over the divisions" Spic. 18, 9 &c. (But also in the sg.: ܘܟܠ ܚܕ ܐܝܟ ܡܐ ܣܒܪ ܣܒܪ "each of them, as has been ordered it (f.), quickly carries out his wish" Aphr. 281, 14, cf. Aphr. 438, 13; Ov. 176, 27). Similarly ܣܟ̈ܠܐ ܘܟܠ ܪܚܘ ܣܒܪ ܠܘܩܒܠ ܚ̈ܕܕܐ ܣܒܪ ܡܬܩ "and all things stand opposed to each other" Aphr. 303 ult.—And thus even a simple ܫܒܪ ܡܢ, ܣܒܪ with a plural following, is frequently construed in negative

Plur. in Phrases with ܣܒܪ.

sentences as a plural: ܘܒܝܢܬܗܘܢ ܕܗܠܝܢ ܚܕܐ ܡܢ ܗܠܝܢ ܠܐ ܗܘܝܐ "and among these there is no single one of them" Spic. 14, 5; ܘܚܕܐ ܡܢܗܘܢ ܠܐ ܥܒܪ ܨܒܝܢܗ "and no one of them resists his will" Aphr. 284, 4; ܕܠܐ ܢܚܙܘܢ ܚܕ ܡܢ ܓܒܪܐ ܗܠܝܢ . . . ܐܪܥܐ "that no one of these men . . . shall see the
☞ p. 360
land" Deut. 1, 35 &c. Farther examples: Philipp. 4, 15; Philox. 543, 26; Apoc. Baruch 83 (fol. 551 *c ult.*); John van Tella (Kleyn) 50, 18; Euseb. Ch. Hist. 260, 4 *ab inf.* (But sing. *e. g.* in ܚܕܐ ܡܢܗܘܢ . . . ܠܐ ܬܦܘܩ "and let none (f.) of them go out" Ov. 177, 11). Similarly in a conditional clause: ܐܢ ܫܪܝܪܝܢ ܠܟ ܚܕܐ ܡܢ ܬܫܥܝܬܗ ܕܚܕ ܡܢ ܐܠܗܝܟ "if any one of the stories about one of thy gods is true for thee" Anc. Doc. 55, 2; ܐܢ ܢܫܒܘܢܝܗܝ ܚܕ ܡܢ ܒܣܝܡܘܬܗ ܕܥܠܡܐ ܗܢܐ "if one of the joys of this world takes him captive" John van Tella 31, 1 (var. ܢܫܒܘܗܝ). Except in Negative, and Conditional clauses, I know of the occurrence of this construction only in ܢܐܬܝܢ ܚܕܐ ܡܢ ܥܠܝܡܬܐ "one of the maidens may come" Land III, 36, 18, and in ܠܡܢܐ ܚܕܐ ܡܢ ܗܠܝܢ ܥܠܝܡܬܐ ܢܫܝܓܢ ܪܓܠܝܟ "why should one of these maids wash thy feet?" *ibid.* line 19, which sentences are
☞ p. 360
translated from the Greek.

In the same fashion as with ܚܕ ܚܕ, we have also ܣܩܘܒܠܝܢ ܘܫܠܝܢ ܫܝܢܐ ܗܢܐ ܠܘܬ ܗܢ "they are opposed, but peaceful, the one toward the other" Moes. II, 84 v. 127; ܘܢܩܝܦܝܢ ܗܘܘ ܗܢܐ ܠܗܢܐ "and they were attached to one another" Moes. II, 100 v. 371.

Prep. with Substantive as Subject.

§ 320. In the rather uncommon case, in which a substantive, dependent upon a preposition, has the position of subject, it is construed according to its gender and number. Thus in ܘܡܢ ܪܘܚܗ ܬܘܒ ܕܡܫܝܚܐ ܡܬܐܫܕܐ ܝܘܡܢܐ ܥܠ ܟܠ ܒܣܪ "and farther there is poured out today of the spirit of Christ upon all flesh" Aphr. 122, 18; ܐܦܢ ܡܢܗܘܢ ܡܢ ܡܠܐ ܠܐ ܫܠܡܢ ܠܡܐܡܪܐ ܐܚܪܢܐ "even should some of the words not agree with those of another speaker" Aphr. 441, 12. So also ܘܡܢ ܥܝܢܝܗܘܢ ܢܦܩܝܢ ܗܘܘ ܒܕܡܘܬܐ ܕܒܪܩܐ ܩܠܝܠܐ "and from their eyes there darted as it were quick flashes of lightning" Sim. 271 *paen.*; ܕܥܡܗ ܓܝܪ ܕܡܟܐ ܗܘܬ ܒܥܪܣܐ ܕܡܘܬܐ ܕܐܢܬܬܐ "for with him there was sleeping in bed the likeness of a woman" Sim. 292 mid.; ܢܚܬ ܕܡܘܬܐ ܕܒܪܩܐ "something like a flash of lightning shot down" Mart. I, 73, 6.

§ 321. In other cases the verb agrees throughout with the subject. *Verb in the Sing.* In particular a plural subject requires a plural verb. (¹) It is no real *with Subj.* exception to this rule that ﻮﻫ ﻞﻳﺍ may stand even with a fem. or pl. *in the Plur.* (§ 304), for the properly-nominal character of the sg. m. ﻞﻳﺍ "existence" still operates here. On the other hand there is an exception in the construction, occurring occasionally, of the uninflected passive Participle with ﻝ indicating the agent, in conjunction with a feminine or plural subject. In this case the language has begun to conceive the form ﻢﻴﺴﺣ ﻞ (§ 279) as quite equivalent to an active verb "I have made". Thus: ﻩﺪﻴﺣ ﻢﻴﺴﺣ ﻞﻳ̈ﺪﻗﺭﻭ ﻼﻴ̈ﺛﻭﻫﻭ "and hymns and psalms he made" Jos. St. 52, 1 (immediately after ﻩﺪﻴﺣ ﻢﻘﺴﻫ ﻼﻴﺛﻣ ﻲﻣ̈ﺪﻟﺑﻣﻭ "by whom many poems had been composed"); ﻢﺴﻣ ﻞﻴﺣ ﻩﻭ ﻞﻴﺣﺪﻫ "I have heard this" Kalilag and Damnag 10, 16; 15, 23; ﻢﻔﻣﻭ ﻼﻴﻧﻣ ﻢﺣ ﻞﻣﺍ̈ﺑﻳﻭ ﻞﺣ ﻢﻴﺴﺣ ﻼﻴﻣﻣ ﻢﺣ ﻞﺣﻣﺜﻣ ﻞ ἐποιήσαμεν διαθήκην μετὰ τοῦ Ἅιδου καὶ μετὰ τοῦ θανάτου συνθήκας [Is. 28, 15] Jac. Ed. in Wright's Catalogue 28 *a*ₗ *inf.*, and often thus in Jac. Ed. But here too agreement is far more usual. Of like construction is ﻼﻴﻧﻮﻳ ﻞﻴ̈ﺪﺣﺛﺪﻣ ﻖﺪ ﺖﻴ̈ﻟﻣﻭ "and on it were Greek characters" Jos. St. 66, 10; ﻞ̣ﻴ̈ﻣﺻﻫ ﻩﻩ ﻩ̇ﻩﺍ ﻢﻴﺴﻣ ﻩﻩﺍ ﺖﻴ̈ﺪﻣﺍﻭ ﻼ̣ﻔﻟ ﺍ "where the things had been consigned to writing and deposited" (Ps.-Eusebius) de Stella 1, 18; ﻼﻴﻣ̈ﻴﻣﺻ ﻞﻴ̈ﻣﺻﻫ ﻞﻴﺪﺣﺛﺪﻣ ﻢﻴ̈ﺪﺣ ﻩﻩﺍ ﺖﻴ̈ﻣﻣﻭ "and upon them were written hieratic characters" Ephr. II, 145 A (Jac. Ed.?).

Rem. The Singular-construction ﻩﻩﺍ ﻞﻴﺸ ﻩﺪﺣ ἐν αὐτῷ ζωὴ ἦν John 1, 4 (but different in C. after another division of the sentence) must rest upon a dogmatic caprice, like the masculine use of ﻼﻴ̈ﻣﻣ, when it signifies "Logos". (²)

Rem. On the Gender of Compounds cf. § 142.

§ 321ᵇ. ﻩﺪﻴ̈ﺣﺸ ﺮﺑ, literally "son of his moment" has wholly stif- ﻩﺪﺣ̈ﻣ ﺮﺑ fened into an adverb and stands unchanged with the fem., with the pl., *&c.*

(¹) Of course orthographical inadvertencies of author, copyist or even editor,— when, for instance, ﺡ̈ﻣﻣ stands for the similarly-pronounced ﺡﻣﺣﻣ,—can form no ground for questioning this rule.

(²) Thus ﻼﻴﻧ̈ ﻩﻩﻭ "is life" Joseph 304, 8 is perhaps correct. Philoxenus (Budge II, CV, 11) ventures upon ﻮﻴﺣ ﺪﺣ "one life".

and even with the 1st and 2nd Persons: ܘܐܝܟܢܐ ܡܢ ܫܥܬܗ ܐܬܐܣܝܬ καὶ ὡς ἰάθη παραχρῆμα (ἡ γυνή) Luke 8, 47 C. S. (P. ܡܚܕܐ), cf. v. 55; ܘܗܢܘܢ ܐܝܟ ܡܢ ܫܥܬܗܘܢ ܟܕ ܚܙܘܗܝ ܥܪܩܘ "but they withdrew, as soon as they saw it" 2 Macc. 14, 44; ܡܢ ܫܥܬܗܝܢ ܣܚܝ̈ ܘܟܚܠ̈ܝ ܥܝܢ̈ܝܗܝܢ "they (the women) forthwith washed themselves and painted their eyes" Ezek. 23, 40; ܘܡܢ ܫܥܬܝ ܫܕܪܬ ܠܘܬܟ ἐξαυτῆς οὖν ἔπεμψα πρός σε Acts 10, 33; ܡܢ ܫܥܬܟ ܣܝܡ "set

☞ p. 361

forth immediately" Clem. 9, 18 &c. It is the same with ܒܝܘܡܗ: ܡܢ ܒܝܘܡܗ ܗܒ ܠܗ ܐܓܪܗ "the same day give him the hire" Deut. 24, 15; ܡܢ ܒܝܘܡܗ . . . ܐܬܝܢ "we came the same day" Clem. 146, 32; ܘܡܢ ܒܝܘܡܗ . . . ܫܩܠܘܗ̇ "they took her away the same day" John Eph. 222, 15.— So also ܗܠܟܘ ܡܢ ܒܣܬܪܐܝܬ "they went backward" Gen. 9, 23.

Gender and Number of a Group of Nouns coupled with ܘ or a like Conjunction.

§ 322. When two or more nouns, connected by means of ܘ or a like conjunction, combine to form one member of a proposition, then, as regards concord, various cases become possible. If the members of the combination are all plural and of the same gender, naturally the connection is construed in accordance therewith. But when there are differences in gender and number, it is sometimes the position, sometimes the assumed importance of one or more of the members, that determines the case. Besides, when several singulars are combined, they are sometimes treated as a singular, sometimes as a plural.

Singular: ܦܫ ܐܪܥܢ ܘܡܕܝ̈ܢܬܢ "our land and our city remained" Jos. St. 31, 3; ܘܠܐ ܦܪܝܫ ܬܡܢ ܕܟܪܐ ܘܢܩܒܬܐ "male and female are not discriminated there" Aphr. 429, 1; ܘܡܠܝܐ ܟܝܠܬܐ ܘܡܢܝܢܐ "and measure and number are full" Spic. 12, 18; ܗܝܕܝܢ ܢܦܩ ܢܘܚ ܘܒܢܘ̈ܗܝ "then went forth Noah and his sons" Aphr. 477, 9; ܗܘ ܘܙܪܥܗ ܐܬܒܪܟ "he and his seed were blessed" Aphr. 328, 16: ܗܘܬ ܗܝ ܘܒܝܬ ܐܒܘܗ̇ ܡܩܒܠܐ ܝܪܬܘܬܐ "she and her father's house received an inheritance" Aphr. 329, 3 (and often thus, when there is a *principal person* concerned); ܡܢ ܟܝܢܐ ܗܘ̣ܐ ܝܠܕܐ ܘܒܢ̈ܝܐ "procreation and children are from nature" Spic. 11, 20; ܒܐܝܕܐ ܓܘܕܐ ܐܘ ܬܓܡܐ "in which troop or order?" Ephr. III, 245 D; ܘܐܡܬܝ ܕܗܘܐ ܙܘܥܐ ܘܟܦܢܐ ܘܡܘܬܢܐ ܘܩܪܒܐ "and when there was earthquake, famine, pestilence and war" Jos. St. 1, 4; ܠܐ ܣܠܩܬ ܥܠ ܠܒܗܘܢ ܚܡܬܐ ܘܛܢܦܘܬܐ "there did not rise in their heart wrath or impurity" Aphr. 428, 6; ܕܒܥܓܠ ܥܩܬܐ ܘܬܘܬܐ ܢܦܩܐ ܡܢ ܠܒܗܘܢ "that quickly grief

and regret of soul overtake them" Sim. 388, 14; ܘܐܣܪ ܗ̇ܘ ܘܐܣܪ ܕܚܫܐ ܗ̇ܘ ܘܐܣܪ
ܘܐܝܐܝܟܐ؛ ܕܚܠܝܘܬܐ ܗܕܐ ܘܒܣܝܡܘܬܐ ܠܐ ܡܬܚܬܐ؛ ܕܐܝܟ ܗܠܝܢ "that such a savour and such a sweet-
ness cannot be set forth in the world" Sim. 272 *ad inf.*; ܡܛܠ ܝܬܝܪܐܝܬ
ܟܡܐ . . . ܘܡܓܢܝܘ ܩܪܝܒܘܬ ܚܙܬܗ؛ ܘܡܦܣܩ ܡܠܝܘܬܗ ܚܠܝܬܐ ܕܥܡܗܘܢ
ܚܦܛ ܐܢܘܢ ܗܘܐ "how much more must near association with his look,
and his charming converse with them, have incited them to all that is
good" Ov. 199, 14.

Plural: ܘܡܡܠܠܝܢ ܗܘܘ ܗ̇ܘ ܘܗܢܘܢ "and he and they spoke" Sim.
340 mid.; ܘܗܦܟܘ ܠܬܡܢ ܦܛܪܝܩܘܣ ܘܗܘܦܛܝܐ [1] "Patricius and Hypatius
returned thither" Jos. St. 54, 3; ܘܪܚܡܬ ܟܣܦܐ ܐܘ ܪܓܬ ܩܢܝܢܐ ܗܠܝܢ
ܘܠܐܡܘܬܢܝ؛ ܠܐܘܪܚܐ ܘܢܡܘܣܢ ܐܦ ܠܐ ܢܬܩܪܝܢ "but avarice and covetousness
[*lit.* 'love of money or longing after possessions'], the which are alien to
our course of life, shall not even be named" Ov. 174, 11; ܒܨܝܪܝܢ ܐܢܘܢ
ܢܡܘܣܐ ܘܢܒܝܐ "the Law and the Prophets are too little" Aphr. 24, 3; ܐܘ
ܕܐܡܗܬܐ ܐܘ ܕܥܒܕܐ ܡܢ ܚܠܡܝܐ "of maid-servants or men-servants out of the laity" Ov.
174, 1; ܕܒܘܪܐ ܘܒܪܩ ܗܘܘ ܡܕܒܪܢ؛ "Deborah and Barak were leaders" Aphr.
481, 12; ܚܛܐ ܘܬܒܢܐ ܣܚܝܦܝܢ ܐܚܕܐ "wheat (f.) and straw are mixed together" Aphr. 152, 10; ܘܡܙܡܘܪܐ ܘܬܫܒܚܬܐ ܪܘܚܢܐ؛ ܘܒܩܛܪܓܡܐ ܗܘܬ "and
psalms and spiritual songs were brought into service" Sim. 392 mid. (Cod.
Lond. ܗܘܘ ܒܬܫܡܫܬܐ).—ܚܦܛ ܠܡܡܠܠܝ P. C. (ܦܪ̈ܣܝܬܐ S.)
οἱ τελῶναι καὶ αἱ πόρναι προάγουσιν ὑμᾶς Matt. 21, 31, cf. 32; ܝܘܣܦ
ܘܡܪܝܡ ܡܟܝܪܬܗ ܬܪܝܗܘܢ ܐܝܢ "Joseph and Mary his betrothed, both—" Aphr.
472, 20; ܒܢܝ ܡܬܘܠܐ ܐܘ ܒܢܬ ܩܝܡܐ ܗܠܝܢ ܕܢܦܠܘ ܡܢ ܕܪܓܗܘܢ؛ ܫܕܪܘ ܐܢܘܢ
"those under vows, of either sex [*lit.* 'sons of the covenant or daughters
of the covenant'], who have fallen from their grade, send ye into convents"
Ov. 218, 19; ܕܥܒܕܘܗܝ . . . ܘܡܠܘܗܝ ܠܟܠܢܫ ܝܬܪ ܗܘܘ "for
his works and words (f.) were profitable to every one" Ov. 178, 22; ܘܡܚܒܨ
ܢܘܪܐ ܒܥܡܝܪܐ ܘܩܢܝܐ ܘܚܒܛܐ ܡܫܬܠܛ؛ ܘܡܬܓܡܪܝܢ "and the fire gains the mastery
over the grass, reeds and brushwood, and they are consumed" Aphr.
16, 12; ܕܗܒܐ ܘܣܐܡܐ ܘܟܐܦܐ ܝܩܝܪܬܐ؛ ܕܒܗܝܢ ܣܠܩ ܒܢܝܢܐ "gold and silver
and precious stones, with which the building rises" Aphr. 16, 13 (where
the two masculine singulars preponderate over the plural feminine) &c.

---

[1] Write the verb thus in accordance with ܗܦܟܘ.

Cf. farther ܠܟ ܩܳܪܝܳܐ ܢܰܦܫܳܐ ܘܦܰܓܪܳܐ ܕܬܶܚܘܣ ܥܠܰܝܗܝ ܟܡ ܕܩܳܝܡܺܝܢ "soul calls to thee and body, that thou shouldst take pity upon them, so long as they endure" Quotation in Barh. gr. 2, 15 *ult.* (where at first the member standing at the beginning exercises its influence, but afterwards, in the pl., the m. predominates). The case is the same as with ܘ, in ܘܟܠܗܝܢ ܪ̈ܓܝܓܳܬܳܐ ܥܡ ܟܠܗܘܢ ܟܘ̈ܒܶܐ ܕܚܛܺܝܬܳܐ ܡܶܬܘܰܩܕܺܝܢ ܒܶܗ "all the lusts, together with all the briars of sin, are burned up therein" Ov. 164, 13.

The different Persons (1st, 2nd, 3rd) when bound together. § 323. In ranking together nouns of different persons, the 1st preponderates over the 2nd and 3rd, and the 2nd over the 3rd: ܐܶܢܳܐ ܡܳܪܳܟ ܘܐܰܢ̄ܬ ܪܰܒܰܝܬܳܐ(1) ܝܳܕܥܺܝܢ "I, thy lord, and thou, the steward, know [1st pl.]" Ov. 303, 13; ܘܩܳܡܢ ܐܶܢܳܐ ܘܗܽܘ "and we rose up, I and he" Jos. St. 29, 13, cf. line 10; ܐܶܢܳܐ ܘܡܰܠܟܽܘܬܝ ܡܚܰܣܝܳܢ ܐܶܢܳܐ "I, with my kingdom, am free from guilt" Jul. 70, 12; ܐܰܢ̄ܬ ܘܡܰܠܟܽܘܬܳܟ ܡܚܰܣܝܳܢ ܐܰܢ̄ܬ *ibid.* 132, 10; ܐܰܢ̄ܬ ܘܒܰܝܬ ܐܳܒܽܘܟ ܬܶܦܠܚܽܘܢ "thou and thy father's house shall serve [2nd pl.] Aphr. 272, 10. The exception ܠܳܐ ܡܰܠܟܳܟ ܘܠܳܐ ܦܽܘܩܕܳܢܶܗ ܘܠܳܐ ܐܰܢ̄ܬ ܘܠܳܐ ܚܰܝܠܳܟ ܘܐܳܦܠܳܐ ܬ̈ܝܪܳܬܰܢ ܡܫܰܟܚܺܝܢ ܦܳܪܫܺܝܢ ܠܰܢ "neither thy king nor his command, neither thou nor thy power, nor even our chastisements, are able to separate us" Mart. I, 155, 8,—has nothing remarkable in it, seeing that the 2nd person in this case is put between two 3rd persons.

ARRANGEMENT OF WORDS.

Position of the Subj. and Pred. § 324. A. The relative arrangement of the principal parts of the sentence is very free. The Subject in the Verbal sentence,—just as in the Nominal sentence, stands sometimes before, sometimes after the Predicate; and sometimes its parts are even broken up or inverted by parts of the predicate.(2) It is of course granted that in purely Verbal sentences, particularly in simple narration, the Predicate stands more

---

(1) = ܪܰܒ ܒܰܝܬܳܐ.

(2) How freely words may be arranged in Syriac, is well demonstrated by comparing passages of Syriac with Arabic translations of them. The Arab in that case is continually *obliged* to alter the arrangement of the words, while the Syrian in almost every instance might have *chosen* that arrangement which is absolutely *binding* upon the Arab.

frequently before the subject; but this is by no means a fast rule,—apart even from the fact that, if a new subject of importance appears, or if the subject has to be brought emphatically into notice, it is more usual to place the subject first. Also in sentences with the participle, the predicate perhaps stands oftener before, than after, the subject. But in purely Nominal sentences the reverse is the case. Still even the predicative adjective very often goes first, particularly in short secondary sentences with ܟܕ. It is farther to be noticed that, in the most diverse kinds of sentences, demonstrative pronouns are commonly placed at the beginning. In none of these cases do absolutely unbending rules prevail; and a Syriac sentence can scarcely be imagined, in which the position of the subject, relative to the predicate, might not be altered, without offending against grammar. Even the rhetorical effect might in most cases be preserved though the order were changed, perhaps by adding or omitting an expletive word like ܗܘ. The diversity of arrangement in sentences standing close together has often indeed a rhetorical purpose; but not seldom the same thing has been brought about quite unconsciously. Instances of all forms of arrangement might be adduced in abundance. It will suffice, however, to illustrate merely the leading cases by supporting-passages, confronting them with one another.

B. *Verbal Sentences, Perf.*: ܐܡܪ ܠܗ ܗܘ ܛܘܒܢܐ ܡܪܝ ܫܡܥܘܢ "the blessed St. Simeon said to him" Sim. 271, 13, immediately following ܗ̇ܘ ܕܝܢ ܛܘܒܢܐ ܡܪܝ ܫܡܥܘܢ ܐܡܪ ܠܗ *ibid.* 1, 3 (where, however, Cod. Lond. reads ܘܐܡܪ ܠܗ ܗܘ ܛ'); ܐܠܘ ܫܒܩܬ ܢܦܫܐ ܠܦܓܪܐ "if the soul abandoned the body" Moes. II, 90 v. 221, beside ܐܠܘ ܚܝܠܗ ܫܒܩ ܠܒܪܝܬܐ "if his power abandoned creation" *ibid.* v. 222; ܘܚܝܠܗ ܕܐܠܗܐ ܐܬܚܙܝ "and the power of God appeared" Aphr. 25, 1, beside ܐܬܚܙܝ ܚܝܠܗ ܕܐܠܗܐ line 4, cf. line 6; ܘܗܘ ܕܢܡܘܣܐ ܠܐ ܐܬܣܝܡ ܠܗ "and he, on whom the law had not been imposed" Aphr. 25, 9, close to ܘܥܠ ܟܐܢܘܬܗܘܢ ܠܐ ܐܬܬܣܝܡ ܢܡܘܣܐ "and on their righteousness the law was not imposed" l. 22; ܚܪܒ ܠܗ ܡܩܕܫܢ ܘܒܝܬ ܨܠܘܬܢ ܐܬܚܪܒ "destroyed is our sanctuary, and our house of prayer is laid waste" Aphr. 491, 1.—*Imperfect*: ܨܒܐ ܡܪܝܐ ܕܒܐܝܕܝܟ ܫܡܗ ܢܫܬܒܚ "for it pleased the Lord that by thee his name should be glorified" [*lit.* "the Lord willed that by thy hands &c."] Sim. 270 mid., close beside ܕܒܐܝܕܝܟ ܢܬܢܛܪܘܢ ܢܡܘ̈ܣܐ ܘܩܢܘ̈ܢܐ ܕܥܕܬܐ ܩܕܝܫܬܐ "that by thy hand the laws and ordinances of the holy Church be maintained"; ܘܢܪܬܚ ܗܘܢܗ ܒܪܘܚܐ ܕܐܠܗܗ ܘܬܒܝܐܝܘܗܝ ܨܠܘܬܗ ܒܝܚܝܕܝܘܬܗ "and let his mind glow in the spirit of his God, and let his praying comfort him in his loneliness" Ov. 185, 12.—*Participle*: ܕܥ . . . ܕܥܠ ܫܬܐܣܘ̈ܗܝ ܕܒܢܝܢܐ ܟܐܦ̈ܐ ܗܘ ܡܬܬܣܝ̈ܡܢ ܘܗܝܕܝܢ ܥܠ ܟܐܦ̈ܐ ܡܬܥܠܐ ܟܠܗ ܒܢܝܢܐ "know . . . that upon the foundations of the building the stones are laid, and then upon the stones the whole building rises" Aphr. 6, 14 (and quite similar in 7, 1); ܗܠܝܢ ܡܬܒܥܝܢ ܥܒ̈ܕܐ ܡܢܗ ܗܝܡܢܘܬܐ "all these things faith demands" Aphr. 9, 10, alongside of ܘܗܠܝܢ ܥܒ̈ܕܐ ܡܬܒܥܝܢ ܠܗ ܠܡܠܟܐ ܡܫܝܚܐ "and these works are required for the king Christ" l. 12 (where the logical parallelism is set above the grammatical, as often happens); ܚܪ̈ܒܘ ܟܘܡܪ̈ܝܢ ܘܪܫܢ ܡܚܦܐ "destroyed are our priests, and our head is veiled" Aphr. 491, 1.—That the verb may also stand a long way after the subject, is shown by cases like ܝܘܒܝܢܘܣ ܗܘ ܕܡܠܟ ܒܬܪܗ ܥܠ ܪ̈ܗܘܡܝܐ ܫܝܢܐ ܓܒܐ ܡܢ ܟܠܡܕܡ ܝܬܝܪ "Jovian, who was Roman Emperor after him, preferred peace to everything else" Jos. St. 8, 17.

C. *Nominal Sentences*: ܫܡܝܐ ܙܥܘܪܐ ܘܡܠܝܐ ܡܢܟ "heaven is small and filled with thee" Moes. II, 80 v. 75, beside ܙܥܘܪ ܠܟ ܥܠܡܐ ܘܠܐ ܣܦܩܝܢ ܠܟ ܐܬܪ̈ܘܬܐ "small for thee is the world, and the parts of the earth are not sufficient for thee" v. 77; ܫܡܫܐ ܡܝܬܪ ܡܢ ܣܗܪܐ ܘܪܒ ܣܗܪܐ ܡܢ ܟܘܟ̈ܒܐ ܕܡܫܡܫܝܢ ܠܗ "the sun is more excellent than the moon, and greater is the moon than the stars which attend it" Aphr. 434, 19 &c. In ܪܒ ܚܝܠܐ ܚܝܠܬܢܐ ܨܐܡ ܗܘ "a powerful commander is fasting" Ov. 99, 19, the subject is postponed in an unusual way, to obtain rhetorical effect.

D. The position of ܗܘܐ results, to a certain extent, from § 299. Apart from certain cases like those noted in §§ 260, 261, 300, it generally follows the most important word of the predicate (cf. even ܥܒ̈ܕܐ ܠܡܗܘܐ "to become servants" Ov. 311, 24); thus it often appears, along with such word, before the subject. It is not common to have it placed at the very beginning, as it is in ܗܘܘ ܥܒ̈ܕܐ ܒܢ̈ܘܗܝ ܕܟܢܥܢ "Canaan's children became slaves" Joseph 43, 4 [Ov. 290, 12]; ܕܢܗܘܘܢ ܥܒ̈ܕܐ ܒܢܝ ܚܐܪ̈ܐ "that free persons become servants" *ibid.* 42 *paen.* [Ov. 290, 8].

E. We have already had cases, in which the subject appears in the middle of the predicate, v. § 312. Thus: ܕܡܫܡܫܢܐ ܚܢܢ ܕܐܠܗܐ "that we are God's servants" Ov. 173, 18; ܙܝܢܐ ܗܘ ܠܘܩܒܠ ܒܝܫܐ "it is a weapon against the wicked one" Aphr. 44, 2; ܕܟܠܒܐ ܐܢܬ ܝܥܢܐ "since thou art a greedy dog" Mart. I, 183 mid. &c. The reverse happens in ܐܒܗܘܗܝ ܕܝܢ ܐܝܬ ܗܘܘ ܠܗ ܡܗܝܡܢܐ "he had, however, believing parents" Mart. II, 268.

§ 325. The *Object* stands most frequently after the governing word, but often too before it, v. § 287 *sqq*. Even in the case of the Inf. with ܠ, it is not uncommon to put the object first, v. § 293. In these cases, at bottom, there is a true Involution.

Position of the Object.

§ 326. In simple, plain speech adverbial qualifications most frequently follow that leading member of the sentence, to which they specially belong, *e. g.* ܟܕ ܡܛܘ ܠܘܬ ܡܕܒܚܐ "when they came to the altar" Sim. 272, 8, but often too they precede it, *e. g.* ܘܒܟܠܗ ܐܪܙܐ ܐܠܗܝܐ ܐܫܬܡܠܝ "and he had been initiated [had been made perfect] in the whole Divine mystery" Ov. 165, 16; ܡܢ ܢܩܦܐ ܕܢܫܐ ܬܗܘܘܢ ܦܪܝܫܝܢ "from intercourse with women ye shall keep yourselves separate" Ov. 173, 24; ܟܕ ܐܦܠܐ ܒܡܐܟܘܠܬܐ ܡܣܬܦܩܢܝܬܐ ܥܠ ܬܘܟܠܬܐ ܕܬܘܪܣܝܗ ܕܦܓܪܐ ܡܫܩܠܘܬܐ ܢܗܘܐ ܠܟܘܢ "while not even about simple fare for the due supply of nourishment to the body, shall ye take any trouble" Ov. 174, 8; ܡܢ ܕܣܟܐ ܡܥܠܐ ܠܢܝܚܐ "whoever expects to enter into rest" Aphr. 107, 18 &c. The position of adverbial qualifications may often be of extreme variety, particularly when several occur in one sentence. The simple sentence ܒܪܘܝܐ ܡܛܝܒ ܚܡܪܐ "the Creator prepares the wine", Ephr. III, 663 A, permits of five other arrangements of the words, which arrangements are all good Syriac; only, in this case, just because of the antithesis to ܚܬܢܐ "the host",—which opens the next sentence, it is most convenient to put the subject first, and the placing of the object last comes readiest to hand. With the adverbial complement, ܒܪܘܝܐ ܡܛܝܒ ܚܡܪܐ ܒܓܘ ܓܘܦܢܐ "the Creator prepares the wine in the vines", the number of possible arrangements is very considerably increased; but, provided that the genitive association of ܒܓܘ ܓܘܦܢܐ is kept together, all other conceivable interchanges of position are permissible, although the placing of the words ܒܓܘ ܓܘܦܢܐ in the very beginning of the sentence, for

Position of Adverbial Qualifications.

instance, would give them a special emphasis (which does not suit the context in Ephr.).

Position of certain Particles. § 327. There are several Particles which can never stand in the beginning of the sentence (v. § 155 C). Their proper place is immediately after the first word, yet they may also take a place farther on; cf. ܣܘܐ ܗܘܐ ܠܗ ܓܝܪ ܣܒܐ ܛܘܒܢܐ ܠܕܘܟܬܐ ܕܡܘܕܝܢܘܬܐ "for the blessed old man longed for the position of confessor" Jul. 55, 21; ܐܡܪ ܠܗܘܢ ܕܝܢ (C. S. ܠܗܘܢ) ܐܦ ܡܬܠܐ ἔλεγεν δὲ παραβολὴν αὐτοῖς Luke 18, 1; ܘܪܫܝܥܐ ܝܘܠܝܢܘܣ ܒܐܝܕܗ ܕܗܢܐ ܕܒܚ ܟܝܬ ܢܦܫܗ ܠܫܐܕ̈ܐ "and the impious Julian through him sacrificed himself in fact to the demons" Ov. 160, 14. In Moes. II, 122 v. 703 *sq.*, ܟܝܬ stands twice at the end of a short sentence, and at the end of the verse. Still, these are exceptions. We have seen in §§ 208 A, 240, that these particles may break up the chain of both genitive and prepositional connection. Thus they may be interposed even between the preposition and the relative clause governed by it: ܩܕܡ ܓܝܪ ܕܢܚܛܐ "for before he sinned" Ov. 81, 8; ܡܢ ܕܝܢ ܕܫܠܡ "but after it was finished" Sim. 283, 11; ܡܛܠ ܕܝܢ ܕ "but because" Jos. St. 7, 21; 80, 20; Ov. 169, 24 &c.; even ܡܢ ܕܚܙܐ ܕܝܢ "but after he saw" Ov. 168, 8; ܡܢ ܕܗܘܐ ܕܝܢ "but after he was" Sim. 269, 6 (otherwise, in Cod. Lond.) &c. Thus too with ܟܠ: ܟܠ ܟܝܬ ܓܝܪ ܕܫܐܠ ܢܣܒ "for every one, it is said, who asks, receives" Ov. 102, 14. Cf. also the usage in other relative clauses: ܡܢ ܓܝܪ ܕܐܟܠ ܦܓܪܗ "for whoever has eaten of his body" Aphr. 222, 3; ܟܠ ܡܢ ܗܟܝܠ ܕܫܡܥܗ "thus every one, who hears it" Jos. St. 66, 21 &c., as set overagainst ܡܛܠ ܕܐܢܫ ܓܝܪ ܐܬܩܪܒ "for if any one draws near" Aphr. 7, 2; ܐܝܟܢ ܕܐܠܗܐ ܕܝܢ ܨܒܐ "but when God wills" Spic. 20, 23 &c.

B. SPECIAL KINDS OF SENTENCES.

NEGATIVE SENTENCES.

ܠܐ and its strengthened Forms. § 328. A. The simple negative ܠܐ is mainly employed in giving a negative meaning to the verb, and then usually stands immediately before it: ܠܐ ܐܫܟܚܘ ܐܢܫܘܗܝ ܕ "his people were not able to . . . " Aphr. 210, 17; ܠܐ ܦܩܝܕ ܗܘܐ ܓܝܪ ܠܡܨܪ̈ܝܐ ܕ "it was not ordered the Egyptians to" *ibid.* l. 13; ܟܕ ܚܢܢ ܡܢ ܓܘܬܝ̈ܐ ܠܐ ܩܛܠ "while he killed none of the Goths" Jos. St. 85, 16; ܡܛܠ ܕܠܐ ܡܣܦܩܐ ܗܘܬ ܡܕܝܢܬܐ ܠܓܘܬܝ̈ܐ "because the city did not suffice for the Goths" *ibid.* 86, 21; ܘܩܪܒܐ ܥܠ ܚܕ̈ܕܐ ܠܐ ܢܬܚܪܘܢ "that they should not stir up war against one another" *ibid.* 90, 6 &c. No essential difference is occasioned by the interposition of particles, as in ܠܐ ܕܝܢ ܡܝܬܘ "but they did not die" Ov. 170, 17; ܠܐ ܓܝܪ ܡܬܘܡ ܐܫܬܥܒܕ ܠܗܕܐ ܕ "for he never submitted to this, that" Ov. 179, 8; ܠܐ ܓܝܪ ܡܢ ܝܘܡ̈ܝ ܒܢܝܬ ܟܠ ܒܢܝܢܐ "for I have not in all my days erected any building" Sim. 271, 4; ܠܐ ܓܝܪ ܡܬܘܡ ܡܬܙܟܝܐ ܛܝܒܘܬܟ ܡܢ ܒܝܫܘܬܢ "for never is thy goodness vanquished by our wickedness" Aphr. 493, 7; ܠܐ ܓܝܪ ܐܝܬ ܗܘܐ ܒܣܪܐ ܟܠܗ ܡܕܝܢܬܐ ܠܓܘ ܡܢ "for there was no flesh (meat) at all within the city" Jos. St. 69, 4. Less common are cases like ܕܠܐ ܥܠܘܗܝ ܐܬܓܠܝܬ ܗܘܬ ܟܕ ܛܢܢܗ ܙܕܝܩܘܬܗ ܕܐܠܗܐ ܗܘܬ ܠܡܪܕܘܬܗ "on whom God's righteousness, in his jealousy, would not have been revealed for his punishment" Ov. 187, 16 &c.

ܠܐ stands also where the predicate is an adjective: ܠܐ ܫܦܝܪ ܕܢܗܘܐ "it is not well that [he] be . . ." Gen. 2, 18; ܠܐ ܫܪܝܪ ܠܗ ܕ "it is not true for him, that" Aphr. 498, 6, 13; ܒܡܕܡ ܠܐ ܫܠܝܛܝܢ "over some things they have no power" Spic. 9, 23; ܠܐ ܫܦܝܪ ܗܕܐ ܐܝܟ ܗܘ "this is not beautiful, like that" Anc. Doc. 87, 9; ܫܘܢܩܝܗܘܢ ܕܝܢ ܡܢ ܣܗܕܘܬܐ ܠܐ ܒܨܝܪܝܢ ܗܘܘ "but their sufferings were not less than [*i. e.* nothing short of] a martyrdom" Ov. 170, 5 (where however ܠܐ ܗܘܘ ܒܨܝܪܝܢ would also be correct).

B. Otherwise, to express negation in the Nominal sentence,—and in the very same way in a Verbal sentence, when a different word from the verb (inclusive of Part. and predicative adj. as well as ܐܝܬ) has to be rendered negative,—ܠܐ is strengthened by means of an enclitic ܗܘܐ (thus ܠܐ ܗܘܐ) or by means of ܗܘ (in that case always written ܠܘ). The first method is the more frequent of the two in ancient writings: some avoid ܠܘ altogether, while others employ the two promiscuously. There is no difference in their signification. Of course an author has often to consider whether he has to negative the whole sentence by means of negativing the verb, or merely to negative a single word or phrase; thus the mere separation of the ܠܐ from the verb may, amongst other effects, account for the appearance of the corroborating Form, while an additional emphasis then falls upon the word immediately following the negative. Examples: ﻸﻮ؛ﻬﻮﺣ ﻼ ﻧﻬﻤﺣ ﻧﻐﻼﻧﻊ ﻣﻊ ﺣﻨﻐﻼ ﻣﻊ ﻟﻮﻫﺣ ﻼ ؛ﻊ ﻼ؛ ἐγὼ δὲ οὐ παρὰ ἀνθρώ- που τὴν μαρτυρίαν λαμβάνω John 5, 34; ﻮﻮﻮﻮ ﻓﻤﺣ ﻣﻊ πάντες μὲν οὐ κοιμηϑησόμεθα 1 Cor. 15, 51; ﻮﺣ ﻼﻮﻮﻮ ﻣﻊ ﻟﻮﻮ ﻼﻮﻮﻮ "this death is no death" Mart. I, 245, 8; ﻼﻸﻟﺣﻮ؛ ﻮﺣ ﺣﻮﺣﻮ؛ ﻼ ﻮﺣ ﻼﻼﻟﺣﻮ ﺣﻤﻊ "he is not God, but God's servant" Sim. 327 *inf.*; ﻮﺣ ﻼﺣﻼﻟ ﻣﺣﻊ؛ "who is no shadow" Moes. II, 166 v. 1392; ﻼ؛ﻬﺣﻮ؛ ﻮﺣ ﺣﻤﻼﺣﺣﻸﺣﻮ؛ﻣﺣﻮ ﻟﻮﺣ ﻼ ... ؛ ﻟﻮ؛ﻮ "this circumstance, that . . . , is not that which sets forth the truth" Ov. 163, 8; ﻟﻮﺣ ﻼﻟ؛ ﻼﻼﻣﺣﻮ ﺣﻮﻣﺣﻮﻮﺣ؛ ﻧﻼ؛ﻮﺣ ﻮﺣﻮ؛ ﻟﻐﻼﻣﻟﺣ؛ﻐﻼﺣ "because not in their murder lies victory for the Romans" Jos. St. 70, 2; ﻼﻮﺣ ﻣﻬﺣ؛ ﻧﺣﻣﻮﻮﺣﺣﻮ؛ ﻧﻐﻼ؛؛ ﻟﻮﺣ ﻼ ﻊﻊ "while she was no observer of the law" Aphr. 48, 18; ﻼﻼﻮ؛ ﺣﻮﻣﻊﻼﻟﺣ؛ ﻮﺣ ﺣﻤﻊﻣﻐﺣﻮ؛ ﻣﻼ؛ ﺣﻮﻣﺣﻊﻊﻊ ﻼﻧﻐﻼ "that men are not equally guided" Spic. 12 *ult.*; ﻼ ﻟﻮﺣ ﺣﻤﻊ ﻣﻮﻼ؛ﻟﻐﻼﺣﻊ ﻣﻼﻟﻮ؛ ﻼ ﻟﻮﻟﻮ ﺣﻮﻓﻮ؛ "for the word was not trifling, but he who applied it was but small" Aphr. 165, 9; ﻊﻊ ﻟﻮﺣ ﻼ ﺣﻤﻼﻣﺣﻼﻣﻮﺣﻮﺣﻮﺣﻮ؛ ﻣﻐﻮ؛ﻟﺣﻮﻣﻼﻟﺣﻮ؛ ﻼﻟ "the freedom [freewill] of the Persians I do not however deny" Jos. St. 6, 18; ﻼﻧﻐﻼ ﺣﻧﻬﻤﺣ ﻼ ﻣﻐﻼﻼﺣﻣﻮ؛ ﻮﻮ ﻟﻮﺣ ﻼ "it is not from fear that I do not go forth" Jos. St. 89, 22; ﺣﻣﻼﻟﻣﻮ؛ ﻮﻮ ﺣﻤﺣﻣﻊﻣﺣﻮ؛ ﻮﻮﺣﻣﻊ ﻟﻣﻊﻟﻼ "that this treachery was by no means brought about at his instigation" Jos. St. 12, 17; ﻣﻐﻼﻧﻮﺣﺣﻣﺣﻊ ﻣﻮﻼﻟﺣﻼﺣ ﻧﻐﻼﻼﺣ؛ "that are not well cared for" Moes. II, 68, 12; ﺣﻤﻊﻣﺣ ﺣﻤﻼﺣ ﻼﻟ ﻣﻮﺣﺣﻣﻊﻮﺣ؛ ﺣﻤﻊﻼ "not only with murder, but also" Moes. II, 65, 23, and thus frequently . . . ﻣﻮﺣﺣﻣﻊﻮﺣ؛ ﺣﻤﻊﻼ, or even ﻣﻮﺣﺣﻣﻊﻮﺣ؛ . . . ﺣﻤﻊﻼ, cf. ﻼﻟ ﻧﻐﻼ؛ﻣﻊﻧﻟﻼ ﻟﻮﻟﻼ ﻟﻮﻮﻼﻮﻮ؛ ﻼﻟ ﻟﻮﺣ ﻼ "not merely to Edessa [Orhāi] came this edict, but" Jos. St. 26, 9; ﺣﻣﻼﻣﺣﻼﺣﻣﻊ ﻮﻮﺣﺣ ﺣﻣﻐﻼﺣﻣﺣﻼﻟﻣﺣﻼﻼﻣﻼﺣﻣﻊﻟﺣﻣﻼﻼﺣﻼﺣﻣﻼﻟﺣﻣﻼﻼ "for not in confidence that they would return to life did they proceed thither" Ov. 170, 2; ﻟﻮﺣ ﻼ ﺣﻣﻊ ﻼﻣﺣﻣﻊﻟﻐﻼﺣﺣﻼﺣﺣ ﻣﻮﻣﻊﻧﻐﺣﺣﻮﻣﻊﻼ ﻼﻣﺣﻊ "he has no foreknowledge" Aphr. 130, 1; ﻣﻮﻮﺣﺣﻮﻣﻊﺣﻣﻊﻼﻣﺣﻮﺣﻼ ﻣﻧﻟﻐﻼﺣﻮﻣﺣﻼﺣ ﺣﻣﻊﻼ "not dumb were they (f.)" Moes. II, 102 v. 393 (in both of which cases, with re-arrangement, ﻼﻣﺣﻼﺣ, ﻣﻼﺣﻣﻼﺣ might also have been used, &c.). Even when complete clauses take the place of parts of a sentence, ﻟﻮﺣ ﻼ, or ﺣﻣﻊﻼ is found: . . . ﺣﻣﺣﻮﻟﻼﺣﻣﻊﻟ ﻮﻣ ﻼﻧﻊﺣﺣﺣﻣﻼ؛ ﻧﻟﻐﻼﻣﻣﻼ؛ﻼﺣﻣﺣﻊﻟﺣﻣﻼﻣﻊﻮﻣﻊ؛ "not merely did he manifest his diligence in uprooting the tares out of his land" Ov. 192, 19; ﻼﻮﺣﺣﻼﺣﻣﺣﺣﻮﻼﺣﻣﻊﻟﺣﺣﺣﺣ؛ ﺣﻣﻊﻼ "I do not seek to boast" Ov. 138, 6; ﻣﺣﻣﻊﻼﺣ ﻣﻬﻟﻐﻼﻼ ﻼﻟﻣﺣﻊﺣﻣﻊﻟﻟﻣﻼﺣﻣﻊﻣﻮﺣﻧﺣﻣﻼﺣﻣﻊﺣﺣﻣﻮﺣ ﻣﺣﻼﻟﻣﺣﻼﺣﻼﻟﺣﻣﻐﻼ ﻼﻧﻊﺣﻣﻊﻼﺣ "and it is not because they are distant as regards the body, that they are no sons of the Church" Ov. 121, 8 (where the two ܠܘ are regular); ܕܐܦ ܗܠܝܢ ܕܐܬܪܥܝܢ ܒܗܘܢ ܠܐ ܗܘܐ ܡܛܠ ܕܨܒܝܢ ܒܗܘܢ ܗܘܝܢ ܠܢ "that even those things, with which we are satisfied, fall to our lot, not because we have pleasure in them" Spic. 10, 18 &c. So ܠܘ ܕܠܐ ܦܬܚ ܐܢܐ ܠܟܘܢ ܐܡܪ "he said not 'I do not open to you'" Frothingham, Stephen Bar Sudaili 18, 1. Even before the Inf. Abs. they come in: ܠܐ ܗܘܐ ܡܘܠܕܘ ܡܘܠܕܝܢ ܒܠܚܘܕ "not merely do they *bring forth*" Spic. 11, 7; ܡܠܦܢܐ ܓܝܪ ܡܫܬܐܠܘ ܗܘ ܡܫܬܐܠܝܢ ܠܐ ܗܘܐ ܡܫܐܠܘ ܡܫܐܠܝܢ "for teachers are *asked* questions; they do not *put* them" Spic. 1, 18; ܕܠܐ ܗܘܐ ܡܕܥ ܝܕܥ ܓܢܒܐ "that the thief does not know" Aphr. 129, 13; ܕܠܘ ܡܥܟܣܘ ܥܟܣ ܐܢܐ ܠܗܘܢ "that I do not calumniate them" Euseb. Ch. Hist. 315, 6. So *ibid.* 180, 9.

C. The simple ܠܐ, however, is retained in several cases. It seems always to stand thus in prohibitive sentences, *e. g.* ܠܐ ܒܥܠܬܐ ܕܟܘܪܗܢܐ ܢܫܒܩܘܢ ܐܚܐ ܕܝܪܬܗܘܢ "the brethren shall not, on the pretext of illness, forsake their cloisters" Ov. 213, 17; ܘܠܐ ܠܒܘܫܐ ܢܩܕܐ ܐܘ ܡܐܢܐ ܫܥܝܥܐ ܢܒܨܪܘܢ ܝܩܪܘܬܗ ܕܨܘܡܟܘܢ "and tidy clothing, or sleek raiment, may not belittle the worth of your abstinence" Ov. 174, 14. And so, generally, in all modal relations,—thus ܕܠܐ "that . . not", "lest" &c.

D. Farther, in repetitions like ܕܠܐ ܚܙܘܗ ܫܦܝܪ ܘܠܐ ܛܥܡܗ ܒܣܝܡ ܘܠܐ ܪܝܚܐ ܒܣܝܡܐ ܐܝܬ ܠܗ "the appearance of which is not good, nor the taste agreeable, and which has no pleasant smell" Aphr. 307, 19; ܠܐ ܒܩܕܡܝܐ ܘܠܐ ܒܐܚܪܝܐ ܢܗܘܐ ܕܪܒ ܡܢܟ "neither among those who have gone before, nor among those who may come after, will one be found who is greater than thou" Sim. 270 *inf.*; ܘܠܐ ܥܘܬܪܐ ܡܫܬܟܚ ܐܠܐ ܠܘܬ ܙܥܘܪܐ ܘܠܐ ܡܫܠܛܢܘܬܐ ܐܠܐ ܠܘܬ ܚܕ ܘܬܪܝܢ ܘܠܐ ܚܘܠܡܢܐ ܕܦܓܪܐ ܠܘܬ ܟܠܗܘܢ ܒܢܝܢܫܐ "and riches are not found except with a few, nor power except with one or two individual men; neither is bodily health found with all men" Spic. 10, 2; ܘܡܐܢܐ ܨܐܝܐ ܐܘ ܒܠܝܐ ܠܐ ܒܗܘܢ ܘܠܐ ܥܠܝܗܘܢ ܡܬܚܙܝܢ ܗܘܘ ܟܠ "and soiled or shabby clothes were not to be seen at all, either among or upon them" Ov. 203, 10; ܠܐ ܦܫ ܗܘܐ ܥܠ ܐܝܕܘܗܝ ܠܐ ܡܫܟܐ ܘܠܐ ܒܣܪܐ "on his hands there remained neither skin nor flesh" Sim. 281 mid., and many such instances. ☞ p. 361

E. Again, in elliptical speech, such as simply ܠܐ "No", and in cases like ܘܒܡܢܗܘܢ ܡܬܪܥܝܢ ܚܢܢ ܘܒܡܢܗܘܢ ܠܐ "and with some of them we are satisfied, and with others not" Spic. 10, 19; ܘܐܢ ܠܐ "but if not, then . . " ☞ p. 361

Aphr. 441, 7, and in other passages; ܕܰܠܘܰܝ ܕܶܝܢ ܠܳܐ "*quod utinam non (fuisset)*" Assem. II, 44*b* (Philoxenus); ܐܢܐ ܟܬܒܬ ܠܒܢܝ̈ ܦܝܣܐ ܘܠܐ ܠܡܒܙܚܢ̈ܐ "I have written for those who are amenable to persuasion [sons of persuasion], not for scoffers" Aphr. 441, 8; ܘܠܐ ܐܝܟ ܣܦܪ̈ܝܗܘܢ *καὶ οὐχ ὡς οἱ γραμματεῖς αὐτῶν* Matt. 7, 29; and, in a similar use, the word often occurs.

F. Again, it constantly presents itself in certain combinations, like
☞ p. 361 ܐܦܠܐ, ܐܠܐ, ܕܠܐ "without" (and "that not", "lest", *ne*). So in Nominal compounds like ܠܐ ܡܝܘܬܐ "immortal"; ܠܐ ܡܬܚܒܠܢܘܬܐ *ἀφθαρσία* 1 Cor. 15, 53 &c.; also in cases like ܐܘ ܥܡܐ ܣܟܠܐ ܘܠܐ ܡܣܬܟܠܐ "O foolish and unintelligent people!" Mart. I, 113 *inf.* So too ܠܐ ܐܢܫ "no one", ܠܐ ܡܕܡ "nothing".

G. Here and there occurs also ܠܐ for ܠܐ ܗܘܐ or ܠܘ. Thus ܠܐ ܓܒܪ̈ܐ ܬܠܬܐ ܐܪܡܝܢ "did we not cast *three* men?" Dan. 3, 24; ܠܐ ܡܨܪ̈ܝܐ ܘܡܘܐܒ̈ܝܐ ܘ . . . ܐܠܨܘܟܘܢ "did not the Egyptians and the Moabites and . . . oppress you?" Judges 10, 11 (and that the fact of interrogation in such cases does not necessarily call for ܠܐ, [instead of ܠܐ ܗܘܐ] is shown by ܠܐ ܗܘܐ ܡܘܫܐ ܝܗܒ ܠܟܘܢ ܢܡܘܣܐ *οὐ Μωϋσῆς δέδωκεν ὑμῖν τὸν νόμον*; John 7, 19); ܘܠܐ ܒܡܪܟܒܬܐ ܐܚܪܢܐ ܡܕܡ ܡܣܬܓܕ ܗܘܐ "and there was nothing else reverenced in the vehicle" Moes. II, 166 v. 1397; ܠܐ ܒܒܢܝ̈ܢܫܐ ܒܠܚܘܕ ܡܗܪܝܢ "not merely men do they injure" Spic. 12, 7; ܠܐ ܒܠܚܘܕ ܐܝܕܐ ܕܓܝܪܐ ܡܬܩܛܠܐ "not merely she who commits adultery is put to death" Spic. 15, 20; ܘܠܐ ܡܛܠ ܕܒܠܚܘܕܘܗܝ ܐܝܬܘܗܝ ܗܘܐ ܠܐ ܐܫܬܡܥ "and he did not, because he was alone, remain unheard" Aphr. 70, 8 &c. These sentences are not all free from a suspicion that the text has been tampered with; and this suspicion applies with special force to the words ܠܘ ܐܬܝܠܕܬ ܐܠܐ ܢܦܩܬ "she was not born, but came forth" Ov. 403, 22, where in a way quite unusual ܠܘ stands immediately before the verb.

Position of the Negative.

§ 329. ܠܐ and its strengthened forms ܠܐ ܗܘܐ, ܠܘ can never come after the word to which they most directly refer. In the simple Verbal sentence, for instance, ܠܐ must stand always before the verb.

Double Negative.

§ 330. That a double negative may even in Syriac have the force of an affirmative, we have seen in several examples which embody restrictions; cf. farther ܠܘ ܓܝܪ ܡܢ ܡܘܬܒܘܬܐ ܕܐܘܪ̈ܚܬܐ ܕܐܠܗܘܬܗ ܒܠܚܘܕ ܠܐ

ܚܣܪ ܐܢܘܢ "for not only did he not deprive them of a share in the alms of his beneficence" Ov. 195, 1 &c. But, in particular circumstances, there may be attached to a negative sentence another ܐܦ ܠܐ, with a noun to be specially negatived; or the negation of several things may be expressly specified, alongside of the leading negation: ܘܡܢ ܓܢܣܐ ܕܕܝܪܝܐ ܠܐ ܐܬܢܟܝ ܐܦܠܐ ܚܕ "and of the race of the monks not even one was injured" Jul. 26, 13; ܒܕܠܐܝܬ ܡܕܡ ܠܐ ܡܟܠܝܐ ܠܨܠܘܬܐ ܘܠܐ ܡܕܡ ܡܕܘܕ ܠܗ ܐܦ ܠܐ ܣܝܦܐ ܐܦ ܠܐ ܢܘܪܐ "for nothing whatever proves a hindrance to prayer, and neither sword nor fire brings it to perplexity" Anc. Doc. 104, 25; ܡܛܠܗܢܐ ܠܐ ܐܗܦܟ ܐܦܠܐ ܡܢ ܥܡܐ ܩܫܝ ܩܕܠܐ ܕܒܢܝ ܐܝܣܪܝܠ "therefore he did not even take his eyes off the stiff-necked people of the children of Israel" Ov. 194, 26; ܫܪܪܐ ܕܐܠܗܢ ܠܐ ܒܚܝܝܢ ܘܠܐ ܒܡܘܬܢ ܠܐ ܡܫܒܩܝܢ ܚܢܢ "the truth of our God, neither in our life nor in our death, do we give up" Mart. I, 186 mid.; ܠܐ ܬܕܚܠ ܘܠܐ ܬܬܪܗܒ ܠܐ ܡܢ ܩܕܡ ܡܠܟܐ ܘܠܐ ܡܢ ܕܝܢܐ "be not thou afraid nor alarmed, either before kings or judges" Sim. 300 mid.; "in such-and-such lands ܠܐ ܐܢܫ ܚܙܐ ܠܐ ܓܠܘܦܐ ܘܠܐ ܨܝܪܐ ܘܠܐ . . . ܘܠܐ . . . ܘܠܐ no man sees sculptors, nor painters, nor . . . nor . . . " Spic. 17, 4 &c. In all these cases other modes of expression might also be used, cf. *e. g.* ܐܠܐ ܘܠܐ ܡܕܡ ܐܘܬܪܗ ܗܘܐ "but this brought him no help at all" Ephr. II, 212 B.

INTERROGATIVE SENTENCES.

§ 331. A. In Syriac there is no special syntactical or formal method of indicating direct questions, as to "whether" the Predicate applies to the Subject. Such interrogative sentences can only be distinguished from sentences of affirmation by the emphasis. ܪܒ ܗܘ ܐܠܗܐ may mean "God is great", quite as well as "Is God great?". Interrogative Sentences.

B. The special interrogative words (which enquire about the subject or its attributes or other relations, or again after individual parts of the predicate), stand mostly at the beginning of the sentence: ܟܡܐ ܬܪܗܛ ܒܬܪ ܡܕܡ ܕܠܐ ܡܫܬܠܡ "how long art thou to keep running after what never stops?" Ov. 119, 10; ܡܢܘ ܡܡܬܘܡ ܚܙܝܬ ܕܥܬܪ ܘܣܒܥ "whom hast thou ever seen, that had grown rich and was satisfied?" Ov. 119, 11; ܘܐܝܟܢܐ ܥܒܕܗ ܚܛܝܬܐ "and how did he make him to be sin?" Aphr. 134, 6; ܐܝܕܐ ܕܚܠܬܐ ܫܪܝܪܐ "which religion is true?" Mart. I, 182, 6 &c. There is no essential divergence in cases like ܥܠ ܐܝܠܝܢ ܗܟܝܠ ܦܘܩܕܢܐ ܘܕܝܢܐ ܐܡܪ ܚܙܩܝܐܝܠ ܕ "of what commands and judgments then did Ezekiel say that...?" Aphr. 318, 11; ܥܕܡܐ ܠܐܡܬܝ ܐܗܘܐ ܠܘܬܟܘܢ ἕως πότε ἔσομαι μεθ' ὑμῶν; Matt. 17, 17; Luke 9, 41, and similar cases. But the interrogative is frequently shifted farther on in the sentence; only it is never permitted to stand after the verb or the copula: ܟܐܦܐ ܗܕܐ ܡܢܘ ܣܡܟ ܠܗ "what supports this stone?" Moes. II, 88 v. 182; ܬܘܪܥܝܬܗ ܐܡܝܢܬܐ ܕܠܘܬ ܩܠܝܪܘܣ ܩܝܡܐ ܕܩܕܝܫܘܬܐ ܡܢܘ ܡܨܐ ܠܡܫܬܥܝܘ "his constant exhortations to the clergy under vows of chastity, who can recount?" Ov. 176, 14; ܠܡܫܘܚܬܐ ܕܝܢ ܪܒܬܐ ܕܡܣܬܪܩܘܬܗ ܡܢܘ ܡܢ ܕܝܪܝܐ ܢܫܘܐ ܢܦܫܗ ܗܘܐ "but to the mighty proportions of his renunciation, which of the monks could compare himself?" Ov. 184, 22; ܒܘܪܟܬܐ ܕ... ܗܝ ܠܡܢܐ ܠܐ ܥܒܪܬ "the blessing, which... (long relative sentence), why has it not passed from me?" Aphr. 469, 1; ܠܥܠ ܡܢ ܫܡܝܐ ܡܢܐ ܐܝܬ "above the heavens what is there?" Aphr. 496, 2; ܗܟܝܠ ܥܠ ܫܐܘܠ ܐܝܟܢܐ ܡܫܟܚܐ ܠܡܬܐܡܪ "how can this apply to Saul?" Aphr. 342, 17; ܫܪܒܬܗ ܐܝܢܐ "what is her race?" Moes. II, 110 v. 538; ܐܝܟܐ ܐܘܪܚܐ ܡܛܠ ܡܢܐ ܘܠܐܝܢܐ ܦܪܨܘܦܐ "wherefore and to what end is the face of the lion?" Moes. II, 104 v. 431; ܗܟܝܠ ܟܬܒܐ ܕܡܢܘ ܐܝܠܝܢ "whose are these books?" Sim. 269 *inf.* &c.

For sentences with ܠܡܢܐ v. § 373.

2. COMBINATION OF SEVERAL SENTENCES OR CLAUSES.

A. COPULATIVE SENTENCES.

Ellipses in Copulative Sentences.

§ 332. Two nouns are strung together by means of ܘ or ܐܘ.(1) If there are more members than two, the conjunction need only appear before the last of them, as in ܐܪܥܐ ܟܪܡܐ ܘܙܝܬܐ ܚܫܚܝܢ ܠܗ ܠܢܛܘܪܘܬܐ "land, the vine, and the olive stand in need of careful attention" Ephr. Nis. p. 8 v. 91 &c. Two or more nouns are combined to form one member of a sentence, while the association of several verbs properly constitutes, on

(1) On ܐܘ in comparisons v. footnote to § 249 E.

all occasions, just so many sentences. But the grammatical sense makes no nice distinction between these cases, as is proved by the circumstance that the same conjunctions are employed for both. The connection of sentences, even with two verbs, is often very intimate, when, for instance, both verbs have the same subject and object, and perhaps even the same adverbial qualifications, as in a sentence of this sort: ܡܛܠ ܗܢܐ ܫܡܥܘܢ ܒܝܬܐ ܫܬܐܣܗ ܘܒܢܐ "on this account Simeon founded and built the house". Gentle transitions gradually lead to a perfectly clear separation of the two clauses, as when I say: ܡܛܠ ܗܢܐ ܫܡܥܘܢ ܒܝܬܐ ܫܬܐܣܗ ܘܡܛܠ ܗܢܐ ܗܘ ܒܢܝܗܝ ܠܒܝܬܐ "on this account Simeon founded the house, and on this account he built the house". But only special reasons could justify such a tedious mode of expression. In most cases, in which there is a combination of clauses thus closely related in contents, some form or other of *Ellipsis* will appear, even though the conjunction fall entirely away. Thus also the proper verb for two closely connected clauses is often omitted in the second position, even though number and gender are different. The possible varieties of expression in such cases are very numerous. Compare the following examples: ܘܐܬܝܠܕܘ ܠܗ ܡܢ ܠܐܐ ܪܘܒܝܠ ܘܫܡܥܘܢ ܘ . . . ܘܡܢ ܪܚܝܠ [ܐܬܝܠܕܘ ܠܗ] ܝܘܣܦ ܘܒܢܝܡܝܢ "and there were born to him of Leah, Reuben, Ṣimeon &c., and of Rachel, Joseph and Benjamin" Aphr. 480, 8; ܘܚܙܘܗܘܢ ܕܡܐ ܗܘܐ ܐܝܟ ܢܘܪܐ ܘܐܦܝܗܘܢ [ܕܡܝܢ ܗܘܘ] ܐܝܟ ܙܠܝܩܐ ܕܫܠܗܒܝܬܐ "and their aspect was like fire, and their faces like gleams of flame" Sim. 271 *inf.*; ܗܢܘܢ ܢܠܦܘܢ ܡܙܡܘܪ̈ܐ ܒ̈ܢܝ ܩܝܡܐ ܘܒ̈ܢܬ ܩܝܡܐ ܕܝܢ ܐܦ ܡܕܪ̈ܫܐ (1) [ܢܐܠܦܢ] "the men who are under vows [sons of the rule, *canonici*] shall learn psalms, but the women [daughters of the rule] hymns also" Ov. 217, 18; ܪ̈ܡܘܬܐ ܘܫܒ̈ܗܪܘܬܐ ܠܐ ܝܐܝܐ ܠܡܟ̈ܝܟܐ ܘܐܦܠܐ [ܝܐܝܐ] ܟܠܝܠܐ ܠܪܝܫܐ ܕܡܣ̈ܟܢܐ "haughtiness and pride do not beseem the lowly, nor does a crown [beseem] the head of the poor" Aphr. 180, 15; ܢܗܘܐ ܒܥܦܪܐ ܗܪܓܟ ܒܛܝܢܐ [ܢܗܘܐ] ܒܘܚܢܟ ܠܐܪܥܐ [ܢܗܘܐ] ܪܗܛܟ "thy contemplation may cleave to the dust, thy search to the mire, thy course to the earth" Moes. II, 96 v. 328; ܐܠܗܘܬܐ ܕܐܒܐ ܘܒܪܘܚܐ ܠܐ ܢܬܩܘܡ ܒܡܢ̈ܝܢܐ ܐܠܐ ܗܘ ܡܢܝܢ

(1) The same tense as that at the beginning of the clause could not stand here (§ 260).

ܘܙܒܢܐ ܠܙܒܢܘܬܗܘܢ ܕܠܣܘܦ ܘܠܐ ܢܫܬܟܚܘܢ [ܕܥܒܕ ܠܗܘܢ ܣܢܝܩܘܬܐ] "wares for purchase and sale must not be found in the convents, except that only which suffices for their needs, without greediness" Ov. 213, 9; ܗܢܘܢ ܡܬܚܦܛܝܢ ܗܘܘ ܕܢܬܚܪܪܘܢ ܡܢ ܟܘܪܗܢܐ ܗܕܐ ܕܝܢ [ܡܬܚܦܛܐ ܗܘܬ ܕܬܬܚܪܪ] ܡܢ ܒܝܫܬܗ̇ "those made every endeavour to free themselves from disease, but this woman [strove to free herself] from her evil doings" Ov. 103, 5; and with ellipsis in the first position: ܗܢܘܢ ܕܝܢ ܠܡܐܣܝܘ ܟܘܪܗܢܝܗܘܢ [ܘܢܬܚܠܡܘܢ ܡܣܬܪܗܒܝܢ ܗܘܘ] ܗܕܐ ܕܝܢ ܠܐܣܝܘܬ ܪ̈ܓܝܓܬܗ̇ ܕܬܬܐܣܐ ܡܣܬܪܗܒܐ ܗܘܬ "now to cure their diseases those hastened, but this woman to cure her desires" Ov. 103, 3 &c. Thus also in parallel clauses, entirely unfurnished with any external mark of union: ܠܘ ܚܫܐ ܦܓܪܢܝܐ ܐܠܨܗ̇ ܐܝܟ ܠܐܚܪ̈ܢܐ ܕܬܣܬܪܗܒ ܠܘܬ ܡܪܢ ܐܠܐ ܥܘܩܣܐ ܕܬܐܪܬܗ̇ ܠܘ ܓܪܒܐ ܕܦܓܪܗ̇ ܐܠܐ ܡܘ̈ܡܐ ܕܢܦܫܗ̇ ܠܘ ܘܫ. "for not bodily pain constrained her, as it did the others, to hasten to our Lord, but the sting of her conscience, not the leprosy of her body but the blemishes of her soul, not . . . &c." Ov. 102, 23 &c. ☞ p. 361

Negation in Copulative Sentences.

§ 333. When the first clause is affirmative, and the attached clause negative, ellipses occur of the kind mentioned in § 328 E. But when the negation has reference to both clauses, it is either repeated,—in which case the emphasised form described in § 330 may appear,—or it merely stands once for all. In the latter case ܐܘ is more usual as a connecting particle than ܘ, unless the second clause is at bottom rather an expansion or inference than a purely parallel clause. Sentences with ܠܐ . . . ܘ . . . instead of ܠܐ . . . ܘܠܐ . . . : ܠܐ ܫܩܠܐ ܐܢܐ ܘܡܣܝܒܪܢܐ ܐܢܐ ܟܠܡܕܡ ܕ "I (f.) am not to bear and endure everything which" Spic. 3, 20; ܠܐ ܬܩܒܠܘܢ ܡܢ ܐܢܫ (1) ܐܓܪܬܐ ܦܠܣܘܢ ܘܡܛܠܬܗ̇ ܬܥܒܕܘܢ ܡܕܡ ܠܒܪ ܡܢ ܟܐܢܘܬܐ "do not ye accept for any one a forged letter (φάλσον *falsum*), and do nothing on that account beyond justice" Ov. 220, 10; ܠܐ ܫܩܠܝܢ ܐܢܬܘܢ ܘܐܙܠܝܢ "you are not to take and go" [*i. e.* "you are not to carry off"] John Eph. 399, 15; ܠܐ ܬܚܛܐ ܘܬܐܡܪܝܢ ܒܝܫܬܐ ܥܠܝ "do not sin and speak evil of me" Mart. I, 75 *inf.*; ܘܠܐ ܟܠܗ ܬܐܡܐ ܘܬܕܓܠ "and by no means swear falsely [*lit.* "swear and be false"]" Ephr. II, ☞ p. 361

(1) V. § 260.

337 E; ܠܐ ܬܒܥܝܢ ܒܝ ܒܘܪ̈ܝ ܘܬܦܪܘܥܝܢܝ ܐܝܟܢܐ (1) ܕܚܘܝܒܝ "search not in me for my faults, so as to requite me as I have deserved" Ephr. III, 522 E; ܠܐ ܬܗܦܐ ܡܪܝ ܡܢ ܕܘܘܢܝ ܘܐܗܘܐ ܥܒܕܐ ܠܣܛܢܐ "turn not away (thine eyes), O Lord, from my wretchedness, and let me not become a servant of Satan" Ephr. III, 523 A &c.

With ܐܘ: ܘܠܐ ܬܟܪܐ ܠܟ ܐܘ ܬܬܦܟܗ ܒܬܪܥܝܬܟ "and grieve not or be desponding in thy thought" Sim. 301, 4 (Cod. Lond. otherwise); and many similar instances. Cf. ܠܐ ܢܗܘܘܢ ܩܫܝܫܐ ܘܡܫܡܫܢܐ ܘܒܢܝ ܩܝܡܐ ܐܦܛܪ̈ܘܦܐ ܐܘ ܦܪ̈ܢܣܝܐ ܠܐܢܫܐ ܥܠܡ̈ܝܐ ܐܘ ܢܣܒܘܢ ܒܝܕܝܗܘܢ ܕܝ̈ܢܐ ܕܒ̈ܢܝ ܓܢܣܗܘܢ ܐܘ ܕܡܢ ܕܢܗܘܘܢ ܐܓܝܪܝܢ ܠܗܘܢ ܕܝ̈ܢܐ ܘܡܬܟܬܫܝܢ ܒܬܪ̈ܥܐ ܕܕ̈ܝܢܐ "Priests, Deacons, and men under vows shall not be curators or agents for laics, or take charge of the lawsuits of their own relatives, or undertake for hire the conduct of the suits of any one whomsoever, or be in constant attendance at the door of the judge" Ov. 218, 8. In this example several prohibitions are comprised, in part by means of ܘ, in part by ܐܘ, while only a single negative is expressed. Of course the negative might have been repeated once or oftener.

§ 334. A. In several of the sentences quoted above, the connection effected by ܘ has figured as a somewhat inexact mode of signifying a relation, which is not quite identical with the one given in the first clause. Such an "and" is also found sometimes when a consequence, or a contemporaneous accessory circumstance, is dealt with: ܡܢܐ ܐܥܒܕ ܗܘܝܬ ܘܐܟܠܐ ܠܫܡܫܐ "what should I have done, to hinder the sun?" ZDMG XXX, 117 v. 235; ܠܐܝܟܐ ܟܠܢ ܐܬܟܢܫܢ ܐܢܫܝܢ ܘܩܡܬ ܐܢܬ "whither had we all withdrawn ourselves, that thou didst arise?" Joseph 227, 4 [Ov. 312, 12]; ܘܠܕܣܡ ܒܢܝܢܗ ܥܠ ܫܘܥܐ ܘܠܐ ܡܬܙܝܥ ܡܢ ܪ̈ܘܚܐ ܘܓܠ̈ܠܐ "and to him who has set his building upon a rock, whereon it is not swayed by winds and waves" Sim. 395, mid.; ܦܘܡܐ ܕܐܡܪ ܐܠܗܐ ܘܪܬܐ ܟܘܠܝ̈ܬܐ ܕܒܪ̈ܝܬܐ "the mouth which said "God", at which the reins of beings created trembled" Ov. 138, 24; ܐܦܝ ܬܪ̈ܥܐ ܕܡܪܝܡ ܘܥܐܠ ܠܗ ܟܘܡܪܐ "the curtain which the priest raises and (through which he then) enters" Apost. Ap. 176, 18 (Gnost. Hymn); ܐܝܟ ܕܐܦܩ ܠܒܘܣ̈ܡܐ ܘܐܬܟܠ ܐܣܛܘܟ̈ܣܐ "as he produced

Copulative Sentence for a Contemporaneous circumstance or for a Consequence.

☞ p. 361

☞ p. 361

(1) V. § 64.

(water) to Hagar, whereof Ishmael drank" Aphr. 314, 6; ܗܠܝܢ ܟܠܗܝܢ ... ܕܟܬܒܬ ܐܥܗܕܬܟ ܚܒܝܒܝ ܘܠܐ ܡܠܐܝܬ ܠܟ "all this that I have written I ☞ p. 361 have reminded thee of, beloved, without being wearied" Aphr. 184, 5; ܡܕܡ ܕܐܣܬܟܠܘܗܝ ܘܐܛܪܦܘܗܝ "something which they imposed upon him, and with which they vexed him" Sim. 280 mid.; ܡܛܠ ܒܝܫܬܐ ܕܥܒܕ ܗܘܐ ܘܥܨܝܢ ܠܣܓܝܐܐ "by reason of the evil which he did, and (through which) he oppressed many" Sim. 317 mid.; ܕܬܫܒܘܩ ܡܢ ܟܠܢ ܘܦܠܓܝ ܠܒܟ "that thou leave us with thy heart in doubt" Ov. 308 *ult.*; ܗܝ ܐܢܬܬܐ ܗܝ ܢܦܩܬ ܘܠܚܡܐ ܥܡܗ "then went out that woman, having bread with her" Acta S. Maris 45, 2. Instances of the latter kind, where the ܘ introduces a pure conditional clause, are rare in original writings in Syriac, as the more distinct ܐܢ is used for this purpose.

B. To the verb ܦܩܕ, ܦܩܕ "to command" the execution of the design is sometimes annexed, without the substance of the order having been announced beforehand; so too with ܨܒܐ "to wish", and occasionally with other verbs besides: ܦܩܕ ܘܐܦܩܘ ܐܢܘܢ "he gave command (to bring them out) and they brought them out" Mart. I, 94, 8; ܘܦܩܕ ܘܐܬܘ ܡܝܐ "and at his command water came" Sim. 353, 11; ܦܩܕ ܠܟܗܢܐ ܘܫܩܠܘܗ ܥܠ ܟܬܦܬܗܘܢ "at his command the priests took it (f.) upon their shoulders" ☞ p. 361 Aphr. 265, 6 &c. (and thus frequently in the Document of 201 in the Chron. Ed.); ܨܒܐ ܡܪܝܐ ܘܐܬܦܨܝܘ "by the will of the Lord they were delivered" Sim. 295, 11; ܝܗܒ ܠܗܘܢ ܡܪܝܐ ܘܚܙܘ ܢܘܗܪܐ "the Lord granted them that they should see the light" Sim. 346, *inf.*; ܘܫܪܝ ܘܒܢܐ "and he began (to build) and built (completing the work)" Land II, 167, 6.

Close Combination of two Verbs by means of "and".

§ 335. Some verbs, which express a quality, very often join the specific verb to themselves in this way, by means of ܘ. In particular we have ܐܡܪܚ, ܐܡܪܚ "to be audacious", ܐܣܓܝ "to multiply": ܕܐܡܪܚ ܗܘܐ ܘܐܡܪ "who had the boldness to say" Mart. I, 19 *inf.*; ܐܡܪܚܬ ܘܐܡܪܬ "thou didst venture to say" Aphr. 82, 11; ܐܣܓܝ ܩܪܐ ܠܗܘܢ "he called often to them" Aphr. 503, 4; ܓܥܪ ܘܐܣܓܝ "he threatened severely" Jul. 64, 3 &c. Not seldom the impersonal ܓܕܫ "it befell", "it came to pass", is dealt with in the same way, *e. g.*: ܓܕܫ ܘܫܐܠܢܝ ... ܓܒܪܐ "it chanced that a man asked me" Aphr. 394, 6. Farther ܡܘܣܦܝܢ ܘܢܣܒܝܢ ☞ p. 361 "they take in addition" Spic. 14, 18; ܠܐ ܬܘܣܦ ܘܬܫܐܠ "but ask no more"

Simeon of Bēth Arshām (Guidi) 11, 4 = Knös, Chrest. 44 *inf.*; ܩܕܡ ܘܚܘܝ "showed before" Aphr. 451, 9; ܩܕܡܘ ܘܡܝܬܘ "died before" Euseb. Ch. Hist. 128 *paen.*; ܡܩܕܡ ܗܘܐ ܘܐܬܐܡܪ "was said beforehand" *ibid.* 14, 14, 18; 275, 6 *ab inf.* (more frequently ܩܕܡ occurs in this application without the ܘ, § 337 A). In these cases, however, subordination of the second clause is permitted, and in certain of them it is much more usual. Thus along with the afore-mentioned ܐܡܪܚܬ ܘܐܡܪܬ, there occurs also ܡܢܘ ܡܡܪܚ ܕܢܐܡܪ "who ventures to say?" Aphr. 430, 12, and ܐܡܪܚ ܠܡܐܡܪ "he ventured to say" Ov. 196, 15. ☞ p. 361

Government of such Combinations. § 336. In the case of two closely combined verbs, the substantive Object, which is governed by both, needs to appear once only, § 332 (*e. g.* ܕܢܓܠܐ ܘܢܘܕܥ ܪ̈ܥܝܢܗ "that he reveal and make known his mind" Jul. 83, 9; ܢܨܚ ܘܐܪܝܡ ܘܫܒܚ ܠܒ̈ܢܝ ܐܢܫܐ "he ennobled, elevated and glorified the sons of men" Aphr. 336, 3, where no fewer than three verbs have only one expressed object). Not only so, but an Object-suffix which belongs to both verbs is occasionally attached to one only: ܚܨܝ ܘܫܕܝܗ ܡܢܟ "ἔξελε αὐτὸν καὶ βάλε ἀπὸ σοῦ" Matt. 5, 29 C. (P. ܚܨܝܗ ܘܫܕܝ ܡܢܟ; S. ܚܨܝܗ ܫܕܝܗ ܡܢܟ); ܘܓܪܘ ܘܫܕܐܘܗܝ "and they dragged and threw him down" Aphr. 471, 12; ܚܓܪ ܘܟܠܐ ܐܢܘܢ "lamed and hindered them" Aphr. 330, 16 &c. And then, two verbs are often so intimately associated that the government of the one, which may not be at all that of the other, operates for the entire combination, and the object stands next to the verb to which it by no means belong: ܟܕ ܟܘ̈ܟܒܐ ܫܡܝܐ ܢܩܘܡ ܘܢܡܢܐ "while he rises up and numbers the stars of heaven" Aphr. 199, 13; ܟܣܐ . . . ܐܡܪܚܬܘܢ ܠܡܓܢܒܗ ܡܢܝ "the cup ye have had the daring to steal from me" Joseph 238, 9 [Ov. 318, 14]; ܗܕܐ ܩܕܡ ܘܚܘܝ ܠܗܘܢ "he referred this to him beforehand" Aphr. 12, 3; ܡܛܠ ܕܥܠܘ ܓܝܪ ܘܩܝܡܘ ܪ̈ܗܘܡܝܐ ܒܗܝܟܠܐ ܢܫܪܐ ܥܡ ܨܠܡܐ ܕܡܠܟܗܘܢ "because the Romans entered and set up the eagle in the temple, together with the image of their emperor" Ephr. II, 222 E; ܘܡܓܒܠ ܥܘܠܐ ܘܡܣܬܪܗܒ "and he hastens to practise iniquity" Isaac I, 266 v. 362; ܚܦܪ̈ܐ ܚܦܪܐ ܐܪܟܢܝܬ ܘܢܟܝܪܘ "they had craftily dug mere pits" Land III, 257, 3; ܡܘܫܐ ܠܡܟܝܟܘܬܐ ܢܚܬ ܠܬܚܬܝܐ ܒܡܨܪܝܢ ܦܨܚܐ ܘܥܒܕ "Moses, here below, brought himself down to the lower people in Egypt and prepared the Passover" ZDMG XXVII, 571 ☞ p. 361

v. 103 (cf. *ibid.* v. 109); ܐܬܝܐ ܘܛܥܝܢܐ ܣܝܥܬܗ̇ "she comes carrying her companions" (f.) *ibid.* 598 v. 274; and ܐܬܐ ܗܘ ܘܛܥܝܢ ܠܣܘܥܪ̈ܢܘܗܝ "he goes bearing his deeds" *ibid.* v. 276 &c. Similarly too with the passive: ܡܐܢ̈ܐ ܕܣܐܡܐ ܕܝܢ ܣܓܝ̈ܐܐ ܕ . . . ܦܬܐܡ ܐܙܕܒܢܘ ܒܦܘܩܕܢܗ "but many vessels of silver, which (—long relative clause . . .), were on a sudden sold at his command" Ov. 172, 20. Cf. with Prep.: ܘܠܩܒܪܐ ܟܒܫܬ ܘܐܪܡܝܬܗ "and I have conquered him and have cast him into the grave" [*lit.* "and into the grave I have conquered and cast him"] Ephr. Nis. p. 106, 39.

☞ p. 361

Close Combination of two Verbs without "and".

§ 337. A. Syriac, however, very frequently indeed combines a pair of verbs, set together without any connecting particle at all, (a) when they denote actions which immediately follow each other or attend upon each other, or (b) when the verbs are such that the one merely gives expression to a modification of the other. Examples: (a) ܓܕܥܘܢ ܥܠ ܛܝܒ "Gideon went in and made ready" Judges 6, 19; ܘܐܢܗܘ ܕܐܬܐ ܐܢܫ ܫܐܠ ܠܟ "and if any man doth come and enquire of thee" Judges 4, 20; ܐܬܐ ܩܡ ἐλθὼν ἐστάθη Matt. 2, 9 P. S. (C. ܘܩܡ 'ܐ); ܢܦܠܘ ܣܓܕܘ ܠܗ πεσόντες προσεκύνησαν αὐτῷ Matt. 2, 11 P. C. (S. 'ܘܣ); ܐܬܐ ܐܢܐ ܒܥܐ ܐܢܐ ἔρχομαι ζητῶν Luke 13, 7; ܩܡ ܕܒܪܗ "he arose and led him away" Ov. 162, 20; ܢܦܩ ܦܣܩ ܪ̈ܫܗܘܢ "he went out and beheaded them" Mart. I, 122, 23; ܩܘܡ ܗܠܟ ܬܐ "up! go and come" Sim. 293 *inf.*; ܕܢܐܙܠ ܢܨܠܐ "that he go and pray" Ov. 163, 25; ܕܢܪܕܐ ܢܚܙܐ ܐܪܥܐ "that he go there and see the land" Aphr. 455, 3, and frequently thus with verbs of motion; ܫܕܪ ܩܛܠ ἀποστείλας ἀνεῖλεν Matt. 2, 16; ܫܕܪ ܐܝܬܝ ܠܒܪܬܗ ܠܢܨܝܒܝܢ "he sent and fetched his daughter to Nisibis" Jos. St. 89, 18, and thus frequently ܫܕܪ ܐܝܬܝ "to send for", "to fetch"; ܠܐ ܓܝܪ ܡܥܠ ܡܘܬܒ ܠܢ ܘܩܐܡ ܥܘܠ ܕܐܢ ܠܢ "for he does not cause us to enter and be seated, just for the purpose of rising and iniquitously judging[1] us" Joseph 205, 1; ܐܚܝܕ ܫܒܝܩ ܥܠܡܐ "the world is laid hold of and abandoned" Aphr. 458, 1. (b) ܩܕܡܬ ܐܡܪܬ προείρηκα Matt. 24, 25; ܩܕܡܘ ܩܪܐܘܗܝ "they named him before" Aphr. 7, 8; ܩܕܡ ܓܝܪ ܐܫܥܝܐ ܐܩܝܡ ܥܠܝܗܘܢ ܕܝ̈ܢܐ "for Isaiah placed judges over them before" Aphr. 97, 6; ܩܕܝܡܝܢ ܗܘܘ ܐܬܝܢ "they had come beforehand" Land III, 350, 7; ܡܩܕܡ ܗܘܐ ܡܚܠܡ

(1) The last couple ܥܘܠ ܕܐܢ ranks rather under (b).

ܘܘܝ "had been promised before" Aphr. 26, 4, and many other verbs with
ܩܕܡ and ܡܩܕܡ, and particularly in translating Greek verbs compounded
with προ-; in passive forms like ܐܬܚܘܝ ܩܕܡ "had been pointed out before"
Aphr. 63, 18, or (more rarely) like ܡܨܛܝܪ ܡܩܕܡ "is prefigured" Isaac
II, 136 v. 600 &c. So too in another sense ܘܢܣܩܘܢ ܒܨܦܪܐ "that they
ascended in the morning (the next morning)" Sim. 293 mid.—ܐܣܓܝ
ܐܪܡܪܡܗ αὐτὸν ὑπερύψωσεν Phil. 2, 4; ܐܣܓܝ ܐܦܝܣܗ "strongly convinced
him" Sim. 279 mid.; ܐܣܓܝ ܪܚܡ "loved much" Ephr. in Wright's Cat.
689 *a*, 14; ܡܡܠܠ ܐܢܬ ܣܓܝܐܬܐ "thou speakest a great deal" Job 15, 4 &c.
This verb too (ܐܣܓܝ) is often put second: ܣܐܡ ܐܬ ܣܓܝ "thou heapest ☞ p. 362
up much treasure" Isaac II, 92 v. 67; ܓܕܦ ܐܣܓܝ "abuse greatly" Joseph
213, 12 [Ov. 305, 8] (var. ܩܥܐ ܐܣܓܝ "exclaim loudly") &c. (cf. *supra*
§ 335).—ܡܬܦܠܚܝܢ ܝܬܝܪ "they are farther cultivated" Aphr. 458,
1 &c.—ܓܕܐ ܢܛܥܐ "he by chance forgets" Aphr. 296, 8.—ܒܢܐ ܐܬܦܢܝ "he
built anew" Land III, 246, 14; ܐܬܬܣܝܡ ܐܬܦܢܝ "was laid down anew" Land
III, 177, 27—ܡܫܪܐ ܡܦܢܐ "he begins again" Aphr. 439, 3 &c.—ܘܚܘܪܢ
ܡܣܪܗܒܐ "they buried him in haste" Ov. 207, 26— ☞ p. 362
"she speedily gained health" Ephr. III, 554 E; ܩܒܠܬ ܚܠܝܡܐ ܒܥܓܠ
"he eagerly flung off every burden" Ov. 166, 7—ܣܡܗ ܒܓܘ "he
placed him in the midst" Ephr. III, 569 A—ܐܦ ܗܢܘܢ ܫܕܘ "they shot, in
corresponding fashion" Mart. I, 79, 12; and so too with other verbs,
particularly in translations from the Greek, like ܦܢܝ, ܥܠ, ܦܣ, ܗܦܟ ☞ p. 362
"again"; ܐܘܚܪ "late"; ܐܘܪܟ "long" &c. Very probably in all these cases
other constructions might have been employed, for instance with ܘ, or
with subordination effected by means of ܠ or ܕ.

B. The construction of ܐܫܟܚ has a special ranking of its own in
this section: ܐܫܟܚ ܓܪܒܘ "they could draw out" ("they were able, they
drew out") Sim. 365 mid.; ܐܫܟܚ ܦܪܩ "has (he) been able to save thee?"
Dan. 6, 20; and even negatively, ܐܝܟܢܐ ܘܠܐ ܐܫܟܚ ܐܢܝܢ ܐܦ ὥστε μηκέτι
χωρεῖν Mark 2, 2; ܠܐ ܐܫܟܚ ܦܣܩܗ "could not cut it (m.)" Mart. I,
129 *ult.*; ܠܐ ܐܫܟܚ ܦܪܩܝܗܝ "could not save him" Jul. 96, 17; ܠܐ ܐܫܟܚܬ ܬܓܘܙ
"she could not cross over" Ov. 12, 19. Additional instances are found
in Ephr. (Lamy) I, 607 str. 19; 617 str. 1; 684 str. 18; Joseph 124, 8 *sq.* &c.
Cf. ܘܒܐܝܕܐ ܐܫܟܚ ܕܒܪ "how could he drive her away?" Joseph 100, 5.

At the same time, such construction of this very common word is relatively rare. So ܠܐ ܫܟܚܘ ܡܩܛܠܘܬܗ "they were not able to put him to death" Ephr. II, 435 B = Lamy I, 23 str. 26. ☞ p. 362

Government of such Combinations.

§ 338. A. Just as in the case of verbs connected by ܘ (§ 336), so when two verbs are placed together without a conjunction, an object which is common to both usually appears only once: ܡܐ ܕܐܥܠܬ ܠܥܘܗܕܢܗ ܒܢܦܫܟ ܘܐܫܪܝܬܗ "when thou dost introduce the memory of him into thy soul, and cause it to dwell there" Ov. 163, 20; ܢܣܒܬ ܠܒܘܫܐ ܠܒܫܬ ܕܐܒܠܐ "she took garments of mourning and put them on" Jac. Sar., Thamar v. 280. With suffixes: ܘܐܣܩ ܐܚܙܝܗ ἀναγαγὼν αὐτόν Luke 4, 5 S.; ܘܟܦܢܘܗ ܐܦܩܘܗ ܘܩܒܪܘܗ καὶ συστείλαντες ἐξήνεγκαν καὶ ἔθαψαν (αὐτὴν) Acts 5, 10; ܫܩܠ ܐܫܕ ܐܢܘܢ "he lifted them up and poured them out" Sim. 273 *inf.*; ܢܣܒܗ ܝܗܒܗ "he took and gave her" Ov. 168, 7; ܘܐܝܬܝܗ ܐܥܠܗ "he brought him and led him in" Sim. 271 mid.; and thus pretty often.

B. When the object belongs only to one of the verbs thus set together, it may yet be separated from it by the other verb, just as in the case of verbs connected by means of ܘ: ܐܪܙܐ ܬܡܝܗܐ ܩܕܡ ܐܚܕ ܒܐܝܕܘܗܝ "a wonderful mystery he held by anticipation in his hands" Aphr. 64, 5; ܘܐܦ ܗܢܐ ܒܪܐܙܐ ܩܕܡ ܥܒܕܗ ܐܒܘܢ "this too our father did beforehand by mystic sign" Aphr. 63, 13; ܝܕܥܬܐ . . . ܕܩܕܡܘ ܐܚܕܘ "the knowledge . . . that they had before" Aphr. 448, 16; ܘܡܪܝܐ ܐܬܐ ܐܪܡܝ ܒܐܪܥܐ ܢܘܪܐ "and the Lord came and cast fire upon the earth" Ov. 124, 14; ܟܣܦܐ ܡܢ ܥܠ ܐܝܬܝ ܠܢ "who has come in and brought us money?" Joseph 229, 7 [Ov. 313, 17]; ܠܐܝܠܝܢ ܕ . . . ܐܫܝܛ ܣܓܝ ܘܨܥܪ "those, who . . ., he subjected to much contempt and humiliation" Ov. 175, 11; ܘܗܕܐ ܗܘܬ ܫܕܪܘ ܐܘܕܥܘ ܒܐܘܪܗܝ "and this they made known in Edessa, by means of messengers" Jos. St. 90, 15; ܕܫܕܪ ܐܝܬܝ "whom he sent for" John Eph. 328, 6 &c. So too ܐܝܟ ܕܠܐ ܫܟܚܘ ܠܝ ܐܒܐܫܘ ܐܠܨܘ ܘܐܝܩܘ "for as they could not afflict or injure me" Sim. 300 *inf.* (cf. § 337 B). So also with prepositions: ܚܠܦܐ ܗܦܟܘ ܐܬܪܥܡܘ ܠܗ "in their turn they found fault with the judge" (1) Isaac I, 220 v. 313; ܡܢ ܡܕܢܚܐ ܒܝܬ ܙܘܕܘ ܐܒܗܝ ܫܕܪܘܢܝ "from the East, our native land, my parents equipped and sent me forth"

---

(1) ܐܬܪܥܡ ܥܠ ܐܢܫ "he found fault with some one".

Apost. Apoc. 274, 11 (Gnostic hymn); (var. ܘܐܢܘܢ) ܐܓܠܘܗ ܐܢܘܢ ܟܬܒܬ ܘܫܕܪܬ ܠܟ ܥܠ ܗܠܝܢ ܪ̈ܫܐ "I am writing and submitting demonstrations to you, my beloved friend, about these leading points" Aphr. 446, 1 &c.

C. There is a Hebraism, which is occasionally imitated in original writings,—the placing of a ܘܗܘܐ (ויהי) devoid of any special meaning, at the beginning of the clause,—and which is followed by a Perf. with or without an ܘ-connection, *e. g.* ܘܗܘܐ ܡܢ ܒܬܪ ܩܠܝܠ ܝܘܡܬܐ ܥܠ ܝܘܒܝܢܘܣ "and, a few days after, Jovianus entered" Jul. 86, 1; ܘܗܘܐ ܠܒܬܪܗ ܕܝܘܡܐ ܒܨܦܪܗ ܕܨܦܪܐ ܘܟܢܝܫ ܟܠܗ ܥܡܐ ܐܟܚܕܐ "and the next day, in the morning season, the whole of the people assembled together" Jul. 95, 9 &c.

§ 339. The conjunction ܘ does not serve the purpose of introducing the apodosis (like the German "so" &c.). Where it seems to stand for this in the O. T., it is a literal translation of the Hebrew ו; in other passages its appearance is due to corruption of the text. ([1]) ܘ has, however, taken possession of nearly the whole compass of the signification of the Greek *καί*, and often means "also", "even" ["auch"], and then it is interchangeable with ܐܦ or ܬܘܒ. Such an ܘ ("auch") may have a place in the most diverse positions of the sentence, and even at the very beginning of the apodosis. Farther ܘ is everywhere allowable in the sense of exclusion before negations, in cases like ܘܠܐ ܚܕ "not even one"; ܘܠܐ ܡܕܡ "nothing at all" &c. In the same sense we find ܐܦ ܠܐ ܚܕ &c.

Note upon ܘ.

☞ p. 362

☞ p. 363

§ 340. In rare cases, when several members of a sentence, or several sentences, are put together, ܘ is placed even before the first of these ("both . . . and"), *e. g.* in ܙܟܬ ܘܠܝܗܘܕܝܐ ܘܠܚܢܦܐ "she conquered both the Jews and the infidels" Ephr. III, 161 B; ܕ . . . ܘܠܢܘܪܟ ܢܕܘܫ ܚܢܢ ܘܠܓܘܙܡܝܟ ܕܝܫܝܢ ܚܢܢ ܘܒܟܘܡܝܢܝܟ ܡܓܚܟܝܢ ܚܢܢ "that . . . we overcome thy fire, trample thy menaces underfoot, mock at thy threatenings" Jul. 48, 1. Cf. *ibid.* 21, 7, 14. So ܘܠܐ—ܘܠܐ "neither—nor" *ibid.* 106, 1. More frequent is ܐܘ—ܐܘ "either—or": ܐܘ ܠܡܪܕܐ ܠܡܘܢܐ ܢܣܒܘ ܐܘ ܠܡܢܝܢܘܬܗ ܕܡܠܬܐ ܦܪܘܫ ܠܡܩܦܣܢܘܬܐ "either chastise to the length of frightening, or

ܘ and ܐܘ doubled.

([1]) Copyists often dealt rather carelessly with these very common particles ܘ and ܕ—of little significance to their minds.

send the erring ones to the civil magistrates" Ov. 219, 10; ܐܘ ܐܝܬܐܘ ܠܢ ܐܘ ܐܘܩܕܘ ܒܢܘܪܐ "either bring to us (the writings of the heretics), or burn them in the fire" Ov. 220, 19; ܕܐܦ ܗܢܘܢ . . . ܐܘ ܢܙܟܘܢ ܐܘ ܢܬܙܟܘܢ "that they also . . . either conquer or are overcome" Spic. 12, 13; cf. *ibid.* 19, 23; Jul. 146, 6; 152, 27 &c. Probably this use of ܘ—ܘ, ܐܘ—ܐܘ was first brought about through *καί—καί*, *ἤ—ἤ*; cf. *e. g.* Luke 16, 13.

B. RELATIVE CLAUSES.

ATTRIBUTIVE RELATIVE CLAUSES.

Relative Pronoun and Referring Form. § 341. What was originally the demonstrative pronoun ܕ has had its signification so much weakened, that in very many cases it serves merely to indicate the connection of the relative clause with the word, of which that clause forms the attribute, while a personal pronoun (or a pronominal suffix), *pointing back* to that word, stands in its regular grammatical connection within the relative clause.

Referring Form in the case of the Subject. § 342. This referring pronoun may even stand as the *Subject*, *e. g.* ܡܠܟܐ ܡܕܝ ܘܦܪܣ ܕܗܘ ܕܪܝܘܫ "the king of Media and Persia, who is Darius" Aphr. 83, 5 (but ܟܪܘܒܐ ܕܡܛܠܠ ܕܐܝܬܘܗܝ ܢܒܘܟܕܢܨܪ "the overshadowing cherub, who is Nebuchadnezzar" Aphr. 87, 2); ܒܝܬܟ ܕܗܘܝܘ ܗܝܟܠܗ ܕܐܠܗܐ "thy house, which is the temple of God" Aphr. 46, 1; ܢܒܝܐ ܗܘ ܕܗܘ ܐܘܕܥܢ ܠܢ ܥܠ ܗܠܝܢ "that prophet, who has informed us of this" Ov. 75, 10; ܠܡܘܫܐ ܕܗܘ ܦܪܫ ܡܐܟ̈ܘܠܬܐ ܠܐܝܣܪܝܠ "to Moses, who separated the kinds of food for Israel" Aphr. 310, 8; ܕܝܬܩܐ ܐܚܪܝܬܐ ܕܗܝ ܩܕܡܝܬܐ "the last testament, which is the first" Aphr. 28, 9; ܘܐܦ ܠܐ ܕܚܠܬܗ ܐܝܬ ܒܗܘܢ ܕܗܝ ܡܦܨܝܐ ܠܗܘܢ ܡܢ ܟܠܗܝܢ ܕܚܠܬܐ "nor even is there in them the fear of Him (God), which delivers them from every (other) fear" Spic. 2, 25; ܡܕܝܢ̈ܝܐ ܕܐܝܬܝܗܘܢ ܒܢܝ ܩܛܘܪܐ "the Midianites, who are the children of Keturah" Aphr. 211, 4 &c. The separation of the referring pronoun from the relative-word gives stronger emphasis in ܗܢܘ ܪܚܡܐ ܕܡܐ ܕܛܥܘܟ ܪ̈ܚܡܐ ܘܐܚܐ ܗܘ ܠܐ ܛܥܐ ܠܟ ܘܠܐ ܫܒܩ ܠܟ ܐܠܐ ܥܡܟ ܡܟܬܪ ܗܘ "that is the (true) friend, who, when friends and brethren forget thee, for his part forgets thee not, and forsakes thee not, but remains with thee" Ephr. III, 305 F. Additional force we find given by a demonstrative, *e. g.* in ܕܗܘ ܗܕܐ ܕܓܕܫ "*id quod accidit*" Ephr. (Lamy) I, 217, 5;

ܕܗܘ ܗܘܐ ܥܡ ܡܠܟܐ ܐܫܬܟܚ ܗܘܐ "which man found himself directly with the king" Jul. 235, 25.

In all these cases, however, the Referring form is necessary only when the relative clause consists merely of ܕ and a substantive, without a copula. Far more frequently it is wanting as the Subject.

Referring Form in the case of the Object.

§ 343. In the majority of cases too the *Objective relation* is indicated without having recourse to a referring pronoun. Thus *e. g.* ܡܘܡܬܐ ܕܝܡܐ ὅρκον ὃν ὤμοσεν Luke 1, 73; ܡܠܬܐ ܕܐܠܗܐ ܕܩܒܠ "the word of God, which he had received" Ov. 166, 9; ܚܘܠܐ ܘܚܛܗ̈ܐ ܕܡܘܠܕܐ ܦܪܝܨܘܬܐ "the wickedness and the sins, which looseness engenders" Ov. 179, 18; and thus very frequently. On the other hand recourse is had to the Referring form in ܗܘ ܕܥܗܕܢܢܝܗܝ "whom we have mentioned" Ov. 164, 17; ܒܥܕܬܗ ܕܐܠܗܐ ܗܝ ܕܩܢܗ̇ ܒܕܡܗ "in the Church of God, which he gained with his blood" Ov. 172, 17; ܠܐܕܡ ܓܝܪ ܕܒܪܟܗ ܐܠܗܐ "for to Adam, whom God blessed" Aphr. 346, 12; ܗܢܘܢ ܓܝܪ ܕܠܐ ܐܦܝܣ ܐܢܘܢ ܚܘܒܗ "for those whom his love did not persuade" Ov. 175, 5 &c. The Referring form is usual with the participle: ܒܢܝ̈ܢܫܐ ܐܝܠܝܢ ܕܥܕܡܐ ܠܗܫܐ ܡܛܥܝܐ ܠܗܘܢ ܪ̈ܓܬܗܘܢ "the sons of men, whom their cupidity still beguiles" Spic. 8, 14; ܐܢܫܐ ܕܩܪܝܐ ܠܗܘܢ ܛܝܒܘܬܐ "people, whom grace calls" Jul. 27, 27 &c. With a dependent Infinitive: ܗܘ ܡܕܡ ܕܠܡܟܬܒܗ ܠܐ ܨܒܝܬ ܗܘܝܬ "that thing, which I did not wish to write" Ov. 21, 7; ܠܘ̈ܛܬܐ ܘܓܘܕܦܝܬܐ ܐܝܠܝܢ ܕܐܦ ܠܐ ܟܬܒܐ ܡܫܟܚ ܠܡܓܠܝܘ ܐܢܝܢ "the curses and revilings, which not even Scripture can reveal" Aphr. 343, 18. Since a verb does not readily take two personal pronouns as its object, the Referring form is left out with double transitives, in cases like ܦܬܟܪ̈ܐ ܕܕܓܠܘܬܐ ܕܐܘܪܬܘܢ ܐܒܗ̈ܝܢ "the false gods [idols of falsity], which our fathers made us heirs to" Jer. 16, 19 (Aphr. 321 *ult.*); ܐܝܠܝܢ ܕܦܩܕܬܢ "that which thou hast commanded us" Sim. 397, 12; ܡܕܡ ܕܐܬܒܥܝܬܢܝ ܘܐܦ ܕܠܐ ܫܐܠܬܢܝ "what thou hast sought from me, and also what thou hast not asked of me" Aphr. 506 *ult.* &c. On the other hand, the Referring form is desirable in cases like ܐܘܣܒܝܘܣ ܛܘܒܢܐ ܗܘ ܕܥܒܕܗ ܗܘܐ ܩܕܝܫܐ ܪܒܘܠܐ ܐܦܣܩܘܦܐ "the blessed Eusebius, whom the holy Rabbūlā made a bishop" Ov. 167, 20. We have a Passive from the double transitive verb, in ܡܕܡ ܕܦܩܝܕ ܐܢܬ "something that was ordered thee" Moes. II, 70, 11; but such an expression perhaps can only occur in brief unequivocal sentences. To this perhaps we may add, that ܡܦܝܣ "(is) satisfied, contented" is sometimes employed like a transitive verb, in a short relative clause: ܕܢܡܠܠ ܡܕܡ ܕܡܦܝܣ "that he should say what he wanted" ("wherewith he was satisfied") Joseph 11 *paen.* [Ov. 275, 5] (var. ܕܪܓܝܢ "what we wished"); ܟܠ ܡܐ ܕܡܦܝܣ Ephr. III, 674 F; ܘܟܡܐ ܕܡܦܝܣ *ibid.* 675 A; ܢܗܘܐ ܦܩܕ ܠܗܘܢ ܟܠ ܕܡܦܝܣ "let him order them whatever he wishes" Sim. 369, 8. Similarly ܙܪܥܐ ܒܪܝܟܐ ܕܝܬܐܒܐ ܗܘܬ "the blessed seed, after which she was longing" Jac. Sar., Thamar v. 279.

Peculiar is the lack of the Referring form with dependent participles (§ 272) in ܛܝܒܘܬܐ ܗܝ ܕܡܒܕܪ ܗܘܐ ܡܦܠܓ "the bounty, which he was wont to dispense" Ov. 205, 19.

Referring Form with Genitive and Prepositions.

§ 344. The Referring form, however, is necessary with the Genitive relation and with Prepositions: ܡܢ ܕܒܝܬܗ ܓܢ̈ܒܐ ܦܠܫܝܢ ܠܗ "one, whose house thieves break into" Aphr. 145, 11; ܗܕܐ ܡܘܗܒܬܐ ܕܦܚܡܗ̇ ܠܝܬܘܗܝ ܒܥܠܡܐ ܟܠܗ "this gift, the like of which does not exist in the whole world" Aphr. 356, 3; ܒܐܬܐ ܙܥܘܪܬܐ ܕܒܗ̇ ܐܬܨܝܕ ܠܚܝ̈ܐ "through a little sign, by means of which he was caught for life" Ov. 162, 1; ܠܡܥܪܬܐ ܕܐܬܝܠܕ ܒܗ̇ "to the grotto, in which he was born" Ov. 165, 3; ܠܐܠܗܐ ܕܣܓܕ ܐܢܬ ܠܗ ܘܣܐܡ ܐܢܬ ܠܗ ܒܣ̈ܡܐ ܘܫܡܝܥܬ ܠܟܬܒ̈ܘܗܝ "God whom thou dost adore, and before whom thou layest sweet odours, and whose scriptures thou hast heard" Sim. 271 mid. &c. The Referring form is attached to a substantive depending on another substantive, in ܒܐܒܗ̈ܬܐ ... ܗܠܝܢ ܕܒܥܬܝܩܬܐ ܘܒܚܕܬܐ ܡܫܬܥܝܢ ܨܠܡ̈ܐ ܕܡܝܬܪܘܬܗܘܢ "in the fathers, the delineations of whose virtues are set forth both in the Old Testament and in the New" Ov. 160, 9; ܐܒܪܗܡ ... ܗܘ ܕܒܡܫܘܚܬܐ ܕܢܘܗܪܐ ܕܚܕܐ ܡܢ ܐܬܘܬܗ ܐܬܢܓܕ ܗܘܐ ܛܘܒܢܐ ܪܒܘܠܐ "Abraham . . ., by the moderate brightness of one of whose signs the blessed Rabbūlā was attracted" Ov. 167, 12—14.

Referring Form in a second clause.

§ 345. The Referring form may, in certain circumstances, occur explicitly or implicitly, only in a farther attributive or dependent clause: ܗܘ ܕܐܢܐ ܠܐ ܫܘܐ ܐܢܐ ܕܐܫܪܐ ܥܪ̈ܩܬܐ ܕܡܣܐܢܘܗܝ οὗ οὐκ εἰμὶ ἐγὼ ἄξιος ἵνα λύσω αὐτοῦ τὸν ἱμάντα τοῦ ὑποδήματος John 1, 27; ܐܪܒܥܝܢ ܘܫܬ ܐܬ̈ܘܢ ... ܗܠܝܢ ܕܐܢ ܡܥܕܪܐ ܛܝܒܘܬܐ ܡܬܟܬܫܝܢ ܚܢܢ ܕܢܦܩ ܐܢܝܢ ܡܢ ܝܘܢܝܐ ܠܣܘܪܝܝܐ "the forty-six letters . . . which, if grace help (*or* with the help of God's grace), we are endeavouring to translate from the Greek into Syriac" Ov. 200, 19;

ܦܘܩܕܢܐ ... ܐܝܠܝܢ ܕܟܠ ܒܪ ܐܢܫܐ ... ܡܫܟܚ ܕܢܥܒܕ ܐܢܘܢ "commandments, such as every one can fulfil" Spic. 5, 24; ܗܠܝܢ ܕܐܦ ܐܝܟ ܡܐ ܕܐܬܗܪܬ ܒܣܘܓܐܗܘܢ ܦܩܕܬ ܠܝ ܐܟܬܘܒ ܐܢܝܢ "which, as they filled thee with amazement through the greatness of their number, thou didst commission me to note down (in letters)" Jos. St. 5, 2; ܬܫܒ̈ܚܬܐ ܡܨܒ̈ܬܬܐ ܕܣܦܪܐ ܥܫܩܢ ܠܗ ܠܡܡܠܠ ܐܢܝܢ "the well-ordered glories, which the book-learned man has a difficulty in describing" Moes. II, 158 v. 1266; ܣܗܪܐ ... ܗܘ ܕܡܣܒܪܝܢ ܕܗܫܐ ܝܬܝܪܐܝܬ ܐܝܬܝܗܘܢ ܠܗ "the moon, to which they think that now they very specially belong" Ov. 70, 3; ܚܕܐ ܐܘܪܚܐ ... ܗܝ ܕܐܦܠܐ ܬܪܝܢ ܐܢܫܝܢ ܕܢܣܩܘܢ ܒܗ ܠܐ ܡܫܟܚܝܢ ܗܘܘ "one path, by which not even two persons could ascend together" Jos. St. 15, 6; ܗܢܘ ܚܘܒܐ ܕܕܪܒ ܡܢܗ ܐܚܪܢܐ ܠܐ ܐܝܬ "*hic est amor, quo qui major sit, non est*" Jac. Sar. in Zingerle's Chrest. p. 375—ܨܒ̈ܘܬܐ ܕܐܡܪܬ ܕܒܦܘܩܕܢܐ ܩܝܡܢ "the things, of which I have said, that they rest upon ordinance" Spic. 4, 17; ܗܢܐ ܡܕܡ ܕܡܦܩܕܝܢ ܐܢܬܘܢ ܕܬܥܒܕܘܢ "this thing, which you have been commanded to do" Spic. 1, 7; ܡܐ ܕܥܬܝܕ ܗܘܐ ܕܢܥܒܕ ܡܪܢ ܥܡܗ "what the Lord was about to do with him" Sim. 309 mid. &c. Cf. ܐܝܟܐ ܕܟܬܝܒ ܕܡܬܝܠܕܝܢ ܓܒܪ̈ܐ "*ubi scriptum est nasci viros*" Spic. 15, 9. Notice farther ܣܘܥܪ̈ܢܐ ... ܗܠܝܢ ܕܠܗܘܢ ܙܒܢܐ ܐܢܐ ܕܐܫܬܥܐ ܠܟ "these doings, which I will recount to thee" Jos. St. 8, 6; ܕܠܗܘܢ ܣܝܡܐ ܠܢ ܕܢܟܬܘܒ "*quae ut scribamus nobis propositum est*" Jos. St. 6, 11,—in which instances also the Referring form belongs to the verb which stands at the close. The sentence ܗܘ ܕܟܒܪ ܠܐ ܢܦܩ ܐܢܫ ܡܢ ܦܟܝܗܘܬܐ ܟܕ ܩܘܐܣܛܝܘܢܪܐ ܕܡܗܝܡ̈ܢܐ ܢܩܪܝܘܗܝ "*quem quis carnificem fidelium vocans forte non fallatur*" Land II, 175, 9 [*lit.*: "he whom perhaps one would not depart from propriety in calling 'the executioner' (*questionarius*) of the faithful"] is no doubt essentially Greek in thought. The clause which should have contained the Referring form, is left out as self-evident, in ܘܐܝܟ ܕܦܐܐ [ܕܢܥܒܕܘܢ] ܢܥܒܕܘܢ "and do what it befits them [to do]" Jos. St. 88, 15.

§ 346. The expression of the Referring form by means of a proper demonstrative is rare, and is limited to special cases. In ܗܘ ܕܢܣܒ ܠܟܘܢ ܡܢ ܗܕܐ "*quod absit a vobis*" Addai 44, 16, the ܢܣܒ—originally belonging to the beginning of the sentence—is but loosely attached to what precedes it. Sentences, again, of a different style, are met with in

Referring Form expressed by a Demonstrative.

ܚܙܐ ܐܢܐ ܓܒܪܐ ܚܕ ܡܫܒܚܐ ܕܐܝܟ ܗܘ ܕܕܡܘܬܗ ܠܐ ܐܬܚܙܝܬ ܠܝ "I see a glorious man, the like of whose form has never yet been seen by me" Sim. 328, 7, and ܐܬܐ ܕܐܝܟ ܗܘ ܠܐ ܗܘܬ ܒܗܠܝܢ ܙܒܢܐ "a sign, the like of which has not happened in these times" Sim. 379, 12.—ܕܡܛܠ ܗܕܐ ܦܩܕܝܢ ܚܢܢ ܕܬܬܪܕܐ "on account of which thing we command thee to be chastised" John Eph. 202, 19, and suchlike expressions, in John Eph. and others, scarcely correspond to true Syriac idiom. The Referring form is strengthened by means of a demonstrative in ܒܢܝ̈ ܛܘܗܡܐ . . . ܕܠܗܘܢ ܠܗܠܝܢ ܐܝܬ ܠܗܘܢ ܚ̈ܝܠܐ "kinsmen . . ., people who possessed an army" Jul. 152, 21; ܕܗܘ ܗܘܐ ܒܗ ܡܚܕܐ ܐܬܦܓܥ ܠܡܠܟܐ ܗܘܐ "who had just met with the emperor" Jul. 235, 25; ܕܐܦ ܗܘ ܗܘܐ ܓܠܝܗ ܠܗ ܡܪܢ "what the Lord likewise revealed to him" Sim. 366 mid. In expressions of locality, the Referring form is more usually contrived by means of the adverb of place, ܬܡܢ "there": ܠܐܬܪܐ . . . ܕܐܦܠܐ ܠܬܡܢ ܡܛܝܐ ܡܠܬܐ "at a place, which even the word does not reach" Moes. II, 156 v. 1247; ܐܬܪܐ ܕܟܠܗܘܢ ܚܛܗ̈ܐ ܬܡܢ ܡܬܚܣܝܢ "there, where all sins are expiated" Aphr. 243, 2; ܥܡ ܒܪ ܓܢܣܗ ܕܐܬܐܣܪ ܬܡܢ "with its own like, where (= in which) it had been fettered" Ov. 63, 10; ܕܠܘܝ ܬܡܢ ܦܘܫ ܗܘܬ "*ubi utinam mansisset mens*" Moes. II, 98 v. 334.

Relative Clauses attached to Adverbial Expressions.

§ 347. Even as several nouns of place, and especially nouns of time, may, without any preposition, stand as adverbs (§ 243), so also, in a relative clause which serves as attribute to a noun of that kind, the mere relative-word [ܕ] may suffice, without any preposition or Referring form, *e. g.* ܥܕܡܐ ܠܝܘܡܐ ܕܥܠ ܢܘܚ ἄχρι ἧς ἡμέρας εἰσῆλθεν Νῶε Matt. 24, 38 P. (= ܕܒܗ; S. merely ܥܕܡܐ ܕܥܠ); ܒܝܘܡܐ ܕ ἐν ἡμέρᾳ ᾗ Matt. 24, 50 (and thus, frequently); ܒܫܥܬܐ ܕ ἐν ὥρᾳ ᾗ *ibid.*; ܒܝܘܡܐ ܬܡܝܢܝܐ ܕܡܬܓܙܪܝܢ "on the eighth day, when they are circumcised" Spic. 19, 17; ܒܗ̇ ܒܫܥܬܐ ܕ "at the very moment, when" Aphr. 129, 6; ܡܢ ܙܒܢܐ ܕܫܬ ܫܥܝܢ ܕܙܩܦܘܗܝ "from the time of the sixth hour, when they crucified him" Aphr. 15, 17; ܥܕܡܐ ܠܫܢܬ ܐܪܒܥ ܕܡܠܟܘܬܗ ܕܫܠܝܡܘܢ ܕܫܪܝ ܠܡܒܢܐ "till the fourth year of the reign of Solomon, when he began to build" Aphr. 482, 9; ܐܠܐ ܗܘ ܝܘܡܐ ܕܙܩܦܘܗܝ ܕܗܘܐ ܚܫܘܟܐ ܒܦܠܓܗ ܕܝܘܡܐ "but that day, when they crucified him, when there was darkness at midday" Aphr. 343, 6; ܟܕ ܡܛܐ ܙܒܢܐ ܕܢܡܘܬ ܡܘܫܐ "when the time came, that Moses was to die" Aphr. 161, 7; ܒܫܢܬܐ ܬܪܬܝܢ ܕܡܠܟܗ ܚܙܩܝܐ "in the

three months, during which they besieged it" Jos. St. 50, 11; ܒܟܠܗܘܢ ܥܣܪܝܢ ܫܢܝ̈ܢ ܫ̈ܢܘܗܝ ܕܗܘܐ ܒܟܘܡܪܘܬܐ "for in all the years of his life, that he was in the priesthood" Ov. 176, 16; and in the same way with many similar expressions of time. Other turns of speech also may take their place here, such as ܒܬܪ ܙܒܢܐ ܣܓܝܐܐ ܕܐܬܒܠܒܠܘ ܠܫܢ̈ܐ "long, after tongues had been confused" Aphr. 463 *ult.*; ܒܬܪ ܚܡܫܝܢ ܫܢܝ̈ܢ ܕܐܬܐ ܠܚܪܢ "fifty years, after he had come to Hāran" Aphr. 465, 9; ܡܢ ܩܕܡ ܚܡܫ ܫܢܝ̈ܢ ܕܢܣܒ ܐܝܣܚܩ ܠܪܦܩܐ "five years, before Isaac had taken Rebecca" Aphr. 479, 16, and many like examples (but ܡܢ ܒܬܪ ܥܣܪܝܢ ܝܘܡܝ̈ܢ ܕܩܘܐ ܒܨܘܡܐ "for after twenty days, during which he had continued fasting" Sim. 273, 8). Thus also ܒܫܢܬܐ ܬܪܬܝܢ ܕܡܠܠ ܥܡܗ ܐܠܗܐ "two years, after God had spoken with him" Aphr. 237, 4 &c.—With expressions of place: ܒܟܠ ܕܘܟ ܕܐܝܬܝܗܘܢ "wherever they are" [*lit.* "in every place that they are"] Spic. 20, 15; ܒܗܿ ܒܕܘܟܬܐ ܗܿܝ ܕܐܬܟܠܠܘ "in the place where they were crowned [*i. e.* suffered martyrdom]" Mart. I, 159 *inf.*; ܐܝܬ ܕܘܟܬܐ ܕ "*est locus, ubi*" Aphr. 69, 12 (but ܠܗܿܝ ܕܘܟܬܐ ܕܐܬܐܚܕ ܒܗܿ "in the place, where he had been laid hold of" Aphr. 222, 3); ܣܓܝܐܢ ܐܬܪ̈ܘܬܐ ܒܡܠܟܘܬܐ ܕܦܪ̈ܬܘܝܐ ܕܩܛܠܝܢ ܐܢܫܐ ܢܫ̈ܝܗܘܢ "there are many districts in the kingdom of the Parthians, where men put their wives to death" Spic. 14, 24; ܒܟܠܗܝܢ ܐܬܪ̈ܘܬ ܘܩܠܝ̈ܡܐ ܕܗܘܘ "in all lands and climes, where they are" Spic. 14, 20 &c.

This mode of expression comes most readily, when the same preposition is found before the words of time and place, that would have had to stand before the Referring form. Under such a condition, even in the case of other words, the Referring form is on rare occasions omitted. Thus particularly in cases like ܒܕܡܘܬܐ ܕ "in the form, that", "just as" Ov. 163, 22; 192, 7; Philox. 531, 19; and ܒܗܿܝ ܕܡܘܬܐ ܕ Sim. 330 *inf.*; Philox. 384, 11, and often in Philox.; ܒܛܘܦܣܐ ܕ "as" *ibid.* 343, 20; ܒܗܿܘ ܣܕܪ ܛܟܣܐ ܕ "in the order, in which" *ibid.* 589, 24; ܒܙܢܐ ܕ "in the way, in which" *ibid.* 573, 19. More remarkable are the following: ܐܢܬ ܚܛܐ ܐܢܬ ܡܛܠ ܗܿܝ ܕܚܛܐ ܐܢܬ ܘܐܢܚܢܢ ܡܝܬܝܢ ܡܛܠ ܗܿܝ ܕܡܝܬܝܢ ܐܢܚܢܢ "thou sinnest, because of that for which (= ܕܡܛܠܬܗ) thou sinnest; and we die, because of that for which we die" Mart. I, 126, 2; ܒܟܠ ܒܝܫܬܐ ܕܐܘܫܛܬ ܐܝܕܐ "in all the evil, to which thou hast set hand" Isaac I,

132 v. 1117; ܒܗܘ ܡܕܡ ܕܫܠܝܛܝܢ "in that matter, over which they have power" Spic. 9, 24 (cf. line 25).

Relative Clauses attached to Adverbs.

§ 348. In the same series with such expressions of place and time, stand the adverbial forms, some of them of frequent occurrence, like ܝܘܡܢܐ ܕ "to-day, when"; ܗܫܐ ܕ "now, when"; ܡܚܕܐ ܕ or ܡܚܕܪܘ ܕ "as soon as"; ܒܪ ܫܥܬܗ ܕ "as soon as" (§ 155 B); ܡܟܝܠ ܕ "now that" Aphr. 484, 14; ܐܡܬܝ ܕ "when", "as often as"; ܡܕܝܢ ܕ "now that", "but now that" Land III, 60, 13; ܐܝܟܐ ܕ "where"; ܡܢ ܐܝܡܟܐ ܕ "from that place, where" Gen. 12, 1; Ex. 5, 11; ܐܝܟܢܐ ܕ "so as"; ܡܐ ܕ "when", "in case that", (§ 258) and others, to which we must to some extent return, farther on. In none of these cases does a Referring form occur; ܠܬܡܢ is only found occasionally, as above, § 346; ܐܬܪܐ ܕܠܐ ܐܝܬ ܠܬܡܢ ܓܘܫܡܐ "where no body is present" Moes. II, 136 v. 939, and ܘܠܐ ܐܝܬ ܐܬܪܐ ܕܠܐ ܠܬܡܢ ܗܝ "and there is no place where it (f.) might not be" Moes. II, 92 v. 239.

Placing before the Relative Clause the Preposition proper to the Referring Form.

☞ p. 363

§ 349. A. The preposition, which of right should have been attached to the Referring form, is sometimes found prefixed to the Noun, to which the relative clause belongs, particularly in the case of the Adverbial Noun of place, ܐܝܟܐ: ܠܐܬܪܐ ܕܫܕܪܬ ܕܗܒܐ ܦܠܛܝܢ ܠܐ ܐܬܒܢܝܬ "the palace has not been built in the place, to which I have sent gold" ZDMG XXV, 340 v. 403; ܠܐܬܪܐ ܕ "there, whither", "whithersoever" 1 Sam. 14, 47, and thus, frequently; ܡܢ ܐܬܪܐ ܕ "there, whence" Matt. 12, 44 (C. S. ܡܢ ܐܬܪ ܕ); Chron. Edess. (Hallier) 145 *paen.* (Doc. of 201); Jul. 242, 22; Sim. 325, 8. So too with the construct state ܒܝܬ (§ 359); ܠܒܝܬ ܕ "whithersoever" Judges 2, 15; 2 Sam. 8, 14 (where there is a var. ܠܐܬܪ ܕ); Aphr. 438, 18; 439, 8; ܡܢ ܒܝܬ ܕ "from whatever place" Aphr. 121, 14; Jul. 21 *ult.* In these cases a referring form is inadmissible. But ܠܒܝܬ ܕ may mean also "to that place, whither" ZDMG XXV, 337 v. 297; Jul. 15, 13; and "to that place, where" Aphr. 46, 15; ܡܢ ܒܝܬ ܕ "from the place, where" Aphr. 222, 1; Ephr. I, 36 B; and ܡܢ ܐܬܪܐ ܕ "from the place, whence" Ephr. II, 117 F. It is the very same in the case of several combinations with ܟܠ: ܨܠܡܐ ܕܡܠܟܐ ܒܟܠ ܐܬܪ ܕܐܙܠ ܡܬܩܒܠ "the image of the king [money] is accepted in all parts it goes to" Aphr. 442, 16, and so Aphr. 302, 1; 438, 14 (but also ܒܟܠ ܐܬܪ ܕܐܙܠܘ ܠܗ ܗܘ "in every place to which they have gone" Spic. 18, 21); ܕܠܟܠ ܐ̱ܝܟܐ ܕܬܗܦܟܝܗ̇ (var. ܢܗܦܟܝܢ) ܚܙܘܐ ܦܐܝܐ ܝܗܒ ܠܗ̇ "which (f.), on every side to which you turn it, presents a beautiful appearance" Aphr. 442, 6; ܠܟܠ ܒܪܢܫܐ ܕܡܬܦܓܥ ܒܗ ܚܟܝܡܐ ܡܢ ܠܫܢܗ ܛܥܡ ܠܕܝܢܗ "whomsoever the wise man meets with, he learns [*lit.* 'tastes'] his judgment from his tongue" Aphr. 186, 4.

B. In translations however, Greek relative constructions, with the preposition before the relative pronoun, are directly copied. Thus even in the N. T.: ܘܠܒܝܬܐ(1) ܐܝܢܐ ܕܥܐܠܝܢ ܐܢܬܘܢ ܬܡܢ ܗܘܘ Luke 9, 4 C. S.; ܘܠܐܝܢܐ ܒܝܬܐ ܕܥܐܠܝܢ ܐܢܬܘܢ ܠܗ ܬܡܢ ܗܘܘ *ibid.* Pesh. = καὶ εἰς ἣν ἂν οἰκίαν εἰσέλθητε, ἐκεῖ μένετε; cf. Mark 6, 10 &c. And completely is this the case in later, slavish translations; in these we have ܕ ܡܢ ܗܘ ἐξ οὗ (instead of ܗܘ ... ܕܡܢܗ); ܠܗܘ ܕ ὅν &c., *e. g.* ܒܪܢܫܐ ܐܢܫ ܐܝܬܘܗܝ ܗܘܐ ܒܐܬܪܐ ܕܥܘܨ ܠܗܘ ܕܫܡܗ ܐܝܘܒ ἄνθρωπός τις ἦν ἐν χώρᾳ τῇ Αὐσίτιδι ᾧ ὄνομα Ἰώβ Job 1, 1 Hex.; ܐܒܥܐ ܥܡ ܗܢܘܢ ܕܡܬܟܢܫ ܐܢܐ ζητήσω μεθ' ὧν συνελεύσομαι ("I shall seek those, with whom") Prov. 23, 35 Hex.; ܥܪܣܐ ܥܠ ܗܝ ܕܣܠܩܬ ܠܬܡܢ ἡ κλίνη ἐφ' ἧς ἀνέβης ἐκεῖ 4 (2) Kings 1, 16 Hex.; ܪܘܟܒܐ ܡܕܡ ܠܗܘ ܕ σύνθεσίν τινα ἥν ... Arist. Hermeneutica (ed. G. Hoffmann) 26, 6 = 27, 7. Such constructions are also imitated by original writers who affect a Greek style, *e. g.* (ܡܠܬܐ) ܠܗܝ ܕ ܐܝܢܐ ... ܠܐ ܚܕܐ ܒܠܚܘܕ ܥܠܬܐ ܢܫܟܚ ܡܫܟܚܐ ܠܗ̇ ܕܐܝܬܝܗ̇ conceived like λόγος ᾧτινι ... μὴ μίαν μόνον εὑρήσει εἶναι αἰτίαν Jac. Ed. Epist. 13 p. 2, 21. Here the Referring form serves at least to clear up the meaning. Compare ܕܠܗܕܐ ܟܕ ܫܡܥܗ̇ "*quod quum audiret*" Hoffmann, Märtyrer 107, 964, and similarly in John Eph.

§ 350. A. When the relative clause refers directly to the first or second Person, then the Referring form also keeps this Person throughout: ܐܢܬܘܢ ܐܝܠܝܢ ܕܐܬܝܬܘܢ ܒܬܪܝ ὑμεῖς οἱ ἀκολουθήσαντές μοι Matt. 19, 28; ܠܢ ܕܡܥܠܝܢܢ ܡܢܗܘܢ "to us, who are higher placed than they" Ov. 184, 17; ܚܢܢ ܕܡܣܟܢܝܢܢ "we, who are poor" Aphr. 119, 22; ܚܢܢ ܕܝܢ ܕܝܕܥܝܢܢ "but we, who know" Aphr. 497, 16; ܐܢܐ ܕܪܗܛܬ "I, who have been running" Ov. 306, 11; ܘܐܣܩܝܢܝ ܕܢܦܠܬ ܒܒܝܫܬܐ "and lift me out, who have fallen into evil" Ephr. III, 429 A; ܐܢܐ ܕܝܢ ܕܒܝ ܚܝܘ ܡܝܬܐ ܣܓܝܐܐ "but I, by whom many dead people lived" Ephr. Nis. p. 68 v. 58; ܠܟܘܢ ܕܡܬܩܪܝܢ ܐܢܬܘܢ "to you,

Relative Clauses referring to the 1st and 2nd Pers.: and to the Vocative. Apposition to the Vocative.

(1) Read thus for ܠܒܝܬܐ also in C.

who believe" Spic. 2, 19; ܠܟ ܡܪܝ ܕܒܪܬܢܝ "to thee, O Lord, who hast
☞ p. 363 created us" Ov. 424, 4 (where there is a whole series of instances) &c.

Rem. The correctness of ܚܢܢ ܕܥܕܝܪܝܢ ܡܢܗܘܢ "we, who have been aided by them" Ov. 184, 20 (instead of ܕܥܕܝܪܝܢܢ) and of ܠܢ ܗܘ ܕܐܝܬ ܫܘܠܛܢܐ "to us, who have power" *ibid.* 19 (instead of ܕܐܝܬ ܠܢ) is very doubtful.

B. The second Person may stand with the vocative: ܐܠܗܐ ܕܦܫܝܩܢ ܠܟ ܟܠܗܝܢ ܥܣܩܬܐ "O God, to whom all difficult things are easy" Sim. 330, 1; ܐܘ ܪܥܝܐ ܣܟܠܐ ܘܫܛܝܐ ܕܫܠܡܬ ܥܢܝ ܠܐܝܕܟ ܕܝܡܝܢܐ ܘܠܥܝܢܟ ܕܝܡܝܢܐ "O stupid and foolish shepherd, to whose right hand and right eye I have committed my sheep" Aphr. 194, 14; ܐܘܪܫܠܡ ܕܩܛܠܬܝ (1) ܠܢܒܝܐ ܘܪܓܡܬܝ (1) ܠܐܝܠܝܢ ܕܐܫܬܠܚܘ ܠܘܬܗ Ἰερουσαλήμ, *ἡ ἀποκτείνουσα τοὺς προφήτας καὶ λιθοβολοῦσα τοὺς ἀπεσταλμένους πρὸς αὐτήν* Luke 13, 34
☞ p. 363 C. S.; cf. ܫܡܥܘ ܥܡܡܐ ܟܠܟܘܢ 1 Kings 22, 28, and ܫܡܥܘ ܥܡܡܐ ܟܠܗܘܢ Micah 1, 2 = שִׁמְעוּ עַמִּים כֻּלָּם. But the third person appears oftener in this case: ܐܘ ܕܟܪܐ ܕܩܪܢܬܗ ܡܬܒܪܢ "O thou ram, whose horns are broken" Aphr. 83, 23; ܡܟܝܠ ܐܘ ܒܢܝ ܐܕܡ ܟܠ ܕܡܘܬܐ ܐܡܠܟ ܒܟܠܗܘܢ ܐܬܪܥܘ ܒܡܘܬܐ "now, ye sons of Adam, all ye whom death reigns over, think upon death" Aphr. 422, 20; ܒܪ ܐܢܫܐ ܕܠܐ ܡܣܬܟܠ "O man, who dost not understand" Aphr. 497, 15; ܐܝܬܝܐ ܕܝܚܝܕ ܗܘ ܠܗ ܠܢܦܫܗ "O Being, who alone knowest thyself" Moes. II, 76 v. 5; ܥܒܪܝܐ ܕܐܬܝܩܪܘ "ye Hebrews, who were honoured" Ov. 304, 13; ܐܘ ܕܝܡܐ ܒܪܫܗ ܘܡܕܓܠ "O thou who swearest by thy head [*lit.* 'his head'], and liest" Aphr. 500, 7 &c.

C. Also when, without any formal relative clause, an indication of reference appears in the detailed determination [or complement] of the
☞ p. 363 Vocative, the third person is then taken: ܐܘ ܪܚܡܝܗ ܠܩܛܝܠܐ ܒܕܡܗܘܢ "ye who love, with your [heart's] blood, him who was put to death" Mart. I, 68, 19, cf. line 21; ܐܘ ܨܝܪ ܨܘܪܬܗ ܒܝܘܣܦ "O thou who dost represent an image of thyself in Joseph" Joseph 4, 12 [Ov. 271, 22]; ܕܥܘ ܟܠܗܘܢ ܟܠܟܘܢ ܐܚܝܢܘܗܝ "know, all of you his kinsmen" Jul. 158, 26; ܓܒܪܐ ܕܫܘܚܢܘܗܝ "O man of wounds" [*lit.* "man of his sores"] (§ 224) Moes.

(1) To be read as Perfects.

II, 162 v. 1324 &c. So Luke 13, 34 in P. [but otherwise in C. and S., see above], in verbal agreement, to be sure, with the original text.

Compare with these examples ܕܠܢ ܡܝ̈ܬܐ ܒܦܓܪܗܘܢ ܡܠܟ ܐܢܬ ܕܢܗܘܐ ܬܘܒ ܡܝ̈ܬܐ ܒܢܦܫ̈ܬܗܘܢ "thou who dost advise us, who are dead in our body (*lit* 'people dead in their body'), that we should farther become people who are dead in their souls" Mart. I, 159 mid., where the Referring form in the Apposition is the same as in the relative clause. ܒܦܓܪܢ would hardly be wrong here. In the same way ܘܡܫܠܛܝܢ ܥܠ ܚܐܪܘܬܗܘܢ ܐܢܬܘܢ "and you are (such as are), the masters of their own freedom" Jul. 73, 13; ܫܥܒܕ̈ܐ ܚܢܢ ܘܠܐ ܡܫܠܛܝܢ ܥܠ ܨܒܝܢܗܘܢ "we are the subjects, and not the masters of our will" Jul. 106, 6.

D. The first or second Person, however, is generally employed directly in the Referring form of an attributive relative clause, attached to a predicate whose subject is in the first or second person respectively: ܐܢܐ ܐܢܐ ܚܒܝܒ ܕܒܥܝܬܘܢܝܗܝ "I am Habib, whom ye have sought" Anc. Doc. 90 *ult.*; ܐܢܬ ܗܘ ܒܪܝ ܘܚܒܝܒܝ ܕܒܟ ܐܨܛܒܝܬ σὺ εἶ[1] ὁ υἱός μου ὁ ἀγαπητός, ἐν ᾧ εὐδόκησα Matt. 3, 17 C. S.; ܠܚܡܐ ܕܚܝ̈ܐ ܐܢܬ ܕܐܟܠܘܗܝ ܡܝ̈ܬܐ ܘܐܬܚܝܝܘ ܒܗ ܘܚܡܪܐ ܛܒܐ ܐܢܬ ܕܒܗ ܡܬܒܝܐܝܢ ܟܠ ܐܒ̈ܝܠܐ "the bread of life art thou, which the dead have eaten, and through which they have been raised to life again; and the good wine art thou, through which all mourning ones are comforted" Jac. Sar. Thamar v. 31; ܐܢܬ ܗܘ ܕܐܘܕܥܬܢ "thou art he, who hast made known to us" Aphr. 492, 18 &c. Cf. ܘܡܫܬܟܚܝܢܢ ܒܢܝ̈ܢܫܐ ܕܡܬܕܒܪܝܢ ܚܢܢ "and we are found to be men who are led" Spic. 10, 20, and ܘܐܢܬܘܢ ܐܝܟ ܐܢܫܐ ܕܣܢܘ ܐܝܩܪܢ ܘܐܬܫܝܛ ܒܥܝ̈ܢܝܗܘܢ ܫܘܠܛܢܐ ܕܝܠܢ ܦܘܩܘ "ye, as men who have hated our honour, and in whose eyes the power wielded by us is despised, go forth" Jul. 73, 11.

And yet the third person is permissible in such cases too: ܘܚܢܢ ܓܦ̈ܬܐ ܕܢܨܝܒܢ ܒܓܘܗ "and we are vines, that have been planted therein" Aphr. 288, 12, and similar examples.

§ 351. Corresponding to what is described in §§ 242 and 319, a substitute for the Subject may occur even in a relative clause, by means

Relative Clauses with ܚܢܢ—ܚܢܢ.

(1) Like Mark 1, 11; Luke 3, 22 (where S. also has ܕܒܟ). Our text here has οὗτός ἐστιν, and P. agrees with it.

of separating it into its parts through ܚܕ—ܚܕ and suchlike forms: ܨܒܘ̈ܬܐ ܕܦܪ̈ܫܢ ܚܕܐ ܡܢ ܚܕܐ "things which are different from one another" Spic. 11, 14 &c. And still more freely: ܬܪܝܢ ܕܝܢ ܐܚܝܢ ܕܫܡܗܘܢ ܗܘܐ ܠܚܕ ܒܪ ܚܕܒܫܒܐ ܘܠܐܚܪܢܐ ܫܡܘܐܝܠ "two brothers, however, of whom the one was called Barḥadhbeshabbā, and the other Samuel" Mart. I, 157 *ult.*; ܕܠܚܕ ܫܡܗ ܗܘܐ ܫܡܘܐܝܠ ܘܠܚܕ ܝܘܢܬܢ "of whom the one was called Samuel, and the other Jonathan" Land II, 277, 14, and thus, frequently, with ܕܠܚܕ . . . ܫܡܗ.

Relative Clause preceding its Noun.

§ 352. A. It is not common to have the attributive relative clause preceding the word, to which it refers. But the following are examples of that arrangement: ܘܕܐܝܬܝܗܘܢ ܒܥܝ̈ܢܝܗܘܢ ܫܝܛܢ ܠܗܘܢ ܨܒܘ̈ܬܐ "and the things, which lie before their eyes, are despised by them" Aphr. 426, 18; ܕܝܬܝܪ ܡܢ ܒܪܗ ܡܢܐ ܗܘܐ ܠܡܬܠ ܠܢ "what should he have given us, that was better than his son?" Aphr. 485, 20, [*lit.* "that was better than his son—what ought he to have given us?"] where a strong rhetorical relief is produced; ܠܝܬ ܕܚܫܒ ܐܢܫ "no man existed, who thought . . " Jul. 194 *ult.* The words ܘܗܘ ܗܢܐ ܕܐܠܦܢ ܦܪܘܩܢ ܒܛܢܢܘܬܐ ܕܚܘܒܗ ܚܘܝ are to be translated "and this very thing, which our Redeemer taught to us,—the zeal of his love,—he showed . . " Aphr. 40 *ult.*, so that ܛܢܢܘܬܐ is an Epexegesis, and not "and just this zeal which he &c.".

B. Very frequently there stand, at the commencement of the clause, only compounds of ܕܐܝܟ with demonstratives or interrogatives: ܕܐܝܟ ܗܠܝܢ ܚܫ̈ܐ "sufferings, which are as these" = "such sufferings" Ov. 168, 1; ܒܕܐܝܟ ܗܢܐ ܣܘܥܪܢܐ "in such a deed" Isaac II, 216 v. 251 and v. 280; ܒܕܐܝܟ ܗܠܝܢ ܓܝܪ ܫܘܦܪ̈ܐ ܫܐܝ̈ܠܐ "for in such borrowed beauties" Ephr. II, 171 E; ܕܐܝܟ ܗܕܐ ܗܟܝܠ ܐܬܐ "such a token, then" Jos. St. 41, 7 &c.; ܕܐܝܟ ܐܝܢܐ ܩܘܒܪܢܝܛܐ "what sort of pilot?" Sim. 384 mid.; ܡܢ ܕܐܝܟ ܐܝܠܝܢ ܡܘ̈ܬܐ "*a qualibus mortibus*" Assem. 2, 44 (Philoxenus) &c. It is, however, permissible to place the demonstrative forms at the end, *e. g.* ܐܘܠܨܢ̈ܐ ܕܐܝܟ ܗܠܝܢ "such afflictions" Jos. St. 4, 17 &c.

Rem. The ܕ may also be wanting here: ܐܝܟ ܗܢܐ ܦܬܓܡܐ "such a word" Aphr. 77, 6; ܐܝܟ ܗܕܐ ܨܒܘܬܐ "such a thing" Sim. 292, 10 &c. ܕܐܝܟ . . . may also stand as a substantive: ܒܗܠܝܢ ܓܝܪ ܘܒܕܐܝܟ ܗܠܝܢ "*per haec enim et talia*" Isaac I, 248 v. 511 &c. After the Greek pattern several combinations are formed, like ܐܝܟ ܐܝܟ οἷον, οἷον ὡς "for example" and many others.

"Whosoever" &c. § 353. Interrogatives with ܕ and the pronoun of the third person are employed adjectively and substantively in the sense of "whosoever, whatsoever", "any (one), any (thing)" &c.: ܡܛܠ ܨܒܘܬܐ ܐܝܢܐ ܕܗܘ "for anything whatsoever" Jos. St. 80, 16; ܒܐܝܢܐ ܐܝܢܐ ܕܗܘ ܐܘ ܐܝܕܐ ܕܗܝ ܥܠܬܐ "in any way or for any cause whatever" Philox. Epist. (Guidi) fol. 10 *a*, 1, 2; ܒܟܠ ܐܝܕܐ ܕܗܝ ܡܕܝܢܬܐ "in any city you please" Land II, 240, 10; ܒܟܠ ܐܘܠܨܢܐ ܘܡܟܐܘܒܐ ܐܝܢܐ ܕܗܘ "in any distress or illness whatsoever" Moes. II, 73, 26; ܘܡܘܬܐ ܐܝܢܐ ܕܗܘ ܕܢܡܘܬ ܢܝܚܐ ܗܘ ܠܢ "and any kind of death whatsoever, that we may die, is for us a comfort" Ephr. II, 175 C; ܟܠ ܐܝܢܐ ܕܗܘ ܩܒܪܐ "any grave whatever" Jos. St. 39, 10; ܘܫܒܩܢܝܗ̇ ܠܐܝܟܐ ܕܗܝ ἐπιδόντες ἐφερόμεθα (*lit.* "we let her go wherever she would") [E. V. "we let her drive"] Acts 27, 15; ܕܡܢ ܕܗܘ "of any one you please" Ov. 218, 11 &c. So frequently ܐܡܬܝ ܕܗܘ "whensoever"; ܐܝܟܐ ܕܗܘ "wherever", and many others. In accordance with these forms we have even ܡܢ ܦܢܐ ܕܗܘ "from whatever quarter" Euseb. Ch. Hist. 332, 12.

Omission of the ܕ. § 354. The omission of the ܕ in a complete attributive relative clause occurs perhaps only as a Hebraism, in the O. T., as in ܐܝܘܒ ܫܡܗ "whose name was Job" Job 1, 1.—Formulae of blessing,—as in ܝܘܫܝܐ ܕܘܟܪܢܗ ܠܒܘܪܟܬܐ "Josiah, whose memory be blessed!" [*lit.* "Josiah—his memory (is) with blessing!"] Aphr. 470, 15 (cf. Sim. 392 mid.); ܡܪܢ ܣܓܝܕ ܠܗ "the Lord—to Him be adoration paid!" Sim. 358, 1; 363 *inf.* (Cod. Lond. ܣ' ܠܣܓܕܬܗ)—are not to be regarded as relative clauses, but as parentheses. They are, besides, comparatively rare in Syriac.

Short Adverbial Qualifications as Relative Clauses. § 355. Short adverbial adjuncts to a noun are generally turned into the form of relative clauses, by means of ܕ; ܒܩܪ̈ܒܐ ܩܫ̈ܝܐ ܕܥܡ ܐܪ̈ܟܘܣ "in hard combats with the powers (of hell)" Ov. 159, 9; ܒܚܟܡܬܐ ܐܠܗܝܬܐ ܕܒܗ "with the Divine wisdom, which (was) in him" Ov. 172, 18; ܥܠ ܛܘܥܝܝܗ ܕܥܕܡܐ ܠܗܫܐ "over his error, which had lasted till then" Ov. 164, 7; ܒܨܦܬܐ ܕܥܠ ܢܦܫܗ ܒܠܚܘܕܘܗܝ "through anxiety solely for himself" Ov. 177, 22; ܠܡܝܩܪܘܬܗܘܢ ܕܥܡܗ "their reverence for him" Ov. 183, 26; ܡܗܠܟܬܗ ܕܠܬܡܢ "his journey thither" Ov. 168, 20, and countless other instances.

Time is not usually specified in such phrases (§ 315). Moreover, when no harshness arises, direct collocation is allowable, and often occurs: ܡܥܒܪܬܗܘܢ ܠܡܨܪܝܢ "their immigration into Egypt" Aphr. 27, 13 &c. But even to adjectives the adverbs ܛܒ, ܣܓܝ "very" are often attached by means of the relative particle: ܡܚܘܬܐ ܪܒܬܐ ܕܛܒ "a very severe blow" Judges 11, 33; ܥܡܠܢ ܪܒܐ ܕܣܓܝ "our very great toil" Ov. 320, 9, where of course the ܕ might be left out.

Relative Clause as Attribute to a whole Sentence. § 356. A relative clause may stand as attribute to a whole sentence even: ܐܡܪ ܕܚܫܘܟܐ ܪܓ ܗܘܐ ܠܢܘܗܪܐ ܗܘ ܕܠܝܬܘܗܝ ܒܟܝܢܐ "he said, that the darkness longed after the light,—a thing which (*id quod*) lies not in nature" Ov. 59, 13; ܘܐܢ ܡܬܚܫܐ ܚܫܘܟܐ ܡܢ ܕܝܠܗ ܗܢܘ ܕܥܣܩ ܠܡܬܩܒܠܘ "and if the darkness is put in pain through what belongs to itself,—a notion which is difficult to accept" Ov. 60, 9; ܗܢ ܕܐܦ ܗܘܐ (after a rather long passage) "a thing which, however, actually happened" Sim. 284 mid.; 290 mid.; ܕܠܡܐ ܡܐܡܪ ܝܩܝܪܐ ܠܗ ܗܘܐ ܕܥܣܩܐ ܕܠܡܬܗܝܡܢܘ "was perhaps burdensome to him,—a thing which is difficult to believe" Joseph 293, 2; ܘܠܐ [ܐܬܦܩܕܢ] ܕܢܒܢܐ ܩܘܪܝܐ ܘܢܫܬܐܣ ܡܕܝܢܬܐ ܐܝܟ ܕܡܠܟܐ ܗܘ ܒܠܚܘܕܝܗܘܢ ܡܫܟܚܝܢ ܠܡܥܒܕܗ "nor (are we ordered) that we should build towns and found cities,—a thing which kings only can do" Spic. 5, 19 (where there are several other examples of ܐܝܟ ܕ). In all these cases, of course, a demonstrative or interrogative will be found as a correlative. Cf. § 346.

Rem. On the correlatives in use or permitted with the attributive relative clause, v. § 236.

CONJUNCTIONAL RELATIVE CLAUSES.

Preliminary Observations. § 357. The relative particle ܕ often serves to indicate that a complete clause,—quite beyond its attributive relation,—is taking the place of an individual part of speech. Between this conjunctional use and the attributive use the contrast is by no means very strongly marked. The language sometimes treats relative clauses, which were originally Conjunctional, as if they were equivalent to Attributive ones (as *e. g.* with ܐܠܐ ܕ, where the relation is properly a genitive one § 359), and transforms Conjunctional clauses into epexegeses of an attributive character, by putting substantives, correlative pronouns, or adverbs, in front of them,— often without altering the sense in the least. We shall accordingly, for convenience' sake, discuss in the present chapter several points, which in strictness belong to the foregoing one.

§ 358. A. A clause may, with the help of ܕ, take the place of *Subject*: ܝܘܬܪܐ ܕܝܢ ܐܝܬܝܗ ܕܢܗܘܐ ܣܘܡܟܐ ܠܡܠܬܐ "it is of advantage that support should be gained for the word from other things" Ov. 162, 19; ܠܗ ܐܝܬ ܚܝܐ ܘܠܢ ܕܢܥܪܘܩ ܡܢ ܡܘܬܐ "to him belongeth life, but to us, that we should flee from death" Aphr. 487, 11; ܗܘ ܕܢܚܫ ܟܝܢܐܝܬ ܠܐ ܘܠܐ ܠܗ "he, to whom it is not by nature fitting that he should suffer" Ov. 198, 3: ܘܕܚܝܘܬܐ ܠܐ ܡܬܗܦܩܢ ܗܘܝ ܡܐ ܕܐܙܠܢ ܗܘܝ ܡܛܠ ܕ . . . "and that the animals were not excited at coming out, was owing to the circumstance that . . ." Moes. II, 126 v. 787; ܡܛܠ ܡܢܐ ܕܝܢ ܚܒܝܒܝ ܕ . . . ܐܬܟܬܒ "but why, dear friend, was it that . . . was written?" Aphr. 26, 20 &c. in countless available forms.

Relative Clause as Subject, Object, Predicate.

Still more frequently a clause with ܕ takes the part of *Object*. To this section belong all constructions with ܨܒܐ ܕ "to be willing, that"; ܒܥܐ ܕ "to seek, that"; ܚܙܐ ܕ "to see, that"; ܐܡܪ ܕ "to say, that"; ܝܕܥ ܕ "to know, that" &c. Even a second Object may be represented in this way, in cases like ܚܙܐܗ ܕܒܟܝܐ *εἶδεν αὐτὴν κλαίουσαν* John 11, 33; ܚܙܬܗ ܐܡܗ ܕܡܫܚܠܦ ܓܘܢܗ "his mother saw (him), that his colour was altered" Ov. 162, 12.

B. In certain circumstances a clause with ܕ (without a copula) may even constitute the *Predicate*; of course it has always in that case a sense of *purpose* (§ 366 A): (1) ܗܕܐ ܕܝܢ ܕܗܘܬ ܕܢܬܡܠܘܢ *τοῦτο δὲ ὅλον γέγονεν ἵνα πληρωθῶσιν* Matt. 26, 56 P. (similarly S.); cf. Matt. 1, 22; ܘܗܠܝܢ ܕܥܠ ܓܒܪܐ (2) ܗܢܐ ܕܐܫܬܥܝܬ ܕܬܚܙܘܢ "and these things have I narrated of this man, that you may see" John van Tella 73, 1; ܗܕܐ ܕܟܬܒܬ ܠܟ ܚܒܝܒܝ ܕܐܢܫ ܢܥܒܕ ܨܒܝܢܗ ܕܐܠܗܐ "this which I have written to thee, dear friend, (is to this end), that one should do the will of God" Aphr. 75, 6; ܘܗܢܐ ܟܠܗ ܕܢܬܩܝܡ ☞ p. 363

(1) [As if it read: "now this which happened, (was) in order that" &c.]

(2) [*Lit.*: "and these things, which I have narrated of this man, (have been) in order that you may see".]

ܘܢܘܫܠܟ ܕܐܚܘܝܟ "and all this, which I have explained and pointed out to thee, (is) that thou mayst know" = I have written to thee for this end only, that thou shouldest &c." Aphr. 213, 15; and thus frequently ܡܛܠܗ ܕ . . . ܕ,—ܕ . . . ܕ ܗܕܐ ܡܛܠܗ, ܕ . . . ܕ ܗܠܝܢ ܡܛܠܗܝܢ, in the meaning "only with this purpose, in order that" [or "only to the end that"] Aphr. 184, 5; Ov. 65, 17; Ephr. Nis. p. 8 v. 109; p. 87 v. 113; Ephr. (Lamy) I, 253 *ult.*; III, 689 str. 13 &c. (cf. § 360 B).

☞ p. 363

Relative Clause in the position of a Genitive.

§ 359. The immediate subordination of a clause, to a noun in the construct state by means of ܕ, is limited to some few cases. ܐܬܪ̈ ܕ and ܒܗ̇ ܕ "in the locality (of the circumstance) that" = "there, where" (מְקוֹם אשר); ܒܙܒܢ ܕ "in the time (of this) that",—are by the speech itself already treated as equivalent to the attributive constructions ܒܐܬܪܐ ܕ, ܒܙܒܢܐ ܕ. Not merely are they interchanged without distinction (cf. ܒܙܒܢ ܕܡܬܒܙܥ "at the time when it is rent in pieces" Aphr. 451, 1, alongside of ܒܙܒܢܐ ܕܡܝܬܬ "at the time when she died" *ibid.* 452, 13), but the Referring form through ܬܡܢ may stand at least with ܐܬܪ and ܒܗ̇ (§ 346), and even the form through ܒܗ with ܐܬܪ: ܐܬܪ ܕܢܝܚܝܢ ܒܗ ܙܕܝܩܐ "in the place where the just are at rest" Aphr. 389, 11; ܠܥܠ ܡܢ ܗܘ ܕܐܝܬܘܗܝ ܗܘܐ ܛܠܝܐ ἐπάνω οὗ ἦν τὸ παιδίον Matt. 2, 9 C. (ܐܬܪ ܕܐܝܬܘܗܝ ܗܘܐ S.). Notice, that after ܐܬܪ ܕ, the mere naming of the Subject is sufficient sometimes to convey the sense of 'existence': ܐܬܪ ܕܣܝܡܬܢ "where our treasure is" Aphr. 506, 15; cf. 176, 19; ܐܬܪ ܕܐܢܘܢ "wherever they are" Spic. 20, 14, 18 (for which 19, 19 ܐܬܪ ܕܐܝܬܝܗܘܢ, cf. 20, 5 ܐܬܪ ܕܐܝܬܝܢ "wherever we are").—ܣܦܩ ܕ "sufficing for this, that", "only for this, that" Aphr. 276, 19; Ephr. I, 66 C; cf. Spic. 47, 16; then directly "in order that" (in translations of ἵνα, ὡς ἄν).—This use of the Constr. st. is illustrated farther in very rare cases only: ܒܙܒܢ̈ ܕܢܦܩܢ "at the time that they (f.) go out" Gen. 24, 11; ܒܥܠܬ ܕ "by reason of this, that", "on this account, that" Aphr. 505, 5; ܡܢܐ ܝܘܬܪܢ ܕ "what gain is there from this, that" Job 22, 3.

☞ p. 363

Relative Clause dependent upon a Preposition.

§ 360. A. Complete clauses are widely rendered dependent upon *Prepositions*, by means of ܕ. Above all, the exceedingly common ܟܕ must be mentioned here (from כ "as", "like", which is no longer extant in Syriac in its uncompounded state, and ܕ) "when, since, while"; constantly implying time (for exceptions v. § 230), often with a causal or conditional secondary meaning.—So too we have ܒܕ, from ܕ + ܒ "while", "through this, that" (Ov. 180, 9), generally "seeing that":—ܡܢ ܕ "from", "from this, that" (Ov. 199, 1 &c.), also in comparisons (§ 249 E ܘܣܓܝܐܬ ܢܟܝܢ ܒܥܠܝܗܘܢ ܢܛܝܪ ܡܢ ܕܗܘܘ ܐܠܨܝܢ "and he has more greed for them, than they had [for riches]" Aphr. 431, 2), usually "since", for which also appears ܡܢ ܒܕ;—ܡܛܠ ܕ "because", also "in order that" (Aphr. 455, 8, and frequently);—ܥܠ ܕ "on this ground, that", "because", also "in the meantime", "while", *e. g.* Land III, 208, 10; so too in incomplete clauses, where we translate the phrase by the preposition "within": ܥܠ ܕܬܪܥܣܪ ܝܘܡܝܢ "within twelve days" Jos. St. 61, 7; so ܥܠ ܕ . . . ܝܘܡܝܢ "in so many days" John Eph. 193, 7; 406, 7; Land III, 206, 24 (cf. Jer. 28, 11 Hex. ܥܠ ܕܬܪܬܝܢ ܫܢܝܢ)—ܡܢ ܒܬܪ ܕ "after that" (conj.) &c. ☞ p. 364

Similarly, ܒܝܕ ܕ "through this, that", "because" Ov. 145, 18; 190, 27 &c., and ܠܦܘܬ ܕ "according as", "just as" Ephr. I, 66 D; II, 27 D; 269 F; 271 A. Farther, ܠܩܘܒ ܕ "towards the time, that—" Qardagh (Feige) 87, 7 (= Abbeloos 97, 1).

B. Clauses with ܡܛܠ ܕ, and the like, appear as predicates,—just as those with ܕ only (§ 358), and convey purpose and cause, in cases similar to ܟܠܗ ܓܝܪ ܕܡܬܐܕܒܝܢ ܒܢܝܢܫܐ ܒܥܠܡܐ ܗܢܐ ܡܛܠ ܕܢܬܟܠܘܢ ܡܢ ܚܛܗܝܗܘܢ "for all that men are punished with in this world, (comes) in order that they may be restrained from their sins" = "is only for this purpose . . . that" &c. Jos. St. 6, 2; ܟܠܗ ܕܠܐ ܐܬܝܗܒܬ ܠܢ ܙܟܘܬܐ ܐܠܐ ܕ "the victory has not been given us, only because" Jul. 199, 22; ܗܕܐ ܕܟܬܒܬ ܠܟ ܡܛܠ ܕܣܒܪܝܢ "I have written this to thee, because they think" Aphr. 359, 1; ܗܢܐ ܟܠܗ ܕ . . . ܡܛܠ ܕ Aphr. 166, 1; ܗܢܐ ܟܠܗ ܡܬܡܪܐ ܕ . . . ܥܠ ܕ Aphr. 403, 10;(1) ܘܗܠܝܢ ܐܚܝ ܕܩܕܡܬ ܐܘܕܥܬܟ ܡܛܠ ܕܢܗܘܐ ܠܟ ܐܬܪܐ "this, my brother, I have informed thee of beforehand, in order that thou mayest have space . . . " Jul. 88, 19. Cf. farther Apost. Apocr. 182 *sq.*; Jul. 219, 18(2); 239, 20. ☞ p. 364

(1) Cf.: ܟܠܗ ܕܦܘܫܓܐ ܗܘܐ ܒܗܠܝܢ ܡܛܠ ܐܠܝܢ ܕ "he allowed this to pass just because of the fact, that . . . " [*lit.* "all the inattention which he showed in these matters was by reason of this, that"] Jul. 54, 23; and ܗܠܝܢ ܕܝܢ ܟܠܗܝܢ ܕܗܘܝ ܒܡܦܪܢܣܘܬܗ ܕܝܘܒܝܢܘܣ "all this happened through the influence of Jovian" Jul. 171, 2.

(2) Read ܡܣܬܟܠ instead of ܡܣܟܠ.

C. Apart from the conditional particles ܐܶܢ and ܐܶܠܘܼ and in many cases ܐܝܟ, ܥܰܕ is the only relative conjunction which stands without ܕ, both in its meaning of "as long as" and in that of "until", "before that". In the latter sense ܥܕ ܠܐ is often employed to bring into prominence the negative force of the conjunction, *e. g.* ܥܕ ܠܐ ܐܙܠ ܐܢܐ "before I go" Ps. 39 *ult.* &c., but also ܥܕ ܡܬܦܬܚ ܬܪܥܐ "before the door is opened" Sim. 366, 25; 377, 8. ܥܰܕ ܕ only occurs in very rare instances, as in ܥܕ ܥܕܟܝ ܠܬܪܥܐ ܐܚܝܕ ܩܕܡ ܐܦ̈ܝܢ ܘܥܕ ܦܬܝܚ ܬܪܥܐ ܕܪ̈ܚܡܘܗܝ ܩܕܡܝܢ "as long as the door of the grave is still shut before our face, and as long as the door of his mercy is still open before us" Ephr. III, 426 E; ܥܕ ܕܐܡܪ ܐܢܐ "till I say" Joseph 322, 10; ܥܕ ܕܠܐ ܡܝܬܐ ܗܝ "before she dies" Simeon of Bēth Arshām (Guidi) 13, 4. ܥܕܡܐ ܕ "until" is more usual.

Abridging-Substantive before Relative Clause.

§ 361. Clauses with ܕ are widely made to serve as explanatory additions [*Epexegeses,*—parenthetical explanations] for abstract substantives; cf. *e. g.* ܐܪܓܫ ܒܡܚܝܠܘܬܝ ܕܠܐ ܡܣܝܒܪܢ ܐܢܐ ܥܘܪ̈ܩܠܐ "he perceived my weakness, (which is *or* consists in this) that I cannot support calamities" Ov. 168, 5; ܠܘܛܬܐ ܕ "the curse, that" Aphr. 447 *ult.* &c. And thus occasionally, to ensure a better connection, the non-significant word ܨܒܘܼܬܐ "thing" ("circumstance", "fact") is joined with the ܕ which is acting as subject; and for this word the clause then forms an Epexegesis: ܘܝܕܝܥܐ ܨܒܘܬܐ ܕܐܦ ܗܘ ܡܢ ܕܡܙܝܥ ܠܗ ܐܝܟ ܕܨܒܐ ܗܘ ܡܙܝܥ ܠܗ "and the fact is well known, that he who moves it, moves it as *he* wills" Spic. 3, 6; ܡܢܐ ܐܠܨܐ ܗܘܬ ܨܒܘܬܐ ܕܢܫܬܒܩ ܒܚܝ̈ܐ "why was it necessary that he should be allowed to live?" Ov. 67, 12; ܕܡܝܬܪܐ ܗܝ ܨܒܘܬܐ ܕ "that it is an excellent thing, that" Aphr. 45, 19; ܠܐ ܡܫܟܚܐ ܗܘܬ ܨܒܘܬܐ ܕܢܗܘܐ ܗܘܝܢ ܠܢ ܡܣܟ̈ܢܐ ܫܪܝܪܐܝܬ "it would not have been possible for us to be truly needy persons" Ov. 25, 25 &c. With ܨܒܘܬܐ placed after the clause: ܕܢܫܒܚ ܐܢܫ ܘܢܒܪܟ ܠܪܚܡܗ ܕܦܫܝܩܐ ܨܒܘܬܐ "it is an easy thing for one to praise and bless his friend" Spic. 6, 14; ܘܕܠܐ ܗܘܐ ܟܠܡܕܡ ܒܨܒܝܢܢ ܗܘܐ ܡܬܚܙܝܐ ܨܒܘܬܐ ܡܢ ܗܕܐ "and that everything does not happen according to our will, is (a fact) seen from this" Spic. 9, 26 &c. (1)

(1) ܨܒܘܬܐ is found with this force even along with the Inf. with ܠ: ܐܢ ܐܠܨܐ ܨܒܘܬܐ ܠܡܦܢܝܘ "if it is necessary to reply" Aphr. 374, 18 &c. So also, put absolutely: ܐܝܟ ܕܡܬܚܙܝܐ ܠܢ ܨܒܘܬܐ "as it appears to us" Aphr. 375 *ult.*, cf. 234, 19.

§ 362. Far more common, however, is the practice of attaching with ܕ the demonstrative pronoun ܗܝ or ܗܕܐ to a clause, which serves in any way as member of a sentence: ܗܕܐ ܕܦܩܕ ܐܢܘܢ ܠܒܢܝ̈ ܐܝܣܪܝܠ ܘܦܪܫ ܠܗܘܢ ܡܐܟܘ̈ܠܬܐ ܡܛܠ ܕܣܛܘ ... "this fact,—that he gave command to the children of Israel, and separated for them the different kinds of food, was brought about because they had swerved ... " Aphr. 310, 10; ܘܬܡܝܡܘܬܗ ... ܗܕܐ ܗܘܬ ܕ "and his integrity consisted in this, that ... " Aphr. 234, 18; ܠܐ ܗܘܬ ܕܝܢ ܪܒܐ ܐܝܟ ܗܕܐ ܗܝ ܕ "but not so great as this, was the circumstance that" Jos. St. 2, 14; ܐܦ ܠܐ ܗܝ ܕܦܪܩܗ ܝܘܢܬܢ ܠܕܘܝܕ ܡܢ ܡܘܬܐ ܡܢ ܐܝ̈ܕܝ ܫܐܘܠ ܫܘܝܐ ܠܬܗܪܐ "nor is the fact that Jonathan saved David from death at the hands of Saul, deserving of wonder" Jos. St. 2, 18; ܒܠܚܘܕ ܗܕܐ ܝܕܥܝܢ ܕ "only this we know, that" Aphr. 496, 6; ܘܕܗܟܢܐ ܐܝܬܝܗܝܢ ܗܠܝܢ ܝܕܝܥܐ ܗܝ ܗܕܐ ܡܢ ... "and that these things are so, is clear from ... " Jos. St. 6, 9; ܐܦ ܕܢܣܡܘܟ ... ܐܦ ܗܕܐ ܡܫܟܚ "even that he should lend support ... this too he can do" Spic. 5, 14; ܚܫܒܬ ܗܝ ܕܗܘ ܡܚܢ ܒܐܝ̈ܕܝܗܘܢ "I have assumed this, that he smote us by their hands" Jos. St. 7, 1; ܟܕ ܠܐ ܢܦܪܘܫ ܗܝ ܕܐܠܗܘܬܗ ܠܐܠܗܐ "while he should not part with this (property),—that he is God" Ov. 197, 26 &c. *Strengthened expressions*:—ܗܝ ܗܕܐ ܕܝܢ ܕܥܒܕܬܢ ܡܪܝ ܗܝ ܗܝ ܥܠܬܐ ܠܛܒܘܬܐ "the very consideration that thou, Lord, hast made us, is a motive for goodness" Ephr. II, 524 C.—Two such clauses are confronted with each other through ܗܝ and ܗܕܐ in ܕܡܠܐ ܕܝܢ ܗܕܐ ܕܐܬܢܝܚ ܐܠܗܐ ... ܠܗܝ ܕܟܕ ܨܒܐ ... ܐܡܪ "for the one fact, that God rested ... has a resemblance to the other fact that, when he wished ..., he said" Aphr. 241, 18. Just as we have in this case ܠܗܝ ܕ, so have we many other combinations of a like nature with prepositions, *e. g.* ܒܗܕܐ ܕ, ܒܗܝ ܕ "in this, or through this, that" frequently (ܠܐ ܗܘܐ ܒܗܕܐ ܕ ... ܐܠܐ ܒܗܝ ܕ "not from the circumstance, that ..., but from this [other circumstance], that" Spic. 4, 21); ܡܛܠ ܗܝ ܕ "for this reason, that" Jos. St. 18, 14; 49, 20; ܥܠ ܙܒܢ ܗܝ ܕ "for meantime that" Ephr. II, 3 B &c. There is a considerable space between the ܗܕܐ and the ܕ in ܐܦ ܡܛܠ ܗܕܐ ܓܝܪ ܗܘܬ ܡܪܕܝܬܗ ܠܐܬܪܐ ܕܬܡܢ ܕܬܪܥܝܬܐ ܕܐܠܗܐ ܡܢ ܢܦܫܗ ܠܐ ܬܬܦܪܫ ܡܢ "for even on this account was his journey (taken) to that place,—that the thought of God might never be separated from his soul" Ov. 168, 19. Much more rarely is the masculine

Abridging-Demonstrative Pronoun before Relative Clause.

ܗܘܐ found with such a clause, as in ܘܗܢܐ ܡܢܝ ܕܘܗܘ ܠܟܠ ܟܐܦܐ ܠܐ ܩܪܝܬ ܠܡܫܝܚܐ "and this,—namely, that I have called Christ a stone,—I have not said from my own thinking" Aphr. 7, 7.

ܘܗܠܝܢ may stand with more than one clause: ܟܠܝ ܡܢ ܟܕ ܫܡܥ ܢܘܚ ܗܕܐ ܕܦܩܕܗ ܐܠܗܐ . . . ܘܕܐܡܪ "when Noah heard this, that God commanded him . . . and that he said . . ." Aphr. 235, 8.

☞ p. 364

ܡܐ ܕ §363. In certain cases also ܡܐ intervenes as correlative between a prep. and the conjunctional ܕ. Thus, frequently ܥܕܡܐ ܕ "until (that)" (= ܥܕ + ܡܐ + ܕ), and in rare instances ܟܡܐ ܕ "while", "when indeed" Jos. St. 69, 19.(¹) Of common occurrence also is ܟܡܐ ܕ "as many as", "as much as", "the more", "as long as" (ܡܐ ܕ "when", "as" &c. § 348).

ܐܝܟ §364. A. ܐܝܟ "as" (originally an interrogative [—"in what way? how?"—] but no longer used as such) may also, with the help of ܡܐ ܕ, introduce a clause: ܐܝܟ ܡܐ ܕܐܝܬܘܗܝ ܗܘܐ "as it actually was" Ov. 172, 20. Of more frequent occurrence is ܐܝܟ ܡܢ ܕ (in imitation of ὡς μέν) "as", "since", e. g. Ov. 83, 8; 185, 25, also "in order that" Jos. St. 8, 6; 12, 10 &c.—ܐܝܟ ܗܘ ܕ occurs always by way of supposition "as if": ܐܝܟ ܗܘ ܕܐܝܠܘܢ ܚܡܣ ܗܝܥܡܠ ܠܟ ܗܘ "as if a bargain with us had been made by him" Ov. 295, 20; cf. Jos. St. 31, 16; 33, 4; 34, 18; 56, 14 and 17; Mart. I, 98 mid.; Sim. 282, 10; Ov. 179, 15 &c.

B. In much larger proportion, however, ܐܝܟ ܕ is found pure and simple. It signifies not merely "as", but often "in order that" and "so that"(²) (= ὡς); also in the negative form ܐܝܟ ܕܠܐ "that not", "lest". Very often too it stands before the Inf. with ܠ, to bring out more strongly the notion of purpose: ܐܝܟ ܕܠܡܒܚܪ "in order to scrutinize" Ov. 252, 4 &c. So also before prepositional phrases, particularly in the statement of design, motive or view (= ὡς): ܐܝܟ ܕܠܐܝܩܪܗ "as a mark of respect to him" Jos. St. 59, 9; ܐܝܟ ܕܠܙܘܗܪܗ "as a warning to him" Sim. 370 mid.; and frequently ܐܝܟ ܕܠ "as a . . . ", but also ܐܝܟ ܕܚܡܣܕܘܬܐ "from ostentation" Sim. frequently; ܐܝܟ ܕܚܝܠܬܐ "with cunning" ZDMG

(¹) Martin 62, 17 reads thus, to all appearance correctly. Wright has ܟܡܐ.

(²) This use, however, is not equally in favour with all Syriac authors; in Aphr. it occurs only a dozen times at the most.

XXV, 335 v. 190; ܐܝܟ ܕܡܛܠܬܗ "for his own sake" Ov. 82, 3; ܐܝܟ ܕܒܣܘܓܐܐ ὡς ἐπὶ τὸ πολύ; ܐܝܟ ܕܒܦܣܝܩܬܐ "shortly", "in few words", often in ancient writings even.

C. ܐܝܟ without ܕ is also found in many references. Thus, first of all, before brief nominal phrases, with the help of which it forms a relative clause: ܐܝܟ ܬܓܪܐ "as (is) a merchant" = "as merchant" Ov. 165, 22: ܐܝܟ ܒܪ ܥܬܝܪ̈ܐ "as a son of wealthy parents" Ov. 160 *paen.*; ܐܝܟ ܙܒܢܐ ܕ κατὰ τὸν χρόνον ὅν Matt. 2, 16 P. (ܠܦܘܬ ܙܒܢܐ ܕ C. S.); ܐܝܟ ܦܘܩܕܢܗ ܕܡܪܝܐ "according to the command of the Lord" Ov. 166, 25; ܐܝܟ ܡܚܝܠܘܬܝ "according to my feebleness" [*or* "in my humble opinion"] Spic, 9, 14; ܐܝܟ ܡܕܡ ܕ "suitably to that which", frequently, &c. Often before numbers ܐܝܟ ܡܐܐ ܫܢܝܢ "as" *i. e.* "about (ὡς כְּ) a hundred years" &c. —So with ܕܡܐ "to be like" and similar words: ܕܡܐ ܗܘܐ ܐܝܟ ܢܘܪܐ "he was like a fire" Sim. 271 *inf.* &c.(1)—If the word with which comparison is made must receive a preposition, then ܐܝܟ ܕ is used, *e. g.* ܐܝܟ ܕܠܐܒܗ̈ܬܐ ܡܥܠܝ̈ܐ "as in the eminent fathers" Ov. 160, 8; ܐܝܟ ܕܥܡ ܓܒܪܐ "as with the man" Ov. 168, 9 &c. Or the preposition is withheld, and the special relation of that with which comparison is instituted is gathered merely from the context: "that great cheapness will prevail" ܐܝܟ ܫܢ̈ܝܐ ܕܡܢ ܩܕܝܡ "as (were) the years before" = "as in earlier years" Jos. St. 41, 16. However, there occurs: ܚܫܒܘ ܠܥܠܡܐ ܐܝܟ ܒܡܫܪܝܬܐ ܒܨܝܪܬܐ ܢܣܒܘܗܝ ܘܠܗܘ ܕܠܗܠ ܐܝܟ ܠܡܕܝܢܬܐ ܕܡܠܝܐ ܫܘܦܪܐ "they considered this world as an insignificant sheltering-place, but that world beyond as a city which was full of beauty" Anc. Doc. 101 *ult.*; ܐܝܟ ܕܢܫܪܐ ܦܪܚ "like an eagle" Sim. 385 mid. (if this is the right reading; Cod. Lond. gives it without ܐܝܟ).

D. An Object or an Adverbial adjunct may stand in the incomplete clause which is introduced by ܐܝܟ: ܘܗܦܟ ܐܢܘܢ ܐܝܟ ܪܥܝܐ ܛܒܐ ܠܓܙܪܗ "and turned them, as a good shepherd (turns) his flock" Aphr. 192, 11; ܘܐܝܟ ܐܡܐ ܠܒܢ̈ܝܗ̇ ܐܟܢܫ ܬܚܝܬ ܟܢ̈ܦܐ ܕܨܠܘ̈ܬܗ ܡܚܒܒ ܗܘܐ ܠܗܘܢ "and as a mother her children, he embraced them under the wings of his prayers" Sim. 389 *inf.*; ܙܟܐ ܒܩܪܒܗ ܐܝܟ ܐܝܘܒ ܒܢܣܝܘܢܘܗܝ "was victorious in his fight, like Job

(1) Compare ܐܝܟܢ ܕܡܐ "how does he look?" Joseph 195, 9; 225, 2.

in his temptations" Sim. 395 *inf.*; ܘܩܕܡ ܐܠܗܐ ܡܕܥܗ ܡܩܘܐ ܗܘܐ ܐܝܟ ܕܡܫܡܫܝܢ ܕܥܝܪ̈ܐ ܒܬܫܡܫܬܗܘܢ ܕܒܫܡܝܐ "and before God his intelligence continued, after the manner of the angels in their service in heaven" Ov. 169, 21 &c. Yet ܐܝܟ ܕ is more usual, at least when the Object is put at the commencement of the clause: ܘܢܓܕܗ ܡܢ ܝܗܘܕܝܘܬܐ ܠܗܝܡܢܘܬܗ ܐܝܟ ܕܐܦ ܪܒܘܠܐ ܡܢ ܚܢܦܘܬܐ ܠܟܪܣܛܝܢܘܬܐ "and carried him off from Judaism to his own faith, as Rabbūlā also from heathenism to Christianity" Ov. 161, 23; (1) ܐܝܟ ܕܒܥܠܕܒܒܐ "as the enemy (acc.)" Anc. Doc. 105, 11.

E. In some cases, however, ܐܝܟ "as if" without ܕ appears also before a short but complete clause. Thus frequently ܐܝܟ ܐܢܫ ܕܐܡܪ "as one says" ("as if one should say"); ܐܝܟ ܬܐܡܪ "as if thou shouldst say" = "that is" Isaac I, 184 v. 129; ܠܐ ܗܘܐ ܐܝܟ ܡܕܡ ܙܕܝܩܘܬܐ ܐܝܬ ܗܘܐ ܠܗܘܢ "not as if they had any righteousness" Aphr. 309, 12; ܠܐ ܗܘܐ ܐܝܟ ܡܕܡ ܐܬܓܠܝ ܠܝ "not as if anything had been revealed to me" Aphr. 101 *paen.*, and with special readiness in the case of Participles and Adjectives: ܘܐܝܟ ܢܛܪ ܚܣܡ ܗܘܐ "and (it was) as if he bore a grudge" Moes. II, 116 v. 635; ܩܪܒܘ ܐܢܫܐ ܐܝܟ ܡܪܚܡܝܢ ܥܠܝܗܘܢ "*accesserunt homines ut qui eos miserarentur*" Mart. I, 197, 15; ܗܘܐ ܠܗ ܓܝܪ ܐܝܟ ܠܐ ܝܕܥ "for he was as if he did not know" Joseph 259, 2 [= Ov. 329, 10]; ܗܘܝ ܐܝܟ ܢܨܐ ܘܡܬܚܡܬ "be as if thou wert quarrelling and wert angry" Ephr. (Lamy) I, 259, 10; ܐܝܟ ܨܒܝܢ "as if they wanted . . . " Jos. St. 56, 19; ܐܝܟ ܚܕܝ ܗܘܐ "he was as if pleased", *i. e.* "he looked pleased" Jul. 143, 2, and thus frequently. We may often render this ܐܝܟ by "as if". Answering thereto, we have ܗܘ ܕܟܕ ܐܝܬܘܗܝ ܐܝܟ ܠܐ ܐܝܬܘܗܝ "who, while he is, (is) as if he were not" (*or* "as though he were not") Ov. 70, 2; and thus often ܐܝܟ ܠܝܬܘܗܝ, ܐܝܟ ܠܝܬܝܗܘܢ; also ܐܝܟ ܠܝܬ ܐܢܝܢ Ephr. II, 339 C. (2)

---

(1) Thus an object may farther be found standing even after ܒܕܡܘܬܐ "in the likeness *or* form of", "as", and its genitive: ܒܕܡܘܬܐ ܕܕܘܝܕ ܠܫܐܘܠ ܐܚܒܬܢܝ "thou hast loved me, as David (did) Saul" Jos. St. 3, 5; ܒܕܡܘܬܐ ܓܝܪ ܕܩܝܣ̈ܐ ܠܒܢܝ̈ܢܐ ܨܠܘܬܗ ܠܒܪܝܬܐ ܡܚܒܩܐ ܗܘܬ "for his prayers held creation together, as rafters do buildings" Sim. 384 *ult.* &c.; cf. ܘܥܐܠܝܢ ܒܕܡܘܬܐ ܐܡܪ̈ܐ ܩܕܡ ܕܝܢ̈ܐ ܠܢܟܣܬܐ "and come in before the judges, as lambs to the slaughter" Ov. 394, 14.

(2) The construction of ܐܝܟ, as the above shows, is very strongly influenced by the Greek ὡς, but it is at the same time founded on a genuine Syriac idiom.

§ 365. As with ܐܝܟ ܕ, so too with ܐܝܟܢܐ ܕ, ܐܝܟܢ ܕ "so as", "so that" and "in order that". The interrogative is in the position of correlative here, just as in ܐܝܟܐ ܕ &c. The demonstrative ܗܟܢ ܕ, ܗܟܢܐ ܕ conveys the meaning "*só* that" with a measure of emphasis: in this case the adverb does not require to stand immediately before ܕ, as is necessary in ܐܝܟ ܕ, ܐܝܟܢܐ ܕ.

Other Adverbs as Correlatives.

A demonstrative often appears overagainst a relative clause which is introduced by an interrogative adverb; and in other cases also such a particle is often added: thus ܗܟܢ overagainst ܐܝܟ ܕ "just as . . ., so"; ܗܝܕܝܢ "at that time", "then", overagainst ܐܡܬܝ ܕ, ܥܕܢܐ ܕ, ܟܕ; and ܬܡܢ "there", overagainst ܐܝܟܐ ܕ &c.

§ 366. A. Following ancient usage, the bare particle ܕ, however, is still very frequently employed to mark the dependence of a clause, without the special kind of subordination being given. Thus, times without number, ܕ stands for "in order that": ܟܐܝܢ ܗܘܘ ܒܗ ܕܢܫܬܘܩ ἐπετίμων αὐτῷ ἵνα σιγήσῃ Luke 18, 39; ܕܢܬܝܕܥܘܢ P. = ܕܢܬܓܠܘܢ C. ἵνα φανερωθῇ (ἔργα) John 3, 21; ܘܗܝܕܝܢ ܐܦܩܗ ܪܘܚܐ ܕܢܬܢܣܐ ܡܢ ܣܛܢܐ "and then the Spirit led him away that he might be tempted of Satan" Aphr. 129, 4, after Matt. 4, 1 (πειρασθῆναι); ܕܠܐ ܢܙܕܟܐ ܡܢ ܒܥܠܕܒܒܐ "that he may not be overcome by the enemy" Aphr. 129, 9; ܗܕܐ ܡܢ ܡܪܢܐ ܐܣܬܥܪܬ ܕܢܚܘܐ "this was done by the Lord, in order to show" Sim. 391 *inf.* &c.

ܕ "in order that", "since", &c.

B. ܕ is also employed very often in a loosely causal connection = "since", "while": ܕܘܒܪܗܘܢ ܕܝܢ . . . ܕܡܘܬܐ ܗܘܬ ܕܥܕܬܐ ܕܫܠܝܚܐ ܕܡܕܡ ܕܐܝܬ ܗܘܐ ܠܗܘܢ ܕܫܘܬܦܐ ܗܘܐ "now their life was a copy of the church of the Apostles, seeing that everything which they had, was in common" Ov. 167, 22; ܠܚܘܕܐܝܬ ܕ "particularly as" Mart. I, 16 *inf.*, and other passages; ܘܝ ܠܝ ܕ "woe is me, that (seeing that)" Ov. 137, 5 &c., and many like instances; cf. § 358 B.

C. ܕ also serves the purpose, sometimes, of setting down a clause as a kind of theme, the meaning of which is explained afterwards, without any proper grammatical connection appearing: ܘܕܚܝܘܬܐ ܠܐ ܡܬܗܦܟܢ ܟܕ ܐܙܠܢ ܗܘܝ ܒܗܘܢ ܒܩܕܡܝܬܐ ܪܫܝܡ ܗܘܐ ܫܡܥܘܢ ܘܫ' "and as regards the circumstance that the animals did not turn round, as they went,—Simon was represented by the first &c." Moes. II, 128 v. 796; ܘܕܐܡܪ ܕܒܟܠܐ

ܐܬܝܢ ܗܘܘ ܘܡܠܚܟܝܢ ܫܘܚ̈ܢܘܗܝ ܟܠܒ̈ܐ ܓܝܪ ܕܐܬܝܢ ܗܘܘ ܚܢ̈ܦܐ ܐܢܘܢ "and as to the fact, that he said that the dogs came and licked his sores,—the dogs indeed that came, are the heathen" Aphr. 382, 18; and thus frequently ܕܐܡܝܪ, ܕܟܬܝܒ, ܕܡܠܬܐ "with reference to the (spoken *or* written) words . . . , then" v. Aphr. 384, 10; Mart. I, 24, 11; Spic. 3, 3 &c. Cf. ܗܫܐ ܕܝܢ ܗܕܐ ܕܐܡܪ ܕܣܕܘܡ ܘܒܢ̈ܬܗ ܢܬܩܢܢ ܐܝܟ ܕܡܢ ܩܕܝܡ ܘܠܐܘܪܫܠܡ ܐܡܪ ܕܐܢܬܝ ܘܒܢ̈ܬܟܝ ܬܗܘܝܢ ܐܝܟ ܕܡܢ ܩܕܝܡ ܗܢܘ ܚܝܠܗ ܕܡܠܬܐ ܕܠܥܠܡ ܠܐ ܢܬܒܢ̈ܝܢ "but now with reference to this fact, that he said: 'Sodom and her daughters shall remain as of old', and that he said to Jerusalem: 'thou and thy daughters shall be as of old',—the force of the expression is this, that they shall never more be inhabited" Aphr. 400, 2.

ܕ before *Oratio Directa.*

§ 367. On ܕ before *Indirect Interrogative Clauses* v. § 372. Farther ܕ often serves to indicate the entirely loose dependence, in which *direct speech* is joined to the words which introduce it. In all cases, in fact, ܕ may be used to introduce direct speech, but it is not absolutely necessary. When however, ܕ is so used, it is very often impossible to determine whether the *oratio* is *directa* or *indirecta*: ܐܡܪ ܕܒܢܐ ܫܡܥܘܢ ܒܝܬܐ may be "he said that Simeon had built a house", and it may be "he said: 'Simeon has built a house'". Again, in ܐܡܪ ܕܒܢܝܬ ܒܝܬܐ the context alone determines whether it must read: "he said 'I have built a house'" (when the person who 'said', is identical with the builder), or on the other hand: "he said that I had built a house" (when the reporter and not the person who 'said' is the builder). ܡܫܬܘܕܐ ܐܢܬ ܕܫܒܩ ܐܢܬ Aphr. 71, 20 is indirect speech: "thou dost promise that thou wilt forgive"; the variant ܐܢܐ for ܐܢܬ makes of it, without any change in the general sense, the *directa oratio*: "thou utterest the promise 'I forgive'".

ܕ left out.

§ 368. The ܕ which expresses the subordination may in many cases be omitted, when that is sufficiently denoted by the context. Thus, frequently, with ܨܒܐ "to be willing", ܐܫܟܚ "to be able", ܫܪܝ "to begin" &c. Cf.—besides what is given in §§ 267, 272—: ܠܐ ܨܒܐ ܗܘܐ ܐܦܠܐ ܥܝ̈ܢܘܗܝ ܢܪܝܡ οὐκ ἤθελεν οὐδὲ τοὺς ὀφθαλμοὺς ἐπᾶραι Luke 18, 13 (S. ܕܐܦܠܐ; C. ܐܪܝܡ . . . ܢܪܝܡ); ܫܠܚܬ ܠܝ ܐܟܬܘܒ ܐܢܝܢ "thou hast sent me a message, that I am to write them" Jos. St. 5, 3; ܗܘ̇ ܕܠܗ ܐܘܕܐ ܚܝܒ ܐܢܐ "whom I am obliged to acknowledge" Ov. 163, 15; ܘܡܘܕܐ ܠܗ

☞ p. 364

ܢܫܩܝܗ̇ "and gave him to drink" Sim. 359 *inf.*; ܫܒܩܝܢ ܗܘܘ ܠܗ ܠܓܘܫܡܐ ܢܬܢܓܕ "they suffered the body to be scourged" Anc. Doc. 105, 11; ܕܢܦܩܘ ܠܡܬܬܣܝܡ "who came forth to be set" Anc. Doc. 95, 1; ܘܠܘ ܕܡܢܗ ܗܘܐ ܠܡܬܦܪܩ ܗܘܐ "nor was it of himself that he was rescued" Anc. Doc. 87, 23; ܐܠܘ ܡܫܟܚ ܐܢܫ ܐܘ ܢܐܩܕ ܐܘ ܠܐ ܢܐܩܕ "if one have the power, either to be burned or not to be burned" Anc. Doc. 87, 16; and many such instances. Also, when the subordinate clause is put at the beginning: ܢܬܕܡܪ ܐܝܬ ܠܗ "he may wonder" Moes. II, 110 v. 521; ܐܢ ܠܡܐܠܦ ܗܘ ܨܒܐ ܐܢܬ "if thou art willing to learn" Spic. 1, 15; ܘܐܢܫ ܕܢܚܛܘܦ ܗܘܐ ܕܘܟܬܗ ܕܣܗܕܐ ܠܐ ܡܫܟܚ ܗܘܐ "and no one was able to snatch the martyr's place" Anc. Doc. 90, 15 &c.

§ 369. On the other hand, particularly in long periods, the relative particle ܕ is kept, and it may even be doubled: ܠܐ ܓܝܪ ܡܫܟܚܐ ܗܘܬ ܨܒܘܬܐ ܕܟܕ ܦܠܚܝܢ ܠܒܥܠܐ ܕܢܛܪܘܢ ܬܫܥܐ ܦܘܩܕܢܝܢ "for it was not a possible thing that, while they worshipped Baal, (that) they should keep the nine commandments" Aphr. 15, 4 (so, a farther similar instance in ܘܠܐ ܡܫܟܚܐ ܨܒܘܬܐ ܕ . . . ܕ Spic. 16, 8); ܡܥܕܕ ܗܘܐ ܓܝܪ ܕܐܡܬܝ ܕܡܫܟܚ ܗܘܐ ܠܢ . . . ܕܢܫܐܠܢ "for he was in the habit, whenever he found us . . ., of asking" [*lit.* "for he was accustomed that, whenever he found us . . ., (that) he asked us"] Spic. 1, 3; ܘܠܐ ܦܐܐ ܠܟ ܐܘ ܒܪ ܐܢܫܐ ܕܒܗܘ ܬܪܥܐ ܕܡܠܟܐ ܥܐܠ ܒܗ ܕܢܦܩܘܢ ܡܢܗ ܙܒܠܐ ܘܣܝܢܐ "and it is not seemly for thee, O man, that through that gate, by which the king entereth, filth and mud should come forth" Aphr. 46, 1 (where there is the additional incongruity that ܒ [in ܒܗܘ ܬܪܥܐ] is taken up by ܡܢ [in ܡܢܗ]). These examples might be held as confirmed. The same may be said of some in Euseb. Ch. Hist. In other places, a case here and there, which appears to belong to this class, may rest on a copyist's error, just as, on the other hand, a few cases of omission may do the same. The representations contained in this and the foregoing section are, for all that, well established.

ܕ repeated.

§ 370. We have already had a few examples, in which a conjunctional ܕ did not appear at the head of its clause. So, farther, ܘܚܝܠܗ ܒܠܚܘܕܘܗܝ ܕܒܝܫ̈ܘܬܗ ܕܢܦܫܗ ܠܡܣܝܒܪܘܬܐ ܠܐ ܣܦܩ "but his power was not suf-

ܕ not at the head of its clause.

ficient to render subject to sin her liberty in Jesus" Ov. 160, 20; ܘܐܢܐ ܠܗ ܗܘ ܠܫܪܪܐ ܕܐܕܥ ܨܒܐ ܐܢܐ "and I wish to know the exact truth" Ov. 163, 10; ܐܦ ܐܪ̈ܓܘܢܐ ܒܙܒ̈ܢܝܢ ܕܢܠܒܫ ܦܣܘ ܗܘܘ ܠܗ ܡܠܟ̈ܐ "at times indeed the emperors permitted him to wear purple" Sim. 349 *inf.*; ܘܠܟܠ ܙܘܥܝܢ ܒܝܫܝܢ ܒܟܠ ܙܘܥܝܢ ܛܒܝܢ ܕܢܐܪܘܥ ܡܛܝܒ ܗܘܐ "and he was ready to meet all wicked emotions with all good emotions" Ov. 169, 8; ܠܐ ܡܫܟܚ ܐܢܐ ܝܘܩܪܐ ܕܫܘܠܛܢܐ ܕܐܛܥܢ ܘܐܣܝܒܪ: "I was not able to bear and endure the weight of power" Ov. 171, 14 &c. In many of these clauses it would be very natural to keep to the same arrangement of the words, using, however, ܠ with the Inf. instead of ܕ with the finite verb. ܡܐ too is occasionally found not at the beginning of its clause: ܡܘܫܐ ܡܐ ܕܢܟܣ ܐܡܪܐ ܐܬܩܛܠܘ ܒܘܟܪ̈ܝܗܘܢ ܕܡܨܪ̈ܝܐ "when Moses slew the lamb, the first-born of the Egyptians were slain" Aphr. 406, 2; ܘܐܦ ܠܐ ܨܗܝܐ ܡܐ ܕܢܫܬܐ ܡܢ ܡܒܘܥܐ ܚܣܪܝܢ ܠܗܘܢ ܡ̈ܝܘܗܝ "and not even when a thirsty person drinks from a fountain, do its waters dwindle away" Aphr. 199, 10 &c. Of course such inversions of the natural order are more frequent in rhetorically elevated discourse, and with the poets, than in homely statement.

Relative Clauses set in a Series.

§ 371. When several relative clauses occur in a series, they may be satisfied with one ܕ, even when they are not constructed alike; for attributive clauses v. above, (§ 344); cf. ܗܢܐ ܕܡܢ ܪܘܚܩܐ ܐܫܬܕܪ ܠܗ ܕܗܒܐ ܘܩܒܠܗ ܒܚܕܘܬܐ "this person, to whom gold had been sent from far, and who had joyfully accepted it" Ov. 199, 17 &c. Conjunctional: ܕܦܩܕܗ ܐܠܗܐ . . . ܘܐܡܪ ܠܗ "that God had enjoined him . . . and had said to him" Aphr. 235, 8 &c. Of course, however, the ܕ may also be repeated after ܘ: this repetition may likewise take place when there is a separation of the divisions of the sentence into their individual members, without necessitating thereby the formation of several complete clauses: ܕܒܪܬ ܐܚܘܗܝ ܐܘ ܕܒܪܬ ܚܬܗ ܢܥܡܪ ܥܡܗ "that he cause a brother's daughter or a sister's daughter to live with him" Ov. 173, 25, where the second ܕ might quite as well be wanting.

☞ p. 364

C. INDIRECT INTERROGATIVE CLAUSES.

Indirect Interrogative Clauses Proper.

§ 372. A. In many cases in Syriac, indirect questions cannot be distinguished from direct. Even the presence of the relative particle ܕ, marking dependence, does not prove that an interrogative clause is indirect, seeing that this ܕ may also stand before the *oratio directa* (§ 367).—Still, the point here is very often determined by the connection, the enfolding of the clauses, and particularly the change of person necessary in many cases of *oratio obliqua*.

B. An interrogation which concerns the entire predicate is denoted in indirect discourse by the conditional particle ܐܢ ("if") "whether". ܢܚܙܐ ܐܢ ܐܬܐ ܡܥܕܪ ܠܟ "we shall see if it comes and helps thee" Sim. 332, 3; ܠܐ (ܐܬܝܕܥ) ܐܢ ܠܬܚܬ ܦܓܪܐ ܕܩܛܝܠܐ ܐܬܛܡܪ. ܘܠܐ ܐܢ ܒܝܡܐ ܫܕܐ ܢܦܫܗ. ܘܠܐ ܐܢ . . . ܘܠܐ ܐܢ . . . "nor (is it known) whether he was buried under the bodies of the slain, nor whether he threw himself into the sea, nor whether . . . nor whether . . . " Jos. St. 11, 6. The alternative question, expressed in the last example by means of the repetition of ܘܠܐ ܐܢ, may also be denoted by ܐܘ: ܠܐ ܗܘܐ ܝܕܥ ܠܗ ܓܢܒܐ ܐܢ ܡܪܗ ܕܒܝܬܐ ܒܓܘܗ ܗܘ ܐܘ ܠܐ "the thief does not know whether the master of the house is within it or not" Aphr. 129, 13 &c. ܐܢܗܘ ܕ often stands for ܐܢ (§ 374 B): ܐܬܒܩܐ ܠܟ ܩܕܡ ܒܡܚܫܒܬܟ ܐܢܗܘ ܕܫܒܩ ܐܢܬ "consider first in thy thoughts whether thou dost forgive" Aphr. 71, 21.

The dependence is more emphatically expressed by prefixing ܕ to ܐܢ: ܘܡܫܐܠܝܢ ܗܘܘ ܠܗ ܘܐܡܪܝܢ ܕܐܢ ܫܠܝܛ ܒܫܒܬܐ ܠܡܐܣܝܘ καὶ ἐπηρώτησαν αὐτὸν λέγοντες εἰ ἔξεστιν τοῖς σάββασιν θεραπεῦσαι Matt. 12, 10 (C. ܕܐܢ ܗܘ ܕ); ܫܐܠܬܢܝ ܬܘܒ ܕܐܢ ܒܟܠܙܒܢ ܡܫܬܟܚܝܢ ܙܕܝܩܐ ܘܟܐܢܐ ܥܠ ܐܪܥܐ "thou hast farther asked me, whether righteous and just persons have at all times been found on the earth" Aphr. 446, 6; ܕܐܬܝܕܥܝܘܗܝ ܠܡܫܝܚܐ ܕܐܢ ܗܘܝܘ ܫܪܪܐ ܢܟܦܬܐ "that I may know Christ, whether he is the pure truth" Ov. 163 14 (where the interrogative clause is a kind of 'epexegesis' or rather second object; v. above, § 358 A, and several examples in what follows).

C. Even when the interrogative concerns the Subject, or individual points in the Predicate, ܕ may precede: ܕܢܬܡܠܟܘܢ ܕܡܢܘ ܢܩܝܡܘܢ ܐܦܣܩܘܦܐ ܒܐܘܪܗܝ "that they deliberate as to whom they should institute as bishop in Edessa" Ov. 170 *ult.*; ܝܕܥܘ ܒ̈ܢܝ ܕܝܪܗ ܕܐܝܟܐ ܘܐܝܟܢ ܐܝܬܘܗܝ "his fellow-monks learned where and how he was" Ov. 169, 23; ܘܝܕܥ ܗܘ ܫܪܪܐ ܕܐܝܟܢܐ ܐܚܝܕ ܠܟ ܠܘܬܗ "and the truth knows, how to hold thee to herself" Ov. 163, 12; ܟܕ ܚܙܐ ܗܘܐ ܢܨܝܚܘܬܗ ܕܒܐܝܠܝܢ ܐܣܟܡܐ ܡܟܝܟܐ ܩܕܡ ܥܡܐ ܩܐܡ ܗܘܐ "while he saw his dignity,—with what a humble demeanour he stood at the head of the people" Ov. 189, 22; ܕܐܐܝܡܬܝ "when" Aphr. 19, 6; 170, 1; ܕܡܢ ܐܝܟܐ "whence" Ov. 190, 4; ܕܟܡܐ ܥܬܝܪ "how rich" Ov. 191, 20 &c. With the interrogative placed in the end of its clause: ܡܢܘ ܕܐܡܪ ܗܘ ܕܡܢ ܓ̈ܝܓܠܐ ܕܡܢ ܐܝܬܝܗܘܢ "who is it that says, what are these wheels?" Moes. II, 104 v. 438; and with the ܕ placed at the same time at the commencement: ܐܘܕܥܟ ܐܦ ܕܗܠܝܢ ܥ̈ܠܠܬܐ ܡܢ ܐܝܡܬܝ ܐܬܚܝܠܝ ܐܠܝܢ "I will make known to thee also, from what time these causes acquired strength" Jos. St. 8, 3. So also in headings of themes, when the governing word is not given: ܕܐܝܟܢ ܗܘܐ ܛܘܒܢܐ ܪܒܘܠܐ ܐܦܣܩܘܦܐ ܒܐܘܪܗܝ ܡܕܝܢܬܐ "How the blessed Rabbūlā became Bishop in the town of Edessa" Ov. 170, 21 &c. (¹)

☞ p. 365

D. But this ܕ may also be wanting: ܬܚܘܝܢܝ ܐܝܠܝܢ ܥܒ̈ܕܐ ܡܬܒܥܝܢ "(that) thou show me, what works are demanded" Aphr. 5, 4; ܢܚܙܐ ܡܢܐ ܦܐܐ ܠܗ ܠܬܫܡܫܬܐ . . . ܘܒܐܝܠܝܢ ܨ̈ܒܘܢ ܢܫܦܪ ܠܗ "let him see, what will be suitable for the service . . . and by what things he will please him" Aphr. 8, 13 (together with ܢܪܦ ܒܪܢܫܐ ܕܡܢܐ ܡܬܒܥܐ ܠܗ . . . "man becomes concerned, as to what is requisite for him (who) . . . " Aphr. 8, 2); ܕܒܗܘܢ ܟܬܝܒ ܡܢܐ "wherein is written, what . . . " Spic. 13, 8; ܠܐ ܝܕܝܥ ܡܢܐ ܗܘܐ ܡܢܗ "it is not known what became of him" Jos. St. 11, 5; ܘܚܙܝ ܐܝܟܢܐ ܐܬܦܪܫܘ "and see thou, how they have distinguished themselves" Aphr. 60, 5; ܕܢܚܘܐ ܟܡܐ ܝܩܪܐ ܦܠܓ "that he may show how great honour he has bestowed [dispensed]" Sim. 391 *inf.* (Cod. Lond. ܕܟܡܐ); ܘܐܢܬ ܕܝܢ ܗܕܐ ܨܒܐ ܐܢܬ ܠܡܠܦ ܡܢ ܐܝܠܝܢ ܥ̈ܠܠܬܐ ܐܬܥܝܪܬ "thou art desirous to learn this thing, by what causes it (the war) was stirred up"

(¹) Notice farther ܠܡܛܠ ܕ, ܥܠ ὅτι "because" John 5, 16 C. S. (P. has merely ܕ).

Jos. St. 7, 22 (notice the demonstrative before the interrogative clause) &c. In all these cases ܕ may also be found.

E. Just as, in many cases, a direct question is really an expression of wonder, so too is it with many an indirect question: ܘܐܬܪܘܡܬ ܢܦܫܗ ܕܐܝܢܐ ܡܪܐ ܚܙܐ ܕܢܗܘܐ ܠܗ "and his soul grows elate, that to such a master [*lit.* 'to what sort of master'] he has become worthy of belonging" Moes. II, 116 v. 639; and quite a similar instance is given *ibid.* p. 164 v. 1384. So ܘܡܫܒܚ ܠܐܠܗܐ ܕܐܝܢܐ ܐܒܐ ܩܫܝܐ ܘܚܛܘܦܐ ܠܐܝܢܐ ܒܪܐ ܟܐܢܐ ܘܢܕܝܒܐ ܘܡܪܚܡܢܐ ܐܘܠܕ "and praised God, that such a stern and rapacious father had begotten such a just, generous and compassionate son" Land II, 159, 24; ܣܓܠܬܗ ܘܝ ܠܗ ܠܡܠܟܘܬܐ ܕܪ̈ܗܘܡܝܐ ܕܐܝܠܝܢ ܡܠܟܐ ܐܘܒܕܬ ܘܐܝܠܝܢ ܚܠܦ ܐܝܠܝܢ ܐܫܟܚܬ "Woe to the empire of the Romans, that it has lost such emperors, and met with such instead (of such)!" Jul. 79, 19; "Edessa is in mourning" ܕܡܢܘ ܚܠܦ ܡܢܘ ܝܬܒ ܥܠ ܟܘܪܣܝܐ ܕܪ̈ܗܘܡܝܐ "that such a man, instead of such, is sitting on the throne of the Roman world" Jul. 123, 2 (*lit.* '*who* instead of *whom*'). ☞ p. 365

The conjoining of two interrogatives in one clause, as we have it in these last cases, is somewhat rare. Another instance, however, is found in ܢܒܩܐ ܐܢܘܢ ܠܬܪ̈ܝܗܘܢ ܕܐܝܢܐ ܚܝܠܬܢ ܡܢ ܐܚܪܐ "try both of them, as to which of them is the stronger" Ephr. (Lamy) III, 681 str. 25. But it is only in translations from the Greek that this construction appears with any considerable frequency.

§ 373. ܕܠܡܐ, ܕܠܡ, originally "for what?", then "if perhaps", "that perhaps" or even, when it is an expression of doubt "lest perhaps" [*ne forte*]—is properly an indirect interrogation. The ܕ here indicates dependence. Moreover a proper governing word is often wanting, and the notion of uncertainty, found in the connection, suffices,—so that we may translate by "perhaps", "perchance". And thus a farther additional ܕ may be prefixed to the ܕ (which has here become grammatically indistinct) in order to express the dependence more clearly. ܠܡܐ is in strictness independent, and introduces at first an independent clause, but we deal likewise with it in this place on account of its being tantamount in meaning to the compound form. Examples: ܚܙܝ ܠܡܐ ܠܐܢܫ ܬܐܡܪ ὅρα, μηδενὶ εἴπῃς Matt. 8, 4 P. (C. S. ܕܠܡܐ); ܠܡܐ ܣܒܪ ܐܢܬ ܠܐܠܗܐ ܕܠܡܐ &c.

ܠܡܐ ܐܡܐ ܘܐܢܬܬܐ ܕܝܗܘܕܝܐ ܗܘ ܒܠܚܘܕ ἢ Ἰουδαίων ὁ θεὸς μόνον Rom. 3, 29; ܛܒ̈ܢ ܠܝ ܡܢ ܐܠܗܐ "are mother and wife haply better to me than God?" Mart. I, 251 *inf.*—"He does this or that" ܕܠܡܐ ܢܬܪܥܐ ܠܘܬܗ "(in the hope) that perhaps he may take him into favour again" Aphr. 150, 5; "are asked ܕܠܡܐ ܚܙܘ ܐܢܘܢ ܕܐܬܝܢ ... ܘܕܐܙܠܝܢ ܕܠܡܐ ܚܙܝܢ ܠܗܘܢ whether those who come may have seen them, and whether those who go may see them" Joseph 193, 9 (var. both times with ܕܕܠܡܐ) [= Ov. 294, 16]; ܕܠܡܐ ܐܝܟ ܐܫܬܟܚ ܠܝ ܕ "would that I were found (thought he) such that &c.!" Ov. 171, 23; ܚܘܪ ܘܐܦ ܐܢܬ ܠܡܘܬܐ ܐܘ ܣܦܪܐ ܚܟܝܡܐ ܕܠܡܐ ܢܬܪܝܡ ܠܒܟ "think upon death thou too, O wise and learned scribe, lest haply thy heart be uplifted" Aphr. 427, 18; "seek ye for him ܕܠܡܐ ܠܗܕܐ ܡܥܪܬܐ ܥܠ ܘܬܡܢ ܡܝܬ ܘܡܬܒܥܝܢܢ ܚܢܢ ܒܚܘܒܬܗ lest haply he may have gone into that cave and be dying there, and we be punished for his guilt" Sim. 283 mid.; ܡܢܐ ܢܐܡܪ ܥܠ ܗܕܐ ܕܠܡܐ ܒܢܝ ܐܝܣܪܝܠ ܩܒܠܘ ܡܠܟܘܬܐ ܕܡܪܝܡܐ ܚܣ ܠܗ ܐܘ ܕܠܡܐ ܗܘ ܥܡܐ ܐܬܐ ܥܠ ܠܥܢ̈ܢܝ ܫܡܝܐ "what shall we say about this? Is it that the children of Israel have received the kingdom of the Highest? God forbid! Or is it that the people have reached somehow to the clouds of heaven?" Aphr. 96, 8 &c.—ܕܝܢ ܣܪܝܩܐܝܬ ܪܗܛܬ ܐܘ ܪܗܛ ܐܢܐ μήπως εἰς κενὸν τρέχω ἢ ἔδραμον Gal. 2, 2; ܘܕܡܐ ܡܚܫܒ ܐܢܬ "it may be thou thinkest" Jul. 47, 1.—ܕܢܐܨܦ ܕܝܠܗܘܢ ܕܕܠܡܐ ܡܛܠ ܣܢܝܩܘܬܗܘܢ ܢܬܛܠܨܘܢ ܠܡܥܒܕ ܡܕܡ ܕܠܐ ܦܐܐ "that we be concerned about them, so that they should not, through their need, be obliged to do anything that is unseemly" Ov. 217, 16; ܕܚܠܝܢ ܗܘܘ ܕܕܠܡܐ ܢܬܒܥ ܕܡܗܘܢ "were afraid that he would take vengeance on them" Jos. St. 19, 21; ܕܚܠ ܡܢܗ ܕܕܠܡܐ ܢܣܓܘܢ ܡܝܐ "is afraid of it, lest the waters should increase" Aphr. 145, 15 (var. ܕܠܡܐ); ܘܢܫܡܥܘܢ ܠܦܘܩܕܢܗ ܕܕܠܡܐ ܡܛܠ ܒܥܘܬܢ ܕܡܢܗ ܢܒܢܐ "and will listen to his command, in order that perhaps, on account of our request of him, he may build" Jul. 110, 1; ܘܐܬܚܫܒ ܕܢܝܐܝܠ ܕܡܛܠ ܚܛܗ̈ܝܗܘܢ ܕܥܡܐ ܕܠܡܐ ܢܫܬܚܪ ܠܗ ... "and Daniel thought, that on account of the sins of the nation, he might perhaps remain . . ." Aphr. 58, 14 (where ܕ is separated from ܕܠܡܐ; var., however, ܕܕܠܡܐ ܡܛܠ, ܕܠܡܐ afterwards) &c.—ܢܒܨܐ ܗܘܐ ... ܕܕܠܡܐ ܒܡܕܡ ܚܝܒܝܢ ܟܘܢܝܐ "let him examine . . . whether in any respect they may be deserving of reproof" Ov. 176, 6; ܦܢܝ ܡܫܡܫܢܘܬܐ ܕܡܫܡܫܢܘܗܝ ܕܕܠܡܐ ܬܬܐܠܨ ܠܗ ܠܗ ܘܬܟܫܠ

ܡܫܘܚܬܐ ܕܚܛܗ̈ܘܗܝ "he shortened the measure of his days, that the measure of his sins might not become too great and overpowering" Jul. 5, 24.

By far the most common of these forms is ܕܠܡܐ (without ܕ before it).

D. CONDITIONAL CLAUSES.

§ 374. A. The condition which is set forth as possible is expressed by ܐܢ. With the negative we say ܐܢ ܠܐ or ܐܠܐ. The ܐܢ which introduces a clause occasions no farther change in its construction. The Act. Part. mostly serves as its verb (§ 271), the Impf. not so often (§ 265). When the past is referred to, which of course occurs much less frequently in these clauses, the Perf. is employed (cf. § 258), or the Part. act. with ܗܘܐ (§ 277), or even, though not often, the Impf. with ܗܘܐ (§ 268 A). Besides, ܐܢ is frequently followed by a Nominal clause. The apodosis may agree with the protasis in time and in construction, but it may also differ from it in many ways, without thereby causing any deviation from the leading rules of clause-formation which have been described above. We give a few examples in support of the most important cases. *Part.* ܘܐܢ ܒܒܢ̈ܝܟ ܡܫܬܒܗܪ ܐܢܬ ܡܬܦܪܫܝܢ ܠܗܘܢ ܡܢܟ "and if thou gloriest in thy sons, they are torn away from thee" Aphr. 84, 13; ܐܠܐ ܢܦܩ ܢܒܚ ܒܗ ܡܪܗ ܕܥܢܐ ܡܚܐ ܠܗ "if he (the dog) does not run out and bark at it, the master of the sheep beats him" Ov. 138, 20 (compare § 271). So with ܐܝܬ and ܠܝܬ, *e. g.* ܐܢ ܠܝܬ ܟܐܢ̈ܐ ܐܒܕܝܢ ܚܛܝ̈ܐ "if there are no righteous persons, (even) the wicked perish" Aphr. 458, 9.—*Impf.*: ܐܢ ܨܐܡ ܐܢܫ ... ܠܐ ܢܚܠܛ ... "for if he is fasting . . ., let him not mingle . . . " Aphr. 45, 22; ܐܢ ܕܝܢ ܠܐ ܬܬܛܦܝܣܘܢ ܘܬܬܟܬܫܘܢ ܗܘܝܬܘܢ ܡܢܢ ܡܬܒܣܝܢ "but if you will not be convinced, but continue to resist, then you will be held in contempt by us" Ov. 175, 3; ܐܢ ܬܬܥܘܪ ܟܠܗ ܦܓܪܐ ܒܛܝܠ "if it becomes blind, the (whole) body has grown useless" Aphr. 457, 11; ܗܘܝܘ ܫܪܪܐ ܡܘܕܥ ܢܦܫܗ ܠܟ ܐܢ ܬܬܟܦܪ ܡܢ ܝܕܥܬܟ "the truth makes itself known to thee, if thou dost renounce thine own knowledge" Ov. 163, 16 (and thus very frequently, a Part. in the principal clause, overagainst an Impf. in the conditional clause; cf. § 265). Both *Impf.* and *Part.* alternating: ܘܐܢ

ܐܢ ☞ p. 365

ܢܘܕܐ ܐܢܫ ܕܒܝ ܗܘ ܐܠܗܐ ܚܕ ܡܚܬ ܦܘܩܕܢܘܗܝ ܘܠܐ ܥܒܕ ܗܠܐ ܫܪܝܪ ܠܗ ܓܝܪܐ ܠܐ ܗܘܐ ܚܕܘ
ܕܒܝ ܗܘ ܐܠܗܐ "and if any one makes confession (Impf.), that there is only one God, but transgresses (Part.) his commandments, and does (Part.) not do them, then it is not true for him that there is only one God" Aphr. 498, 5 (cf. line 12; v. 301, 17; 339, 1).—*Perf.* ܢܩܬܐ ܐܚܘܕ ܐܒܘܟ ܠܝ ܗܒ ܠܝ ܚܡܫ ܠܝܛܪ̈ܝܢ "if thy father has brought fish, give me five pounds (of them)" Sim. 273 mid.; ܐܢ ܕܝܢ ܚܒܠܬ݀ ܗܝܡܢܘܬܐ ܒܚܢܦܘܬܐ ܐܘܒܕܬ݀ ܢܦܫܐ "but if faith has been injured by unbelief, then the soul is lost" Anc. Doc. 98, 12; ܐܢ ܡܫܝܚܐ ܐܬܬܣܝܡ ܡܫܬܐܣܬܐ ܐܝܟܐ ܗܟܝܠ ܥܡܪ ܐܦ ܡܫܝܚܐ ܒܒܢܝܢܐ "if Christ has been laid as the foundation, how then dwelleth Christ also in the building?" Aphr. 9, 14 &c. Cf. ܐܢ ܟܡ ܡܬܩܕܙ ܘܟ̇ܗ̈ܢܐ . . . ܡܬܡܥܕܝܢ ܗܘܘ ܟܗ̈ܢܐ ܕܐܝܣܪ̈ܝܠ ܠܡܦܠܚ ܬܫܡ̈ܫܬܐ . . . "if the priests of Israel were accustomed to perform the service, how much more is it fitting for us . . .!" Ov. 172, 14 &c. For examples with the *Impf. and* ܗܘܐ v. 268 A. *Nominal clauses*: ܐܢ ܟܗܪܐ ܗܘ ܠܟ . . . ܕ . . . ܚܙܝ . . . "if it is a disgraceful thing for thee that . . . , then see . . ." Ov. 162, 8; ܐܢ ܡܢܡ ܕܡܝ̈ܬܐ ܕܦܬܟܪܐ ܩܝ̈ܡܝܢ ܒܐܬܪܐ ܡܕܡ ܢܬܥܩܪ̈ܢ "if even the remains of an idol's temple are standing in any place, they shall be destroyed" Ov. 220 *paen.* &c. We have several cases together in . . . ܐܢ ܒܝ ܗܘ ܐܠܗܐ . . . ܘܝܗܒ ܒ̈ܢܝ ܐܢܫܐ ܟܝܢܗܘܢ ܘܚܕܐ ܒܗܕܐ . . . "if God is one (Nominal clause) . . . and has given men their nature (Perf.), and takes pleasure in this (Part.) . . . , why then did he not give them such a nature, that . . . ?" Spic. 1, 6.

☞ p. 365

B. For ܐܢ there often stands ܐܢ ܗܘ ܕ, ܐܢܗܘ ܕ "if it (is) that" e. g. ܐܢܗܘ ܕܡܬܒܥܐ ܠܗܘܢ "if there is necessary for them" Jos. St. 13, 18; ܐܢ ܗܘ ܕܢܙܟܘܢ "if they should conquer" Jos. St. 13, 13; ܐܢ ܗܟܝܠ ܒܪܝ ܐܝܬ ܠܟ . . . ܐܡܪ̈ܝܗܝ "if thou therefore, my son, hast . . . , then tell it" Spic. 2, 3 &c.

C. We have already seen that several clauses connected by ܘ may stand after ܐܢ. It is true that ܐܢ may also be repeated with ܘ: in that case conditional clauses are often elliptical: ܐܢ ܠܡܘܬܐ ܘܐܢ ܠܚܝ̈ܐ "be it for death, or for life" Jul. 169, 19; ܐܢ ܒܡܠܬܐ ܘܐܢ ܒܥܒܕܐ ܒܙܒܢܐ ܘܕܠܐ ܒܙܒܢܐ "be it word or work, in season or out of season" Ov. 181, 22, and manifold cases resembling these (cf. e. g. Jos. St. 50, 19). How ܘ and ܐܘ "or" may be exchanged here, is shown by the following example: ܐܢ ܓܐܪܘܦܐ ܐܢܬ ܐܘ ܓܪ̈ܝܕܐ ܐܘ ܚܣܦܐ ܐܘ ܚܣܦܝ̈ܗ ܐܘ ܚܝ̈ܢܙܪܝܐ ܐܘ ܚܠ̈ܝܡܐ ܐܘ ܡܚܝܠܐ ܘܟܠ ܕܡܕܡ

ܒܬܝܡܢ ... "whether they are in Edom or in Arabia, in Greece or in Persia, whether in the North or whether in the South, they observe this law" Spic. 19, 14.

D. We have another ellipsis in ܘܶܐܠܳ ܠܳܐ or ܘܶܐܠܳܐ "if not" *e. g.* ܘܐܠ ܠܐ ܐܝܬ ܠܝ ܠܡܐܡܪ (var. ܘܐܠܐ) "if not, I have to say" Aphr. 441, 7; so 117, 14; Ov. 214, 11. Cf. ܘܐܠܐ ܠܐ ܥܒܕ݂ ܗܘܝܬ "otherwise (if it were not so,) I would not have done it" Jul. 245, 26.

After ܐܠܐ "if not", "excepting", "except that", "other than", sentences which are incomplete are very common. In this application a farther ܐܢ often comes in after ܐܠܐ. Examples: ܠܐ ܓܝܪ ܐܬܦܩܕܘ ܒܢܝ ܐܢܫܐ ܠܡܥܒܕ ܐܠܐ ܗܘ ܡܕܡ ܕܡܫܟܚܝܢ ܠܡܥܒܕ "for men have not been commanded to do anything, except that which they are able to do" Spic. 5, 2; ܘܡܛܠ ܡܢܐ ܕܝܢ ܚܒܝܒܝ ܕ... ܐܬܟܬܒ ܠܗܘܢ ܐܪܒܥܡܐܐ ܘܬܠܬܝܢ ܫܢܝܢ ܐܠܐ ܡܛܠ ܕ "and why is it, dear friend, that ... there was written for them 'four hundred and thirty years', except because ...?" Aphr. 26, 20; ܘܚܕܐ ܡܢ ܨܠܡ̈ܐ ܠܐ ܥܒܕܘ ܠܗܘܢ ܠܡܣܓܕܬܐ ܐܠܐ ܨܠܡܐ ܕܥܓܠܐ "and not one image made they for themselves to worship, excepting the image of the calf" Aphr. 312, 20; ܠܐ ܫܠܝܛ ܗܘܐ ܠܗ ܒܟܠ ܐܬܪ ܠܡܟܣܘ ܦܨܚܐ ܐܠܐ ܩܕܡ ܚܕ ܡܰܕܒܚܐ ܒܐܘܪܫܠܡ "it was not permitted to him to slay the Paschal lamb in any place, except before one altar at Jerusalem" Aphr. 218, 22, while line 12 has ܠܐ ܫܠܝܛ ܗܘܐ ܠܗ ܕܢܥܒܕ ܦܨܚܐ ܐܠܐ ܐܢ ܒܐܘܪܫܠܡ ܒܠܚܘܕ "it was not permitted him to prepare the Paschal lamb, save at Jerusalem only"; ܘܠܐ ܐܢܫ ܝܕܥ ܠܒܪܐ ܐܠܐ ܐܢ ܐܒܐ *καὶ οὐδεὶς ἐπιγινώσκει τὸν υἱὸν εἰ μὴ ὁ πατήρ* Matt. 11, 27; ܠܝܬ ܛܒܐ ܐܠܐ ܐܢ ܚܕ ܐܠܗܐ *οὐδεὶς ἀγαθὸς εἰ μὴ εἷς θεός* Luke 18, 19; ܘܡܢܐ ܐܝܢ ܗܢܝܢ ܟܐ̈ܦܐ ܕܢܘܪܐ ܐܠܐ ܐܢ ܒܢ̈ܝ ܨܗܝܘܢ "and what are the stones of fire but the children of Zion?" Aphr. 85, 7, where there is a var. ܐܠܐ ܒܢ̈ܝ without the ܐܢ; ܡܢ ܐܢܘܢ ܒܢ̈ܝܐ ܐܠܐ ܐܢ ܟܗ̈ܢܐ "who are the builders except the priests?" Aphr. 10, 18; ܠܐ ܦܫ ܐܢܫ ܡܢܗܘܢ ܚܝܐ ܐܠܐ ܐܢ ܐܦܝܣܩܘܦܐ ... ܘܬܪܝܢ ܐܢܫܝܢ ܐܚܪܢܝܢ "no one of them remained alive but the bishop ... and two other men" Jos. St. 29, 4; ܒܡܢܐ ... ܐܠܐ ܐܢ ܒ' "in what ... except in ...?" Aphr. 57, 11; ܡܢܘ ܝܕܥ ... ܐܠܐ ܐܢ ܓܡܝܪ̈ܐ "who understands ... except the perfect?" Ov. 185, 19; and thus frequently. *With these Particles beginning the sentence*: ܘܐܠܐ ܐܢ ܚܕܐ ܐܘܪܚܐ ܒܠܚܘܕ ܗܘܬ ܕܡܣܩܐ ܠܗ "and only one way was there, which led up to it" Jos. St. 15, 5. An entire clause stands after ܐܠܐ ܐܢ in ܘܐܢܐ ܠܐ ܡܫܟܚ ܐܢܐ ܠܡܗܝܡܢܘ ܐܠܐ ܐܢ ܐܬܦܝܣܬ "and I cannot believe, without being convinced" Spic. 2, 14; ܠܐ ܡܫܟܚ ܐܢܬ ܠܡܣܬܟܠܘ . . . ܐܠܐ ܐܢ ܝܕܥܬ "thou canst not understand . . ., if thou ☞ p. 365 hast not known" Ov. 162, 26.

☞ p. 365 From the meaning "if not" is developed the adversative meaning "however, but, yet", in which sense ܐܠܐ is oftenest met with.

E. After the concessive particle ܐܶܦܶܢ = ܐܶܦ ܐܶܢ "even if, if even" a complete clause may follow, *e. g.* ܐܦܢ ܠܛܘܪܐ ܗܢܐ ܬܐܡܪܘܢ . . . ܬܗܘܐ *κἂν τῷ ὄρει τούτῳ εἴπητε . . . γενήσεται* Matt. 21, 21 (C. S. merely ܐܢ); ܐܦܢ ܡܐܬ ܢܚܐ S., ܐܦܢ ܢܡܘܬ ܢܚܐ P. *κἂν ἀποθάνῃ ζήσεται* John 11, 25; ܘܐܦܢ ܣܓܝ ܢܣܓܘܕ . . . ܠܐ ܡܬܐܪܥ "for even though he worships . . ., still he is not found fault with" Aphr. 335, 18; ܘܐܦ ܒܚܛܐ ܐܬܢܛܪ ܡܢܗ ܙܪܥܐ ܕܙܕܝܩܐ "and even if he has sinned, yet the seed of the righteous has been preserved by him" Aphr. 462 *ult.*; ܐܦ ܣܓܝ ܢܗܘܐ ܕ . . . ܐܠܐ ܬܗܘܐ ܠܢ ܒܢ̈ܝ ܡܗܝܡܢܐ ܘܫܪܝܪܐ ܠܢ ܕ . . . "for even if it happens that . . ., let it yet be firm and sure for us, my sons, that . . . " Jul. 8, 27 *sqq.* (where ܐܠܐ, as frequently happens, occurs at the beginning of the apodosis) &c. But very often ܐܦ is followed by a mere fragment of a clause, *e. g.* ܘܟܠܐ ܐܦ ܚܕ ܒܪܢܫܐ ܡܢ ܨܠܘܬܐ "and thou hinderest from prayer though it were but one man" Sim. 328 mid. &c.; cf. ܕܚܠ ܐܢܐ ܕܝܢ ܐܦ ܕܐܥܗܕܘ "I am afraid even to mention" Ov. 196, 14. Often it signifies "though it were only", "at least" (like *κἄν* = *καὶ ἐάν*), *e. g.* ܘܒܥܝܢ ܗܘܘ ܡܢܗ ܕܐܦ ܠܟܢܦܐ ܕܠܒܘܫܗ ܢܩܪܒܘܢ *καὶ παρεκάλουν αὐτὸν ἵνα κἂν τοῦ κρασπέδου τοῦ ἱματίου αὐτοῦ ἅψωνται* Mark 6, 56; ܕܐܦ ܡܛܠ ܡ̈ܠܝ ܢܬܕܟܪܘܢܢܝ ܝܕ̈ܘܥܝ "that my acquaintances might remember me, for the sake of my words at least" Ov. 137, 5; ܐܶܥܡܪ ܐܦ ܡܢ ܒܪ ܠܡܪܥܝܬܐ "let me dwell at least on the outskirts of the pasture ground" Ephr. III, 576 D; ܛܘܒܘܗܝ ܠܡܢ ܕܙܟܐ ܕܢܚܣܢܝܗ̇ ܐܠܐ ܒܟܐܢܘܬܐ ܐܦ ܒܛܝܒܘܬܐ ܘܐܠܐ ܡܢ ܥܒ̈ܕܐ ܐܦ ܡܢ ܪ̈ܚܡܐ "Blessed is he who has been found worthy to obtain it (Paradise), if not through righteousness, at least through grace,—if not by works, yet by (Divine) compassion" Ephr. III, 576 A &c.

F. We have, in the following sentence, an example of an ellipsis in the principal clause being made up for, by the contents of the conditional clause: ܐܢ ܠܡܫܝܚܐ ܪܕܦܘ ܐܦ ܠܢ "if they persecuted Christ, so also (will they persecute) us" Aphr. 484, 15; v. also farther sentences there of like character. Other ellipses occur in ܐܢ ܐܝܩܪܐ ܕܝܠܢ ܗܘ ܘܐܢ ܫܝܛܐ ܠܘܬ ܬܪ̈ܝܢ "if (there is) honour, it is ours, and if discredit, it is also on both sides" Ov. 151, 17.

G. ܐܢ is found almost always at the beginning of its clause. Very seldom do we meet with cases like ܥܠ ܪ̈ܝܫܬܐ ܕܟܠܗܘܢ ܪ̈ܘܡܐ ܐܢ ܩܐܡ ܐܢܐ "if I stand upon the summit of all heights" Moes. II, 82 v. 83; and thus also 80 v. 79 and 81.

Exceptionally ܐܢ is set down twice in ܐܢ ܓܝܪ ܟܠ ܡܐܟܘ̈ܠܝܢ ܕ . . . ܐܢ ܡܢ ܗܠܝܢ ܢܐܟܘܠ ܒܪܢܫܐ "for if of all kinds of food which . . ., if man eats of them" Aphr. 307, 11, where the sentence is taken up anew.

Rem. The insertion of ܐܢ in relative clauses to express the indeterminate ("any", "somehow") is an imitation of the later Greek style, *e. g.* ܗܘ ܐܝܢܐ ܕܐܢ ܢܣܬܡܟ *ὅστις ἐὰν ἐπιστηρίχθῃ* Is. 36, 6 Hex.; ܡܕܡ ܕܐܢ ܐܡܪ ܠܟܘܢ *ὅ τι ἐὰν λέγῃ ὑμῖν* John 2, 5 Hark.; ܠܒܪ ܡܢ ܗܘ ܕܐܢ . . . ܢܬܟܠܐ *ἐκτὸς εἰ μὴ . . . ἐμποδίζοιτο* Lagarde, Reliquiae 57, 5 &c., and similarly, here and there, even in ancient original writings. Thus in particular ܟܡܐ ܐܢ "how much soever", "although"; ܟܡܐ ܐܢ ܡܚܪܐ "however much he exerts himself" Jul. 9 *ult.*; ܟܡܐ ܐܢ ܕܘܝܐ ܠܚܙܝܐ "however pitiful he might be to the eye" Ov. 188, 20; cf. Philox. 47, 16; 54, 21; 264 &c. Instead of this expression we have also ܘܐܢ ܟܡܐ, Land III, 210, 19, 21; 211, 6 &c.; and even ܐܢ ܟܡܐ ܐܢ Philox. Epist. fol. 13 *a*, 1, 4.

§ 375. A. The condition which is set forth as impossible is expressed by ܐܠܘ. This particle is generally followed by the Perf. which is so much in use for hypothetical clauses (§ 259), or by the Part. with ܗܘܐ (§ 277); the Perf. is also strengthened occasionally by ܗܘܐ. In the principal clause the Part. with ܗܘܐ is very generally found. There is no sharp distinction between what is represented, by way of Condition, as still unfinished (*si faceret*), and what is represented as completed (*si fecisset*). Examples: ܘܐܠܘ ܠܐ ܐܬܟܪܝܘ ܝܘ̈ܡܬܐ ܗܢܘܢ ܠܐ ܚܝܐ ܗܘܐ ܟܠ ܒܣܪ *καὶ εἰ μὴ ἐκολοβώθησαν αἱ ἡμέραι ἐκεῖναι οὐκ ἂν ἐσώθη πᾶσα σάρξ* Matt. 24, 22; ܐܠܘ ܫܒܩܬ ܢܦܫܐ ܠܦܓܪܐ ܠܐ ܩܐܡ ܗܘܐ "if the soul abandoned the body, it (the body) would not continue in existence" Moes. II, 90 v. 221; ܐܠܘ ܢܡܘ̈ܣܐ ܕܩܠ̈ܝܡܐ ܗܘܘ ܗܢܐ ܠܟܠܗܘܢ ܠܐ ܡܫܟܚܐ ܗܘܬ "if laws belonged to climes, this would be

ܐܠܘ ☞ p. 365

impossible (to be)" Spic. 18, 25; ܐܠܘ ܝܗܒ . . . ܠܐ ܝܩܕ ܗܘܐ "if he had given a sign . . ., he would not have been burned" Anc. Doc. 87, 22; ܐܠܘ ܓܝܪ ܬܒܘ ܐܝܬ ܗܘܐ ܬܝܒܘܬܐ "for if they had been converted, there would have been penitence" Aphr. 54, 5; ܐܦ ܒܢܝܐ ܐܠܘ ܐܘܠܕ ܗܘܐ ܡܦܨܐ ܗܘܐ "even the children, if he had begotten them, he would have rescued" Aphr. 352, 10; ܐܠܘ ܓܝܪ ܐܬܥܒܕ ܗܘܐ ܐܝܟܢܐ ܕ . . . ܛܒܬܐ ܐܦ ܠܡܥܒܕ . . . ܠܐ ܗܘܐ ܕܝܠܗ ܗܘܬ "for if he had been made so, that . . ., then the good even (that he would do) . . . would not be his" Spic. 4, 4; ܐܠܘ ܒܟܠܙܒܢ ܥܡܗ ܐܝܬܝܗ ܗܘܬ ܠܐ ܫܒܩܐ ܗܘܬ ܠܗ "if it (f.) had always been with him, it would not have allowed him . . . " Aphr. 128, 3; ܐܠܘ ܝܕܥ ܗܘܐ . . . ܡܬܬܥܝܪ ܗܘܐ εἰ ᾔδει . . . ἐγρηγόρησεν ἄν Matt. 24, 43; ܐܠܘ ܓܝܪ ܡܛܪܐ . . . ܡܬܚܠܫ ܗܘܐ . . . ܢܗܝܪܐ ܗܘܬ "for if the rain had weakened . . ., it would be clear . . . " Aphr. 450, 14; ܐܠܘ ܠܟܠܡܕܡ ܡܫܬܡܫܘ ܡܫܬܡܫܝܢ ܗܘܐ ܡܢܘ ܗܘ ܕܡܫܡܫ ܗܘܐ "if everything were ministered unto, who would he be that ministered?" Spic. 3, 24; ܦܩܚ ܗܘܐ ܠܗ ܐܠܘ ܠܐ ܐܬܝܠܕ καλὸν ἦν αὐτῷ εἰ οὐκ ἐγεννήθη Matt. 26, 24, cf. Mark 14, 21; ܦܩܚ ܗܘܐ ܠܗܘܢ ܐܠܘ ܠܐ ܩܡܝܢ ܗܘܘ "it would be better for them, if they did not rise" Aphr. 169, 12; ܐܠܘ ܡܫܟܚܐ ܗܘܬ "if it had been possible" Ov. 201, 1; ܐܠܘ ܗܟܢ ܗܘܐ ܗܘܐ ܒܪܢܫܐ ܗܘ ܠܢܦܫܗ ܠܐ ܐܝܬܘܗܝ ܗܘܐ ܐܠܐ ܡܐܢܐ ܗܘܐ "if man had been made in that way, he would not have been for himself, but would have been an instrument" Spic. 3, 4.

Occasionally, with the naturally definite ܐܠܘ, the suggestion of unreality, given by the Perf., remains quite in abeyance, and the particle is then followed by a clause with the Impf. or Part., or by a Nominal clause: ܕܐܠܘ ܢܫܡܥܝܘܗ ܠܗ ܓܒܠܐ ܚܘܒܠܐ ܗܘܬ ܠܢ "which, if we listened to it (f.), would bring us woe" Jul. 210, 7; ܐܦܠܐ ܐܠܘ ܢܗܘܐ ܕܗܘ ܠܛܘܪܢܐ ܐܘܦܢܝ ܘܡܫܒܩܢܝ "not even if it should happen that the tyrant let me go free" (where the hypothetical Perf. is in the dependent clause) Jul. 84, 7; ܐܠܘ ܓܝܪ ܡܚܐ ܪܝܚܗ ܕܚܛܝܐ ܠܡܩܪܒ ܠܗ ܐܢܬܘܢ ܟܠܟܘܢ ܥܪܩܝܢ ܐܢܬܘܢ "for if the odour of the sinner were to strike one who approached him, then you would all flee" Ov. 140, 20 (where there is a var. ܐܢܬܘܢ ܗܘ ܥܪܩܝܢ ܗܘܝܬܘܢ); ܐܠܘ ܒܥܝܬܗ ܝܡܐ ܘܝܒܫܐ ܙܡܪܘ ܠܫܘܒܚܟ "if thou didst seek it, sea and land would sing thy praise" Moes. II, 78 v. 45; ܐܠܘ ܨܒܝܬ "if thou didst wish" *ibid.* v. 39. Cf. ܐܠܘ ܠܐ ܡܬܛܪܢܘܬܐ

ܕܐܠܘܠܐ ܚܒܝܫܐ ܠܗ ܠܥܠܡܐ ... ܡܟܝܠ ܕܝܢ ܐܬܦܣܩܘ ܚܝܐ "if the protection of God did not embrace the world, life would no doubt have come to an end" Jos. St. 4, 14; ܐܠܘ ܠܐ ܐܝܬܝܗܘܢ ܒܗ ܒܥܠܡܐ ܡܫܬܪܐ ܥܠܡܐ "if they were not in the world, it would dissolve" Aphr. 457, 14 (where there is a var. ܡܫܬܪܝܐ ܗܘܐ); ܐܠܘ ܐܝܬ ܠܢ ܢܦܫܐ ܕܟܝܬܐ ... ܬܗܪܗ ܗܘܐ ܠܢ ܡܫܬܩܢܘ "if we had a pure soul ..., astonishment thereat would strike us dumb" Moes. II, 160 v. 1307 (and so 164 v. 1357, while 166 v. 1385 has ܐܠܘ ܐܝܬ ܗܘܐ); ܘܐܠܘ ܫܦܝܐ ܥܝܢܐ ... ܬܗܪܗ ܗܘܐ ܠܢ ܟܢܫܐ "and were the eye clear ..., the throng would astonish us" Moes. II, 164 v. 1355; ܐܠܘ ܫܠܝܛ ܐܢܫ ... ܗܢܐ ... ܪܡ ܗܘܐ "if one had power ..., then would this (one) ... be higher" Anc. Doc. 87, 16. ☞ p. 365

B. The clause with ܐܠܘ is subjected to a certain dependence in cases like ܘܡܢܐ ܨܒܐ ܐܢܐ ܐܠܘ ܡܢ ܟܒܪ ܐܬܕܠܩܬ *καὶ τί θέλω εἰ ἤδη ἀνήφθη* Luke 12, 49 (P. ܘܨܒܐ ܐܢܐ); ܨܒܐ ܐܢܬ ܗܫܐ ܐܠܘ ܚܙܝܬܝܗܝ "thou wishest now, thou hadst seen him" Moes. II, 160 v. 1319 (and so v. 1320); ܘܟܡܐ ܨܒܝܬܘܢ ܗܘܝܬܘܢ ܐܠܘ ܡܢ ܟܒܪ ܥܪܒܬ "and how much you wished, it had already gone down" Jul. 23, 22. Cf. *ibid.* 81, 25; 104, 26. The notion of a hypothesis has in these cases passed over into that of a wish.

C. With ܐܠܘ ܠܐ, accompanied by a noun, the idea of existence does not need to be expressly denoted: ܘܐܠܘ ܠܐ ܡܪܝܐ ܕܟܪܝ ܝܘܡܬܐ ܗܢܘܢ ܠܐ ܚܝܐ ܗܘܐ ܟܠ ܒܣܪ *καὶ εἰ μὴ κύριος* (ὃς) *ἐκολόβωσεν τὰς ἡμέρας* (*ἐκείνας*) *οὐκ ἂν ἐσώθη πᾶσα σάρξ* Mark 13, 20 (S. differently); ܐܠܘ ܠܐ ܣܘܪܚܢܐ ܕܥܒܕܘ "had it not been the offence, which they committed" Jul. 50, 27; ܘܐܠܘ ܠܐ ܗܘ ܘܠܐ ܓܠܝܢܐ ܕܢܦܩܘ ܡܢ ܐܒܘܗܝ "and had he not been, then neither would there have been (§ 339) any revelations from his Father" Moes. II, 118 v. 654. The construction of ܐܠܘ ܠܐ ܕ = ܐܠܘ ܠܐ is exactly like the latter in syntax: ܐܠܘ ܠܐ ܕܐܥܫܢ ܟܦܢܐ ܕܐܪܥܐ ܥܡܢ ܠܐ ܫܒܩܗ "if the famine had not become severe, he would not have allowed him to come with us" Joseph 242, 9 (Ov. 320, 15); ܐܠܘ ܠܐ ܕܠܡܠܟܐ ܕܦܪܣܝܐ ܡܫܥܒܕ ܐܢܐ ܐܦ ܐܢܐ ܣܠܩ ܗܘܝܬ "had I not been made subject to the king of the Persians, I too would have gone up" Sim. 328 *inf.*(¹)

(¹) I would not like to maintain confidently that even in ܐܠܘ ܕ ... ܠܐ ܐܬܪܥܝܬ "if I did not ... think" Jul. 132, 12, the ܕ is correct.

ܐܢ for ܐܠܘ

§ 376. In rare cases ܐܢ occurs instead of ܐܠܘ with conditions clearly assumed as impossible, *e. g.* in ܐܶܢ ܓܹܝܪ ܡܶܕܶܡ ܝܘܬܪܵܢܵܐ ܐܝܬ ܠܗ ܠܒܥܝܪܵܐ ܡܶܢ ܢܛܳܪ ܫܒܬܐ ܠܡܩܕܡ ܡܢ ܗܠܝܢ ܛܢ̈ܦܬܐ ܟܠܐ ܗܘܐ ܠܗ ܢܵܡܘܣܐ "for if cattle had any advantage in keeping the sabbath, the law would have hindered them from these impure things before" Aphr. 233, 8 (only one Codex); ܘܐܶܢ ܡܕܡ ܠܐ ܫܠܝܛ ܗܘܐ ܠܐܝ̈ܕܝܢ ܠܡܥܒܕ ܡ̈ܐܢܐ ܗܘܝܢ ܕܐܚܪ̈ܢܐ "for if it were not in the power of our hands to do anything, we would be the instruments of others" Spic. 20, 22 (in the parallel clause ܐܠܘ).

Clauses which resemble Conditional Clauses.

§ 377. The great variety of Conditional Clauses could only be represented here by a few leading types. But, besides, there are associated more or less with Conditional Clauses proper, the Disjunctive Conditional, with ܐܘ—ܐܘ (§ 258), the Temporal Conditional, with ܡܐ ܕ (§ 258), as well as the Temporal, with ܡܐ, ܐܡܬܝ ܕ (§§ 258; 265 &c.) and many others. ܡܐ takes a concessive meaning by the addition of ܐܦ, more rarely ܣܓܝ "much, greatly, even" ("even while")—"however much", "although", *e. g.* ܘܐܦ ܡܐ ܕܒܢܐ ܠܗ ܬܘܒ ܬܪܥܘܬܐ ܡܬܩܪܝܐ "and although he builds it up, it is still called a crack" Aphr. 145, 10; ܡܐ ܐܦ ܒܐܘܪܗܝ ܐܟܣܢܝܐ ܗܘܐ ܐܦܝܣܩܘܦܐ "although Xenāyā [Philoxenus] was at the time in Edessa" Jos. St. 25, 11 and frequently thus.—ܘܡܐ ܣܓܝ ܒܚܢ ܘܪܕܐ ܐܢܘܢ ܠܐ ܐܬܬܩܢܘ "however much he tried and punished them, still they did not do well" Aphr. 402, 13.

* * *

STRUCTURE OF PERIODS. INVOLUTION AND OTHER IRREGULAR FORMS.

Structure of Periods.

§ 378. The fondness of the Syrians for the construction of rather long *Periods*, founded on the genius of their language—has been not a little fostered by the model which the Greek Style presented. Those periods are produced by the co-ordination and subordination of such clauses as have been already described, or others like them. The number of possible ways, in which the known elements may in these individual cases be combined, is unbounded.

§ 379. The license given in the arrangement of words in a clause is in part also extended to the arrangement of the clauses, which serve as members of a period. For the purpose of being brought into stronger relief, the governed clause is occasionally placed a long way before the governing; and not seldom an express *Involution* or enclosing of one clause within another, makes its appearance. Cf. ܡܢ ܝܘܡܐ ܓܝܪ ܕܫܡܗ ܕܡܫܝܚܐ ܐܬܩܪܝ ܥܠܘܗܝ ܕܢܣܒܥ ܟܦܢܘܬܗ ܡܢ ܡܕܡ ܠܐ ܢܣܒ ܕܢܬܛܦܝܣ "for, from the day on which the name of Christ was named over him, by nothing was he persuaded to resolve to satisfy his hunger" Ov. 182, 12; ܡܢܘ ܕܝܢ ܢܫܟܚ ܫܘܚܠܦܐ ܕܬܕܡܪܬܐ ܕܒܗܢܐ ܫܠܝܐ ܓܢܝܒܐ ܕܝܘܡܬܐ ܩܠܝܠܬܐ ܕܨܠܘܬܗ ܕܡܢ ܪܘܚܐ ܕܐܠܗܐ ܒܓܘ ܢܦܫܗ ܡܬܚܕܬܝܢ ܗܘܘ "but who can describe the wonderful changes, which, in this stolen quiet of the few days of his prayer, were renewed in his soul by the spirit of God?" Ov. 185, 18; ܠܡܢ ܕܨܒܐ ܐܡܪܬ ܘܐܡܪ ܐܢܐ ܕܦܫܝܩܝܢ ܐܢܘܢ "*ei, qui vult, dixi et dico eos faciles esse*" Spic. 6, 4; ܘܟܕ ܗܠܝܢ ܠܬܕܡܪ̈ܬܐ ܪ̈ܘܪܒܬܐ ܫܡܥܬ ܕܥܒܕ ܐܢܬ "*et quum haec mirabilia magna audiverim te facere*" Addai 3, 3 *ab inf.*; ܓܠܘܣܩܡܐ ܕܡܝ̈ܬܐ ܐܝܠܝܢ ܕܨܒܝܢ ܡܢ ܕܝܪ̈ܝܐ ܕܢܥܒܕܘܢ ܠܗܘܢ "those of the monks, who wish to make for themselves stone chests for the dead" Ov. 214, 12; ܐܠܐ ܠܘ ܗܫܐ ܕܢܕܘܫ ܐܬܝܢ ܕܒܪܕܝܨܢ ܗܘܦܐ "but we have not now come to stir up the mud of Bardesanes" Ov. 64, 12; ܡܛܠ ܕܐܦ ܐܢܬܘܢ ܡܡܠܠܐ ܡܥܕܪܢܐ ܚܙܐ ܐܢܐ ܕܪܗܝܛܝܢ ܐܢܬܘܢ ܠܡܫܡܥܗ "for I see that you too are eager to hear profitable speech" Philox. 120, 2, and many similar instances.

Involution, or Enclosing of one Clause within another.

§ 380. *Parentheses*, like the following one, are seldom met with: ܟܡܐ ܚܟܝܡܝܢ ܐܢܬܘܢ ܣܒܪܝܢ ܐܒܛܠܘ ܢܡܘ̈ܣܐ ܡܢ ܐܬܪ̈ܘܬܗܘܢ "how many wise men, think you, have abrogated laws in their several countries?" Spic. 19, 1. More frequently are parentheses found in quotations of sayings: *e. g.* ܕܚܠ ܐܢܐ ܐܡܪ ܥܒܕܐ ܕܐܡܪ ܡܕܡ ܕܓܢܒܬܘܢ "I am afraid, says the servant, to mention what you have stolen" Joseph 218, 3 [= Ov. 307, 14] &c.

Parenthesis.

§ 381. The construction of the Nominative Absolute (§ 317) belongs at bottom to the *Anacoluthon*, and the same may be said of several other constructions which we have met with above. But true Anacolutha,— *i. e.* those which are felt to be such,—are not very common. They belong, moreover, rather to the department of rhetoric than that of grammar.

Anacoluthon.

§ 382. The range of the *Ellipsis* is very extensive. We have already in foregoing sections dealt with various instances of its employment, cf. *e. g.* §§ 374 E; 375 C. To the Ellipsis belongs the omission of
individual words and groups of words, which may be supplied from the
contents of corresponding clauses (§§ 332; 374 F); thus farther ܐܝܣܝܐ
ܐܢ̈ܫܐ ... ܗܘ ܐܢ̣ܬ ܘܗܘ ܗܘ "it is one thing for a
man to write with pathos, and another thing (for him to write) with
truth" Jos. St. 5, 7; ܘܐܡܬܝ ... ܘܗܘ ... ܢܦܩܝܢ
ܢܦܫ̈ܐ "and whenever they [the teachers] do put a question, (they do so)
that they may direct the mind of the questioner [the pupil], so that he
may ask properly" Spic. 1, 18; ܘܐܫܬ̈ܪ ... ܡܥܒܪܐ
ܘܕܝܪ̈ܬܐ ܘܡܚ̈ܣܢ̈ܐ ... ܚܒ̈ܐ ܘܐܦ ... ܩܕ̈ܝܫ̈ܐ
"and sent others, who conveyed his kindness (*i. e.* his gifts) to the
monasteries of the West and the South . . . , so that even to the needy
saints who dwell in the wilderness of Jerusalem (he sent gifts)" Ov.
205, 22 &c. Bursts of *Exclamation* produce other ellipses, which do not
admit of being formed into complete sentences. Others, again, are produced by the peculiar style of *Adjuration-formulae.* In fact living speech
is very elliptical; but of course the proportion, in which the individual
man may avail himself of this form of expression, is not a matter to be
settled by grammar.

Ellipsis.

APPENDIX.

ON THE USE OF THE LETTERS OF THE ALPHABET
AS CIPHERS.

The letters, which are noted on p. 2, may take numerical values.
A line drawn above them, or some other distinguishing mark, is wont
upon occasion to make them significant as ciphers. In compound numerals the higher order takes the right hand place. The *hundreds* from
500 to 900, for which the alphabetical characters do not suffice, are
represented by the corresponding tens, ܢ, ܣ, ܥ, ܦ, ܨ, over which a

point is placed for distinction's sake. This point, however, is often wanting; yet the numerical value is generally quite clear from the mere order of the ciphers, or from the context. For the hundreds from 500—800, combinations with ‾ܠ = 400 frequently appear also, thus: ‾ܠܩ = 500; ‾ܠܖ = 600; ‾ܠܡ = 700; ‾ܠܠ 800. For the *thousands* the units may be placed, where the order of the ciphers gives them to be recognised as indicating thousands; a small oblique stroke is sometimes set below them as a distinguishing mark.

Examples: ‾ܟܓ = 23; ‾ܖܛ = 209; ‾ܫܥܕ = 394; ‾ܢܩܡ (‾ܢܩܡ) or ‾ܠܩܡܡ = 527; ‾ܐܦܣܒ (‾ܐܦܣܒ, ‾ܐܘܣܒ) = 1862; ‾ܘܢܗ = 5550 &c.

Farther, the thousands are very often written out in full, with numeral letters accompanying, *e. g.* ‾ܐܠܦܝܢ ܘܬܫܥ ‾ܡܐܐ ܘܡܕ = 1944; ‾ܬܪܝܢ ‾ܐܠܦܝܢ ܘܡܐܐ ܘܢܒ = 2152 &c. And, besides, there occur combinations of numerals written out in full and numerals represented by letters, *e. g.* ‾ܐܠܦܐ ܘܬܫܥܡܐܐ ܘܣܙ = 1967; ‾ܫܬ ‾ܡܐܐ ܘܠ = 630 &c.

Rem. In certain MSS. a very ancient system of ciphers is found, resting upon quite a different principle.

ADDITIONS AND CORRECTIONS.

P. 2, l. 2 from foot, 3rd last col.; after—*sh*—, insert—(ܐ).

P. 16, l. 15 from top; read—Exception.

P. 23, l. 19; for—"there"—, read—"then".

P. 45, l. 4 from foot of text; for ܐܢܒܝ, read—ܐܢܒܝ.

P. 46, l. 4 of § 66; for—f. ܣܒ—, read—f. ܣܒ.

P. 52, l. 11 from top; read last word—ܢܒܝܗܘܢ.

P. 64, l. 10; for ܐܘܓܠ, read—ܐܘܓܠ.

P. 64, l. 11; for ܓܙܓܠ, read—ܓܙܓܠ.

P. 74, l. 4; for—syllables—, read—letters.

P. 87. l. 11; for—ܣܦ—, read—ܣܦ.

P. 87, l. 20, 2nd col.; for—ܐܣܒܝ, read—ܐܣܒܝ.

P. 87, l. 26, 2nd col.; for—ܐܬܢܣܒܝ, read—ܐܬܢܣܒܝ.

P. 88, 4th footnote; for—ܐܓܪܘܦ, read—ܐܓܪܘܦ.

P. 94, l. 9 from foot; for—ܐܩܪܡܠ, read ܐܩܪܡܠ.

P. 95, l. 3 from foot of text; for—ܡܐܝܠܚܡܝ, read—ܡܐܝܠܚܡܝ.

P. 97, margin; for—months—, read—month.

P. 98, l. 2 from foot of text; after—"ill";—, insert—ܟܝ "well", "much" (adv.);—.

P. 103, margin; for—Preposition—, read—Prepositions.

P. 107, l. 8; read first word as—ܐܚܢܒܝ.

P. 114, 1st line of footnote; for—ܡܬܢܒ—, read—ܡܬܢܒ.

P. 128, l. 2; read last word as—ܝܟܦܪ.

P. 128, l. 9; for—ܘܓܚܠ—, read—ܚܓܠ.

P. 128, *ult.*, mid. col.; for—ܢܟܦܪ—, read—ܝܟܦܪ.

P. 133, *ult.*; for—ܢܫܠ—, read—ܝܫܠ.

P. 140, l. 10; for—ܝܣܦܘܢܣܒ—, read—ܢܐܣܦܘܢܣܒ

P. 144, last column; read 3rd word as—ܣܓܒܚܝ.

P. 182, l. 16; read last word as—ܩܝܨ.

P. 209, l. 8; read 3rd Syriac word as—ܝܐܪܘܦ.

P. 212, ll. 10 & 9 from foot; read—Sentences.

P. 222, l. 11 from top; after—§ 283—, insert—A.

P. 229, l. 15; for—ܐܝܦܘܗܘ—, read—ܐܝܦܘܗܘ.

P. 232, l. 5 from foot; for—ܐܝܐ̈ܚ—, read—ܐܚܝܨܝܚ.

P. 240, l. 2 from foot; from the words—"who are you Christians"—, delete—you.

P. 244, l. 5 from top; read first word as—ensample.

P. 255, l. 15; for—28 *ab inf.*—, read—28 *a, inf.*

P. 255, l. 19; read—consigned to writing.

P. 257, l. 16; for—ܘܗܘ, read—ܘܗܘ.

P. 271, l. 9 from foot; for—XXX—, read—XXIX.

Note.—A vowel-mark, or a point or other sign, has fallen out in the Syriac portion of the type, much oftener than could have been wished. It would appear that the occasional occurrence of such an accident, immediately before the final impression, is exceedingly difficult to avoid in this particular type, however careful the manipulation may be; and, happening when it does, it is of course beyond the control of any proofreading. In the above list of "Additions and Corrections", only those instances of such a fault have been pointed out, which stand in Paradigms or similarly important situations. The others are left to the discernment of the reader to discover and correct, and to his indulgence to condone.

INDEX OF PASSAGES.

(THE REFERENCES ARE TO THE PAGES OF THIS EDITION)

A. SCRIPTURE.

(a) OLD TESTAMENT.

21

(b) APOCRYPHA.

(c) NEW TESTAMENT.

B. AUTHORS AND WORKS MENTIONED IN THE PREFACE, AS WELL AS THE FOLLOWING:

PHILOX. = Discourses of Philoxenus, Bishop of Mabbogh (Budge);
JOHN VAN TELLA (Kleyn);
EUSEB. CH. HIST. = Eusebius' Church History;
BEDJAN, MART. = Acta Martyrum et Sanctorum (Bedjan).

C. OTHER AUTHORS, WORKS AND DOCUMENTS,

OCCASIONALLY REFERRED TO.

Printed by W. Drugulin, Leipzig.

Appendix

The Handwritten Additions in Theodor Nöldeke's Personal Copy
edited by Anton Schall (1966)
translated by Peter T. Daniels

Preface

Not one treatment of Syriac grammar has appeared since Theodor Nöldeke's (1880, 2d ed. 1898) that either is not based on it, or does not at least acknowledge it, aside from Rubens Duval's meritorious *Traité de grammaire syriaque* (Paris, 1881), though the latter does not achieve Nöldeke's heights. Like the Mandaic grammar of 1875, the *Compendious Syriac Grammar* is a work of art in every part, which called forth the admiration of his contemporaries.[1] Nöldeke satisfied "the need for a Syriac grammar that is both convenient and comprehensive." He "used good native sources throughout, but applied strict criteria in evaluating them" and especially "for the first time presented Syriac syntax according to the usage of good, old texts."[2]

Thus, acting on a suggestion by Enno Littmann, commissioned by the Wissenschaftlichen Buchgesellschaft, I undertook to edit for an Appendix Nöldeke's handwritten notes in his interleaved personal copy[3] of the second edition of 1898. The examples noted by Nöldeke have been taken over only after preliminary examination. Some observations that upon careful study of the relevant Syriac textual context proved to be unsound have not been repeated. The additions themselves appear here in edited form, so that sufficient space remained for the

1. The review by Georg Hoffmann (1845–1933), himself an eminent Syriac scholar, may stand for all, in *Literarisches Centralblatt* 1882, cols. 318–22.
2. Quotations from Nöldeke's own remarks on the first edition in *GGA* 1880: 1629–32.
3. Held by the Tübingen University library under the call number Ci VIII 40a H.

insertion of more recent resources and the occasional addition. In order to make the additions readable in themselves and to spare the user page-flipping, I have limited myself to the abbreviations listed on pp. XV f. of the Preface. Alongside the generally known abbreviations, Nöldeke added the following:

Efr., *Nis.* followed by a number without p. (page) refers to the number of the poem.

Jos. sometimes occurs instead of the usual abbreviation *Jos. Styl.*

Philox. = The Discourses of Philoxenus, Bishop of Mabbôgh, A.D. 485–519. Edited . . . with an English Translation by E. A. Wallis Budge. 2 Vols. London (1893). 1894.

[Schall now describes the citation index he provided on the model of that added by Crichton, but] in contrast to the citation index of the English edition, I endeavored to provide the full titles and bibliographical information for the cited texts and other sources, and hope thereby also to create a sense of Theodor Nöldeke's impressive breadth of reading, with whose name the rise and most productive epoch of Syriac studies remains inseparably connected.[4]

I am grateful to the Tübingen University Library for the generosity with which it allowed me to keep Nöldeke's own copy at home on indefinite loan. For her valuable assistance in preparing the citation index I must thank my wife.

Heidelberg, December 1964   Anton Schall

The translator wishes to express his gratitude to Prof. Robert D. Hoberman for his careful reading and improvements.

The additions are keyed to the main text by page and section (and subsection) number; in the text, a siglum is inserted alongside the line to which the note applies (☞ plus the

---

4. The place of the *Compendious Syriac Grammar* in the history of the discipline is sketched by Franz Rosenthal in his book *Die aramaistische Forschung seit Th. Nöldeke's Veröffentlichungen*, Leiden 1939 (repr. 1964), p. 189, in the following review: "With the appearance of the second edition of Nöldeke's grammar, a detailed presentation of the work done since then and the results achieved should be inserted. Yet already at this point in time the most productive epoch of Syriac studies had come to a close, and despite the profusion of problems to be solved, a major decrease in productive activity as well as a shrinking of the circle of Orientalists among whom Syriac studies found sympathetic consideration cannot be denied. This is especially clear in the field of grammatical and lexical studies. . . ."

appropriate page number in the appendix). Estrangelo type is used for the forms that in Schall's Anhang exhibit the eastern vocalization system. References are generally cited by page and line (joined by a period), and despite Schall's misgiving, the following abbreviations for new materials have been employed.

Acts of Thomas, Sinai Codex	ed. F. C. Burkitt in *Studia Sinaitica* 9 (London, 1900)
Aḥiḳar	F. C. Conybeare, J. Rendel Harris, and A. S. Lewis, *The Story of Aḥiḳar*, 2d ed. (Cambridge, 1913)
Balai, *Dichtung*	*Beiträge zur Kenntnis der religiösen Dichtung Balai's*, ed. and trans. K. V. Zetterstéen (Leipzig, 1902)
Bar Bahlūl, *Lexicon Syriacum*	ed. R. Duval (Paris, 1901)
Bar Hebraeus, Book of Rays	*Le Livre des Splendeurs*, ed. A. Moberg (Lund, 1922)
Bar Hebraeus, *Ethicon*	*Ethicon seu moralia*, ed. P. Bedjan (Paris, 1898)
Bar Hebraeus, *Nomocanon*	ed. P. Bedjan (Paris, 1898)
Brockelmann, *GVG*	*Grundriß der vergleichenden Grammatik der semitischen Sprachen* (Berlin, 1908–13)
Brockelmann, *Syrische Grammatik*	8th ed. (Leipzig, 1960)
Budge, *Blessed Virgin Mary*	*The History of the Blessed Virgin Mary and the History of the Likeness of Christ which the Jews of Tiberias made to mock at, the Syriac texts edited with English translations* by E. A. W. Budge (London, 1899)
Chabot, *Synodicon*	J. B. Chabot, *Synodicon orientale* (Paris, 1902)
Drijvers, *Inscriptions*	*Old-Syriac (Edessean) Inscriptions*, ed. H. J. W. Drijvers (Leiden, 1972)
Drijvers–Healey, *Old Syriac Inscriptions*	H. J. W. Drijvers and J. F. Healey, *The Old Syriac Inscriptions of Edessa and Osrhoene: Texts, Translations and Commentary* (Leiden, 1999)
Ephraem, *Hymni et sermones*	*S. Ephraem Syri hymni et sermones*, ed. Th. J. Lamy (Mechelen, 1882–1902)
Ephraem, *Prose Refutations*	*S. Ephraim's Prose Refutations of Mani, Marcion, and Bardaisan*. Vol. 1 publ. by C. W. Mitchell (London, 1912); vol. 2 transcribed by C. W. Mitchell and completed by A. A. Bevan and F. C. Burkitt (London, 1921)
Ephraem, "Testament"	R. Duval, "Le Testament de St. Éphrem," *JA* **9**/18 (1901)
GGA	*Göttingische gelehrte Anzeigen*
Išōᶜyahb III Patriarcha, *Liber epistularum*	ed. R. Duval (CSCO Scr. Syri, ser. 2, vol. 64; Paris & Leipzig, 1904)
JA	*Journal asiatique* (**series**/volume)
JAOS	*Journal of the American Oriental Society*

Jacob of Sarug, *Homiliae selectae* *Homiliae selectae Mar-Jacobi Sarugensis*, ed. P. Bedjan (Paris & Leipzig, 1905–10)

Kugener–Cumont, *Manichéisme* M.-A. Kugener and F. Cumont, *Recherches sur le Manichéisme*, vols. 2/3 (Brussels, 1912)

Lagarde, *Apocryphi* *Libri Veteris Testamenti apocryphi Syriacae* e recognitione P. A. de Lagarde (Leipzig & London, 1861)

Mingana, *Bar-Penkayé* A. Mingana, *Sources syriaques*, vol. 1, *Bar-Penkayé* (Leipzig, 1908)

Mingana, *Mšiḥa-Zkha* A. Mingana, *Sources syriaques*, vol. 1, *Mšiḥa-Zkha* (Leipzig, 1907)

Nöldeke, *Beiträge* Th. Nöldeke, *Beiträge zur semitischen Sprachwissenschaft* (Strasbourg, 1904)

Nöldeke, *Mandäische Grammatik* Th. Nöldeke, *Mandäische Grammatik* (Halle, 1875)

Nöldeke, *Neue Beiträge* Th. Nöldeke, *Neue Beiträge zur semitischen Sprachwissenschaft* (Strasbourg, 1910)

Philoxenus, *Letters* *Three Letters of Philoxenus Bishop of Mabbôgh*, ed. A. A. Vaschalde (Rome, 1902)

Pognon, *Inscriptions sémitiques* H. Pognon, *Inscriptions sémitiques de la Syrie, de la Mésopotamie et de la région de Mossoul* (Paris, 1907)

Pseudo-Callisthenes *The History of Alexander the Great, being the Syriac Version of Pseudo-Callisthenes*, ed. E. A. W. Budge (Cambridge, 1889)

Sachau, *Berlin* E. Sachau, *Verzeichnis der syrischen Handschriften der K. Bibliothek zu Berlin* (Berlin, 1899)

SBAW *Sitzungsberichte der Berliner Akademie der Wissenschaften*

Schulthess, *CPA* F. Schulthess, *Grammatik des christlich-palästinischen Aramäisch* (Tübingen, 1924)

Testamentum *Testamentum Domini Nostri Jesu Christi*, ed. Ignatius Ephraem II Rahmani (Mainz, 1899)

Theophile of Edessa, *Acta Sancti* *Acta Ss. Conff. Guriae et Shamonae exarata Syriaca lingua a Theophilo Edesseno anno Christi 297*, ed. Ignatius Ephraem II Rahmani (Rome, 1899)

Thomas of Edessa, *De Nativitate* *Tractatus de Nativitate Domini Nostri Christi*, ed. et Lat. redd. S. J. Carr (Rome, 1898), Phil. Diss. Cath. Univ. of America

Wright W. Wright, *A Grammar of the Arabic Language*, 2 vols. (Cambridge, 1896–98)

Wright, *British Museum* W. Wright, *Catalogue of Syriac Manuscripts in the British Museum* (London, 1870–72)

Wright, *Cambridge* W. Wright, *A Catalogue of the Syriac Manuscripts of the University of Cambridge* (Cambridge, 1901)

ZA *Zeitschrift für Assyriologie*

Additions

X For XXIII, read XXXIII.

XIII The appearance that the Vatican manuscript of the Life of Simeon Stylites represents a more original text than that of the British Museum is contested and in fact reversed by C. C. Torrey in *JAOS* 20 (1899) 275.

XIII Nöldeke admits to having overlooked the revision of a large number of pages of the Codex Sinaiticus by A. Smith Lewis, *Some Pages of the Four Gospels Re-transcribed from the Sinaitic Palimpsest* (London, 1896), though in fact without too much damage.

XVI The various discrepancies in orthography and even form found in the late Melkite liturgical songs (cf. E. Sachau, *SBAW* 1889: 502ff. and earlier already F. Baethgen, *ZDMG* 33 [1879] 666ff.) do not belong in a grammar of Classical Syriac. For the most part they are simple inaccuracies, showing a slight influence of the modern dialect. Only the latter is of linguistic interest. Cf. once again Sachau, *Berlin*, no. 295 and facsimile VIII.

3 § 1 C [The note that ܐ and ܘ are not sufficiently discriminated refers to the typeface in which the German editions were set, rather than to the Oxford font used in the English edition and emulated in this Appendix.—PTD]

5 § 4 Also ܠܚܡܐ Matt 18:23 S. vs. the correct reading for ܠܚܡܘ.

14 § 21 C ܒܪܝܬܐ 'streets' does not belong here, since it is a loanword from Akkadian, cf. W. von Soden, *Akkadisches Handwörterbuch* (Wiesbaden, 1959–83), p. 128b, *birītu(m)* at the end, and H. Zimmern, *Akkadische Fremdwörter*, 2d ed. (Leipzig, 1917), p. 43 [and S. Kaufman, *The Akkadian Influences on Aramaic* (Assyriological Studies 19; Chicago, 1974), p. 44 —RDH].

15 § 23 A In the *Kitāb at-Tanbīh wa-l-išrāf* (345 A.H./956 A.D.), ed. M. J. de Goeje (Bibl. geogr. ar. 8; Leiden, 1894), p. 91.2, al-Masʿūdī denies that the Syrians have the sound *f*. Thus by the middle of the 10th century A.D. the East Syrians whom he knew no longer had *f*.

15 § 22 n. 2 Likewise ܓܘܚܟܐ 'laughter', in which as in ܩܕܡܘ and L are not in direct contact and so L is not assimilated to ܛ, cf. Brockelmann, *Syrische Grammatik*, § 19 Anm.

25 § 36 For § 177 D, read § 177 B.

29 § 42 The Syriac *ā* was probably open and therefore tended to *ɔ*. The Syriac *ē*

at an earlier time was probably sometimes open and remains so in the western pronunciation, sometimes close and easily becoming *ī*. The Syriac *ō* was probably close and tended toward *ū*. Jacob of Edessa (d. 708 A.D.) in the vowel signs for West Syriac that he created on the Greek model to be organically inserted into the consonantal text still distinguished two different *o*-sounds, one represented by omicron in e.g., ܣܦܘܓܐ < σπόγγος 'sponge', and one which according to A. Merx probably was based on omega in words like ܢܣܪܬܐ 'sawdust', ܨܠܘܬܐ 'prayer'. Cf. A. Merx, *Historia artis grammaticae apud Syros* (Leipzig, 1889), pp. 50f., 58f., and J. B. Segal, *The Diacritical Point and the Accents in Syriac* (London, 1953), pp. 42ff.

31 § 43 E   Read ܡܘܗ, cf. R. Payne Smith, *Thesaurus Syriacus*, 2495.

31 § 44   F. Nau shows in *JA* **10**/17 (1911) 185f. that in the 7th century in the West Syrian area the *ā* preserved in East Syriac was still pronounced. This is determined from the Greek transcription of a Syriac phrase in Leontios of Neapolis's Life of Simeon Salos: Λαδεχρε λιχεμ ܐܘܟ ܠܟܚ ܠܐܬܝ ܠܐ = μὴ λυποῦ, μῆτερ, where Nau properly corrects δεχρε to ϑεχρε.

32 § 45   Such as ܦܚܘܬܐ for ܦܚܐ 'chasm', ܢܗܡܠ for ܢܗܠ 'neigh', ܬܗܪܐ for ܬܗܪ 'astonishment', to which Bar Hebraeus refers in the Book of Rays, 237.22ff.—As in Christian Palestinian Aramaic (cf. Schulthess, *CPA* § 42), in the Syrus Sinaiticus *a* assimilates to *u* (*o*?) before *ḇ* or *b*, e.g., Mark 8:5, 6 ܣܘܒܪ (elsewhere ܣܒܪ), Luke 10:17 ܣܘܒܪܝܢ (elsewhere ܣܒܪ), 13:14 ܣܘܒܐ (elsewhere ܣܒܐ).

32 § 46   We are unable to carry through the distinction between open and close *ē*, which certainly must have existed. Serious consideration, at least, must be given to Brockelmann's opinion, *GVG* 1: 37, that the East Syriac *ē*s that correspond to West Syriac *ī* were close, and the others open. Open *ē* is indicated e.g., by the frequent representation of [ת]יב in Aramaic place names by Arabic ط. Moreover, the question of close and open also comes into consideration for *o*-sounds. Note Jacob of Edessa's complicated provision for vowels. Finally, all this holds not just for the long *e*, *o*, but also for the short ones. [Cf. J. Blau, "The Origins of Open and Closed *e* in Proto-Syriac," *Bulletin of the School of Oriental and African Studies* 32 (1969) 1–9.]

42 § 59   Also ܡܫܢܐ 'whetstone', Bar Bahlūl, *Lexicon Syriacum*, 1174, which in the Arabic–Syriac dictionary of Elias of Nisibis, specifically in ms. Gotha

arab. 1091, described by Nöldeke as "transferred from the Nestorian to the
Jacobite tradition," is found as ܪܟܝܟܪ, cf. Nöldeke's description of the ms.
in W. Pertsch, *Die orientalischen Handschriften der Bibl. zu Gotha, An-*
hang (1893), pp. 58f. The edition printed in Hebrew by P. de Lagarde,
Praetermissorum libri duo (Göttingen, 1879), as usual forgoes indication
of the vowels on ܡܚܣܡ on p. 31.97. The variants ܪܟܝܟܪ or ܪܟܝܟܪ in Bar
Bahlūl are scarcely legitimate. For ܡܚܣܡ cf. also § 126 B.

45 § 64   In Philoxenus, *Letters*, p. 140.5ff., Codex A has these forms close to
each other:

ܣܪܒ ܐܠܣܠܡ ... ܣܠܡܝ ... ܣܠܡ ... ܡܣܠܡ ... ܚܩܣܡ ܐܠܣܠܡ ... ܡܣܠܡܡ
ܣܠܡ ... ܡܚܬܪܠܡ

Cod. C: ܣܪܒ ܣܠܡ ... ܣܠܡܝ ... ܐܠܣܠܡ ... ܚܩܣܡܝ ... (!) ... ܡܣܠܡܣܝ ܡܚܬܪܒ
ܐܠܣܠܡ

but Cod. B always has the forms written together.

45 § 64 n. 3   The cited passage ܚܚܒ ܘܐ ܡܣܚܡ is a quotation from 1 Thess
4:10: ܚܠܐ ܐܠܐ. The underlying Greek, however, has παρακαλοῦμεν 'we
beseech'.

46 § 64   ܡܚܟܒܡ Sachau, *Berlin*, p. 192b (Narses) 'I am forsaken' (fem.).

47 § 67   ܗܝ = *hi* is also to be read in Balai, *Dichtung*, 3.7, where the editor
wrongly changes ܠܡܣܐܘܗܕ to ... ܠܕܗܘ.

49 § 71   And even once after *ān* belonging to the root in ܛܢܝܢܐܝܬ 'zealously',
Jacob of Sarug, *Homiliae selectae*, 2: 363.6. Cf. Brockelmann, *GGA* 1909:
586.

49 § 71   Yet Apost. apocr. 315.7 up has ܛܢܝܢܐܝܬ, perhaps a mistake of the editor, W. Wright.

49 § 71   Also ܡܬܦܘܠܐ 'rebellious', Prov 7:11; cited in *Didascalia apostolorum*
Syriacae, ed. P. de Lagarde (repr. Göttingen, 1911), p. 6.1. On the emph. st.
fem. sg. cf. § 107.

51 § 75   In the abs. st. also ܚܠܒ ܕܠܐ 'without hindrance', Mingana, *Mšiḥa-*
Zkha, pp. 48.9 and 53 ult.—Read "But in the **true** adjectives . . .".

51 § 74 n. 3   By all appearances, ܚܣܘܡܐ 'villages' is originally also *plurale tan-*
tum.—Here also belongs the plural ܝܪܩܘܢܐ 'greens, vegetables' (for ܝܪܩܘܢܐ)
from the singular ܝܪܩܐ.

52 § 76 A   But ܢܒܝܘܬܐ 'prophecies' 1 Cor 13:8; 1 Tim 1:18 (corresponding
to ܢܒܝܘܬܐ *Novum Testamentum Syriacum* cura et studio J. Leusden et

C. Schaaf, 2d ed. [Leiden, 1717]), whose pronunciation Brockelmann, *GGA* 1914: 690, finds confirmed by the meter in the passage Jacob of Sarug, *Homiliae selectae*, 5: 616.18.

52 § 77 n. 3 ܟ݂ܢܛܐ is a borrowing from Akkadian *kinattu*, cf. H. Zimmern, *Akkadische Fremdwörter*, 2d ed. (Leipzig, 1917), p. 46 [and S. Kaufman, *The Akkadian Influences on Aramaic* (Assyriological Studies 19; Chicago, 1974), p. 64—RDH].

53 § 79   The singular ܡܚܠܐ (so probably better than ܡܚܠܐ) is rare, as is the plural ܡܚܠܬܐ beside the usual ܡܚܠܐ.

54 § 79 B   Namely ܨܦܪ̈ܘܬܐ 'dawns', Lagarde, *Analecta Syriaca* (London, 1858), p. 179.4 beside ܨܦܪ; ܪ̈ܡܫܐ 'evenings', Bar Bahlūl, *Lexicon Syriacum*, 1905, cf. R. Payne Smith, *Thesaurus Syriacus*, 3935. Also ܪ̈ܡܫܐ = أَطْرَاف النبات 'tips of plants', Bar Bahlūl, ibid., 1918, is surely the plural of ܪܫܐ, if it is set alongside the Mandaic plurals רישואתא or רישאואתא 'heads' (Nöldeke, *Mandäische Grammatik*, p. 167).

54 § 80   As well as the plural ܒܙܬܐ of the singular ܒܙܪܐ 'booty'.

55 § 81   Strikingly, for the singular ܟܠܬܐ 'bride', the plural ܟܠܠܐ Ov. 146.12 and Ephraem, "Testament," p. 264.6, where Codices FG have the usual ܟܠܠܬܐ. From this is formed the abstract ܟܠܠܘܬܐ 'bridehood', Chabot, *Synodicon*, p. 158.26, and *Histoire de Mar-Jabalaha, de trois autres patriarches, d'un prêtre et de deux laïques, nestoriens*, ed. Paul Bedjan (Paris & Leipzig, 1895), p. 455 n. 2. See also the addition to p. 84 below.

To the singular ܡܢܬܐ 'hair' corresponds the plural ܡܢܐ (variant in Bar Hebraeus ܡܢܬܐ), parallel to Babylonian Talmudic בינתא and its plural ביני.

55 § 82   Constr. st. ܩܘܡܐ e.g., in an Old Edessan inscription *JA* 10/7 (1906) 283ff., ܠܚܡܐ ܩܘܡܐ (= ܩܘܡܬܐ ܠܚܡܐ) [= Drijvers–Healey, *Old Syriac Inscriptions*, no. Am2 (Drijvers, *Inscriptions*, no. 45)].

55 § 83   Read ܟܘܒܚܐ according to Nöldeke, *Beiträge*, p. 116, esp. n. 5.

55 § 83   Beside ܠܘܦܐ, East Syriac ܦܘܦܐ. A third bird name belongs here, the dialectal ܙܘܦܐ = ܙܘܦܐ 'perh. kite or vulture', see Nöldeke, ibid., p. 51 n. 3.

56 § 84   The usual plural of ܕܠܦܐ 'spring' is ܕܠܦܐ, ܕܠܦܐ Gen 14:10; 26:15, 18. The plural ܕܠܦܬܐ is attested in *Legends of Eastern Saints*, ed. A. J. Wensinck (Leiden, 1911–13), 2: 26.10, 27.4 with variant ܕܠܦܐ in both places.

57 § 84   Also ܠܩܦܬ, byform ܠܩܦܬ 'tripod, hearth', feminine also Bar Hebraeus, *Ethicon*, p. 264.1; plural ܠܩܦܬܐ (§ 79 A) and ܠܩܦܬ.

58 § 84 n. 1   ܩܪܠܐ according to Nöldeke "certainly" from Latin *cracli*, vulgar form of *clatri, -orum* m. 'latticework' (the Appendix Probi, see *Archiv für lateinische Lexikographie*, ed. E. Wölfflin, 11 [1900] 329), which in turn goes back to the Doric plural κλᾷϑρα.

59 § 87   The feminine gender of ܩܢܘܡ appears to be Nestorian, cf. *The Book of the Bee by Salomon of Basra*, ed. with an English transl. by E. A. W. Budge (Oxford, 1886), p. 49 n. 16, p. 50.2 (Syriac text).

60 § 87   Also ܩܢܐ 'nest', which is frequently also attested as feminine, see Brockelmann, *Lex. Syr.*, 2d ed., 674, and R. Payne Smith, *Thesaurus Syriacus* 3650f. The word is feminine moreover in the Jewish Aramaic of Targum Onkelos as well, Deut 22:6 (*The Bible in Aramaic*, ed. A. Sperber, 1 [1959] 327), and also in Mandaic (M. Lidzbarski, *Johannesbuch der Mandäer*, part 1 [Giessen, 1905], p. 12.11, 13).

63 § 93   Also ܙܠܝܩ 'brightness, ray': ܙܠܢܝ (East Syriac); ܦܠܓ 'half': ܦܠܓ (East Syriac).

66 § 98 C   For "deaf," read "mute."

67 § 101   Also ܓܒܝܬ 'election', plural ܓܒܝܬܐ 'collection (of tribute, etc.)'.

67 § 103   Read ܐܘܪܟ 'length'.

70 § 109   Here also ܐܣܕ in ، ܐܣܕܝ ܡܣ 3 Esdras 3:8 (Lagarde, *Apocryphi*, p. 144.7) ὑπὸ τὸ προσκεφάλαιον . . . , otherwise always with suffix ܐܣܕܘܗܝ etc.

70 § 109   Some other names of bodily ailments, namely ܙܪܒ 'head cold'; ܟܐܒ, ܣܟܠ, ܣܟܠܘܬ 'unable to swallow', cf. Nöldeke, *Beiträge*, p. 32.

70 § 109   These adjectives can be multiplied (Nöldeke, ibid., p. 33 n. 2): ܩܡܦ 'flabby, feeble'; ܚܘܪ 'blind'; ܣܪܝܡ 'flat-nosed, with nose or lip cut off'; ܚܨܡ 'parti-colored'; ܦܪܛܡ 'snub-nosed'.

70 § 109   As for example ܓܪܘܬ 'shaving', ܩܪܘܬ 'amber waste', corresponding to the Arabic nominal form *fuʿālatun*, cf. Nöldeke, *Beiträge*, p. 31.

70 § 111 n. 3   Read ܡܡܘܠ 'flood'.

72 § 115   Also ܫܡܫ 'servant' (ܫܡܫ 'serve').

75 § 125   Read ܙܘܪܢ.

77 § 128   Also ܐܟܠ 'devouring'; ܣܘܦ 'end, downfall'.

78 § 129   Also ܦܪܣ 'hoofed' (ܡܦܪܣ ܘܩܪܢ Ps 69:31), from ܦܪܣܬ 'hoof'.

79 § 129   Also ܣܰܝܳܕܐ 'hunter' in "Mēmrā über die Geschichte des Klosters Bēt Qōqā am großen Zāb," Mingana, *Mšiḥa-Zkha*, Appendice, p. 191.9 from ܣܰܝܕܐ 'hunt' (< Pers. *naxčīr*); ܡܰܚܝܠܐ 'powerful' from ܡܰܚܝܠ 'power'; ܟܡܳܐܢܐ 'lying in wait' from ܟܡܐܢܐ 'ambush'.

79 § 130[b]   The suffix *-īn* of the words listed in § 130[b] ܡܰܘܦܰܢܐ 'file', ܡܰܘܓܢܐ 'turtledove', ܡܰܘܦܓܐ 'lark' according to Brockelmann, *GVG* 1: 395, could have arisen via dissimilation of the suffix *-ōn*.

80 § 135   Note the formations which are to some extent only late: ܐܠܨܰܝ 'necessary', ܘܡܨܐ 'similar', ܘܠܚܐ 'seemly', ܘܦܐܝ 'right', ܠܚܡܐ 'suitable', ܝܳܐܠܰܝ 'appropriate', ܝܳܐܠܐ ditto, whose original participial forms, for which in the case of ܘܠܐ, ܘܐܝ, ܠܚܝ the finite verb surely no longer existed, could be used more comfortably as adjectives with the ending *-āi*

82 § 135   From ܚܕܝܒ 'Adiabene' in Mingana, *Mšiḥa-Zkha*, Appendice, p. 203.18, is formed ܚܕܝܒܝܐ (four syllables), pp. 191.11, and 205.10 likewise four-syllable ܚܕܝܒܝܘ, from time to time in metrical discourse.

82 § 135   But ܘܪܝܐ Ephraem, "Testament," p. 266.8.

82 § 135   ܠܝܐ 'belonging to the monastery of Dālyātā (ܕܝܐܬܐ ܘܘ ܘܝ)', Wright, *Cambridge*, p. 467 penult.

84 § 138   Likewise ܟܠܠܘܬܐ 'bridehood', cf. the addition to p. 55 § 81 above.

85 § 140   Nöldeke sees the same kind of formation in ܢܣܝܢܝܐ 'nasienia', Bar Bāhlūl, *Lexicon Syriacum*, 1257, which is glossed with ܢܣܝܘܢܐ. Brockelmann, *GVG* 1: 52, on the other hand, explains forms like ܐܚܝܒܐ from within Semitic without relying on a foreign model.

85 § 141   Nonetheless, also ܚܢܝܟ ܡܟܝܘܦ P. Zingerle, *Chrestomathia Syriaca* (Rome, 1871), p. 194.5.

86 § 142   ܐܝܕܐ ܣܡܡ 'laying on of hands' is feminine, Bar Hebraeus, *Nomocanon*, p. 25.17, as is ܡܚܦܐ ܚܘܪܐ 'apology' Thomas of Edessa, *De Nativitate*, p. 9.14.

Finally, ܢܚܬܝܐܬܐ 'the lowest part' is also construed with the feminine of the verb in Ephraem, *Prose Refutations*, 2: 226.24.

87 § 145   The use of the plural pronominal suffixes formed with *ai* for the singular as well that is common in Babylonian Talmudic, Mandaic, and especially Modern East Aramaic (Nöldeke, *Mandäische Grammatik*, p. 174, and *Grammatik der neusyrischen Sprache* [Leipzig, 1868], p. 78), appears in ܚܙܝܟܘܢܝܘܢ (four syllables), Mingana, *Mšiḥa-Zkha*, Appendice,

p. 193.19 instead of the usual ܚܡܪ̈ܟܘܢ or ܚܡܪ̈ܝܟܘܢ. Here a colloquial form has snuck in on the author, who probably lived in the ninth
century. Thus, as in Mandaic, Talmudic, and Modern East Aramaic, at that
period, throughout the Tigris region, the masculine plural ending had likely
already been introduced before the suffixes in such forms (cf. *ZA* 30 [1915/
16] 119).

90 § 145 J   For abs. st., read emph. st.

91 § 145 L   So also ܐܣܟܘܠܐ σχολή 'school' in ܚܕ ܣܟܘܠܗ̇ ܕܝܠܗ 'in his very
own school', Barḥadbšabba ᶜArbaya, *Cause de la fondation des écoles* (pub.
by Addai Scher, *Patrologia Orientalis* 4 [1908]), p. 374.12 and ܘܪܕܐ
ܠܐܣܟܘܠܗ 'he conducted his school', ibid., 371.11; ܚܕ ܐܣܟܘܠܝܗ̇ 'his
classmates', Wright, *British Museum*, 424b.2 up. Th. Nöldeke believes he
has now dealt with all such words that take pronominal suffixes.

91 § 146   The plural ܢܙ̈ܐ is avoided in the Peshitta as well as Rev 18:24, but is
found in the Hexaplaric recension and elsewhere in late authors, cf.
Nöldeke, *Neue Beiträge*, p. 117.

92 § 146   It has a later plural ܣܠܘܬ̈ܐ Budge, *Blessed Virgin Mary*, p. 116 ult.,
cf. Nöldeke, *Neue Beiträge*, p. 151, esp. n. 5.

93 § 146   ܠܠܝܐ 'night' is nonetheless found with a suffix in Jonah 4:10 ܠܠܝܗ.

96 § 148 n. 2 end   . . . pretty late manuscripts. Bar Bahlūl, *Lexicon Syriacum*,
2020, punctuates ܙܕܩ ܗܕܟ.

96 § 149   In any case ܨܐܕܝ is the earlier form, e.g., without variants in John
21:8, *Tetraevangelium sanctum juxta simplicem Syrorum versionem*, ed.
G. H. Gwilliam (Oxford, 1901), while the New York edition and G. H.
Bernstein, *Das hl. Evangelium des Johannes* (Leipzig, 1853), have ܨܐܕܝ.
Cf. Nöldeke, *Neue Beiträge*, p. 152, esp. n. 4.

96 § 149   Abs. st. pl. ܨܕ̈ܘܬ Nöldeke, ibid., 152.

96 § 149   Note ܚܠܫ̈ܝܢ ܬܠܬܐ ܐܠܦ̈ܝܢ '6000' ܐܠܦܐ ܬܠܬܐ 'with suppression of the
Ālaf', thus probably pronounced ܬܠܬ ܠܦ̈ܝܢ, Bar Bahlūl, *Lexicon Syriacum*, 2020.

96 § 149 n. 1   Bar Hebraeus, *Nomocanon*, always has ܟܪܦܬܝܢ. ܟܪܦܬܝܢ in
Wright, *Cambridge*, 422.6 up (end of the 17th century).

97 § 151   This formation is of course already found in Palmyrene, where עשרתא
'council of ten' serves as the counterpart of Greek δεκάπρωτοι (Fr. Rosenthal, *Die Sprache der palmyrenischen Inschriften* [Leipzig, 1936], p. 82),

and also in Christian Palestinian Aramaic (Schulthess, *CPA*, p. 54), so it must be **old**.

98 § 154   Only ܐܠܘܬ, ܪܘܚܟ, ܣܒܘܐ are attested early; ܬܘܕܝܐ and ܟܚܘܡܐ not until Bar Hebraeus. ܣܘܪܘܣ '⅙' from Arabic سُدُس also in Wright, *Cambridge*, 601.11 (somewhat earlier than Bar Hebraeus). ܬܘܣܐ '⅑' Bar Hebraeus, *Nomocanon*, p. 355.1.

99 § 155 B   ܠܐܝܠܝܢ ܠܟܕܐ Ephraem, *Hymni et sermones*, 4: 175.12.

100 § 155 B   ܠܚܝܡܘ, lit. relative clause 'for him who (then still) lives' (Brockelmann, *GVG* 1: 494, 665), has an exact equivalent in Modern Arabic لِنْسَلِم 'a next year' in Ḥaḍramaut, see D. C. Phillott and R. F. Azoo, "Some Arab Folk Tales from Ḥazramaut," *Journal and Proceedings of the Asiatic Society of Bengal* NS 2 (1906) 400.

100 § 155 B   Cf. ܡܢ ܐܝܟܐ John 7:27.

100 § 155 B   Add ܟ ܬܘܒ 'again'.

100 § 155 C   Additionally, ܟ ܠܐ = אַף כִּי 'to say nothing of, let alone, much less', 1 Kgs 8:27; Ephraem, *Prose Refutations*, 2: 90.16 and XLI n. 4. ܕܠܡܐ is postposed (by analogy with ܐܝܟ?) in Mingana, *Mšiḥa-Zkha*, p. 39.11 (ܪ̈ܝܟ ܗܘܐ ܟܝܒܪܕ), and *Bar-Penkayé*, pp. 140.8, 159.19, etc.

100 § 155 C   ܟ "on very rare occasions heading a clause," e.g., Budge, *Blessed Virgin Mary*, p. 102.12f. According to F. Schulthess, *ZA* 24 (1910) 51f., ܟ doubtless owes its placement as second word in the clause to the influence of ἄρα, while clause-initial ܟ is a false translation of ἄρα. ܕܠܡܐ thus probably conforms to γέ and ܟܚܘܐ to οὖν.

102 § 156   Rare ܐܬܬܘܝܬ Kugener–Cumont, *Manichéisme*, p. 101.4.

103 § 156   e.g., ܣܣܘ ܠܟܐ in the Old Edessan column inscription, cf. Pognon, *Inscriptions sémitiques*, no. 118, p. 204 [= Drijvers–Healey, *Old Syriac Inscriptions*, no. As1 (Drijvers, *Inscriptions*, no. 27)].

103 § 157   So also ܡܚܠܒ, ܡܚܠܒܘܦ ܡܚܠܒ etc.

104 § 158 C   The [second] oldest dated Syriac inscription, or at any rate the [second] oldest one assignable to the Edessan linguistic sphere, the epitaph of Maꜥnū from the neighborhood of Serrīn from 73 A.D., has the forms ܐܬܐ (יֵאתֶא) 'comes', ܣܚܒܠ 'destroys', ܗܘܐ 'becomes', ܢܪܡܐ 'throw', ܐܠܟܣܘ 'are found', all with a clear ܘ and none with ܝ, see Pognon, *Inscriptions sémitiques*, no. 2 [= Drijvers–Healey, *Old Syriac Inscriptions*, no. Bs2 (Drijvers, *Inscriptions*, no. 2)]. But every other Old Edessan

inscription has only *n*-forms, and since they are proven by Mandaic and Babylonian Talmudic to be old and widespread, therefore this inscription probably represents a historical accommodation to the West Aramaic literary language, not a genuinely Edessan or some other sort of local form; cf. Nöldeke, *ZA* 21 (1908) 152.

104 § 158 E   This ܝ is already found in a few forms in the Codex Sinaiticus, Mark 16:4f. S., namely ܐܪܝܠܝ — ܚܝܠܝ — ܘܗܝܠܝ. Some of these forms appear well established.

105 § 159   Also ܐܠܚܡܕ Ethpeel as reflexive-passive of ܐܚܡܕ Aphel 'baptize'.

106 § 160 B   ܣܘܩܗ Ephraem, *Hymni et sermones*, 4: 219.15, is untrustworthy, cf. Nöldeke, *Wiener Zeitschrift für die Kunde des Morgenlandes* 17 (1903) 199f.

107 § 163   For § 23 F, read § 23 I.

112 § 170   ܕܪܨ is not entirely certain. ܘܕ probably means literally 'be behind (cf. Arabic دَبَرَ), push'. In Syriac ܕܪܒܠ ܢܐܚܕ, to which Hebrew יְשַׁבֵּר, Arabic يَثْبِر, and Ge‘ez subjunctive ይትባር correspond, analogy has probably been at work.

112 § 170   Imperative ܗܦܘܩܘ Išō‘yahb III Patriarcha, *Liber epistularum*, pp. 148.17, 151.5, 272.20. Also P. Bedjan, *Acta martyrum et sanctorum* (Paris, 1890–97), 3: 272.6 up and two examples in R. Payne Smith, *Thesaurus Syriacus*, 3337.

115 § 173   ܠܥܙܝܕܬ Mingana, *Bar-Penkayé*, p. 135.2, belongs here too.

116 § 174 A   Besides in Wright, *Cambridge*, more often ܐܟܚܕܗ = ܐܚܕܐ, e.g., 121.3, 186 penult.

117 § 174 B   A noteworthy imperative with apocope of the first radical is formed from ܐܚܕ 'take care' in Išō‘yahb III Patriarcha, *Liber epistularum*: singular ܚܕ pp. 110.17 and 244.11; plural ܚܕܘ p. 157.11 for ܐܚܕ etc. Influence from verbs *primae* ܝ is not to be postulated, since there imperatives of this kind are limited to ܠ and ܘ.

117 § 174 B   Namely ܐܦܓܥ 'encounter', ܦܓܘܥܠ; ܐܣܪ 'bind', ܣܘܪܗ.

125 § 177 B   Exceptionally, in verbs *primae* **L**, three **L**s may be written in a row: ܐܠܠܠ, Wright, *British Museum*, 583a.5 up.

126 § 177 G   For ܡܝܬ 'die' cf. the verbal adjective ܡܝܬܐ ܡܝܬܐ 'dead' § 118.

130 § 179 D   Add ܚܕܝ 'be joyful', Bar Hebraeus, Book of Rays, 105.25, where still more verbs of this type are listed.

132 § 181   Also ـمܠܚܣܐ(ἐξάσκησον S. *Gregorii Theologi liber carminum iambicorum, versio Syriaca antiquissima*, pars 2, ed. H. Gismondi (Beirut, 1896), p. 23.21. On the other hand, *Testamentum*, p. 104.12 has (ܐܣܚـ(and Bar Hebraeus, *Ethicon*, p. 106.10, has ܐܪܬܚـܐ (without variants).

132 § 182   ܐܬܚـܓـܡܠ Bar Bahlūl, *Lexicon Syriacum*, 924 ult.

133 § 183 (2)   Once (ܐ(as imperative Luke 16:2 S.

133 § 183 (4)   In the Codex Sinaiticus a few times as imperative ܐܠ(Matt 9:6 and ܐܠ(Luke 7:22, but mostly ܐܠ and ܐܠ.

138 § 186   Also ܢـܣܦܣܡ (Pael) 'they abused me' Apost. apocr. 112.10.

139 § 188   Also ـ(ܘܣܪܣ('that I destroy him' Apost. apocr. 302 n. c and 306 n. b. There is not much to be said about ـ(ܘܠܣܝܡ 'and we comfort him' (= ـ(ܘـܠـܣܝܡ) Jul. 26.26, since with (and ـ interference is easily possible.

140 § 188   Here perhaps ـ(ܘܣܦܪ 'they pierce him', I. Guidi, "Textes orientaux inédits du martyre de Judas Cyriaque, évêque de Jérusalem," *Revue de l'Orient chrétien* 9 (1904) 94.24 from a manuscript probably of the 6th century.

140 § 189   In the quasi-Maqāme of the supplement to the Book of the Dove (*Ktābā d-yaunā*), by analogy with ـ(ܘܣܠܠܣܡ etc. Bar Hebraeus creates the forms ـܝـ(ܘܪܠ 'may she nourish me', ـܝـ(ܘܕܠ 'may she judge me', *Ethicon*, p. 603.10, to rhyme with ـܝـܣܡܪܬܚ(!) and ـܝـܣܝـܓܬܚ(!). Properly, i.e., in earlier times, these forms scarcely belong to ـܝـ.

142 § 190 D   Bar Hebraeus also reads ـ(ܘܣـܢܣܐ('suckle him' in the scholia commentary on Exod 2:9 (*Barhebraeus' Scholia on the Old Testament*, Part 1, ed. M. Sprengling and W. Cr. Graham [Chicago, 1931], p. 100.30) explicitly ـܝـܣ ܣܠܚ 'with vowellessness of the nūn'.

141 § 190 B n. 1   Brockelmann refers to the form ـܝـܣܐ (monosyllabic) 'protect (m.) her', Jacob of Sarug, *Homiliae selectae*, 5: 641.16 to confirm the pronunciation doubted by Nöldeke ـ(ܘܣܣܘܐ 'give it', see *GGA* 1914: 690.

142 § 190 F   Cf. Ephraem, "Testament," p. 251.10 ـ(ܘܣܦܚـܠ(with the variants ـܝـ(ܘܕـܚـܠ(and ـܝـ(ܘܣܚـܣܐܠ, as well as p. 251.12 ـ(ܘܪܣܣܡ with the variant ـ(ܘܦܘܣܡ.

142 § 190 G   For (§ 84 B), read (§ 49 B).

144 § 193   Alongside the fully certain form ـܝـܪܣܦܠܚ Prov 7:15, Luke 8:20, 2 Tim 1:4, ـܝـܣܡܦܠܚ 'to blame thee' without ـ is attested in Išōᶜyahb III *Patriarcha, Liber epistularum*, p. 131.6.

146 § 194 But J. P. N. Land, *Anecdota Syriaca* (Leiden, 1862–75), 2: 26.11 ܡܚܰܐܘܽܗܝ 'they struck him'.

146 § 195 ܐܝܠܘܗܝ also in the Acts of Thomas, Sinai Codex, p. 32.11 = Apost. apocr. 315.8 ܐܝܠܘܗܝ; ܠܡܚܐܘܗܝ 'thou strikest him', Sachau, *Berlin*, facsimile VI line 6 (dated 1568 A.D.); ܢܚܐܠܘܗܝ 'we make him related', Kugener–Cumont, *Manichéisme*, p. 95.1; ܠܚܐܝܘܗܝ 'she sees him', ibid., 114.5 and ܢܡܢܐܘܗܝ 'we count him', ibid., 109.5.

147 § 196 Forms without ܘ, e.g., ܒܚܝܗ 'examine it (scil. ܚܣܡܐ)', Apost. apocr. 314.4 up, immediately adjacent to the regular ܐܒܕܗ. By analogy to the strong verb (cf. § 195 *Rem.*) are formed ܘܐܪܡܝܗ 'and throw him', which because of the meter is to be read trisyllabically, ܘܐܪܡܝܗ, Ephraem, *Hymni et sermones*, 4: 109 penult., as well as ܘܐܫܪܝܗ 'and absolve him', Jacob of Sarug, *Homiliae selectae*, 2: 252.4.

147 § 196 Also ܣܪܒܝܗ 'look at her', Jacob of Sarug, *Homiliae selectae*, 3: 864.9; cf. Brockelmann, *GGA* 1909: 586.

147 § 197 Instead of "were stubborn against him," read "embittered him."

148 § 197 Variant ܩܐܠܡܗ 'complete it (f.)' instead of ܩܐܠܡܗ, *Testamentum*, p. 98.16.

152 § 202 B E.g., ܠܩܛܠܬܐ, see generally Nöldeke, *Beiträge*, p. 49, esp. n. 2.

153 § 202 D Also ܟܠ ܟܝܢ̈ܐ (better thus than ܟܝ̈ܢܐ) 'all beings', Ephraem, *Prose Refutations*, 2: 199.5.

153 § 202 D "Along with numerals; (a) when the numeral precedes": ܚܒܪ̈ ܘܒܝ ܐ̇ܘ ܚܣ ܠ ܣܘܡ̈ 'in one rank or in one boundary', Ephraem, *Prose Refutations*, 2: 226.28f.; ܐܪܒܥ ܟܝܢ̈ (better ܟܝ̈ܢ) 'four beings', ibid., 203.1f.; ܚܕ ܟܝܢ ܐܝܬ ܡܚܡ 'they are of one nature', Ephraem, *Prose Refutations*, 1: 167.38f.; ܠܚܘܫܒܝ ܬܪ̈ܝܢ 'two inclinations', ibid., 167.41; ܬܪ̈ܝܢ ܟܝܢ̈ܐ 'two beings', ibid., 140.32; ܬܪ̈ܝܢ ܐܬܪ̈ 'two places', ibid., 72.24. Noteworthy is the effect on the following genitive in the expression ܬܪ̈ܝܢ ܐܡ̈ܗܬܐ ܘܡܕܝ̈ܢܬܐ 'two μητροπόλεις', Išōᶜyahb III Patriarcha, *Liber epistularum*, p. 75.20f.

154 § 202 E ܟܡܐ ܚܒܪ̈ܐ 'how many companions', Efr. 2: 553 D.

155 § 202 F (Emph. st.) ܘܚܛܝܬܐ (Abs. st.) ܘܠܐ ܡܪܚܡ ܥܕܠܐ 'and no sin and (no) censure', Afr. 313.17f.

155 § 202 F But also ܘܐܢ ܐܡܚܐ ܠܣܟܠܐ ܣܘܓܐܐ ܕܡܚܘ̈ܬܐ ܠܐ ܡܣܬܟܠ 'for (even) if you smite the fool with many blows, he will not understand', *Aḥikar*,

p. 44.10f.

155 § 202 H Also ܓܪܒܝ ܡܕܢܚ 'northeast', Ezek 40:23; ܓܪܒܝ ܡܥܪܒ 'northwest', Ephraem, *Prose Refutations*, 2: 214.36f.; ܐܠܗܐ ܐܚܪܢ 'another god', ibid., 59.11, 17; ܐܠܗܐ ܢܘܟܪܝ 'a strange god', ibid., 59.41 (Marcionite).

156 § 202 I And in other combinations with ܐܚܪܢ, e.g., ܦܘܠܚܢ ܐܚܪܢ Josh 22:23; ܠܓܒܪ ܐܚܪܢ Gen 29:19; ܐܢ ܕܝܢ ܡܢ ܐܬܪ ܗܘ ܐܚܪܢ ܐܬܝܐ ܗܕܐ ܚܝܠܬܐ 'but if this energy comes from another place', Ephraem, *Prose Refutations*, 1: 89.24ff. See also the addition to p. 158 below.

156 § 202 I But ܠܝܘܡܐ ܐܚܪܢܐ, John 1:35, 12:12; Acts 4:5.

156 § 202 I Also Luke 7:19.

156 § 202 I Abs. st. appears because of the influence of the predicate adjective Spic. 8.20 ܐܢ ܓܢܒ ܐܘ ܕܓܠ ܐܘ ܥܒܕ ܢܟܠܐ ܐܘ ܡܚܪܫ 'if he is a thief or a liar or a cheater (ܥܒܕ ܢܟܠܐ) or poisoner . . .'—under the influence of the Imperial Aramaic original, ܐܠܗܝܢ appears for אֱלָהִין in Dan 2:11, 47; 3:25; 5:11, also ܐܠܗܝܢ ܩܕܝܫܝܢ Dan 4:5(8), 6(9), 15(18); 5:11 and depending on it Jul. 34.11f. for אֱלָהִין קַדִּישִׁין 'holy gods'. Dan 7:25 (= Afr. 95.7 up) ܥܕ ܥܕܢ ܥܕܢܝܢ ܘܦܠܓܘܬ ܥܕܢ belongs here, which follows the Imperial Aramaic עַד־עִדָּן (וְ)עִדָּנִין וּפְלַג עִדָּן 'until time and times and half a time', also ܘܡܢ ܛܘܪܐ ܐܬܓܙܪܬ ܟܐܦܐ ܕܠܐ ܒܐܝܕܝܢ, Dan 2:45 corresponding to the original דִּי מִטּוּרָא אִתְגְּזֶרֶת אֶבֶן דִּי־לָא בִידַיִן '(as you have seen,) that a stone was torn loose from the mountain without human hands'. So also Col 2:11 ܘܒܗ ܐܬܓܙܪܬܘܢ ܓܙܘܪܬܐ ܕܠܐ ܒܐܝܕܝܢ 'and in him you were circumcised with a circumcision not by human hands'.

157 § 202 K Also ܒܗ ܥܕܢ 'at this time', Ephraem, *Hymni et sermones*, 4: 115.6.

158 § 203 Cf. also ܘܒܐܚܪܢ ܫܡܐ 'and with another name', Efr. 2: 555 A. In ibid., 555Aff. ܐܚܪܢ is more often found alone. See the first two additions to p. 156.

162 § 205 A Nöldeke here refers to the parallel formation עִקֵּשׁ שְׂפָתָיו 'one with perverted lips', Prov 19:1. H. S. Nyberg adduced the Syriac formations described by Nöldeke on pp. 94f., and one of the just-mentioned similar Hebrew constructions on p. 103, of his article "Zur Entstehung der Bahuvrīhikomposita," *Strena philologica Upsaliensis: Festskrift tillägnäd Per Persson* (Uppsala, 1922) and works out their originally clausal character in a fundamental investigation.

164 § 206 Also ܡܒܙܚ̈ܢܝ ܒܫܡܫܘܢ ‘those who mocked Samson’, Ephraem, *Prose Refutations*, 1: 172.24f.

165 § 207 Here belongs ܩ̈ܝܡܝܢ ܫܦܝܪ ܒܪܝܫ ܒܢ̈ܝܗܘܢ ܘܒ̈ܬܝܗܘܢ ‘présidant convenablement à la tête de leurs fils et de leurs maisons (sic)’, Chabot, *Synodicon*, p. 57.15, which renders 1 Tim 3:12 τέκνων καλῶς προϊστάμενοι καὶ τῶν ἰδίων οἴκων.

167 § 209 B A further example for the construal of ܦܢܐ with ܕ: Ephraem, *Hymni et sermones*, 4: 251.16.

167 § 209 B Also found in Isaac II 56 verse 11 ܕܦܓܪܗ ܡܦܢܐ ܣܟܠܐ ‘of his own body the fool takes care’. In Thomas of Edessa, *De Nativitate*, we read ܘܠܐ ܐܬܦܢܘ ܠܗܘܢ ܕܦܘܩܕܢܐ ܕܡܠܦܢܘܬܗܘܢ ‘and take no care for that which their instruction requires’, p. 31.12, and ܟܕ ܠܐ ܐܬܦܢܝܬ ܠܗ ܕܘܠܬܐ ‘while you did not concern yourself with duty’, p. 34.13.—Brockelmann, *Syrische Grammatik*, § 192 p. 106, explains the construal of ܟܪܝ ‘sorrow’ with ܕ as the old demonstrative ܕ governing only the genitive, similar constructions being ܕܓܘܐ ‘in common’, ܕܒܝܬ ܡܪܩܝܘܢ ‘the followers of Marcion’.

171 § 217 Instead of “on rare occasions,” read “on some occasions.” Further examples of this usage: ܕܟܠ ܟܠܗ ܫܦܝܪܬܐ ܗܘܝܬܘܢ ܪܗܛܝܢ ‘that you always pursue the good’, Addai 46.4f.; ܟܠܟܠ ܒܐܪܥܐ ܚܪܐ ܗܘܐ ‘ever looked on earth’, Apost. apocr. 176.6 and 178.5 (Acts of Thomas).

171 § 217 Cf. also ܕܢܩܪܘܢ ܟܠ ܠܡܫܬܘܬܐ ܚܘܒܗ ‘that they all called to the banquet of his love’, Narsai in Sachau, *Berlin*, p. 194b.2.

176 § 223 The citation ܒܩܢܘܡܗ ܐܝܬ ܗܘܐ Ov. 281.23 is wrong. Replace it with ܒܩܢܘܡܗ ἐν ἑαυτῷ ‘in himself’, John 5:26 (absent from S.).

176 § 223 Cf. the parallels ܢܦܫܗ and ܩܢܘܡܗ in: ܐܝܟܢܐ ܕܐܦ ܠܐ ܕܐܒܐ (ܐܝܬ ܣܩܘܒܠܐ) ܒܢܦܫܗ ܐܦ ܠܐ ܐܪܝܐ ܒܩܢܘܡܗ ‘thus, just as the wolf is not (an opponent) himself, the lion too is not one himself’, Ov. 60.16.

177 § 224* Here probably also belongs ܡܪܝ ܕܟܠܒ̈ܘܗܝ ‘Mâr(ī) with the dogs’, an Aramaic deity known from Jacob of Sarug’s Mēmrā on the destruction of idols (ed. P. Martin, *ZDMG* 29 [1876] 107–47), p. 110.55 = Jacob of Sarug, *Homiliae selectae*, 3: 795–823, p. 798.1. On the form, cf. especially Nöldeke, *ZDMG* 42 (1888) 473, and B. Vandenhoff, “Die Götterliste des Mar Jakob von Sarug in seiner Homilie über den Fall der Götzenbilder,” *Oriens Christianus* NS 5 (1915) 234–62, p. 242.—On the syntax of the examples gathered in § 224*, see Brockelmann, *GVG* 2: 40.

178 § 225 We even find ܐܬܠܝ ܠܝ ܕܠܝ ܐܢܐ ܬܠܝܬܝܐ 'let **me**, the Tertia, come', Apost. apocr. 319.13.

180 § 227 A further example: ܐܢܘܢ ܪ̈ܡܐ (probably to be read ܗ̇ܢܘܢ) ܗ̣ܢܘܢ ܐܘܕܥܘ ܘܐܠܦܘ ܐܢܘܢ ܠܡܟܝ̈ܟܐ 'those high ones informed and instructed the low ones', Anc. doc. 68.6 (Barsamyā).

181 § 231 ܕܡ̈ܢܐ ܬܘܟ̈ܠܐ ܘܣܘܚ̈ܦܢܐ ܘܪ̈ܕܘܦܝܐ ܘܐܘܠ̈ܨܢܐ ܗܘܘ ܒܥܕܬܐ 'what sort of injuries and damages and persecutions and calamities the church has suffered', Chabot, *Synodicon*, p. 52.21. Likewise ܡ̇ܢ ܚܝܠܐ 'what sort of power', *Aḥiḳar*, p. 50.12.

183 § 235 Cf. also ܐܠܐ ܕܒܟܠܙܒܢ ܕܛܒ ܗܘܘ ܥܒܕܝܢ 'unless at every moment you do what is good', Spic. 1.9; ܩܘܕܡܝ ܕܣܡܝܟܝܢ 'before those who recline at table', Balai, *Dichtung*, 17.25 (no. XXXIV, strophe 3).

183 § 236 ܡ̇ܢ ܕ already in the Old Syriac inscription from the year 73 A.D., see Pognon, *Inscriptions sémitiques*, no. 2, p. 17 [= Drijvers–Healey, *Old Syriac Inscriptions*, no. Bs2 (Drijvers, *Inscriptions*, no. 2)]. Inscription no. 44, p. 80, has ܘܡܢ ܕܪܥܠ [= Drijvers–Healey, *Old Syriac Inscriptions*, no. As20 (Drijvers, *Inscriptions*, no. 35 A)]. E. Sachau, "Edessenische Inschriften," *ZDMG* 36 (1882) 142–67, no. 8, has the incorrect reading ܘܡܢ ܪܥܠ 'but who trembles'.

183 § 236 The cumbersome piling up of personal pronouns and demonstratives is especially beloved among the Syrians, cf. the cumbersome German expressions 'derjenige, welcher', etc., where 'wer' would often suffice.

187 § 242 This expression is occasionally found in Hebrew, e.g., אֶחָד בְּאֶחָד יִגַּשׁוּ Job 41:8 'they approach one to the other', somewhat differently in Isa 27:12 וְאַתֶּם תְּלֻקְּטוּ לְאַחַד אֶחָד בְּנֵי יִשְׂרָאֵל 'and you will be gathered one by one, O people of Israel'. Job 41:9, on the other hand, has אִישׁ־בְּאָחִיהוּ יְדֻבָּקוּ 'they are joined one to another'. In Arabic this formation appears to occur only in negative clauses in the meaning 'none to the others'; cf. Abū ᶜUbaid al-Bakrī, *Kitāb Simṭ al-laᵓāliᵓ fī šarḥ al-Amālī*, ed. ᶜAbdalᶜazīz al-Maimanī (Cairo, 1354/1935–36), p. 800.10 *wa-kunnā ka-ġuṣnai bānatin laisa wāḥidun * yazūlu ᶜalā l-ḥālāti ᶜan raᵓyi wāḥidin* 'and we were like the two branches of a bān-tree, in that neither diverged from the opinion of the other in the vicissitudes (of time)'. Also H. Reckendorf, *Die syntaktischen Verhältnisse des Arabischen* (Leiden, 1898), p. 399, marks the use of *aḥadun* to express the reciprocal relationship as rare.

188 § 242 Cf. also ܘܐܝܟ ܗܕܡ̈ܐ ܕܓܘܫܡܐ ܕܐܝܬܝܗܘܢ ܒܢ̈ܝ ܟܝܢܐ ܕܚ̈ܕܕܐ ܘܕܠܗ 'and as the members of the body are of the same nature as each other and as the body itself', A. L. Frothingham, *Stephen Bar Sudaili, the Syrian Mystic and the Book of Hierotheos* (Leiden, 1886), p. 30.17f.

190 § 243 In *GGA* 1909: 589, Brockelmann adds the following examples: ܐܦ ܠܟܠܗ ܫܒܘܥܐ ܕܠܐ ܣܝܒܪܬܐ ܢܥܒܪ ܗܘܐ 'he even passed the entire week without nourishment', Mart. 2: 170.6; ܗܟܢ ܢܦܩܘܗܝ. ܠܝܘܡܐ ܟܠܗ 'so let the whole day pass', Jacob of Sarug, *Homiliae selectae*, 4: 844.15; ܘܗܟܢ ܢܦܩܘܗܝ. 'and let it (scil. the day ܠܝܘܡܐ) pass so', ibid., 4: 846.13.

191 § 246 Also ܡܛܠ ܡܪܝ ܕܫܡܥܬ 'because I have heard, O Lord', *JAOS* 20 (1899) p. 263.17 and also the first addition to p. 293 below.

192 § 247 Instead of Philoxenus, Epistola (Guidi) fol. 29*a*, 2 mid., read fol. 28b,2,14.

193 § 247 The following very striking examples may be added: ܠܥܡܐ ܕܐܬܢܟܬ ܠܚܘ̈ܘܬܐ 'the population that was bitten by snakes', Balai, *Dichtung*, 37.13 (no. IV strophe 3); ܬܪ̈ܬܝܢ ܐܝܬ ܕܡܬܐܟ̈ܠܢ ܠܐܢܫ 'there are two things that serve as food for a person' correctly in F. Schulthess, *Kalila und Dimna, syrisch und deutsch* (Berlin, 1911), 1: 57.1 and 2: 194 n. 215, see also Nöldeke, *ZDMG* 65 (1911) 586; ܢܬܠܛ ܠܡܪܠܗܐ 'may he be cursed by ܡܪܠܗܐ'[5] in the Old Syriac inscription Pognon, *Inscriptions sémitiques*, p. 80 [= Drijvers–Healey, *Old Syriac Inscriptions*, no. As20 (Drijvers, *Inscriptions*, no. 35 A)].

193 § 248 A usage of the preposition ܒ that Nöldeke found nowhere else, even for the verb ܐܟܠ, appears in Ephraem, *Hymni et sermones*, 4: 17.27 ܦܝܢܟܐ . . . ܕܒܗ ܠܚܡ ܗܘܐ 'a salver **from** which he ate', ibid., 43.14 with the variant ܐܟܠ for ܠܚܡ.

193 § 248 In Arabic this would be a *tamyīz*-accusative (accusative of specification) or more likely a partitive *min*.

195 § 249 D On the combination ܡܢ ܟܠ, cf. the addition to p. 197 below.

195 § 249 E Multiplication of ܡܢ in comparative expressions is avoided in the following examples, which are extracted from the Syriac translation of Plutarch's tract *De capienda ex inimicis utilitate*: ܕܢܚܘܬ ܐܢܫ ܡܐ ܕܢܚܬ ܡܢ

5. On this deity, cf. above p. 93 s.v. ܡܪܐ and J. B. Segal, "Pagan Syriac Monuments in the Vilayet of Urfa," *Anatolian Studies* 3 (1953) 97–119, pp. 115f.

ܒܒܥܠܕܒ̈ܒܘܗܝ ܛܠܝ ܡܢ ܪ̈ܚܡܘܗܝ 'that anyone who transgresses shames himself more before his enemies than before his friends', E. Nestle, *A Tract of Plutarch . . . The Syriac Version* (Studia Sinaitica 4; London, 1894), p. 6.10f.—ܗܟܢܐ ܘܡܦܘܩܢ̈ܐ ܓܠܝ̈ܐ ܘܡܦܘܩܢܐ ܕܡܛܫܝ̈ܢ ܒܒܥܠܕܒ̈ܒܐ ܠܗܘܢ ܦܫܝܩ ܠܡܬܝܕܥܘ ܝܬܝܪ ܡܢ ܪ̈ܚܡܐ ܘܒ̈ܢܝ ܒܝܬܐ 'so it is easier to come to know not only the public errors but also the clandestine errors of the enemies than of the friends and intimates', ibid., 12.13ff.—In both cases the doubled ܡܢ (properly ܡܢ ܕܡܢ) is avoided.

196 § 250 n. 1 After Matt 11:24 P. C. S., insert Matt 19:24 P. C. S.

197 § 250 Note also ܡܢ ܥܠ ܐ̈ܦܝ ܐܪܥܐ 'out from the surface of the earth' in Mingana, *Mšiḥa-Zkha*, p. 32.8f.

198 § 252 ܬܚܝܬ ܫܡܝܐ 'what is under heaven' is similarly used as a substantive in the construction ܒܟܠܗ ܬܚܝܬ ܫܡܝܐ 'in the entire (realm) under heaven' = 'on the whole earth', Chabot, *Synodicon*, pp. 167.28, 192.21 (which has ܒܟܠܗ̇).

202 § 254 The fem. is also retained in ܕܢܠܡܐ . . . ܢܬܐܪ̈ܝ ܒܟܠܗܘܢ ܠܡܦܠܓܗ̇ 'it might befall him to have to divide' Išōᶜyahb III Patriarcha, *Liber epistularum*, p. 31.19.

204 § 258 The passage is also attested in Carl Hunnius, "Das syrische Alexanderlied hrsg. und übers.," *ZDMG* 60 (1906) 188, verse 144, where ܣܚܪܬܗ should be read. Cf. ܠܐ ܐܝܬ ܦܘܪܣܐ ܐܠܐ ܒܟܠܗ̇ ܣܚܪܬ ܐܥܘܠ 'I must enter and see the entire region', ibid., 190, verse 171.

204 § 259 This example belongs here as well: ܡܢ ܕܝܢ ܢܣܡܐ ܡܢ ܥܝ̈ܢܝ ܚܕܐ. ܘܥܝ̈ܢܝܟܝ ܕܝܢ ܕܠܟܝ ܢܚܪ̈ܝ ܒܝ ܐܝܟ ܥܝܕܗܝܢ. ܡܢ ܕܝܢ ܢܦܣܘܩ ܕܪܥܝ ܕܝܡܝܢܐ. ܘܐܓܦܟܝ ܕܝܢ ܕܣܡܠܐ ܒܓܦܠܝ. 'O that someone might blind one of my eyes and thine eyes look on me as is their wont. O that someone might cut off my right arm that I might embrace thee with my left arm', Apost. apocr. 286.12ff.—Desiderative clauses in the form of a question are occasionally also found in Modern Arabic dialects, e.g., in the Algerian Arabic dialect of Tlemcen . . . مارًا لي بنتك تطيح في 'who informed me (= مَنْ أَرَى) your daughter succeeded at . . .' = 'O that your daughter may succeed at . . .' in M. Gaudefroy-Demombynes and ᶜAbd El ᶜAziz Zenagui, "Récit en dialecte tlemcénien," *JA* **10**/4 (1904) 45–116, p. 58.5. Another example from Tlemcen and a general discussion are found in Brockelmann, *GVG* 2: 33.

205 § 259 Just as in Arabic, however, the bare perfect appears usable in a precative sense: ܫܡܥܟ (var. ܢܫܡܥܟ) ܐܠܗܗ ܕܐܒܪܗܡ 'may the God of Abraham hear you!' Ephraem, "Testament," p. 263.17, also ܫܡܥܘܢ ܫܡܥܟ ܐܠܗܐ (var. ܢܫܡܥܟ) 'Simon, may God hear you!' ibid., 264.4.

205 § 261 Instead of Chron. Ed. (ed. Hallier 147, 16), read . . . 146, 16.

206 § 261 To the examples given we may add: . . . ܦܐܫ ܠܢ . . . ܕܢܦܠܚܝܘܗܝ ܘܗܘܝ̈ ܡܢܟܪ̈ܝܢ ܡܢܢ ܟܠܗܘܢ ܗܠܝܢ ܦܓܪ̈ܢܝܬܐ 'it becomes us . . . that we serve him . . . and (that) all these fleshly (lusts) are foreign to us', Apost. apocr. 296.14ff.

207 § 265 After "in" insert: ܘܐܢ ܢܒܨܐ ܢܬܢܟܐ 'and if we investigate, we will be harmed'. The passage from Ov. 175.3 cited on p. 307.8–6 up can also serve as an example here: . . . ܐܢ ܕܝܢ ܠܐ ܬܬܦܫܩܘܢ.

213 § 272 Further examples of the use of the participle in place of the imperfect in dependent clauses: ܦܩܘܕ ܕܙܩܦܝܢ ܠܝ 'order them to crucify me', *Aḥiḳar*, p. 56.17 (according to Nöldeke's comment, so also in the Berlin Codex)—ܕܒܢ̈ܝܢܫܐ ܠܬܡܢ ܠܐ ܐܙܠܝܢ ܘܠܐ ܡܚܕܐ ܐܟܠܝܢ ܠܗܘܢ ܚܘ̈ܘܬܐ 'so that the people not go in there, lest the serpents devour them forthwith', Pseudo-Callisthenes, p. 266.3.

214 § 272 Cf. also ܓܪܘܪ ܢܐܙܠ 'drag (him) out, so that he go', Apost. apocr. 140.2; ܓܪܘܪܗ ܢܐܙܠ 'drag (him) out, so that he go', ibid., 306.20. The construction is found elsewhere in this text as well.

214 § 272 Instead of Statuti della Scuola di Nisibi 13.8, read 14.8.

214 § 272 . . . with "can" and "begin": according to information from Siegmund Fraenkel, also with "know, understand," e.g., ܕܝܕܥ ܦܠܓ 'that he understands to divide', Moes. 1: 98.2.

216 § 276 Here also belongs ܡܢܐ ܡܟܝܠ ܥܒܕܝܢ 'so what should we do?' Apost. apocr. 116.16.

221 § 282 Cf. as well ܒܥܠܝ ܛܒܬܗ (= ܒܥ̈ܠܝ ܛܒ̈ܬܗ) 'his benefactors' in the old inscription no. 5 in Pognon, *Inscriptions sémitiques*, p. 28 [= Drijvers–Healey, *Old Syriac Inscriptions*, no. As47 (Drijvers, *Inscriptions*, no. 5)]—ܡܝ̈ܬܝܢ ܡܘܬܐ ܒܝܫܐ 'those who should suffer a bad death' Sachau, *Berlin*, p. 108b.31—ܐܝܟܢܐ ܓܝܪ ܕܠܘ ܦܩܘܕ ܟܠ ܗܘ ܐܢ ܡܬܦܩܕ ܗܟܢܐ ܠܘ ܡܣܝܟ ܟܠ ܗܘ ܐܢ ܡܣܬܝܟ 'for as He is not the commander of all if He is commanded, so is He not the limiter of all if He has limits', Ephraem, *Prose Refutations*, 1: 133.38–43.

222 § 282 n. 1 Cf. the first addition to § 283.

222 § 283 Note 1 on p. 222 needs to be qualified to the extent that abstracts in ܘܬܐ are generally not formed from the active participles of the various verb classes. However, such derivations do occur corresponding to the use of these participles in the construct state in a few cases, e.g., ܡܡܠܠܘܬ ܐܠܗܘܬܐ θεολογία, ܡܟܬܒܘܬ ܫܡܗܐ ὀνοματογραφία 3 Esdras 6:11 (Lagarde, *Apocryphi*, p. 151.30), ܡܟܬܒܘܬ ܙܒܢܐ χρονογραφία (?) beside ܡܟܬܒܢܘܬ ܙܒܢܐ and so probably a few other items such as ܡܩܕܡܘܬ ܝܕܥܬܐ πρόγνωσις and other combinations with ܡܩܕܡܘܬ.

222 § 283 ܡܣܝܟ ܟܠ 'limiter of all' has already been cited in context in the addition to p. 221 § 282.

222 § 283 Also ܐܢܬܝܢ ܡܘܣܣ ܘܐܣܬܪܬܐ ܕܝܬܒܬܝܢ ܥܠ ܣܦ ܝܡܐ ܘܥܡܝܪܢ ܒܐܘܠܘܡܦܘܣ 'you Muses (Μοῦσαι) and Astartes who sit on the shore of the sea and dwell in Olympus', Bar Bahlūl, *Lexicon Syriacum*, 168.25ff. and 1037.24ff., cited from the ܟܬܒܐ ܕܚܢܦܐ.

223 § 283 ܡܣܦܪܐ 'razor' has fully become a noun, as seen from its plural, at least in Nestorian, ܡܣܦܪ̈ܝܢ.

224 § 286 Instead of ܡܥܪܒܐ, read ܡܥܪܒܐ in the Aphel.

225 § 286 Striking is ܡܛܠ ܒܘܚܢܐ ܕܨܒܘ̈ܬܐ ܥܕܬܢܝ̈ܬܐ ܘܡܛܠ ܡܕܢ ... ܕܝܢܐ 'because of the examination of the ecclesiastical concerns and in order to judge . . .' , Chabot, *Synodicon*, p. 104.25 (554 A.D.).

226 § 286 Cf. Hebrew אֵין לַעֲמוֹד 'none can stand' Ezra 9:15.

226 § 286 So also ܠܡܬܕܡܪܘ ܕܝܢ ܒܗܕܐ ܪܘܚܐ 'but one must wonder at this Wind', Ephraem, *Prose Refutations*, 1: 57.4.

226 § 287 n. 1 Eberhard Nestle, *Syrische Grammatik*, 2d ed. (Berlin, 1888), § 49d, counts exactly 15 occurrences of ܠܘ in the Syriac Old Testament, or 14, since the suffixed instance in Song 1:7 should not count.

230 § 288 In Hebrew, כָּל־מְאוּמָה, for example, is treated as definite in Gen 39:23, אֵין שַׂר בֵּית־הַסֹּהַר רֹאֶה אֶת־כָּל־מְאוּמָה בְּיָדוֹ 'the keeper of the prison paid no heed to anything that was in his (Joseph's) care'. Here the Urmia Old Testament has ܠܐ ܚܙܐ ܗܘܐ ܡܕܡ ܒܐܝܕܗ . . . . Other languages too consider and construe such examples as definite like Hebrew, where כֹּל is inherently definite, see C. Brockelmann, *Hebräische Syntax* (Neukirchen, 1956) § 96, p. 88. Nöldeke gives Mandaic examples in the *Mandäische*

Grammatik, p. 392, along with additional Syriac examples.

231 § 228 n. 1 Cf. ܘܐܝܕܥܬܘܢ ܒܝܫܘܥ ܐܢܫ ܗܘ ܕܙܩܦܘܗܝ . . . '. . . and you knew a certain Jesus, whom they crucified', "Acta Mar Ḳardaghi . . . Syriace . . . cum versione Latina," ed. J. B. Abbeloos, *Analecta Bollandiana* 9 (1890) 5–106, p. 74.10f. = *Die Geschichte des Mâr ᶜAbhdîšôᶜ und seines Jüngers Mâr Qardagh*, ed. and trans. H. Feige (Kiel, 1890), pp. 63.16–64.1.

236 § 296 After "Spic. 2, 13," insert: Luke 8:50 C. has ܒܠܚܘܕ ܗܝܡܢܘ ܗܝܡܢ and so does Aphr. 21.1. S. and P. here only have ܒܠܚܘܕ ܗܝܡܢ. Mark 5:36 P. likewise has ܒܠܚܘܕ ܗܝܡܢ, where C. and S. are missing. On the other hand, the Acts of Thomas, Apost. apocr. 239.2, has ܐܠܐ ܒܠܚܘܕ ܗܝܡܢܘ ܗܝܡܢ ܒܝܫܘܥ 'but believe only in Jesus', and the Acts of Thomas, Sinai Codex, p. 28b.7f., leaves out ܐܠܐ and has a minor transposition: ܗܝܡܢܘ ܗܝܡܢ ܒܠܚܘܕ ܒܝܫܘܥ.

237 § 298 Cf. also ܘܡܢ ܢܕܡܟ ܗܫܐ 'who then will sleep?' Ephraem, *Hymni et sermones*, 4: 733.4f. and nine more times as a refrain.

238 § 298 Instead of ܐܬܢܝܚܘ Mart. 1, 197 mid., read ܐܬܢܝܚܘ Mart. 1, 197, 20.

238 § 298 So also in ܐܢ ܬܡܚܐ ܠܣܟܠܐ ܫܘܛܝܢ ܣܓܝܐܝܢ ܠܐ ܢܪܓܫ 'for even if you treat the fool to many beatings, he will not understand', *Aḥiḳar*, p. 44.10f. Cf. מֵהַכּוֹת כְּסִיל מֵאָה 'than a hundred blows into a fool', Prov 17:10. ܘܡܚܝܗܝ ܚܕ ܡܚܘܐ ܘܬܒ ܠܐ ܬܢܝܗ 'and he killed him with a single swordthrust and did not repeat it (= without repeating it)', Theophile of Edessa, *Acta Sancti*, p. 24.8, 11.

240 § 300 The imperative of ܗܘܐ before participle is attested in Apost. apocr. 120.14: ܗܘܝ ܡܚܐ ܠܗ ܥܠ ܦܘܡܗ 'strike him on his mouth'.

240 § 302 Instead of Ephr. Nis. p. 62 v. 88, read v. 87.

243 § 304 Cf. also ܐܝܬ ܗܘܐ ܕܝܢ ܡܢܗܘܢ ܕܐܡܪܝܢ ܗܘܘ ܠܗ 'but there were some among them who said to him', F. C. Burkitt, *Euphemia and the Goth, with the Acts of Martyrdom of the Confessors of Edessa* (London, 1913), pp. 30.22f. and 30.24–31.1.

244 § 305 As in ܕܗܟܢܐ ܬܗܘܘܢ ܐܝܬܝܟܘܢ 'that you are thus', Išōᶜyahb III Patriarcha, *Liber epistularum*, p. 56.28, but ܐܦ ܢܗܘܐ ܐܝܬ ܠܢ ܠ 'it will also be for us to . . .', ibid., p. 188.27 and ܢܗܘܐ ܐܝܬ 'will be', ibid., 230.16.

244 § 307 Cf. also ܗܘ ܕܠܫܘܝܘܬ ܡܘܕܝܢܘܬܐ ܕܥܡ ܐܒܘܗܝ ܒܩܢܘܡܐ ܡܫܡܠܝܐ ܐܝܬ ܠܗ 'qui ὁμολογίαν cum Patre suo in hypostasi perfecta

. . . possidet' (Duval), Išō^cyahb III Patriarcha, *Liber epistularum*, p. 125.3.

245 § 308 Also ܕܐܢܬܘܢ ܫܦܝܪ ܬܗܘܘܢ ܘܫܦܝܪ ܬܡܠܠܘܢ 'ut bene agatis et bene loquamini' (Duval), Išō^cyahb III Patriarcha, *Liber epistularum*, p. 34.9 from a manuscript perhaps of the end of the eighth century and so even ܐܠܝܢ ܕܐܚܪܢܐܝܬ ܐܝܬܘܢ 'those who are otherwise', ibid., p. 237.6.

247 § 312 A Also ܡܢܐ ܝܬܒܝܢ ܐܢܬܘܢ ܘܢܛܪܝܢ ܠܝ 'why are you sitting there and watching me?' Apost. apocr. 331.13. Here also belong the example clauses in Nöldeke, *Mandäische Grammatik*, p. 381 n. 2, and the passage Acts 1:11 ܡܢܐ ܩܝܡܝܢ ܐܢܬܘܢ ܘܚܝܪܝܢ ܒܫܡܝܐ 'why do you stand looking into heaven?'

253 § 318 Thus the orthography of the British Museum Syriac manuscript Add. 14484 fol. 91 r° col. a may be correct with its ܘܐܢܫ ܡܢ ܢܘܟܪܝܐ ܠܐ ܝܕܥܗ 'and none of the strangers knew (it)'. Mart. 2: 304.23, on the other hand, has ܘܐܢܫ ܡܢ ܩܫܝܫܐ ܠܐ . . . ܝܕܥ ܗܘܐ. Cf. § 319 and the additions to p. 254.

254 § 319 Philipp 4:15 reads: ܐܦܠܐ ܚܕܐ ܡܢ ܥܕܬܐ ܐܫܬܘܬܦܬ ܠܝ ܒܚܘܫܒܢ ܡܘܗܒܬܐ ܘܡܣܒܬܐ ܐܠܐ οὐδεμία μοι ἐκκλησία ἐκοινώνησεν εἰς λόγον δόσεως καὶ λήμψεως 'no church entered into partnership with me in the reckoning of giving and receiving'.

254 § 319 Philox. 543.26 reads: . . . ܘܠܐ ܡܬܠܩܦ ܥܠ ܠܒܗ ܚܕܐ ܡܢ ܗܠܝܢ '. . . and not one of them comes into his mind', *The Discourses of Philoxenus Bishop of Mabbôgh,* A.D. *485–519*, ed. with an English trans. E. A. W. Budge (London, [1893] 1894), 1: 543.26f.—Wording of Apoc. Baruch 83 (= Epistle of Baruch to the tribes of Israel living in exile): ܡܟܝܠ ܗܟܝܢ ܠܐ ܬܥܘܩ ܥܠ ܠܒܟܘܢ ܚܕܐ ܡܢ ܗܠܝܢ ܕܡܬܩܦܢ 'so let not one of these (now) occurring things affect your spirit' (= Lagarde, *Apocryphi*, p. 90.20; cf. E. Kautzsch, *Die Apokryphen und Pseudepigraphen des Alten Testaments* 2: 444).

254 § 319 To be added to these two examples: ܗܘ ܕܠܗ ܘܠܐ ܚܕ ܡܢ ܡܠܟܐ ܕܦܠܛ ܡܢ ܕܝܢܗ 'he whose judgment cannot escape from a single one of the kings', Theophile of Edessa, *Acta Sancti*, p. 21.16f.—Contrary to its frequency in Syriac, Nöldeke, *Zur Grammatik des classischen Arabisch*, p. 83.3 and n. 1, characterizes the parallel construction in Sura 69:47 as "unusual." In n. 1 of that citation, the reference to Nöldeke's *Syrische Grammatik* should be corrected from p. 223 to p. 243 [p. 254 of the English edition].

256 § 321 Read: "It is the same with ܒܝܬ ܢܦܫܗ, which is less common than ܒܝܬ ܦܓܪܗ."

265 § 328 D Also ܠܐ ܚܫ ܠܗ ܚܫܐ ܥܠܝ ܠܝ ܘܐܦܠܐ ܡܚܫܒ ܚܫܒܢܝ 'neither did he feel sorry for me nor did he think of me (otherwise)' *Aḥiḳar*, p. 54.12.

265 § 328 E Read ܡܬܦܪܓܝܢ (Ethpaal).

266 § 328 F ܕܠܐ 'without' in ܕܠܐ ܐܢܐ 'without me' Apost. apocr. 268.13 and in ܕܠܐ ܐܢܬ 'without you', ibid., 258.10. The construction really belongs under "Relative Clauses."

270 § 332 Another example of elliptical expression: ܒܢܐ ܠܢ ܥܠܡܐ ܘܐܢܚܢ ܒܝܬܐ 'he built the world for us and we (built for him) a house', Balai (Ov.) 254.15.

270 § 333 The sentence already cited above p. 247 § 312 A end reads in full ܐܡܪ ܠܗܘܢ ܕܬܘܒ ܡܢ ܡܠܟܘܬܐ ܠܐ ܬܦܩܘܢ ܐܠܐ ܘܐܙܠܘ ܕܠܐ ܩܢܝܢ. ܘܡܢܝ ܡܕܡ ܠܐ ܬܣܒܘܢ ܐܠܐ ܘܐܙܠܘ 'he (Emperor Justinus) said to them: "Carry nothing more out of the kingdom and go away without any possessions, and from me you receive nothing, and depart"', John Eph. 399.13ff.

271 § 334 A For *ZDMG* 30, read *ZDMG* 29.

271 § 334 A Instead of ܥܡܝܐ, read ܥܦܝܐ.

272 § 334 A Aphr. 415.12ff. reads ܘܪܘܚܐ ܕܐܪܝܟܘܬܐ ܕܐܬܝܗܒܬ ܠܝܫܘܥ ܒܪ ܢܘܢ. ܟܕ ܣܡ ܡܘܫܐ ܐܝܕܗ ܥܠܘܗܝ. ܘܡܢܗ ܘܣܦܘ ܡܢ ܩܕܡܘܗܝ ܥܡܡܐ ܕܪܕܦܘܗܝ 'and the spirit of insight that was given to Joshua son of Nun when Moses laid his hand upon him, and **as a result** the peoples who persecuted him met their end and perished'.

272 § 334 B Cf. also ܘܒܡܐܡܪܗ (ܕܡܠܟܐ) ܥܠܝܬ ܩܕܡܘܗܝ 'and upon his (the king's) order I went before him', *Aḥiḳar*, pp. 60.12, 62.4.

272 § 335 The example ܡܘܣܦܝܢ ܘܢܣܒܝܢ 'they take in addition' belongs, according to the context, after "ܠܐ ܬܣܒܘܢ ܘܬܦܩܘܢ . . ." in the next line.

273 § 335 Also ܡܐ ܕܐܫܪܝ ܣܗܪܐ ܡܚܣܪܘ 'when the moon had begun to wane', Ov. 152.26 = Ephraem, "Testament," p. 275.9f.

273 § 336 Also ܘܓܪܘܗܝ ܗܘܘ ܘܐܦܩܘܗܝ ܡܢ ܢܘܪܐ 'and pulled him out of the fire', Anc. doc. 84.17—ܘܟܢܫܘ ܗܘܘ ܘܩܒܪܘܗܝ 'and they collected (his remains or his ashes) and buried him', ibid., 84.20.

274 § 336 Also ܕܢܦܩܘ ܠܗܘܢ ܚܫܘܟܐ ܘܟܠܝܗ ܐܢܘܢ 'whom the darkness came

forth and swallowed' Ephraem, *Prose Refutations*, 1: 128.7—ܐܠܐ ܠܗܢܐ ܕܒܪܐ ܘܐܬܒܠܝܬ ܨܒܐ ܡܚܕܬܘ 'but this (world) which he had created and which had grown old, he wished to renew', Philoxenus, *Letters*, p. 164.4—ܘܗܕܐ ܨܒܐ ܐܢܐ ܕܐܦܘܩ ܘܐܚܙܝܘ 'and I will go out and see this', Pseudo-Callisthenes, p. 256.3.

275 § 337 Cf. also ܕܠܐ ܢܬܫܢܩ ܝܠܘܕܐ ܗܘ ܕܡܬܝܠܕ ܘܕܠܐ ܬܬܠܐܐ ܣܓܝ ܬܘܠܥܬܐ ܐܦ ܗܝ ܕܝܠܕܐ 'and thus the child is not in much torment, nor is the mother much exhausted', Ov. 68.24f. = Ephraem, *Prose Refutations*, 1: 17.3ff.

275 § 337 Also ܐܢ ܕܝܢ ܡܣܪܗܒ ܫܡܥܢ ܠܢ 'but if he grants us a swift hearing', Ephraem, *Hymni et sermones*, 4: 405.12f.

275 § 337 So also ܕܢܬܘܒ ܢܨܪܘܗܝ 'that he rend (his tunic) again' Ephraem, *Prose Refutations*, 1: 141.18—ܐܢܗܘ ܕܡܘܚܪ ܫܡܥܢ ܠܢ 'if he delays our hearing' Ephraem, *Hymni et sermones*, 4: 405.8f.

276 § 337 This construction even connects to ܗܢܘܢ ܕܠܐ ܨܒܘ ܡܩܒܠܘ 'those who would not accept', Išōᶜyahb III Patriarcha, *Liber epistularum*, p. 269.19.

277 § 339 On the so-called Waw apodosis, A. A. Bevan wrote to Th. Nöldeke on 31 October 1898: ". . . A few days ago I chanced to speak with F. C. Burkitt on exactly this phenomenon, namely the admissibility of the ܘ at the beginning of the apodosis, a matter he found especially interesting because he has concerned himself much with the Old Syriac translation of the Gospels. He has now made me aware that there are passages where the ܘ under consideration is found in both C. and S., e.g., Luke 12:45, 46 (ܘܢܦܠܓ) and 13:12 (ܘܩܪܝܗ), the latter passage in Lewis's 1910 edition of the Syrus Sinaiticus. It is especially important that the Pšīttā sometimes avoids this construction by altering the protasis; in John 4:1–3, for instance, S. has ܟܕ ܕܝܢ ܝܕܥ . . . ܘܫܒܩܗ, but the Pšīttā ܝܕܥ ܕܝܢ . . . ܘܫܒܩܗ. It can also be seen that the redactors of the Pšīttā really found the reading ܘܫܒܩܗ in their model, but in order to avoid the difficulty left out the ܟܕ at the beginning, although the originality of the ܟܕ is guaranteed by the ὡς of the Greek text."

Numerous additional examples from S. are gathered in *Evangelion da-Mepharreshe, the Curetonian Version of the Four Gospels, with the readings of the Sinai Palimpsest and the early Syriac Patristic evidence*, edited, collected and arranged by F. Crawford Burkitt, vol. 2 (Cambridge, 1904), pp. 69ff. In "good" Syriac original writers, the rule seems to be correct. However, this ‌o must not be seen as purely a Hebraism. Already in more colloquial writings, which generally appear to be influenced by the Old Testament, this ‌o appears to occur. In the Marian texts edited by Budge, this sort of ‌o often appears, namely ‌ܘܗܘ in the apodosis to ‌ܟ, see Budge, *Blessed Virgin Mary*, pp. 10.13, 18.7, 104.17 (Virgin Mary) and 169.12 (Likeness of Christ). P. 25.3, though, has bare ‌ܗܘ. ‌ܘܗܘ ‌ܘܟܕܡܘ is found in n. 1 on p. 75, ‌ܗܘ ‌ܘܗܕ ‌ܘܟܣܘ in the text. In Mandaic, by the way, a Waw apodosis is unknown.

277 § 339 An example for ‌ܘܠܐ ‌ܟܪܡܟ is found on p. 267 § 330 end. According to Nöldeke, *Zur Grammatik des classischen Arabisch*, p. 91 n. 1, this expression is not uncommon in Aramaic. But also Arabic وَلَا 'not at all, not once' in the later language "is not so very rare," see addition 91/8 in the appendix edited by A. Spitaler in the 1963 Darmstadt reprint.

284 § 349 ‌ܘ ‌ܠܐܝܟܐ 'there, whither', Apost. apocr. 229.21.

286 § 350 A Also ‌ܢܫܡܗ ‌ܠܥܠ ‌ܡܢ ‌ܕܩܫܝܡ ‌ܐܝܠܝܢ ‌ܣܒ 'we whose names are inscribed above', Chabot, *Synodicon*, p. 63.14. — ‌ܐܝܠܝܢ ‌ܗܘ ‌ܕܟܠܐܘܗܝ ‌ܐܘܢܟ ‌ܐܝܠܟ, 'you whose ear is inclined to this one' Apost. apocr. 222.20—in object relation ‌ܘܠܟ ‌ܐܝܠܝܢ ‌ܘܐܚܡܒܪܐܝ ‌ܐܝܕܐ ‌ܘܐܝܪܓܝܐ, 'you whom the hand of the one you sent baptized', Sachau, *Berlin*, p. 48.21 — ‌ܫܕܟ ‌ܐܝܠ ‌ܦܚܡ ‌ܐܘ ‌ܚܒܝ ‌ܪܘܝܚ ‌ܩܫܝܡܐ ‌ܘܠܪܚܡ ‌ܡܝܠܐ ‌ܐܝܕܣܕܐ ‌ܘܚܠܝܕ ‌ܐܝܣܣܟܐ 'I leave you, O my beautiful spouse, whom I found after a long time and before whom I sat down', Apost. apocr. 215.6ff.

286 § 350 B The section from "cf. ‌ܘܟܚܕ" to "שִׁמְעוּ" perhaps fits better in § 350 C.

286 § 350 C Read "the third person is **usually** then taken."

291 § 358 ‌ܘܗܘܟ ‌ܘܐܝܠܟ ‌ܡܪܡܚܕܗ, ‌ܘܠܘܝܚܗ 'and that which I recited before you (is that) which you know', Addai 16.24.

292 § 358 Also ‌ܐ ‌ܘܒ ‌ܠܐܚܕܗ, ‌ܘܕܣܘܟܕܗ ‌ܘܐܝܣܠܟܠܐܝ ‌ܠܚܕܐ : ‌ܘܐܪܕܐ ... ‌ܐܝܢܣܡܗ ‌ܘܗܠܘܐܝ ‌ܘܚܣܡܒ 'but if they say that the purpose for which the Good was mingled (with the evil) is that it (the Good) may overcome the great quantity of the Evil . . .', Ephraem, *Prose Refutations*, 1: 167.10–14.

292 § 359 Cf. also ‌ܚܒ ‌ܚܓܠ ‌ܚܒܪ, ‌ܘܐܝܢܗ ‌ܘܐܝܢܗ 'at the time when he desired his reward from you' Ephraem, *Hymni et sermones*, 4: 129.25f. and ‌ܚܒܝ

ﻞﺋﻭ 'at the time when he comes', ibid., 451.4. Cases are also found like ﻮﻫ 'at the exact moment when he died' Ephraem, *Prose Refutations* 2: 162.40f. and ﻮﻫ 'at the exact moment when he was raised from the dead', ibid., p. 163.4f.

293 § 360 A   Sometimes the preposition is separated from the following conjunctional clause introduced by ؟ by e.g., ﻮﻣ 'O Lord' or ﻯ and ﻮ؟, cf. § 246 with the addition to p. 191 and § 327.

293 § 360 B   Further examples of the use of ﻼﻗ illustrated here: ﻮﻠﻗﻮ ﻮﻟﻮﺟﻭ ﻼﺣ ﻱﻭﻩ ﻩﻟﻮﺟﻭ 'this befell her only because she apostasized' Addai 12.23—ﻮﻠﻭ ﻮﻠﻗﺣ ﻮﻠﺟﻮﻠﺟ ﻮﻣ ﻭﺋﻟﻭ ﻮﺣﻣ ﻮﻠﺣﻮﻛﻟﻣ 'for our Lord came to the world only to instruct us' Addai 23.4—ﻮﺋﻟﻭ ﻮﻣ ﻮﻠﺣﺣﻣﻟ ﻭﻟﻭ ﻟﻮﻣ ﻮﻣﻟ ﻮﻣ ﻮﻠﺣﺣ ﻮﺋﻟ 'our Lord came to the world only that thereafter creatures not be worshiped and revered', Addai 44.3ff.—ﻮﻠﺣﻣ ﻮﺣﺣﻣ ﻮﻠﻣ ﻼﻟﻣ ﻩﻭﻩ ﻟﻭ . ﻮﻠﺣﻣﺣﻭ ﻮﺣﺣ ﻮﻠﻣ ﻭﻣﺣﺣﻭ ﻮﺣﺣﺣ ... ﻼﻟﻣ ﻩﻭ ﻟﻭ : ﻮﻠﺣﺣﺣ ﻮﻣﻭﺣﺣﻭ 'therefore I am already made shepherd of mankind, not just those present, but also for . . .'s sake', Anc. doc. 66.1 (Barsamyā).

296 § 362   Delete "that he" and read "when Noah heard that God commanded him . . . and said. . . ."

300 § 368   ﻮﺣﻣ 'is (was) able' is handled the same way. The particle ؟ can also be omitted with ﻮﻗﻣ **before** and **after** the dependent verb (or participle), thus ﻟﻭﻣ ﻮﻣﻠﻟﻟ ﻟﻭﻣﻭ 'nor is she much exhausted', Ephraem, *Prose Refutations*, 1: 17.5f.—ﻮﻣﻟ ﻟﻭﻩ ﻟﻮﻣﻟﻭ 'that she take much', ibid., p. 17.38—ﻮﻣﺣﻣﻭ ﻮﻗﻣﻭﻣ ﻮﺣﻣ ﻮﻗﻣﻭﻭ 'who (f. pl.) have sinned and blasphemed greatly', ibid., 87.38 and so quite often in this work of Ephraem's, but beside clauses with ؟ or beside ﻼ with infinitive.

Other cases: ؟ ﻟﻮﺋﻟ ﻮﻣﺣﺣﻣ ﻮﻠﻭﺣﺋ ﻼﻟﻮﺣﻭ ﻟﻟ,ﻟ 'I beg your fatherliness to pray that . . .', Išōᶜyahb III Patriarcha, *Liber epistularum*, p. 47.20 = 59.21, 67.2, 91.21—ﻮﻗ,ﻣﺣﻭ ﻮﻠﺣﺋﻭ 'that he rend (his tunic) again', Ephraem, *Prose Refutations*, 1: 141.18 — ﻮﺣﻣ ﻮﺣﺣ ﻮﺣﻣﻟ ﻮﻠﺣﻗﻭ ﻮﻠﻗﺣﻣﺣ ﻮﻣﺣﻗﻗ,ﻣﻟﻭ ﻮﻟ,ﻣ 'the evil one had all its dogs barking to bite them', Anc. doc. 100.20.

302 § 371   Something more should be said here about "pleonastic" negation in dependent clauses. Examples and basics are found in Brockelmann, *GVG* 2: 665 § 458c and *GGA* 1914: 690.

304 § 372 C Note also ܥܠ ܕܐܝܟܢܐ 'about how', Išō^c^yahb III Patriarcha, *Liber epistularum*, pp. 4.18, 238.10.

305 § 372 E On Greek models like . . . ἀλλὰ τὴν ἐμαυτοῦ τύχην (ἀπέκλαον), οἵου ἀνδρὸς ἑταίρου ἐστερημένος εἴην '. . . (I was weeping for) myself, not for him—for my misfortune in being deprived of such a comrade', Plato, *Phaedo* 117c [trans. G. M. A. Grube, ed. J. M. Cooper (Indianapolis, 1997)].

307 § 374 A Noteworthy is ܐܢ ܕܠܗ = 'if not', Išō^c^yahb III Patriarcha, *Liber epistularum*, p. 281.10 = *The Book of Governors; The Historia Monastica of Thomas Bishop of Margâ* A.D. *840*, ed. and trans. E. A. W. Budge, vol. 2 (London, 1893), p. 173.4, where instead of the form found in the manuscript one would expect the constructions ܐܢ ܠܗ or ܐܢ ܗܘ ܕܠܗ.

308 § 374 B ܐܝܢܗܘ not followed by ܕ is found in Mingana, *Mšiḥa-Zkha*, pp. 22.20, 33.3. There are some doubts about its legitimacy.

310 § 374 D Note also ܐܠܐ ܐܢ ܐܡܪ܂ ܕܐܦܝܣܩܘܦܐ ܢܦܩܘܕ 'except when the bishop decrees', Chabot, *Synodicon*, p. 153.26 (585 A.D.).—ܐܠܐ is used rather like in Arabic oath clauses with إِلَّا, as in نَشَدْتُكَ اللّٰهَ إِلَّا فَعَلْتَ 'I beseech thee by God to do it' (Wright 2: 339 D) in the epistle of Mārā bar Serapion Spic. 48.25: ܒܚܝܝܟ ܡܪܐ ܐܠܐ ܐܡܪܬ ܠܝ '(I beseech you) on your life, O Mārā, to say to me . . .' (lit. if you do not say to me, then . . .).

310 § 374 D To be mentioned here is also the "peculiar" (Nöldeke) ܐܠܐ ܘܐܝܟ for the simple ܐܠܐ ܐܝܟ 'but as' in Mingana, *Mšiḥa-Zkha*, pp. 30.13, 34.6, 9. Because it occurs three times, the accuracy of the text is assured. ܐܠܐ followed by ܘ (ܐܠܐ ܘܚܡܬܗ ܫܒܩܗ) in *The Book of Kalīlah and Dimnah, transl. from Arabic into Syriac*, ed. W. Wright (Oxford & London, 1884), e.g., p. 189.23f., on the other hand, is according to Nöldeke, *GGA* 1884: 683, an Arabism corresponding to Arabic إِلَّا و, Wright 2: 339 B, C.

311 § 375 Insert: "The condition which is set forth as impossible **(irrealis)** . . . ."

313 § 375 A Also ܐܠܘ ܐܝܬ ܦܘܡܐ ܠܐܪܥܐ ܡܟܣܢܐ ܗܘܬ ܠܢ ܡܥܠܝܐܝܬ 'if the earth had a mouth, it would rebuke us severely', Ephraem, *Hymni et sermones*, 4: 371.22f.